The Holt, Rinehart and Winston Accuracy Commitment: From Manuscript to Bound Book

As a leading textbook publisher in foreign languages since 1866, Holt, Rinehart and Winston recognizes the importance of accuracy in foreign language textbooks. In an effort to produce the most accurate introductory foreign language program available we have added two new stages to the development of *¡Dímelo tú!,* Third Edition — **double proofing** in production and a **final accuracy check** by experienced teachers.

The outline below shows the unprecedented steps we have taken to ensure accuracy:

Author	Writes and proofs first draft.
1st Round of Reviews	Review of first draft manuscript. Independent reviewers check for clarity of text organization, pedagogy, content, and proper use of language.
Author	Makes corrections/changes.
2nd Round of Reviews	Review of second draft manuscript. Independent reviewers again check for clarity of text organization, pedagogy, content, and proper use of language.
Author	Prepares text for production.
Production	Copyediting and proofreading. The project is **double-proofed** — at the galley proof stage and again at the page proof stage.
Final Accuracy Check	The entire work is read one last time by experienced instructors, this time to check for accurate use of language in text, examples, and exercises. The material is read word for word again and all exercises are worked to ensure the most accurate language program possible. The accompanying workbook/lab manual, tapescript, and video are proofed simultaneously.
Final Textbook	Published with final corrections.

Holt, Rinehart and Winston would like to acknowledge the following instructors who, along with others, participated in the final accuracy check for *¡Dímelo tú!,* Third Edition: Tom Fonte, El Camino College; Elaine Rees, Cosumnes River College; Ricardo Castells, Florida International University; Rigo Ibarra, Long Beach City College; Maria Fleck, University of California—Riverside; Paola Bianco, Wilkes University; Maria Villamil, University of Nebraska—Omaha; Lee Daniels, Texas Christian University; Fernando Palacios, University of Alabama—Tuscaloosa; and Yolanda Rivera-Castillo, University of Houston—Downtown.

AMÉRICA DEL SUR
MAR CARIBE
OCÉANO ATLÁNTICO
OCÉANO PACÍFICO
BELICE
HONDURAS
NICARAGUA
Lago de Managua
EL SALVADOR
GUATEMALA
COSTA RICA
PANAMÁ
Maracaibo
Caracas
Barranquilla
Cartagena
Lago de Maracaibo
Río Magdalena
San Cristóbal
Río Orinoco
VENEZUELA
Medellín
Bogotá
Cali
COLOMBIA
Georgetown
GUAYANA
Paramaribo
SURINAM
Cayena
Boa Vista
GUAYANA FRANCESA
ECUADOR
ISLAS GALÁPAGOS
Quito
ECUADOR
Guayaquil
Cuenca
Iquitos
Río Amazonas
AMAZONAS
PERÚ
LOS ANDES
BRASIL
Lima
Machu Picchu
Ayacucho
Cuzco
BOLIVIA
Lago Titicaca
La Paz
Santa Cruz
Brasilia
Sucre
Potosí
Río Paraná
Río de Janeiro
São Paulo
CHILE
PARAGUAY
Asunción
Iguazú
Río Uruguay
Córdoba
URUGUAY
Montevideo
Viña del Mar
Valparaíso
Santiago
Buenos Aires
ARGENTINA
Río de la Plata
Concepción
Bahía Blanca
Viedma
ISLAS MALVINAS (Br.)
Estrecho de Magallanes
TIERRA DEL FUEGO
0 250 500 750 1,000 MILLAS
0 500 1,000 1,500 KILÓMETROS
NIGERIA
ÁFRICA
Malabo
CAMERÚN
GUINEA ECUATORIAL
GABÓN
ÁFRICA
0 MILLAS 500
0 KILÓMETROS 750

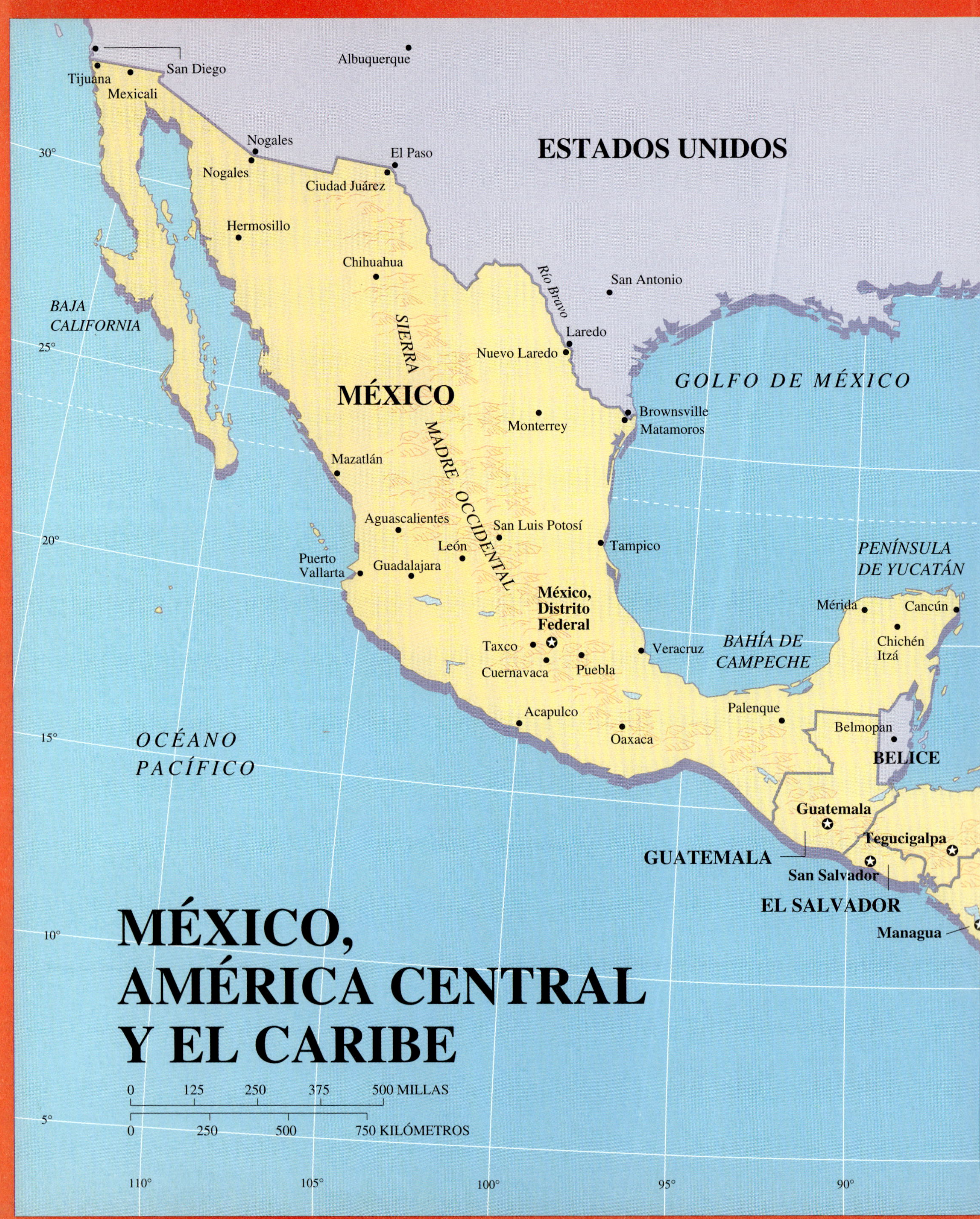
MÉXICO, AMÉRICA CENTRAL Y EL CARIBE
ESTADOS UNIDOS
MÉXICO
GOLFO DE MÉXICO
OCÉANO PACÍFICO
BAJA CALIFORNIA
SIERRA MADRE OCCIDENTAL
PENÍNSULA DE YUCATÁN
BAHÍA DE CAMPECHE
BELICE
GUATEMALA
EL SALVADOR
Río Bravo
San Diego
Tijuana
Mexicali
Albuquerque
Nogales
Nogales
El Paso
Ciudad Juárez
Hermosillo
Chihuahua
San Antonio
Laredo
Nuevo Laredo
Brownsville
Matamoros
Monterrey
Mazatlán
Aguascalientes
San Luis Potosí
Tampico
León
Puerto Vallarta
Guadalajara
México, Distrito Federal
Taxco
Cuernavaca
Puebla
Veracruz
Mérida
Cancún
Chichén Itzá
Palenque
Acapulco
Oaxaca
Belmopan
Guatemala
Tegucigalpa
San Salvador
Managua
0 125 250 375 500 MILLAS
0 250 500 750 KILÓMETROS
30°
25°
20°
15°
10°
5°
110°
105°
100°
95°
90°

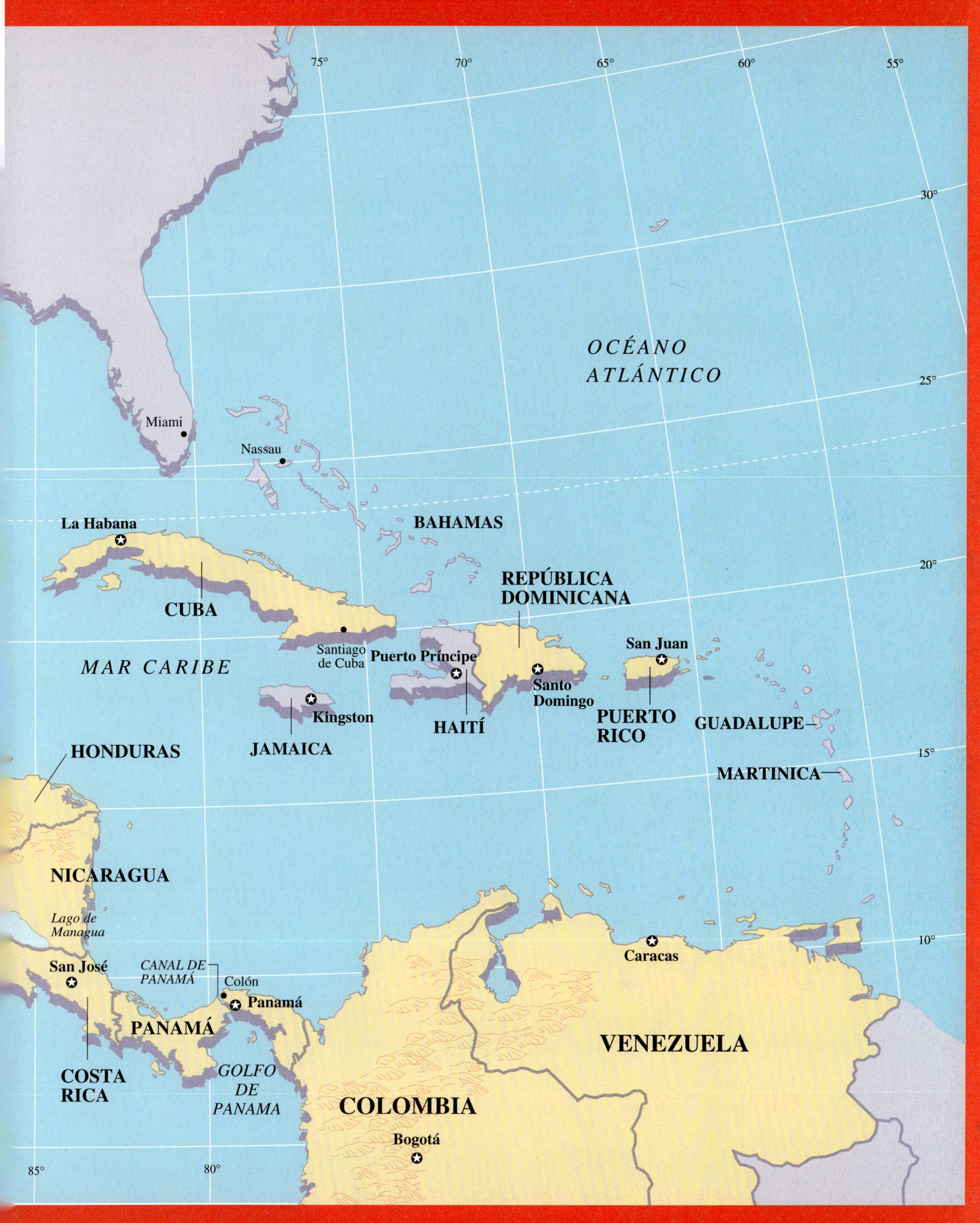

75°
70°
65°
60°
55°
30°
25°
20°
15°
10°
85°
80°
OCÉANO
ATLÁNTICO
Miami
Nassau
BAHAMAS
La Habana
CUBA
Santiago
de Cuba
REPÚBLICA
DOMINICANA
Puerto Príncipe
HAITÍ
Santo
Domingo
San Juan
PUERTO
RICO
GUADALUPE
MARTINICA
MAR CARIBE
Kingston
JAMAICA
HONDURAS
NICARAGUA
Lago de
Managua
San José
COSTA
RICA
CANAL DE
PANAMÁ
Colón
Panamá
PANAMÁ
GOLFO
DE
PANAMA
COLOMBIA
Bogotá
Caracas
VENEZUELA

EL MUNDO
GROENLANDIA
OCÉANO ÁRTICO
RUSIA
Alaska (EE.UU.)
CANADÁ
NORTEAMÉRICA
ESTADOS UNIDOS
OCÉANO PACÍFICO
OCÉANO ATLÁNTICO
Hawai (EE.UU.)
TRÓPICO DE CÁNCER
MÉXICO
BELICE
CUBA
JAMAICA
BAHAMAS
REPÚBLICA DOMINICANA
PUERTO RICO
HAITÍ
AMÉRICA CENTRAL
GUATEMALA
EL SALVADOR
HONDURAS
NICARAGUA
PANAMÁ
COSTA RICA
VENEZUELA
GUAYANA FRANCESA
COLOMBIA
GUYANA
SURINAM
ISLAS GALÁPAGOS (ECUADOR)
ECUADOR
PERÚ
SUDAMÉRICA
BRASIL
BOLIVIA
PARAGUAY
TRÓPICO DE CAPRICORNIO
CHILE
ARGENTINA
URUGUAY
ISLAS MALVINAS
VANUATU
TUVALU
KIRIBATI
SAMOA
TONGA
NUEVA ZELANDA
0 500 1,000 1,500 2,000 MILLAS
0 1,000 2,000 3,000 KILÓMETROS
195° 180° 165° 150° 135° 120° 105° 90° 45° 30°
75° 45° 30° 15° 0° 15° 30° 45°

SUECIA
FINLANDIA
NORUEGA
MAR DE NORUEGA
ISLANDIA
1 LA REPÚBLICA CHECA
2 ESLOVAQUIA
3 AUSTRIA
4 HUNGRÍA
5 ESLOVENIA
6 CROACIA
7 BOSNIA Y HERZEGOVINA
8 YUGOSLAVIA
9 ALBANIA
10 MACEDONIA
RUSIA
ESTONIA
LETONIA
LITUANIA
REINO UNIDO
DINAMARCA
HOLANDA
REPÚBLICA DE IRLANDA
BÉLGICA
ALEMANIA
POLONIA
BIELORRUSIA
UCRANIA
MOLDAVIA
FRANCIA
SUIZA
RUMANIA
EUROPA
BULGARIA
ITALIA
ESPAÑA
PORTUGAL
GRECIA
ASIA
ARMENIA
TURKMENISTÁN
KAZAJSTÁN
UZBEKISTÁN
MONGOLIA
COREA DEL NORTE
GEORGIA
TURQUÍA
AZERBAIYÁN
KIRGUIZISTÁN
TADJIKISTÁN
AFGANISTÁN
REPÚBLICA POPULAR CHINA
REP. ÁRABE SAHARAUI DEMOCRÁTICA
TÚNEZ
CHIPRE
LÍBANO
ISRAEL
SIRIA
IRAQ
IRÁN
NEPAL
BHUTÁN
JAPÓN
MARRUECOS
ARGELIA
JORDANIA
KUWAIT
QATAR
PAKISTÁN
LAOS
COREA DEL SUR
ISLAS CANARIAS (ESPAÑA)
LIBIA
EGIPTO
BAHREIN
EMIRATOS ÁRABES UNIDOS
INDIA
VIETNAM
TAIWÁN
MAURITANIA
ÁFRICA
ARABIA SAUDITA
BANGLADESH
MALÍ
NÍGER
CHAD
ERITREA
YEMEN
OMÁN
TAILANDIA
SENEGAL
GAMBIA
BURKINA FASO
SUDÁN
CAMBOYA
GUINEA
NIGERIA
MYANMAR
FILIPINAS
REP. CENTRO-AFRICANA
ETIOPÍA
JIBUTI
GUINEA-BISSAU
UGANDA
SOMALIA
CAMERÚN
SRI LANKA
MALASIA
PAPÚA-NUEVA GUINEA
GABÓN
ZAIRE
KENIA
SIERRA LEONA
R.P. DEL CONGO
RUANDA
ECUADOR
SINGAPUR
LIBERIA
BURUNDI
TANZANIA
ZAMBIA
COSTA DE MARFIL
INDONESIA
GHANA
OCÉANO ÍNDICO
TOGO
ANGOLA
BENÍN
MALAWI
GUINEA ECUATORIAL
NAMIBIA
BOTSWANA
MADAGASCAR
AUSTRALIA
ZIMBABUE
LESOTO
MOZAMBIQUE
SUDÁFRICA
SUAZILANDIA

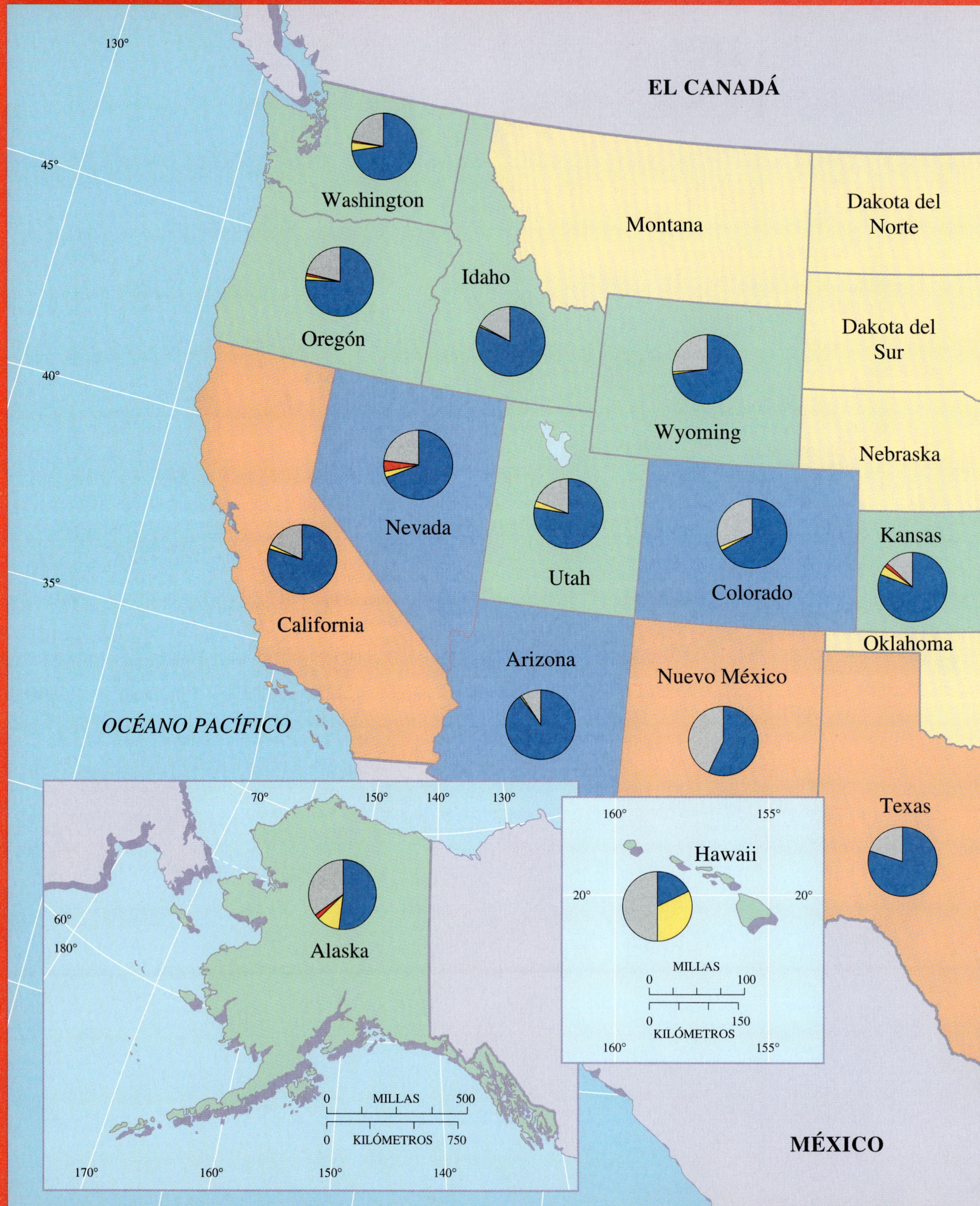

EL CANADÁ
Washington
Oregón
Idaho
Montana
Dakota del Norte
Dakota del Sur
Wyoming
Nebraska
California
Nevada
Utah
Colorado
Kansas
Oklahoma
Arizona
Nuevo México
Texas
OCÉANO PACÍFICO
Alaska
Hawaii
MÉXICO
MILLAS
KILÓMETROS
130°
45°
40°
35°

LOS HISPANOHABLANTES EN LOS ESTADOS UNIDOS

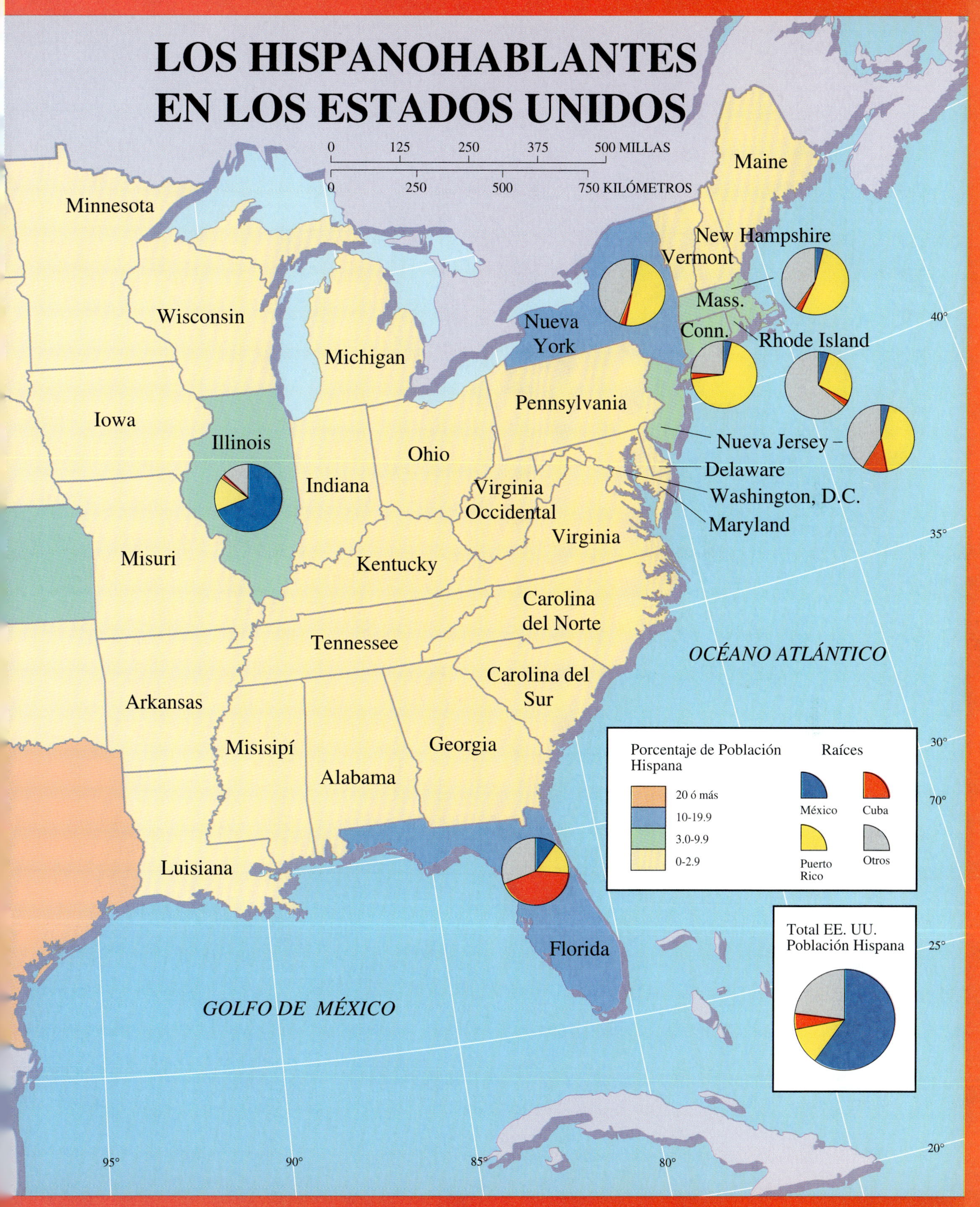

ESPAÑA
0 50 100 150 200 MILLAS
0 100 200 300 KILÓMETROS
OCÉANO ATLÁNTICO
MAR CANTÁBRICO
FRANCIA
ANDORRA
PORTUGAL
PRINCIPADO DE ASTURIAS
GALICIA
CANTABRIA
PAÍS VASCO
NAVARRA
CASTILLA Y LEÓN
LA RIOJA
ARAGÓN
CATALUÑA
MADRID
CASTILLA-LA MANCHA
COMUNIDAD VALENCIANA
EXTREMADURA
MURCIA
ANDALUCÍA
CORDILLERA CANTÁBRICA
PIRINEOS
Río Ebro
SIERRA DE GUADARRAMA
Río Tajo
Río Guadalquivir
SIERRA NEVADA
Santiago
Santander
Bilbao
Pamplona
Zaragoza
Lérida
Gerona
Barcelona
Valladolid
Salamanca
Segovia
Madrid
Toledo
Ciudad Real
Valencia
Alicante
Murcia
Cartagena
Córdoba
Sevilla
Granada
Málaga
Cádiz
Lisboa
Costa Brava
MENORCA
MALLORCA
Palma
IBIZA
ISLAS BALEARES
MAR MEDITERRÁNEO
Costa del Sol
Estrecho de Gibraltar
GIBRALTAR (Br.)
CEUTA (Sp.)
MELILLA (Sp.)
Tanger
MARRUECOS
ISLAS CANARIAS
0 MILLAS 100
0 KILÓMETROS 150
LA PALMA
TENERIFE
GRAN CANARIA
Las Palmas
LANZAROTE
FUERTEVENTURA
HIERRO
GOMERA
ÁFRICA
10° 8° 6° 4° 2°
44° 42° 40° 38° 36°
18° 16° 14° 12° 28°

Third Edition

Fabián A. Samaniego
Emeritus, University of California—Davis

Thomas J. Blommers
California State University—Bakersfield

Magaly Lagunas-Carvacho
University of California—Davis

Viviane Sardán
University of California—Davis

Francisco Rodríguez
Santa Barbara City College

Holt, Rinehart and Winston
Harcourt Brace College Publishers

Fort Worth Philadelphia San Diego New York Orlando Austin San Antonio
Toronto Montreal London Sydney Tokyo

Publisher	Rolando Hernández-Arriessecq
Acquisitions Editor	Terri Rowenhorst
Developmental Editor	Elke Herbst
Project Editor	Mary K. Mayo
Art Director	David A. Day
Production Manager	Debra A. Jenkin

Cover credit:

Background	© Digital Stock
Man and woman walking	© Corel
Mother and daughter at Mayan ruin	Macduff Everton/The Image Works
Couple in Seville	Odyssey/Frerck/Chicago
Street dancing at festival	Odyssey/Frerck/Chicago
Festival	Odyssey/Frerck/Chicago

ISBN: 0-03-020078-4

Library of Congress Catalog Card Number: 97-74837

Address for Editorial Correspondence: Holt, Rinehart and Winston, 301 Commerce Street, Suite 3700, Fort Worth, TX 76102.

Address for Orders: Harcourt Brace & Company, 6277 Sea Harbor Drive, Orlando, FL 32887-6777. 1-800-782-4479.

Web site address: http://www.hbcollege.com

Holt, Rinehart and Winston will provide supplements or supplement packages to those adopters qualified under our adoption policy. Please contact your sales representative to learn how to qualify. If as an adopter or potential user you receive supplements you do not need, please return them to your sales representative or send them to: Returns Department, Troy Warehouse, 465 South Lincoln Drive, Troy, MO 63379.

Printed in the United States of America

9 0 1 2 3 4 5 6 032 9 8 7 6 5

Holt, Rinehart and Winston
Harcourt Brace College Publishers

Preface To the Student

 Teaching for Competency

To develop fluency in Spanish, you must learn to perform a wide variety of communicative language tasks, such as asking and answering questions, describing, narrating, making comparisons, expressing opinions, and hypothesizing. You must learn to perform these tasks in multiple contexts: home, school, department stores, restaurants, travel agencies, traveling abroad, hotels, concerts, lectures, movie theaters, or night clubs. Finally, you must learn to perform these tasks within an appropriate range of accuracy. *¡Dímelo tú!* will help you accomplish this by having you *interact* in Spanish with your classmates and with your instructor on a daily basis.

Organization of ¡Dímelo tú!, Third Edition

As with the previous edition, the third edition consists of a preliminary lesson **(Antes de empezar),** a model lesson **(Para empezar),** and fifteen chapters.

Antes de empezar In this preliminary lesson you will complete a series of group activities that will help you see the global importance of studying the Spanish language and Hispanic culture. You will also receive specific advice on how to study a foreign language and learn about the overall format of the third edition.

Para empezar Here you will learn to greet people, make introductions, and say good-bye. You will also be exposed to all major components of each *Paso* (Step) in the third edition.

Each of the fifteen chapters of *¡Dímelo tú!* are divided into three *Pasos* with the following components:

Lo que ya sabes... This set of questions refers to the photos on the two-page chapter opening spread. The photos have been selected to introduce the chapter theme and/or the country of focus. The questions are designed to help access knowledge you might already have regarding the chapter theme and/or country to be studied in the chapter.

¿Eres buen observador? This section introduces the theme of a *Paso* and challenges you to make cross-cultural comparisons and intelligent guesses about some aspect of the theme by looking at a specific photo, a drawing, or a variety of advertisements from all over the Spanish-speaking world. Then you will be asked to answer some comprehension questions.

¿Qué se dice...? Built into the illustrated narratives and dialogues in this section are the new lesson vocabulary and language structures. The first narrative in every *Paso* is recorded on the audio CD that accompanies the text. You are expected to listen to it and answer the questions in the text **before** beginning the *Paso* in class. Your instructor will use the drawings to help you understand as he or she narrates the remaining parts of the story or dialogue. In class, you are expected to listen carefully to the narration; you are not expected to understand every word, but you should be able to grasp the main point of the narrative.

Ahora, ¡a hablar! In this section you will be guided through your first productive efforts with the structures and vocabulary that you learned to understand in the previous *¿Qué se dice... ?* section.

Y ahora, ¡a conversar! In this section you will do a variety of pair/group cooperative activities designed to encourage creativity with the language and develop fluency in speaking Spanish. By interacting with other students in such activities as finding differences in look-alike pictures, conducting interviews and creating interview grids, resolving cooperative crossword puzzles, and playing language Bingo, you will accomplish this goal.

¡Luz! ¡Cámara! ¡Acción! In this section you will be asked to perform two or three role plays that will allow you to see for yourself if you have mastered the communicative language tasks of the *Paso*.

¿Comprendes lo que se dice? The first two *Pasos* in each chapter have this listening section. In *Paso 1* of Chapters 1–10, you will listen to such materials as brief dialogues, short radio and television news reports, and weather reports. In *Paso 2* of Chapters 1–10, you will view a wide variety of television programs. In the last five chapters of the text, you will watch a complete soap opera, *La dinastía del amor*.

Noticiero cultural The first two *Pasos* of each chapter present these short cultural readings. In *Paso 1,* the text focuses on a specific Hispanic country or region (*Lugar*); *Paso 2* either highlights a noteworthy Hispanic person of that country (*Gente*), or presents a cross-cultural miscommunication that you will be asked to identify and explain (*Costumbres*).

El español en otras disciplinas... In this section at the end of *Paso 1* you will see how Spanish has applications that go beyond the classroom. You will actually do a wide variety of tasks involving other disciplines—geography, art, history, music, mathematics, and so on.

¿Te gusta escribir? This section at the end of *Paso 2* teaches you to write in Spanish the same way you are taught to write any kind of document in English. Each writing task begins with initial planning and brainstorming. Then you write a first draft that is shared, reviewed, and edited by your peers. A final draft that incorporates your peers' suggestions and corrections is then prepared and turned in for grading.

¿Te gusta leer? This section, which occurs only in *Paso 3,* has a reading selection preceded by specific reading strategies and pre-reading activities called *Antes de leer*. The reading selections are taken from Hispanic magazines and newspapers, literary works, and cultural essays written by the authors.

Viajemos por el ciberespacio a... In this section you are encouraged to travel through cyberspace to every Spanish-speaking country featured in your book. You may choose to read the headlines in some of the world's most prestigious newspapers or find out what is happening in the Hispanic world of sports, movies, or theaters in such cities as Buenos Aires, Lima, Madrid, or Mexico City. Through the World Wide Web you can directly communicate with the people in Hispanic cities across the globe.

En preparación All major grammar explanations appear in this section at the end of each chapter. For easy reference, grammatical points are numerically keyed to each *Paso* of the text. Before beginning each *Paso,* you are asked to study the corresponding grammar sections at home and come to class prepared to ask questions about anything you did not understand.

¿Sabías que...? These sections appear whenever appropriate in each chapter. They provide specific cultural information on many aspects of contemporary life in Latin America and Spain.

A propósito... These sections appear wherever appropriate in each chapter and have two functions: they present grammar structures as needed to perform specific communicative tasks, and they preview major grammar structures explained in later chapters.

Appendixes Besides the Spanish/English and English/Spanish vocabularies, the appendixes include accentuation; charts of regular, stem-changing, and irregular verbs; a brief explanation of supplemental grammar points, an index of grammar, and a separate index of culture and functions.

Visual Icons Used Throughout the Text

The Pair Work Icon is used throughout each **Paso**, in particular in the **Ahora, ¡a hablar!**, **Y ahora, ¡a conversar!,** and **¡Luz! ¡Cámara! ¡Acción!** sections, to help students and the instructor readily identify activities designed for paired work.

The Group Work Icon is used throughout each **Paso**, in particular in the **Y ahora, ¡a conversar!** and **¡Luz! ¡Cámara! ¡Acción!** sections, to help students and the instructor readily identify activities designed for work in groups of three or more.

The Listening Icon is used in the **¿Qué se dice...?** sections to indicate that students must listen to the Student CD before coming to class. This icon is also used in the **¿Comprendes lo que se dice?** section in **Paso 1** to indicate that students will be listening to an audio CD or cassette in class.

The Video Icon is used in the **¿Comprendes lo que se dice?** section in **Paso 2** to indicate that students will be viewing and listening to a videotape in class.

The Writing Icon is used in the **Ahora, ¡a hablar!** and **Y ahora, ¡a conversar!** sections whenever the activities require the students to do some writing. This icon is also used in the **¿Te gusta escribir?** section to indicate when students will be writing rather than planning, organizing, or revising.

The Reading Icon is used in the **Noticiero cultural** and **¿Te gusta leer?** sections to inform students that these are reading activities.

Cuaderno de actividades/Manual de laboratorio

The *Cuaderno de actividades/Manual de laboratorio* is an integral part of the *¡Dímelo tú!* program. This material provides you with the additional reading, writing, and listening comprehension practice necessary to attain competency in Spanish.

The activities workbook provides numerous vocabulary-building activities, writing activities, and cultural readings, all keyed to the specific structures and vocabulary being presented in each chapter.

In the audio program you will listen to radio programs and advertisements, public address announcements, and phone conversations, and you will actively participate by marking the correct responses, taking notes, drawing the person or thing being described, and so on. These listening activities are carefully keyed to the structures and vocabulary presented in each chapter.

Cuaderno para hispanohablantes

The *Cuaderno para hispanohablantes* was developed to meet the unique needs of Spanish native speakers enrolled in a first-year course. This workbook provides alternative listening, speaking, reading, and writing activities to complement the textbook. A listening component tailored to the specific needs of native speakers also accompanies this workbook.

Tutorial Software

The *Tutorial Software* correlated directly to *¡Dímelo tú!* allows you to do grammar homework and practice grammar exercises in the language lab or at home. This software provides immediate feedback, error analysis, and scoring.

The Web Site

The *¡Dímelo tú! Home Page* provides a range of interactive web activities, linked to each chapter of the text, that make it easy for you to explore the Hispanic world on the Internet. Additional support materials and links to other resources on the web can also be found at http://www.hrwcollege.com.

Encuentros en español CD-ROM

The *Encuentros en español* CD-ROM takes you on a mystery adventure that unwinds in sixteen different locations in the Spanish-speaking world. Along the way, you will face situations that require many basic Spanish language functions you have learned in the *¡Dímelo tú!* program. You will progress through the adventure by using listening, reading and writing skills, and by completing interactive exercises integral to the story. Activities also build vocabulary and practice grammar structures. Rich cultural material and geographic information introduce each new country where the story is set. The story and cultural material are illustrated with video, audio, photos, realia, original animation and graphics. Glossary and grammar tools are available throughout the program.

Acknowledgments

A revision of this magnitude cannot be completed without the help and participation of many individuals. We wish to express our sincere appreciation to all who supported us in preparing the third edition, in particular to the many users of both the first and second editions. Without their continued support and input this third edition would not have been possible.

We wish to express a very special and heartfelt thank you to our developmental editor, Elke Herbst, for her insightful input, careful guidance, and willingness to listen and to try something new. We would also like to thank Miriam Bleiweiss, developmental editor, for her expert supervision and guidance in the development of the extensive ancillary package that accompanies this text.

We further appreciate the support throughout the project from both Rolando Hernández-Arriessecq, vice president/publisher of Holt, Rinehart and Winston, and Terri Rowenhorst, program director.

A special word of thanks goes to David A. Day, senior art director, who so efficiently handled the extensive art program of this edition, to Debra Jenkin, senior production manager, as well as our project editors Mary Kathryn Mayo and Claudia Gravier who ever so patiently made sure we met all our production deadlines.

We gratefully acknowledge those instructors who reviewed the third edition manuscript. Their insightful comments and constructive criticism were indispensable in the development of this edition. In particular, we thank

Suan Navey-Davis, North Carolina State University; Lynda J. Jentsch, Samford University; Fausto Avendaño, California State University—Sacramento; Alice Ruth Reckley, University of Missouri—Kansas City; Octavio de la Suaree, William Patterson College; Sonia López Blakely, Colorado State University—Fort Collins; Estelita Calderón-Young, Collin County Community College; Olga Berrios Winston, California State University—Bakersfield; Domenico Sottile, College of the Desert; Raquel Oxford, University of North Texas; Catherine M. Barrette, Wayne State University; and Carmen Chaves Tesser, University of Georgia.

Finally, we wish to express heartfelt thanks to Tom Wetterstrom, Jorge Yviricu, Omar Carvacho, and Janet B. Rodríguez, who through their patience and encouragement have supported us throughout this project.

Contenido

Third Edition

Antes de empezar

In this section, you will ...

- answer the question, "Why study a foreign language?"
- learn about Spanish as a global language.
- learn how Spanish can help you in your future career.
- be advised on how to study Spanish in *¡Dímelo tú!*

La Calle Olvera, Los Ángeles

El patio de los leones, la Alhambra, Granada

Las cataratas de Iguazú, Paraguay/ Argentina/Brasil

Las ruinas de Tikal en Guatemala

Panamá, ciudad capital

La biblioteca, Universidad Nacional Autónoma de México

Lo que ya sabes...

1. How many of these places do you recognize? In what countries are they located?
2. Can you describe the importance of each of these places?
3. Have you traveled to other well-known sites in the Spanish-speaking world? If so, what are they?

Why study a foreign language?

Students often ask themselves why they should study a foreign language, but many have difficulty responding. To help you understand the importance of foreign language study, let's explore the many reasons for learning Spanish.

- ▲ EXPERIENCIA MINIMA 2 AÑOS A NIVEL DIRECCION (INDISPENSABLE)
- ▲ EDAD DE 25 A 35 AÑOS
- ▲ INGLES MINIMO 70%
- ▲ MANEJO DE PC: WINDOWS, WORD, EXCEL, ETC.
- ▲ PREFERENTEMENTE CASADA
- ▲ EXCELENTE PRESENTACION (INDISPENSABLE)
- ▲ BUENA ORTOGRAFIA Y MECANOGRAFIA

JEFE DE PRODUCCION

- ▲ QFB, QFI, PASANTE O TITULADA
- ▲ SEXO FEMENINO
- ▲ EDAD: 25-35 AÑOS
- ▲ EDO. CIVIL: INDISTINTO
- ▲ EXCELENTE PRESENTACION
- ▲ EXPERIENCIA INDISPENSABLE COMPROBABLE EN:
  - AREA MEDICINAL
  - PROCESOS DE FABRICACION DE SOLIDOS
  - CONOCIMIENTOS EN VALIDACION DE PROCESOS
  - MANEJO DE TIEMPOS Y MOVIMIENTOS
  - TRATO CON PERSONAL SINDICALIZADO

PARA AMBOS PUESTOS OFRECEMOS: SUELDO COMPETITIVO, PRESTACIONES SUPERIORES A LAS DE LA LEY, DESARROLLO GARANTIZADO.

INTERESADOS PRESENTARSE EN: AMORES No. 1750, COL. DEL VALLE (METRO COYOACAN) CON CURRICULUM Y FOTO RECIENTE EL LUNES 5 Y MARTES 6 DE 9:00 A 13:00 HRS. AT'N. LIC. RICARDO DIAZ FERRER

PRESENTARSE UNICAMENTE SI REUNE LOS REQUISITOS

¿BILINGÜE?

Compañía americana ambiental en crecimiento solicita personal:

- ☆ Excelente presentación.
- ☆ Ingresos en dólares, capacitación.

No entrevistas por teléfono. Citas: **661-81-65**, con **licenciada NICOLE**

Spanish as a Global Language

Spanish is one of the official languages of the United Nations and the fifth most widely spoken language in the world. As advances in world communications bring us in closer contact with other countries, Spanish is destined to assume a major role. To gain a more global perspective on the importance of Spanish, work in groups of four and respond to the following.

1. Spanish is the official language in . . .
   a. five countries.
   b. eleven countries.
   c. fifteen countries.
   d. twenty-one countries.

2. List as many Spanish-speaking countries as you can.

3. Spanish is spoken by approximately . . .
   a. 100 million people.
   b. 200 million people.
   c. 300 million people.
   d. 400 million people.

Spanish in the United States

The influence of Spanish culture and language in the United States is most evident in the Southwest and Florida because these regions were first settled by the Spaniards. The first permanent European settlement in the continental United States was founded in 1565 at St. Augustine, Florida, by the Spaniards. (The Mayflower did not arrive at Plymouth Rock until 1620.) In Santa Fe, New Mexico, the Palace of the Governors, the oldest government building still in use in the continental United States, was built in 1610. In Texas, the first Spanish mission was established in 1690. By 1776, when the thirteen colonies declared their independence, the Spaniards had established seven missions along the California coast.

Today, one does not need to look far to see the influence of Spanish culture in this country. Again, working in groups of four, see how much you know about the influence of Spanish on U.S. culture by answering the following.

Palacio de los gobernadores en Santa Fe, Nuevo México

1. Name seven states that have Spanish names.

2. How many major cities in the U.S. can you list that have Spanish names?

3. Are there any eating establishments in your hometown that serve Spanish or Spanish-American cuisine? What are they?

4. The population of the U.S. is approximately 254 million. The number of Spanish speakers in the United States is approximately . . .
   - a. 12 million.
   - b. 22 million.
   - c. 32 million.
   - d. 42 million.

5. If you were stuck in an elevator with sixteen people in downtown Los Angeles, how many of them do you think would speak Spanish?
   - a. two
   - b. four
   - c. six
   - d. eight

6. Match the U.S. cities with the major Spanish-speaking population that has settled there.

(1) Cubans	a. San Francisco
(2) Mexicans	b. Miami
(3) Puerto Ricans	c. Los Angeles
(4) Nicaraguans and Salvadorans	d. New York

7. Which of the following words have been borrowed from the Spanish language?

potato chili canoe patio
rodeo hurricane tobacco chocolate
sherry
bronco lasso canasta
tomato conquistador MACHETE
ranch corral

How can learning Spanish help me?

HISPANIC BUSINESS, July/August 1996

One obvious way learning Spanish can help is in traveling. Learning to speak Spanish will open the doors to twenty-one different countries for you. It will also help you appreciate the valuable contributions made by Hispanic people in the fields of art, music, literature, and Western civilization in general.

Knowing the language can also help you in the business world. Working in groups of four, decide how knowing Spanish could help a person in the following professions. Explain your answers.

hotel management	law or law enforcement
journalism or publishing	photography
real estate	teaching
social or health services	library science
politics	international business
government	international communications

Learning Spanish will also make you more aware of your native language and will help you realize that when you speak or write, you do so to communicate ideas, not words alone. As you learn Spanish you will learn that ideas are communicated in different ways in different languages, and that there are few exact word-for-word relationships between languages.

How should I study Spanish?

Learning Spanish, like learning to play the piano or to play tennis, requires daily practice. Your ability to understand and to communicate in Spanish will increase each day if you are willing to use the language. Take advantage of every minute you are in the classroom. Do not be afraid to make mistakes when speaking, as this is a normal part of the learning process.

Here is a list of recommendations for how to study Spanish.

1. Practice every day. In class, make every effort to use what you already know. Outside of class, practice what you are learning with classmates or find a student who speaks the language to practice with you. Repeated use of Spanish will help you internalize the language.

2. Learn to make intelligent guesses. Spanish has hundreds of cognates, words that look or sound similar to their English equivalents. Learn to recognize and use them. For example, what do the following mean in English?

   repite **universidad** **grupo**
   clase **información** **conversación**

3. Experiment to find your own learning style and use what works best for you! Some possibilities are: make vocabulary cards with Spanish on one side and English translations or a picture on the other, write the answers to all textbook exercises, say words aloud as you study them, use the tapes that go with the text at home, look at pictures in magazines or newspapers and try to describe them in Spanish.

4. Organize your study time. When planning your schedule, decide on a certain time to study Spanish each day and stick to it. If you miss a day, make it up! It is much easier to learn a foreign language in small segments each day, rather than trying to study an entire chapter in a few hours.

5. Participate! Create learning opportunities for yourself. Don't wait to be called on or until someone else in class takes the initiative. Be aggressive.

6. Don't panic because you don't know a particular word. Listen to what you do understand and guess at the unknown.

7. Draw on your own life experience. Listen to the context and try to anticipate what you will hear. For example, if talking about McDonald's, what would you expect the following to mean?

   hamburguesa **mostaza**
   lechuga **salsa de tomate**
   tomate **cebolla**
   mayonesa **patatas fritas**

8. Listen to Spanish radio and/or Spanish T.V. programs. Learn the lyrics to songs in Spanish you like, and be daring, get involved with one of the many soap operas, called **telenovelas,** currently being transmitted on T.V. in the United States.

9. When reading, don't expect to understand every word you see. You will often be asked to work with authentic materials, such as this advertisement, that clearly have some language that you can understand and some that you are not expected to know. Always focus on what you do know and use that information to make intelligent guesses at the words you do not know. For example, in this advertisement, you probably know the meaning of the five words that are repeated three times because they look very similar to their English equivalents. Beyond that, you probably recognize that a fax number is given and what are most likely two other phone numbers. All other information probably is not within reach for you at this time. That is perfectly okay. In the questions about a reading such as this, you might be asked to consider the information that is within reach and try to guess at the rest. The questions are likely to guide you toward correct answers, for example, you might be asked the following:

> The line below the title states that **DÓNDE** is **La llave maestra** or *the master key* to something. What do you think this master key opens? In English there is an expression that in Spanish would be **Las llaves de la ciudad.** What is the expression in English?

If you guessed that **DÓNDE** is the master key to Mexico City and that the English expression is *The keys to the city* you guessed correctly and should pat yourself on the back because you are already reading authentic materials in Spanish!

Working with *¡Dímelo tú!*

Discover for yourself how ***¡Dímelo tú!*** is organized and what the purpose of each section of the text is. Working in groups of four, look for the section titles in the pages indicated for each set and match them with their descriptions. Be prepared to explain to the class, with examples, the purpose of each section.

Set 1: Pages 27–29

1. Lo que ya sabes	a. *Samples of authentic language*
2. Paso 1	b. *Visual introduction to lesson theme*
3. Tarea	c. *Challenges your critical thinking skills*
4. ¿Eres buen observador?	d. *The first of three lessons that make up each chapter.*
5. ¿Qué se dice… ?	e. *Specifies homework assignments*

Set 2: Pages 30–32 and 38

6. ¿Sabías que… ?	f. *More creative, open-ended speaking activities*
7. A propósito…	g. *Controlled speaking activities for early production*
8. Ahora, ¡a hablar!	h. *Previews structures that will be taught later*
9. Y ahora, ¡a conversar!	i. *Role plays*
10. ¡Luz! ¡Cámara! ¡Acción!	j. *Cross-cultural information*

Set 3: Pages 32–35 and 42

11. ¿Comprendes lo que se dice?	k. *Short cultural reading*
12. Noticiero cultural	l. *Writing*
13. El español en otras disciplinas	m. *Prewriting activities*
14. Antes de escribir	n. *Interdisciplinary connections*
15. ¿Te gusta escribir?	o. *Listening activities*

Set 4: Pages 48–53

16. Antes de leer	p. *Provides grammar explanations*
17. ¿Te gusta leer?	q. *Internet activities*
18. Viajemos por el ciberespacio a…	r. *Prereading activities*
19. En preparación	s. *Practice grammar exercises for homework*
20. ¡A practicar!	t. *Chapter reading selection*

Useful Classroom Expressions

Following are three lists of useful classroom expressions that you should learn to recognize. The first list consists primarily of cognates. Guess the meaning of these expressions.

- Dramatiza esta situación.
- En tu opinión, ¿quién… ?
- No comprendo.
- Prepara una lista por escrito.
- Selecciona una respuesta apropiada.
- En grupos pequeños…

The meaning of these expressions is less obvious, although there are a couple of cognates. What are the three cognates? What do they mean? Match each expression with its translation.

1.	Comparte la información.	a.	*Read this advertisement.*
2.	Contesta la(s) pregunta(s).	b.	*Describe the drawing.*
3.	Escucha la conversación.	c.	*What do you do . . . ?*
4.	Lee este anuncio.	d.	*In pairs*
5.	Describe el dibujo.	e.	*Answer the question(s).*
6.	¿Qué haces… ?	f.	*Listen to the conversation.*
7.	En parejas	g.	*Share the information.*

The following three expressions all have the same cognate, **compañero**. What do you think it means? Why do you suppose there is an (**a**) after the word? The remaining words in these expressions mean *Interview, Ask,* and *Tell*, respectively. Can you guess what the complete expressions mean?

- Entrevista a un(a) compañero(a)...
- Pregúntale a un(a) compañero(a)...
- Dile a un(a) compañero(a)...

Cultural Topics

- **Noticiero cultural**
  Costumbres: *Saludos*

Writing Strategies

- Punctuation

En preparación

- PE.1 **Tú** and **Usted** and Titles of Address
- PE.2 The Spanish Alphabet and Pronunciation: Vowels and Diphthongs

Para empezar: Saludos, presentaciones y despedidas

In this chapter, you will learn how to ...

- greet people at different times of the day.
- introduce yourself and others.
- address people formally and informally.
- say good-bye in formal and informal situations.

Tres estudiantes saludándose en Guadalajara, México

Dos jóvenes se despiden en el campo de fútbol.

Dos hombres se dan la mano en Argentina.

Lo que ya sabes...

1. How do the students in the first photo greet each other? What similarities and differences with how you greet your friends do you observe?
2. Do you observe any differences in how the two men shake hands compared with how men in the United States shake hands? What are they?
3. How do you think the two men saying good-bye are going to wave their hands—up and down or from side to side? Why do you think that?

¡Hola! ¡Mucho gusto! ¡Adiós!

TAREA Before beginning this **Paso**, study **En preparación PE.1** and **PE.2**, and do the **¡A practicar!** exercises. Also listen to the **Paso modelo: ¿Qué se dice...?** on your Audio CD.

¿Eres buen observador?

Un beso al saludarse en México, D.F.

Dos jóvenes se dan la mano en Cuzco, Perú.

Ahora, ¡a analizar!

1. How do people in the U.S. greet each other in formal and informal situations? How do the Spanish-speaking people in the photos greet each other? What similarities and differences do you observe?
2. The men in the photo above are shaking hands. Why do you think that they do not extend their arm out as men in the United States do when shaking hands?
3. What are some gestures you use to say good-bye to your parents, relatives, friends, instructors?

¿Qué se dice...?

Al saludar / presentar / despedirse de una persona

Students' names: ____________________
____

"Hello." ____________________
"What's your name?" ____________________

ELVIRA	Hola, Carlos. ¿Cómo estás?
CARLOS	Bastante bien, ¿y tú?
ELVIRA	¡Excelente! Carlos, te presento a mi amigo Andrés.
CARLOS	Mucho gusto, Andrés.
ANDRÉS	Igualmente, Carlos.

GABRIEL	Profesor Gómez, le presento a mi amiga Teresa.
TERESA	Encantada, profesor.
PROFESOR	El gusto es mío, Teresa.

PROFESORA Buenas tardes.
MATÍAS Buenas tardes, profesora.
PROFESORA ¿Cómo se llama usted?
MATÍAS Matías Suárez. Y usted es la profesora Torres, ¿no?
PROFESORA Sí, soy Angélica Torres. Mucho gusto, Matías.
MATÍAS El gusto es mío, profesora Torres.

RAÚL ¿Qué tal, Mario?
MARIO Bien, Raúl, ¿y tú?
RAÚL No muy bien. No... ¡terrible!

SUSANA Hasta luego, Pepe.
PEPE Hasta pronto, Susana. Adiós, Lisa.
LISA Adiós. Hasta mañana.

A propósito...

Notice that when introducing a person who is a friend or family member you use **te presento**, but when introducing a person who is outside your circle of friends or family, such as your teachers, boss or manager, you use **le presento**.

Ahora, ¡a hablar!

A. Saludos, despedidas y respuestas. Selecciona una respuesta apropiada para cada saludo y despedida.

Modelo

TÚ **¡Hola!**
TU AMIGO(A) **Buenos días.**

Saludos	Respuestas	Despedidas	Respuestas
¿Qué tal?	¡Terrible!	Hasta la vista.	Hasta luego.
¿Cómo te llamas?	Me llamo Antonia.	Adiós.	Hasta pronto.
¿Cómo estás?	Buenas tardes.	Hasta pronto.	Adiós.
¡Hola!	Buenos días.	Hasta luego.	Hasta mañana.
Buenas tardes.	Bastante bien.	Hasta mañana.	Hasta la vista.
Buenos días.	Bien, gracias.		
	Muy bien, gracias.		
	Excelente.		

B. Un estudiante muy popular. ¿Cómo saludas a estas personas en la universidad? (*Role-play greeting these people with a classmate.*)

Modelo una amiga a las nueve (9:00) de la mañana

TÚ **¡Hola, Irene! ¿Cómo estás?**
AMIGA **Bien, ¿y tú?**
TÚ **Bastante bien.**

1. el profesor de español a las ocho (8:00) de la mañana
2. un amigo a las dos (2:00) de la tarde
3. una amiga a la una (1:00) de la tarde
4. un amigo en la clase de español
5. una amiga en la cafetería a las nueve (9:00) de la mañana
6. una profesora a las tres (3:00) de la tarde

C. Amigos nuevos. Pregúntales a tres (3) amigos nuevos cómo se escriben sus nombres.

Modelo

TÚ **¿Cómo se escribe tu nombre?**
AMIGO **S C O T T R A Y (ese, ce, o, te, te; ere, a, i griega)**

D. Presentaciones. Presenta a estas personas.

Modelo papá / profesora Luna
Papá, te presento a la profesora Luna.

1. profesor Durán / amigo John
2. amiga Carmen / amigo Matt
3. mamá / amiga Rosita
4. papá / señora Guzmán
5. profesor Trujillo / amigo José Antonio
6. mamá / profesora Franco

E. ¿Presentaciones o respuestas? Selecciona una respuesta apropiada para cada presentación. *(Then explain when you would use the remaining "respuestas.")*

Presentaciones	Respuestas	Presentaciones	Respuestas
Te presento a…	Igualmente.	Le presento a…	Mucho gusto.
	¡Encantada!		El gusto es mío.

Y ahora, ¡a conversar!

A. ¡Hola! Identifica a cuatro (4) personas que no conoces en la clase y preséntate. Escribe los nombres de las cuatro personas.

Modelo

TÚ	**¡Hola! Soy... ¿Cómo te llamas?**
COMPAÑERO(A)	**Me llamo Andrea Chávez.**
TÚ	**¿Cómo te escribe tu nombre?**
COMPAÑERO(A)	**A N D R E A C H A V E Z**
	(a, ene, de, ere, e, a; ce, hache, a, ve, e, zeta)

B. ¡Encantado(a)! Presenta a dos personas de la clase.

Modelo

TÚ	**Carlos, te presento a mi amiga Susana.**
CARLOS	**Mucho gusto, Susana.**
SUSANA	**Encantada.**

C. ¡Hasta mañana! Practica los saludos y las despedidas en español con tu profesor(a) y tus compañeros de clase todos los días. Usa varios saludos y despedidas.

¡Luz! ¡Cámara! ¡Acción!

A. Te presento a mi familia. Un amigo mexicano, Andrés Salazar, te presenta a su familia. Dramatiza esta situación con tres (3) compañeros de la clase. *(One plays the role of Andrés, the others of his parents. Take turns playing the different roles.)*

B. ¡Mi profesor(a)! Tú, tu papá y tu mamá están en la cafetería de la universidad. Tu profesor(a) de español también está. Tú decides presentar a tus padres a tu profesor. Dramatiza la situación con tres (3) compañeros de clase. *(Let your partners play the role of your parents and professor first. Then alternate roles.)*

¿Comprendes lo que se dice?

Estrategias para escuchar. *When listening to people speak, it is not necessary to understand every word spoken in order to comprehend the gist of what is being said. As you listen to these dialogues, don't worry if you do not understand every word. Simply try to understand enough to answer the questions below.*

¿Formal o informal? Escucha estos dos diálogos y luego selecciona la respuesta correcta a las preguntas que siguen.

1. ¿Cuál de las conversaciónes es más formal? ¿más informal?
   a. La conversación número 1.   b. La conversación número 2.
2. ¿Cómo se llama la amiga de Julio y Rubén?
3. En la conversación número 1, ¿son las personas estudiantes o profesores? ¿Y en la conversación número 2?

NOTICIERO CULTURAL

COSTUMBRES

Antes de empezar, dime...

1. ¿Qué saludos usas con tus amigos en inglés? ¿con tus profesores?
2. ¿Son idénticos o diferentes los saludos?
3. Si son diferentes, explica la diferencia.

Saludos. Julio Hurtado, un cubanoamericano, y Rick Henderson son estudiantes en la Universidad del Estado de Florida en Tallahassee. Rick está en la clase de Español 101 y practica español con su amigo Julio. Ellos conversan cuando el rector (presidente) de la universidad los saluda.

JULIO Buenas tardes, Rick. ¿Cómo estás?
RICK Muy bien, gracias. ¿Y tú?
JULIO Bastante bien. Ah, mira, el rector de la universidad.
RECTOR Buenas tardes, señores.
JULIO Buenas tardes, rector.
RICK Buenas tardes. Ahh,... ¿Cómo estás?
RECTOR ¿Qué? ¡Hmmm! ¡Adiós!

Y ahora, dime...

¿Por qué reacciona el rector negativamente al saludo de Rick?

1. Porque el saludo de Rick fue muy informal.
2. Porque el rector no tiene tiempo para hablar con Rick y Julio.
3. Porque Rick no habla español muy bien.

Lee el número que corresponde a la respuesta que seleccionaste en el Apéndice A.

Antes de escribir
Estrategias para escribir: Puntuación

¡Pobre Rick! Estudia la puntuación en este diálogo. ¿Es idéntica a la puntuación en inglés? Explica las diferencias.

NATALIA	¡Hola, Rick! ¿Cómo estás?
RICK	¿Qué tal, Natalia? No estoy muy bien.
NATALIA	¿No? ¿Por qué? ¿Qué te pasa?
RICK	¡El rector está furioso conmigo!

Ahora, ¡a escribir!

A. Al empezar. Prepárate para escribir un diálogo donde Julio le presenta a Rick el rector de la universidad en una recepción para estudiantes nuevos. Haz (*Make*) una lista del vocabulario que necesitas para escribir el diálogo.

B. El primer borrador. Prepara un primer borrador *(first draft)* de tu diálogo.

C. Ahora, a compartir. Comparte *(Share)* tu diálogo con dos o tres compañeros. Haz comentarios sobre el estilo y la estructura. ¿Es lógico el diálogo? ¿Es formal o informal la presentación? ¿Y cómo contesta Rick, formalmente o informalmente? ¿Hay errores de puntuación o de ortografía *(spelling)*?

D. Ahora, a revisar. Lee tu diálogo una vez más. Si necesitas hacer cambios basados en los comentarios de tus compañeros, hazlos ahora.

E. La versión final. Prepara una versión final de tu diálogo y entrégalo *(turn it in)*.

F. Publicación. En grupos de 4 ó 5 lean los diálogos corregidos que su profesor(a) les da *(gives you)* y decidan cuál es el mejor *(best)*. Prepárense para hacer una lectura dramatizada del mejor diálogo en su grupo.

Vocabulario

Saludos y respuestas

Buenos días.	*Good morning.*
Buenas tardes.	*Good afternoon.*
Buenas noches.	*Good evening.*
¿Cómo estás?	*How are you? (fam.)*
¡Hola!	*Hello!*
¿Qué tal?	*How are you?*
Bastante bien.	*Well enough.*
Bien, gracias.	*Fine, thank you.*
¡Excelente!	*Excellent!*
Muy bien, gracias.	*Fine, thank you.*
No muy bien.	*Not very well.*
¡Terrible!	*Terrible!*

Presentaciones y respuestas

¿Cómo se llama usted?	*What's your name? (form.)*
¿Cómo te llamas?	*What's your name? (fam.)*
Me llamo…	*My name is . . .*
Mi nombre es…	*My name is . . .*
Te presento a…	*I'd like you to meet . . . (fam.)*
Le presento a…	*I'd like you to meet. . . (form.)*
El gusto es mío.	*The pleasure is mine.*
Encantado(a).	*Delighted.*
Igualmente.	*Likewise.*
Mucho gusto.	*Pleased to meet you.*

Despedidas y respuestas

Adiós.	*Good-bye.*
Hasta la vista.	*Good-bye. See you.*
Hasta luego.	*See you later.*
Hasta mañana.	*See you tomorrow.*
Hasta pronto.	*See you soon.*

Universitarios

amigo(a)	*friend*
compañero(a) de cuarto	*roommate*
estudiante	*student*
profesor(a)	*professor*
rector	*president (of a university)*

Palabras y expresiones útiles

clase	*class*
conversación	*conversation*
mi	*my*
no	*no*
soy	*I am*
tú	*you (fam.)*
universidad	*university*
¿Y tú?	*And you?*
¿Yo?	*Me? (In all other instances* **yo = I***)*

En preparación PE

PE.1 *Tú* and *Usted* and Titles of Address

Addressing people

A. *TÚ* and *USTED*

Spanish has two ways of expressing *you:* **tú** and **usted. Tú** is a familiar form generally used among peers, acquaintances, or friends. **Usted** is a more polite, formal form used to show respect and to address anyone with a title such as Mr., Mrs., Ms. or Miss, Dr., Prof., or Rev. It is also used to address individuals you do not know well. Students generally use **tú** when speaking to each other and **usted** when addressing their teachers. Note that in the **¿Qué se dice…?** section, **te llamas** and **estás** are in the familiar **tú** form and **se llama** and **está** are in the more polite, formal **usted** form.

¡A practicar!

¿Tú o usted? Indicate whether you should use **tú** or **usted** to address the following people.

1. your professor
2. your brothers and sisters
3. a stranger
4. your dog
5. your clergyman
6. your roommate
7. your doctor
8. your girlfriend / boyfriend
9. a bank clerk
10. a waitress

B. Titles of Address

The most frequently used titles in Spanish are

señor	*Mr.*	profesor(a)	*professor*
señora	*Mrs.*	doctor(a)	*doctor*
señorita	*Miss*		

The definite article, **el** or **la,** must precede a title when talking about someone.

Es la doctora Sánchez.	*She is Dr. Sánchez.*
El profesor Díaz es bueno.	*Professor Díaz is good.*

¡A practicar!

¿El o la? Complete the following introductions by indicating if a definite article should be used with each person's name as you introduce the people to your mother.

Modelo Mamá, __________ señor Pérez y mi amigo __________ José.
Mamá, el señor Pérez y mi amigo José.

1. Mamá, mi amiga ______________ Rosa María.
2. Mamá, ______________ profesor González.
3. Mamá, ______________ señorita Perea, la directora del laboratorio.
4. Mamá, *(name)* ______________ mi mejor *(best)* amigo(a).
5. Mamá, ______________ señor Padilla.
6. Mamá, ______________ José Aguilar.

PE.2 The Spanish Alphabet and Pronunciation

Spelling and forming vowel sounds

The Spanish Alphabet

a	a	k	ka	rr	erre
b	be, be larga	l	ele	s	ese
c	ce	m	eme	t	te
d	de	n	ene	u	u
e	e	ñ	eñe	v	ve, ve corta, uve
f	efe	o	o	w	doble ve, uve doble
g	ge	p	pe	x	equis
h	hache	q	cu	y	i griega
i	i	r	ere	z	zeta
j	jota				

The Spanish alphabet includes two letters that are not part of the English alphabet: **ñ** and **rr**. The **ch** and **ll** were considered single letters in the alphabet until 1994 when the **Real Academia** decided to eliminate them to accommodate the computer age. The letters **k** and **w** appear only in words borrowed from other languages. Learn the Spanish alphabet so that you can spell words in Spanish.

¡A practicar!

A. ¡Ahora el examen de la vista! You are getting your driver's license renewed. Take the eye test for your license. What do you say?

E

c n d

z m o p h

m r l y x v u w

a l j g s a ñ h rr f z b i

B. Su nombre completo, por favor. You are on the phone with your local bank and want to know the current balance in your checking account. The bank teller asks you to spell out your name, as it appears on your account, and your mother's maiden name. First, write them out. Then spell them in Spanish.

Modelo You write: **J O E S M I T H**
You say: **jota, o, e; ese, eme, i, te, hache**

Pronunciation: Vowels

The Spanish vowels—**a, e, i, o, u**—are pronounced in a short, clear, and tense manner. Unlike English vowels, their sound is hardly influenced by their position in a word or sentence, nor by the stress they receive. English speakers must avoid the tendency to lengthen and change the sound of Spanish vowels. Note the difference in length and sound as you recite the vowels in English first and then repeat them after your instructor in Spanish.

¡A practicar!

A. Las vocales. Repeat the following sounds after your instructor, being careful to keep the vowels short and tense.

a = *hop*	e = *hep*	i = *heep*	o = *hope*	u = *hoop*
ma	me	mi	mo	mu
na	ne	ni	no	nu
sa	se	si	so	su
fa	fe	fi	fo	fu

Very few sounds are identical in Spanish and English. Therefore, the comparisons given here between English and Spanish vowels are to be used merely as a point of reference. To develop "native" pronunciation, you should listen carefully and imitate your instructor's pronunciation and that of the native speakers on the recordings.

B. Vocales en palabras. Escucha y repite. *(Listen and repeat.)*

Ana	él	ir	otro	uno
llama	mente	así, así	como	gusto
mañana	excelente	dividir	ojo	Uruguay

C. Vocales en oraciones. Lee en voz alta. *(Read aloud.)*

1. Ana llama a la mamá de Carmen mañana .
2. Elena es de Venezuela.
3. Gullón es otro crítico literario famoso.
4. La profesora Uribe es una mujer uruguaya.

Pronunciation: Diphthongs

A diphthong is the union of two vowel sounds pronounced as one in a single syllable. In Spanish, diphthongs occur in syllables containing two weak vowels **(i, u)** or a combination of a strong vowel **(a, e, o)** with a weak vowel.

¡A practicar!

A. Diptongos. In diphthongs consisting of a strong vowel and a weak vowel, the strong vowels are more heavily stressed.

Escucha y repite.

ai	**ei**	**oi**	**ia**	**ie**	**io**
baile	ley	soy	gracias	bien	Mario
airoso	afeitar	oigo	especial	viejo	diosa
gaita	veinte	Goytisolo	Colombia	miedoso	miope

ua	**ue**	**au**	**eu**
Paraguay	buenas	auto	Eugenia
Ecuador	cuentista	Paula	Europa
lengua	abuelo	pausar	deuda

B. Dos vocales débiles. When two weak vowels occur together in a word, the emphasis falls on the second vowel.

Escucha y repite.

ui	**iu**
ruido	veintiuno
Luisa	viuda
cuidar	ciudad

C. Dos sílabas. When two strong vowels occur together, or when there is a written accent over the weak vowel in a syllable containing both a strong and a weak vowel, the vowels are pronounced as two separate syllables.

Escucha y repite.

caos	idea	día	baúl
leal	crear	lío	paraíso
cacao	Rafael	comían	continúa

D. Diptongos en oraciones. Lee en voz alta.

1. Luisa baila muy bien.
2. Eugenio y Mario viajan a la ciudad.
3. Mi tía siempre viene a las cuatro.
4. Hay nueve nuevos estudiantes.

CAPÍTULO 1

Cultural Topics

- **¿Sabías que… ?**
  Comparison of U.S. and Hispanic universities: *La semana universitaria*
- **Noticiero cultural**
  Lugar: *Un viaje por las Américas*
  Costumbres: *¿Peruano, venezolano o guatemalteco?*
- **Lectura:** *Para una educación única... UNITEC*

Writing Strategies

- Listing

Reading Strategies

- Recognizing Cognates

En preparación

- 1.1 Subject Pronouns and the Verb **ser:** Singular Forms
- 1.2 Gender and Number: Articles and Nouns
- 1.3 Adjectives: Singular Forms
- 1.4 Infinitives
- 1.5 Subject Pronouns and the Verb **ser:** Plural Forms
- 1.6 Gender and Number: Adjectives
- 1.7 Present Tense of **-ar** Verbs
- 1.8 The Verb **ir**

¡Bienvenidos a la universidad!

In this chapter, you will learn how to . . .

- *describe yourself, your friends, and your professors.*
- *tell where people are from.*
- *name your favorite classes and activities.*
- *describe your classes.*
- *talk about your activities during the first week of the semester.*

La Universidad de Salamanca, España, fundada en 1215

La Universidad Nacional Autónoma de México (UNAM), México, D. F., fundada en 1553

La Universidad de Santo Domingo, República Dominicana, fundada en 1538

Lo que ya sabes...

1. How many years after the arrival of Christopher Columbus was the first university in the New World established? Where is it located?
2. When was the first university in the continental United States established?
3. When was your university established?
4. Name three universities that, in your opinion, are the most important in the United States. Which is the most important in your state?
5. How does your campus compare with the ones pictured here?

LAS AMÉRICAS

¿Mi compañero de cuarto?

TAREA Before beginning this **Paso**, study **En preparación** 1.1, 1.2, and 1.3, and do the **¡A practicar!** exercises. Also listen to the **Paso 1 ¿Qué se dice... ?** on your Audio CD.

¿Eres buen observador?

NOMBRE: Yolanda Ramírez
PAÍS DE ORIGEN: Costa Rica
DEPORTES FAVORITOS: béisbol y voleibol
PERSONALIDAD: simpática, inteligente, sociable
CIUDAD NATAL: San José

NOMBRE: Mónica Fernández
PAÍS DE ORIGEN: Chile
DEPORTES FAVORITOS: tenis y baloncesto
PERSONALIDAD: elegante, seria, paciente
CIUDAD NATAL: Santiago

NOMBRE: Carlos Enrique Rodríguez
PAÍS DE ORIGEN: México
DEPORTES FAVORITOS: fútbol, béisbol, tenis
PERSONALIDAD: inteligente, atlético, paciente, sincero, popular, sociable
CIUDAD NATAL: Guadalajara

Ahora, ¡a analizar!

1. ¿De dónde son estos estudiantes?
2. ¿Cuáles son los deportes favoritos de Yolanda? ¿de Mónica? ¿de Carlos?
3. ¿Cómo es Carlos? ¿Mónica? ¿Yolanda?
4. ¿Es norteamericano Carlos? ¿Mónica? ¿Yolanda?

¿Qué se dice...?

Al describir a nuevos amigos

Origen: ______________________

Universidad: ______________________

Personalidad de Julio: ______________________

de Matón: ______________________

Te quiero presentar a mi amigo Paco. Es de España, de Salamanca. Es estudiante de la Universidad de Salamanca. Es interesante y muy simpático... y algo liberal. También es atlético.

Te quiero presentar a Elena. Ella es una amiga de Venezuela, de Caracas. Ella es elegante, seria y muy paciente. Es también un poco conservadora.

ELENA Allí, mira. Es el libro de español, ¿no?
JULIO Sí, y aquí también hay cuadernos, papel, lápices y bolígrafos... y lo más importante, mochilas.

¿Y tú? ¿Cómo te llamas?
¿De dónde eres? ¿Eres norteamericano(a)?
¿Eres estudiante? ¿De qué universidad?
¿Eres inteligente y estudioso(a)?
¿Eres conservador(a) o liberal? ¿paciente o impaciente?
¿Eres muy popular?

A propósito...

The verb **hay** has only one form which means *there is* and *there are*. When used in a question, **¿Hay... ?** means *Is there . . . ?* or *Are there . . . ?* Be careful not to confuse it with **ser** which, when conjugated, means *is* or *are*.

Ahora, ¡a hablar!

A. Mi mejor amigo(a). Describe a tu mejor amigo(a).

Mi mejor amigo(a) se llama (*nombre*). Él (Ella) es (inteligente / tonto). También es (liberal / conservador). Es (paciente / impaciente) y muy (popular / tímido). Ah, también es un poco (serio / divertido).

B. ¡Qué popular! Pablo Ramírez es muy popular y tiene muchas amigas. ¿Cómo son sus amigas? Selecciona las palabras (*words*) que las describen.

1. Ramona es (estudiosa, tímido, serio).
2. María es (romántico, simpática, serio).
3. Gloria es (tímido, tonto, atlética).
4. Ángela es (elegante, estupendo, conservador).
5. Carmen es (inteligente, atlético, serio).
6. Cecilia es (simpática, interesante, tonto).

C. ¿Muchos? Nombra todos los objetos en...

1. tu escritorio.
2. tu mochila.
3. el escritorio del (de la) profesor(a).
4. el escritorio de un(a) amigo(a).

D. ¿Quién es y de dónde es? ¿Quiénes son estos estudiantes y de dónde son?

Modelo Antonio Pino Quintana, Lima

Él es Antonio Pino Quintana. Es del Perú.

1. Carlos Menéndez Suárez, Madrid
2. Patricio Carrillo Sánchez, Bogotá
3. Ramona Téllez Baca, Montevideo
4. Jorge Castillo Díaz, Santiago
5. Emma Luna Linares, Managua
6. Andrés Salazar Trujillo, San Juan
7. Lupita López Chávez, Quito

E. Diversidad. Pregúntale a tu compañero(a) cómo son estos estudiantes.

Modelo Lupita López / inteligente / conservador

COMPAÑERO(A) **¿Cómo es Lupita López?**

TÚ **¿Ella? Es muy inteligente y conservadora.**

1. Jorge / impaciente / activo
2. Yolanda / serio / estudioso
3. Paco / inteligente / trabajador
4. Ramona / inteligente / simpático
5. Andrés / tímido / serio
6. Eva / activo / divertido
7. Yo / ¿... y... ?
8. Tú / ¿... y... ?

Y ahora, ¡a conversar!

A. ¿Quién es? Identifica a personas famosas (políticos, actores, artistas, deportistas, cómicos, etc.) con las características indicadas.

Modelo **Jim Carrey es muy divertido.**

1. muy divertido
2. elegante y conservador
3. tímido
4. muy serio
5. muy atlético
6. muy divertida
7. elegante y conservadora
8. tímida
9. muy seria
10. muy atlética

B. ¿Qué hay? Pregunta lo que hay en la mochila (o en el escritorio en casa) de tu compañero(a).

Modelo

TÚ **¿Hay un lápiz?**

COMPAÑERO(A) **Sí, hay un lápiz.** o

No, hay un lápiz.

C. ¿Son los mismos? Alicia, Carmen, José y Daniel son estudiantes de la clase de español de tu compañero de cuarto. Tú tienes unos amigos que se llaman Alicia, Carmen, José y Daniel. La descripción de tus amigos aparece (*appears*) la siguiente página. La descripción de los amigos de tu compañero aparece en el apéndice A. ¿Son los mismos? *(To decide if they are the same, ask your partner questions. Do not look at each other's descriptions until you have finished this activity.)*

Modelo **¿Es Alicia de Venezuela?**

Alicia Es una amiga venezolana. Es de Caracas. Es estudiosa, tímida y muy seria. También es muy paciente.

Carmen Es muy seria. También es tímida, inteligente y muy estudiosa. Es de Caracas. Es sociable pero algo conservadora.

José Es de Quito. Es muy activo y muy simpático. Es sociable y chistoso. No es muy serio.

Daniel Es del Ecuador, de la capital. Es muy atlético, pero es un poco tímido. Es activo y estudioso. También es algo serio.

D. ¡Anuario! ¿Cómo eres tú? Prepara una descripción de tu persona por escrito. Usa el modelo del **¿Eres buen observador?** de este **Paso**.

¡Luz! ¡Cámara! ¡Acción!

A. ¿Cómo es? Hay un estudiante latinoamericano en la clase de historia de tu compañero(a) de cuarto. Pregúntale a tu compañero(a)...

- el nombre del estudiante.
- el país y la ciudad de origen del estudiante.
- algunas características del estudiante.
- qué hay en la mochila del estudiante.
- la opinión de tu compañero(a) del estudiante.

B. Mejor amigo(a). ¿Cómo es el (la) mejor amigo(a) de tu compañero(a): nombre, origen, universidad y características? Pregúntale.

¿Comprendes lo que se dice?

Estrategias para escuchar. *A frequent first reaction when listening to spoken Spanish is to assume it is spoken "too fast" and that you "don't understand anything." In fact, it is probably being spoken at a normal rate of speech and you probably understand much more than you think. Most likely, you won't understand every word you hear, but you are not expected to do so. Simply listen for those words that you do understand and don't worry about the others. In this section, you should understand enough to get the gist of what is being said.*

Now listen as your instructor plays a dialogue in which Gloria and Rita talk about Alberto Lozano, a new student in their chemistry class. Then answer the questions that follow.

¿Cómo es Alberto Lozano según Rita? ¿según Gloria?

Según Rita:	Según Gloria:
1.	1.
2.	2.
3.	3.

NOTICIERO CULTURAL

LUGAR... LAS AMÉRICAS

Antes de empezar, dime...

1. ¿Cuáles son tres países de Norteamérica?
2. En tu opinión, ¿cuáles son los tres sitios naturales más impresionantes de Norteamérica?
3. En tu opinión, en toda la historia de Norteamérica, ¿quiénes fueron los indígenas más importantes?

Las Américas

El continente de América se divide en América del Norte, América Central y América del Sur. El continente ofrece muchos contrastes naturales como, por ejemplo...

hermosas costas y playas como ésta en Cancún, . . .

una gran variedad de aves como este hermoso quetzal. . .

e impresionantes lagos y volcanes.

También hay ruinas del glorioso pasado indígena, como...

las ruinas mayas en el sur de México y Centroamérica y. . .

las ruinas incaicas del Perú, como éstas de Machu Picchu.

Los contrastes se reflejan también en la gente de las Américas, como...

los indígenas: aztecas, toltecas, mayas, taínos, quechuas, araucanos y muchos más;

los de descendencia europea: los españoles, italianos, alemanes, portugueses,...

y la nueva raza, los mestizos: la combinación de indígena y europeo.

Y ahora, dime...

1. Con España y Guinea Ecuatorial, hay 21 países donde el español es la lengua oficial del país. Nómbralos.
2. Hay muchos contrastes en las Américas. ¿Cuáles son los más impresionantes, en tu opinión?

El español en otras disciplinas: Geografía

Las Américas. Los estudiantes en los Estados Unidos con frecuencia saben muy poco de geografía. Para mostrar (*To show*) que están bien informados de la geografía del mundo (*world*) hispano, formen grupos de cuatro y túrnense (*take turns*) en nombrar la capital o el país de estas naciones y ciudades hispanas.

1. Buenos Aires
2. La Paz
3. Colombia
4. Costa Rica
5. Cuba
6. Santiago
7. Ecuador
8. San Salvador
9. Estados Unidos
10. Guatemala
11. Tegucigalpa
12. México
13. Nicaragua
14. Panamá
15. Asunción
16. Lima
17. Santo Domingo
18. Uruguay
19. Venezuela
20. España
21. Puerto Rico

Proyecto: *Using the maps in the front of the book, draw outline maps of North America, Central America and the Caribbean, and South America. Label each map with the names of the countries and their capitals. Draw a star to show the approximate correct location of each capital. Memorize the names and location of all the countries and capitals and be prepared to label outline maps of North, Central, and South America on the chapter exam.*

¡Son estupendos!

TAREA Antes de empezar este **Paso,** estudia **En preparación** 1.4, 1.5, y 1.6, y haz por escrito los ejercicios de **¡A practicar!** También escucha el **Paso 1 ¿Qué se dice... ?** del Capítulo 1 en el CD.

¿Eres buen observador?

Ahora, ¡a analizar!

You are not expected to understand every word you see on this advertisement. Simply focus on cognates, words that look alike in both Spanish and English. By doing this, you should be able to get the gist of the message and answer the questions that follow. Then pat yourself on the back! You are already reading authentic documents after just a couple of weeks of studying Spanish!

1. ¿Cómo se llama la universidad?
2. En tu opinión, ¿qué significa «Licenciaturas»?
3. ¿Cuántos de los programas que ofrece esta universidad puedes *(can you)* nombrar en inglés?
4. Explica las actividades del 25 y del 27 de abril.

Licenciaturas en la Anáhuac:

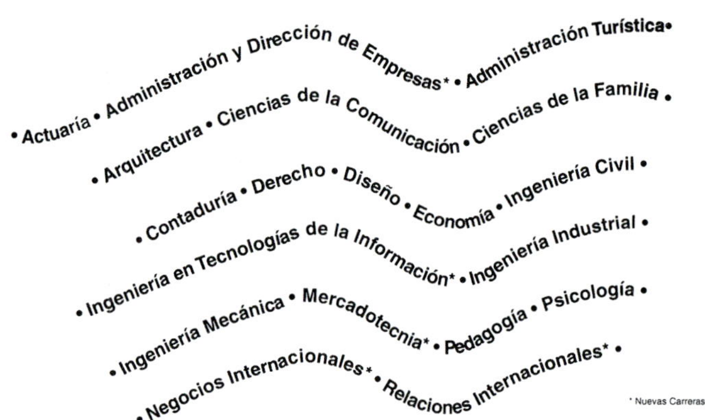

Proceso de admisión:
Examen Orientación Vocacional:
25 de Abril
Prueba de Aptitud Académica:
27 de Abril

Entregar los siguientes documentos en el Departamento de Admisiones: Solicitud de admisión, 6 fotos tamaño infantil, copia de acta de nacimiento y copia del certificado de preparatoria o constancia académica con promedio final.

Fortaleciéndonos para fortalecer tu futuro

Informes Dpto. de Atención Preuniversitaria Universidad Anáhuac Norte, Av. Lomas Anáhuac S/N, Lomas Anáhuac, C.P. 52760. Tels.: 328-80-12 ó 627-02-10 ext. 8238.

¿Qué se dice...?

Al hablar de las clases y los profesores

Personalidad del profesor González: ______________________

____

Mis pasatiempos favoritos: ______________________

____

La clase de física no es fácil; es muy difícil.

Los estudiantes en la clase de ciencias políticas son trabajadores y muy estudiosos. No son perezosos.

¿Sabías que... ?

In Spanish, universities are headed by a **rector**, not a **presidente**. The various schools, such as the School of Engineering, are called **facultades**. The faculty of a university is referred to as **el profesorado**. Finally, **colegio** does not mean *college* but *school,* as in elementary or secondary school.

Ahora, ¡a hablar!

A. ¿Cómo son? Describe tus clases, profesores y amigos.

Modelo mis clases (divertido / aburrido)
Mis clases son divertidas.

1. mis clases (difícil / fácil)
2. los estudiantes (interesante / aburrido)
3. los profesores (paciente / impaciente)
4. unos profesores (divertido / aburrido)
5. mis amigos y yo (trabajador / perezoso)
6. mis amigos (inteligente / tonto)

B. Amigos. Describe a tus amigos de la universidad.

Modelo Mi amigo…
Mi amigo Tomás es divertido y perezoso.

1. Mi amiga…
2. Mi amigo…
3. Mis amigos… y…
4. Mis amigas… y…
5. Mis compañeros de la clase de español…
6. Mis compañeros de la clase de…

C. Mis clases. ¿Cómo son las clases de tu compañero(a)? Pregúntale cuál es su clase…

Modelo más divertida

TÚ **¿Cuál es tu clase más divertida?**
COMPAÑERO(A) **Economía es la clase más divertida.**

Vocabulario útil

arte	economía	francés	inglés	matemáticas
biología	educación física	historia	latín	química
ciencias políticas	física	ingeniería	literatura	teatro

1. favorita
2. más interesante

3. más fácil
4. más difícil
5. más aburrida
6. más divertida

D. ¡Somos muy activos! ¿Cuál es el pasatiempo (la actividad) favorito(a) de estas personas?

Modelo Silvia y Andrea / bailar
El pasatiempo favorito de Silvia y Andrea es bailar.

1. Roberto / hablar por teléfono
2. Lupe y Alfredo / nadar
3. Patricia / escuchar música
4. Cristina / ver la tele
5. José Antonio / estudiar español
6. mis amigos y yo / comer
7. Jaime y Héctor / leer
8. Oscar / comprar discos compactos

Y ahora, ¡a conversar!

A. ¡Son estupendos! Describe a estas personas y estas clases. Menciona tres o cuatro características.

1. mi clase de español
2. mi compañero(a) de cuarto y yo
3. mis amigos
4. mi novio(a)
5. mis profesores
6. la clase de historia

B. Pasatiempos favoritos. ¿Cuáles son los pasatiempos favoritos de tu compañero(a)? Pregúntale y contesta sus preguntas.

Modelo

TÚ **¿Cuáles son tus pasatiempos favoritos?**
COMPAÑERO(A) **Mis pasatiempos favoritos son…**

Vocabulario útil

bailar	escuchar música	leer
comer	estudiar	nadar
escribir cartas	hablar por teléfono	ver la tele

C. Mis clases y yo. ¿Cómo eres tú? ¿Cuáles son dos adjetivos que describen tu personalidad? ¿Cuáles son tus clases favoritas? Escríbelos *(Write them down)*.

D. ¡A escribir! Completa este formulario con tus datos (información) personales.

Nombre: ______________________________

Dirección: ______________________________

Edad: ______________________________

Características: ______________________________

____

Pasatiempos: ______________________________

____

Clase favorita: ______________________________

¡Luz! ¡Cámara! ¡Acción!

A. Nuevos amigos. Es el primer día de clases y tú te presentas a nuevos amigos en la clase de español. Dramatiza la situación con un(a) compañero(a).

Tú	**Nuevo(a) amigo(a)**
■ Saluda a tu nuevo(a) amigo(a) y preséntate.	■ Responde y preséntate también. Pregunta de dónde es.
■ Contesta y pregunta de dónde es él o ella.	■ Menciona de dónde eres tú.
■ Pregunta sobre sus pasatiempos favoritos.	■ Describe tus pasatiempos favoritos y pregunta sobre sus pasatiempos.
■ Responde y pregunta cuál es su clase favorita.	■ Responde y pregunta cuál es su clase favorita.

B. Mi universidad. Tú y un(a) amigo(a) describen sus universidades: los profesores, sus nuevos amigos y las clases. Dramatiza esta situación.

¿Comprendes lo que se dice?

Estrategias para ver y escuchar. *Remember that you are not expected to understand every word you hear. Just listen for those words that are familiar to you and try to get the gist of the message using the visual images on the screen. Then answer the questions that follow.*

1. ¿Qué es **Decuador**?
2. ¿Qué es lo especial de este producto?
3. ¿Cómo es **Decuador**?
4. ¿De dónde es **Decuador**?
5. ¿Porqué es interesante el nombre del producto?

NOTICIERO CULTURAL

COSTUMBRES... LAS AMÉRICAS

Antes de empezar, dime...

1. ¿Qué tipo de inglés hablan en los Estados Unidos?
2. ¿Cuál es la diferencia entre el inglés de Texas y el inglés de Boston o el inglés de otras partes de los Estados Unidos?
3. ¿Qué problemas de comunicación hay entre personas que hablan el inglés de Texas y el de Boston? Explica.

¿Peruano, venezolano o guatemalteco?

Dos estudiantes en una clase de español en Dallas, Texas, conversan sobre sus futuras vacaciones en tres diferentes países de Sudamérica y Centroamérica.

PATRICIA ¿Qué tipo de español hablan en el Perú? ¿y en Venezuela? ¿y en Guatemala?

CAROL Probablemente hablan peruano, venezolano y guatemalteco.

PATRICIA ¡Ay! En la clase no hablamos ni peruano, ni venezolano ni guatemalteco. ¿Cómo vamos a hablar con la gente?

Y ahora, dime...

¿Cómo van a hablar Patricia y Carol con la gente del Perú, Venezuela y Guatemala?

1. En inglés porque todo el mundo (*everyone*) habla inglés.
2. Es imposible porque el español de la clase no es como el español del Perú, Venezuela y Guatemala.
3. Fácilmente porque el español de la clase es como el español del Perú, Venezuela y Guatemala.

Verifica (*Check*) si seleccionaste la respuesta correcta en el Apéndice A.

Antes de escribir
Estrategias para escribir: Sacar listas

Prepárate para escribir. Prepara una lista de las características de un estudiante perfecto.

Vocabulario útil

aburrido	divertido	liberal	simpático
activo	estudioso	paciente	tímido
atlético	impaciente	popular	trabajador
conservador	inteligente	romántico	
difícil	interesante	serio	

Ahora, ¡a escribir!

A. El primer borrador. Prepara una lista de todas las características del (de la) «amigo(a) ideal». ¿Eres tú un(a) amigo(a) ideal? Indica con una marca (√) todas las características que ya tienes (*already have*). Indica con un signo interrogativo (?) las características que no deseas tener (*you do not wish to have*). Indica con un asterisco (*) todas las características que deseas desarrollar (*to develop*).

B. Ahora, a compartir. Compara tu lista con las listas de dos o tres compañeros.

C. Ahora, a revisar. Lee tu lista una vez más. *(Make any changes you wish to make based on what you saw on your classmates' lists. Also, correct any spelling errors you may have noticed.)*

D. La versión final. Prepara una versión final de tu lista y entrégala (*turn it in*).

E. Publicación. Tu profesor(a) va a poner todas las listas en la pared (*wall*) para que tú y tus compañeros de clase decidan si eres un(a) amigo(a) ideal o no.

¡La clave es la organización!

TAREA

Antes de empezar este **Paso,** estudia **En preparación** 1.7 y 1.8 y haz por escrito los ejercicios de **¡A practicar!** También escucha el **Paso 3 ¿Qué se dice... ?** del Capítulo 1 en el CD.

¿Eres buen observador?

En el
CENTRO CULTURAL UNIVERSITARIO
JUSTO SIERRA

PREPARATORIA
ELIGE TU PLANTEL

Contamos con LICENCIATURAS EN:

- Administración • Contaduría
- Derecho • Diseño Gráfico
- Relaciones Industriales
- Ciencias de la Comunicación
- Administración y Finanzas
- Sistemas Computacionales
- Estomatología (Cirujano Dentista)
- Médico Cirujano • Psicología
- Informática • Turismo

Unidad de Lenguas Extranjeras

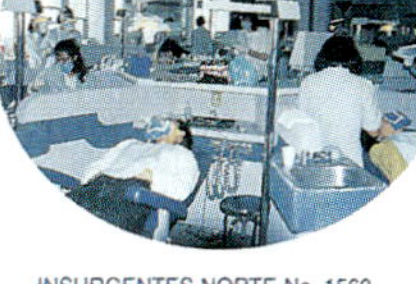
INICIAMOS SEPTIEMBRE

Av. Acueducto 914 casi esq. Avenida IPN
Col. Laguna Ticomán C.P. 07340, México D.F.
Tels. 754-66-77 752- 07-81 752-50-43
FAX 752-59-31

INSURGENTES NORTE No. 1560
COL. LINDAVISTA
TEL. 577-34-00 577-34-04

Ahora, ¡a analizar!

1. ¿Cómo se llama la universidad?
2. ¿Cuál es el significado de «licenciatura»?
3. ¿Cuáles de las licenciaturas mencionadas puedes nombrar en inglés? ¿Cuáles no sabes qué son?
4. ¿Te interesan algunas de estas licenciaturas? ¿Cuáles?
5. ¿Cuándo empiezan las clases? ¿Cuántos planteles (*campuses*) hay?
6. ¿Es posible comunicarse con todos los planteles por fax? Explica.

¿Qué se dice...?

Al describir actividades

Dormitory: ____________________

Nombres: ____________________

____

____

Actividad: ____________________

Ricardo y Hugo miran su programa favorito en la tele. Hugo toma un refresco. Ricardo prepara la cena, unas hamburguesas muy buenas. ¡Mmm!

Mari Carmen escucha unos discos nuevos mientras Cristina y Bárbara bailan con la música.

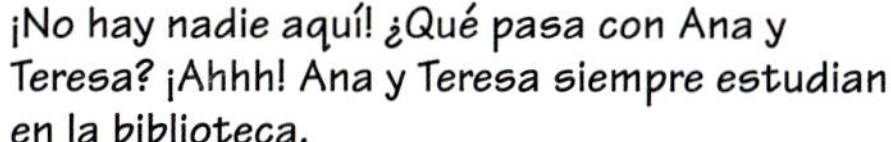

¡No hay nadie aquí! ¿Qué pasa con Ana y Teresa? ¡Ahhh! Ana y Teresa siempre estudian en la biblioteca.

Alfonso escucha la radio y Daniel estudia para un examen.

¿Sabías que... ?

Muchas universidades latinoamericanas celebran **la semana universitaria**—la última semana del primer mes de clases. Durante esta semana hay distintas actividades para los estudiantes cada día. Un día se dedica a practicar deportes, otro a asistir al teatro o a un concierto, otro día se dedica a hacer actividades benévolas, como visitar a personas en hospitales y asilos de ancianos (*rest homes*), otro a participar en actividades juveniles y el último día hay un baile en honor de la estudiante nombrada reina (*queen*) de **la semana universitaria**. El propósito (la razón) de todas estas actividades es recibir a los estudiantes nuevos e iniciarlos en la vida universitaria.

Ahora, ¡a hablar!

A. ¡Qué ocupado estoy! ¿Qué haces la primera semana de clases?

Modelo hablar / con amigos
Hablo con amigos.

1. buscar / mis clases
2. escuchar / a los profesores
3. comprar / los materiales
4. llamar / a mis padres
5. estudiar / las lecciones
6. hablar / con los profesores
7. tomar café / en la cafetería
8. preparar / la cena

B. ¡Tanto que hacer! Al final del primer día de clases, ¿qué hacen tú y tus nuevos amigos?

Modelo yo / llamar a mis padres
Llamo a mis padres.

1. mis amigos y yo / hablar
2. nosotros / escuchar la radio
3. un(a) compañero(a) de cuarto / mirar la tele
4. una amiga / estudiar
5. yo / bailar

6. mis compañeros(as) de cuarto / preparar la cena
7. ellos / tomar café con mis amigos
8. ellos(as) / tomar refrescos

C. ¿Adónde vas? Pregúntale a tu compañero(a) adónde va si necesita hacer estas cosas.

Modelo comprar cuadernos

TÚ **¿Adónde vas si necesitas comprar cuadernos?**
COMPAÑERO(A) **Si necesito comprar cuadernos, voy a la librería.**

1. tomar café
2. estudiar
3. escuchar cintas en español
4. comer
5. comprar lápices
6. escribir cartas

D. ¿Con qué frecuencia? Pregúntale a tu compañero(a) con qué frecuencia hace estas cosas.

Modelo llamar a tus padres

TÚ **¿Con qué frecuencia llamas a tus padres?**
COMPAÑERO(A) **Llamo a mis padres a veces.** o
Llamo a mis padres todos los días. o
Nunca llamo a mis padres.

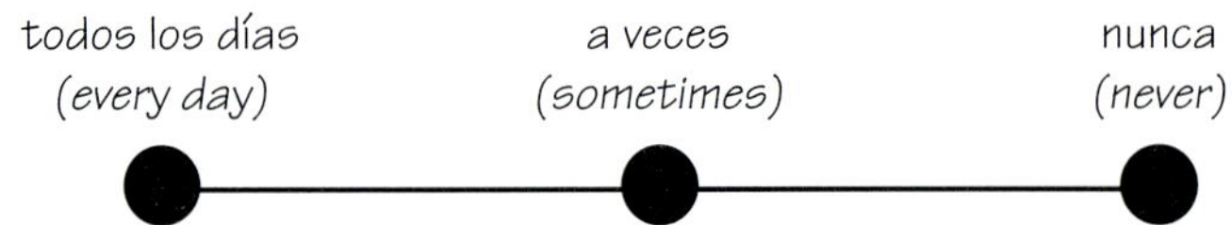

1. hablar por teléfono
2. escuchar a los profesores
3. comprar libros
4. ir a la biblioteca
5. estudiar mucho
6. mirar la tele
7. bailar con amigos

Y ahora, ¡a conversar!

A. ¡Fin de semana! Es el fin de semana y tú y un(a) amigo(a) hablan de sus planes. ¿Qué dicen?

Modelo **Por la mañana yo voy a tomar café con mis amigos. Luego voy a la librería para comprar…**

B. ¿Cierto o falso? Prepara diez oraciones **ciertas** y **falsas** sobre estos dos dibujos. Luego pregúntale a tu compañero(a) si son **ciertas** o **falsas**. Si son falsas, que las corrija *(have him/her correct them).*

Modelo **Un estudiante toma un refresco.** ***(cierto)***
Un estudiante habla por teléfono y baila. ***(falso)***

C. ¿Son diferentes? Estos dibujos y los dibujos en el Apéndice A son similares pero hay cinco diferencias. Descríbele estos dibujos a tu compañero(a) y él / ella va a describirte los otros dibujos hasta encontrar las diferencias. No se permite ver los dibujos de tu compañero(a) hasta terminar esta actividad.

1.

2.

3.

4.

5.

¡Luz! ¡Cámara! ¡Acción!

A. Rin, rin. Estás hablando por teléfono con un(a) amigo(a) que asiste a otra universidad. Te pregunta sobre tu rutina de los días en que no hay clases. Dramatiza esa situación con un(a) compañero(a).

Tú	**Amigo(a)**
■ Saluda a tu amigo(a) y pregúntale cómo está.	■ Responde y pregunta cómo está él (ella).
■ Responde.	■ Pregunta cómo es un día típico cuando no hay clases.
■ Describe un día típico. Algunas posibilidades: mirar la tele, hablar por teléfono, ir a la biblioteca, comprar libros, preparar la cena,... Pregúntale cómo es un día típico para él (ella).	■ Responde. Dile adiós y menciona cuando vas a llamar otra vez.

B. Rin, rin, rin. Ahora estás hablando por teléfono con un(a) amigo(a) de tu escuela secundaria. Él (Ella) te pregunta sobre tus compañeros(as) de cuarto. Dramatiza la situación con un(a) compañero(a) de clase. Menciona:

- sus nombres
- sus personalidades
- sus pasatiempos favoritos
- sus actividades cuando no hay clases

Antes de leer
Estrategias para leer: Palabras afines

Palabras afines (*Cognates*). *Cognates are words that look alike in both languages and have the same meaning. The ability to recognize cognates can help expand your reading vocabulary and comprehension. But beware, there are also false cognates, words that look alike in two languages but have different meanings.*

1. How many cognates in the advertisement on page 49 do you recognize? Write them and their English equivalents.
2. You already know that **facultad** is a false cognate. Can you find any others? What are they? Can you guess what they probably mean?

Now read about **UNITEC** *and answer the questions that follow.*

Lectura

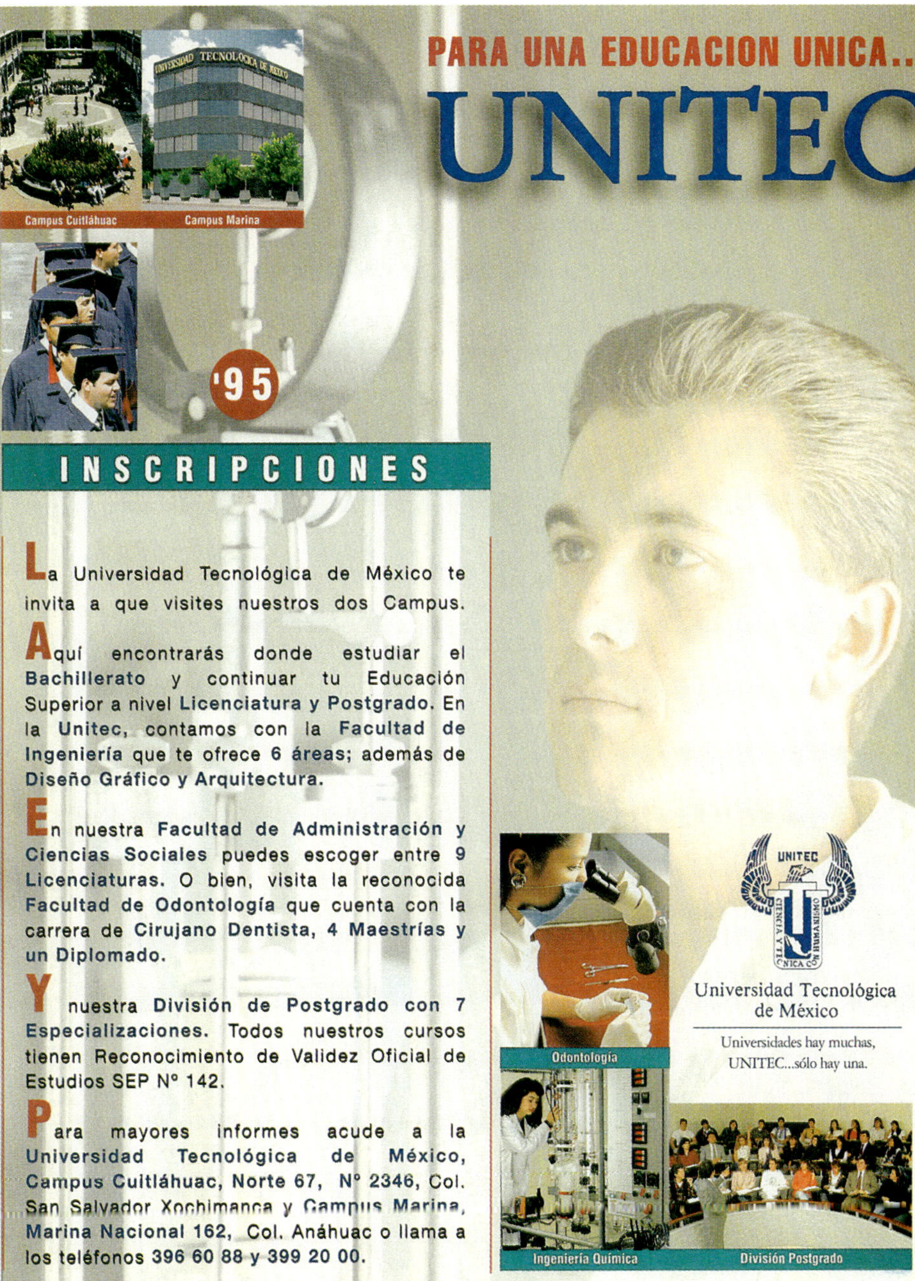

A ver si comprendiste

1. ¿Qué es UNITEC?
2. ¿Qué títulos ofrece UNITEC?
3. Nombra tres (3) divisiones de UNITEC.
4. ¿Cómo es posible obtener más información sobre UNITEC?

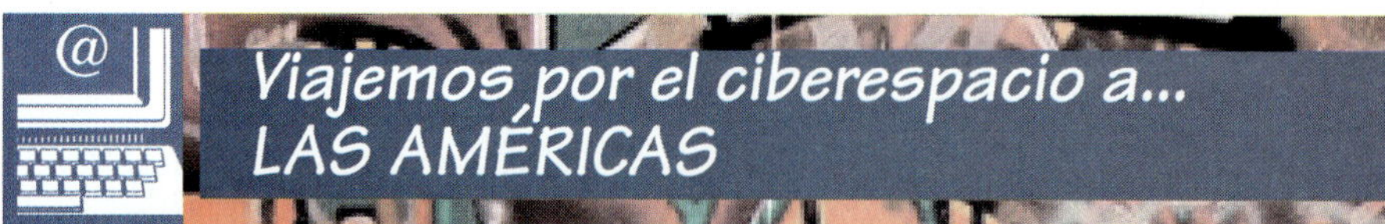

Expand your horizons! *Let's travel through cyberspace to **Las Américas*** and discover that you can . . .

- visit the magnificent land of the Americas, which extends from Alaska in the north to Tierra del Fuego, the tip of South America.
- learn about and appreciate the diversity of the multiethnic people and cultures of this land.
- contact a number of Latin American organizations fighting for a better and more democratic future.
- visit some of the oldest universities of the world.

If your are a cyberspace browser, join us in **Viajemos por el ciberespacio a... Las Américas** by trying the following important addresses:

Cumbre Iberoamericana
http://www.oei.es/vicumbre.htm

http://www.cumbre.cl/

Cumbre de las Américas
http://www.oas.org/SP/PROG/RED/summits.htm

http://www.cumbre-summit.org/cumbre/eng/antes.html

Nuestra América
http://www.latinoweb.com/nuestram/

Amigos de las Américas
http://www.amigoslink.org/index.htpl

Diario Las Américas
http://www.diariolasamericas.com/

Organización de Estados Americanos
http://www.oas.org/

http://www.oas.org/SP/PINFO/charters.htm

http://www.oas.org/SP/MSTATES/bckgrdms.htm

Because addresses are likely to change without notice, the following key words will guarantee that **Viajemos por el ciberespacio a... Las Américas** will get you to your desired destination:

Amigos de las Américas
Constituciones latinoamericanas
Cumbre de las Américas
Cumbre Iberoamericana
LatinoLink
LatinoWeb
Museos Latinoamericanos
Turismo Ecológico en América Latina

http://www.hrwcollege.com

Vocabulario

Descripción de personalidad

aburrido(a) *boring*
activo(a) *active*
atlético(a) *athletic*
bueno(a) *good*
chistoso(a) *funny*
conservador(a) *conservative*
desorganizado(a) *unorganized*
difícil *difficult*
divertido(a) *fun*
elegante *elegant*
especial *special*
estudioso(a) *studious*
estupendo(a) *stupendous*
fácil *easy*
famoso(a) *famous*
favorito(a) *favorite*
grande *big*
impaciente *impatient*
inteligente *intelligent*
interesante *interesting*
liberal *liberal*
paciente *patient*
perezoso(a) *lazy*
popular *popular*
romántico(a) *romantic*
serio(a) *serious*
simpático(a) *pleasant, likeable*
tímido(a) *timid, shy*
tonto(a) *foolish, dumb*
trabajador(a) *hard-working*

Pasatiempos y actividades

bailar *to dance*
buscar *to look for*
comer *to eat*
comprar *to buy*
escribir cartas *to write letters*
escuchar música *to listen to music*
estudiar *to study*
hablar por teléfono *to talk on the phone*
leer *to read*
llamar a tus padres *to call your parents*
mirar *to look at, watch*
mirar la tele *to watch T.V.*
nadar *to swim*
necesitar *to need*
preparar la cena *to prepare dinner*
tomar *to drink; to take*

Clases

arte ***(m.)*** *art*
biología *biology*
ciencias políticas *political science*
economía *economics*
educación física *physical education*
física *physics*
historia *history*
ingeniería *engineering*
inglés ***(m.)*** *English*
literatura *literature*
matemáticas *mathematics*
química *chemistry*
teatro *theater*

Materiales

bolígrafo *ballpoint pen*
calculadora *calculator*
cuaderno *notebook*
diccionario *dictionary*
escritorio *desk*
  del maestro(a) *teacher's desk*
  del estudiante *student's desk*
goma *pencil eraser*
lápiz ***(m.)*** *pencil*
libro *book*
mochila *backpack*
papel ***(m.)*** *paper*
pizarra *chalkboard, blackboard*
silla *chair*
tiza *chalk*

Lugares

banco *bank*
biblioteca *library*
cafetería *cafeteria*
cine *movie theater*
cuarto *room*
laboratorio *laboratory*
librería *bookstore*
teatro *theater*

Expresiones de frecuencia

a veces *sometimes, at times*
fin de semana ***(m.)*** *weekend*
nunca *never*
semana *week*
siempre *always*
todos los días *every day*

Palabras y expresiones útiles

café ***(m.)*** *coffee*
cena *dinner*
con *with*
hamburguesa *hamburger*
maleta *suitcase*
mucho(a) *much, a lot*
muy *very*
novio(a) *boyfriend/girlfriend*
radio ***(f., m.)*** *radio*
refresco *soft drink*
también *also*
teléfono *phone*
un poco *a little*

En preparación 1

1.1 Subject Pronouns and the Verb *ser:* Singular Forms

Clarifying, emphasizing, contrasting, and stating origin

Subject Pronouns

Singular	
I	**yo**
you (familiar)	**tú**
you (formal)	**usted**
he	**él**
she	**ella**

A. Subject pronouns are usually omitted in Spanish because the verb endings indicate the person. Subject pronouns are used for clarity, emphasis, or contrast.

clarity — **Usted** es de México, ¿verdad?
emphasis — No, **yo** soy de Panamá.
contrast — Ah, entonces **tú** eres panameña y **ella** es mexicana.
BUT: — Sí, soy latinoamericana.

B. The subject pronoun **it** in English is NEVER expressed in Spanish.

Es muy importante. *It is very important.*
No es hoy, es mañana. *It is not today, it's tomorrow.*

C. In **Para empezar,** you learned that **tú** is a familiar form generally used among friends, and **usted** is a more polite, formal form used to show respect or to address individuals you do not know well and those whom you address with a title. Note that in Spanish, as in English, titles are frequently abbreviated in writing when used with a last name.

señor	Sr.	*Mr.*	señorita	Srta.	*Miss*	doctor(a)	Dr. / Dra.	*Dr.*
señora	Sra.	*Mrs.*	señores	Sres.	*Mr. and Mrs.*			

The Verb *ser*

Singular	
I am	yo **soy**
you are	tú **eres**
you are	usted **es**
he is	él **es**
she is	ella **es**

A. In Spanish, there are two verbs that mean *to be*: **ser** and **estar**. These two verbs differ greatly in usage. In this chapter, you will learn various uses of **ser**.

B. **Ser** is used to define or identify. It tells who or what the subject of the sentence is. It acts as an equal sign (=) between the subject and the noun that follows. In this context, it is used to express nationality or profession.

Soy norteamericano.	Yo = norteamericano
Ella **es** estudiante.	Ella = estudiante
Tú **eres** inteligente.	Tú = inteligente

C. Just as **ser** is used to express nationality, **ser de** is used to express origin.

García Márquez es colombiano. **Es de** Colombia.
El Sr. Acuña **es de** México.

Remember that it is not necessary to use subject pronouns unless clarity, emphasis, or contrast is desired.

¡A practicar!

A. ¿Quién es? Indicate who is being spoken about by matching each statement with its subject pronoun.

Modelo Es el profesor de español. **él**

1. Es americano. — yo
2. Me llamo Matías. — tú
3. La profesora se llama Elena. — usted
4. Perdón, señor, ¿cómo se llama? — él
5. ¿Cómo te llamas? — ella

B. ¿Tú? ¿Usted? What subject pronouns would the Spanish department receptionist use when speaking directly to the following people?

1. el Sr. Ríos Menéndez, the department chairperson
2. el Sr. Gaitán Rojas, a professor
3. Pedro, a good friend
4. Ana, a roommate
5. la Sra. López Ríos, your counselor

What subject pronouns would the receptionist use when speaking about the following people?

6. el Sr. Ríos Menéndez
7. el Sr. Gaitán Rojas
8. herself
9. Ana
10. Pedro
11. la Sra. López Ríos

C. ¿De dónde es... ? Students come to your campus from different states. Tell from which states these students came.

1. José / Texas
2. Teresa / Ohio
3. el profesor Meza / Nevada
4. tu compañero de cuarto / Florida
5. yo / Nuevo México
6. ¿Y tú?

1.2 Gender and Number: Articles and Nouns

Indicating specific and non-specific people and things

A. There are two kinds of articles: definite and indefinite. Both the definite article (*the* in English) and the indefinite articles (*a, an* [singular] and *some* [plural] in English) have four forms in Spanish.

Singular

	Masculine	Feminine
the	**el**	**la**
a, an	**un**	**una**

Plural

	Masculine	Feminine
the	**los**	**las**
some	**unos**	**unas**

Definite and indefinite articles must agree in number (singular/plural) and gender (masculine/feminine) with the nouns they accompany.

Necesito **un** bolígrafo y **una** calculadora. *I need a ballpoint pen and a calculator.*

Los cuadernos y **las** mochilas están en **el** escritorio.	*The notebooks and the backpacks are on the desk.*

B. A noun is the name of a person, place, or thing. In Spanish, all nouns are either masculine or feminine, even when they refer to inanimate objects. The following rules will help you predict the gender of many nouns; however, the gender of nouns is not always predictable. You should always learn the gender with every new noun.

1. Nouns that refer to males are masculine, and nouns that refer to females are feminine. Many nouns referring to people and animals have identical forms except for the masculine **-o** or feminine **-a** endings.

el hermano	*the brother*	la hermana	*the sister*
el perro	*the male dog*	la perra	*the female dog*

A few nouns that refer to people and animals have completely different masculine and feminine forms.

el hombre	*the man*	la mujer	*the woman*
el padre	*the father*	la madre	*the mother*

2. Generally, nouns that end in **-o** are masculine and those that end in **-a**, **-dad**, and **-ción** or **-sión** are feminine.

el libr**o**	la activi**dad**
el bolígraf**o**	la universi**dad**
la mochil**a**	la educa**ción**
la sill**a**	la televi**sión**

Some important exceptions to this rule are:

la mano	*the hand*	el sistema
el día		el poema
el problema		el programa
el tema		el drama

3. Sometimes the same noun is used for both genders. In these cases, gender is indicated by the article that precedes the noun.

el / la turista	el / la periodista	*the newspaper reporter*
el / la dentista	el / la artista	

4. Many nouns, especially those ending in **-e** or a consonant, do not have predictable genders and must be memorized.

el café	*the coffee*	la clase	*the class*
el arte	*the art*	la tarde	*the afternoon*

C. All plural nouns end in **-s** or **-es.** The plural forms of nouns are derived in the following manner.

1. Singular nouns that end in a vowel form their plural by adding **-s.**

el diccionario	*the dictionary*	los diccionarios	*the dictionaries*
una silla	*a chair*	unas sillas	*some chairs*

2. Singular nouns that end in a consonant form their plural by adding **-es.**

el papel	*the paper*	los papeles	*the papers*
una universidad	*a university*	unas universidades	*some universities*

3. A final **-z** always changes to **c** before adding **-es.**

el lápiz	*the pencil*	los lápices	*the pencils*
una vez	*one time*	unas veces	*a few times*

¡A practicar!

A. ¿Qué busca Micaela? Indicate what Micaela is looking for in the bookstore by changing the definite articles to indefinite articles.

1. la mochila
2. los cuadernos
3. el bolígrafo
4. el papel
5. los libros
6. la calculadora

B. Es de... Now tell who the following items belong to.

Modelo papel / Carlos
Es el papel de Carlos.

1. tiza / profesora
2. calculadora / Julia
3. diccionario / Andrés
4. bolígrafo / Raúl
5. silla / profesora
6. lápiz / Carla

1.3 Adjectives: Singular Forms

Describing people, places, and things

Adjectives are words that tell something of the nature of the noun they describe (color, size, nationality, affiliations, condition, and so on). Spanish adjectives usually follow the noun they describe.

A. Adjectives may be masculine or feminine. Masculine singular adjectives that end in **-o** have a feminine equivalent that ends in **-a**.

Singular

Masculine	Feminine
alt**o** simpátic**o**	alt**a** simpátic**a**

B. Adjectives that end in **-e,** and most adjectives that end in a consonant (except those denoting nationality and personality traits) do not have separate masculine / feminine forms.

el coche grande — el vestido azul
la casa grande — la camisa azul
BUT:
un español trabajador
una española trabajadora

C. Adjectives of nationality that end in a consonant add **-a** to form the feminine singular, **-es** the masculine plural, and **-as** the feminine plural.

Singular		Plural	
Masculine	**Feminine**	**Masculine**	**Feminine**
alemán	aleman**a**	aleman**es**	aleman**as**
inglés	ingles**a**	ingles**es**	ingles**as**
español	español**a**	español**es**	español**as**

¡A practicar!

A. Solamente chicas. María is studying at a private girls' school. How does she describe her new friends?

1. Mi amiga Rosa es ______________ (atlético).
2. Mi amiga Josefina es ______________ (divertido).
3. Mi compañera de cuarto es ______________ (inteligente).
4. Carmen es ______________ (conservador).
5. La profesora de español es ______________ (bueno).
6. La directora es ______________ (trabajador).

B. ¡Qué guapos somos! A six-year-old is showing pictures and talking during her first show-and-tell report at school. Substitute the word in parentheses for the underlined word to see what she is saying.

Modelo **Mi <u>hermana</u> es activa y atlética. (hermano)**
Mi hermano es activo y atlético.

1. Él es mi <u>papá</u>. Es serio y trabajador. (mamá)
2. Él es mi <u>hermano</u>. Es divertido y simpático. (hermana)
3. Ella es mi <u>amiga</u>. Es estudiosa y tímida. (amigo)
4. Ella es mi <u>mamá</u>. Es elegante y especial. (papá)
5. Él es mi <u>vecino</u> (*neighbor*). Es impaciente y perezoso. (vecina)
6. Es mi <u>perro</u>. Es bueno y tonto. (perra)

C. Gente famosa. Identify the nationalities of the following people.

1. Bill y Hillary Clinton son __________. Su hija Chelsea es __________ también.
2. El príncipe Carlos de Inglaterra es __________ y su ex esposa Diana es __________.
3. El rey Juan Carlos de España y su esposa la reina Sofía son __________. Sus hijos (*children*) son __________ también.
4. Ryutaro Hashimoto, el Primer Ministro del Japón, es __________. Su familia también es __________.

PASO 2

1.4 Infinitives

Naming activities

Spanish verbs fall into three categories: **-ar, -er,** and **-ir.** The verb form that ends in **-ar, -er,** or **-ir** is called an infinitive. **Necesitar** *(to need),* **ser** *(to be),* and **vivir** *(to live)* are three examples of Spanish infinitives. Notice that English infinitives are formed by *to + verb.*

Some frequently used **-ar, -er,** and **-ir,** verbs from Chapter 1 are:

bailar	*to dance*	mirar (la tele)	*to watch (T.V.)*
buscar	*to look for*	nadar	*to swim*
comprar	*to buy*	necesitar	*to need*
escuchar	*to listen*	preparar	*to prepare*
estudiar	*to study*	tomar	*to drink; to take*
hablar	*to talk*	comer	*to eat*
llamar	*to call*	leer	*to read*
mirar	*to look at, watch*	ir	*to go*

¡A practicar!

A. ¿Ahora o antes? Indicate by checking the appropriate column **ahora** (*now*) or **antes** (*before*) if these activities are typical of your life now or before as a high school student.

	Ahora	Antes
1. tomar leche (*milk*)	_____	_____
2. hablar por teléfono	_____	_____
3. ir a conciertos	_____	_____
4. estudiar mucho	_____	_____
5. mirar la televisión	_____	_____
6. leer libros	_____	_____
7. preparar la cena	_____	_____
8. llamar a los padres	_____	_____
9. comer en restaurantes	_____	_____
10. escuchar la radio	_____	_____

B. ¿Qué necesitas hacer? From the list of infinitives above, select those that express what you need to do or like to do before, during, and after giving a party.

Modelo Antes de la fiesta **Necesito buscar los discos.**
Durante la fiesta **Necesito hablar con amigos.**
Después de la fiesta **Necesito limpiar el apartamento.**

1. Antes de la fiesta
2. Durante la fiesta
3. Después de la fiesta

1.5 Subject Pronouns and the Verb *ser:* Plural Forms

Stating origin of several people

Subject Pronouns

Plural	
we	nosotros, nosotras
you (familiar) *you* (formal)	vosotros, vosotras ustedes
they	ellos ellas

In **Para empezar**, you learned that **tú** is a familiar form generally used among friends, and **usted** is a more polite, formal form used to show respect or to address individuals you do not know well. **Vosotros(as)**, the plural of **tú,** and **ustedes,** the plural of **usted,** are used in the same way. In the Americas, there is a strong preference to use **ustedes** in place of **vosotros(as).**

The Verb *ser*

Singular		Plural	
yo	**soy**	nosotros(as)	**somos**
tú usted	**eres** **es**	vosotros(as) ustedes	**sois** **son**
él, ella	**es**	ellos, ellas	**son**

¡A practicar!

A. ¿De todas partes? Classes begin next week and foreign students are starting to arrive on campus. Tell what countries they are from.

Modelo Roberto Rojas y José Antonio Méndez / Colombia
Roberto Rojas y José Antonio Méndez son de Colombia.
Son colombianos.

1. Isabel y Julia Martínez / Venezuela
2. José Trujillo y Marta Cabezas / Cuba
3. Cecilia y Pilar Correa / Paraguay
4. Carlos Barros y tú / Costa Rica
5. Sonia Urrutia y Tomás Arias / Perú
6. Tú y yo / México

B. Presentaciones. What does Pepe say about his friends when he introduces them to his roommate?

Modelo Víctor y Daniel ___________ de Nuevo México.
Víctor y Daniel ___son___ de Nuevo México.

1. Rafael y Lalo ___________ mis amigos de Texas.
2. Teresa ___________ estudiante de biología.
3. Ángela y Manuel ___________ estudiantes de literatura.
4. Jaime y yo ___________ de Chicago.
5. Todos nosotros ___________ muy buenos amigos.

1.6 Gender and Number: Adjectives

Describing people

You have learned that adjectives are words that describe a person, place, or thing. Unlike English, Spanish adjectives usually follow the noun they describe.

A. Masculine singular adjectives that end in **-o** have four forms.

Singular

Masculine	Feminine
alt**o** simpátic**o**	alt**a** simpátic**a**

Plural

Masculine	Feminine
alt**os** simpátic**os**	alt**as** simpátic**as**

B. Except for adjectives denoting nationality and personality or physical traits, most other adjectives have only two forms, a singular form and a plural form. The plural is formed by adding **-s** to adjectives ending in a vowel other than **-o** and **-es** to adjectives ending in a consonant.

Singular	**Plural**
grande	grande**s**
azul	azul**es**
BUT:	
español	español**es**
español**a**	español**as**

C. When one adjective describes two or more nouns, one of which is masculine, the masculine plural form of the adjective is used.

Ana y José son muy serios. — *Anna and Jose are very serious.*

Gloria, Isabel y Pepe son muy desorganizados. — *Gloria, Isabel and Pepe are very disorganized.*

¡A practicar!

A. Mis amigos. How does Romelia describe her friends at school? Select the appropriate adjective.

1. Gilberto es muy (atlético / atlética).
2. Mi amiga Mari Carmen es (estudioso / estudiosa) y (serio / seria).
3. Mi amiga Tomasa es (simpático / simpática) y popular.
4. Andrés es (activo / activa), (divertido / divertida) y (estupendo / estupenda).
5. ¿Y yo? Yo soy (trabajador / trabajadora) y muy especial.

B. ¿Cómo son? People usually select friends that are similar to themselves. Tell what the following pairs are like.

1. Julio es divertido. (Julio y José)
2. Elena es alemana. (Elena y Pilar)
3. Paco es impaciente. (Paco y yo)
4. Lupita es liberal. (Lupita y tú)
5. Eduardo es muy atlético. (Eduardo y Carmen)
6. El perro Canela es simpático. (Canela y Matón)
7. La perra Muñeca es inteligente. (Muñeca y Matón)
8. Tú eres... (Tú y yo)

1.7 Present Tense of *-ar* Verbs

Stating what people do

A. Spanish verbs are conjugated by substituting personal endings for the **-ar, -er,** or **-ir** endings of the infinitive. In this chapter, you will learn the **-ar** personal verb endings. Notice that the **-ar** endings always reflect the subject of the sentence, or the person or thing doing the action of the verb.

-*ar* Verb Endings and the Verb *necesitar*

Singular			Plural		
yo	**-o**	necesit**o**	nosotros(as)	**-amos**	necesit**amos**
tú usted	**-as** **-a**	necesit**as** necesit**a**	vosotros(as) ustedes	-**áis** **-an**	necesit**áis** necesit**an**
él, ella	**-a**	necesit**a**	ellos, ellas	**-an**	necesit**an**

B. The present indicative of any Spanish verb has two possible equivalents in English statements and questions.

Compro ropa nueva.	*I buy new clothes.* *I am buying new clothes.*
¿Compras ropa nueva?	*Do you buy new clothes?* *Are you buying new clothes?*

Note that **ser** is never used in combination with another present-tense verb to express that someone is doing something. Also the English auxiliary verb forms *do* and *does* do not exist in Spanish. When asking questions, the conjugated verb by itself communicates the idea of *do* or *does.*

C. As in English, a Spanish present-tense verb may have a future meaning.

Mañana pago las cuentas.	*Tomorrow I will pay (I pay) the bills.*
¿Cuándo lavamos el coche?	*When will we (do we) wash the car?*

D. Some frequently used **-ar** verbs are:

bailar	*to dance*	llevar	*to carry; to take; to wear*
buscar	*to look for*	mirar	*to look at, watch*
comprar	*to buy*	nadar	*to swim*
escuchar	*to listen to*	necesitar	*to need*
hablar	*to speak*	pagar	*to pay*
lavar	*to wash*	preguntar	*to ask (a question)*
limpiar	*to clean*	preparar	*to prepare*
llamar	*to call*	tomar	*to drink; to take*

¡A practicar!

A. El fin de semana. Complete each of the following sentences with the appropriate form of the verb in parentheses to see what Francisco and his friends do on a typical Saturday.

1. Tomás ____________ (preparar) unos sandwiches.
2. Yo ____________ (mirar) la televisión.
3. Ángela y Olga ____________ (escuchar) la radio.
4. Pablo y yo ____________ (tomar) Coca-Cola.
5. Carlos ____________ (hablar) por teléfono.
6. Carlos, Olga y Tomás ____________ (comprar) mucho.

B. ¡Los domingos siempre son especiales! Why are Sundays so special for Enrique? To find out, complete the following paragraph with the correct form of the verbs in parentheses.

Por la mañana, ____________ (yo / llamar) a mi amiga Cecilia. Nosotros ____________ (hablar) casi una hora. Yo ____________ (invitar) a Cecilia a almorzar (*to have lunch*) en mi apartamento. Ella siempre ____________ (aceptar). Entonces, yo ____________ (limpiar) el apartamento rápidamente y ____________ (preparar) mi especialidad, ¡hamburguesas!

1.8 The Verb *ir*

Stating destination **Ir**

to go	
voy	vamos
vas	váis
va	van
va	van

When a destination is mentioned, **ir a** is always used.

Yo **voy a** la librería. *I'm going to the bookstore.*
Ella **va a** un banco. *She is going to a bank.*

Contractions in Spanish: *al, del*

Whenever **a** or **de** are followed by the definite article **el**, they contract and become **al** or **del**. These are the only contractions in the Spanish language. In this lesson you will practice with **al.** Practice with **del** will come in a later chapter.

Vamos **al** teatro.	*We're going to the theater.*
La profesora va **al** laboratorio.	*The professor is going to the laboratory.*
Es Pepe. Llama **del** banco.	*It's Pepe. He's calling from the bank.*

¡A practicar!

A. Un día típico. Today is like every other school day. Everyone is rushing around. Where does Alicia say everyone is going?

Gloria y Teresa ____________ a la cafetería. Julio ____________ a la biblioteca a estudiar para un examen. Beatriz y Humberto ____________ al cine. Yo ____________ al cuarto de Virginia. Ella y yo ____________ al Café Roma a tomar un refresco. Y tú, ¿adónde ____________?

B. Perdón, voy a... Where is everyone really going? How do you correct yourself when you realize you've given the wrong destination?

Modelo Yo voy al teatro. (la biblioteca)
Perdón, voy a la biblioteca.

1. Marta va a la cafetería. (el restaurante)
2. Ángela va a la discoteca. (el teatro)
3. Carlos y José van al laboratorio. (la biblioteca)
4. El profesor va a la librería. (el banco)
5. Olga y yo vamos al restaurante. (la fiesta)
6. Julio y Ana van a San Francisco. (Los Ángeles)

C. ¿Adónde van todos? It is Saturday morning and your roommate wants to know where everyone is rushing off to. What do you say?

Modelo Ernesto / librería
Ernesto va a la librería.

1. Gabriela / San Francisco
2. profesor / laboratorio de biología
3. Paco y Mateo / biblioteca
4. Adela y Tomás / librería
5. Mariana y yo / restaurante
6. Julio y Julia / banco

CAPÍTULO 2

¡Ahora hay tanto que hacer!

Cultural Topics

- **¿Sabías que…?**
  Dorm life in Hispanic universities: Does it exist?
- **Noticiero cultural**
  Lugar: *El estado libre asociado de Puerto Rico*
  Costumbres: *Chinas y la guagua*
- **Lectura:** *Buena de corazón*

Writing Strategies

- Knowing your audience and brainstorming

Reading Strategies

- Using visual images to predict content

En preparación

- 2.1 Present Tense of **-er** and **-ir** Verbs
- 2.2 Numbers 0–199
- 2.3 Possessive Adjectives
- 2.4 Three Irregular Verbs: **tener, salir, venir**
- 2.5 Telling Time
- 2.6 Days of the Week, Months, and Seasons
- 2.7 Verbs of Motion

In this chapter, you will learn how to …

- name and describe some jobs open to students.
- describe your dorm, apartment, or house.
- talk about roommates and dorm life or apartment living.
- describe vacation plans.
- talk about spring / summer / fall / winter break.

Trabajo en un restaurante en San Juan, Puerto Rico.

¡Nuestro apartamento es estupendo!

¡De vacaciones en Puerto Rico!

Lo que ya sabes...

1. En tu universidad, ¿trabaja la mayoría de los estudiantes?
2. ¿Es fácil o difícil encontrar trabajo donde tú estudias?
3. ¿Vives en las residencias de la universidad, en un apartamento o en casa con tu familia?
4. Generalmente, ¿pasas las vacaciones universitarias con tu familia o con amigos de la universidad? ¿Qué hacen?

PUERTO RICO

¿Dónde trabajas?

TAREA

Antes de empezar este **Paso,** estudia **En preparación** 2.1 y haz por escrito los ejercicios de **¡A practicar!** También escucha el **Paso 1 ¿Qué se dice... ?** del Capítulo 2 en el CD del estudiante.

¿Eres buen observador?

Compañía japonesa solicita inmediatamente
Secretaria bilingüe
Requisitos:
- Magnífica presentación
- Tener experiencia
- Ser soltera
- Edad de 18 a 25
- Inglés 80% (sepa traducir)

Interesadas favor de acudir a AV. de Las Palmas No. 239 3er Piso Col. Lomas de Chapultepec TEL. 202-21-08

Importante institución financiera solicita
CHOFER
Requisitos:
- Con experiencia
- Edad 20 años
- Disponibilidad inmediata
- Excelente presentación
- Que viva en el sur de la ciudad
- Recomendaciones indispensables

Ofrecemos:
- Sueldo altamente competitivo

Interesados comunicarse a los teléfonos
598 75 78 598 82 76 598 03 26

Solicitamos
Programador de Computadora
Experiencia en DBASE III para el desarrollo de nuevos programas.
Inglés–Español
Dispuesto a radicarse en Puerto Vallarta.
203-76

SEÑORITA
Para Vendedora
EN TIENDA DE ROPA
Trabajo en el centro.
Sueldo más comisiones.
Tel. 542 67 58
MISS GEORGETTE
Flamencos 12, Local B,
entre 20 de Noviembre y Pino Suárez

Ahora, ¡a analizar!

1. ¿Para qué tipo de trabajo son estos anuncios?
2. ¿Son apropiados algunos de estos puestos para estudiantes universitarios que necesitan empleo? ¿Por qué?
3. ¿Es posible trabajar tiempo completo y asistir a la universidad a la vez? Explica.
4. Explica «Magnífica presentación».

¿Qué se dice...?

Al hablar del trabajo

Estela y Mónica

Ocupación: ______________________

¿Dónde trabajan? ______________________

¿Qué venden? ______________________

____

Julio Pesquero es secretario y trabaja en la computadora todo el día. Escribe en el teclado mientras mira la pantalla y escucha música en los parlantes. También usa el ratón que está en la almohadilla. Sus documentos salen de la impresora.

Alicia Guzmán busca trabajo. Pero, ¿quiénes son los dos señores? «Somos gerentes y entrevistamos a los empleados nuevos».

Antonio Durán es administrador. Él decide qué hacen los otros empleados.

Soy Gilberto. Soy el cocinero aquí. Yo abro el café a las seis de la mañana y trabajo hasta las dos de la tarde.

Javier y Carmen son periodistas. Ellos escriben excelentes artículos todos los días. Por la mañana, al llegar a la oficina, ellos siempre leen sus artículos en el periódico del día.

Ahora, ¡a hablar!

A. ¿Qué es? Lee estas descripciones para que tu compañero(a) identifique qué es la persona que se describe: profesor, secretario, gerente, cocinero, dependiente o periodista.

1. Trabaja en una oficina. Escribe mucho y lee mucho. Generalmente escribe artículos para un periódico.
2. También trabaja en una oficina. No lee mucho pero sí escribe mucho. Generalmente escribe en la computadora.
3. Trabaja en una oficina o en un restaurante o un café. Es una persona muy importante. Esta persona decide qué hacen los otros empleados.
4. No trabaja ni en una oficina, ni en un restaurante, ni en un café. Trabaja en una universidad. Prepara muchas clases y es muy inteligente.
5. Trabaja en una tienda de ropa. Vende ropa al público. Generalmente es una persona muy simpática.
6. Trabaja en un café o un restaurante. Generalmente abre por la mañana y prepara comida para mucha gente.

B. En el trabajo. ¿Qué hacen estas personas en el trabajo?

Modelo Elisa (vender) ropa en una tienda.
Elisa vende ropa en una tienda.

1. Pascual y Dolores (escribir) en una computadora en la oficina.
2. Bárbara (abrir) la puerta en un café.
3. Andrea (escribir) artículos en un periódico.
4. Cristina y David (entrevistar) a estudiantes en la universidad.
5. Gilberto (preparar) la comida en un café.
6. Teresa y yo (vender) libros en una librería.
7. Tú (confirmar) reservaciones en un hotel.
8. Mari Carmen (cocinar) en un restaurante.

C. Ocupaciones. En tu opinión, ¿qué hacen estas personas en el trabajo? Contesta formando frases con palabras de cada columna.

Modelo **Unos gerentes entrevistan a los empleados nuevos.**

		los exámenes
gerentes	entrevistar a	los estudiantes
periodista	vender	al autobús
estudiante	preparar	la tienda
cocinero(a)	escribir	los artículos
dependiente	leer	el café
profesor(a)	correr	los empleados nuevos
secretario(a)	comer	la comida
		a máquina

D. Los fines de semana. Pregúntale a tu compañero(a) si hace estas cosas los fines de semana.

Modelo hablar por teléfono

TÚ ¿Hablas por teléfono?
COMPAÑERO(A) Sí, hablo por teléfono. o
No, no hablo por teléfono.

1. trabajar en una oficina
2. estudiar en la biblioteca
3. correr
4. abrir el libro de español
5. escribir en la computadora
6. leer mucho
7. comer en un restaurante
8. vender ropa en una tienda

Y ahora, ¡a conversar!

A. ¿A quién describe? Selecciona tres de estos puestos y, sin decir cuáles, descríbelos para ver si tu compañero(a) adivina *(guesses)* cuáles describes.

administrador(a)	secretario(a)	gerente
cocinero(a)	dependiente	periodista

B. ¿Trabajas? ¿De veras? En grupos pequeños describan su trabajo. Si no trabajan, inventen un puesto. Luego, después de describir todos los trabajos, decidan quiénes de veras *(really)* trabajan y quiénes probablemente no trabajan.

C. ¿Nosotros? ¿Qué tipo de trabajo hay para estudiantes universitarios en tu universidad y en tu ciudad? Con un(a) compañero(a) prepara una lista de trabajos que los estudiantes universitarios hacen.

Modelo Vendemos ropa.

D. Profesión ideal. En una hoja de papel, escribe el nombre de tu clase favorita. Luego escribe las dos características más representativas de tu personalidad. En grupos de tres o cuatro, diles a tus compañeros cómo eres y cuál es tu clase favorita. *(They are going to tell you what the ideal profession is for you based on your characteristics and favorite class.)*

¡Luz! ¡Cámara! ¡Acción!

A. ¡Ya no busco trabajo! Ahora estás en casa de tus padres. Son tus primeras vacaciones del año escolar. Tú y tus padres están hablando de tu nuevo empleo (trabajo). Dramaticen esta situación.

Mamá y papá	**Hijo**
■ Pregunten dónde trabaja.	■ Responde.
■ Pregunten qué hace.	■ Describe tu trabajo.
■ Pregunten cómo son los otros trabajadores.	■ Descríbelos.
■ Díganle buena suerte.	■ Responde.

B. Consejero(a). Tú necesitas trabajar y vas a hablar con un(a) consejero(a) *(advisor)* de la universidad. Necesitas saber qué tipo de puestos hay. Dramatiza esta situación con un(a) compañero(a).

¿Comprendes lo que se dice?

Estrategias para escuchar. *Knowing what people are talking about or anticipating what they are going to say makes it much easier to understand a foreign language. When listening to spoken Spanish, you should always try to determine what the conversation is about as you listen. In the* **¿Qué se dice... ?** *section of this* **Paso** *you met several working students. Now you are going to listen to two of them talk about how busy they are. Write down*

three things that you think they might say, then check to see if you anticipated correctly after you listen to the recording.

Now listen as your instructor plays the dialogue between Julio and Estela and, working in pairs, answer the questions that follow.

1. ¿Qué hacen Julio y Estela? Indica quién hace las actividades con una **E (Estela)** o con una **J (Julio).**

   _______ prepara la cena

   _______ lee en la biblioteca

   _______ ayuda a su mamá

   _______ escribe en la computadora

   _______ vende ropa

   _______ trabaja de secretario

   _______ abre la tienda

   _______ trabaja en una tienda

2. ¿Cómo son los profesores de Julio y Estela? (Marca uno.)

   ❑ divertidos

   ❑ aburridos

   ❑ fáciles

   ❑ difíciles

NOTICIERO CULTURAL

LUGAR... PUERTO RICO

Antes de empezar, dime...

En tu opinión, ¿son ciertos **(C)** o falsos **(F)** estos comentarios? *(After completing the reading, check to see if your perceptions were correct.)*

C F 1. La isla de Puerto Rico fue descubierta por Estados Unidos en 1898.
C F 2. Todos los puertorriqueños son ciudadanos de Estados Unidos.
C F 3. La moneda oficial de Puerto Rico es el peso.
C F 4. Los puertorriqueños votan en todas las elecciones de Estados Unidos.
C F 5. Los puertorriqueños no pagan impuestos *(taxes)* a Estados Unidos.

El Estado Libre Asociado de Puerto Rico

La hermosa isla de Puerto Rico está situada junto con Cuba, con Haití, y la República Dominicana y Jamaica en el mar Caribe. Con una extensión de 9.000 km. cuadrados, es la más pequeña de estas cuatro islas. Fue descubierta por Cristóbal Colón en 1493. Fue gobernada por España hasta el final de la guerra de 1898 (entre EE.UU. y España) cuando pasó a dominio de los Estados Unidos.

El viejo San Juan, Puerto Rico

El Morro en San Juan, Puerto Rico

En 1917 los Estados Unidos declaró a todos los puertorriqueños ciudadanos de los Estados Unidos. Por esa razón, los puertorriqueños no necesitan ni visa ni pasaporte para viajar a los Estados Unidos. La moneda oficial de Puerto Rico es el dólar estadounidense y los puertorriqueños sirven en el ejército militar de los Estados Unidos, votan en todas las elecciones de los Estados Unidos menos en la presidencial y, lo más importante de todo, ¡no pagan impuestos federales!

En 1952 Puerto Rico se convirtió en el Estado Libre Asociado de Puerto Rico, su nombre oficial actual. En 1993 los puertorriqueños votaron para decidir entre tres opciones: 1) continuar como Estado Libre Asociado; 2) convertirse en el estado número cincuenta y uno de los Estados Unidos, ó 3) convertirse en una nación totalmente independiente. El resultado del voto fue: 4.4% a favor de la independencia, 46.2% a favor de convertirse en el estado número cincuenta y uno y 48.4% a favor de continuar como Estado Libre Asociado.

Y ahora, dime...

¿Similares o diferentes? Compara a Puerto Rico y los Estados Unidos en las categorías indicadas.

	Puerto Rico	Estados Unidos
Tamaño *(Size)*		
Servicio militar		
Moneda oficial		
Derechos de votar		
Ciudadanía *(Citizenship)*		

El español en otras disciplinas: Geografía

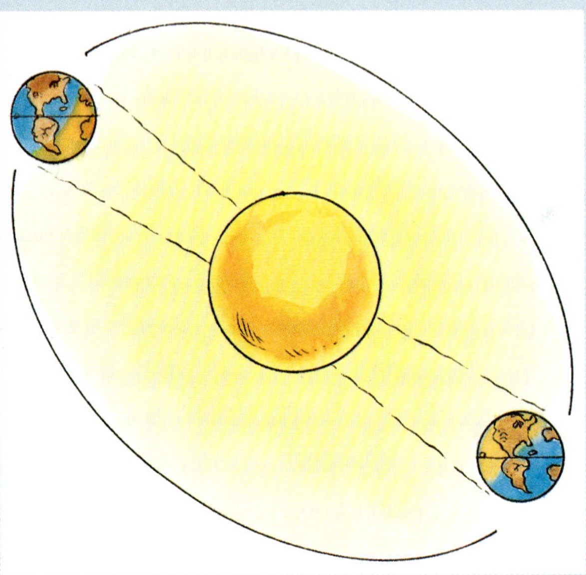

La línea ecuatorial. *Given the movement of the Earth and its position in relation to the sun during the 365 days of a year, climatic changes associated with the four seasons depend entirely on whether a country lies north or south of the equator.* Por esa razón, con excepción de Venezuela y Colombia, las estaciones *(seasons)* en toda Sudamérica son exactamente opuestas a las de Centroamérica y Norteamérica. Las cuatro estaciones son:

otoño	*autumn*	primavera	*spring*
invierno	*winter*	verano	*summer*

Contesta estas preguntas con un(a) compañero(a).

1. ¿Qué estación es en Perú cuando en los Estados Unidos es verano?
2. ¿Qué estación es en México cuando en Chile es invierno?
3. ¿Qué estación es en Argentina cuando en Ecuador es primavera?
4. ¿Qué estación es en Bolivia cuando en Guatemala es otoño?

Proyecto: Divide una hoja de papel en cuatro columnas. En las dos primeras escribe el nombre y el país de una ciudad capital de Norteamérica, dos de Centroamérica y tres de Sudamérica. En la tercera y la cuarta columna escribe una fecha *(date)* y la estación correspondiente en cada ciudad. Varía *(Vary)* las fechas para incluir todas las estaciones. En grupos de cuatro o cinco, túrnense *(take turns)* en nombrar las ciudades y fechas que seleccionaron. Sus compañeros deben nombrar *(must name)* el país y la estación de cada ciudad y fecha nombrada.

Y tú, ¿dónde vives?

TAREA

Antes de empezar este **Paso,** estudia **En preparación** 2.2, 2.3 y 2.4 y haz por escrito los ejercicios de **¡A practicar!** También escucha el **Paso 2 ¿Qué se dice... ?** del Capítulo 2 en el CD del estudiante.

¿Eres buen observador?

DÚPLEX
Sin ruidos
Llenos de luz
2 Dormitorios u$s 1.500
3 Dormitorios u$s 3.000
2 baños, Cocheras
Departamentos impecables
Av. Santa Fe 831
V-15:30–18:30 hrs.
771-8824

¿POR QUÉ PAGAR RENTAS CARAS?
ESPECIAL DE OTÕNO
1 Recámara $395
2 Recámaras $495
Sin depósito o limpieza
Cerca de la universidad
Bastantes áreas verdes
VENGA HOY MISMO
1823 W. MONTECITO
333-6968

$199 PARA MUDARSE
Con crédito aprobado. Apartamentos con jardines, jacuzzi, cuarto de ejercicios y billares. Llame al gerente para más detalles.
764-6917

ALQUILO DEPARTMENTO
temporario en:
SAN ISIDRO y CERVIÑO
Excelentes departamentos, tenis, sauna, cocheras, balcones, vistas panorámicas.
Desde 1.800 Tel. 979-3233

Ahora, ¡a analizar!

1. Dos de estos anuncios clasificados son de periódicos de barrios hispanos en los Estados Unidos y dos de un país latinoamericano. ¿Puedes identificarlos?
2. **Departamento** es un cognado falso. ¿Qué significa en español?
3. ¿Qué diferencias notas en la manera de escribir el precio de los apartamentos en los Estados Unidos y los países latinos?
4. ¿Qué influencias del inglés notas en el español de los anuncios de barrios hispanos en los Estados Unidos?

¿Qué se dice...?

Al hablar de dónde viven los estudiantes

Alicia compra ______________________________.

Patricio vive en ______________________________.

El alquiler es ______________________________.

ALICIA ¿Es grande el apartamento?

PATRICIO Tiene cuatro habitaciones si incluimos la cocina, pero son grandes. Lo peor es el baño... solamente tiene un baño que compartimos entre todos. Cuando uno sale, otro entra.

ALICIA ¿Quién prepara la comida? Porque,... tú no cocinas, ¿verdad?

PATRICIO No. Mi amigo Tomás es nuestro cocinero, más o menos. No es como en casa, pero... por lo general cocina bien.

ALICIA ¿Cómo dividen las otras responsabilidades?

PATRICIO Es fácil. Yo lavo la ropa y mis otros compañeros limpian el apartamento. Todos somos muy responsables. Y para ir a las clases tomamos el autobús o caminamos. En diez a quince minutos llegamos. ¡Ya ves! ¡Es un apartamento ideal!

¿Sabías que... ?

En la mayoría de los países hispanos, los estudiantes universitarios no viven en residencias. Por lo general viven en casa de sus padres, si no está muy lejos de la universidad, o en apartamentos o casas privadas. Normalmente, los estudiantes universitarios no trabajan para pagar sus gastos. Dependen de la ayuda financiera de sus padres. Claro que siempre hay excepciones, en particular cuando la situación económica lo demanda. Sin embargo, la mayoría de los estudiantes universitarios viven en casa de sus padres aún después de graduarse. No se mudan a su propio apartamento a menos que consigan trabajo en otra ciudad o hasta después de casarse (del matrimonio).

A propósito...

Notice that Spanish uses the word **a** before a direct object that refers to a person or persons: **Yo llamo a mis padres.** This **a,** called the personal **a,** has no equivalent in English.

Ahora, ¡a hablar!

A. Nuestro apartamento. Alberto vive con dos compañeros, Andrés y José Antonio, en un apartamento. Ellos comparten algunas cosas y otras no. ¿Qué contesta Alberto cuando le preguntan de quién son estas cosas?

Modelo los discos de salsa / yo
Son mis discos.

1. el baño / nosotros
2. la televisión / Andrés
3. la computadora / José Antonio
4. la radio / Andrés y José Antonio
5. los discos de jazz / nosotros
6. los libros / tú

B. ¿Cuánto cuesta? Siempre hay cosas que necesitamos comprar para las clases. Indica cuánto cuestan las siguientes cosas.

Modelo un buen bolígrafo
Un buen bolígrafo cuesta doce dólares y cuarenta y cinco centavos.

1. un libro de química
2. *¡Dímelo tú!*
3. el *Cuaderno de actividades*
4. un disco flexible *(floppy disk)*
5. una mochila
6. papel para la computadora
7. un cuaderno
8. ¿... ?

C. Nuevos amigos. Alberto estudia en la universidad y tiene nuevos amigos. ¿Cuál es el número de teléfono de sus amigos?

Modelo María Rodríguez: 5–42–14–58

El número de María Rodríguez es cinco, cuarenta y dos, catorce, cincuenta y ocho.

1. Guadalupe Montenegro: 6–83–22–99
2. Alberto y Paula Sánchez: 4–35–56–73
3. Carmen Martínez: 4–35–68–13
4. Pablo Enríquez: 6–85–24–12
5. Sofía Meléndez: 5–42–10–08
6. Arturo y Rodrigo: 7–19–33–11

D. ¡Bienvenidos! Alberto y Lupe están organizando una fiesta de bienvenida para todos los estudiantes que viven en las residencias de la universidad. ¿Qué dice Alberto de la fiesta?

	viene a mi casa primero.
yo	tengo la lista de los invitados.
Lupe	tenemos que preparar los últimos detalles.
Jorge	sale a comprar refrescos.
Lupe y yo	vienen a la fiesta con sus amigos.
los invitados	no tienen que pagar nada.
	vienen de todas las residencias.

E. Una semana típica. Hazle estas preguntas a tu compañero(a) para saber cómo es su semana típica.

1. ¿Vienes a la universidad en carro (auto), bicicleta o a pie *(on foot)*?
2. ¿Qué clases tienes este semestre?
3. ¿Tienes que estudiar mucho?
4. ¿Tienes más clases por la mañana, por la tarde o por la noche?
5. ¿Sales de noche? ¿Adónde vas?
6. ¿Para qué clases tienes que estudiar más?
7. ¿Tienes que estudiar los fines de semana?
8. ¿Vienen tus amigos a estudiar a tu apartamento?

Y ahora, ¡a conversar!

A. ¡Aló! Escribe tu número de teléfono en un papelito. Tu instructor(a) va a recoger los números y redistribuirlos. Ahora lee el número que tienes en el papelito. La persona que reconoce su número debe decir **¡Aló!**

B. ¡Bingo! Prepara tu propia tarjeta de «BINGO». Escribe uno de estos números en cada cuadrado: **B** 1–19, **I** 20–39, **N** 40–59, **G** 60–79, **O** 80–99. Escribe los números arábigos y deletréalos *(spell them out)* porque vas a tener que decirlos en voz alta si ganas. Luego toda la clase va a jugar.

B (1–19)	I (20–39)	N (40–59)	G (60–79)	O (80–99)
Número____ ________	Número____ ________	Número____ ________	Número____ ________	Número____ ________
Número____ ________	Número____ ________	Número____ ________	Número____ ________	Número____ ________
Número____ ________	Número____ ________	Número____ ________	Número____ ________	Número____ ________
Número____ ________	Número____ ________	Número____ ________	Número____ ________	Número____ ________
Número____ ________	Número____ ________	Número____ ________	Número____ ________	Número____ ________

C. ¿Quién lo hace? Pregúntales a tus compañeros de clase si hacen las actividades de estos cuadrados *(grid)*. Cada vez que uno diga que sí, pídele que firme (escriba su nombre) en el cuadrado *(square)* apropiado. La idea es tener una firma en cada cuadrado, **¡Ojo!** No se permite que una persona firme más de un cuadrado.

correr todos los días ________ *Firma*	lavar la ropa ________ *Firma*	caminar a la universidad ________ *Firma*	comer en la cafetería ________ *Firma*
vivir en un apartamento ________ *Firma*	leer el periódico todos los días ________ *Firma*	estudiar en la biblioteca ________ *Firma*	escribir cartas a tus padres ________ *Firma*
no comprar libros usados ________ *Firma*	preparar la comida ________ *Firma*	escuchar la radio con frecuencia ________ *Firma*	mirar videos con la familia ________ *Firma*
escribir en la computadora ________ *Firma*	limpiar su cuarto todos los días ________ *Firma*	escuchar música clásica ________ *Firma*	salir con su familia ________ *Firma*

¡Luz! ¡Cámara! ¡Acción!

A. ¡Hola! ¿Cómo te va? Son los primeros días de clases y ves a un(a) amigo(a) de tu escuela secundaria que asiste a tu universidad. Con un(a) compañero(a), dramatiza su conversación.

Tú	**Amigo(a)**
■ Saluda a tu amigo(a).	■ Responde.
■ Pregúntale si vive en apartamento o en las residencias.	■ Responde y repite la pregunta.
■ Contesta y comenta sobre el costo de tus libros.	■ Describe tus costos.
■ Menciona que tienes una clase en cinco minutos.	■ Pídele su número de teléfono y dale el tuyo.
■ Despídete.	■ Despídete.

B. ¡Necesito una habitación! Unos amigos de otra universidad están de visita en tu universidad. Tú los invitas a tu apartamento. Ellos hacen muchas preguntas sobre tus compañeros(as) de cuarto, la división de responsabilidades, el costo de los libros, etc. Dramatiza la situación con dos compañeros.

¿Comprendes lo que se dice?

Estrategias para ver y escuchar. *In the first* **Paso** *of this chapter you learned that anticipating what you will hear aids comprehension considerably. You are now going to see an advertisement for housing that caters to university students. Write down three things you expect the advertisement to mention. After viewing the video, check to see if you anticipated correctly.*

Ahora mira el video. Luego, marca las expresiones que mejor completan cada oración.

1. Las Palmas es...
   ❑ una casa. ❑ un edificio de apartamentos. ❑ una residencia.
2. Las Palmas tiene salas...
   ❑ modernas. ❑ grandes. ❑ pequeñas.
3. Las Palmas tiene cocinas...
   ❑ modernas. ❑ grandes. ❑ pequeñas.
4. En Las Palmas el alquiler es...
   ❑ razonable. ❑ muy caro. ❑ imposible.

NOTICIERO CULTURAL

COSTUMBRES...

PUERTO RICO

Antes de empezar, dime...

Los ingleses y los norteamericanos se comunican bien en inglés pero a veces tienen problemas de vocabulario. Por ejemplo, si un inglés dice esto, ¿qué significa?

1. *I put it in the "boot."*
   a. *It's in a suitcase.* b. *It's in a shoe.* c. *It's in the car.*
2. *May I borrow half a "capsicum"?*
   a. *fifty cents* b. *half a bell pepper* c. *a half-dozen eggs*
3. *Lower the "bonnet," please. I can't see.*
   a. *hood of a car* b. *window shade* c. *ladies' hat*

¡Por fin, la guagua!

¡Vendo chinas!

Lectura. Ahora lee sobre una miscomunicación que tienen un estudiante puertorriqueño y una española.

Chinas y la guagua

Dos estudiantes esperan el autobús en un barrio de San Juan de Puerto Rico. Mario es puertorriqueño y Teresa es española.

TERESA ¿A qué hora viene el autobús?

MARIO En unos cinco minutos. Ay, no tengo tiempo para pasar por el supermercado. Mi mamá necesita unas chinas esta noche.

TERESA ¿Chinas? ¿En el supermercado? No comprendo.

MARIO Ay chica, tú nunca comprendes… Pero mira. Ahí viene la guagua.

TERESA ¿Viene quién?

Y ahora, dime…

¿Por qué tiene problemas Teresa en comprender lo que dice Mario?

1. Porque Teresa no comprende el español muy bien.
2. Porque el español de España es totalmente diferente del español de Puerto Rico.
3. A veces Mario, que es de Puerto Rico, usa vocabulario típico de Puerto Rico que no se usa en España.

Mira si seleccionaste la respuesta correcta en el Apéndice A.

Antes de escribir
Estrategias para escribir: Grupo de ideas

A. Preparándose. Antes de escribir, hay tres preguntas que el escritor siempre debe contestar.

- ¿Para quién escribo?
- ¿Por qué escribo?
- ¿De qué escribo?

Ahora, lee esta carta y contesta las tres preguntas.

Mi querida Nati:

19 de octubre de 1997

¡Mi apartamento es fenomenal! No es muy caro. Somos cuatro compañeras de cuarto y cada una paga sólo ciento setenta y cinco dólares al mes. Mi habitación no es muy grande pero no necesito mucho espacio. Y no necesito tomar el autobús a la universidad. Camino a mis clases y llego en unos diez o quince minutos. ¡Es estupendo!

¿Cómo es tu apartamento? ¿Tienes compañeras de cuarto? Escribe pronto, y recibe besos y abrazos de...

Tu mejor amiga,

Tere

B. Para concebir ideas. *When getting ready to write, it is a good idea to brainstorm, that is, to collect as many thoughts as possible about what you are going to write.*

Ésta es la lista de ideas que preparó Tere antes de escribir su carta a Natalia:

apartamento	poco espacio
compañeras de cuarto	estéreo estupendo
baño grande	sofá grande
caminar a clases	no caro
supermercado cerca	habitación no muy grande

1. ¿Incluyó Tere toda la información en su lista de ideas? Si no, ¿qué información no se usó?
2. ¿Usó información extra? ¿Cuál o cuáles?

Ahora, ¡a escribir!

A. En preparación. Prepárate para describir tu apartamento o casa en una carta a tu mejor amigo(a). Usa la carta de Tere como modelo. *(Before starting, answer the three questions that a good writer always asks himself or herself before writing. Then brainstorm a list of everything you might say in your letter.)*

B. El primer borrador. Usa la lista que preparaste en **A** para escribir un primer borrador *(first draft).*

C. Ahora a compartir. *(Share your first draft with two classmates.)* Comenta sobre el contenido y el estilo de tus compañeros(as) y escucha los comentarios de ellos sobre tu carta. Si hay errores de ortografía *(spelling)* o gramática, corrígelos.

D. Ahora a revisar. Decide si es necesario hacer cambios en tu carta. *(Keep in mind your classmates' comments as you decide.)*

E. La versión final. Prepara una versión final de tu carta y entrégala.

F. Ahora a publicar. En grupos de tres, lean sus cartas y decidan cuál es la mejor. *(Have the person with the best letter in your group read it to the entire class.)*

...y en verano, ¡vacaciones!

TAREA Antes de empezar este **Paso,** estudia **En preparación** 2.5, 2.6 y 2.7 y haz por escrito los ejercicios de **¡A practicar!** También escucha el **Paso 3 ¿Qué se dice... ?** del Capítulo 2 en el CD del estudiante.

¿Eres buen observador?

primavera

marzo
abril
mayo

verano

junio
julio
augusto

otoño

septiembre
octubre
noviembre

invierno

diciembre
enero
febrero

Ahora, ¡a analizar!

1. ¿Cuáles son las cuatro estaciones?
2. ¿Cuáles son los meses de cada estación?
3. ¿Qué estación asocias con esquiar? ¿las vacaciones? ¿la playa? ¿los exámenes finales? ¿el fútbol americano? ¿el béisbol? ¿el principio de las clases? ¿el final del año escolar? ¿el amor?

¿Qué se dice...?

Al hablar de las próximas vacaciones

Un grupo de estudiantes en la cafetería de la universidad habla de los planes para sus próximas vacaciones.

TERESA: Margarita, Silvia y yo también vamos a pasar las vacaciones de verano en San Juan. Salimos un lunes y regresamos un domingo. Una semana entera. ¡Pero una semana intensa! Comer, caminar, comprar y dormir... ¡nada más!

ROSA: Pues, en diciembre José y yo vamos de vacaciones a San Juan, Puerto Rico. Salimos inmediatamente después del último día de clases y no regresamos hasta el día antes de empezar las clases.

Pedro está muy ________________.

El 20 de julio Pedro ________________ para España.

El 30 de agosto ________________.

JOSÉ: Sí. Yo soy fanático del ejercicio. De día voy a caminar y correr por la playa. Y por las noches, salgo con Rosa a beber, comer y bailar.

A propósito...

In Spanish, the word **vacaciones** is always used in the plural. The singular **vacación** is rarely used.

Ahora, ¡a hablar!

A. ¡Vacaciones! Según el **¿Qué se dice… ?**, ¿adónde van y qué van a hacer estas personas?

	Sale el 20 de julio para España.
José	Regresan de San Juan un domingo.
Teresa, Margarita y Silvia	De noche sale con su amiga Rosa.
Pedro	Regresa de las vacaciones el 30 de agosto.
Rosa	Van a comer, caminar, comprar y dormir.

B. Adivinanzas. Completa estas oraciones.

Vocabulario útil

día(s)	semana(s)	mes(es)	año(s)	estacíon(es)
invierno	otoño	primavera	verano	

1. Hay cuatro ____ en un ____.
2. En una ____ hay siete ____.
3. Hay doce ____ en un ____.
4. Hay cincuenta y dos ____ en un ____.
5. Vamos a esquiar en el ____.
6. Las vacaciones más largas son en el ____.
7. Hay muchas flores en la ____.
8. Septiembre, octubre y noviembre son los meses del ____.

C. ¿Y tu compañero(a)? Pregúntale a tu compañero(a) qué planes tiene para las vacaciones de invierno o verano.

1. ¿Cuándo es tu último día de clase?
2. ¿Cuándo sales? ¿A qué hora?
3. ¿Adónde vas?
4. ¿Cuándo llegas? ¿A qué hora?
5. ¿Cuándo regresas? ¿A qué hora?

D. Las cuatro estaciones. ¿Qué hacen tú y tu familia cuando tienen un fin de semana largo de vacaciones durante cada estación?

Modelo **En la primavera, mi familia y yo vamos a la playa.** o
En la primavera, mi familia y yo no salimos de la casa.

	esquiar
la primavera	visitar a familiares
el verano	ir a las montañas
el otoño	no salir de la casa
el invierno	ir a la playa
	ir a Europa
	¿… ?

Y ahora, ¡a conversar!

A. Vacaciones de primavera. Tu tío Bruce, el millonario, te va a regalar unas vacaciones de primavera para ti y tres amigos(as). Habla con tus amigos(as) ahora y decidan adónde van, cuándo salen y cuándo llegan, qué van a hacer allí y cuándo regresan. Informen a la clase de su decisión.

B. Actividades. Prepara una lista de tus tres actividades favoritas para cada estación. Luego en grupos pequeños, pregúntales a tus compañeros(as) cuáles son sus actividades favoritas y diles las tuyas.

C. Las próximas vacaciones. Pregúntale a tu compañero(a) adónde va y qué va a hacer durante las próximas vacaciones escolares. Pregúntale si va solo o con alguien, cuándo sale(n), cuándo llega(n) y cuándo regresa(n). Dile a tu compañero(a) tus planes también.

¡Luz! ¡Cámara! ¡Acción!

A. Mi viaje soñado. Tú y tus compañeros(as) de cuarto van a las montañas por cuatro días para esquiar. Ahora, tú hablas por teléfono con tus padres y les explicas por qué vas a faltar a clases el viernes y el lunes. Ellos tienen muchas preguntas acerca del viaje. Dramatiza la conversación con tu padre o madre.

B. ¿Qué planes tienen? Tú y unos(as) amigos(as) toman un refresco y hablan de sus planes para el verano. Dramatiza esta situación con dos o tres compañeros(as) de clase.

Antes de leer
Estrategias para leer: Anticipar con imágenes visuales

A. Imágenes visuales. *Before reading any text, it helps to have some idea about the context. There are various clues that can aid you in anticipating information about a selection. Visual images, for example, can help convey a preliminary idea.*

Mira las imágenes visuales en «Buena de corazón» y contesta estas preguntas.

1. En este anuncio hay sólo una imagen visual principal. ¿Qué es? ¿una fruta cítrica? ¿arte moderno? ¿otra cosa?
2. También hay una ilustración muy pequeña. ¿Qué es? ¿una fruta cítrica? ¿arte moderno? ¿otra cosa?
3. En tu opinión, ¿cuál va a ser el tema principal de esta lectura? ¿una fruta cítrica? ¿arte moderno? ¿otra cosa? ¿Por qué opinas eso?

B. Para anticipar. Antes de leer el anuncio, escribe dos preguntas que, en tu opinión, esta lectura va a contestar. *(Then read the advertisement and check to see if you predicted correctly.)*

Lectura La china, uno de los frutos favoritos de los puertorriqueños, llegó a la isla en épocas antiguas desde el país que lleva su mismo nombre, China. Esta deliciosa fruta que se cultiva mayormente en los pueblos montañosos de Puerto Rico, es una rica fuente de vitamina C. Entre la familia de la china podemos encontrar: la chironja, nebo, mandarina, valencia y la china criolla.

A ver si comprendiste

1. Lee la(s) pregunta(s) que escribiste en **Para anticipar** y verifica si anticipaste correctamente o no.
2. ¿Por qué llaman los puertorriqueños «china» a esta fruta cítrica ?
3. ¿Es importada esta fruta cítrica en Puerto Rico? Explica tu respuesta.
4. ¿Por qué dicen los puertorriqueños que: «La china buena de verdad es la china de aquí»?
5. En tu opinión, ¿por qué hace el Departamento de Agricultura de Puerto Rico esta propaganda?

¿Sabías que... ?

The orange was introduced in Europe in the sixteenth century by the Portuguese traveling in China. Records show that Christopher Columbus took orange, lemon, and apple seeds to Haiti, on his second voyage to America. The name for oranges in Puerto Rico comes from street vendors calling out: **«Traigo naranjas de la China... de la China... de la China».** This call was eventually abbreviated to **«Traigo chinas».**

Viajemos por el ciberespacio a... PUERTO RICO

Expand your horizons! *Let's travel through cyberspace to Puerto Rico* and discover that you can . . .

- travel through seven ecosystems in one day.
- visit a mountain from which you can view the ocean, the desert, and the rain forest.
- experience the hospitality and openness of the **borinqueños.**
- discover the fascinating secrets of Taíno hieroglyphs.
- learn about the Puerto Ricans' commitment to justice and to maintaining their ties to the United States.
- stroll through the streets, plazas, and patios of **El viejo San Juan, Ponce,** and other areas of the so-called **Isla del encanto.**

If you are a cyberspace browser, join us in **Viajemos por el ciberespacio a... Puerto Rico** by trying the following important addresses:

Universidades de Puerto Rico
Universidad de Puerto Rico
http://www.upr.clu.edu/home.html

Universidad de Puerto Rico - Humacao
http://cuhwww.upr.clu.edu/

Universidad de Puerto Rico - Ponce
http://cutpo.cu-online.com/

Universidad de Puerto Rico-Mayagüez Campus (UPRM)
http://www_rum.upr.clu.edu/

Museo de cultura taína
http://www.amdatel.com/cb/taino.htm

Puerto Rico, Isla del encanto
http://www.coqui.com/IsladelEncanto.html

Noticias
Noticentro Puerto Rico
http://noticentro.coqui.net/pp.htm

Because addresses are likely to change without notice, the following key words will guarantee that **Viajemos por el ciberespacio a... Puerto Rico** will get you to your desired destination:

Palabras clave

Puerto Rico	Ponce
Borinquen	Taínos
El Morro	Radio en vivo Puerto Rico
Viejo San Juan	Universidades de Puerto Rico

http://www.hrwcollege.com

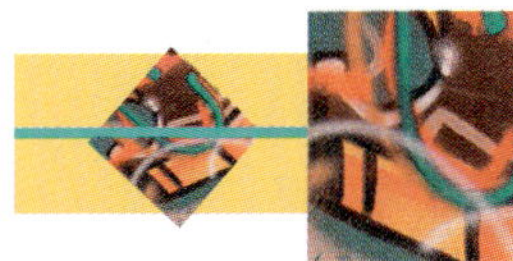

Vocabulario

Empleos

administrador(a)	*administrator*
cajero(a)	*cashier*
chófer *(m. / f.)*	*chauffeur, driver*
cocinero(a)	*cook*
dependiente *(m. / f.)*	*store clerk, salesperson*
empleado(a)	*employee*
gerente *(m. / f.)*	*manager*
lavaplatos *(m. / f.)*	*dishwasher*
mesero(a)	*waiter / waitress*
periodista *(m. / f.)*	*newspaper reporter*
secretario(a)	*secretary*
vendedor(a)	*seller, salesclerk*

En la oficina

computadora	*computer*
almohadilla	*mouse pad*
impresora	*printer*
parlantes *(m. pl.)*	*speakers*
ratón *(m.)*	*mouse*
teclado	*keyboard*
controlar	*to control*
decidir	*to decide*
dividir	*to divide*
empezar	*to begin*
entrevistar	*to interview*
escribir	*to write*
organizar	*to organize*
pagar	*to pay*
trabajar	*to work*
trabajo	*work*

Lugares

apartamento	*apartment*
café *(m.)*	*café*
casa	*house*
edificio	*building*
habitación	*dwelling, room*
hotel *(m.)*	*hotel*
montaña	*mountain*
oficina	*office*
playa	*beach*
residencia	*residence, dorm*
restaurante *(m.)*	*restaurant*
tienda	*store*

Personas

chico(a)	*boy / girl*
familia	*family*
familiares *(m. pl.)*	*extended family members*

Meses

enero	*January*
febrero	*February*
marzo	*March*
abril	*April*
mayo	*May*
junio	*June*
julio	*July*
agosto	*August*
septiembre	*September*
octubre	*October*
noviembre	*November*
diciembre	*December*

Estaciones

estación *(f.)*	*season*
invierno	*winter*
otoño	*autumn*
primavera	*spring*
verano	*summer*

Días

lunes	*Monday*
martes	*Tuesday*
miércoles	*Wednesday*
jueves	*Thursday*
viernes	*Friday*
sábado	*Saturday*
domingo	*Sunday*
día *(m.)*	*day*
de día	*during the day*
de noche	*at night*
día de la semana	*weekday*
todo el día	*all day*
fin de semana *(m.)*	*weekend*

Verbos

abrir	*to open*
aprender	*to learn*
ayudar	*to help*
beber	*to drink*
caminar	*to walk*
compartir	*to share*
correr	*to run*
hacer	*to make; to do*
invitar	*to invite*
lavar	*to wash*
limpiar	*to clean*
pasar	*to pass, spend time*
regresar	*to return*
salir	*to leave, go out*
tener	*to have*
vender	*to sell*
venir	*to come*
visitar	*to visit*
vivir	*to live*

Adjetivos

barato(a)	*inexpensive*
caro(a)	*expensive*
fanático(a)	*fanatic*
feliz	*happy*
feo(a)	*ugly*
nuevo(a)	*new*
otro(a)	*other, another*
próximo(a)	*next*
tanto(a)	*so much, so many*
último(a)	*last, ultimate*

Sustantivos

alquiler *(m.)*	*rent*
autobús *(m.)*	*bus*
baño	*bathroom*
carta	*letter*
comida	*food*
examen *(m.)*	*exam*
hora	*hour, time*
periódico	*newspaper*
puerta	*door*
vacaciones *(f. pl.)*	*vacation*

Palabras útiles

cada	*every, each*
cuántos(as)	*how many*
hasta	*until*
inmediatamente	*immediately*
lo peor	*the worst thing*

En preparación 2

2.1 Present Tense of *-er* and *-ir* Verbs

Stating what people do

The personal endings of **-er** and **-ir** verbs are identical, except for the **nosotros** and **vosotros** forms. As with **-ar** verbs, the personal endings of **-er** and **-ir** verbs always reflect the subject of the sentence.

-er, -ir **Verb Endings**

Subject Pronouns	Singular Endings *-er, -ir*	Subject Pronouns	Plural Endings *-er*	*-ir*
yo	**-o**	nosotros(as)	**-emos**	**-imos**
tú	**-es**	vosotros(as)	**-éis**	**-ís**
usted	**-e**	ustedes	**-en**	
él, ella	**-e**	ellos, ellas	**-en**	

Sample *-er* Verb:

COMER	
com**o**	com**emos**
com**es**	com**éis**
com**e**	com**en**
com**e**	com**en**

Sample *-ir* Verb:

ESCRIBIR	
escrib**o**	escrib**imos**
escrib**es**	escrib**ís**
escrib**e**	escrib**en**
escrib**e**	escrib**en**

Remember that the present indicative in Spanish has three possible equivalents in English.

Los niños **comen** chocolate.	*The children **eat** chocolate.*
Dos pasajeros **leen** el periódico.	*Two passengers **are reading** the newspaper.*
Una azafata **toma** café.	*One flight attendant **does drink** coffee.*

Some frequently used **-er** and **-ir** verbs are:

beber	*to drink*	escribir	*to write*
comer	*to eat*	recibir	*to receive*
correr	*to run*	salir	*to leave, to go out*
leer	*to read*	vivir	*to live*

¡A practicar!

A. ¡Cuánta actividad! It is only 8:00 AM and everyone is out doing something. What is everyone doing?

1. Matías __________________ (beber) un café.
2. Tú __________________ (escribir) una composición.
3. Pedro y Pablo __________________ (comer) en la cafetería.
4. María Isabel __________________ (abrir) la tienda.
5. Nosotros __________________ (correr) en el parque.
6. Yo __________________ (leer) mi libro de español.

B. ¡Qué día! It is now 8:00 PM. What is everyone doing?

1. Matías / estudiar / biblioteca
2. tú / comer / pizza / restaurante
3. Pedro y Pablo / leer / libro
4. María Isabel / ver / televisión / residencia
5. nosotros / beber / refresco
6. yo / correr / por la universidad

2.2 Numbers 0–199

Counting, solving math problems, and expressing cost

0	cero	**16**	dieciséis	**40**	cuarenta
1	uno	**17**	diecisiete	**42**	cuarenta y dos
2	dos	**18**	dieciocho	**50**	cincuenta
3	tres	**19**	diecinueve	**53**	cincuenta y tres
4	cuatro	**20**	veinte	**60**	sesenta
5	cinco	**21**	veintiuno	**64**	sesenta y cuatro
6	seis	**22**	veintidós	**70**	setenta
7	siete	**23**	veintitrés	**75**	setenta y cinco
8	ocho	**24**	veinticuatro	**80**	ochenta
9	nueve	**25**	veinticinco	**86**	ochenta y seis
10	diez	**26**	veintiséis	**90**	noventa
11	once	**27**	veintisiete	**97**	noventa y siete
12	doce	**28**	veintiocho	**100**	cien
13	trece	**29**	veintinueve	**101**	ciento uno
14	catorce	**30**	treinta	**178**	ciento setenta y ocho
15	quince	**31**	treinta y uno	**199**	ciento noventa y nueve

A. The number **uno (veintiuno, treinta y uno...)** changes to **un** before masculine nouns and **una** before feminine nouns.

Es **un** número muy difícil.	*It's a very difficult number.*
Hay cincuenta y **una** camas dobles en el hotel.	*There are fifty-one double beds in the hotel.*
La reservación es para **una** persona.	*The reservation is for one person.*

B. The numbers 16 to 29 are usually written as one word: **dieciocho, veintidós.** They may, however, be written as three words: **diez y ocho, veinte y dos, veinte y tres,** etc.

C. Numbers from 31 to 99 must be written as three words.

D. **Cien** is an even hundred. Any number between 101 and 199 is expressed as **ciento** and the remaining number.

101 ciento uno	**149** ciento cuarenta y nueve
110 ciento diez	**199** ciento noventa y nueve

Note that **y** never occurs directly after the number **ciento.**

E. Use the following expressions for solving math problems.

y *or* más (+)	menos (–)	es / son (=)
por (×)	dividido por (÷)	

¡A practicar!

A. Matemáticas. Solve these math problems. Then write out the problems in Spanish.

1. 4 + 9 = ?
2. 90 + 10 = ?
3. 28 – 12 = ?
4. 17 + 50 = ?
5. 42 ÷ 6 = ?
6. 11 + 152 = ?
7. 3 × 5 = ?
8. 175 – 30 = ?

B. ¿Cuánto cuesta? Tell how much the following items cost.

Modelo una hamburguesa
Cuesta tres dólares, noventa y nueve centavos.

1. el libro de español
2. una mochila
3. un bolígrafo
4. un sandwich y un refresco
5. una pizza para ocho personas
6. un libro de ciencias

2.3 Possessive Adjectives

Indicating ownership

A. Unlike English, possessive adjectives in Spanish must agree in number with the person, place, or thing possessed. **Nuestro** and **vuestro** must also agree in gender.

Possessive Adjectives

Singular Possessor	1 Thing Possessed	2+ Things Possessed	Plural Possessor	1 Thing Possessed	2+ Things Possessed
yo	**mi**	**mis**	nosotros(as)	**nuestro(a)**	**nuestros(as)**
tú usted	**tu** **su**	**tus** **sus**	vosotros(as) ustedes	**vuestro(a)** **su**	**vuestros(as)** **sus**
él, ella	**su**	**sus**	ellos, ellas	**su**	**sus**

Tu apartamento es estupendo y **tus** amigos son muy simpáticos. — *Your apartment is stupendous and your friends are very nice.*
Nuestra casa es nueva. — *Our house is new.*
Nuestras habitaciones son muy grandes. — *Our rooms are very big.*

Note that these possessive adjectives are always placed *before* the noun they modify.

B. Usually the context will clarify any ambiguity that may result with **su / sus** *(your, his, her, their, its)*. However, when ambiguity does occur, one of the following combinations of **de** + *pronoun* is used in place of **su / sus.**

su / sus =
- de usted — *your*
- de él — *his*
- de ella — *her*
- de ustedes — *your*
- de ellos — *their*
- de ellas — *their*

¿Es más grande el apartamento **de ustedes?** — *Is your apartment bigger?*
Sí, pero la casa **de ellos** es más elegante. — *Yes, but their house is more elegant.*

¡A practicar!

A. ¡Carísimo! ¿Cómo son los apartamentos o casas de estos estudiantes?

Modelo Alicia: cuarto / grande
Su cuarto es grande.

1. Andrés: apartamento / elegante
2. tú y Carlos: casa / grande
3. Teresa y Cecilia: residencia / nuevo
4. yo: cuarto / especial
5. Francisco y Mateo: amigas / simpático
6. Marta y yo: cuarto / estupendo

B. Nuestra clase. ¿De quién son estas cosas en la clase de español?

Modelo la computadora: de ella
Es su computadora.

1. la tiza: de ella
2. el lápiz: de él
3. los bolígrafos: de ella
4. la sala de clase: de nosotros
5. la pizarra: de nosotros
6. los exámenes: de ustedes
7. la mochila: de ella
8. el cuaderno: de ellos

C. Compañeros de cuarto. Completa este párrafo con la forma apropiada del adjetivo posesivo para saber qué le escribe Julio a una nueva amiga.

Querida amiga:

______________ compañeros de cuarto, Carlos y Toni, son muy simpáticos. Carlos es español. ______________ familia vive en Madrid. Toni es mexicano. ______________ padres viven en Guadalajara con ______________ abuelos *(grandparents)*. ¿Y yo? ______________ papás son de San Antonio, Texas. ______________ casa está en un barrio hispano de la ciudad. ¿Y tú? ¿Dónde viven ______________ padres?

2.4 Three Irregular Verbs: *tener, salir, venir*

Expressing obligations, departures, and arrivals

Tener		Salir		Venir	
to have		to leave		to come	
tengo	tenemos	salgo	salimos	vengo	venimos
tienes	tenéis	sales	salís	vienes	venís
tiene	tienen	sale	salen	viene	vienen
tiene	tienen	sale	salen	viene	vienen

A. When followed by an infinitive (the **-ar, -er**, or **-ir** form of a verb), **tener** becomes **tener que** and implies obligation.

Tengo que organizar mi apartamento.	*I have to organize my apartment.*
Tenemos que comprar muchas cosas.	*We have to (must) buy many things.*

B. When followed by an infinitive, **salir** and **venir** become **salir a** and **venir a.**

Salgo a correr a las 10:00.	*I go running at 10:00.*
Yo **vengo a** estudiar, y Eva **viene a** ayudarme.	*I come to study, and Eva comes to help me.*

¡A practicar!

A. Muy ocupados. University life is not easy. Everyone's busy all the time. Select the correct form of each verb to tell what these students do.

1. Patricia (tengo / tiene) que lavar el auto.
2. Clara y Eva (salen / salimos) a las 8:00 para la universidad.
3. Felipe y yo (venimos / vienen) a estudiar con ustedes.
4. ¿Y tú? ¡Ah! Tú (vengo / vienes) a trabajar con la computadora.
5. Sí, todos los estudiantes (tiene / tienen) que trabajar mucho.
6. Yo siempre (vengo / vienes) tarde a esta clase.

B. ¿Dónde están? Tell your roommate where everyone is this morning.

1. Juan y Mateo / tener clases
2. Patricio siempre / salir a / caminar
3. Oscar / tener que / trabajar hoy
4. Héctor / venir / más tarde
5. Yo / salir a / correr
6. Nicolás / venir / con Yolanda

C. ¡Tanto que hacer! Tomorrow is the first day of class. Teresa and her friends, Anita and Olga, still have a lot of things to do. What problems are they having? Form at least five sentences, using one element from each column.

Teresa	(no) tener	el horario de las clases
Olga	tener que	lavar la ropa
Anita		todos los libros necesarios
Olga y Anita		problemas con la computadora
nosotras		comprar la comida para la semana
		llamar a sus padres

2.5 Telling Time

Stating at what time things occur

A. The word for *time* (referring to clock time) in Spanish is **hora,** which is always feminine. To tell the hour, **es la** is used only with **una;** otherwise **son las** followed by the hour is used.

¿Qué hora es?	*What time is it?*
Es la una.	*It's one o'clock.*
Son las doce en punto.	*It's twelve sharp.*

B. Minutes from the hour to the half hour are added to the hour and connected with **y.** Between the half hour and the next hour, minutes are subtracted from the next hour and connected with **menos.**

1:24	Es la una **y** veinticuatro.
6:10	Son las seis **y** diez.
1:40	Son las dos **menos** veinte.
12:42	Es la una **menos** dieciocho.

Digital clocks have changed this more traditional way of stating time. Now, one also hears **Son las doce y cuarenta y dos** instead of **Es la una menos dieciocho.**

C. **Cuarto** means *quarter hour* and **media** is used to express *half past the hour.*

Vienen a la una y **cuarto.**	*They are coming at a quarter past one.*
Mañana salen a las siete y **media.**	*Tomorrow they leave at 7:30.*

D. **Mediodía** and **medianoche** are used to express **noon** and **midnight.**

Tengo una cita al **mediodía.**	*I have an appointment at noon.*
El autobús sale a (la) **medianoche.**	*The bus leaves at midnight.*

E. To state that something happens at a particular time, Spanish uses **a las...** This should not be confused with **son las...,** which means *It is* a specific time.

¡Apúrese! **Son las** siete menos cuarto y él llega **a las** siete en punto.	*Hurry up! It's a quarter to seven and he arrives at seven sharp.*
El concierto es **en** el teatro **a las** nueve.	*The concert is at the theater at nine.*

Note that **a las...** means *at* only when speaking about specific clock time. In most other instances *at* is translated by **en.**

F. The phrase **de la mañana / tarde / noche** is used only when a *specific* time in the morning / afternoon / evening is being stated.

El avión llega a las dos **de la mañana.**	*The plane arrives at 2:00 AM.*
Salgo a la una y diez **de la tarde.**	*I leave at 1:10 in the afternoon.*
Son las once **de la noche.**	*It's 11:00 PM.*

The phrases **en** or **por la mañana / tarde / noche** are used to express a general time (not specific clock time).

Por la mañana tengo que cancelar mi reservación.	*In the morning I have to cancel my reservation.*
Llegamos **en la tarde.**	*We arrive in the afternoon.*

¡A practicar!

A. ¿Qué hora es? Write out the following times.

1. 6:00 AM
2. 11:15 AM
3. 12:00 noon
4. 1:22 PM
5. 2:45 PM
6. 1:05 PM
7. 9:40 PM
8. 12:50 AM

B. Mis clases. Contesta las preguntas.

1. ¿A qué hora sales para la universidad por la mañana?
2. ¿A qué hora comienza tu clase de español? ¿A qué hora termina *(does it end)*?
3. ¿Tienes más clases por la mañana, por la tarde o por la noche? ¿A qué hora es tu primera clase? ¿y tu última *(last)* clase del día?
4. ¿Tomas el almuerzo *(lunch)* al mediodía?
5. ¿Con qué frecuencia te acuestas *(go to bed)* a medianoche?

2.6 Days of the Week, Months, and Seasons

Giving dates and stating when events take place

A. The days of the week are *not* capitalized in Spanish, and they are all masculine.

Los días de la semana

lunes	*Monday*	viernes	*Friday*
martes	*Tuesday*	sábado	*Saturday*
miércoles	*Wednesday*	domingo	*Sunday*
jueves	*Thursday*		

B. The months of the year also are *not* capitalized in Spanish and are also masculine.

Los meses del año

enero	mayo	septiembre
febrero	junio	octubre
marzo	julio	noviembre
abril	agosto	diciembre

C. As in English, the four seasons also are not capitalized.

Las estaciones

el otoño	*fall*	la primavera	*spring*
el invierno	*winter*	el verano	*summer*

D. To indicate that something happens on a particular day, Spanish always uses the definite article, never the preposition **en.**

Hay una fiesta **el** lunes.	*There's a party on Monday.*
No hay clases **los** sábados ni **los** domingos.	*There are no classes on Saturdays and Sundays.*

E. The preposition **en** is used to indicate that something happens in a particular month or season.

No hay vuelos **en** enero.	*There are no flights in January.*
En verano hay dos excursiones.	*In the summer there are two excursions.*

F. Dates **(las fechas)** in Spanish are given using the formula **el + (número) + de + (mes) + de + (año).**

El concierto es **el 5 de julio de 1998.**	*The concert is on July 5th, 1998.*

¡A practicar!

A. Fechas. Escribe en español estas *(these)* fechas.

1. la fecha de Navidad *(Christmas)*
2. la fecha de la independencia de Estados Unidos
3. la fecha de tu cumpleaños *(birthday)*
4. la fecha del cumpleaños de tu madre y de tu padre
5. las fechas del primer *(first)* día de primavera, verano, otoño, invierno

B. Días, meses y estaciones. Contesta las preguntas.

1. ¿Cuántos meses hay en un año? ¿Cuántos días hay?
2. ¿En qué meses hay nieve *(snow)*?
3. ¿Qué días hay clases de español? ¿Qué días no hay clases?
4. ¿En qué estaciones hay clases? ¿no hay clases?

2.7 Verbs of Motion

Telling where people are going

Any verb that indicates movement, such as *to walk, to leave, to run, to arrive,* is a verb of motion. Some common verbs of motion are:

andar	*to walk*	ir	*to go*	regresar	*to return*
caminar	*to walk*	llegar	*to arrive*	salir	*to leave*
correr	*to run*				

In Spanish, these verbs always use the preposition **a** to indicate movement *to* or arrival *at* a place, and **de** to indicate movement *from* a particular place.

El autobús **sale de** San Diego a las nueve y **llega a** Palo Alto a las once y veinte.	*The bus leaves San Diego at 9:00 and arrives at Palo Alto at 11:20.*
El lunes **regresamos de** Lima **a** Cuzco.	*On Monday we return from Lima to Cuzco.*

¡A practicar!

A. ¿Qué pasa? What is happening at the bus station in San Diego? To find out, form sentences, using the following words.

1. un niño / correr / la cafetería para comer
2. una chica / ir / los servicios
3. un autobús / llegar / Mazatlán
4. una persona / regresar / tienda / para comprar un recuerdo
5. una familia / viajar / Guadalajara
6. un señor / ir / cafetería para tomar café

B. Necesito un cambio. Isabel needs your advice. Complete the following paragraph with the appropriate form of each verb so that you may understand her problem.

Mi vida es terrible. Todas las mañanas yo ____ (correr) por veinte minutos. Luego ____ (ir) a la universidad. Allí ____ (estudiar), ____ (trabajar) y ____ (comer). Generalmente yo ____ (regresar) a casa a las 9:00 de la noche. A veces yo ____ (salir) y ____ (caminar) con el perro media hora. Pero mi problema es que nunca ____ (tener) energía. ¿Qué me recomiendan?

CAPÍTULO 3

Cultural Topics

- **¿Sabías que…?**
  Birthday Celebrations for Fifteen-Year-Old Girls
- **Noticiero cultural**
  Lugar: *Barcelona*
  Gente: *Joan Miró*
- **Lectura:** *Enrique Iglesias: Deseado por todas*

Writing Strategies

- Brainstorming and Using Clusters

Reading Strategies

- Scanning

En preparación

- 3.1 The Verb **estar**
- 3.2 Interrogative Words
- 3.3 Present Progressive Tense
- 3.4 Superlatives
- 3.5 **Ser** and **estar** with Adjectives
- 3.6 Two Irregular Verbs: **saber** and **conocer**

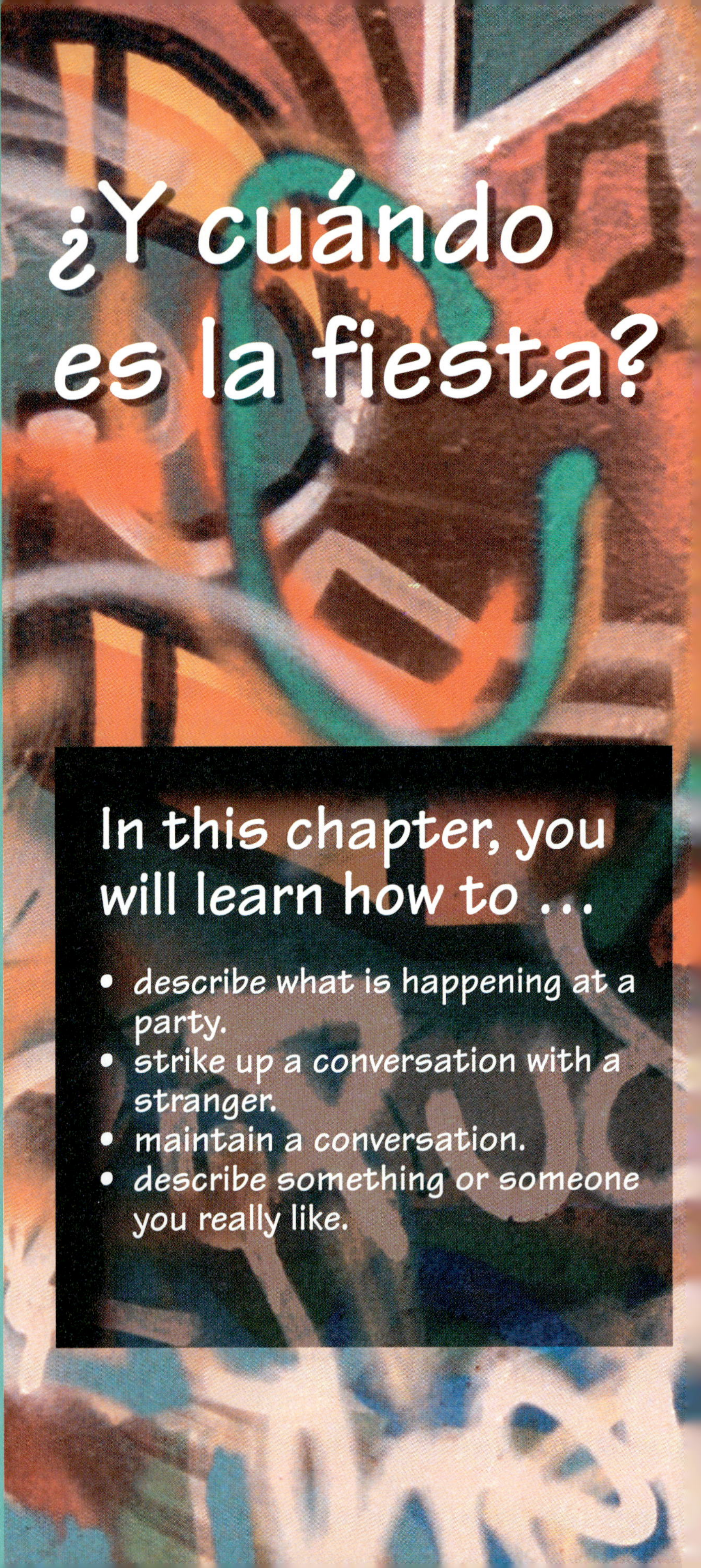

¿Y cuándo es la fiesta?

In this chapter, you will learn how to …

- describe what is happening at a party.
- strike up a conversation with a stranger.
- maintain a conversation.
- describe something or someone you really like.

«La sardana», baile folklórico típico de Cataluña

Club nocturno popular en Madrid

Una boda en España

Lo que ya sabes...

1. Los bailes folklóricos son muy populares en todo el mundo hispanohablante. ¿Cuáles son algunos de los bailes folklóricos populares en los Estados Unidos?
2. ¿Adónde vas tú a bailar? ¿Vas a clubes nocturnos o a fiestas de amigos?
3. ¿Qué haces en las fiestas? ¿Bailas mucho o prefieres comer, beber y conversar?
4. ¿Asistes a bodas familiares? ¿Qué hacen en las bodas familiares: bailan, comen, cantan? ¿Quiénes asisten?

ESPAÑA

¡En casa de Natalia, el sábado!

TAREA Antes de empezar este **Paso,** estudia **En preparación** 3.1 y 3.2 y haz por escrito los ejercicios de **¡A practicar!** También escucha el **Paso 1 ¿Qué se dice...?** del Capítulo 3 en el CD del estudiante.

¿Eres buen observador?

Ahora, ¡a analizar!

1. Ésta es la cubierta *(cover)* de una revista. ¿Qué tipo de información hay en la revista?
2. La revista incluye un poster: ¿De quién es el poster? ¿A quiénes les interesaría tener el poster?
3. La cubierta menciona a dos grupos musicales. ¿Cuáles son? ¿Qué tipo de música tocan?
4. ¿Cuál es tu música favorita? ¿la clásica? ¿el rock? ¿el jazz? ¿la popular? ¿la música ranchera (*country music*) de los Estados Unidos?
5. Un artículo en esta revista presenta las opiniones de ciertas personas sobre un tema algo controversial. ¿Cuál es el tema? ¿Quiénes expresan sus opiniones? ¿Qué crees que van a decir?

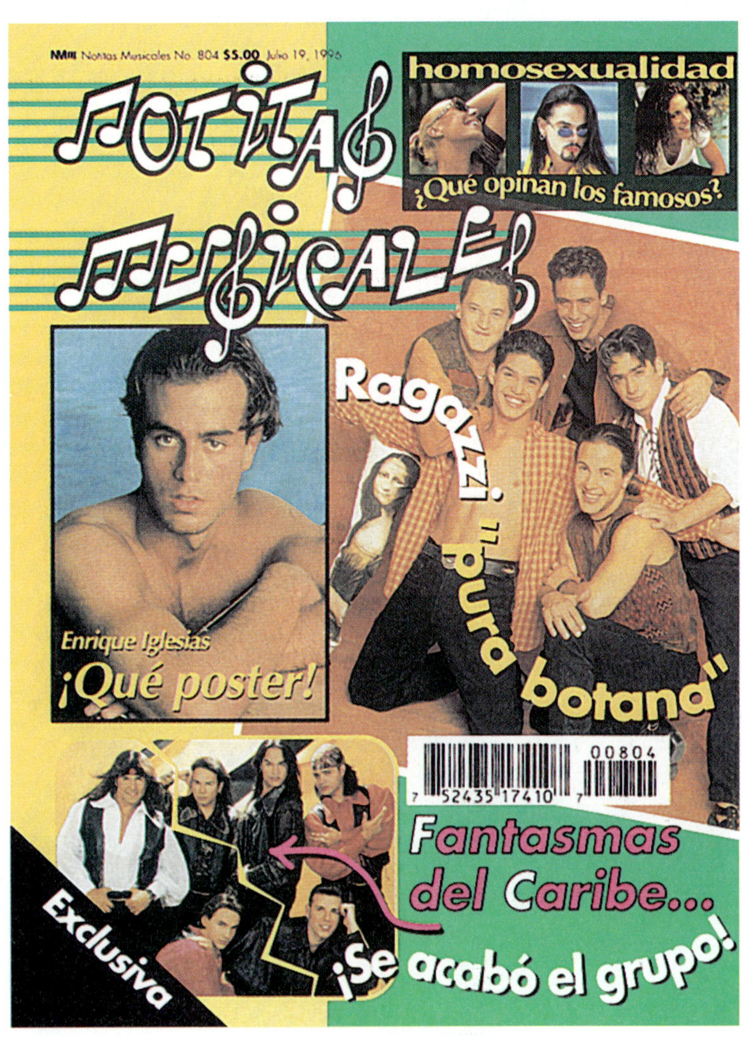

¿Qué se dice...?

Al describir una fiesta

Hay una fiesta esta noche en casa de Natalia Alarcón.

¿Qué preocupa a la señora Alarcón?

❑ los invitados	❑ los nachos	❑ los refrescos
❑ el casete de Jon Secada	❑ la comida	❑ la cerveza
❑ la persona en la alcoba	❑ la hora	❑ su hija Elisa

Ya están todos los invitados en la fiesta de Natalia. Toda la gente está muy contenta, excepto la señora Alarcón. Ella está en la sala con sus hijos. Está muy preocupada y muy nerviosa. Tiene mil preguntas para sus hijos. ¿Está la comida en la cocina? ¿Tienen el casete de Jon Secada? ¿Dónde están los nachos? ¿Quién está en la alcoba? ¿Está enfermo? ¿Está borracho? ¿Por qué está triste Nicolás? Para distraerla, Diego, su hijo, invita a su mamá a bailar.

Ahora, ¡a hablar!

A. ¿Dónde está? Tu amiga acaba de llegar a la fiesta. ¿Qué pregunta?

Modelo Alicia / cocina

TU AMIGA **¿Dónde está Alicia?**
TÚ **Está en la cocina.**

1. Enriqueta / sala
2. la comida / cocina
3. los invitados / patio
4. los refrescos / sala
5. el perro / patio
6. Eduardo y Arturo / alcoba

B. Es muy interesante. En la fiesta de Natalia hay una persona muy interesante. ¿Qué le preguntas?

Modelo Hola, ¿ _____________ te llamas?

TÚ **Hola, ¿cómo te llamas?**

COMPAÑERO(A) **Hola, soy [*nombre*]. o Me llamo [*nombre*].**

1. ¿ _____________ estás hoy?
2. ¿ _____________ eres?
3. ¿ _____________ vives ahora?
4. ¿ _____________ estudias en la universidad?
5. ¿ _____________ clases tomas este semestre, cinco o seis?
6. ¿ _____________ es tu profesor(a) de español?
7. ¿ _____________ es más fácil, español o historia?
8. ¿ _____________ vas después de la fiesta? ¿a la residencia?
9. ¿ _____________ tienes que regresar a la residencia?
10. ¿ _____________ no vamos a un café? Yo invito.

C. ¿Cómo están? Dile a tu compañero(a) cómo estás tú y cómo están estas personas en las situaciones indicadas. Selecciona la palabra apropiada para cada una.

aburrido	borracho	contento	enfermo
furioso	nervioso	preocupado	triste

Modelo Estás en el examen final de química.
Estoy muy nervioso(a).

1. Un amigo está en el hospital.
2. Tú estás en un concierto de música clásica.
3. Tus amigos están estudiando para un examen difícil.
4. El novio de tu amiga sale para otra universidad. ¿Cómo está tu amiga? ¿Cómo está su novio?
5. En una fiesta, hablas con una persona que siempre bebe mucho. ¿Cómo estás tú? ¿Cómo está la persona con quien hablas?
6. Hay una fiesta el sábado pero tú tienes que estudiar para un examen de español.

D. ¿Yo? ¿Interesante? Ahora una persona cree que tú eres muy interesante. Contesta las preguntas de tu compañero(a). *(Keep the conversation going as long as possible by ending each response with a question.)*

Modelo

COMPAÑERO(A) **Hola. ¿Qué tal?**
TÚ **Bien gracias, ¿y tú?**

Y ahora, ¡a conversar!

A. Gente interesante. En la clase hay mucha gente interesante. Conversa con tres personas hasta descubrir sus nombres, su origen, sus clases favoritas y menos favoritas, los nombres de sus profesores favoritos y los menos favoritos, etc.

B. ¡Mímica! En grupos pequeños, dramaticen, sin decir una sola palabra, la situación que su profesor(a) les va a dar. Sus compañeros tienen que adivinar la situación.

Modelo Estás muy preocupado(a). Hay un examen en la clase de español mañana.
Acción: *Act worried. Open and close your Spanish book pretending to be studying / memorizing certain vocabulary and grammar, etc.*

C. ¿Quién lo hace? Pregúntale a tus compañeros de clase si hacen las actividades en este cuadro. Cada vez que uno diga que sí, pídele que firme (escriba su nombre) en el cuadrado (*square*) apropiado. La idea es tener una firma en cada cuadrado. **¡Ojo!** No se permite que una persona firme más de un cuadrado.

comer nachos con frecuencia ________ *Firma*	vivir con sus padres ________ *Firma*	estar furioso(a) con frecuencia ________ *Firma*	estar frustrado(a) ahora ________ *Firma*
estar nervioso(a) ahora ________ *Firma*	ir a México en el verano ________ *Firma*	ir a una fiesta esta semana ________ *Firma*	salir todas las noches ________ *Firma*
ir al cine con frecuencia ________ *Firma*	trabajar los sábados ________ *Firma*	tener clases los martes y jueves ________ *Firma*	no tener clases aburridas ________ *Firma*
visitar a sus padres cada fin de semana ________ *Firma*	no ser de los Estados Unidos ________ *Firma*	tener una clase de historia ________ *Firma*	preparar la comida todos los días ________ *Firma*

¡Luz! ¡Cámara! ¡Acción!

A. ¡Es un gran éxito! Tú estás en una fiesta fantástica cuando ves a dos personas muy interesantes que deseas conocer. Dramatiza la situación con dos compañeros(as) de clase.

Tú	**Dos personas**
■ Preséntate.	■ Respondan.
■ Pregunta si son estudiantes.	■ Respondan y pregunten qué hace él o ella.
■ Responde y pregunta sobre sus clases.	■ Respondan y pregunten sobre sus clases.
■ Contesta y menciona que uno de ellos está preocupado. Pregunta por qué.	■ Explica por qué.

B. ¡Es estupenda! Estás en una fiesta y ves que un(a) estudiante nuevo(a) que tú quieres invitar a salir está hablando con tu amigo(a). Cuando terminan de hablar, tú corres a pedirle información a tu amigo(a) sobre la nueva persona. Como no conoces a esta persona, preguntas acerca de su nombre, edad, origen, residencia, horario de clases, clase y profesor(a) favorito(a), etc. Dramatiza esta situación con un(a) compañero(a).

¿Comprendes lo que se dice?

Estrategias para escuchar. *In a previous chapter you learned that knowing what people are talking about or anticipating what they are going to say makes it easier to understand a foreign language. Knowing what to listen for, or listening for specific information also aids listening comprehension considerably. In these recorded sections and on the tests, you can always get a good idea of what to listen for if you read the questions at the end of the listening section* before *you listen to the recording. Read those questions now and write down four things that you know you have to listen for. Check to see if you anticipated correctly after you listen to the recording.*

Now listen as your instructor plays the dialogue between two guests at Natalia Alarcón's party.

¿Fumar o beber? Estamos en la fiesta de Natalia. Escucha la conversación que Paco tiene con Cristina cuando llega a la fiesta. Luego contesta las preguntas a continuación.

1. ¿Dónde están los invitados?
   a. en el patio b. en la sala c. en la cocina
2. ¿Qué desea tomar Cristina?
   a. un refresco b. una cerveza c. No desea tomar nada.
3. ¿Qué opina Paco sobre el fumar?
   a. Cree que no es bueno para la salud.
   b. Cree que está bien fumar en el patio pero no en la casa.
   c. Cree que está bien fumar porque él fuma.
4. ¿Qué opina Cristina sobre el tomar bebidas alcohólicas?
   a. Cree que está bien tomar porque ella toma.
   b. Cree que no es bueno fumar ni tomar bebidas alcohólicas.
   c. Cree que el alcohol no es bueno para la salud.

NOTICIERO CULTURAL

LUGAR... ESPAÑA

Antes de empezar, dime...

Contesta estas preguntas para saber algunas de tus opiniones sobre el arte y edificios o monumentos simbólicos.

1. Nombra una ciudad antigua y una moderna en tu estado. ¿Hay alguna ciudad que sea *(is)* moderna y antigua?
2. ¿Qué opinas del arte moderno? ¿del arte realista? En tu opinión, ¿cuál es mejor? ¿Por qué?
3. ¿Conoces un edificio o monumento excéntrico en tu ciudad o estado? ¿Por qué lo consideras excéntrico?
4. En Washington, D.C., hay varios edificios y monumentos que son símbolos de la ciudad. ¿Hay algún edificio o monumento que sea *(is)* símbolo de tu ciudad? ¿Cuál es?

A propósito...

Be aware when reading in Spanish that, although you have only learned the present tense so far, you will be able to recognize other tenses just from the context. Find three past tense verbs in the reading that follows. Can you find any other tenses in this reading?

Joan Miró, *Una joven en fuga*, 1968.

Barcelona

Si visitas la ciudad de Barcelona algún día, vas a observar que es una ciudad antigua pero también es una de las ciudades más cosmopolitas e internacionales de España.

Barcelona ha inspirado a grandes artistas que nacieron o vivieron en esa región, como Salvador Dalí, Pablo Picasso, Joan Miró y el gran arquitecto Antonio Gaudí.

Gaudí, por ejemplo, combinó elementos tan contradictorios como el expresionismo modernista, el esplendor gótico-cristiano y el misticismo árabe. Su arquitectura es un arte que combina la temática formal con la imaginación más espontánea.

El edificio más importante de Gaudí es el Templo de la Sagrada Familia. Se inició en 1883, pero todavía no se ha completado. En el Templo de la Sagrada Familia, Gaudí combinó el pasado con el presente, antiguos exteriores con interiores abstractos.

Dicen que el Templo de la Sagrada Familia es el símbolo de Barcelona, así como el edificio Empire State es el símbolo de Nueva York.

Templo de la Sagrada Familia en Barcelona

Y ahora, dime...

Contrastes. Contesta estas preguntas para ver por qué muchas personas dicen que Barcelona es una ciudad de contrastes.

1. ¿Cuáles son algunos de los contrastes que observamos en Barcelona?
2. ¿Es válido decir que Antonio Gaudí es una persona de contrastes? ¿Por qué?
3. ¿Por qué se dice que el Templo de la Sagrada Familia une el pasado con el presente? Explica.
4. Compara el Templo de la Sagrada Familia y el Empire State Building. ¿En qué son similares? ¿En qué son diferentes?

El español en otras disciplinas: Arte

Arte mundial. El arte es una parte esencial de todas las culturas del mundo. ¿Cuánto sabes tú de arte? Con un(a) compañero(a) prepara una lista de todos los artistas que ustedes dos conocen. Indica para cada artista su país de origen. Tienen sólo cinco minutos para hacer esto.

Diego Velázquez, *Las Meninas*, 1656, Museo del Prado, Madrid.

Proyecto: Trae (*Bring*) a la clase un libro de arte con tu cuadro favorito y explícale a la clase por qué es tu favorito... ¡en español, claro!

Pablo Picasso, *Guernica*, 1937, Centro de Arte Reina Sofía, Madrid.

¿Con quién está bailando Nicolás?

TAREA Antes de empezar este **Paso,** estudia **En preparación** 3.3 y 3.4 y haz por escrito los ejercicios de **¡A practicar!** También escucha el **Paso 2 ¿Qué se dice...?** del Capítulo 3 en el CD del estudiante.

¿Eres buen observador?

Super 1

Master Plan, Clack, Scanner, La Bomba, Caribó, Drack y Carlos Izaga participan este año en la gira del Super 1. Entre julio y agosto, un camión-escenario recorrerá más de 50 ciudades españolas. En anteriores Super 1 participaron Alejandro Sanz y Sergio Dalma, y Whigfield y Paco Pil se hicieron novios allí... ¡No se te ocurra perdértelos!

PRÓXIMOS CONCIERTOS SUPER 1

FECHA	CIUDAD	DIAL 40
16-M	Murcia	91.3
17-X	Cartagena	102.3
18-J	Elda	100.5
19-V	Alicante	91.0
20-S	Elche	94.8
21-D	Alcoy	96.3
22-L	DESCANSO	
23-M	Onteniente	95.3
24-X	Valencia	94.2
25-J	DESCANSO	
26-V	Santa Ponsa (Mallorca)	94.1
27-S	Alcudia (Mallorca)	94.1
28-D	DESCANSO	
29-L	Gandía	96.5

Dani lleva desde los 14 años trabajando como modelo, José Luis trabaja como actor en la serie *Médico de familia* y Rubén está colaborando en la composición y programación del nuevo disco de Kike Boy. Junto a Luis y Julio César forman el grupo Clack!. Su single debut, *El morbo que me das*, es el tema perfecto para una noche veraniega.

20 Clack!

Fotos: Gabowicz, Jesús Aparicio, Pablo Plaza. Texto: J. Orge.

Ahora, ¡a analizar!

1. ¿Qué es el **Super 1**? ¿Qué es un camión-escenario? ¿En qué país es la gira del **Super 1**?
2. ¿Quiénes van a participar en el **Super 1** este año? ¿En cuántas ciudades van a estar?
3. Durante este mes, ¿cuántos días de descanso van a tener? ¿Cuántas ciudades van a visitar los lunes? ¿En qué ciudades van a estar los miércoles?
4. Tres de los miembros del grupo musical Clack también trabajan en otros puestos. ¿Qué hacen?

¿Qué se dice...?

Al describir lo que está pasando

¿Con quién habla Patricia? ______________

¿Dónde está Patricia? ______________

Marca quiénes están:

❑ Diego	❑ Luis	❑ Estela
❑ Carmen	❑ Mercedes	❑ Dolores
❑ José Luis	❑ Lola	❑ Nicolás

ALICIA ¿Qué están haciendo?

PATRICIA Estoy decorando un pastel buenísimo. Ahora están tocando mi disco favorito. Y en el patio José Luis está tocando la guitarra y cantando. Canta tan bien.

ALICIA Y Nicolás, ¿qué está haciendo Nicolás?

PATRICIA Nicolás está bailando con Natalia. Ella está hermosísima esta noche. Y él está guapísimo también.

ALICIA ¡Ay, y yo enferma! ¿Por qué hoy... cuando necesito tanto estar en la fiesta?

¿Sabías que... ?

El quincenario o cumpleaños de quince años es un día muy importante en la vida de una joven hispana de México o del suroeste de los EE.UU. Ese día, la quinceañera invita a sus parientes y amigos a una gran celebración que incluye una misa (servicio religioso) especial en la iglesia, una recepción donde sirven mucha comida y un gran baile donde todos llevan vestidos y trajes muy elegantes.

Ahora, ¡a hablar!

A. Todos están trabajando. Teresa y sus amigos están haciendo los últimos preparativos para una fiesta de cumpleaños. ¿Qué están haciendo?

Modelo **Paula está decorando el pastel.**

Paula		preparar / comida
yo		hacer / limonada
Tomás	estar	decorar / pastel
Alicia		comprar / cervezas
Francisco y María		mirar / televisión
Rafael		hablar / Paula

B. ¡Fiesta! Hoy es la fiesta de tu clase de español. Es en casa de uno de los estudiantes. ¿Qué están haciendo todos?

Modelo **Mis amigos *Ken* y *Greg* están hablando con la profesora.**

1. Mis amigas… y…
2. Mi amigo…
3. El (la) profesor(a)…
4. Yo…
5. Mi amiga…
6. Mis amigos… y…

C. ¡Está divertidísima! Todo el mundo está contentísimo en la fiesta de Natalia. ¿Por qué?

Modelo música / buena

La música está buenísima.

1. Nicolás / guapo
2. Teresa / hermosa
3. pastel / rico
4. comida / buena
5. invitados / contentos
6. refrescos / buenos

D. ¡Qué exagerado! You have a friend who always exaggerates when talking about himself. Following is what his friends say about him. How would he describe himself?

Modelo Es alto.

Soy el estudiante más alto de la clase.

1. Es un estudiante inteligente.
2. Es un chico interesante.
3. Es un muchacho popular.
4. Es un estudiante serio.
5. Es guapo.
6. Es un chico estupendo.

Y ahora, ¡a conversar!

A. ¡Yo soy simpatiquísimo(a)! En tu opinión, ¿cuál es tu cualidad más significativa? Decídelo y luego habla con varios compañeros de clase. Diles cómo eres y escucha cómo son ellos.

Modelo

You choose: inteligente
You say: **Soy inteligentísimo(a).** o
Soy el (la) estudiante más inteligente de la clase.

B. Excusas. ¿Qué excusas das cuando alguien te invita a correr y tú no tienes ganas de (no quieres) correr? Prepara una lista de todas las excusas que puedes usar. Luego compara tu lista con las de otras dos o tres personas.

Modelo **Lo siento, pero estoy comiendo.**

C. ¿Qué están haciendo? ¿Cuántas diferencias hay entre este dibujo y el de tu compañero(a) en el Apéndice A? Háganse preguntas para determinar cuáles son las diferencias. Recuerda que no se permite mirar el dibujo de tu compañero(a) hasta terminar esta actividad.

Modelo **¿Cuántas personas están bailando?**

¡Luz! ¡Cámara! ¡Acción!

A. ¡Qué fiesta! Estás en una fiesta buenísima y decides llamar a un(a) amigo(a) que está enfermo(a). En parejas dramaticen esta situación.

Tú	Amigo(a) enfermo(a)
■ Saluda a tu amigo(a) y pregúntale cómo está.	■ Responde. Pregunta sobre la fiesta, los invitados y sus actividades.
■ Responde. Da muchos detalles.	■ Pregunta si tu amigo(a) especial está allí y qué está haciendo.
■ Responde y despídete. Explica por qué tienes que irte.	■ Responde y despídete.

B. ¡Estoy furioso(a)! Tú estás en una fiesta después de un partido de fútbol. Estás muy frustrado(a) porque la persona que te gusta y que quieres conocer está hablando con todo el mundo e ignorándote a ti. Tu amigo(a) quiere saber por qué estás tan frustrado(a). Dramatiza la situación con un(a) compañero(a).

¿Comprendes lo que se dice?

Estrategias para ver y escuchar. *In the first* ***Paso*** *of this chapter you learned to anticipate what you will hear by reading the questions you will be asked* before *you listen to the recording. You can anticipate what you will see and hear on video the same way, by reading the questions first. Read those questions now and write down three things that you expect to see and hear on the video. After viewing the video, check to see if you anticipated correctly.*

Su fiesta privada de San Fermín. Todos los años en julio vienen a Pamplona turistas de todas partes del mundo para participar en la fiesta de San Fermín que incluye los famosas corridas de toros por las calles de la ciudad. Mira ahora el anuncio para **Su fiesta privada de San Fermín** y luego contesta las preguntas a continuación.

1. ¿Qué es la Agencia Gorostiaga?
2. Nombra por los menos tres cosas que hace la Agencia Gorostiaga por sus clientes.
3. El anuncio dice que es una fiesta "privada." ¿Por qué? Explica.
4. Según el anuncio, ¿por qué es necesario llamar al 8–05–23–40?

NOTICIERO CULTURAL

GENTE… JOAN MIRÓ

Antes de empezar, dime...

Contesta estas preguntas para ver cuánto sabes de las influencias en los artistas y del surrealismo.

1. En tu opinión, ¿qué influye más en un artista: su familia, su ciudad o su país? ¿Por qué crees eso?
2. Hay otras cosas que influyen en los artistas también. Nombra algunas.
3. ¿Qué es el arte surrealista? Descríbelo.

Joan Miró, *Pajaro y mujer a la luz de la luna*, 1949, Galería Tate, Londres.

A propósito...

Be aware that the simple present tense will be used as historical present to narrate past time. For example, in the reading that follows you will see:

Su arte antes de 1920 está influido por los colores brillantes.
Su estilo florece después de 1920, en París.

Joan Miró (1893-1983)

Como Salvador Dalí, Joan Miró, gran artista español, es uno de los hijos pródigos de la región de Cataluña.

Su arte antes de 1920 está influido por los colores brillantes de Fauves—el artista francés—el cubismo, el arte del folklore catalán y el arte de los frescos romanos de su España nativa.

Su estilo florece después de 1920, en París. El artista usa la memoria, la fantasía y lo irracional para crear las analogías visuales de la poesía surrealista. Así, en su obra aparecen por ejemplo animales de formas distorsionadas o extrañas figuras geométricas. La complejidad de líneas contrasta con una simplificación de colores.

El arte que Miró produce incluye no sólo pinturas sino también esculturas de cobre (*copper*) y masonita, litografías y murales en cerámica. Sus dos grandes murales son los de la UNESCO en París: *La muralla de la Luna* y *La muralla del Sol* (1957-1959).

Y ahora, dime...

1. ¿Por qué crees que esta lectura habla de Joan Miró como «hijo pródigo de Cataluña»?
2. Compara la obra de Miró antes y después de 1920.

La obra de Joan Miró

Antes de 1920	Después de 1920
1.	1.
2.	2.
3.	3.

3. ¿Qué es un mural? Si hay murales en tu ciudad, descríbelos. Describe los murales *La muralla de la Luna* y *La muralla del Sol* de Miró, según tu imaginación.

Antes de escribir
Estrategias para escribir: Agrupar ideas

A. Preparándote. Contesta estas preguntas para ver cuánto sabes de la música latina.

1. ¿Conoces a algunos músicos latinos? Prepara una lista de todos los músicos latinos que puedes nombrar.
2. Prepara una lista de los distintos tipos de música latina que tú conoces.

B. Grupos. *When brainstorming to gather ideas for writing on a specific topic, it is helpful to organize those ideas into various groups called clusters. Brainstorming clusters are listings of closely related ideas.*

If you had brainstormed a list of ideas to write about university life, you might have organized your list in clusters similar to the following. Can you fill in the blank bubbles?

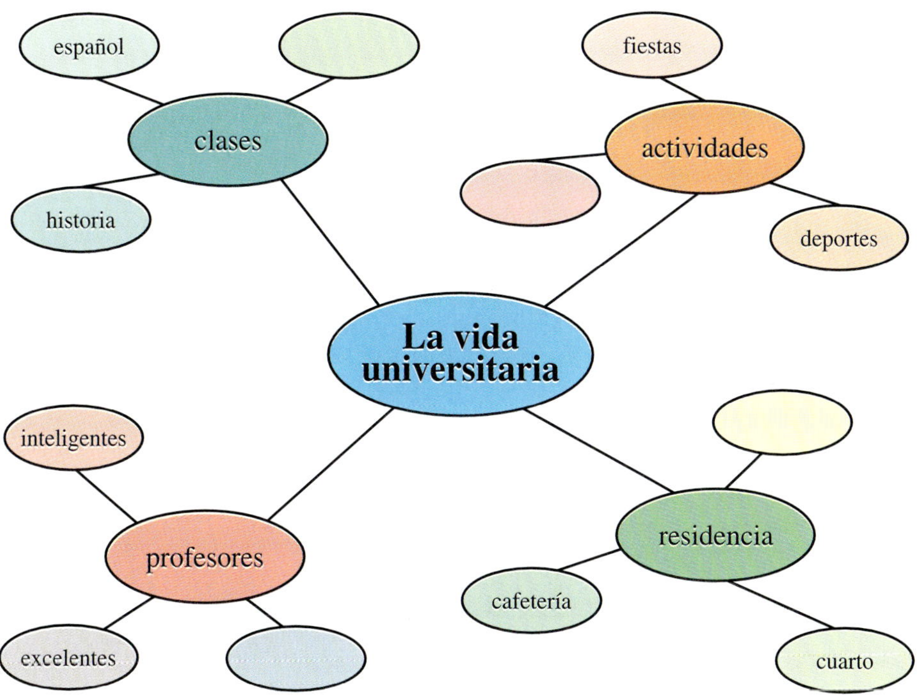

Ahora, ¡a escribir!

A. Agrupar ideas. Prepara ideas para escribir un breve artículo sobre tu cantante latino(a) favorito(a). Si no conoces a cantantes latinos, agrupa ideas sobre tu cantante norteamericano(a) favorito(a).

B. Grupos. Organiza tu lista de ideas en grupos de ideas parecidas (similares). Cada grupo debe incluir varias ideas relacionadas con tu cantante favorito(a).

C. El primer borrador. Usa la lista de ideas que preparaste para escribir un primer borrador (*first draft*) de tu artículo, con uno o dos párrafos sobre tu cantante favorito(a). Pon toda la información que tienes de un grupo en un párrafo.

D. Ahora, a compartir. Comparte tu primer borrador con dos o tres compañeros. Comenta sobre el contenido y el estilo del artículo de tus compañeros y escucha los comentarios de ellos sobre tu artículo. Si hay errores de ortografía o gramática, menciónalos.

E. Ahora, a revisar. Si necesitas hacer unos cambios basados en los comentarios de tus compañeros, hazlos ahora.

F. La versión final. Prepara una versión final de tu artículo en la computadora o escrita a máquina y entrégala.

G. Publicación. En grupos de cinco, lean los artículos que su instructor les da y seleccionen el mejor para ser leído a la clase entera.

¿Sabes bailar salsa?

TAREA Antes de empezar este **Paso,** estudia **En preparación** 3.5 y 3.6 y haz por escrito los ejercicios de **¡A practicar!** También escucha el **Paso 3 ¿Qué se dice...?** del Capítulo 3 en el CD del estudiante.

¿Eres buen observador?

La salsa se viste de mundo

Desde Japón y Escandinavia, la música afrocubana conquista nuevos públicos

Orquesta de la Luz, formada hace más de cinco años, es una curiosidad: una docena de japoneses tocando y cantando música afrocubana con una calidad que tiene poco que envidiar a las bandas locales.

Hot Salsa de Suecia es una banda fundada por un peruano con un nombre que suena sueco: Wilfredo Stevenson. En su primera visita exploratoria a Nueva York, la banda pasó su bautizo de fuego en una noche memorable en el club SOB's.

Ahora, ¡a analizar!

1. ¿Qué son *Orquesta de la Luz* y *Hot Salsa*? ¿Por qué son interesantes?
2. ¿Por qué se habla de la salsa como «música afrocubana»?
3. La música salsa es muy popular en todo el mundo latino. ¿Cuántos otros bailes latinos populares puedes nombrar?
4. Explica el título de este artículo.

¿Qué se dice...?

Al iniciar una conversación

¿Qué opina Andrés de la fiesta? ______________.

¿Qué opina Luisa? ______________.

Luisa sabe bailar ______________.

OFELIA ¿Conoces a mucha gente aquí?
PABLO Conozco a varias personas. Y tú, ¿conoces a muchas?
OFELIA No conozco a nadie. ¿Quiénes son ellas? ¿Y quién es el muchacho rubio y delgado? Es guapísimo.

FRANCISCO ¿Qué más hay para tomar?
GABRIEL Hay refrescos en la cocina. ¿Quieres una bebida?
FRANCISCO Sí, gracias. ¿Por qué no invitas a Luisa a bailar? Está muy bonita esta noche.

JUAN ¿Estudias aquí? ¿Cuál es tu especialización?
MARIO Estudio ingeniería mecánica. Y tú, ¿estudias aquí también?
JUAN Sí. Estudio inglés. ¿Qué clases tienes este semestre?

Ahora, ¡a hablar!

A. ¡No te reconozco! Con frecuencia, cuando asistimos a una fiesta, nuestra personalidad cambia. ¿Cómo son estas personas generalmente y cómo cambian cuando están en una fiesta?

Modelo Andrés: perezoso / activo

Andrés generalmente es perezoso pero en la fiesta está muy activo.

1. Carmen: activa / tranquila
2. Javier: serio / loco
3. Alejandro: simpático / aburrido
4. Teresa y Olga: felices / tristes
5. tú y Juan: arrogantes / simpáticos
6. yo: ¿… ?

B. Mi mejor amigo(a). Tú acabas de recibir una foto de tu mejor amigo(a) de la escuela secundaria. Describe la foto a tus compañeros(as) de cuarto.

Modelo **Mi amigo [Sebastían] es muy listo.**

		español(a)
		en Barcelona
		estudiando…
mi amigo(a) [*nombre*]	es / está +	tocando la guitarra
		guapo(a)
		simpático(a)
		un poco gordo(a) ahora
		contento(a) en esta foto

C. ¿Qué tenemos en común? Estás en una fiesta, hablando con una persona muy interesante. ¿Qué le preguntas para saber si tienen algunos intereses en común?

Modelo bailar salsa

TÚ **¿Sabes bailar salsa?**

AMIGO(A) **Sí, sé bailar salsa.** o **No, no sé bailar salsa.**

1. cocinar comida mexicana
2. tocar la guitarra
3. cantar
4. jugar tenis
5. hablar español
6. ¿… ?

D. ¡Qué popular! Carmen es una chica muy inteligente y popular. Ella tiene muchos talentos y conoce a mucha gente. ¿Por qué es Carmen tan popular?

Modelo **Carmen sabe tocar la guitarra.**

	Gloria Estefan
	hablar tres idiomas
	cantar muy bien
Carmen sabe / conoce +	bailar salsa
	Jon Secada
	tocar la guitarra
	todo el mundo en la fiesta

Y ahora, ¡a conversar!

A. Enlaces amorosos. Tú necesitas ayuda para encontrar a la persona ideal. Decides usar un servicio de computadora que se llama **«Enlaces amorosos»**. Para usar este servicio, primero tienes que describirte completamente. Escribe una descripción de ti, de tu apariencia física y de tu personalidad.

Vocabulario útil

aburrido(a)	feliz	modesto(a)
arrogante	frustrado(a)	simpático(a)
borracho(a)	furioso(a)	tímido(a)
contento(a)	inocente	tonto(a)
enamorado(a)	miserable	triste

B. ¡Qué cambiados están! Éstos son Daniel y Gloria antes de estudiar un año en la Universidad de Salamanca. En el Apéndice A, tu compañero(a) tiene un dibujo de Daniel y Gloria después de regresar de España. Describan a las personas en sus dibujos para saber cómo han cambiado. No se permite mirar el dibujo de tu compañero(a) hasta terminar esta actividad.

C. ¡Encuesta! Usa este cuadro para entrevistar a tres compañeros de clase. Escribe sus respuestas en los cuadrados apropiados.

Modelo

TÚ **¿Tocas el piano?**
AMIGO 1 **No, no toco el piano.**
YOU WRITE: **[*Name*] no toca el piano.**

	Amigo(a) 1	Amigo(a) 2	Amigo(a) 3
tocar el piano			
su bebida favorita ser agua mineral			
conocer a una persona famosa			
saber bailar salsa			
escuchar música latina en la radio			
¿... ?			

¡Luz! ¡Cámara! ¡Acción!

A. ¡Está guapísima! Imagínense que están en una fiesta en casa de su profesor(a) de español y que están hablando de los invitados. Trabajando en grupos de tres o cuatro, preparen su diálogo.

Modelo —Nuestro(a) profesor(a) está muy elegante esta noche.
— Sí, pero, ¿quién es la persona que está bailando con... ?
— Creo que es su novio(a). Es guapísimo(a), ¿no?...

B. No conozco a nadie. Estás en una fiesta y no conoces a nadie. Decides presentarte a un grupo de tres personas que parecen ser interesantes. Ellos te aceptan cortésmente y mantienen una buena conversación contigo. Dramatiza esta situación con tres compañeros de clase.

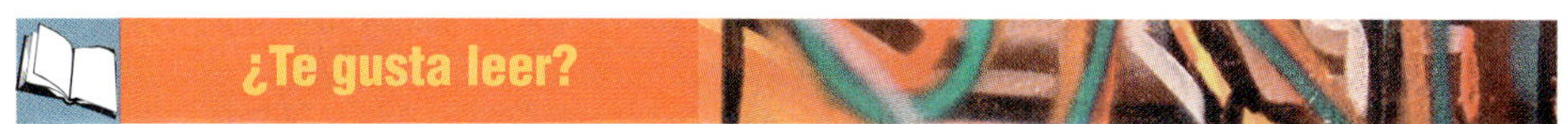

Antes de leer
Estrategias para leer: Dar un vistazo

A. Dar un vistazo. *To scan* **(dar un vistazo)** *is to look for and locate specific information by quickly reading a text. It is an especially useful strategy when reading reference texts such as indexes, road maps, dictionaries, classified ads, long lists, and interviews because their format allows the reader to concentrate on the information needed and to ignore extraneous material.*

Da un vistazo a la entrevista con Enrique Iglesias para contestar estas preguntas. No es necesario leer palabra por palabra; simplemente da un vistazo rápido hasta encontrar la información que necesitas.

1. ¿Tiene novia Enrique Iglesias?
2. ¿Es feliz?
3. ¿Hay mucha competencia entre Enrique y su padre Julio Iglesias?

B. Prepárate para leer. Expresa tu opinión al contestar estas preguntas sobre los hijos de personas famosas.

1. ¿Crees que es fácil ser hijo de una persona famosa? ¿Por qué?
2. ¿Sienten envidia (*envy*) los padres famosos por la juventud y éxitos de sus hijos? Explica tu respuesta.
3. ¿Quién crees que critica más a sus hijos, un padre famoso o una madre famosa? ¿Por qué?

Lectura

Enrique Iglesias

Es un ligón, un conquistador y todo lo consigue a través de una simpatía desbordante y unas melodías que nos suben hasta otras galaxias. En estos momentos ya se debe haber metido en el bolsillo a la italianas, pero antes de cruzar el Mediterráneo, se dió un paseo por Madrid y allí fue donde lo pillamos. Nos lo confesó: ¡¡aún no tiene novia y pronto se irá a vivir solo!!

Deseado por todas

22

—¿Ya se ha cruzado en tu camino la chica de tu vida?

—No. Bueno, he tenido novias, pero ahora estoy muy tranquilo, muy solo en esta parcela de la vida. Y no me preocupa estarlo. Tengo mucho tiempo por delante para alcanzar la felicidad sentimental.

—¿Alguna de tus admiradoras es más especial que otra?

—No quiero mezclar trabajo y amor. Lo que más protejo es a esas admiradoras tan fieles que se merecen mi respeto.

—¿Eres un chico feliz?

—Hago casi siempre lo que quiero, no me falta nada. Sería injusto que me quejara habiendo tantos chicos como hay con tantas necesidades. Paso mis pequeñas «depres», pero son eso, pequeñas.

—¿Sintió envidia sana tu padre al saber que llevas vendidos más de dos millones y medio de discos?

—Me dijo que está super contento con mi éxito y que ojalá que venda igual de bien mis siguientes elepés. Mi padre y yo somos muy felices porque nos va estupendamente a los dos como cantantes.

—De quién recibes más críticas, ¿de tu padre o de tu madre?

—A nivel musical mi padre es el que más me critica porque él es el entendiso y el que siente la música de un modo muy especial. Mi madre es mi fan número uno, todo le parece bien. Más que criticarme me da consejos familiares.

—¿Cuántas veces has soñado que Isabel Presley y Julio Iglesias se habían reconciliado?

—Lo de mi madre y mi padre está muerto. Y lo bueno es que siempre se llevaron bien después de divorciarse. Es mucho mejor ver a unos padres separados y en buena amistad, que unidos y peleándose todos los días. Los dos son muy sensatos e inteligentes.

—¿Te das cuenta de la cantidad de dinero que has ganado en poco tiempo?

—Yo no trabajo por dinero. El dinero, el poder y la fama no me importan, porque si me preocupara todo eso me convertiría en un imbécil, en un caprichoso y en un tonto. Psicológicamente sigo siendo un chico sencillo y normal.

—¿Eres ahorrador?

—Sí y por eso ahora me podré comprar una casa para vivir con mi perro y quien sabe, algún dia… con alguien más, pero eso lo dirá el tiempo. De momento, nada de nada, sólo mi perro.

A ver si comprendiste

Ambos Enrique Iglesias y su padre Julio son cantantes de fama internacional. Después de leer este artículo, ¿cómo crees que son diferentes y cómo son similares padre e hijo? Usa este diagrama «mente abierta» para indicar lo que padre e hijo Iglesias opinan del amor, de la felicidad, de la música, del divorcio y del dinero. Escribe las opiniones de cada uno en el diagrama apropiado.

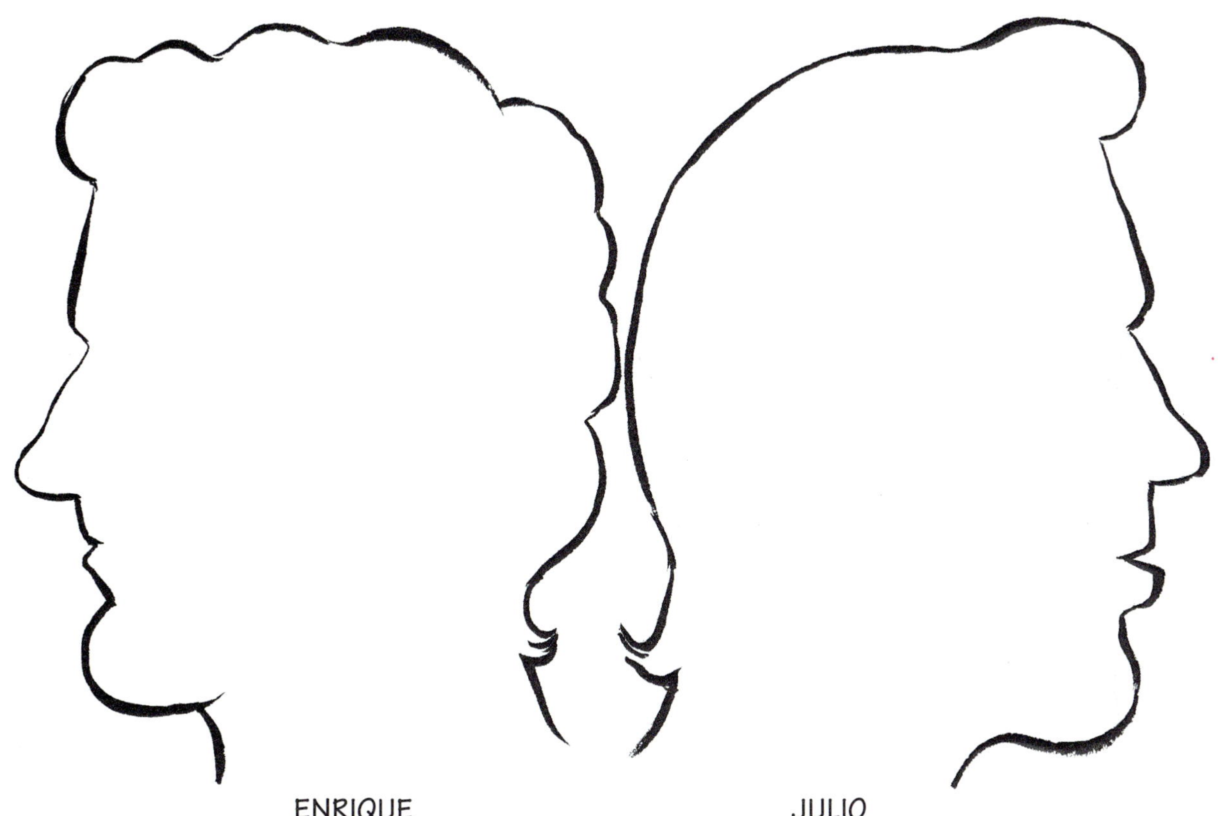

Expand your horizons! *Let's travel through cyberspace to España* and discover that . . .

- in Cadaqués, you can stroll through the **Museo Dalí**; in Madrid, the **Museo del Prado** and the **Museo Reina Sofía**; in Toledo, the **Museo del Greco**.
- in Madrid, you will also be able to browse through the exceptional **Biblioteca Nacional** and in Sevilla, the **Archivo de Indias.**
- through the Internet, you have immediate access to Spain's most prestigious newspapers: ***El País, ABC,*** and ***Mundo.***
- you also have access to **Agencia EFE** (Spain's equivalent to the Associated Press), the most important news agency in the country.

If you are a cyberspace browser, join us in **Viajemos por el ciberespacio a... España** by trying the following important addresses.

Biblioteca nacional
http://www.bne.es/

Canal Sur
http://www.canalsur.es/ram/csur.ram

Cadena Cope
http://www.cope.es/

Onda Cero
http://ondacero.adam.es/index_0.htm.

El Museo Joan Miró
http://www.bcn.fjmiro.es/

Periódicos
http://www.abc.es/
http://www.elpais.es/
http://www.el-mundo.es/

Because addresses are likely to change without notice, the following key words will guarantee that **Viajemos por el ciberespacio a... España** will get us to our desired destination. Type any of these key words in your favorite search engine.

Palabras clave
Museo del Prado
Archivo de Indias
El País
Diario ABC
Barcelona
Sevilla
Segovia
Toledo

Radio en directo España
Cadena Cope
Canal Sur
Onda Cero

http://www.hrwcollege.com

Vocabulario

Domicilio

alcoba *bedroom*
cocina *kitchen*
patio *patio*
sala *living room*

Diversiones

canción (*f.*) *song*
casete (*m.*) *cassette*
cerveza *beer*
cine (*m.*) *movie theater*
coche (*m.*) *car*
cumpleaños (*m. sing.* or *pl.*) *birthday*
¡Feliz cumpleaños! *Happy birthday!*
disco *record*
disco compacto *compact disc*
fiesta *party*
foto (*f.*) *photo*
guitarra *guitar*
llamada *phone call*
música *music*
novela *novel*
pastel (*m.*) *cake, pie*
piano *piano*
salsa *type of Puerto Rican dance and music*

Personas

gente (*f.*) *people*
hombre (*m.*) *man*
invitado(a) *guest*
mujer (*f.*) *woman*
pareja *pair, couple*

Descripción

alto(a) *tall*
antipático(a) *disagreeable*
bajo(a) *short*
borracho(a) *drunk*
contento(a) *happy*
delgado(a) *thin*
enamorado(a) *in love*
enfermo(a) *sick*
fenomenal *phenomenal; great*
frustrado(a) *frustrated*
furioso(a) *furious*
gordo(a) *fat*
guapo(a) *good-looking*
hermoso(a) *beautiful*
importante *important*
loco(a) *crazy*
modesto(a) *modest*
moreno(a) *dark-complexioned*
nervioso(a) *nervous*
pequeño(a) *small, little*
preocupado(a) *preoccupied, worried*
rico(a) *rich; delicious*
rubio(a) *blond*
tranquilo(a) *tranquil, peaceful*
triste *sad*

Palabras interrogativas

¿Cómo? *How? What?*
¿Cuál(es)? *Which one(s)? What?*
¿Cuándo? *When?*
¿Dónde? *Where?*
¿Adónde? *To where?*
¿Por qué? *Why?*
¿Cuánto? *How much?*
¿Cuántos(as)? *How many?*
¿Qué? *What? Which?*
¿Quién(es)? *Who?*

Verbos

cantar *to sing*
conocer *to know (people); to be acquainted with*
decorar *to decorate*
descansar *to rest*
esperar *to wait for; to expect*
estar *to be*
practicar *to practice*
saber *to know (facts); know how*
tocar *to play (an instrument)*

Palabras y expresiones útiles

aquí *here*
especialización (*f.*) *specialization, major*
idioma (*m.*) *language*
Lo siento. *I'm sorry.*
nadie *no one, nobody*
naturalmente *naturally*
pregunta *question*
todo el mundo *everyone, everybody*

En preparación 3

3.1 The Verb *estar*

Giving location and indicating change

Estar

to be	
estoy	estamos
estás	estáis
está	están
está	están

Estar is used to tell where someone or something is located and to describe how one is feeling or one's condition. It is also used with the present participle to form the present progressive tense. (See **En preparación 3.3**).

A. Location

La comida está en el comedor.	*The food is in the dining room.*
¿Dónde están los nachos?	*Where are the nachos?*
Están en la cocina.	*They are in the kitchen.*
¿No está tu papá?	*Isn't your father here?*
No. Está en Nueva York.	*No. He's in New York.*

B. Conditions and feelings

La fiesta está muy aburrida.	*The party is very boring.*
Roberto está enfermo otra vez.	*Roberto is sick again.*
Está borracho.	*He's drunk.*
Natalia está muy preocupada (triste, nerviosa, contenta).	*Natalia is very worried (sad, nervous, happy).*

¡A practicar!

A. ¿Dónde están? Give the location of the following people and things.

Modelo discos / sala

Los discos están en la sala.

1. refrescos / cocina
2. Natalia / su casa

3. nosotros / fiesta
4. Patricia / patio
5. comida / cocina
6. Natalia y los invitados / sala
7. tú / sala
8. yo / mi habitación

B. ¿Cómo está...? Describe Natalia's party.

Modelo La música está fantástica.

	fenomenal
la señora Alarcón	muy contento y activo
Natalia y yo	excelente
Nicolás	fantástico
la comida y los refrescos	muy nervioso
la música	muy tranquilo
¿… ?	aburrido
	¿… ?

C. ¡Fiesta! In order to find out what is happening at Roberto's house tonight, complete the following paragraph with the correct form of the verb **estar.**

Hay una fiesta en mi casa esta noche porque mis padres ______________ en Europa. Yo ______________ muy contento porque todos mis amigos ______________ aquí. También ______________ muy ocupado con los invitados. Mi amigo Gonzalo ______________ muy nervioso porque su ex novia ______________ en la fiesta también. Mi amiga Amalia ______________ furiosa porque Juan Carlos, su novio, no baila con ella. Los otros invitados ______________ contentos porque hay mucha comida y la música ______________ buena.

3.2 Interrogative Words

Asking questions

¿Cómo?	*How? What?*	¿Cuánto(a)?	*How much?*
¿Cuál(es)?	*Which one(s)? What?*	¿Cuántos(as)?	*How many?*
¿Cuándo?	*When?*	¿Qué?	*What? Which?*
¿Dónde?	*Where?*	¿Quién(es)?	*Who?*
¿Por qué?	*Why?*	¿Adónde?	*Where to?*

A. *All* interrogative words require a written accent, even when used in a statement rather than a question.

No sabemos **dónde** vive.	*We don't know where she lives.*
Necesito saber **qué** es.	*I need to know what it is.*

B. When these words do not have a written accent, they lose their interrogative meaning.

Siempre escucho música **cuando** estudio.	*I always listen to music when I study.*
Yo creo **que** vive cerca.	*I believe that he lives nearby.*
Donde yo vivo hay más gente joven.	*Where I live there are more young people.*

C. **¿Cuál(es)?** meaning *what* is used instead of **qué** before the verb **ser** when the verb is followed by a noun, except when a definition of a word is being requested.

¿Cuál es tu dirección?	*What's your address?*
¿Cuál es tu especialización?	*What's your major?*
¿Qué es la enología?	*What's enology?*

D. When used before a noun, **¿qué?** usually requires an explanation or definition. **¿Cuál?** followed by a verb indicates a choice.

¿A **qué** restaurante vamos?	*What restaurant are we going to?*
¿Cuál prefieres tú, El Moro o La Toledana?	*What (Which one) do you prefer, El Moro or La Toledana?*

E. In English, when asking someone to repeat a question, one frequently says "What?" In Spanish, one would never say «**¿Qué?**» but rather «**¿Cómo?**» when making a one-word response. **¿Qué?** is used only in a complete-sentence response.

¿Cómo? No te oigo.	*What? I can't hear you.*
¿Qué dices?	*What are you saying?*
¿Qué me preguntas?	*What are you asking me?*

¡A practicar!

A. Preguntas. Diego has just met a new classmate. Match the words in **A** with those in **B**, in order to know what he asks her.

A	B
	tal?
¿Con quién	te llamas?
¿Qué	estudias?
¿Cómo	clases tomas?
¿Dónde	son tus profesores?
¿Cuál	vives?
	es tu número de teléfono?

B. Acepto tu invitación. Antonio has just accepted Victoria's invitation to a party, but needs to know the specifics. What does he ask her?

Antonio	Victoria
¿__________ es la fiesta?	Es el sábado.
¿__________ es?	A las 9:00.

¿__________	es?	En mi casa.
¿__________	es tu dirección?	La calle Bolívar, número 10.
¿__________	personas van?	Veinte, más o menos.
¿__________	son tus amigos?	Son de Ecuador.
¿__________	van a la fiesta?	Enriqueta, Víctor Mario, Luz María, Enrique y muchos más.

3.3 Present Progressive Tense

Describing what is happening now

A. In English, the present participle is the verb + *-ing: talking, walking, buying.* In Spanish, the present participle is formed by dropping the infinitive ending and adding **-ando** to **-ar** verbs, and **-iendo** to **-er** and **-ir** verbs.

trabajar:	trabaj**ando**	*working*
bailar:	bail**ando**	*dancing*
poner:	pon**iendo**	*putting*
escribir:	escrib**iendo**	*writing*

NOTE: Present participles of stem-changing verbs are presented in **En preparación 6.3.**

B. Some present participles are irregular. For example, the **-iendo** ending becomes **-yendo** whenever the stem of the infinitive ends in a vowel.

leer:	le**yendo**	*reading*
traer:	tra**yendo**	*bringing*

C. In English, the present progressive is formed with the verb *to be* and an *-ing* verb form: *I am eating; He is driving.* In Spanish, the present progressive is formed with **estar** and a present participle.

¿Qué están haciendo?	*What are they doing?*
Todos están bailando.	*Everyone is dancing.*
Estamos comiendo.	*We're eating.*

D. In Spanish as in English, the present progressive tense is used *only* to describe or emphasize an action that is taking place *right at the moment.*

Estoy escribiendo una carta.	*I'm writing a letter.*
Pablo y Ana están leyendo el periódico.	*Pablo and Ana are reading the newspaper.*

¡A practicar!

A. ¿Qué están haciendo? What is everyone doing just before the guests arrive?

Modelo Yo (decorar) el pastel
Yo estoy decorando el pastel.

1. Francisco (preparar) unas hamburguesas.

2. Ricardo y yo (abrir) unos refrescos.
3. Tú y Teresa (descansar) un poco.
4. Elisa y su novio (hablar) por teléfono.
5. Ahora yo (esperar) a mis amigos.
6. Natalia (recibir) a los invitados.

B. ¿Y ahora? Everybody is having fun at Natalia's party. Form sentences using the following words to find out what they are doing now.

1. Gonzalo y Ramón / beber / refrescos
2. nosotros / comer / hamburguesas
3. yo / poner / música / favorita
4. Nicolás / abrir / puerta
5. Andrea / escribir / mi número de teléfono
6. Tomás / comprar / más refrescos

3.4 Superlatives

Stating exceptional qualities

A. In English, the superlative is formed by adding *-est* to adjectives of one or two syllables or by using *the most* or *the least* with longer adjectives. To form the superlative in Spanish, place the definite article **el, la, los,** or **las** and **más** or **menos** before the adjective.

Sin duda, este libro es **el más** interesante.	*Without a doubt, this book is the most interesting.*
Esta casa es **la más** grande.	*This house is the biggest.*
Teresa e Isabel son **las más** populares.	*Teresa and Isabel are the most popular.*
Pascual y Felipe son **los menos** activos.	*Pascual and Felipe are the least active.*

1. Whenever the person, place, or thing being emphasized is stated, it always precedes **más** and **menos.**

Es la clase más difícil.	*It is the most difficult class.*
El apartamento más grande es el primero.	*The biggest apartment is the first one.*
Estudié la información menos importante.	*I studied the least important information.*

2. To express a superlative quality as a part of the total, the preposition **de** must be added after the adjective.

Roberto es la persona más simpática **de** la clase.	*Roberto is the nicest person in the class.*
Este apartamento es el más caro **de** la ciudad.	*This apartment is the most expensive in town.*

B. The superlative of nouns is expressed with the definite article + **mayor/menor** or **mejor/peor.**

Ernesto es **el mayor** y Yolanda es **la menor.**	*Ernesto is the oldest and Yolanda is the youngest.*
El mejor libro para aprender español es *¡Dímelo tú!*	*The best book for learning Spanish is* ¡Dímelo tú!
Ésta es **la peor** fiesta del año.	*This is the worst party of the year.*

C. The absolute superlative is used to express a high degree of a quality, or exceptional qualities. It is formed by adding **-ísimo(a, os, as)** to the singular form of an adjective. Final vowels are always dropped before adding the **-ísimo** endings. The English equivalents are *extremely, exceptionally,* or *very, very.*

El pastel está **buenísimo.**	*The cake is exceptionally good.*
Estoy **nerviosísimo.**	*I'm extremely (very, very) nervous.*

¡Ojo! Whenever the singular form of the adjective ends in **-co** or **-go**, a spelling change occurs in the absolute superlative form.

c	→	qu	g	→	gu
rico	→	**riquísimo**	largo	→	**larguísimo**

¡A practicar!

A. ¡Son los más populares! Mónica is pointing out the most popular students at her school. Why does she say they are so popular?

Modelo Natalia / divertido / clase
Natalia es la más divertida de la clase.

1. Jorge y Antonio / sociable / universidad
2. Tina / romántico / todas las muchachas
3. nosotros / inteligente / universidad
4. ustedes / sincero / todos mis amigos
5. tú / divertido / clase
6. Marta y Cristina / hermoso / universidad
7. Andrés / atlético / universidad
8. yo / normal / todos(as) mis amigos(as)

B. ¡Son excepcionales! Name exceptional people who fit the following descriptions.

Modelo divertido
Whoopi Goldberg es la mujer más divertida del mundo.

1. inteligente
2. alto
3. guapo / hermosa
4. generoso
5. atlético
6. difícil
7. interesante
8. divertido

C. ¡Mi universidad es la mejor! Gloria Morales is talking on the phone with her ex-boyfriend, Roberto. He is attending a new university and is determined to impress her. Fill in the blanks to see how far he goes to create a good impression.

Modelo Este campus es _______________ (grande) de todos.
Este campus es el más grande de todos.

ROBERTO ¡Aló! ¿Gloria?
GLORIA Sí, soy yo, Roberto. ¿Cómo estás? ¿Y cómo es el campus allá?
ROBERTO Estoy feliz. Este campus es _______________ (popular) de todos.
GLORIA ¿Cómo es la gente?
ROBERTO La gente es _______________ (sociable) de todo el mundo.
GLORIA ¿Cómo son tus compañeros de cuarto?
ROBERTO ¿Mis compañeros de habitación? ¡Oh! Son ideales. Miguel y José son _______________ (estudioso) de todos mis amigos. También son _______________ (divertido) y son muy simpáticos.
GLORIA ¿Y tus profesores?
ROBERTO Mis profesores son __________ (exigente) de la universidad, pero también son __________ (bueno). Todo es perfecto. Y lo más importante: ¡Esta universidad no es __________ (caro) de todas!

D. ¡Qué exagerado eres! Your friend always uses superlatives when talking about others. What does he say about the following people?

1. David es (guapo).
2. Amalia y María son (simpáticas).
3. Marcos es (rico).
4. Estela es (hermosa).
5. Pedro y Virginia son (listos).
6. Teresa es (interesante).

PASO 3

3.5 *Ser* and *estar* with Adjectives

Describing attributes and indicating changes

A. Ser is used with adjectives to describe attributes such as

1. physical characteristics, essential traits, and qualities.

Nicolás es guapísimo.	*Nicolás is very handsome.*
Cecilia es delgada.	*Cecilia is thin.*
Los nachos son deliciosos.	*Nachos are delicious.*

2. personality.

Eva es simpatiquísima.	*Eva is very nice.*
Teresa es inteligente.	*Teresa is intelligent.*
Héctor es perezoso.	*Héctor is lazy.*

3. inherent characteristics.

La nieve es blanca.	*Snow is white.*
El cielo es azul.	*The sky is blue.*
El edificio es muy alto.	*The building is very tall.*

B. **Estar** is used with adjectives to indicate a more subjective, temporal evaluation of

1. appearance, taste, and physical state of being.

Estos nachos están deliciosos.	*These nachos are (taste) delicious.*
Carlos está delgado.	*Carlos is (looks) thin.*
Teresa, ¡estás hermosa!	*Teresa, you are (look) lovely!*

2. behavior.

Estás muy antipático hoy.	*You are (being) very disagreeable today.*
Estela, estás perezosa.	*Estela, you are (being) lazy.*

3. conditions.

Victor está cansado.	*Victor is tired.*
Todos están contentos.	*Everyone is happy.*
La nieve está negra.	*The snow is black. (It's dirty.)*

¡A practicar!

A. ¡Son excelentes! Pilar is describing her classmates to a new student. What does she say?

1. Elisa / romántica y muy estudiosa
2. Sara e Isabel / divertidas y muy simpáticas
3. Carlos / un poco perezoso
4. Marta y Javier / muy sociables
5. todos nosotros / muy sinceros
6. tú / honesta y muy guapa

B. ¡Están diferentes! It's Pilar's first visit home since she went away to college. She finds that everybody has changed considerably. What does she say about the following people?

1. ¡Mamá, tú __________ muy diferente!
2. Victor __________ más grande.

3. Patricia y Lucía __________ más trabajadoras.
4. Eduardo y yo __________ muy activos.
5. Papá __________ más paciente.
6. Todos ustedes __________ muy bien.

C. En una boda. Carlos and Pepe are commenting on the guests at Carlos's sister's wedding. Complete the following dialogue with the appropriate form of **ser** or **estar** to find out what they are saying.

CARLOS La señora Durán ______________ hermosa hoy.
PEPE Sí, y el señor Durán ______________ muy delgado, ¿verdad?
CARLOS Tienes razón. Creo que ______________ enfermo.
PEPE Pobre. Y en tu opinión, ¿cómo ______________ el novio de tu hermana?
CARLOS ______________ muy simpático. También ______________ muy inteligente y, ¡______________ rico!
PEPE Sí, pero ahora ______________ nervioso y ______________ muy cansado.

D. ¡Rin-rin! Marta is having a wonderful time at her own birthday party when the phone rings. Complete the following paragraph with the appropriate form of **ser** or **estar** to see what she has to say about the party.

¿Bueno? ¡Hola, Elisa! ¿Dónde ______________ ? Todo el mundo ______________ aquí. Todos ______________ bailando. En este momento, Carlos y yo ______________ preparando más ponche. No, no ______________ alcohólico. ______________ de jugo de frutas y ______________ delicioso. ¿Conoces a Jaime? Él ______________ el amigo de Roberto. Él ______________ muy guapo y muy rico . . . y no tiene novia. ¿Por qué no vienes? Todos aquí te ______________ esperando.

3.6 Two Irregular Verbs: *saber* and *conocer*

Stating what you know and what you are familiar with

Conocer

to know, to be acquainted with	
conozco	conocemos
conoces	conocéis
conoce	conocen
conoce	conocen

Saber

to know (how)	
sé	sabemos
sabes	sabéis
sabe	saben
sabe	saben

Spanish has two verbs that mean *to know:* **saber** and **conocer.** Both have an irregular *yo* form but are regular in all other persons.

A. **Saber** is used when speaking of knowing specific, factual information. When followed by an infinitive, **saber** means *to know how to do something.*

No sé si es estudiante.	*I don't know if she's a student.*
Pero sabes dónde vive, ¿no?	*But you know where she lives, don't you?*
¿Sabes bailar?	*Do you know how to dance?*

B. **Conocer** is always used when speaking of knowing a person or being familiar with a place or thing. When speaking of knowing people, *conocer* is always followed by the personal «a».

¿Conoces a Guillermo?	*Do you know Guillermo?*
No lo conozco muy bien.	*I don't know him very well.*
¿Conocen ustedes este libro?	*Are you familiar with this book?*

¡A practicar!

A. ¡Sí, pero... ! You are talking with your friend about what you know and don't know. What do you say to her?

1. Yo ______________ francés, pero no ______________ Francia.
2. Yo ______________ a tu amiga, pero no ______________ su nombre.
3. Yo ______________ su auto, pero no ______________ si es un Mercedes o un Porsche.
4. Sí, yo ______________ quién es Viviana, pero no la ______________ bien.
5. No, yo no ______________ su casa, pero ______________ su dirección.

B. ¡Impresionante! Julián Chacón y sus amigos tienen mucho talento artístico. Completa estas oraciones con la forma apropiada de **saber** o **conocer** para conocerlos.

1. Julián ______________ bailar mejor que todos sus amigos.
2. Pepe y yo ______________ tocar la guitarra.
3. María ______________ a artistas famosos en París, Londres, Madrid y Roma. ______________ hablar francés, español e italiano.
4. Ángela ______________ cantar ópera. Ella ______________ a Victoria de Los Ángeles, la famosa cantante de ópera española.
5. Armando ______________ muy bien a Julio Iglesias. Él ______________ dónde vive Julio en Miami.
6. Jorge ______________ a Bill Clinton.

CAPÍTULO 4

¿Qué hacemos hoy?

Cultural Topics

- **¿Sabías que…?**
  - *Los servicios*
  - *Unidades monetarias de los países de habla hispana*
  - *¿Agua con o sin gas?*
- **Noticiero cultural**
  - **Lugar:** *México*
  - **Gente:** *Diego Rivera (1886)*
- **Lectura:** *Déjate conquistar por México*

Writing Strategies

- Identifying key words and phrases

Reading Strategies

- Skimming

En preparación

- 4.1 Demonstrative Adjectives
- 4.2 Present Tense of **e** → **ie** and **o** → **ue** Stem-changing Verbs
- 4.3 Numbers above 200
- 4.4 Comparisons of Equality
- 4.5 **Tener** Idioms
- 4.6 **Hacer** in Time Expressions

In this chapter, you will learn how to …

- describe the physical appearance and character traits of people.
- express preferences.
- discuss prices.
- make comparisons.
- shop in the clothing section of a department store.
- order a drink in a café.

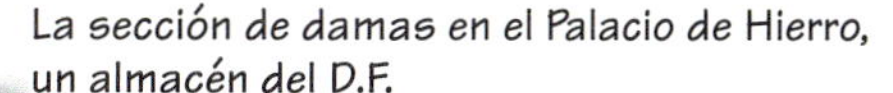

La sección de damas en el Palacio de Hierro, un almacén del D.F.

Una tienda de moda en la Zona Rosa, México, D.F.

De compras en el Mercado de San Ángel, México, D.F

Lo que ya sabes...

1. ¿Conoces la Zona Rosa? Basado en esta foto, ¿qué es la Zona Rosa? ¿Hay una zona similar en la ciudad donde tú vives?
2. En base a estas fotos, ¿cómo es el Palacio de Hierro comparado con las tiendas de la Zona Rosa? ¿Hay una tienda similar al Palacio de Hierro en tu ciudad? ¿Cómo se llama?
3. ¿Sabes qué es un mercado al aire libre? ¿En qué es diferente el Mercado de San Ángel de la Zona Rosa? ¿del Palacio de Hierro? ¿Quiénes van de compras a la Zona Rosa? ¿al Palacio de Hierro? ¿al Mercado de San Ángel?

MÉXICO

¡Al Museo de Antropología!

TAREA

Antes de empezar este **Paso**, estudia **En preparación** 4.1 y 4.2 y haz por escrito los ejercicios de **¡A practicar!** También escucha el **Paso 1 ¿Qué se dice...?** del Capítulo 4 en el CD del estudiante.

¿Eres buen observador?

El calendario azteca es un excelente ejemplo del conocimiento científico-astrológico de esta civilización precolombina. El calendario, llamado la Piedra del Sol, pesa más de 24 toneladas. Fue esculpido en el año 1479 y colocado en el Templo Mayor de Tenochtitlán, la capital de los aztecas. El calendario gregoriano, que es el calendario que todavía usamos, no fue creado hasta 103 años más tarde, en el año 1582.

Ahora, ¡a analizar!

1. El calendario azteca tiene 18 meses de 20 días cada uno más 5 días religiosos al final de cada año. ¿Cuántos días hay en un año?
2. Los 20 días de un mes aparecen en el calendario en un círculo con 20 símbolos distintos. Encuéntralos.
3. Identifica a las dos personas que salen de la boca de dos serpientes. Se llaman los cuates *(twins)* y representan el día y la noche.
4. ¿Dónde crees que está el símbolo del sol que representa el centro del universo azteca y al que llaman «tonatiuh»?

Al describir a personas y expresar preferencias

¿En qué idiomas hay visitas?

__________ __________ __________

__________ __________

Hora de la próxima visita en francés: __________

Frida Kahlo, *Frida & Diego Rivera*, 1931, Museo de Arte Moderno, San Francisco.

Diego Rivera, *Dos Mujeres y un niño*, 1926, Museos de Bellas Artes, San Francisco.

¿Sabías que... ?

Cuando viajamos, una de las necesidades básicas es encontrar los servicios públicos. En inglés preguntamos por *the men's* o *ladies' room, the lavatory, the restroom, the bathroom,* etc. Así también en español hay diferentes maneras de referirse a los servicios. Algunas de las más comunes son: **el servicio o los servicios, el aseo o los aseos, el baño, el excusado, el retrete, el wáter o el WC** *(water closet),* **el inodoro o el tualé** ***(toilet).***

A propósito...

En español, el nombre de una lengua casi siempre es idéntico a la forma masculina singular del adjetivo de nacionalidad: **alemán, árabe, español, francés, hebreo, inglés, italiano, japonés, ruso, …**

Ahora, ¡a hablar!

A. En el museo. Guadalupe y su amiga Victoria visitan el Palacio de Bellas Artes en México. Victoria está muy impresionada con todo lo que ve. ¿Qué dice?

Modelo esta / señoras / ser / muy elegante
Estas señoras son muy elegantes.

1. este / museo / ser / muy interesante
2. ese / cuadros / tener colores / muy violento
3. este / audífono / no funcionar
4. ese / guía / saber / mucho / arte
5. esta / niñas / entender / francés
6. ese / señores / hablar / alemán

B. ¿Quién es? Identifica a las personas de la clase que tu profesor(a) va a describir.

Modelo **Esta persona lleva una blusa amarilla.**
Esta persona lleva una camisa anaranjada.

C. Preferencias. Cuando visitan la ciudad de México, estas personas tienen sus propias preferencias individuales. ¿Qué prefieren hacer estas personas?

Modelo Victoria / visitar el Palacio de Bellas Artes
Victoria prefiere visitar el Palacio de Bellas Artes.

1. los señores Martínez / comprar recuerdos
2. Sandra / sacar fotos de la ciudad
3. yo / mirar a la gente
4. Sandra y Elena / caminar por la ciudad
5. Valentín y yo / visitar el Museo Nacional de Antropología
6. yo / ver los salones *(halls)* de cultura maya
7. Valentín / ver el calendario azteca

D. Primero quiero ver... En el Museo Nacional de Antropología en México, todo el mundo quiere ver ciertos objetos inmediatamente. ¿Qué quieren ver estas personas primero?

Modelo yo / querer ver / calendario azteca
Yo quiero ver el calendario azteca.

1. nosotros / querer ver / tocado *(headdress)* de Moctezuma
2. yo / querer ver / piedra *(stone)* de los sacrificios
3. perdón, mis amigas / no encontrar / a Tláloc, el dios de la lluvia *(rain god)*
4. mi familia / pensar ir / salones de cultura tolteca
5. mi esposa y yo / preferir ir / salones de cultura maya
6. mi padre / querer pasar / todo el día / el salón de códices *(writings)* precolombinos

Y ahora, ¡a conversar!

A. Una encuesta. Tú eres reportero(a) de la sección de modas *(fashion column)* de tu periódico escolar. Entrevista a cuatro compañeros(as) de clase para saber qué llevan *(wear)* en estas ocasiones.

Modelo ¿... al teatro?

TÚ **¿Qué llevas al teatro?**

COMPAÑERA **Llevo una blusa blanca y una falda negra larga.**

1. ¿... a clase?
2. ¿... a un partido de fútbol? ¿de béisbol?
3. ¿... a un baile?
4. ¿... para jugar al tenis? ¿al fútbol?
5. ¿... a una fiesta?

B. ¿A quién describo? Sin decir a quién describes, describe en detalle a un(a) compañero(a) de clase. Tu pareja *(partner)* debe adivinar *(guess)* a quién describes. Luego, que tu pareja describa y tú puedes adivinar.

C. ¡Robo! *(There was a theft in the* Palacio de Bellas Artes *in Mexico City and you were the only witness.)* Usa el dibujo *(drawing)* en el Apéndice A para describir a los ladrones *(thieves)*. Tu compañero(a), un(a) artista que trabaja para la policía, va a dibujar a las personas que tú describes.

D. Preferencias. Pregúntales a tus compañeros de clase si hacen las cosas indicadas en este cuadro. Si contestan afirmativamente, pídeles que firmen el cuadrado apropiado. Recuerda que no se permite que la misma persona firme más de un cuadrado.

entender dos idiomas ________ *Firma*	preferir tener pelo rubio ________ *Firma*	querer ir a otra universidad ________ *Firma*	no encontrar sus libros hoy ________ *Firma*
preferir estudiar en la biblioteca por la noche ________ *Firma*	pensar ir a España este verano ________ *Firma*	poder hablar tres idiomas ________ *Firma*	querer visitar el Museo de Antropología ________ *Firma*
volver a casa tres veces al día ________ *Firma*	dormir en una clase ________ *Firma*	entender español muy bien ________ *Firma*	empezar las clases a las ocho de la mañana ________ *Firma*
pensar estudiar español otro año ________ *Firma*	tener cuatro clases en un día ________ *Firma*	almorzar a las 11:30 todos los días ________ *Firma*	querer ir a bailar esta noche ________ *Firma*

¡Luz! ¡Cámara! ¡Acción!

A. ¡Una ciudad fascinante! Tú trabajas de recepcionista en un hotel o motel de tu ciudad. Un(a) turista quiere información sobre museos, excursiones, lugares interesantes para visitar, buenos restaurantes, etc. Dramatiza esta situación con un(a) compañero(a). Tu compañero(a) puede hacer el papel de turista.

B. Nuevos amigos. Estás en casa durante las vacaciones y tus padres tienen muchas preguntas acerca de la apariencia y la personalidad de tus nuevos amigos y tu nuevo(a) novio(a). Dramatiza esta situación con dos compañeros(as) de clase.

¿Comprendes lo que se dice?

Estrategias para escuchar. *In a previous chapter you learned that identifying cognates when reading helped you better understand what you read. Recognizing cognates can also help you to understand when listening. However, even cognates that are spelled similarly in Spanish and English are often not pronounced the same. This is often because accentuation (the emphasis or stress) in Spanish is different from that of English. For example, the word* total *in English is stressed on the first syllable (TO-tal) while in Spanish it is stressed on the last syllable (to-TAL).*

Now listen as your instructor plays the first three sentences of this narrative. Note how the following cognates are pronounced in Spanish, and draw a circle around the stressed syllable. Then go back and write the English equivalent and underline the syllable that is stressed in the English word. Note how the pronunciation varies.

Cognates

museo	____________________	**arquitecto**	____________________
nacional	____________________	**estilo**	____________________
antropología	____________________	**contemporáneo**	____________________

Museo Nacional de Antropología. *Listen now to a guide in a tour bus talking about the* Museo Nacional de Antropología *as the bus arrives at the museum. As you listen, check all the facts and places that are mentioned by the guide.*

- ❑ fecha de construcción
- ❑ nombre del director
- ❑ tesoro de arte
- ❑ salida del museo
- ❑ patio central
- ❑ tienda del museo
- ❑ popular con los turistas
- ❑ estilo contemporáneo
- ❑ Parque de Chapultepec
- ❑ entrada del museo
- ❑ dos pisos
- ❑ cafetería del museo

NOTICIERO CULTURAL

LUGAR... MÉXICO

Antes de empezar, dime...

Contesta estas preguntas para reflexionar un poco en las ciudades más históricas de tu estado.

1. ¿Qué determina la importancia de una ciudad? ¿su historia? ¿su población? ¿su tamaño *(size)*? Explica tu respuesta.
2. ¿Cuál es la ciudad más importante de tu estado o región? ¿Por qué es importante?
3. En tu ciudad, ¿dónde se junta *(get together)* la gente para festivales patrióticos, reuniones políticas o demostraciones?

El Zócalo, México, D.f.

El Zócalo

La Ciudad de México, con su población de treinta millones de habitantes, es ahora la ciudad más grande del mundo. Como los otros grandes centros urbanos (Tokio, Londres, Sao Paulo, Nueva York, Moscú y Shangai), la Ciudad de México ofrece de todo: hoteles elegantes, museos excelentes, cines y teatros innovadores, una tremenda variedad de restaurantes, centros de estudio, establecimientos industriales, tráfico y contaminación.

En el centro de la ciudad está el Zócalo, que es una plaza cuadrada. Todos los edificios que rodean esta plaza están en contacto con la rica historia mexicana: los templos sagrados del Tenochtitlán de los aztecas, recientemente descubiertos por arqueólogos, como también la Catedral y los edificios de gobierno de los tiempos coloniales en la Nueva España.

Antes de llegar los españoles en el siglo XV, Tenochtitlán ya era una gran ciudad muy poblada y el Zócalo era su centro ceremonial rodeado de pirámides, templos y palacios.

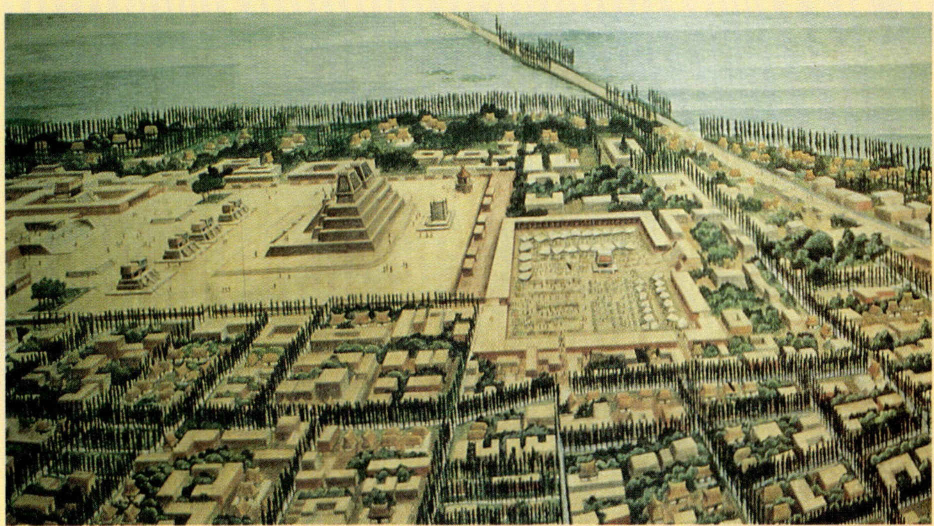

El Zócalo en tiempos precolombinos

Los españoles destruyeron las construcciones aztecas y en el mismo sitio construyeron su catedral y edificios de gobierno. Después de varias transformaciones, el Zócalo es ahora una plaza abierta que permite una vista directa de la catedral y de los hermosos edificios coloniales. Es también el sitio de festivales, reuniones políticas y manifestaciones (demostraciones).

Y ahora, dime...

Contrastes. Compara Tenochtitlán con la Ciudad de México del siglo XXI y compara el Zócalo precolombino con el colonial y el del siglo XXI. En una hoja de papel, haz una copia de estos diagramas y complétalos.

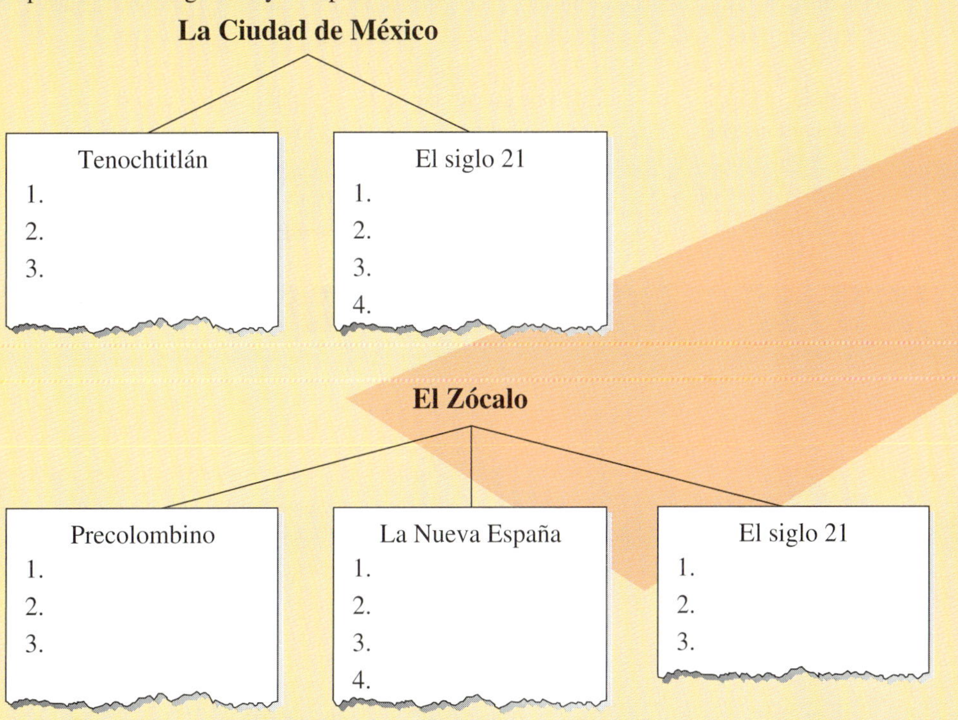

El español en otras disciplinas: Historia

Anónimo, Cristóbal Colón al descubrir «Las Américas».

El descubrimiento. El descubrimiento de las Américas por los españoles es uno de los períodos más interesantes y controversiales en la historia del mundo. Todavía continúa la polémica: ¿Fue el descubrimiento de nuevas culturas o la destrucción de antiguas culturas? ¿Fue un período de muchos héroes o de muchos villanos? ¿Cuáles son tus opiniones? En grupos de tres o cuatro, contesten estas dos preguntas e informen a la clase de sus conclusiones.

Proyecto: Prepara un informe por escrito en inglés o español sobre uno de estos personajes históricos. Explica la controversia que rodea a la persona que selecciones.

Cristóbal Colón	Hernán Cortez	Pedro de Alvarado
Malinche	Moctezuma	Atahualpa

¡Vamos de compras!

TAREA

Antes de empezar este **Paso**, estudia **En preparación** 4.3 y 4.4 y haz por escrito los ejercicios de **¡A practicar!** También escucha el **Paso 2 ¿Qué se dice...?** del Capítulo 4 en el CD del estudiante.

¿Eres buen observador?

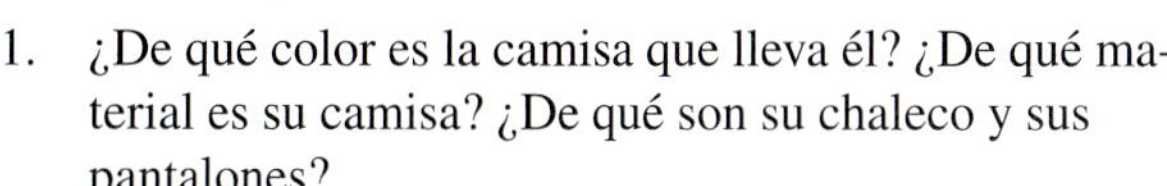

Ahora, ¡a analizar!

1. ¿De qué color es la camisa que lleva él? ¿De qué material es su camisa? ¿De qué son su chaleco y sus pantalones?
2. ¿Cuánto cuesta la camisa? ¿el chaleco? ¿los pantalones?
3. La camisa de él es de mangas largas. ¿Es de mangas largas su chaleco? ¿De qué material son los botones del chaleco?
4. ¿Es de mangas largas la blusa de ella? ¿Es de algodón su blusa?
5. ¿Cuáles pantalones cuestan más, los de él o los de ella?

¿Qué se dice...?

Al hablar de precios y hacer comparaciones

Ropa en oferta: ______________________________

____

____

VENDEDORA ¿Qué se le ofrece, señorita?

MARTINA Busco suéteres de lana. También necesito un impermeable, pero... ¡qué caros son!

VENDEDORA Los impermeables van a estar en oferta en septiembre. Aquí están los suéteres. Son lindos, ¿no?

MARTINA Sí, verdad. Pero, ¿podría decirme por qué cuestan los suéteres de algodón tanto como los de lana? Los de lana siempre son más caros, ¿no?

VENDEDORA Es que los suéteres de lana están en rebaja esta semana.

MARTINA Ah, ¡con razón!

¿Sabías que... ?

Unidades monetarias de los países de habla hispana

Argentina	**peso**	Honduras	**lempira**
Bolivia	**boliviano**	México	**peso**
Colombia	**peso**	Nicaragua	**córdoba**
Costa Rica	**colón**	Panamá	**balboa**
Cuba	**peso**	Paraguay	**guaraní**
Chile	**peso**	Perú	**nuevo sol**
Ecuador	**sucre**	Puerto Rico	**dólar**
El Salvador	**colón**	República Dominicana	**peso**
España	**peseta**	Uruguay	**peso nuevo**
Guatemala	**quetzal**	Venezuela	**bolívar**

Ahora, ¡a hablar!

A. La sección de varones. En el Palacio de Hierro, las rebajas están en efecto ahora. ¿Cuánto pagaría *(would pay)* usted por los siguientes artículos en la sección de varones?

Modelo un suéter de lana
Pagaría quinientos veintinueve pesos.

1. un par de zapatos
2. tres corbatas
3. dos pantalones
4. dos camisas
5. un traje completo
6. un pijama

B. La sección de damas. Alicia decide llevar de compras a su prima española Mari Carmen. Van al Palacio de Hierro porque hay rebajas hoy en la sección de damas. ¿Cuánto tendría que *(would have to)* pagar Alicia por esta ropa y cuánto es eso en pesetas, según Mari Carmen? (1 peso = 19 pts)

Modelo un suéter de lana (8.341 pts)

ALICIA **Tendría que pagar cuatrocientos treinta y cinco pesos.**

MARI CARMEN **En España yo tendría que pagar siete mil ochocientas pesetas.**

1. una falda de lana (5.510 pts)
2. una blusa de seda (8.265 pts)
3. un impermeable (20.064 pts)
4. un par de botas (17.955 pts)
5. un traje (21.432)

C. Comparaciones. Tú estás comparando los precios en el Palacio de Hierro con los de una tienda de ropa de mujer muy popular, Vitros de México. ¿Cómo son los precios?

Modelo las medias
Las medias en Vitros son tan caras como en el Palacio de Hierro. o
Las medias en Vitros son más baratas. o
Las medias en Vitros son más caras.

Vitros de México		Palacio de Hierro
$945	1. botas	$945
$1.099	2. impermeables	$1.056
$445	3. suéteres	$439
$475	4. pantalones	$475
$549	5. zapatos	$584
$289	6. faldas	$290
$439	7. blusas	$435
$1.569	8. trajes de noche	$1.128

D. ¡Es carísimo! Tú trabajas para la Asociación de Estudiantes de tu universidad. Tu responsabilidad en el mes de agosto es servirles de guía a estudiantes nuevos. ¿Qué contestas cuando un(a) estudiante de México, representado(a) por tu compañero(a), te hace estas preguntas?

1. ¿Cuánto es el alquiler de un apartamento aquí? ¿de un cuarto en las residencias?
2. ¿Es tan cara la ropa aquí como en México? ¿Cuánto cuesta un par de jeans? ¿un vestido? ¿un par de zapatos?
3. Y la comida, ¿es cara? ¿Cuánto gastas *(do you spend)* tú en comida en una semana? ¿en un mes? ¿Gastas tanto en comida como en ropa?
4. ¿Cuánto pagas en el metro? ¿en el autobús? ¿en un taxi? ¿Son caros los coches? ¿Cuánto costaría un coche usado? ¿uno nuevo? ¿una bicicleta?
5. ¿Son tan baratos los libros aquí como en México? ¿Cuánto pagas por los libros cada semestre?

Y ahora, ¡a conversar!

A. ¿Tú? ¿Tan bueno(a) como...? Compárate con compañeros de clase o con personas famosas. En una hoja de papel, escribe las comparaciones en estas categorías.

Modelo **Luis Miguel es tan guapo como yo.**

1. alto
2. bueno
3. simpático
4. guapo
5. listo
6. elegante
7. interesante
8. ¿… ?

B. ¡Fanáticos en el vestir! ¿Eres un(a) fanático(a) en el vestir? Para contestar, primero prepara por escrito una lista de toda la ropa en tu ropero *(closet)*. Incluye la cantidad de cada prenda *(number of each item)*. Luego en grupos pequeños, pregúntales a tus compañeros cuántas prendas tienen en su ropero y compara sus respuestas con lo que tú tienes.

Modelo

TÚ **¿Cuántos pares de zapatos tienes?**
COMPAÑERO(A) **Tengo cuatro pares de zapatos.**
TÚ **Ah, tienes tantos zapatos como yo.** o
Yo tengo más zapatos que tú. o
Yo no tengo tantos zapatos como tú.

C. En el escaparate. Tú estás de compras en la Ciudad de México y quieres comprar todas las prendas de esta lista. Desafortunadamente, muchas prendas no tienen etiqueta *(price tag)*. Pídele a tu compañero(a) los precios que quieres saber y dale los precios que él o ella necesita basándote en el dibujo de la siguiente página. El escaparate *(store window)* de tu compañero(a) está en el Apéndice A. No se permite mirar el escaparate de tu compañero(a) hasta terminar esta actividad.

Tú quieres comprar:

1. una blusa para tu mamá
2. una corbata para tu papá
3. zapatos para ti
4. una camisa para tu hermano
5. un sombrero para tu hermana

¡Luz! ¡Cámara! ¡Acción!

A. Día de las Madres. El Día de las Madres es dentro de una semana y tú tienes que comprar un regalo para tu madre. Vas al almacén y hablas del precio de varias prendas de ropa para señoras con el (la) dependiente. Dramatiza esta situación con un(a) compañero(a).

B. ¡Es guapísimo(a)! Este fin de semana vas a salir a bailar con una persona muy especial. Decides comprar ropa nueva para esta ocasión. El (La) dependiente en el almacén es muy simpático(a) y te ayuda *(helps you)* a comparar varias prendas. Dramatiza la situación con un(a) compañero(a).

¿Comprendes lo que se dice?

Estrategias para ver y escuchar. *In the first* **Paso** *of this chapter you learned to recognize cognates by listening for changes in accentuation. Listen now as your instructor plays the first three sentences of this video advertisement. Note how the following cognates are pronounced in Spanish and draw a circle around the stressed syllable. Then go back and write the English equivalent and underline the syllable that is stressed in the English word. Note how the pronunciation varies.*

Cognates

introduce ____________________

precios ____________________

línea ____________________

femenina ____________________

democráticos ____________________

Ropa de Felena. Mira ahora el anuncio sobre una nueva línea de ropa para damas. Luego escribe el precio de cada prenda, según el anuncio.

1. zapatos ______
2. suéteres ______
3. vestidos ______
4. trajes ______
5. blusas ______
6. faldas ______

NOTICIERO CULTURAL

GENTE... DIEGO RIVERA

Antes de empezar, dime...

Contesta estas preguntas para ver cuánto sabes del arte mural.

1. Si un «muro» es una pared *(a wall)*, ¿qué es el «arte mural»?
2. ¿Hay ejemplos de arte mural en la ciudad donde vives ahora? Descríbelos.
3. ¿Cuál es la diferencia entre el arte mural y el grafiti?

Mural de Diego Rivera

Diego Rivera (1886–1957)

Diego Rivera es un famoso pintor muralista mexicano que empieza a pintar durante la época de la Revolución mexicana de 1910. Él, como otros artistas, usa el arte para comunicarse con su pueblo. En sus murales, Rivera representa la miseria, las malas condiciones de trabajo, los problemas de la reforma y sus víctimas directas: el hombre, la mujer y el niño campesino, el obrero, el indio.

Rivera pinta excelentes murales, la mayoría ejemplos del arte social revolucionario en edificios públicos de la Ciudad de México. En el Palacio Nacional de México, por ejemplo, hay una excelente colección de murales que representan el conflicto entre el indio y el español.

Pero es en el Museo Diego Rivera, o «Anahuacalli», al que Rivera donó más de 60.000 piezas de arte antes de morir, donde podemos ver la colección más grande de este artista. El museo fue diseñado *(designed)* por el artista mismo, y representa uno de los edificios más importantes de la Ciudad de México.

Y ahora, dime...

Compara al muralista mexicano Diego Rivera con el artista español Joan Miró según esta lectura y la lectura sobre Miró del Capítulo 3, página 118.

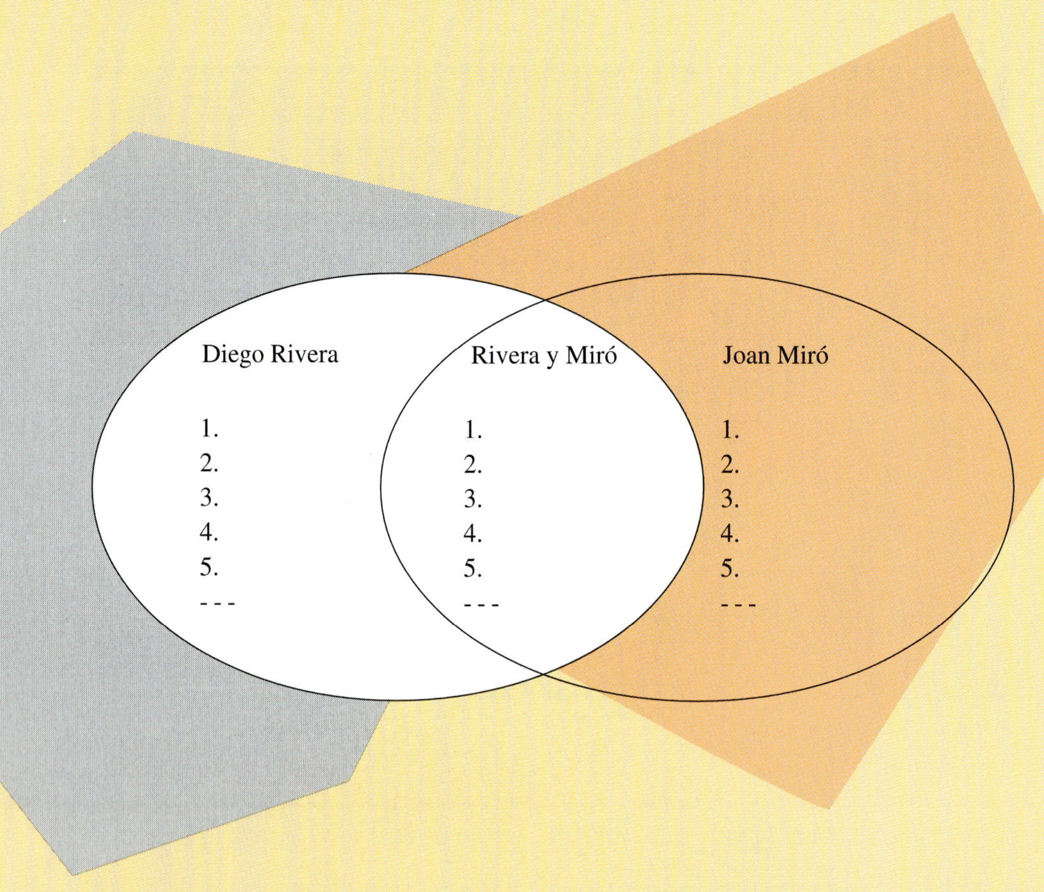

¿Te gusta escribir?

Antes de escribir
Estrategias para escribir: Palabras y frases clave

When writing advertisements, it is necessary to have a list of key words and phrases (palabras y frases clave) *that must be worked into the advertisement. These key words or phrases usually contain the essence of the message to be conveyed.*

Mira el anuncio de la Secretaría de Turismo de México en la página 165. En este anuncio hay cinco palabras o frases clave que mencionan los aspectos más atractivos de México. ¿Puedes identificarlas? ¿Cuáles son? ¿Qué llama la atención a estas palabras en el diseño del anuncio?

Ahora, ¡a escribir!

A. Agrupar ideas. Prepara una lista de palabras y frases clave que puedes usar en un anuncio las atracciones de tu ciudad o estado. Tu anuncio va a ser para atraer a más turistas a tu estado. Debe llamar la atención a las atracciones más importantes de tu ciudad o estado.

B. El primer borrador. Usa la lista que preparaste en el grupo de ideas para escribir un primer borrador de tu anuncio sobre las atracciones de tu ciudad o estado. Tal vez decidas escribir una o dos oraciones para explicar cada palabra o frase clave de tu anuncio.

C. Ahora, a compartir. Comparte tu primer borrador con dos o tres compañeros. Comenta el contenido y el estilo del anuncio de tus compañeros y escucha los comentarios de ellos sobre tu anuncio. Si hay errores de ortografía o gramática, menciónalos.

D. Ahora, a revisar. Si necesitas hacer unos cambios, basados en los comentarios de tus compañeros, hazlos ahora.

E. La versión final. Prepara una versión final de tu anuncio y entrégala. Si quieres, puedes usar fotos o dibujos para hacer tu anuncio más atractivo.

F. Publicación. Tu profesor(a) va a poner todos los anuncios en la pared. Léelos y con dos o tres compañeros de clase decidan cuál va a atraer a más turistas. Informen a la clase de su decisión.

¿Dónde prefieres comer?

TAREA

Antes de empezar este **Paso**, estudia **En preparación** 4.5 y 4.6 y haz por escrito los ejercicios de **¡A practicar!** También escucha el **Paso 3 ¿Qué se dice...?** del Capítulo 4 en el CD del estudiante.

¿Eres buen observador?

Ahora, ¡a analizar!

1. ¿Para qué es esta propaganda? ¿Para una bebida alcohólica? ¿Para un refresco? ¿Para un jugo?
2. ¿Cuántas variedades de Jumex hay? ¿Cuáles son? ¿Cuál prefieres tú?
3. ¿Por qué dicen que Jumex es «light»?
4. ¿Cuántos preservantes tiene Jumex?
5. ¿Adónde puedes llamar para conseguir más información sobre Jumex?

¿Qué se dice...?

Al pedir algo en un café

¿Cuánto tiempo hace que esperan? ________________

¿Qué necesita tomar el niño? ________________

¿Por qué no ordenan? ________________

MESERA ¿Qué desean tomar?

RAMÓN Yo no tengo hambre. Sólo quiero algo para beber.

ANTONIO Pues yo tengo mucha sed. ¿Qué me recomienda para beber?

MESERA Tenemos limonada, cerveza, vino, café, té, chocolate y leche.

ANTONIO Una cerveza, por favor.

RAMÓN Y un café para mí. Tengo sueño ahora.

¿Sabías que... ?

En los países hispanos, como en la mayoría de los países europeos, los restaurantes, por lo general, no sirven agua del grifo *(tap water)*. Si deseas agua para beber, usualmente hay que pedir agua mineral embotellada. Casi siempre, el mesero pregunta: **¿Agua con gas o sin gas?** Algunos meseros simplemente dicen: **¿Gaseosa?**

Ahora, ¡a hablar!

A. Tengo sed. Quiero un... En un café al aire libre tú y unos jóvenes universitarios dicen que tienen mucha sed. ¿Qué quieren tomar?

Modelo mi amigo / tener prisa / limonada
Mi amigo tiene mucha prisa; sólo quiere una limonada.

		agua sin gas
tú	tener sueño	café negro
mi amigo(a)	tener sed	agua mineral
ellas	tener prisa	café con leche
yo	tener calor	tomarme una pastilla
nosotros	tener que	limonada
		cerveza grande

B. ¿Cuándo? ¿Cuándo tomas estas bebidas o comidas en un café?

Modelo **Tomo cerveza cuando tengo sed.**

1. refresco bien frío	a. tener sed
2. café	b. tener hambre
3. té caliente	c. tener calor
4. cerveza	d. tener frío
5. sandwich	e. tener prisa
6. agua mineral	f. tener que tomar una aspirina
7. chocolate	g. tener sueño
8. hamburguesa	

C. ¡Mozo, por favor! Son las nueve de la noche y hay muchos clientes en el Café Malinche, un café al aire libre. Muchos están cansados de esperar. ¿Qué dicen?

Modelo nosotros / hambre / una hora
¡Mozo, por favor! Tenemos mucha hambre. Hace una hora que esperamos.

1. yo / examen en 15 minutos / una hora
2. mis hijos / sed / mucho tiempo
3. mi esposa(o) y yo / hambre / media hora
4. el señor / prisa / veinte minutos

5. nosotros / hambre y sed / un cuarto de hora
6. yo / una cita / una hora

D. ¿Cuánto tiempo hace? Pregúntale a tu compañero(a) cuánto tiempo hace que (no) hace estas cosas.

Modelo tocar el piano

TÚ **¿Cuánto tiempo hace que tocas el piano?**
COMPAÑERO(A) **Hace cinco años que toco el piano.** o **No toco el piano.**

1. vivir donde vives ahora
2. asistir a la universidad
3. estudiar español
4. tener un coche
5. no visitar a tus padres
6. no hablar por teléfono
7. no comer en un restaurante
8. no ver a tus maestros de la secundaria

Y ahora, ¡a conversar!

A. ¡Tantas cosas que hacer! Prepara dos listas: una de responsabilidades y obligaciones que tienes para el fin de semana y otra con lo que te gustaría *(you would like)* hacer con tu tiempo libre. En grupos pequeños, compara tu lista con la de tus compañeros.

Modelo **Tengo que estudiar para un examen de inglés.**
Quiero ir a la playa el domingo.

B. En un café. En grupos pequeños, escriban una descripción de esta escena. Mencionen lo que todo el mundo está pensando, cómo se siente cada persona y lo que probablemente van a decirle al mesero.

C. Obligaciones y... Pregúntales a tus compañeros de clase si tienen las obligaciones o sienten lo indicado en este cuadro. Cada vez que respondan afirmativamente, pídeles que firmen en el cuadrado apropiado. Recuerda que no se permite que una persona firme más de un cuadrado.

siempre tener hambre en la clase de español __________ *Firma*	tener mucha sed ahora __________ *Firma*	tener que tomar pastillas todos los días __________ *Firma*	tener mucha prisa después de esta clase __________ *Firma*
hacer tres horas que no comer __________ *Firma*	tener ganas de tomar una cerveza __________ *Firma*	siempre tomar agua mineral __________ *Firma*	tener sueño ahora __________ *Firma*
tener frío ahora __________ *Firma*	tener miedo de los exámenes de español __________ *Firma*	simpre tener razón __________ *Firma*	tener calor ahora __________ *Firma*
tener más años que el profesor (la profesora) __________ *Firma*	hace tres años que asiste a la universidad __________ *Firma*	tener ganas de dormir ahora __________ *Firma*	tener que hacer mucha tarea __________ *Firma*

¡Luz! ¡Cámara! ¡Acción!

A. ¡Estoy muerto! Tú y dos amigos(as) andan de compras y deciden entrar a un café porque tienen sed, calor y mucha hambre. Cuando el mesero viene, cada uno pide algo de beber y comer. Uno también pide un vaso de agua para tomarse una pastilla. En grupos de cuatro, dramaticen esta situación.

B. ¿Un refresco? Tú y dos amigos(as) van a la cafetería de la universidad. Primero piden algo para tomar y luego hablan un poco de sus compañeros de la clase de español. Dramatiza esta situación con tres compañeros(as) de clase.

Antes de leer
Estrategias para leer: Examinar ligeramente

A. ¡Rápidamente! *Often, before deciding to read an article or short passage, we skim it, that is, we glance through it quickly, focusing only on clues that will give us a general idea of its content.*

When you skim (examinar ligeramente), *read only selected sentences or phrases that may give you the main idea. Focus on textual clues such as highlighted words, headlines, photos, and subtitles, and special spacing and formatting. Do not read every word or sentence.*

Ahora examina ligeramente el anuncio y escribe una o dos oraciones sobre lo que crees que va a ser el tema principal de este anuncio.

B. Prepárate para leer. Miles y miles de turistas de otros países visitan los Estados Unidos cada año. Una cosa que motiva este turismo es la propaganda que hace la Oficina de Turismo del gobierno estadounidense. Imagínate que tú trabajas para la Oficina de Turismo y tienes que preparar un anuncio para atraer *(attract)* más turismo a los Estados Unidos.

1. En tu opinión, ¿cuáles son las atracciones más grandes de los Estados Unidos?
2. Escribe una o dos oraciones para describir cada una de esas atracciones.
3. Escribe una o dos palabras clave *(key words)* como subtítulo para cada una de las descripciones.

Ahora, vas a examinar un anuncio sobre el turismo en México. Ten en cuenta *(keep in mind)* las tres preguntas de arriba.

Lectura

A ver si comprendiste

Prepara un grupo de ideas para cada una de las cinco atracciones principales de México. Mira cómo parte de la primera ya está completada.

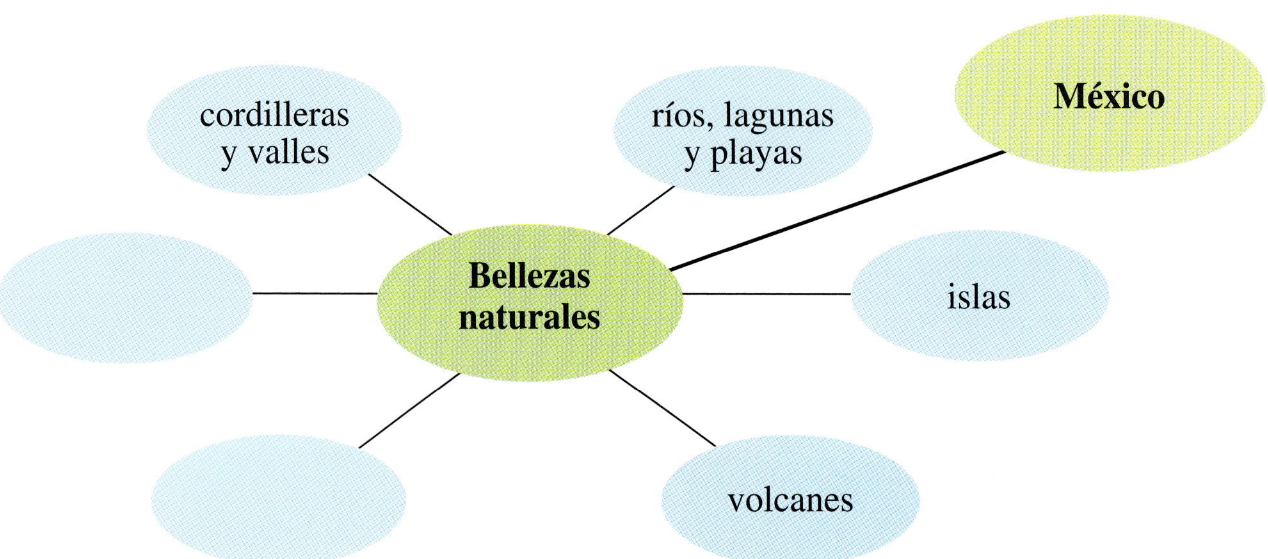

Viajemos por el ciberespacio a... MÉXICO

Expand your horizons! *Let's travel through cyberspace to México* where, through the Internet, you can . . .

- plan a weekend in **México, D.F.,** by checking magazines like ***Tiempo Libre*** that provide detailed information about the events taking place in the city.
- visit the **Museo Nacional de Antropología** and others displaying the works of **Diego Rivera, Frida Kahlo,** and many other great Mexican artists.
- have immediate access to Mexico's most prestigious newspapers: ***Excelsior, Jornada, El Norte, El Imparcial,*** and ***Mundo.***

If you are a cyberspace browser, join us in **Viajemos por el ciberespacio a... México** by trying the following important addresses.

Museos del INBA
http://www.internet.com.mx/bartes/

Universidad Nacional Autónoma de México
http://serpiente.dgsca.unam.mx/

Periódicos
http://www.imparcial.com.mx/
http://worldnews.net/excelsior/
http://www.infosel.com.mx/reforma
http://serpiente.dgsca.unam.mx/jornada/
http://148.246.247.123:80/elnorte/
http://www.planet.com.mx/tiempolibre/

Because addresses are likely to change without notice, the following key words will guarantee that **Viajemos por el ciberespacio a . . . México** will get you to your desired destination.

Palabras clave
Museo del Palacio de Bellas Artes
Museo de Arte Moderno
Museo Nacional de Antropología
Museo Nacional de Arte
Museo Mural Diego Rivera
Museo Estudio Diego Rivera
Periódicos de México
Revista Tiempo Libre
Radio en vivo, México

http://www.hrwcollege.com

 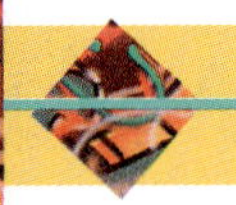

Vocabulario

Bebidas

agua	*water*
gaseosa	*carbonated drink*
leche *(f.)*	*milk*
limonada	*lemonade*
té *(m.)*	*tea*
vino	*wine*

Nacionalidades

alemán, alemana	*German*
francés, francesa	*French*
japonés, japonesa	*Japanese*

Excursiones

audífono	*headphone*
cámara	*camera*
cuadro	*painting*
excursión *(f.)*	*tour*
fotografía	*photograph*
película	*film*
servicios	*bathroom*
visita	*tour*

Liquidación

en oferta	*on special*
en rebaja	*reduced*
ganga	*bargain*
liquidación *(f.)*	*sale*

Colores

amarillo(a)	*yellow*
anaranjado(a)	*orange*
azul	*blue*
blanco(a)	*white*
gris	*gray*
negro(a)	*black*
rojo(a)	*red*
verde	*green*

Ropa

algodón *(m.)*	*cotton*
blusa	*blouse*
botas	*boots*
camisa	*shirt*
camiseta	*tee shirt*
chaqueta	*jacket*
corbata	*necktie*
falda	*skirt*
impermeable *(m.)*	*raincoat*
lana	*wool*
medias	*stockings*
pantalones *(m.)*	*pants, trousers*
pantalones cortos / shorts	*shorts, short pants*
par *(m.)*	*pair*
pijama *(m.)*	*pajamas*
seda	*silk*
suéter *(m.)*	*sweater*
traje *(m.)*	*suit*
vestido	*dress*
zapatos	*shoes*

Personas

dama	*lady*
esposa	*wife*
esposo	*husband*
guía *(m. / f)*	*guide*
joven *(m. / f)*	*young man / woman*
niño(a)	*child*
señora	*lady, Mrs.*
varón *(m.)*	*male, man*

Demostrativos y comparaciones

ese(a)	*that*
eso	*that*
esos(as)	*those*
este(a)	*this*
esto	*this*
estos(as)	*these*
tan... como	*as ... as*
tanto como	*as much as*
tantos como	*as many as*

Adjetivos

corto(a)	*short (length)*
largo(a)	*long*
lindo(a)	*pretty*

Modismos

tener... años	*to be ... years old*
tener calor	*to be hot*
tener éxito	*to succeed*
tener frío	*to be cold*
tener ganas de	*to feel like*
tener hambre	*to be hungry*
tener miedo de	*to be afraid of*
tener prisa	*to be in a hurry*
tener que	*to have to*
tener razón	*to be right*
tener sed	*to be thirsty*
tener sueño	*to be sleepy*
tener suerte	*to be lucky*

Verbos

almorzar (ue)	*to have lunch*
asistir	*to attend*
beber	*to drink*
cerrar (ie)	*to close*
costar (ue)	*to cost*
desear	*to desire*
dormir (ue)	*to sleep*
encontrar (ue)	*to find*
entender (ie)	*to understand*
ir de compras	*to go shopping*
pensar (ie)	*to plan; to think*
poder (ue)	*to be able, can*
preferir (ie)	*to prefer*
querer (ie)	*to want*
recomendar (ie)	*to recommend*
sacar fotografías	*to take pictures*
usar	*to use*
ver	*to see*
volar (ue)	*to fly*
volver (ue)	*to return*

Palabras y expresiones útiles

año	*year*
aspirina	*aspirin*
botella	*bottle*
casi	*almost*
pagaría	*I would pay*
recuerdos	*souvenirs*
sandwich *(m.)*	*sandwich*
tarea	*homework*
tendría	*I would have*
¡Apúrese!	*Hurry up!*
¡Con razón!	*No wonder!*

En preparación 4

4.1 Demonstrative Adjectives*

Pointing out specific people, places, events, or things

A. Demonstrative adjectives in English and Spanish are used to point out a specific person, place, or thing. The Spanish equivalents are:

este niño	*this*	**esta** niña
estos señores	*these*	**estas** señoras
ese hombre	*that*	**esa** mujer
esos chicos	*those*	**esas** chicas

B. In Spanish, demonstrative adjectives must agree in NUMBER and GENDER with the nouns they modify.

Esas niñas son altas y delgadas.	*Those girls are tall and slim.*
Este señor es mi papá.	*This man is my father.*
Esta joven baja y hermosa es mi hermana.	*This short and beautiful young woman is my sister.*

C. In Spanish, when the person, place, event, or thing being pointed out is perceived to be physically a far distance from the speaker and the listener, the following demonstratives are used.

aquel hombre	*that*	**aquella** mujer
aquellos chicos	*those*	**aquellas** chicas

*Note: Demonstrative pronouns are explained in Appendix F.

¡A practicar!

A. ¡Nunca satisfecho! You are at a restaurant with a friend who is a constant complainer. What does your friend say?

Modelo **Estos niños son terribles.**

	refrescos son muy caros.
Este	sillas no son cómodas.
Esta	restaurante es muy caro.
Estos	comida está muy fría.
Estas	mesero es antipático.
	señoras hablan constantemente.

B. ¡Mira! You are giving your parents a guided tour of the campus. What do you say as you point to various people and buildings?

Modelo ____________________ edificio es la biblioteca.
Ese edificio es la biblioteca.

1. ____________________ señor es el profesor de italiano.
2. ____________________ estudiantes son mis compañeras de cuarto.
3. ____________________ casa es la Casa Internacional.
4. ____________________ personas trabajan en el Club Social.
5. ____________________ lugar es la administración.
6. Y ____________________ autobús va a mi casa.

C. ¡Qué guapos somos! A ten-year-old is showing pictures and talking during her first show-and-tell report at school. Replace the underlined word with the word in parentheses and make all other necessary changes.

1. Este señor es mi papá. Él es alto y simpático. (mamá)
2. Esa chica es mi amiga. Es baja y delgada. (chicos)
3. Estas muchachas muy guapas son mis hermanas. (amiga)
4. Esos edificios son muy modernos y originales. (casa)
5. Esta perra es mi amiga. (perros)
6. Ese auto rojo es de mi profesora de español. (bicicleta)

4.2 Present Tense of *e* → *ie* and *o* → *ue* Stem-changing Verbs

Describing activities

Certain Spanish verbs undergo an **e** → **ie** or **o** → **ue** vowel change in all persons, except the **nosotros** and **vosotros** forms, whenever the stem vowel is stressed.

e → ie
Cerrar

to close	
cierro	cerramos
cierras **cie**rra	cerráis **cie**rran
cierra	**cie**rran

o → ue
Poder

to be able; can	
puedo	podemos
puedes **pue**de	podéis **pue**den
puede	**pue**den

Other frequently used stem-changing verbs:

empezar (ie)	*to begin*	almorzar (ue)	*to have lunch*
entender (ie)	*to understand*	contar (ue)	*to count*
pensar (ie)	*to think; to plan*	dormir (ue)*	*to sleep*
perder (ie)	*to lose*	encontrar (ue)	*to find*
preferir (ie)*	*to prefer*	volar (ue)	*to fly*
querer (ie)	*to want*	volver (ue)	*to return*

Note that in this text stem changes will always appear in parentheses after the verb when listed in the vocabulary section and in the appendix.

---

*All-**ir** stem-changing verbs also undergo a one-vowel change **e** → **i** or **o** → **u** in the present participle form of the verb: **prefiriendo, durmiendo.**

¡A practicar!

A. ¡Qué diferente! Has your life changed as much as this student's since you came to the university?

Modelo Yo ______________________ (preferir) mi vida en casa.
Yo prefiero mi vida en casa.

1. Mis clases ______________________ (empezar) a las ocho de la mañana.
2. Yo ______________________ (dormir) tres o cuatro horas al día.
3. Yo ______________________ (almorzar) sólo un sandwich.
4. En la mañana yo no ______________________ (encontrar) estacionamiento *(parking)*. Es muy difícil.
5. Por eso, yo ______________________ (preferir) usar mi bicicleta.
6. Mis profesores ______________________ (pensar) que soy un buen estudiante.

B. De vacaciones en México. Mr. and Mrs. Acuña are on vacation in Mexico City. Find out what they have planned for the day by completing the paragraph with the correct form of the verbs in parentheses.

Hoy nosotros ______________________ (pensar) ir al Museo Nacional de Antropología. Yo ______________________ (querer) aprender algo de la cultura azteca. Mi esposo ______________________ (preferir) estudiar la cultura de Oaxaca. Él ______________________ (pensar) que si nosotros ______________________ (empezar) muy temprano ______________________ (poder) ver todo lo que deseamos. Él no ______________________ (entender) que es imposible ver todo en un día. Pero no importa, mañana él ______________________ (volver) a pasar todo el día aquí en el museo y yo ______________________ (poder) ir de compras.

C. Somos guías. Get to know Felipe and David, guides in a museum in Mexico City, by completing the paragraph with the correct form of the verbs in parentheses.

Me llamo Felipe y mi amigo es David; somos guías aquí en el museo. David y yo hablamos inglés, francés y, por supuesto, español. Muchas personas no ____________________ (entender) el español y ____________________ (preferir) una excursión en otro idioma. Nosotros ____________________ (empezar) a trabajar a las diez de la mañana. Las visitas ____________________ (empezar) a las diez y media de la mañana. A las dos de la tarde yo ____________________ (almorzar) en la cafetería del museo. David no ____________________ (almorzar) hasta las tres. Nosotros ____________________ (volver) al trabajo una hora y media después de almorzar. El museo ____________________ (cerrar) a las seis y media.

PASO 2

4.3 Numbers above 200

Counting and writing checks

200	doscientos
225	doscientos veinticinco
300	trescientos
400	cuatrocientos
500	quinientos
600	seiscientos
700	setecientos
800	ochocientos
900	novecientos
1.000	mil
1.005	mil cinco
2.000	dos mil
7.000	siete mil
12.045	doce mil cuarenta y cinco
99.999	noventa y nueve mil novecientos noventa y nueve
154.503	ciento cincuenta y cuatro mil quinientos tres
1.000.000	un millón
25.100.900	veinticinco millones cien mil novecientos

A. When the numbers between 200 and 900 precede a feminine noun, they must end in **-as**.

300 camisas	trescient**as** camisas
450 blusas	cuatrocient**as** cincuenta blusas

Remember that the numbers between 30 and 90 *always* end in **-a.**

ciento treinta hombres
cuatrocientos cincuenta libros

B. **Mil** means *one thousand* or *thousand.* It is never preceded by **un.** Its plural, **miles,** meaning *thousands,* is never used when counting.

1994	mil novecientos noventa y cuatro
100.000	cien mil

C. An even million is expressed as **un millón.** Two or more million are expressed with the plural form **millones.** When a number in the millions precedes a noun, it is always followed by **de.**

1.000.000	un millón
2.000.000	dos millones
4.000.000 habitantes	cuatro millones **de** habitantes

¡A practicar!

A. ¡A pagar cuentas! Imagine that you are spending your junior year abroad at the **Universidad de las Américas** in Puebla, Mexico. Today you are writing checks to pay your bills. Write out the following amounts.

1. alquiler: 630,00
2. comida con la Sra. Rocha: 269,00
3. matrícula *(registration):* 4.579,00
4. libros: 315,00
5. lavandería / tintorería: 119,00
6. préstamo *(loan)* del Banco Nacional: 7.753,00

B. ¡Presupuesto! How much do you (or your parents) spend on your education? Work out a budget for an academic school year by indicating how much you spend in each of the following categories. Then write out each number as if you were writing a check to cover that amount. (**¡En español, por supuesto!**)

1. habitación
2. comida
3. auto
4. libros
5. ropa
6. matrícula
7. diversión

4.4 Comparisons of Equality

Stating equivalence

Comparisons of equality fall into two categories: comparisons of nouns and comparisons of adverbs or adjectives.

A. **Tanto(a, os, as)... como** *(as much / many . . . as)* is used to compare nouns. In these expressions, **tanto** is an adjective and always agrees with the noun being compared. The noun itself may be expressed or implied.

Pago **tantas** cuentas **como** tú.	*I pay as many bills as you do.*
Pero no pagas **tantas** (cuentas) **como** tu hermano.	*But you don't pay as many (bills) as your brother does.*

B. **Tan... como** *(as . . . as)* is used to compare adjectives or adverbs. **Tan** precedes the adjective or adverb, and **como** follows it.

Esta falda es **tan cara como** la de seda.	*This skirt is as expensive as the silk one.*
Pero en ésta no te ves **tan bien como** en la de seda.	*But in this one you don't look as good as in the silk one.*

¡A practicar!

A. ¡Son iguales! Tomás selects friends that are very much like him. Tell him what he has in common with the following people.

Modelo tú / activo /Juan
Tú eres tan activo como Juan.

1. María / atlético / tú
2. tus amigos / popular / tú
3. tú / divertido / tus amigos
4. tu papá / rico / el papá de Isabel
5. tu mamá / guapo / la mamá de Juana
6. tú / conservador / Antonio

B. ¡Tanto como tú! María always wants to keep up with her friends. What does she do to be exactly like her friends?

Modelo María / comprar / zapatos / Carmen
María compra tantos zapatos como Carmen.

1. María / comprar / ropa / Beatriz
2. María / leer / libros / Isabel
3. María / tener / amigos / José
4. María / trabajar / horas / Miguel
5. María / ganar / dinero / Samuel
6. María / organizar / fiestas / Paco

C. Son gemelas. Tere and Pepa are identical twins. Their parents have been very careful not to favor one over the other. Compare the two of them.

Modelo ropa
Tere tiene tanta ropa como Pepa.
simpático
Tere es tan simpática como Pepa.

1. zapatos	4. alto
2. inteligente	5. blusas y faldas
3. rubio	6. libros

4.5 *Tener* Idioms

Expressing feelings, obligations, and age

An idiom is a group of words with a clear meaning in one language that, when translated word for word, does not make any sense or sounds strange in another language. For example, in English the expression *to be tied up at the office* means "to be busy" and not "to be tied up with ropes." Many ideas, both in English and in Spanish, are expressed with idioms and simply must be learned. Literal translation does not work with idioms.

Following is a list of idioms with the verb **tener** that are frequently expressed with the verb *to be* in English.

tener calor	*to be hot*
tener éxito	*to succeed; to be successful*
tener frío	*to be cold*
tener hambre	*to be hungry*
tener miedo de	*to be afraid of*
tener prisa	*to be in a hurry*
tener razón	*to be right*
no tener razón	*to be wrong*
tener sed	*to be thirsty*
tener sueño	*to be sleepy*
tener suerte	*to be lucky*
tener... años	*to be ... years old*

Tengo mucha prisa ahora.	*I'm in a big hurry right now.*
Tenemos mucho calor y los niños **tienen mucha sed.**	*We're very hot, and the children are very thirsty.*

Other frequently used **tener** idioms are:

tener que + *infinitive*	*to have to do (something)*
tener ganas de + *infinitive*	*to feel like (doing something)*

Tengo que estudiar ahora.	*I have to study now.*
No tengo ganas de comer.	*I don't feel like eating.*

¡A practicar!

A. Asociaciones. Write the **tener** idioms you associate with each of the following.

Modelo 1 + 4 = 7
No tiene razón.

1. Frankenstein
2. Alaska
3. hamburguesa
4. 115°F
5. 5 − 5 = 0
6. Las Vegas o Atlantic City
7. 2:30 de la mañana

B. ¿Qué les pasa? Select the response that best explains each description.

1. La señora Rivera dice que necesita su suéter inmediatamente.
   a. Tiene frío. b. Tiene miedo. c. Tiene suerte.
2. El señor González necesita agua bien fría, ¡pronto!
   a. Tiene hambre. b. Tiene razón. c. Tiene sed.
3. Hace tres días que los niños no comen nada.
   a. Tienen prisa. b. Tienen hambre. c. Tienen éxito.
4. ¡Mi autobús sale en un minuto!
   a. Tengo que dormir. b. Tengo que leer. c. Tengo prisa.
5. Mi profesora insiste en que América se descubrió en 1492.
   a. Tiene prisa. b. Tiene razón. c. Tiene miedo.
6. ¡El señor Peña regresa de Las Vegas con cinco mil dólares!
   a. Tiene sueño. b. Tiene suerte. c. No tiene ganas.

4.6 *Hacer* in Time Expressions

Describing what has been happening

To describe an action that began sometime in the past and is still going on, Spanish uses the formula that follows.

Hace + (length of time) + **que** + (present tense verb)

Hace dos horas **que** esperamos.	*We have been waiting for two hours.*
Hace mucho tiempo **que** viven aquí.	*They have been living here for a long time.*

Note that the English equivalent is: *to have been* + (-ing verb) + (length of time).

¡A practicar!

A. ¡Tenemos prisa! The hostess at a very popular restaurant is explaining to her boss how long people have been waiting for a table. What does she say?

Modelo la señora Cárdenas: 35 minutos
Hace treinta y cinco minutos que ella espera.

1. el señor Santiago Domínguez y su familia: una hora
2. Miguel y Teresita Alarcón: 25 minutos
3. el señor Téllez y sus dos hijos: media hora
4. los señores Apodaca: 45 minutos
5. los jóvenes del Club de Exploradores: 15 minutos

B. ¿Cuánto tiempo hace? How long has it been that you have been doing or not doing the following?

Modelo no llamar a tu novio(a)
Hace ocho horas que no llamo a mi novio(a).

1. conocer a tus amigos
2. estudiar español
3. hablar inglés
4. no hablar con tus padres
5. no recibir dinero de tus padres
6. no visitar a tus padres

CAPÍTULO 5

¡Hogar, dulce hogar!

Cultural Topics

- **¿Sabías que… ?**
  Hispanic last names
- **Noticiero cultural**
  Lugar: *Argentina*
  Gente: *«Evita»*
- **Lectura:** *La Nación*

Writing Strategies

- *Precisos*

Reading Strategies

- *Dar un vistazo*

En preparación

- 5.1 Adverbs of Time
- 5.2 Prepositions
- 5.3 **Ir a +** *Infinitive* to Express Future Time
- 5.4 **Ser** and **estar:** A Second Look
- 5.5 Comparisons of Inequality
- 5.6 **Por** and **para:** A First Look

In this chapter, you will learn how to …

- *describe your family.*
- *inquire about renting an apartment.*
- *describe an apartment and its furnishings.*
- *describe how you and people you know have changed.*

El barrio "La Boca" en Buenos Aires

El barrio "La Recoleta" en Buenos Aires

Un barrio moderno de Buenos Aires

Lo que ya sabes...

1. Describe la primera foto. ¿Qué te llama la atención? En tu opinión, ¿qué tipo de gente vive en este barrio? ¿Hay barrios parecidos en los EE.UU.? ¿en tu ciudad?
2. Compara la foto de la casa en el barrio "La Recoleta" con la primera foto. ¿Cómo crees que es la gente que vive en este barrio?
3. Describe el barrio moderno. En tu opinión, ¿cómo es la gente que vive en este barrio? ¿Crees que los edificios donde vivimos dicen algo de nuestras personalidades? ¿Qué dice la casa de tus padres de tu personalidad?

ARGENTINA

¡Por fin en la «U»!

TAREA

Antes de empezar este **Paso**, estudia **En preparación** 5.1 y 5.2 y haz por escrito los ejercicios de **¡A practicar!** También escucha el **Paso 1 ¿Qué se dice...?** del Capítulo 5 en el CD del estudiante.

¿Eres buen observador?

Ahora, ¡a analizar!

1. ¿Para qué producto es esta propaganda?
2. ¿Qué es una bombilla? ¿Por qué son especiales las DULUX EL?
3. Explica cómo es posible ahorrar 29.400 ptas. en el dormitorio principal con la DULUX EL. ¿Cuánto puedes ahorrar en el otro dormitorio? ¿en el salón? ¿en la cocina? ¿en la entrada?
4. Explica la garantía que acompaña la DULUX EL.

Al buscar un apartamento

Dibuja *(Draw)* el edificio rojo y la iglesia. También escribe el nombre de la calle del edificio de apartamentos.

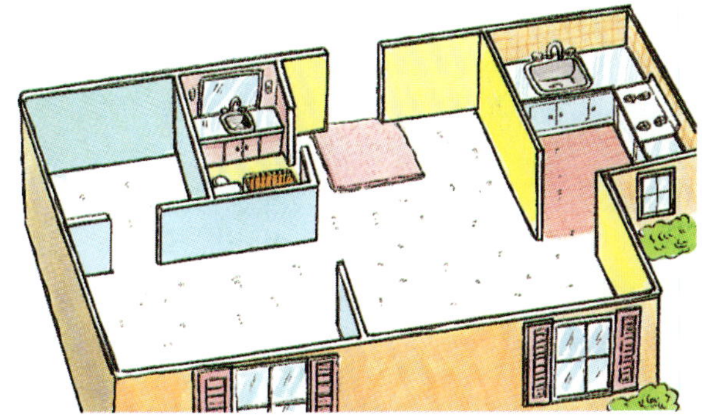

DOLORES ¿Cuántas habitaciones tiene?

SEÑOR P. Cuatro: un dormitorio, sala, comedor y cocina... y un baño, por supuesto.

DOLORES ¿Está amueblado?

SEÑOR P. No, no incluye muebles.

DOLORES ¿Cuánto es el alquiler?

SEÑOR P. Es barato, sólo $495,00 dólares al mes. Eso incluye garaje.

DOLORES ¿Está desocupado y disponible ahora?

SEÑOR P. Está desocupado y puede mudarse a fines de este mes.

DOLORES ¡Ah! Una pregunta más. ¿Permite animales domésticos? Tengo una linda gatita.

SEÑOR P. Lo siento, pero no permito ni gatos ni perros.

DOLORES ¿No? Entonces, no me interesa. ¡Adiós!

Ahora Dolores está con sus amigas Claudia y Beatriz, la hermanastra de Claudia. Dolores está contándoles los problemas que tiene para encontrar un apartamento.

DOLORES ¡Es terrible! Busco y busco y no encuentro nada. Nadie permite tener animales domésticos... y yo no puedo vivir sin mi gatita.

CLAUDIA Tranquila, tranquila, Dolores. No te preocupes. Vas a encontrar algo.

BEATRIZ Claudia, papá tiene un edificio de apartamentos y...

CLAUDIA ¡Tienes razón, Beatriz! Dolores, mi padrastro siempre tiene apartamentos disponibles, y él sí acepta animales domésticos pequeños.

DOLORES ¿De veras? ¡Pues, vamos a llamarlo en seguida!

A propósito...

Hay varias maneras de decir **apartamento** en español. Algunas son el **departamento,** el **domicilio,** la **residencia,** la **habitación** o el **piso.** El cuarto donde se duerme es el **dormitorio,** la **habitación,** la **recámara,** la **alcoba,** la **pieza** o simplemente el **cuarto.**

¿Sabías que... ?

En los países hispanos es común usar dos apellidos *(last names)*, por ejemplo, **Castillo Torres.** El primer apellido, en este caso **Castillo,** siempre es el apellido del padre; el segundo, **Torres,** es el apellido de la madre.

Ahora, ¡a hablar!

A. ¿Quién es quién? En la familia de Dolores, ¿cómo están relacionadas las siguientes personas? (La relación indicada entre paréntesis es la de cada persona con Dolores.)

Modelo Andrés con Dolores, Elodia y Antonio

Andrés es el primo de Dolores, el hermano de Elodia y el primo de Antonio.

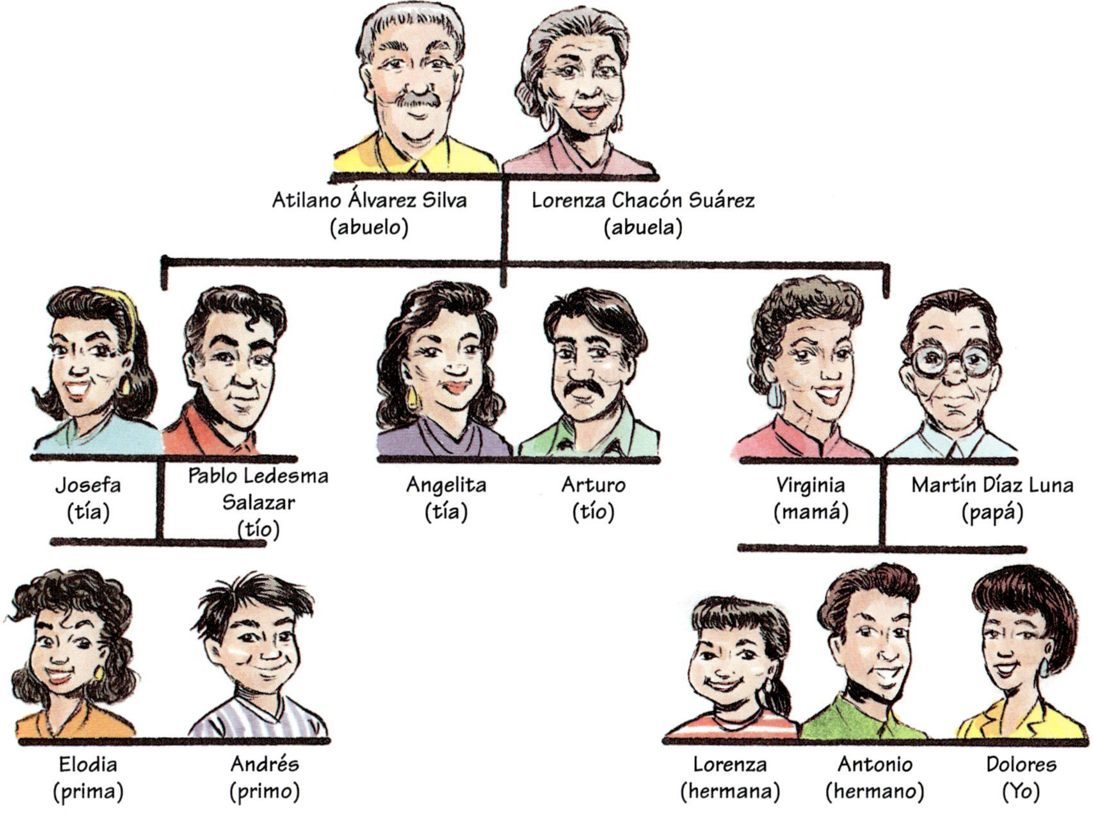

1. Pablo con Elodia, Andrés y la joven Lorenza
2. Josefa con Angelita, Virginia y Atilano
3. Lorenza la mayor con Arturo, Andrés y Lorenza la joven
4. Virginia con Josefa, Elodia y Dolores
5. Atilano con Arturo, Andrés y Antonio
6. Angelita con Arturo, Atilano y Elodia

B. ¿Mi habitación? Te interesa mucho alquilar un apartamento en el edificio donde vive tu compañero(a). Hazle preguntas para conseguir toda la información que necesitas sobre el apartamento.

1. ¿Dónde está el apartamento? ¿Cuál es la dirección exacta?
2. ¿Está lejos / cerca de la universidad? ¿del centro?
3. ¿Está cerca de una parada de autobús?
4. ¿Cuántas habitaciones tiene?
5. ¿Está amueblado? ¿Qué muebles hay?
6. ¿Son nuevos o viejos los muebles?
7. ¿Es caro? ¿Cuánto es el alquiler?
8. ¿Está desocupado ahora?
9. ¿Permiten animales domésticos?

C. ¿Con qué frecuencia? Pregúntale a un(a) compañero(a) con qué frecuencia hace estas cosas.

Modelo ir al banco

TÚ **¿Con qué frecuencia vas al banco?**

COMPAÑERO(A) **Voy al banco una vez a la semana.**

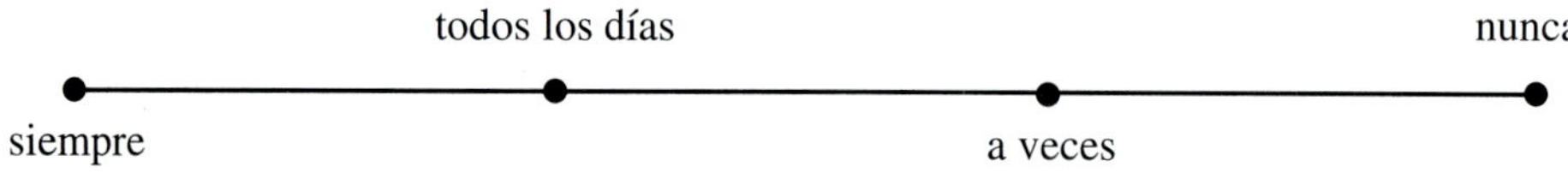

1. organizar fiestas en su casa
2. ir a clase
3. hacer fiestas
4. dormir
5. estudiar
6. ir a la biblioteca

D. ¿Dónde está la gatita? Perla es una gatita muy activa. ¿Puedes decir dónde está ahora?

Modelo

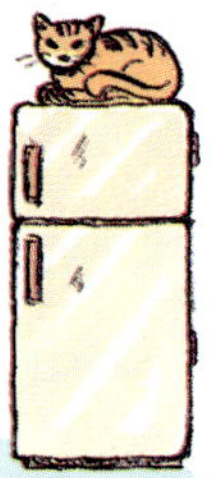

La gatita está encima de la nevera.

1. ______________________________

3. ______________________________

2. ______________________________

4. ______________________________

5. ______________________________ 7. ______________________________

6. ______________________________ 8. ______________________________

Y ahora, ¡a conversar!

A. ¿Mi familia? Dibuja el árbol genealógico de tu familia siguiendo el modelo del árbol en el ejercicio **A** de la sección anterior. Luego, sin permitir que nadie lo vea, describe tu árbol a un(a) compañero(a) mientras él (ella) lo dibuja. Cuando termines de describir, compara tu dibujo con el dibujo de tu compañero(a) para ver si lo explicaste bien. Finalmente, repite el proceso pero esta vez tú debes dibujar mientras tu compañero(a) describe.

B. La casa de tus padres. Describe la casa / el apartamento de tus padres. Di dónde está cada cuarto en relación con los otros.

Modelo cocina / baño

La cocina está lejos del baño.

1. cocina / sala
2. comedor / cocina
3. sala / baño
4. recámara / sala
5. entrada / cocina
6. garaje / comedor

C. Mi habitación. Dibuja tu habitación. Incluye todos los muebles, ventanas, closet, televisor, etc. Luego, en una segunda hoja de papel dibuja un esquema *(outline)* de tu habitación e indica el sitio de la cama, nada más. Dale el esquema a tu compañero(a) y mientras tú describes tu habitación, mencionando el sitio de cada objeto, tu compañero(a) va a dibujarla, poniendo todos los muebles en su lugar. Al terminar, compara tu dibujo original con el de tu compañero(a) para ver si explicaste bien. Repitan el proceso, pero esta vez tu compañero(a) describe y tú dibujas.

¡Luz! ¡Cámara! ¡Acción!

A. ¡Es demasiado caro! Tú y un(a) amigo(a) necesitan un apartamento para el próximo semestre. Van a hablar con el dueño de unos apartamentos. Hacen muchas preguntas para conseguir toda la información que necesitan. En grupos de tres, dramaticen la situación.

B. Un perrito encantador. Un matrimonio *(married couple)* joven necesita un apartamento para tres: ellos dos y Chuchi, un perrito encantador. En grupos de tres, el matrimonio y el (la) dueño(a), dramaticen esta situación.

¿Comprendes lo que se dice?

Estrategias para escuchar. *In Chapter 4 you learned to listen for stress variations (accents) in English and Spanish cognates. You will recognize many more cognates if you learn to listen for corresponding suffixes or word endings. For example,* -mente *in Spanish corresponds to -ly in English. Following is a list of three corresponding suffixes in Spanish and English. Recognizing these suffixes makes many more cognates easier to understand.*

Español	Inglés	Español		Inglés
perfecta**mente**	*perfect**ly***	**-mente**	=	***-ly***
generosi**dad**	*generosi**ty***	**-dad**	=	***-ty***
urg**ente**	*urg**ent***	**-ente**	=	***-ent***

Escucha la conversación de Guillermo, un estudiante universitario, con el dueño de un apartamento. *(With a partner, see how many* **-mente, -dad,** *and* **-ente** *cognates you can recognize. Write them down and share your list with the rest of the class.)*

¿Está disponible? Vuelve a escuchar la conversación de Guillermo con el dueño del apartamento. Luego compara el lugar donde tú vives ahora con el nuevo apartamento de Guillermo. Describe tu alojamiento en la columna de la izquierda, el de Guillermo en la columna de la derecha y lo que tienen en común en la columna del medio.

Lugar donde yo vivo	Ambos lugares	Apartamento de Guillermo
1.	1.	1.
2.	2.	2.
3.	3.	3.
4.	4.	4.
5.	5.	5.
...	...	...

NOTICIERO CULTURAL

LUGAR... ARGENTINA

Antes de empezar, dime...

Contesta estas preguntas para reflexionar un poco sobre las ciudades más históricas de tu estado.

1. ¿Cuál es la población de los EE.UU.? ¿Qué porcentaje de sus habitantes son de origen europeo? ¿de origen indígena?
2. ¿Ha tenido los EE.UU. un dictador en control del gobierno alguna vez en su historia? Explica tu respuesta.
3. ¿Qué papel *(role)* o control tienen los militares en los EE.UU.? ¿Imponen su voluntad o fuerza en el gobierno estadounidense? Explica tu respuesta.
4. ¿Qué papel tienen las mujeres en la política estadounidense? ¿Ha tenido los EE.UU. una mujer como presidenta? ¿una mujer como vicepresidenta?
5. ¿Qué probabilidades hay que una mujer llegue a ser presidenta de los EE.UU. en el futuro cercano? Explica tu respuesta.

Las madres de la Plaza de Mayo, Buenos Aires

Argentina

Argentina es un país con una superficie de 2.808.602 kilómetros cuadrados, cuatro veces más grande que el estado de Texas, y con una población que sobrepasa los 30.000.000 de habitantes.

El 97 por ciento de la población argentina es descendiente de italianos, españoles u otros grupos europeos. Se considera uno de los países más avanzados de Latinoamérica.

La Casa Rosada, Buenos Aires

Políticamente, como la mayoría de los países del continente, sufrió las consecuencias de una dictadura militar por muchos años. Una junta militar suspendió las elecciones generales y tomó el control del gobierno desde 1976 hasta 1983. En octubre de este último año, Argentina volvió a la democracia con el presidente Raúl Alfonsín en «La Casa Rosada» (que es «La Casa Blanca» de Argentina).

Las mujeres argentinas son una fuerza importante en el país y así, todos los jueves, todavía se reúnen Las Madres de la Plaza de Mayo, exactamente en ese lugar para reclamar y recordar a sus hijos y familiares desaparecidos durante el período militar.

Argentina se destaca también por tener en su historia a una de las primeras mujeres al mando del gobierno, la presidenta María Estela (Isabel) Perón que, como vicepresidenta del país, asumió el cargo al morir su esposo, el presidente Juan Domingo Perón, en 1975.

Y ahora, dime...

Contesta estas preguntas con un(a) compañero(a) de clase.

1. Prepara un esquema como el siguiente y complétalo con información de la lectura.

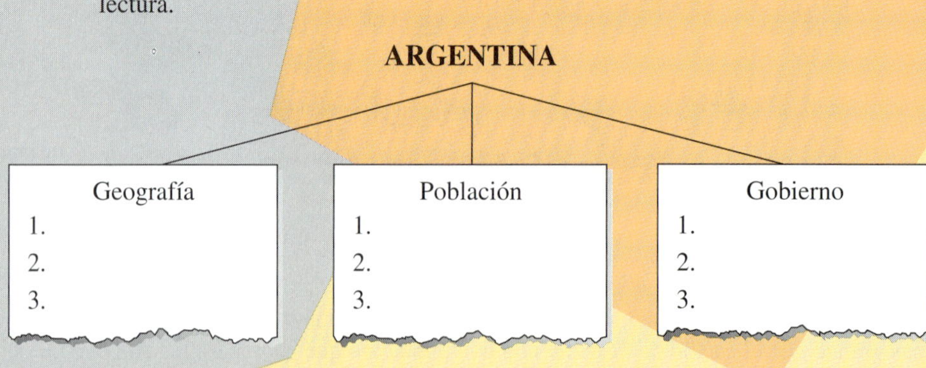

2. ¿Conoces otros países que tengan una mujer como presidenta o vicepresidenta en su historia?

El español en otras disciplinas: Matemáticas

El sistema métrico. Hay dos sistemas que usamos para hablar de longitud, peso y volumen: el sistema inglés y el sistema métrico. A continuación presentamos algunas medidas *(measures)* de ambos sistemas.

Longitud

Sistema inglés	Sistema métrico
1 pulgada	2,54* centímetros
1 pie	30,48 centímetros
1 yarda	91,44 centímetros
	1 metro = 100 centímetros ó† 1000 milímetros
0,62 milla	1 kilómetro
1 milla	1,609 kilómetros

Peso

Sistema inglés	Sistema métrico
0,035 onza	1 gramo
1 libra	453,59 gramos
2,2046 libras	1 kilogramo

Volumen

Sistema inglés	Sistema métrico
1 onza	0,02957 litro
0,2642 galón	1 litro
1 galón	3,785 litros

Conversiones. Contesta las siguientes preguntas usando medidas del sistema inglés primero y luego conviértelas a medidas del sistema métrico.

1. ¿Cuál es la velocidad máxima permitida en las carreteras de los EE.UU.?
2. ¿Cuánto mides tú? ¿Y tu compañero(a)? ¿Cuánto pesan?
3. ¿Cuántos galones de gasolina necesitas para llenar el tanque de tu auto? ¿Cuántos litros?

Proyecto: Pregúntales a tus padres, a dos hermanos o a dos amigos cuánto miden y cuánto pesan y anótalo. Convierte la información al sistema métrico. En grupos de tres, comparte tus medidas métricas para ver si tus compañeros pueden adivinar las medidas exactas en el sistema inglés.

*In most Spanish-speaking countries the use of the comma and period in numbers is reversed. Thus, **2,54 centímetros** is expressed in English as 2.54 centimeters, and a number like 3,000,000 (three million) is written as **3.000.000** in Spanish.

† When the Spanish word **o** (*or*) is used between or next to numerals, it is written with an accent to distinguish it from a zero: **5 ó 6 alumnos** as opposed to 506 alumnos.

PASO 2 ¡Tu cuarto es un desastre!

TAREA Antes de empezar este **Paso**, estudia **En preparación** 5.3 y 5.4 y haz por escrito los ejercicios de **¡A practicar!** También escucha el **Paso 2 ¿Qué se dice... ?** del Capítulo 5 en el CD del estudiante.

¿Eres buen observador?

Y en nuestro próximo número...

ESPECIAL BAÑOS
Baños bien zonificados, con revestimientos de mármol y madera, de colores luminosos y con soluciones modernas y elegantes.

MOBILIARIO DE DORMITORIO
Mesitas, cabezales, cómodas, galanes, baúles, etc. Todo lo necesario para darle el toque final al dormitorio.

SILLAS DE COMEDOR
Las mejores reproducciones de modelos clásicos, cómodas y con un toque de calidad que ennoble el espacio.

RINCONES DE LECTURA
Ocho propuestas diferentes, con sus presupuestos, de butacas, librerías y complementos.

TODO SOBRE CHIMENEAS
Explicamos todas las posibilidades, desde frontales para chimeneas hechas, hasta chimeneas falsas, con todos los complementos necesarios para crear un espacio muy personal y cálido.

Y ADEMÁS

MUEBLES TAPIZADOS
Cabezales, banquetas, cómodas, butacas... Muebles tapizados que ofrecen más calidad y confort.

MESAS Y SILLITAS PARA NIÑOS
Llenas de color y con motivos y dibujos que introducen notas de alegría en las habitaciones de los niños.

CÓMO COMBINAR EL AZUL Y EL VERDE
Dos colores que ofrecen muchas posibilidades decorativas.

Ahora, ¡a analizar!

1. ¿Para qué crees que es esta propaganda? ¿para una fábrica de muebles? ¿para una tienda de muebles? ¿para una revista de muebles? ¿para otra cosa? Explica tu respuesta.
2. ¿A qué se refiere el «ESPECIAL BAÑOS»? ¿a ideas para decorar baños? ¿a precios especiales? ¿a otras cosas? Explica.
3. ¿Cuáles de los muebles mencionados en «MOBILIARIO DE DORMITORIO» tienes en tu dormitorio en casa? ¿Necesita tu dormitorio un toque final? ¿Por qué?
4. ¿Cómo se comparan estas sillas de comedor con las sillas de comedor en la casa de tus padres? ¿Son más o menos elegantes?
5. ¿Qué es una chimenea falsa? ¿Tiene chimenea la casa de tus padres? ¿Es una chimenea falsa o una que funciona?

Al describir la habitación

Indica con una **M** si la madre dice lo siguiente y con una **H** si la hija lo dice.

1. _______ ¡Es un desastre!
2. _______ Está sucio.
3. _______ Son de bonitos colores.
4. _______ Son muy cómodos.
5. _______ Están en malas condiciones.
6. _______ ¡Son de plástico!

MADRE Por Dios, Dolores. La habitación es tan pequeña y tan oscura. ¡No hay ni una ventana!

DOLORES Así duermo mejor, mamá.

MADRE	¡Ay, hija! El baño está muy sucio.
DOLORES	¡Pero qué difícil estás hoy, mamá! No está sucio. Simplemente es tan viejo que es imposible limpiarlo.
MADRE	Es que no comprendo cómo puedes vivir aquí, hija.
DOLORES	Estoy muy cómoda aquí. El apartamento está en el centro, cerca de todo. Y mamá, con el dinero que tú y papá me dan, es imposible alquilar uno mejor.

Ahora, ¡a hablar!

A. ¡Fiesta de despedida! Mañana por la mañana Dolores Chacón sale para la universidad. Hoy es su fiesta de despedida y todos sus parientes van a ayudar en los preparativos. ¿Qué dice Dolores que van a hacer?

Modelo Mis tías Josefa y Angelita van a hacer un pastel para mí.

mi hermano Gilberto		preparar el ponche
mis tías Josefa y Angelita		hacer mis maletas
mamá y yo		comprar unos zapatos
papá	+ ir a +	hacer un pastel
mis primos		ir al banco
mi hermano Antonio		lavar mi auto
mi abuela		traer los discos compactos

B. ¿Recuerdas? ¿Recuerdas cuando decidiste asistir a la universidad? ¿Recuerdas todas las buenas intenciones que tenías? En parejas, imagínense que es el día antes de ir a la universidad por primera vez. Digan qué piensan hacer y no hacer para ser excelentes estudiantes universitarios.

Modelo Voy a estudiar cuatro horas todos los días. No voy a ir a fiestas durante la semana. Voy a...

C. ¡No soporto ni un día más aquí! Tú acabas de alquilar *(just rented)* un apartamento, pero después de una semana, quieres dejarlo porque encuentras muchos inconvenientes. ¿Cuáles son algunos de los problemas?

Modelos cocina / sucia
La cocina está muy sucia.
alquiler / demasiado caro
El alquiler es demasiado caro.

1. apartamento / muy oscuro
2. muebles / malas condiciones
3. apartamento / lejos de todo
4. cama / no cómoda
5. cocina / demasiado pequeña
6. alfombras / muy viejas

D. ¡Pero fíjese que...! El dueño del apartamento no quiere cancelar el contrato y habla de las ventajas que el apartamento ofrece. ¿Cuáles son?

Modelos apartamento / limpio
El apartamento está limpio.
edificio / moderno
El edificio es moderno.

1. apartamento / cerca / supermercado
2. alquiler / barato
3. habitaciones / grandes
4. sala y habitaciones / muy limpias
5. cama / nueva
6. edificio / cerca / parada de autobús

E. ¿Y tu apartamento? Entrevista a un(a) compañero(a), luego que él (ella) te entreviste a ti.

Pregúntale...

1. cómo es su apartamento / habitación / casa.
2. en qué condición está hoy.
3. qué muebles hay en su cuarto.
4. en qué condición están los muebles.
5. dónde está el apartamento / habitación / casa.
6. qué es lo mejor de su apartamento / habitación / casa.
7. qué no soporta.

Y ahora, ¡a conversar!

A. ¡Mi futuro! ¿Cómo ves tu futuro? ¿Qué vas a hacer en los próximos cinco años? Escribe una lista de tus planes futuros. Después, comparte tus planes con el resto de la clase para ver si tienen metas en común.

B. ¡Una casa ideal! Trabajas para una agencia de bienes raíces *(real estate).* Tu compañero(a) está buscando una casa para comprar. Tú quieres encontrar la casa ideal para tu cliente. Para eso, vas a tener que conocer a tu cliente muy bien. Pregúntale sobre su profesión, sus pasatiempos, su personalidad y el tipo de casa que prefiere.

C. Encuesta. Usa este formulario para entrevistar a cinco compañeros acerca de sus habitaciones. Anota toda la información que te den. Al completar el formulario, formen grupos de cuatro o cinco y comparen sus resultados. Traten de decidir el promedio *(average)* de su grupo en cada categoría e informen a la clase.

Modelo ¿Dónde vives, en un apartamento, en una casa o en las residencias?

Nombre	Habitación	Número de cuartos	Número de baños	Condición general	Alquiler por mes	Ventajas y desventajas
1.						
2.						
3.						
4.						
5.						

¡Luz! ¡Cámara! ¡Acción!

A. ¡Ay, mis padres! ¿Recuerdas cuando tus padres te visitaron por primera vez en la universidad? Dramatiza esta situación con dos compañeros(as).

B. El nuevo apartamento. Suena el teléfono. Tú contestas. Es tu mejor amigo(a) que ahora asiste a otra universidad. Él (Ella) quiere saber, con detalle, cómo es tu apartamento y qué planes tienes para el verano. Dramatiza la conversación con un(a) compañero(a).

¿Comprendes lo que se dice?

Estrategias para ver y escuchar. *In the previous* **Paso** *you learned a number of simple and compound prepositions. As you listen to this commercial the first time, mark an* **X** *by every preposition you hear.*

❑ debajo de	❑ a	❑ de
❑ enfrente	❑ detrás de	❑ al lado de
❑ a la derecha	❑ a la izquierda	❑ después de

El Churrasco del Gaucho. Este anuncio comercial usa los sentidos de olfato y sabor *(smell and taste)* para llamar la atención del público. Aunque no sabes algunas de estas palabras, mira el anuncio y marca las palabras que se refieren al olfato con **O** y las que se refieren al sabor con **S**.

_______ huele	_______ hambre	_______ Hmmm...
_______ rico	_______ olor	_______ Ahhh...
_______ churrasco	_______ sabroso	_______ delicioso

NOTICIERO CULTURAL

GENTE... EVA PERÓN

Antes de empezar, dime...

1. ¿Sabes quiénes son los actores principales de la película *Evita*? ¿Quién hace el papel de «Che» Guevara, el revolucionario argentino?
2. ¿Dónde conoce Perón a Evita?
3. ¿Cómo reacciona el pueblo argentino a la esposa del presidente Perón?
4. ¿Por qué hay oposición a Madonna en el papel de Evita?

Eva Perón

«Evita»

Eva Perón es una figura de mucha controversia en la historia de Argentina. La gente la rechaza con pasión extrema o la adora con fervor casi religioso. Era una ex actriz, con un anterior estilo de vida algo escandaloso, que acabó por enamorarse de y casarse con Juan Domingo Perón, el presidente de la República. Muchos, en particular los de alta sociedad, no la aceptaron como esposa del presidente de la República. Pero ella nunca olvidó *(forgot)* su origen, ni al pueblo de trabajadores quienes sí la aceptaron. Éstos la querían mucho y fueron quienes le dieron el nombre de «Evita» para mostrar el cariño *(affection)* que le tenían.

«Evita» fue responsable de grandes cambios sociales en Argentina. Con ella como aliada, las mujeres argentinas obtuvieron el derecho al voto en 1947. Dos años después, por primera vez en la historia de Argentina, se nombró a siete mujeres al senado y a veinticuatro mujeres a la cámara de diputados. Desde la era de «Evita» la mujer argentina continúa teniendo gran fuerza política en el país.

Su vida es objeto de la ópera-rock que lleva el nombre de Evita. La película de Evita, como el personaje que representa, también ha sido objeto de muchas controversias. Entre otras cosas, hubo *(there was)* mucha oposición a la actriz americana Madonna en el papel de la venerada Eva Perón. Los argentinos que todavía la adoran con fervor decían *(said)* que una actriz con la personalidad, historia y fama de Madonna no debía *(should)* representar a su «Evita». También decían que un actor hispano y no inglés, debía hacer el papel del ex presidente Juan Domingo Perón.

Madonna en la película "Evita"

Y ahora, dime...

Usa estos cuadros para resumir los eventos más importantes en la vida de Eva Duarte de Perón.

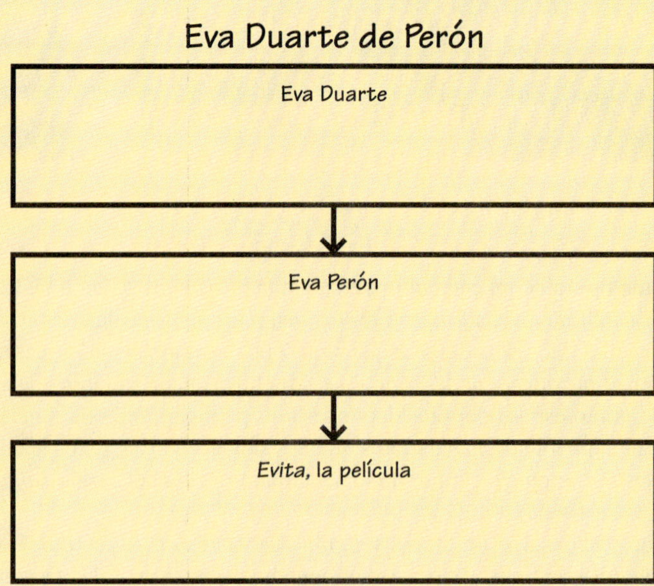

¿Te gusta escribir?

Antes de escribir
Estrategias para escribir: Precisar

In the previous chapter you learned that when writing advertisements, it is necessary to have a list of key words and phrases that must be worked into the advertisement. These key words or phrases usually contain the essence of the message to be conveyed. When writing advertisements, especially when writing classified ads, it is very important to be precise. Since space is limited and very costly in newspapers, classified ads must be expressed in very few words.

Estudia estos modelos y luego contesta las preguntas a continuación.

RECOLETA-S-piso Parisino elegante L y C bcón corr 3 dorm 2 bños coc com-drio dep TE categoría U$$ 175.00 Montevideo 1722 2°A ver hoy y mañana 15–18 hrs 801-1823/7797	**AV SANTA-FE 1179 piso 11° tel amplio 170m 3 dom (1 suite) ampl recep balc corr palier priv entr serv 2 bñ dep serv ap prof U$$ 195.00 v 15–18 476–1384**

1. ¿Cuál departamento está en el segundo piso? ¿En qué piso está el otro?
2. ¿Cuál no tiene comedor?
3. ¿Cuál tiene más dormitorios? ¿más baños?
4. ¿Tienen chimeneas los dos? ¿Tienen balcón?
5. ¿A qué hora se pueden ver estos departamentos?

Ahora, ¡a escribir!

A. Para precisar. Prepara una lista de toda la información esencial que debes incluir en un anuncio clasificado para alquilar el apartamento donde vives ahora. Prepara una segunda lista de toda la información esencial que incluirías en un anuncio para alquilar la casa o el apartamento de tus padres.

B. El primer borrador. Ahora prepara un primer borrador de dos anuncios clasificados: uno para alquilar tu apartamento y otro para alquilar la casa o apartamento de tus padres. Compara tus anuncios con las listas originales para asegurarte que incluiste toda la información esencial. Para precisar, usa abreviaturas como en los dos modelos.

C. Ahora, ¡a compartir! Comparte tu primer borrador con dos o tres compañeros. Comenta sobre el contenido y el estilo de los anuncios de tus compañeros y escucha los comentarios de ellos sobre tu anuncio. Si hay errores de ortografía o gramática, menciónalos.

D. Ahora, ¡a revisar! Si necesitas hacer unos cambios basados en los comentarios de tus compañeros, hazlos ahora.

E. La versión final. Prepara la versión final de tus anuncios en limpio y entrégala. Escribe la versión final a máquina o en la computadora con un estilo periodístico, usando columnas de seis centímetros.

F. ¡A publicar! Cuando ya esté calificado, pon tus anuncios en la página de anuncios clasificados que tu profesor(a) va a proveer.

¡Qué delgada estás, hija!

TAREA

Antes de empezar este **Paso,** estudia **En preparación** 5.5 y 5.6 y haz por escrito los ejercicios de **¡A practicar!** También escucha el **Paso 3 ¿Qué se dice... ?** del Capítulo 5 en el CD del estudiante.

¿Eres buen observador?

ronda AUSTRAL ronda AEROLINEAS ARGENTINAS

Hay 480.000 pasajeros esperando su aviso.

¿Usted que espera para publicarlo?

*Publicando hoy en **Ronda**, la revista de **Aerolíneas Argentinas** y **Austral**, usted puede llegar todos los meses a más de 480.000 consumidores potenciales, de muy buen poder adquisitivo y con hábitos muy favorables al consumo.*

*Porque con **Ronda** su mercado crecerá rápidamente entre quienes vuelan dentro y fuera del país.*

Reserve su espacio hoy.

Sus productos tienen un público que no puede esperar.

NINGUN OTRO MEDIO LLEGA TAN ALTO NI TAN LEJOS.

Vedia 1971 - (1429) Buenos Aires - Argentina
Tel / Fax: 703-0080 y líneas rotativas.

Ahora, ¡a analizar!

1. ¿Para qué es esta propaganda? ¿para suscribirse a una revista de viajeros? ¿para vender espacio comercial en una revista? ¿para invitar a escritores a publicar con MANZI Editores?
2. ¿Qué es *Ronda*? ¿Qué es *Austral*?
3. ¿Cuántas personas leen la revista de Aerolíneas Argentinas y Austral cada mes? ¿cada año?
4. Explica el lema: «Ningún otro medio llega tan alto ni tan lejos».

¿Qué se dice...?

Al hablar de cambios físicos o de personalidad

Indica con una **M** si lo siguiente se refiere a Marta o con una **I** si se refiere a Irene.

1. _______ Está más delgada que su hermana.
2. _______ Es la hermana mayor.
3. _______ Necesita comer en casa.
4. _______ Es más gordita.
5. _______ Está más alta que su hermana.
6. _______ No está en el aeropuerto.

MADRE Ya conoces a tu hermana. Siempre está con su novio. Cuando no están juntos, se pasan la vida hablando por teléfono.

MARTA ¿Así que tiene novio ahora? ¿Quién es?

MADRE Es el primo de tu amigo Marco. No recuerdo cómo se llama.

MARTA ¡Javier! ¿El hijo menor de don Anselmo que siempre pasa por la casa para ayudar a papá?

MARTA No lo puedo creer. ¡Javier! Pero es más feo que una rana, ¡qué horror!

MADRE ¡No seas mala y exagerada! Para mí, Javier es bastante bien parecido. ¿Y tú? ¿Ya tienes novio?

MARTA No, pero tengo muchos amigos.

Ahora, ¡a hablar!

A. Datos personales. Usa estos datos personales para comparar a Marta con su hermana Irene.

Modelo pasatiempos: Marta / Irene
Marta es más activa que Irene.

Datos personales

	Marta	Irene
Fecha de nacimiento:	10.11.77	29.8.75
Estatura:	1 metro 65	1 metro 60
Peso:	54 kilos	57 kilos
Pelo:	castaño	rubio
Ojos:	verdes	negros
Pasatiempos:	tenis	leer
	fútbol	escuchar música
	béisbol	pasear
Películas favoritas:	películas de aventuras	películas de amor

1. peso: Marta / Irene
2. estatura: Marta / Irene
3. edad: Marta / Irene
4. peso: Irene / Marta
5. estatura: Irene / Marta
6. edad: Irene / Marta
7. pasatiempos: Marta / Irene
8. películas: Marta / Irene

B. ¿Y tú? Compárate con tu hermano(a) en las siguientes categorías. [Si eres hijo(a) único(a) *(only child),* compárate con tu mejor amigo(a).]

1. edad
2. estatura
3. número de amigos
4. pasatiempos favoritos
5. peso
6. paciencia
7. organización
8. personalidad

C. Vamos de compras. Dos amigas están hablando de sus planes para el fin de semana. Para saber qué dicen, completa el diálogo con **por** o **para.**

TINA ¿(Por / Para) qué no vamos de compras esta tarde?

LISA ¡Qué buena idea! Si quieres, paso (por / para) tu casa a la una y media. ¿Adónde vamos?

TINA Al centro comercial San Martín. ¿Sabes cómo llegar?

LISA Bueno, siempre voy allí (por / para) autobús. Hay tanto tráfico. Pero, a ver,... (por / para) llegar a San Martín, primero tenemos que pasar (por / para) el parque central en la calle Gertel. Luego si vamos (por / para) la calle Rayuela una buena distancia, llegamos, ¿no?

TINA No me preguntes a mí. (Por / Para) mí, es siempre un misterio cómo llegar allí.

LISA Mira, Tina, ¿(por / para) qué no vamos (por / para) autobús? Es más fácil.

D. ¿Vienes a estudiar? Tú vas a estudiar en casa de un amigo esta noche pero no sabes cómo llegar a su casa. Ahora tu amigo te explica cómo llegar. Completa el párrafo con **por** o **para** si quieres saber lo que dice.

_______________ venir a mi casa debes caminar _______________ la calle Solano hasta el parque. Luego pasa _______________ el parque y camina al hospital. Ya sabes cómo llegar de allí. Si prefieres, puedes venir _______________ autobús. No es nada caro. El autobús pasa _______________ todo el parque y va directamente al hospital. _______________ mí, es más práctico venir en bus.

Y ahora, ¡a conversar!

A. ¡Qué cambios! ¿Has cambiado mucho desde hace diez años? Explica cómo has cambiado.

Modelo **Ahora estoy más delgado(a). También estoy más alto(a) y menos…**

B. ¿Quién es? Compárate con otro(a) estudiante de la clase sin mencionar el nombre de esa persona. Continúa la comparación hasta que tu compañero(a) adivine con quién te estás comparando. Repitan el proceso al revés, tu compañero(a) hace la comparación y tú adivinas.

Modelo **Es más alta y más rubia que yo. Pero yo soy más…**

C. ¡Más que yo! Usa este formulario para compararte en detalle con dos compañeros de la clase. Primero completa la primera columna y luego entrevista a dos compañeros para completar las otras dos. Informa a la clase de los resultados.

	Yo	Amigo(a) 1	Amigo(a) 2
edad			
estatura			
personalidad			
pasatiempos			
clases			
trabajo			

¡Luz! ¡Cámara! ¡Acción!

A. ¡Qué cambiado(a) estás! Tú regresas a la casa de tus padres para las vacaciones de Navidad. Ellos reaccionan frente a tus cambios físicos y de personalidad. Tú también reaccionas frente a ciertos cambios en la casa y en la familia. En grupos de tres, dramaticen esta situación.

B. Vacaciones de verano. Tú estás hablando con dos amigos que no ves desde hace más de un año. Primero, ellos comentan cómo has cambiado en un año y tú comentas los cambios físicos que notas en ellos. Luego tú invitas a tus dos amigos a cenar en un restaurante nuevo. Ellos no saben dónde está y tienes que darles instrucciones para llegar allí.

Antes de leer
Estrategias para leer: Dar un vistazo

In Chapter 3 you learned that "to scan" is to look for and locate specific information by quickly reading a text. In this reading you will practice scanning the table of contents of an Argentine newspaper.

Da un vistazo al contenido de *La Nación,* uno de los periódicos más respetados de Buenos Aires, para luego contestar estas preguntas. No es necesario leer palabra por palabra; simplemente dale un vistazo rápido hasta encontrar la información que necesitas.

1. ¿En qué página puedes leer algunas noticias sobre los EE.UU.? ¿Sobre Brasil? ¿Sobre el IRA?
2. ¿De qué vas a informarte si lees la primera sección?
3. ¿En qué sección y en qué página puedes encontrar información sobre el fútbol?

Lectura

En esta sección

EE. UU.: el candidato republicano Bob Dole repunta en las encuestas, pero aún está a considerable distancia de Clinton. **Pág. 5**

Manchester: una bomba del IRA en las proximidades de un centro comercial dejó doscientos heridos. **Pág. 5**

Brasil: la situación de los campesinos nordestinos amenaza la gestión del presidente Cardoso. **Pág. 7**

Amira Yoma: la cuñada del Presidente volvió a la función pública como asesora de Octavio Frigerio para los cascos blancos. **Pág. 16**

Caso Carrasco: la Justicia sospecha que el ocultamiento del crimen no termina en la brigada de Neuquén y puede involucrar a esferas superiores. **Pág. 17**

Discotecas: la comuna porteña clausuró ayer cinco locales que no cumplían con las normas de habilitación. **Pág. 20**

Facundo Suárez: el ex titular de la SIDE dijo que los autores del robo de las manos de Perón estaban vinculados con la extrema derecha. **Pág. 23**

Dole

Amira

Suárez

Otras secciones

Clasificados
Empleos
Espectáculos
a la vista
Deportiva
Cultura
Turismo
Las dos ciudades de BORGES
LA NACION Revista
CUATRO POR UNA

Clasificados Circulación nacional.

Indice

	Sec.	Pág.
Agenda cultural	4ª	9
Cine, teatro y música	4ª	1
Culto católico	1ª	19
Deportes	3ª	1
Economía	2ª	1
Farmacias de turno	4ª	9
Información general	1ª	20
Loterías y quinielas	1ª	23
Movimiento de aviones	4ª	9
Política	1ª	12
Servicios	4ª	9
Transp. fluvial de pasajeros	4ª	9
Televisión y FM	4ª	8
Avisos fúnebres	1ª	22
Remates	2ª	8

LA NACION

Bouchard 557, C.P. 1106
Tel. 319-1600 Fax 319-1611/12/13
E-mail: **lanacion@starnet.net.ar**
LA NACION On Line:
Argentina: **www.lanacion.com.ar**
EE.UU.: **www.lanacion.com**

Precio del ejemplar

Domingo	$	2,50
En Uruguay	$U	20,00
En Paraguay	₲	5000
En Brasil	R$	3,50
En Chile	$	1200
Recargo envío al interior	$	0,20

A ver si comprendiste

Practica el «dar un vistazo» al contestar las siguientes preguntas.

1. Según esta edición, ¿en qué noticias de los EE.UU. está interesado el público argentino?

2. ¿De qué vas a informarte si lees la tercera sección? ¿la cuarta? ¿la quinta? ¿la sexta?
3. ¿En qué sección y en qué página puedes encontrar información sobre asuntos religiosos? ¿sobre las olimpiadas? ¿sobre programación en la tele? ¿sobre una película que quieres ver? ¿sobre una persona que acaba de morir?
4. ¿Cómo se llaman las dos secciones especiales en esta edición de domingo?

Expand your horizons! *Let's travel through cyberspace to* ***Argentina*** where, through the Internet, you can . . .

- visit **Buenos Aires** and go sightseeing in this elegant, cosmopolitan city of irresistible European charm and hospitality.
- access Argentina's extremely varied landscapes and climates: the extensive **pampa**, the cold turquoise waters of the southern lakes area, the breathtaking beauty of **Iguazú** Falls, and the awe-inspiring glaciers of **Patagonia** and **Tierra del Fuego**.
- visit **Punta Tombo**, the world's most important breeding colony of Magellanic penguins.
- view the **Perito Moreno** glacier, one of the few advancing glaciers in the world.

If you are a cyberspace browser, join us in **Viajemos por el ciberespacio a... Argentina** by trying the following important addresses

Universidad de Buenos Aires
http://www.uba.ar/

Secretaría de turismo
http:www.pccp.com.ar/

Periódicos
http://www.clarin.com.ar/
http://www.lanacion.com.ar/
http://us.pinos.com/Los Andes/LosAndes.Html

Museo Nacional de Bellas Artes
http://www.startel.com.ar/bellas artes/mnba.htm

106.3FM-Buenos Aires
http://www.rockpop.com/

93.1-Rosario
http://www.allcomm.com/oasis/

93.3FM-Mar del Plata
http://www.argenet.com.ar/atlantica/.

(Ver página siguiente)

Because addresses are likely to change without notice, the following key words will guarantee that **Viajemos por el ciberespacio a... Argentina** will get you to your desired destination.

Palabras clave

Aerolíneas Argentinas
Bariloche
Buenos Aires
Calle Caminito
Glacial Perito Moreno
Iguazú
Paisajes Pampa
Palermo Viejo
Postales de Argentina
Punta Tombo

Radio en vivo Argentina

106.3FM-Buenos Aires
93.1-Rosario
93.3FM-Mar del Plata

http://www.hrwcollege.com

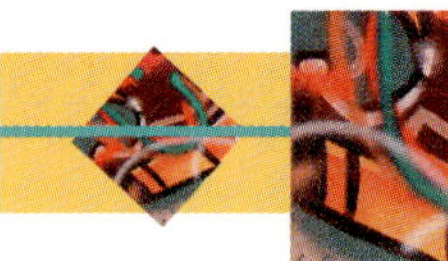

Vocabulario

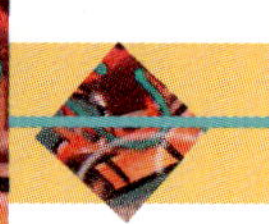

Apartamento

alfombra	*carpet*
amueblado(a)	*furnished*
cama	*bed*
chimenea	*fireplace*
comedor *(m.)*	*dining room*
condición	*condition*
cuarto de baño	*bathroom*
disponible	*available*
dormitorio	*bedroom*
dueño(a)	*landlord / lady*
entrada	*entrance*
garaje *(m.)*	*garage*
lámpara	*lamp*
mueble *(m.)*	*(piece of) furniture*
nevera	*refrigerator*
piscina	*swimming pool*
recámara	*bedroom*
sofá *(m.)*	*sofa*
televisor *(m.)*	*T.V. set*
ventana	*window*

Ciudad

avenida	*avenue*
calle *(f.)*	*street*
centro	*downtown*
centro comercial	*shopping center*
cuadra	*city block*
iglesia	*church*
parada de autobús	*bus stop*
parque *(m.)*	*park*
supermercado	*supermarket*
tráfico	*traffic*

Datos personales

apellido	*last name*
dirección	*address*
edad *(f.)*	*age*
estatura	*height*
ojos	*eyes*
pelo	*hair*
peso	*weight*

La familia

abuela	*grandmother*
abuelo	*grandfather*
abuelos	*grandparents*
hermana	*sister*
hermano	*brother*
hermanos	*siblings*
hija	*daughter*
hijo	*son*
hijos	*children*
madre *(f.)*	*mother*
padre *(m.)*	*father*
padres	*parents*
hermanastra	*stepsister*
hermanastro	*stepbrother*
madrastra	*stepmother*
padrastro	*stepfather*
pariente *(m.)*	*relative*
primo(a)	*cousin*
tía	*aunt*
tío	*uncle*

Descripción

cómodo(a)	*comfortable*
desocupado(a)	*unoccupied*
fuerte	*strong, loud*
malo(a)	*bad*
mayor	*older*
mejor	*better*
menor	*younger*
oscuro(a)	*dark*
sucio(a)	*dirty*
viejo(a)	*old*

Animales

gatito(a)	*small cat*
gato(a)	*cat*
perro(a)	*dog*
rana	*frog*

Preposiciones: sitio

a la derecha	*to the right*
a la izquierda	*to the left*
al lado	*beside*
cerca de	*near*
debajo de	*under*
delante de	*in front of*
después de	*after*
detrás de	*behind*
en	*on*
encima de	*on top of*
enfrente de	*in front of*
entre	*between*
lejos de	*far from*
sobre	*over, on top of*

Otras preposiciones

a	*to*
para	*for, (in order) to*
por	*for, by, through*
sin	*without*

Verbos

permitir	*to permit*
poner	*to put*
prometer	*to promise*
recordar (ue)	*to remember*

Adverbios

ahora	*now*
con frecuencia	*frequently*
entonces	*then*
hoy	*today*
junto	*next to, by*
mensual	*monthly*
sólo	*only*
tan	*so*
tarde	*late*
temprano	*early*

Palabras y expresiones útiles

cosa	*thing*
dólar (m.)	*dollar*
fecha	*date*
paciencia	*patience*
plástico	*plastic*
¡Ay!	*Oh!*
por supuesto	*of course*
¡Qué desastre!	*What a mess!*

En preparación 5

5.1 Adverbs of Time

Expressing time and frequency

Adverbs are words that qualify or modify an adjective, a verb, or another adverb. There are many types of adverbs. Some common adverbs of time are:

ahora	anoche/de noche	todos los días	tarde
temprano	nunca	siempre	a veces

Ahora necesito ver la casa. — *I need to see the house now.*
Siempre pedimos el alquiler con un mes de adelanto. — *We always ask for the rent one month in advance.*

¡A practicar!

A. ¿Cuándo? Answer the following questions telling when you do these things.

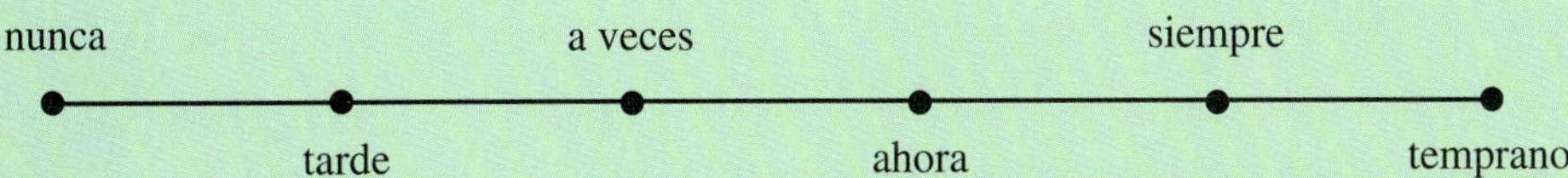

1. ¿Vas al cine?
2. ¿Estudias en la biblioteca?
3. ¿Almuerzas en la universidad?
4. ¿Preparas tu comida?
5. ¿Llamas a tus padres?
6. ¿Preparas tu lección de español?
7. ¿Regresas a casa después de una fiesta?

B. ¿Cuándo puedo verlo? You are interested in seeing some apartments. When can you see them?

1. today at 10:30 AM
2. Saturday, early in the morning
3. tonight at 8:30 PM
4. today early, at 2:00 PM
5. today late, at 8:00 PM

5.2 Prepositions

Describing the position of things

Prepositions express relationships with respect to time, place, material, possession, among others. The relationships may be between things or between nouns or pronouns and the adjectives or verbs that refer to them. Following are some of the most commonly used prepositions. Note that compound prepositions are always two or more words while simple prepositions always consist of one word.

Compound Prepositions

a la izquierda de (derecha)	*to the left (right)*
al lado de	*next to, beside*
antes de	*before*
cerca de	*near*
debajo de	*under*
delante de	*in front of*
después de	*after*
detrás de	*behind*
encima de	*on top of*
enfrente de	*facing, opposite*
lejos de	*far from*

Simple Prepositions

a	*to, at*
con	*with*
de	*of, from*
en	*in, at*
entre	*between*
para	*for, in order to*
por	*for, by*
sobre	*on, above*

El apartamento está **detrás del** supermercado. — *The apartment is behind the supermarket.*
También está **cerca de** la universidad. — *It's also near the university.*

¡A practicar!

A. A estudiar. Julia is walking out of her apartment. To find out what she plans to do, complete this paragraph with appropriate prepositions.

Ahora voy _______________ la biblioteca. Voy _______________ estudiar _______________ Inés. Necesito el libro _______________ física que está _______________ mi mochila. Por la tarde tengo una hora libre *(free)* _______________ la clase de química y la de física. La cafetería está _______________ el gimnasio pero _______________ del laboratorio de química. Pero, ¿dónde está la clase de español? ¡Ah! Está _______________ la clase de inglés.

B. ¿Dónde está? Jorge is looking for an apartment. Right now he is calling three apartment owners to find out where their buildings are located. What do they tell him?

1. El edificio está *(at 162 Alvarado Street, behind the library and to the right of the supermarket).*
2. El apartamento está *(in front of the tall building at 1449 Velázquez Avenue, not far from downtown).*
3. La residencia está *(at 927 Trujillo Street, to the left of the new supermarket).*
4. La oficina está *(to the right, near the park).*
5. El hospital está *(next to the office).*

5.3 *Ir a + Infinitive* to Express Future Time

Describing future plans

In **Capítulo 1**, you learned that when a destination is mentioned, a form of the verb **ir + a** is always used. The combination **ir a +** *infinitive* is used to express future actions.

Voy a estudiar en la Universidad de San Marcos.	*I'm going to study at the University of San Marcos.*
Vamos a regresar en un mes.	*We will return in a month.*
¿Van a ir contigo?	*Will they go with you?*

¡A practicar!

A. Futuros profesionales. What professional plans for the future do these students have?

Modelo Iván: estudiar genética.
Iván va a estudiar genética.

1. Matilde: trabajar en la Organización de los Estados Americanos
2. Cecilia y Alfredo: estudiar en Argentina
3. tú: trabajar en la compañía de tu papá
4. Rubén y tú: continuar los estudios
5. yo: ser profesor(a) de francés
6. nosotros: ser excelentes profesionales

B. Proyectos. Three friends are getting ready to leave for the university. They are discussing what they will do to have a successful first semester. What do they say?

Modelo Luis (estudiar) alemán, francés y español.
Luis va a estudiar alemán, francés y español.

1. Yo (estudiar) cuatro horas cada día.
2. Anita y yo (hacer) la tarea juntos cada día.
3. Luis (trabajar) mucho para sacar buenas notas *(grades).*
4. Ramón y Luis (vivir) en la residencia.
5. Anita (hacer) los ejercicios de español conmigo todos los días.
6. Ramón y yo (leer) las lecciones en la biblioteca los fines de semana.

5.4 *Ser* and *estar*: A Second Look

Describing people and things and telling time

A. **Ser** is used

- with adjectives to describe physical traits, personality, and inherent characteristics.
  Tu habitación es grande.
  Mamá es muy particular.
  Los muebles viejos son más cómodos.
- to identify people or things.
  Yo soy estudiante de química y éstos son mis libros de texto.
- to express origin and nationality.
  Somos de Bariloche; somos argentinos.
- to tell of what material things are made.
  ¡Los muebles son de plástico!
- to tell time.
  ¡Ya son las nueve!
- with impersonal expressions.
  ¿Es necesario vivir aquí?

B. **Estar** is used

- with adjectives to describe temporal evaluation of states of being, behavior, and conditions.
  Hijo, estás imposible hoy. *(behavior)*
  El baño está sucio. *(condition)*
- to indicate location.
  El apartamento está cerca del centro.
- to form the progressive tense.
  Carlos está limpiando el apartamento.

¡A practicar!

A. ¡Pobre Eva! Complete the following paragraph with the appropriate form of **ser** or **estar** to see why Eva is so miserable today.

Eva y Ramón ______________ en la cafetería. ______________ hablando de su vida en Albuquerque. Ellos ______________ de Argentina pero ahora ______________ en Nuevo México. Ellos ______________ estudiantes en la universidad. Eva ______________ inteligente y generalmente ella ______________ muy simpática pero hoy ______________ antipática. Eva ______________ furiosa porque Ramón ______________ muy ocupado y no puede salir con ella esta noche. Ramón tiene un examen importante mañana y él ______________ muy nervioso. ¡Pobre Eva!

B. ¡Qué desastre! Complete the following paragraph with the appropriate form of **ser** or **estar** to see why Mario is so nervous.

Mario ______________ un estudiante de filosofía. Él ______________ de Buenos Aires; ______________ argentino. Hoy ______________ muy nervioso porque sus padres vienen a visitarlo en media hora. Ahora ______________ las diez de la mañana y Mario y sus compañeros de cuarto ______________ muy ocupados. Todos ______________ limpiando la casa porque ______________ muy sucia. ______________ difícil porque la casa ______________ bastante grande. Ahora Mario ______________ en la cocina y sus dos compañeros _______________ limpiando los baños.

5.5 Comparisons of Inequality

PASO 3

Comparing and contrasting

A. With the exception of four irregular forms, comparisons are made with **más** and **menos** in Spanish**. Más** is the comparative of superiority, and **menos** is the comparative of inferiority.

más / menos + (adjective / noun / adverb) + **que**

Mi hermana es **más alta que** yo.	*My sister is taller than I.*
Tú pagas **menos alquiler que** nosotros.	*You pay less rent than we do.*
Sí, pero tu apartamento está **más cerca** de todo.	*Yes, but your apartment is closer to everything.*

Note that **más** and **menos** always precede the adjective, noun, or adverb being compared.

B. There are four adjectives with irregular comparatives.

mayor *older*	mejor *better*
menor *younger*	peor *worse*

¿Conoces a mi hermano **menor?**	*Do you know my younger brother?*
Este apartamento es **peor** que el otro.	*This apartment is worse than the other one.*
¿Quién es **mayor,** tú o yo?	*Who's older, you or I?*

¡A practicar!

A. Los Estados Unidos. Complete the following comparisons of cities and states in the United States.

1. California es ______________ grande ______________ Texas.
2. Chicago es ______________ interesante ______________ Nueva York.

3. Hay _______________ tráfico en Los Ángeles _______________ en Denver.
4. La población de Wyoming es _______________ numerosa _______________ la población de Illinois.
5. El número de méxicoamericanos en California es _______________ grande _______________ el número de méxicoamericanos en Delaware.
6. Hay _______________ puertorriqueños en Nueva York _______________ en la Florida.

B. Mi apartamento. Compara tu apartamento o habitación de ahora con la casa o apartamento de tus padres.

Modelo ¿Cuál es más pequeño?

Mi apartamento es más pequeño que la casa de mis padres.

1. ¿Cuál es más grande?
2. ¿Cuál está menos desordenado?
3. ¿Cuál es más cómodo?
4. ¿Cuál es más moderno?
5. ¿Cuál es más limpio?

5.6 *Por* and *para:* A First Look

Expressing direction and means

The prepositions **por** and **para** have many English equivalents, including *for.* **Por** and **para** are *not* synonymous, however. Study the following English equivalents of **por** and **para.**

Por

- *By, by means of*
  ¿Es preferible viajar **por** tren?
  Siempre se comunican **por** teléfono.
- *Through, along, on*
  Tengo que pasar **por** el parque.
  ¿Sigo **por** la avenida Godoy?
  Voy **por** esta calle.

Para

- *In order to*
  Para llegar allí, ¿necesito tomar el bus?
  Voy a tomar café **para** no dormirme.
- *For,* as in *compared with* or *in relation to others*
  Para mí, es mejor ir caminando.
  Para ellos no es bueno.

¡A practicar!

A. ¡Viajes! Fernando has family spread all over the country. How does he keep in touch with everyone? To find out, complete his ideas with **por** or **para.**

1. ______________ ir a visitar a mis primos, ______________ mí, es mejor ir ______________ tren.
2. Tengo primas que viven cerca de la universidad. ______________ ir a su casa el camino es más corto si paso ______________ el parque.
3. Tengo que comunicarme ______________ teléfono con mis padres. Ellos viven muy lejos.
4. Cuando mis padres me visitan, ______________ ellos es más fácil viajar ______________ avión *(airplane)*.
5. ______________ mis tíos el viaje es más fácil. Ellos sólo necesitan tomar el autobús ______________ llegar a mi apartamento.

B. Paso por ahí. ¿Cómo va Guadalupe a la universidad? Para saberlo, completa el párrafo con **por** o **para.**

______________ llegar a la universidad tomo el autobús que pasa ______________ la avenida San Pedro. Siempre viajo ______________ autobús porque es más barato que manejar *(driving)*. Después de bajar del autobús tengo que pasar ______________ el parque. Tomo la calle Sucre y continúo ______________ la calle San Simón.

CAPÍTULO 6

Cultural Topics

- **¿Sabías que…?**
  El paseo
- **Noticiero cultural**
  Lugar: *Colombia: la esmeralda de Sudamérica*
  Gente: *Gabriel García Márquez*
- **Lectura:** *Consultorio sentimental de la doctora Dolores del Corazón*

Writing Strategies

- *Dar consejos*

Reading Strategies

- *Pistas de contexto*

En preparación

- 6.1 Direct Object Nouns and Pronouns
- 6.2 Irregular **-go** Verbs
- 6.3 Present Tense of **e** ⟶ **i** Stem-Changing Verbs
- 6.4 Review of Direct Object Nouns and Pronouns
- 6.5 Review of **saber** and **conocer**

¡Te invito a cenar!

In this chapter, you will learn how to . . .

- *ask for a date.*
- *accept or refuse a date.*
- *express preferences.*
- *express emotions.*

Dos jóvenes de Bogotá, Colombia

Dos enamorados en crisis

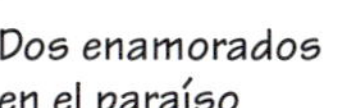

Dos enamorados en el paraíso

Lo que ya sabes...

1. ¿Cómo están relacionados los dos jóvenes de Bogotá? ¿Son hermanos? ¿primos? ¿otra cosa? Explica tu respuesta.
2. ¿Qué emociones se comunican los dos jóvenes de Bogotá? ¿Cómo se comunican si no están hablando?
3. ¿Qué opinas de las personas en las otras dos fotos? ¿Crees que sólo son amigos? ¿Por qué?
4. ¿Qué opinas de personas que muestran sus emociones abiertamente en la calle? ¿Cuáles de las emociones que ves en estas fotos son más aceptable mostrar públicamente? ¿Por qué?

COLOMBIA

¿A qué hora te paso a buscar?

TAREA

Antes de empezar este **Paso**, estudia **En preparación** 6.1 y 6.2 y haz por escrito los ejercicios de **¡A practicar!** También escucha el **Paso 1 ¿Qué se dice...?** del Capítulo 6 en el CD del estudiante.

¿Eres buen observador?

Ahora, ¡a analizar!

1. ¿Dónde y cuándo puedes conseguir estas dos películas?
2. ¿Qué tienen en común estas dos películas?
3. ¿Por qué cree la protagonista de *Nadie me quiere* que nadie la quiere? ¿Qué edad tiene? ¿Es casada? ¿Busca esposo?
4. ¿Crees tú que «Cuando pasas los 30, es más fácil que te caiga encima una bomba que un hombre»? ¿Por qué?
5. ¿Entre quiénes es la amistad en *Nanuk el esquimal*? ¿en *Nadie me quiere?*

¿Qué se dice...?

Al pedir una cita

Horacio quiere ____.

Judas quiere ____.

En mi opinión, Angélica va a ___________________________________.

JUDAS Oye, guapa. Me vas a acompañar al baile el sábado, ¿verdad? Mira, aquí traigo dos boletos de entrada. ¿Qué me dices? ¿Vas conmigo?

ANGÉLICA Muchas gracias, pero no puedo. Tengo otros planes. Además, este sábado salgo de la ciudad.

JUDAS No importa, preciosa. En ese caso puedes acompañarme al cine el viernes. ¿Qué te parece?

ANGÉLICA No, gracias.

HORACIO	Hola, Angélica. ¿Puedo ayudarte con los libros?
ANGÉLICA	Gracias, Horacio.
HORACIO	Angélica, si estás libre el viernes me gustaría invitarte al teatro. Y después, tal vez podamos ir a cenar.
ANGÉLICA	¡Cómo no! Me encantaría acompañarte. ¿A qué hora me pasas a buscar?
HORACIO	Después te digo. Necesito revisar mi horario. ¿Te puedo llamar esta noche?
ANGÉLICA	Claro que sí. Puedes llamarme después de las 9:00. Te espero entonces.

Ahora, ¡a hablar!

A. ¿Y tú? Pregúntale a tu compañero(a) si hace lo siguiente cuando sale en una cita.

Modelo

TÚ **¿Compras flores para la otra persona?**
COMPAÑERO(A) **Sí, las compro.** o **No, no las compro.**

1. ¿Alquilas películas?
2. ¿Miras la televisión?
3. ¿Escuchas música romántica?
4. ¿Compras boletos para el cine?
5. ¿Invitas a amigos?
6. ¿Preparas una cena especial?

B. ¡Te invito! Alguien te invita para una primera cita. No sabe dónde llevarte ni qué hacer. ¿Qué le recomiendas tú?

Modelo

AMIGO(A) **¿Deseas ver la nueva película?**
TÚ **Bien, vamos a verla.** o **No, no la quiero ver.**

1. ¿Quieres ver la nueva obra de teatro?
2. ¿Deseas escuchar música clásica?

3. ¿Quieres visitar la exposición de arte?
4. ¿Deseas ver la exhibición de fotos?
5. ¿Me acompañas al cine?
6. ¿Te llamo por la mañana?

C. Buenos modales. Horacio es un chico muy educado que sabe impresionar a todos. ¿Haces tú como él? ¿Qué haces para impresionar a otras personas?

Modelo Horacio hace muchas cosas para su novia.
Yo también hago muchas cosas para mi novia(o). o
Yo no hago nada para mi novia(o).

1. Horacio siempre trae bebidas a las fiestas.
2. Él siempre dice la verdad.
3. Él hace todo con sus amigos.
4. Él no pone los pies (*feet*) en la mesita.
5. Horacio nunca viene tarde a cenar.
6. Horacio nunca sale demasiado tarde de la casa de su novia.

D. ¡Qué afán! Esta noche el jefe de tu padre viene a cenar a tu casa. ¿Qué hacen todos para impresionarlo?

Modelo mamá / hacer / cena especial
Mamá hace una cena especial.

1. mamá / poner / flores / la mesa
2. papá / traer / vino especial
3. yo / hacer / pastel de chocolate
4. mis hermanos / poner / la mesa
5. mi hermana y yo / decir / que vamos a lavar / platos
6. yo / hacer / café

Y ahora, ¡a conversar!

A. ¡Paso a paso! Trabajando en parejas, supongan que no se conocen *(don't know each other)* y están hablando por primera vez. Conversen un poco para llegar a conocerse.

Pregúntense...

1. cuáles son sus deportes favoritos. ¿Con qué frecuencia los practican?
2. cómo pasan el tiempo libre. ¿Qué hacen?
3. si miran la tele con frecuencia. ¿Cuáles son sus programas favoritos? ¿Con qué frecuencia los miran?
4. quiénes son sus profesores favoritos. ¿Los ven los fines de semana?
5. si visitan a sus padres con frecuencia. ¿Los visitan cada fin de semana? ¿una vez al mes?
6. si conocen a... (*nombre de un amigo*). ¿Lo conocen muy bien?

B. Citas. ¿Qué hacen tus compañeros de clase cuando salen a una cita? Para saberlo, entrevístalos usando este cuadro. Encuentra a compañeros que puedan contestar afirmativamente a cada pregunta y pídeles que firmen en el cuadrado apropiado. No olvides que una persona no debe firmar más de un cuadrado.

Antes de salir	Durante la cita	Después de la cita
no espera, invita a la otra persona ________ *Firma*	lo paga todo ________ *Firma*	invita a su amiga(o) a tomar un café en casa ________ *Firma*
siempre acepta invitaciones para salir ________ *Firma*	controla la conversación ________ *Firma*	inmediatamente planea otra cita ________ *Firma*
prefiere salir en grupo ________ *Firma*	siempre lleva su auto ________ *Firma*	siempre promete llamar a su amiga(o) por teléfono ________ *Firma*
decide qué actividades hacer ________ *Firma*	bebe bebidas alcohólicas ________ *Firma*	siempre se despide con un beso ________ *Firma*

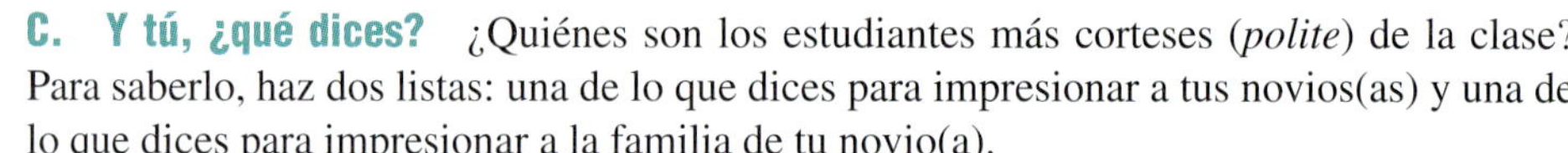

C. Y tú, ¿qué dices? ¿Quiénes son los estudiantes más corteses (*polite*) de la clase? Para saberlo, haz dos listas: una de lo que dices para impresionar a tus novios(as) y una de lo que dices para impresionar a la familia de tu novio(a).

D. ¿Cuáles son las diferencias? Tú debes usar este dibujo y tu compañero(a) el dibujo en el Apéndice A. Ambos son similares, pero no son idénticos. Describan sus dibujos para descubrir las diferencias. No mires el dibujo de tu compañero(a) hasta descubrir todas las diferencias.

¡Luz! ¡Cámara! ¡Acción!

A. En una discoteca. Estás en una discoteca con unos amigos cuando ves a una persona que quieres conocer.

- Preséntate.
- Pregúntale si es estudiante y habla un poco de tus clases.
- Invítalo(la) a salir este fin de semana.
- Si te dice que no puede, sugiere otra alternativa.

B. ¿Qué les digo? Tú, tu novio(a) y dos amigos están imaginando la primera visita de tu novio(a) a casa de tus padres. Dramatiza esta situación con tres compañeros. Díganle a tu novio(a) qué puede hacer para impresionar a tus padres. También hablen de temas de conversación apropiados y no apropiados para tu novio(a) y tus padres.

¿Comprendes lo que se dice?

Estrategias para escuchar. *In previous chapters you learned to listen for stress variations in English and Spanish cognates. Listening to intonation, that is, the rise and fall of a speaker's voice, can be very helpful when distinguishing between questions and statements in Spanish. Questions in Spanish usually have one of the following two intonation patterns.*

1. In questions requiring yes/no answers, the voice rises on the last word of the question.

   ¿Te gustaría ir conmigo? **¿Viven cerca de aquí?**

2. In questions requesting information, the speaker's voice usually drops on the last word of the question.

   ¿Qué vas a hacer el sábado? **¿A qué hora vienes por mí?**

Being aware of these intonation patterns for questions will help you better understand a conversation.

Escucha la conversación entre Manolo, un joven muy tímido, y Carmen, una chica muy atractiva. (*As you listen the first time, indicate how many yes/no questions you hear and how many information questions are asked.*)

_______________ **Sí / No** _______________ **Que piden información**

¿Está disponible? Vuelve a escuchar la conversación de Manolo y Carmen e indica con un círculo las palabras que mejor completen cada frase.

El sábado por la noche

1.	Carmen piensa...	estudiar.	mirar la tele.	visitar a una amiga.
2.	Manolo piensa...	estudiar.	mirar la tele.	ir al cine.
3.	Manolo...	la invita.	la acepta.	no la acepta.
4.	Carmen...	lo invita.	lo acepta.	no lo acepta.
5.	Manolo va por Carmen...	a las 6:00.	a las 7:00.	a las 7:10.

NOTICIERO CULTURAL

LUGAR... COLOMBIA

Antes de empezar, dime...

Contesta estas preguntas para reflexionar un poco sobre algunas de las características más sobresalientes *(outstanding)* de tu país.

1. ¿A cuántos océanos tiene salida los EE.UU.? ¿Cuáles son?
2. ¿Cuántas cordilleras de montañas que cruzan los EE.UU. puedes nombrar?
3. En tú opinión, ¿cuáles son los productos más importantes de los EE.UU.? ¿Por qué? Explica tu respuesta.
4. ¿Cuáles son algunas de las atracciones más grandes de la capital de los EE.UU.?
5. ¿Por qué crees que tantos turistas visitan los EE.UU. cada año? ¿Qué los atrae?

Un collar con una esmeralda colombiana en el centro

Colombia: la esmeralda de Sudamérica

Colombia es el único país del continente que tiene salida al Pacífico y al Atlántico (Caribe). Además, tres cordilleras montañosas de los Andes cruzan el país de norte a sur. Desafortunadamente este país ha sufrido la violencia producida por el narcotráfico, problema conocido internacionalmente, pero Colombia es mucho, mucho más que eso.

Gracias a un clima generalmente tropical los principales productos del país son su sabrosísimo café, una gran variedad de flores —entre ellas, hermosas orquídeas—, bananas y caña de azúcar. De fama mundial son también las esmeraldas que se producen en el país —de allí el nombre de «Colombia, la esmeralda de Sudamérica».

La capital, Bogotá, tiene todo lo que se espera de una ciudad moderna: rascacielos, hoteles lujosos, oficinas elegantísimas, tiendas fascinantes, excelentes restaurantes y una gran diversidad de actividades culturales. Allí puedes visitar, entre otras maravillas, la Catedral de Sal y el famoso Museo de Oro, que es un verdadero tesoro de colecciones de oro prehispánico.

En tu próxima visita a Sudamérica... ¡Colombia te espera!

Artefacto precolombino en el Museo de Oro, Bogotá

Y ahora, dime...

Contesta estas preguntas con un(a) compañero(a) de clase.

1. Explica el título de esta lectura.
2. Prepara un esquema como el siguiente y complétalo con información de la lectura.

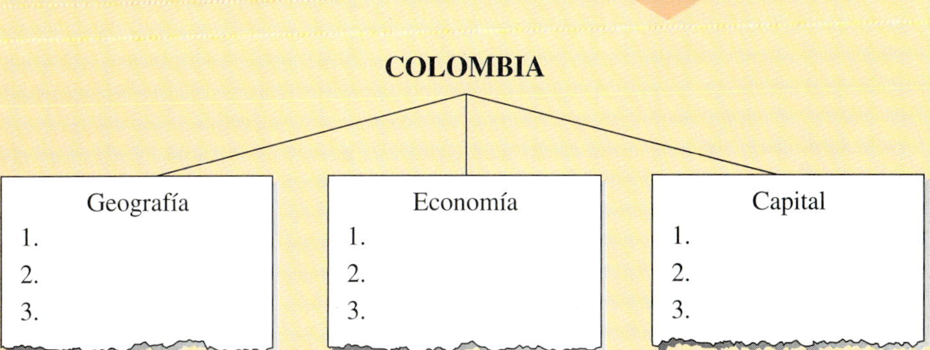

El español en otras disciplinas: Literatura y cine

Literatura y cine. Los libros y el cine son medios de comunicación importantísimos en el mundo ahora. A continuación vas a encontrar los títulos de obras escritas por autores latinoamericanos que han inspirado una versión cinematográfica. En grupos de tres, identifiquen al autor de cada obra y, si pueden, digan de qué país es cada autor. También preparen un resumen oral de las películas que conocen.

___ 1. Laura Esquivel	a. *Gringo viejo*
___ 2. Carlos Fuentes	b. *La casa de los espíritus*
___ 3. Gabriel García Márquez	c. *El beso de la mujer araña*
___ 4. Isabel Allende	d. *Como agua para chocolate*
___ 5. Manual Puig	e. *Cien años de soledad*

Proyecto: Busca más información sobre uno de estos escritores y escribe un breve resumen sobre el (la) autor(a) y su obra.

¿Qué quieres hacer, mi amor?

TAREA	Antes de empezar este **Paso**, estudia **En preparación** 6.3 y haz por escrito los ejercicios de **¡A practicar!** También escucha el **Paso 2 ¿Qué se dice...?** del Capítulo 6 en el CD del estudiante.

¿Eres buen observador?

1. Ésta es la portada de una revista. ¿Qué tipo de revista es *Dónde?* ¿Qué tipo de información hay en *Dónde?*
2. ¿Con qué frecuencia se publica *Dónde*? ¿Cómo lo sabes?
3. ¿Cuáles son los tres artículos principales de esta edición? ¿A qué pasatiempos están relacionados estos artículos?
4. ¿Incluye esta revista información de varios países o sólo de uno? Explica.
5. ¿Es *Dónde* una revista que tú podrías (*you could*) usar? ¿Cuándo? ¿Dónde?

¿Qué se dice...?

Al decidir qué hacer en una cita

Horacio recomienda ________________________ o ________________________.

Angélica sugiere ____.

HORACIO	Aquí viene el mesero. ¿Deseas tomar algo, vida mía?
ANGÉLICA	¿Sirven buen helado aquí?
HORACIO	Sí, cómo no, es muy bueno.
ANGÉLICA	Entonces quiero un helado de chocolate y es todo.
HORACIO	¿No pides un café?
ANGÉLICA	Sí, claro. ¿Y tú? ¿Qué vas a pedir?
HORACIO	Un coñac, nada más.

Ahora, ¡a hablar!

A. ¿Qué preferimos? Unos amigos están tratando de decidir qué van a hacer esta tarde. ¿Qué dice cada uno que prefiere hacer?

Modelo Fernando: ir al cine
Fernando dice que prefiere ir al cine.

1. Víctor Mario y yo: ir a un café
2. yo: cenar en un restaurante
3. Elvira: ir a bailar
4. Angélica: ver una obra de teatro
5. Ana María: escuchar discos
6. Fernando y Alicia: jugar béisbol

B. ¡Aquí sirven bebidas riquísimas! Tú y unos amigos celebran tu cumpleaños en tu restaurante favorito. ¿Qué hacen todos?

Modelo **Gerardo pide las bebidas.**

Vocabulario útil

pedir	servir	traer	preferir
traer	decir	conseguir	¿... ?

1. Jesús
2. Antonio y Alicia
3. el mesero
4. tú y yo
5. yo

C. Somos diferentes. Eduardo y Margarita salen juntos frecuentemente. Cuando tú sales con alguien, ¿haces lo mismo que él (ella) o haces algo diferente?

Modelo Eduardo y Margarita prefieren ir a un restaurante.
Nosotros preferimos ir a un café. o
Nosotros también preferimos ir a un restaurante.

1. Ellos siempre salen los sábados por la noche.
2. Ellos siempre dicen «Buenas tardes, señores».
3. Ellos consiguen boletos para el teatro y el ballet.
4. Ellos piden cerveza en un restaurante.
5. Ellos siguen una rutina.
6. Ellos nunca repiten la misma actividad.

Y ahora, ¡a conversar!

A. Entrevístense. Entrevista a un(a) compañero(a) y luego que él (ella) te entreviste a ti.

1. ¿Con qué frecuencia tienes citas?
2. ¿A qué hora sales para una cita generalmente?
3. ¿Qué días prefieres salir usualmente?

4. ¿Prefieres salir con la misma persona o con diferentes personas?
5. ¿Qué prefieres hacer cuando sales para una cita? Nombra tres actividades favoritas.
6. Por lo general, ¿quién paga?
7. ¿A qué hora crees que debe terminar una cita?

B. ¿Eres buen(a) amigo(a)? ¿Cómo actúas con tus amigos? ¿Eres egoísta? ¿generoso(a)? ¿demasiado bueno(a)? Toma este examen primero. Luego tu profesor(a) te va a decir cómo sumar (*add up*) los puntos para que puedas determinar qué tipo de amigo(a) eres.

1. Cuando un(a) amigo(a) tiene problemas con su tarea, tú...
   a. le das (*give him or her*) las soluciones.
   b. le explicas cómo llegar a la solución.
   c. no le dices nada. Es su problema, no tu problema.

2. Cuando dos de tus amigos se pelean *(fight)*, tú...
   a. tratas de separarlos.
   b. ayudas al más débil *(weak)*.
   c. no haces nada.

3. Cuando alguien te acusa de algo que tú no hiciste (*did*) pero que uno de tus amigos hizo *(did)*, tú...
   a. aceptas la acusación sin decir nada.
   b. hablas con la persona responsable y le dices que tiene que decir la verdad.
   c. dices que no eres la persona responsable y nombras a tu amigo(a).

4. Cuando un(a) amigo(a) te dice un secreto, tú...
   a. no repites el secreto.
   b. repites el secreto solamente a tu mejor amigo(a).
   c. repites el secreto a tus compañeros.

5. Cuando tu amigo(a) quiere comprar un libro pero no tiene bastante dinero, tú...
   a. le das el dinero que necesita.
   b. le prestas *(lend)* el dinero.
   c. no le das ni le prestas nada.

6. Cuando un(a) amigo(a) te dice sus problemas, tú...
   a. haces todo lo posible para ayudarle.
   b. lo escuchas y lo consuelas.
   c. le hablas de tus problemas.

10 ó más puntos Tú eres un(a) amigo(a) excelente. Siempre ayudas a tus amigos. **¡Ojo!** Alguien puede abusar de tu gentileza.

5–9 puntos Usualmente tú piensas primero en ti, después en los otros, pero ayudas a tus amigos a veces.

0–4 puntos Tú das la impresión que los amigos no son importantes. **¡Ojo!** Tú puedes perder a tus amigos.

C. ¡No es fácil decidir! Tú y tres amigos deciden que pueden divertirse más si juntan *(gather)* todo su dinero. Ahora tienen que decidir qué van a hacer el sábado por la noche. Tienen sólo un total de $35,00 para gastar.

D. Sílabas. Combina las sílabas en la primera columna con las de la segunda columna para formar palabras relacionadas con pasatiempos apropiados para citas.

Modelo **r e s t a u - r a n t e**

ca-	**ran-te**
te-a-	**si-ca**
dis-co-	**cier-to**
res-tau-	**ne**
de-	**tro**
mú-	**te-ca**
ci-	**fé**
con-	**por-tes**

¡Luz! ¡Cámara! ¡Acción!

A. La primera cita. Con un(a) compañero(a) de clase, dramatiza tu primera cita. Decidan quién invita a quién, cuándo van a salir, adónde van a ir, qué van a hacer, cómo van a viajar, quién va a buscar a quién, cuánto dinero van a necesitar y a qué hora piensan regresar.

B. ¡Esta noche! Tienes una cita esta noche con una persona muy especial. Ahora estás hablando con tus dos compañeros(as) de cuarto. Ellos(as) quieren saber con quién vas a salir y qué planes tienes. Contesta sus preguntas con muchos detalles.

¿Comprendes lo que se dice?

Estrategias para ver y escuchar. *In the previous* **Paso** *you learned that by listening to intonation you can easily distinguish between statements and questions in Spanish. You also learned that questions in Spanish usually have different intonation patterns depending on whether they are yes/no questions or information questions. As you view this commercial for* **Casa de Novias Elizabet,** *you will find that all of the questions asked are of the same type. What type are they? What intonation pattern do they use?*

¡Una boda poco tradicional! Esta boda es poco tradicional. No incluye ciertas prácticas que siempre se incluyen e incluye otras no muy comunes. Vuelve a ver el video y con un(a) compañero(a), preparen dos listas de lo tradicional y lo no tradicional en esta boda.

UNA BODA POCO TRADICIONAL

Tradicional	No tradicional
1.	1.
2.	2.
3.	3.
- - -	- - -

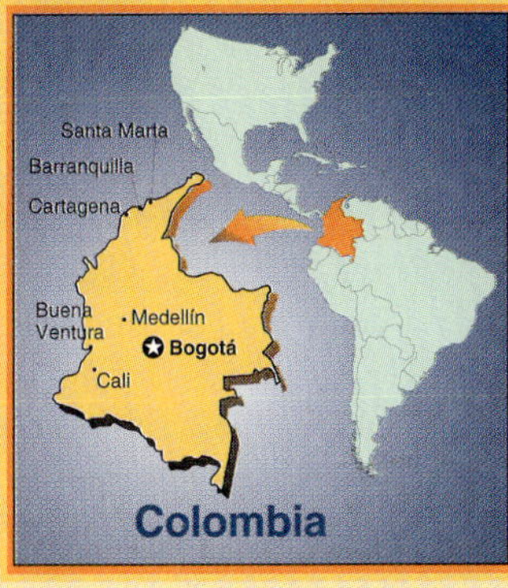

NOTICIERO CULTURAL

GENTE... GABRIEL GARCÍA MÁRQUEZ

Antes de empezar, dime...

Contesta estas preguntas sobre tus gustos literarios.

1. ¿Qué tipo de literatura te gusta leer?
2. ¿Quién es tu autor(a) favorito(a)? ¿Sabes cuándo y dónde nació?
3. ¿Cuál es la obra principal de tu autor(a) favorito(a)? ¿De dónde crees que viene la idea original de tu obra favorita? ¿de una experiencia personal? ¿de un viaje que hace? ¿de su imaginación?
4. ¿Ha recibido algunos premios tu autor(a) favorito(a)? ¿Cuáles?

Gabriel García Márquez

Nació en Colombia en el año 1928. Estudió leyes en Bogotá y Cartagena. Trabajó como periodista para diferentes periódicos de Colombia, Cuba y otros países latinos. En 1961 se fue a vivir a México donde, según dijo él mismo, en un viaje que hizo con su familia a

Acapulco, tuvo la idea para una de sus novelas más famosas: *Cien años de soledad.* Publicó esta novela en el año 1967, dos años después de su viaje a Acapulco. *Cien años de soledad,* según dicen la mayoría de los críticos, se considera la novela más importante de Hispanoamérica por su temática y técnica creativa.

García Márquez recibió el Premio Nóbel de Literatura en el año 1982. Entre sus obras más conocidas podemos nombrar: *El otoño del patriarca, Crónica de una muerte anunciada, El amor en los tiempos del cólera, La increíble y triste historia de la cándida Eréndira y de su abuela desalmada* (cuentos).

Y ahora, dime...

Siempre es interesante saber algo de la vida de los grandes escritores del mundo. Usa estos cuadros para resumir los datos (*facts*) más importantes en la vida de Gabriel García Márquez.

DATOS MÁS IMPORTANTES

Datos personales	Datos profesionales
1.	1.
2.	2.
3.	3.
- - -	- - -

¿Te gusta escribir?

Antes de escribir
Estrategias para escribir: Dar consejos

Cartas de consejo. Cuando escribimos cartas de consejo *(advice)*, hay que usar ciertas estructuras. La más sencilla es usar ciertos verbos que ya conoces con el infinitivo.

necesitar + *infinitivo*	**Necesitas ser** más activa.
deber ***(should)*** + *infinitivo*	**Debes hablar** con tu novia.
tener que + *infinitivo*	**Tienes que decidir** qué quieres.

Otra forma de dar consejos es usar mandatos *(commands)* directos. Se pueden dar mandatos directos familiares **(tú)** simplemente usando el presente indicativo de la forma **Ud. / él / ella** de la mayoría de los verbos.

Practica un deporte como el fútbol.	*Practice a sport, like football.*
Habla con tu novia.	*Talk to your girlfriend.*
Decide qué quieres hacer.	*Decide what you want to do.*

Ahora piensa en un(a) amigo(a) que está teniendo problemas de amor y prepara una lista de sus problemas. Incluye lo que dice tu amigo(a) y lo que dice su novia(o). Si no tienes un amigo con problemas, invéntalo.

Ahora, ¡a escribir!

A. Ahora, a organizar. Prepárate para escribirle una carta a tu amigo(a) con problemas amorosos. Empieza por crear un grupo de ideas para aconsejar *(advise)*. Escribe todas tus ideas en las dos formas de dar consejos: ciertos verbos más el infinitivo y mandatos familiares (tercera persona singular del presente indicativo). Organiza tus ideas en grupos que puedan elaborarse en párrafos.

B. El primer borrador. Ahora prepara un primer borrador de tu carta de consejo. Incluye la información de la lista de ideas que preparaste en la sección previa.

C. Ahora a compartir. Comparte tu primer borrador con dos o tres compañeros. Comenta sobre el contenido y el estilo de las cartas de consejo de tus compañeros y escucha los comentarios de ellos sobre tu carta. ¿Comunican bien los consejos? ¿Hay bastantes consejos o necesitan más? ¿Es lógica la organización de la carta?

D. El segundo borrador. Haz los cambios necesarios basándote en los comentarios de tus compañeros de clase. Luego prepara un segundo borrador.

E. A compartir, una vez más. Comparte tu segundo borrador con dos o tres compañeros. Esta vez comenta sobre los errores de estructura, ortografía o puntuación. Concéntrate específicamente en cómo da los consejos. ¿Usa los mandatos correctamente? ¿Da consejos usando **necesitar, deber** y **tener que** correctamente? Indica todos los errores de las cartas de tus compañeros y luego decide si necesitas hacer cambios en tu carta en base a los errores que ellos te indiquen a ti.

F. La versión final. Prepara la versión final de tu carta de consejo y entrégala. Escribe la versión final a máquina o en la computadora siguiendo el formato recomendado.

G. Ahora, a publicar. En grupos de cuatro o cinco, lean sus cartas y decidan cuál da los mejores consejos. Léanle esa carta a la clase.

¡Estoy loco por ti!

TAREA

Antes de empezar este **Paso**, estudia **En preparación** 6.4 y 6.5 y haz por escrito los ejercicios de **¡A practicar!** También escucha el **Paso 3 ¿Qué se dice... ?** del Capítulo 6 en el CD del estudiante.

¿Eres buen observador?

Ahora, ¡a analizar!

1. Ésta es la portada de una revista. ¿Qué tipo de revista es? Explica.
2. ¿Quién crees que es Lety Calderón? ¿Por qué hay tanto interés en su boda?
3. Explica el escándalo de Roberto Cantoral. ¿Quién crees que es él?
4. ¿Conoces al boxeador Julio César Chávez? Es un boxeador de los EE.UU. ¿Por qué crees que hay tanto interés en ver su casa—hasta su recámara? ¿De qué te imaginas consiste su colección de autos?
5. ¿Podrías usar esta revista para seleccionar programas de televisión en tu ciudad? Explica tu respuesta.

NM No. 56 N$ 8.00 Julio 26, 1995
te damos toda la televisión
TVNOTAS
Se casó Lety Calderón
Fotos exclusivas
¡Sólo nosotros cubrimos TODA la boda!
Ale Avalos culpa a Carina Ricco del fracaso de Morir dos veces
Ahora te presentamos la casa de JC Chávez
Roberto Cantoral y su escándalo en Perú: ¡Se enamoró de una joven actriz y se la trajo a México!
¡Entramos hasta su recámara y vimos su colección de autos!

¿Qué se dice...?

Al expresar emociones

ANGÉLICA	¿Conoces a mi amiga Margarita?
HORACIO	La conozco muy bien y la admiro aún más. Es hermosísima.
ANGÉLICA	¡A veces te odio, Horacio!
HORACIO	Querida, digo que la conozco y la admiro; no digo que la amo. ¡Tú sabes cuánto te amo a ti!

HORACIO	¿Quién es ese muchacho que está contigo en la foto?
ANGÉLICA	¿Cuál? Ah, ése. Es Judas Maleza, tu amigo.
HORACIO	Ah, ¿sí? ¡Es obvio que no es buen amigo!
ANGÉLICA	Ay, Horacio. Tú sabes que te amo.
HORACIO	Sí, sí. Y yo te adoro.

¿Sabías que... ?

Ya sabes que hay muchos «cognados» en español y que el reconocerlos aumenta mucho tu vocabulario. Pero **¡ojo!**, porque también hay «cognados falsos» que como los amigos falsos te pueden crear problemas serios. Un «cognado falso» es una palabra que se escribe casi idénticamente en dos lenguas pero que tiene un significado totalmente diferente en las dos lenguas. Algunos «cognados falsos» en inglés y español son:

«COGNADOS FALSOS»

español	inglés	inglés	español
molestar	*to bother*	*molest*	violar
embarazada	*pregnant*	*embarrassed*	avergonzado(a)
parientes	*relatives*	*parents*	padres
colegio	*school*	*college*	universidad
lectura	*reading*	*lecture*	conferencia
nota	*grade*	*notes*	apuntes

Ahora, ¡a hablar!

A. Sentimientos. ¿Qué sentimientos sientes tú hacia estas personas y cosas?

Modelo mamá

Yo la admiro, la respeto y la amo mucho.

Vocabulario útil

amar	respetar	admirar	odiar
detestar	fascinar	querer	adorar

1. mejor amigo(a)
2. compañeros(as) de cuarto
3. novio(a)
4. universidad
5. tarea
6. políticos
7. policías
8. profesores

B. Somos muy unidos. La unidad familiar es muy fuerte en la familia de Mari Carmen. ¿Qué dice ella de su familia?

Modelo yo / saber que mamá / querer muchísimo (a mí)
Yo sé que mamá me quiere muchísimo.

1. papá / saber que mamá / adorar (a él)
2. mis abuelos / saber que papá / respetar mucho (a ellos)
3. mis hermanos / decir que mis abuelos / adorar (a ellos)
4. nosotros / saber que mi tío / querer mucho (a nosotros)
5. yo / saber que mis hermanos / respetar (a mí)
6. mamá / saber que papá / adorar (a ella)

C. Amar, querer, respetar, odiar... Di algo sobre las relaciones entre las siguientes personas o animales.

Modelo tus amigas: tu novio
Mis amigas lo admiran y lo respetan.

1. tú: los animales domésticos
2. los gatos: los perros
3. los republicanos: los demócratas
4. los estudiantes: los profesores
5. tu hermano(a): tú
6. tu profesor(a) de español: tú y tus compañeros de clase

Y ahora, ¡a conversar!

A. Datos personales. Entrevista a un(a) compañero(a) para obtener algunos datos personales.

1. ¿Es fácil o difícil para ti expresar tus sentimientos? ¿Por qué?
2. ¿Quién es la persona que más admiras? ¿que más amas? ¿Por qué?
3. ¿Odias a alguna persona? ¿Por qué?
4. ¿Te odia alguien a ti? ¿Por qué?
5. ¿Eres una persona básicamente sociable o no? ¿Por qué?
6. ¿Cuáles son los ingredientes necesarios para tener una relación ideal?

B. Compañeros(as) de cuarto. Tú y tu compañero(a) de cuarto están hablando de sus novias(os). Tu compañero(a) dice que tiene un problema: no sabe si su novia(o) lo (la) ama. ¿Qué preguntas puedes hacerle para ayudarle a solucionar su problema?

Modelo **¿Te invita a su apartamento?**
¿Acepta tus invitaciones?

C. ¿Tienes una buena personalidad? Para saberlo, contesta a estas preguntas y sigue el orden de las flechas → hasta llegar al final.

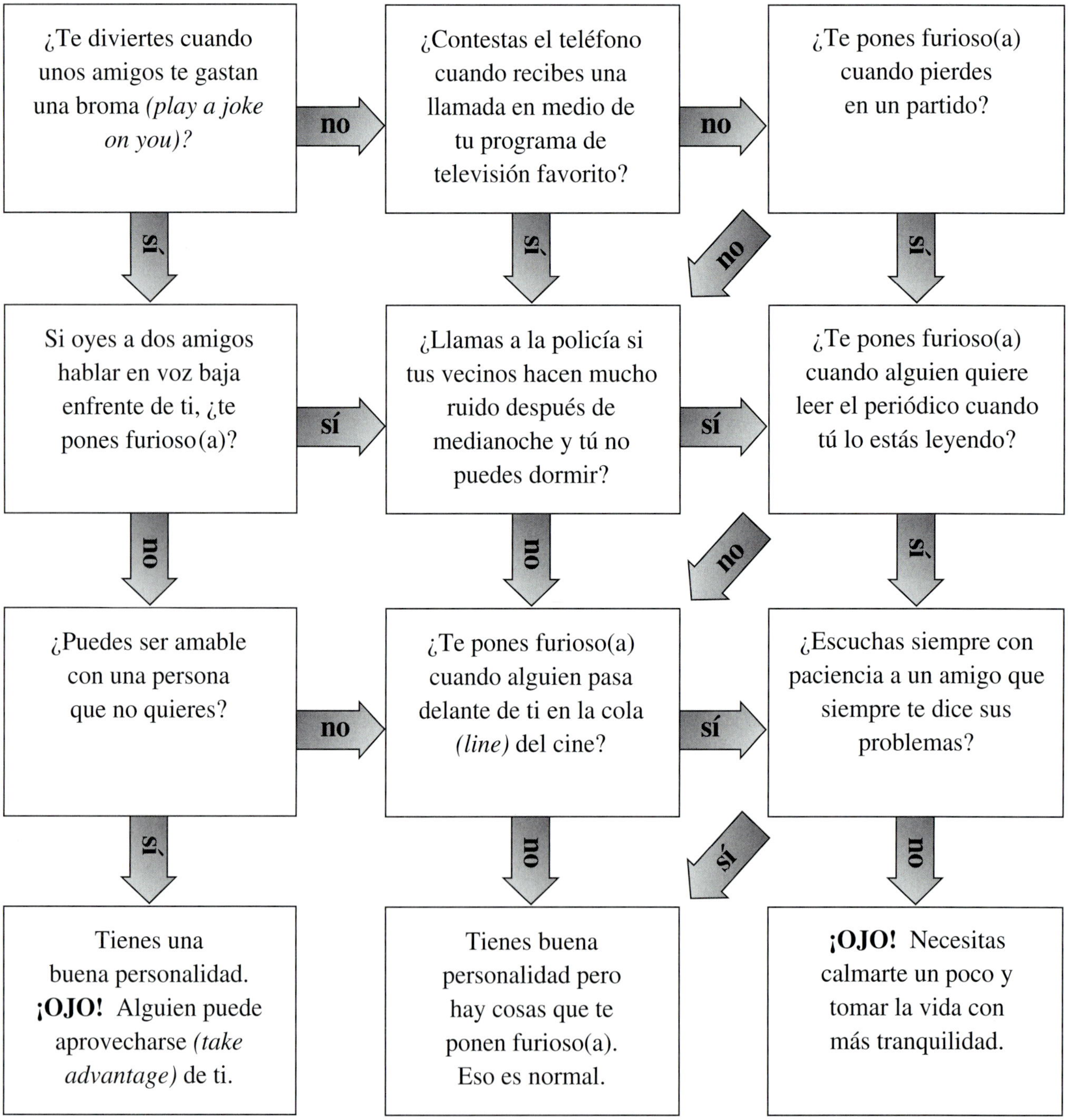

¿Te diviertes cuando unos amigos te gastan una broma *(play a joke on you)*? → no →	¿Contestas el teléfono cuando recibes una llamada en medio de tu programa de televisión favorito? → no →	¿Te pones furioso(a) cuando pierdes en un partido?
↓ sí	↓ sí ↙ no	↓ sí
Si oyes a dos amigos hablar en voz baja enfrente de ti, ¿te pones furioso(a)? → sí →	¿Llamas a la policía si tus vecinos hacen mucho ruido después de medianoche y tú no puedes dormir? → sí →	¿Te pones furioso(a) cuando alguien quiere leer el periódico cuando tú lo estás leyendo?
↓ no	↓ no ↙ no	↓ sí
¿Puedes ser amable con una persona que no quieres? → no →	¿Te pones furioso(a) cuando alguien pasa delante de ti en la cola *(line)* del cine? → sí →	¿Escuchas siempre con paciencia a un amigo que siempre te dice sus problemas?
↓ sí	↓ no ↙ sí	↓ no
Tienes una buena personalidad. **¡OJO!** Alguien puede aprovecharse *(take advantage)* de ti.	Tienes buena personalidad pero hay cosas que te ponen furioso(a). Eso es normal.	**¡OJO!** Necesitas calmarte un poco y tomar la vida con más tranquilidad.

¡Luz! ¡Cámara! ¡Acción!

A. ¡Ay, amor! Tú estás completamente enamorado(a) de tu novia(o) pero no sabes si ella (él) todavía te ama a ti. Acabas de saber que sale con otra persona. Decides pedir consejos a tu mejor amigo(a). Dramatiza esta situación con un(a) compañero(a).

B. Telenovela. En grupos de tres o cuatro, dramaticen una escena de su telenovela favorita. Puede ser un triángulo amoroso o dos parejas que tienen una relación que vacila entre el amor y el odio.

Antes de leer
Estrategias para leer: Pistas de contexto

A. Pistas de contexto. *A good reader uses a variety of problem-solving techniques. Using context clues when you do not know the meaning of a specific word is one such strategy. The context referred to here is the sentence in which the unknown word occurs. Although there is no easy formula to help you always guess the correct meaning of unknown words, the following suggestions can be very helpful:*

1. *Use the meaning of the rest of the sentence to reduce the number of meanings the unknown word may have.*
2. *Be satisfied with getting at the general meaning of unfamiliar words. More often than not, the exact meaning is not necessary in order to get the gist of what you are reading.*
3. *Look for help in punctuation and grammar. Knowing the relationship between various parts of a sentence can help you understand the sentence.*
4. *Don't feel you have to know the meaning of every unfamiliar word. Learn to recognize key words needed to understand the sentence, and don't worry about other unfamiliar words.*

B. Prepárate para leer. Busca las palabras de la columna **A** en la lectura y estudia el contexto de las oraciones donde las encuentres. Luego selecciona según el contexto, la palabra o palabras de la columna **B** que mejor completen las oraciones. No olvides que la gramática y la puntuación también ayudan a entender el contexto de la oración.

A	B
1. se queja	a. es muy pequeña para mí
2. me deja solo	b. darme
3. prestarme	c. enamorar
4. vacío	d. me abandona
5. no me queda	e. objeta
6. conquistar	f. sin nada

Lectura

Consultorio sentimental de la doctora Dolores del Corazón

La tengo prisionera

Cuando vamos a fiestas, mi novia se queja de que la tengo prisionera. Tan pronto como llegamos, ella corre a conversar con sus amigas y me deja solo, plantado en la puerta. Yo no la quiero tener prisionera pero creo que debe prestarme más atención. La amo mucho pero ya no tolero esta situación. ¿Qué hago?

Plantado en México

Entre dos hermanas

Estoy bastante confundido. Mi novia es dulce, simpática, tranquila y, si voy a ser honesto, un poco aburrida. Yo siempre sé todo lo que está pensando o lo que va a hacer y decir. Ella tiene una hermana que es todo lo opuesto: es agresiva, interesante, impredecible. Yo la encuentro fascinante. Pero ahora no sé qué hacer. ¿Debo abandonar a mi novia y tratar de conquistar a su hermana?

Confundido en Perú

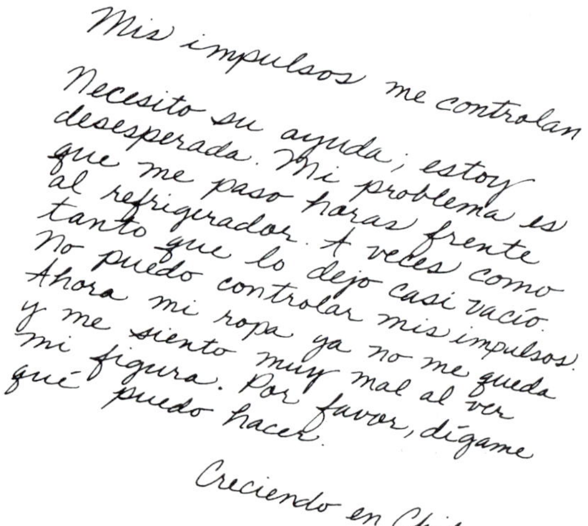

Mis impulsos me controlan

Necesito su ayuda; estoy desesperada. Mi problema es que me paso horas frente al refrigerador. A veces como tanto que lo dejo casi vacío. No puedo controlar mis impulsos. Ahora mi ropa ya no me queda y me siento muy mal al ver mi figura. Por favor, dígame qué puedo hacer.

Creciendo en Chile

A ver si comprendiste

Identifica a las personas que se describen aquí.

1. Plantado
2. novia de Plantado
3. Creciendo
4. Confundido
5. novia de Confundido
6. hermana de la novia de Confundido

a. Prefiere a la hermana de su novia.
b. Quiere más atención de su novia.
c. Abandona a su novio para visitar a sus amigas.
d. Le gusta comer.
e. Le gustan las mujeres independientes.
f. Cree que su novio es muy posesivo con ella.
g. Necesita ropa nueva.
h. Es fácil saber cómo piensa.
i. Es fascinante.

Expand your horizons! Let's travel through cyberspace to ***Colombia*** where . . .

- through the Internet, you can discover the exuberance and rich contrast between the three main areas in Colombia: the **Andes,** the **Caribbean,** and **Amazon** regions.
- you can visit the magnificent **Nueva Catedral de Sal** in Zipaquirá.
- you can admire some of the 33,000 pieces found at the **Museo del Oro**, displayed in Bogotá and other Colombian cities.
- you will become familiar with the work of prestigious author **Gabriel García Márquez** and the humorous art of **Fernando Botero**.

If you are a cyberspace browser, join us in **Viajemos por el ciberespacio a... Colombia** by trying the following important addresses.

Universidad de los Andes
http://www.uniandes.edu.co

Radio Caracol
http://latina.latino.net.co/
empresa/caracol/caracol.htm

Periódicos y revistas
http://www.elespectador.com/
http://www.semana.com.co/
http://www.sinycia.com.co/
Clientes/dgrafic

Because addresses are likely to change without notice, the following key words will guarantee that **Viajemos por el ciberespacio a... Colombia** will get you to your desired destination.

Palabras clave

Bogotá	Nueva Catedral de Sal
Fernando Botero	Turismo Colombia
Gabriel García Márquez	Radio en vivo Colombia
Museo de Oro	Radio Caracol

http://www.hrwcollege.com

El amor

admirar	*to admire*
adorar	*to adore*
amar	*to love*
corazón *(m.)*	*heart*
detestar	*to detest*
estar enamorado(a) de	*to be in love with*
estar loco(a) por	*to be crazy about*
expresar	*to express*
fascinar	*to fascinate*
impresionar	*to impress*
odiar	*to hate*
respetar	*to respect*
sentimientos	*feelings, sentiments*

Citas

aceptar	*to accept*
acompañar	*to accompany*
cita	*date*
cenar	*to eat dinner*
conducir	*to drive*
explicar	*to explain*
flores *(f.) (pl.)*	*flowers*
planes *(m.) (pl.)*	*plans*

Lugares y diversiones

baile *(m.)*	*dance*
bebida	*drink*
boleto	*ticket*
concierto	*concert*
evento	*event*
exhibición *(f.)*	*exhibition*
obra de teatro	*play (as in theater)*
programa *(m.)*	*program*

Verbos

conseguir (i)	*to get, obtain*
deber	*to ought to, should*
decir (i)	*to say*
firmar	*to sign*
imaginar	*to imagine*
llevar	*to take*
oír	*to hear*
parecer	*to seem, to appear like*
pedir (i)	*to ask for*
poner la mesa	*to set the table*
querer (ie)	*to love; to want*
rechazar	*to reject*
servir (i)	*to serve*
traer	*to bring*

Adjetivos

aficionado(a)	*fan (of sporting events)*
clásico(a)	*classical*
demasiado(a)	*too much*
libre	*free*
primero(a)	*first*
todo(a)	*all*

Otras palabras y expresiones

algo	*something*
gasto	*expense*
mesa	*table*
momento	*moment*
ocasión *(f.)*	*occasion*
plato	*plate*
pero	*but*
¡Claro que sí!	*Of course!*
¡Cómo no!	*Why not!*
Me encantaría.	*I would love to.*
¡Oye!	*Listen!*

En preparación 6

6.1 Direct Object Nouns and Pronouns

Agreeing and disagreeing, accepting and refusing

A. Direct object nouns and pronouns answer the questions *Whom?* or *What?* in relation to the verb of the sentence.

I'll see her tonight (*Whom* will I see? Her.)
They have my tickets. (*What* do they have? My tickets.)

Identify the subjects and direct objects in the following sentences and check your answers.*

1. She doesn't know my address.
2. Can you hear them now?
3. Shall I put flowers on this table?
4. Bring it tomorrow.

B. In Spanish, whenever the direct object is a specific person or persons, an **a** is *always* placed before it. This "personal **a**" is never translated into English.

No conozco **a** tus padres. *I don't know your parents.*
Pero sí conozco Nueva York. *But I do know New York.*
Siempre traen **a** Gloria. *They always bring Gloria.*

C. Direct object pronouns replace direct object nouns. The direct object pronouns in Spanish are as follows.

Singular		Plural	
me	**me**	**nos**	us
you *(fam.)*	**te**	**os**	you *(fam.)*
you *(formal, m./f.)*	**lo/la**	**los/las**	you *(formal, m./f.)*
him, it *(m.)*	**lo**	**los**	them *(m.)*
her, it *(f.)*	**la**	**las**	them *(f.)*

***Answers: 1.** She / address **2.** you / them **3.** I / flowers **4.** you / it

D. Direct object pronouns must be placed *directly* in front of a conjugated verb.

Te amo.	*I love you.*
¿Sabes cuánto **me** quiere?	*Do you know how much she loves me?*
Yo ni **la** conozco.	*I don't even know her.*

E. The direct object pronoun *may* follow and be attached to an infinitive or a present participle.

Voy a traer**los** mañana. **Los** voy a traer mañana.	*I'm going to bring them tomorrow.*
Está esperándo**me** ahora. **Me** está esperando ahora.	*He's waiting for me now.*

Note that when a direct object pronoun is attached to a present participle, a written accent is required to maintain the original stress: **esperando** ⟶ **esperándome.**

¡A practicar!

A. Examen. Juanita is taking the foreign language placement exam. How does she answer the examiner's questions?

PROFESOR ¿Me ves bien de allí?
JUANITA Sí, profesor. ____________ veo bien.
PROFESOR ¿Tienes un lápiz No. 2?
JUANITA Sí, ____________ tengo.
PROFESOR ¿Escuchas bien la cinta *(tape)*?
JUANITA Sí, ____________ escucho muy bien.
PROFESOR ¿Me escuchas bien a mí y a la profesora Salas?
JUANITA Sí, ____________ escucho muy bien a los dos.
PROFESOR ¿Entiendes bien las instrucciones?
JUANITA Sí, sí, ____________ entiendo.
PROFESOR Bien, entonces empecemos.

B. ¡Qué casualidad! Two people have just met at a party and realize that they both come from the same town. What do they ask each other? How do they respond?

Modelo Gloria Gutiérrez
— ¿Conoces a Gloria Gutiérrez?
— Sí, la conozco muy bien. o **No, no la conozco.**

1. Lucas Trujillo
2. Josefa y Elodia Ledesma
3. el padre Francisco
4. los señores Villegas
5. mi hermana Delia Cortez
6. los Díaz

C. ¿Qué hacen ustedes? Do you and your date do any of the following things together? Answer using direct object pronouns.

Modelo ¿Ven videos juntos *(together)*? ¿Dónde?
Sí, los vemos en mi apartamento.

1. ¿Ven la televisión juntos? ¿Dónde?
2. ¿Escuchan discos juntos? ¿Dónde?
3. ¿Leen novelas juntos? ¿Leen periódicos juntos? ¿Dónde?
4. ¿Preparan comidas juntos? ¿Dónde?
5. ¿Hacen sus tareas juntos? ¿Dónde?
6. ¿Lavan el auto juntos? ¿Dónde?

6.2 Irregular *-go* Verbs

Telling what people do, say, or hear

In **Capítulo 2,** you learned the irregular verbs **tener, salir,** and **venir**. Following are several other Spanish verbs that have the same irregular ending in the **yo** form: **-go.** Note that some of these verbs also have stem changes.

Hacer	**Traer**	**Poner**	**Decir**	**Oír**
to do, make	to bring	to put	to say, tell	to hear
hago	traigo	pongo	digo	oigo
haces	traes	pones	dices	oyes
hace	trae	pone	dice	oye
hacemos	traemos	ponemos	decimos	oímos
hacéis	traéis	ponéis	decís	oís
hacen	traen	ponen	dicen	oyen

¡A practicar!

A. ¡Ay, los postres! What does this person do when he is feeling a little depressed? To find out, complete the following paragraph with the appropriate form of the verb in parentheses.

Cuando yo estoy deprimido, siempre ______________ (tener) mucha hambre y generalmente______________ (hacer) un postre *(dessert)*. Todo el mundo ______________ (decir) que los postres no son buenos para la salud *(health)* pero yo ______________ (decir) que son ideales para la depresión. Nunca ______________ (poner) demasiado azúcar *(sugar)* en mis postres. Cuando yo______________ (traer) un pastel de chocolate a las fiestas, siempre ______________ (oír) lo que dicen todos: —¡Mmm! ¡Está delicioso!

B. Buena impresión. María is dating Raúl. To find out what she and her family do to impress him, complete the following paragraph with the appropriate form of the verb in parentheses.

Cuando Raúl _______________ (venir) a nuestra casa, siempre _______________ (traer) unas rosas para mi mamá. Ella siempre _______________ (decir) que las rosas son lindísimas. Yo _______________ (poner) la mesa y _______________ (hacer) una torta especial para Raúl. Mi mamá y mi abuelo _______________ (hacer) su refresco preferido, ponche. Mi papá _______________ (decir) que nosotros queremos impresionarlo.

C. ¡Qué caballero! Raúl also tries to impress María's family. Complete the following paragraph with the appropriate form of the verb in parentheses to see his point of view.

Cuando yo _______________ (venir) a tu casa siempre _______________ (hacer) todo lo posible para impresionar a tu familia. A veces _______________ (traer) flores para tu mamá. Otras veces _______________ (traer) algo para tu papá. Yo _______________ (saber) que ellos lo agradecen *(appreciate)* porque _______________ (oír) sus comentarios. Yo siempre _______________ (decir) que la cortesía es muy importante.

PASO 2

6.3 Present Tense of *e* → *i* Stem-Changing Verbs

Stating what people do

In **Capítulo 4**, you learned that some Spanish verbs have an **e** → **ie** or an **o** → **ue** vowel change whenever the stem vowel is stressed. Other verbs have an **e** → **i** vowel change.

Pedir

to ask for	
pido	pedimos
pides	pedís
pide	**piden**
pide	**piden**

Seguir

to follow	
sigo	seguimos
sigues	seguís
sigue	**siguen**
sigue	**siguen**

Other frequently used **e** → **i** stem-changing verbs are: **decir** *(to say, tell)*, **repetir** *(to repeat)*, **vestir** *(to dress)*, and **servir** *(to serve)*. Note that derivatives of these verbs will also be stem-changing: **conseguir** *(to get, obtain)*, **despedir** *(to fire, dismiss)*. Remember that all **-ir** stem-changing verbs undergo a one-vowel change in the present participle: **pidiendo, siguiendo, diciendo.**

¡A practicar!

A. Dietas. What do these people think about dieting?

1. Yo siempre (pedir) fruta, nunca (pedir) postres.
2. Yo (seguir) una dieta que me permite comer de todo.
3. Mi médico (repetir) constantemente: «No es necesario estar a dieta, pero sí es

necesario hacer ejercicio».

4. Pues yo sólo voy a restaurantes donde (servir) comida vegetariana.
5. Yo no (seguir) los consejos de nadie. ¡Yo como lo que quiero, cuando quiero!

B. En un bar. Miguel has invited several of his friends to have a drink with him to celebrate the end of the semester. Complete the following paragraph with the appropriate form of the verb in parentheses to find out what they do when they get to the local pub.

Nosotros _______________ (seguir) a Miguel a una mesa grande. Él _______________ (conseguir) sillas para todos y _______________ (pedir) las cervezas. Pedro y María _______________ (decir) que prefieren margaritas. Cuando la mesera _______________ (servir) las bebidas, todos _______________ (decir): —¡Salud!

C. Una cita con Miguel. Virginia Salazar always enjoys going out with Miguel. Complete the following paragraph with the appropriate form of the verb in parentheses to find out why.

Cuando Miguel y yo _______________ (salir), siempre es divertido. Él siempre _______________ (vestir) elegantemente. Nosotros nunca _______________ (repetir) las mismas actividades; siempre _______________ (hacer) algo diferente. Por ejemplo, vamos a un restaurante donde _______________ (servir) comida exótica y él _______________ (pedir) comidas que yo no conozco. Todos los meseros conocen a Miguel y _______________ (servir) la comida inmediatamente. Yo _______________ (repetir): salir con Miguel es muy divertido.

6.4 Review of Direct Object Nouns and Pronouns

Referring to people and things indirectly

A. Direct object nouns answer the question *Whom?* or *What?* in relation to the verb. Identify the subjects and direct objects in the following sentences.*

1. Te adoro, Rodolfo. Y tú, ¿me amas?
2. Yo no lo puedo creer. Dice que ya no me quiere.

B. Direct object pronouns are always placed directly in front of a conjugated verb, but may be attached to the end of an infinitive or a present participle. They are always attached to an affirmative command. Identify the direct object pronouns in the following sentences.†

1. ¿Bebidas alcohólicas? ¡Las detesto!
2. Mis abuelos me quieren mucho pero no me permiten salir de noche.
3. — Llámanos al llegar, por favor.
   — Sí, los llamo. Lo prometo.

Note that, as with the case of present participles, when a direct object pronoun is attached to an affirmative command a written accent is required to maintain the original stress: **Llama → Llámanos.**

---

* **Answers:** 1. subjects **Yo / tú;** direct objects **Te / me** 2. subjects **yo / Él** (or **Ella**); direct objects **lo / me**

† **Answers:** 1. **Las** 2. **me / me** 3. **nos / los / Lo**

¡A practicar!

A. ¿Quién va a traerlos? Your Spanish teacher is throwing a party this weekend for everyone in your class. Of course, all of you volunteered to help out! Answer these questions by telling who in your class is doing these things.

Modelo ¿Quién va a traer los discos? (Francisco)
Francisco va a traerlos. o
Francisco los va a traer.

1. ¿Quién va a traer la torta?
2. ¿Quién va a hacer los nachos?
3. ¿Quiénes van a preparar la comida?
4. ¿Quién va a tocar la guitarra?
5. ¿Quiénes van a comprar las cervezas?
6. ¿Quién va a limpiar la casa después de la fiesta?

B. ¿Qué piensan de ti? How do the following people feel about you?

Vocabulario útil

amar	odiar	respetar	admirar	fascinar
querer	detestar	adorar	molestar	no querer

1. tus padres
2. tus hermanos
3. tu perro o gato
4. tu profesor(a) de español
5. tu novio(a)
6. tu abuelo(a)

6.5 Review of *saber* and *conocer*

Stating what you know and what you are acquainted with

A. Saber is used when speaking of knowing specific, factual information.
B. Conocer is used when talking about knowing a person or being familiar with a place or a thing.

¡A practicar!

A. ¿Quién es? Enrique is trying to find out as much as he can about the new girl at the party. Complete the following sentences with the appropriate form of **saber** or **conocer** to find out what his friends say.

NATALIA	Yo no la ____________ pero ____________ que vive en la residencia.
VÍCTOR	Mi novia ____________ a su hermana.
ROSA	Julio y Roberto ____________ su número de teléfono.
GLORIA	Mis padres ____________ a sus padres.
ROBERTO	Yo no ____________ quién es pero ella ____________ bailar el tango muy bien.
ANTONIO	Si la quieres ____________, te puedo presentar.

B. ¡No conozco a nadie! It's not easy when you are the new person in town. What would you say if you wanted to know who the following people are?

Modelo Pablo y Antonio

¿Quiénes son esos chicos? No los conozco.

1. Jacobo
2. Ángela y Matilde
3. tú
4. Esteban y Luisa
5. Víctor Mario y tú
6. Luz María

C. ¡Lo siento, pero... ! What do these people say when asked for specific information?

Modelo **Sí, yo <u>conozco</u> a su hermana, pero no <u>sé</u> su nombre.**

1. Yo la ____________ muy bien, pero no ____________ su número de teléfono.
2. Yo ____________ la casa de Andrés, pero desafortunadamente, no ____________ su dirección.
3. Lo siento, yo ____________ francés, pero no ____________ Francia.
4. Nosotros no ____________ San Francisco muy bien, pero ____________ dónde está ese restaurante.
5. Mamá no ____________ cómo se llama ese libro.
6. Ustedes ____________ México, ¿verdad? ¿ ____________ cuáles son las playas más bonitas?

CAPÍTULO 7

Un comunicado especial

Cultural Topics

- **¿Sabías que?**
  El *Popol Vuh*
- **Noticiero cultural**
  Lugar: *Guatemala*
  Gente: *Rigoberta Menchú*
- **Lectura:** *Avisos limitados*

Writing Strategies

- *Orden cronológico*

Reading Strategies

- *Adelantarse al tema*

En preparación

- 7.1 Preterite of Regular Verbs
- 7.2 Preterite of Verbs with Spelling Changes
- 7.3 Preterite of **ir, ser, decir,** and **hacer**
- 7.4 The Pronoun **se:** Special Use

In this chapter, you will learn how to ...

- talk about the news.
- discuss what you read in the newspaper.
- tell what happened in your favorite TV program.
- prepare want ads.

María Elena Salinas y Jorge Ramos, locutores de Univisión

Pasatiempo internacional: leer las noticias del día

Lo que ya sabes...

1. ¿Con qué frecuencia miras las noticias en la tele?
2. ¿Cuál sección de las noticias prefieres? ¿las noticias nacionales e internacionales? ¿las noticias regionales? ¿las noticias del tiempo? ¿las de deportes?
3. ¿Conoces a los locutores en las fotos de arriba? ¿Quiénes son? ¿Quiénes son tus locutores favoritos? ¿Por qué te gustan?
4. ¿Con qué frecuencia lees el periódico? ¿Lo lees de cabo a rabo o sólo lees ciertas secciones? ¿Cuáles? ¿Por qué?

GUATEMALA

Aquí en su Tele * Guía

TAREA

Antes de empezar este **Paso**, estudia **En preparación** 7.1 y haz por escrito los ejercicios de **¡A practicar!** También escucha **Paso 1 ¿Qué se dice... ?** del Capítulo 7 en el CD del estudiante.

¿Eres buen observador?

Domingo

AGO. 4 MAÑANA

EL PERSONAJE DE NORA SALINAS PIERDE LA VIRGINIDAD EN CONFIDENTE DE SECUNDARIA.

Domingo

4 San Eleuterio

XXVI JUEGOS OLIMPICOS. ATLANTA 96. CARTEL DE EVENTOS. Decimosexto y último día de Actividades. ATLETISMO, a las18:05 horas: Prueba de la Maratón, Varonil, desde la salida, recorrido y llegada a la Meta. BASQUETBOL, 09:30: Encuentros por las Medallas, Femenil. BOX,13:30: Encuentros por las Medallas en todos los pesos. CANOTAJE, KAYAK, 09:00: Pruebas Finales en distintas especialidades, Varonil y Femenil. EQUITACION, 10:00: Salto de Obstáculos, Prueba Semifinal y Final, Individual, Abierto. GIMNASIA RITMICA,13:00: Prueba Final, individual, Femenil. HANDBOL (Balón Mano), 15:00: Encuentros por las Medallas, Varonil. VOLIBOL, 12:00: Encuentros por las Medallas, Varonil.

LO MEJOR DEL DIA

Atletismo, a las: 18:05 horas. prueba de la maratón, varonil (se espera la excelente participación de los mexicanos Dionocio Cerón, Benjamín Paredes y de Germán Silva).
10:00 horas. Equitación, salto de obstáculos (es posible que participa por la presea de oro el alemán Ludyer Beerbaum), prueba semifinal y final, individual y abierto.
13:00 Gimnasia rítmica femenil, prueba final, individual. (La candidata para el oro es María Petrova de Bulgaria).
12:00 Volibol varonil, encuentros por las medallas. (Estarán presentes los italianos y los holandeses).
Ceremonia de clausura a las 20:00 horas.

7:00 2 **EN FAMILIA.** Tres horas de concursos y diversión infantil, con: Javier López "Chabelo".
MAÑANA 4 **XXVI JUEGOS OLIMPICOS. ATLANTA 96.** Transmisión, comentarios y reseña, en forma "Local" (México, Distrito Federal), hasta las 09:00 horas.
5 **RAYITO EL MAGO DE LOS SUEÑOS.** Dibujos animados.
7 **CAPSULAS C.V.G.** Ventas por televisión.
9 **ODISEA BURBUJAS.** Fantasía infantil. Tema: "Operación Teledesastre II".
13 **APOLON EL REY.** Dibujos animados.
22 **A, B, C. DEL DEPORTE.** Reportajes. Judo.
7:30 5 **MR. BOGUS.** Dibujos animados.
11 **VENTANA DE COLORES.** Dibujos animados. Bolek y Lolek, Juega Otra Vez, Pacha y los Gatos, Las Aventuras de Ric, El Cocodrilo Christopher, El Bosque Mágico, Capitán Oso Azul, Penny Crayon, Inspector Truquini.
13 **AVENTURAS EN EL MISSISIPI.** Dibujos animados.
22 **LA BELLA Y LA BESTIA.** Teatro Infantil.
8:00 5 **LA VUELTA AL MUNDO EN 80 DIAS.** Dibujos animados.
7 **XXVI JUEGOS OLIMPICOS, ATLANTA 96. Actividades Matutinas.** Desde los escenarios de los Juegos del Centenario. Comentarios y análisis del Ultimo día de Actividades.
9 **EL TESORO DEL SABER.** Fantasía infantil.
13 **PARTIDOS POLITICOS.** P. C.
22 **HISTORIETA DE LA CIENCIA.** Reportaje. Vida y Muerte de una Estrella.
8:30 5 **FLASH GORDON.** Aventuras.
9 **CHIQUILLADAS.** Comedia.
13 **KISSYFUR.** Dibujos animados.
22 **LABORATORIO DE CIENCIAS NATURALES.** Reportaje. Gracias por el Suelo.

CHARLIE ES ENGAÑADO POR SU NOVIA, QUIEN LE PINTA EL CUERNO EN "CONFIDENTE".

9:00 4 **XXVI JUEGOS OLIMPICOS. ATLANTA 96.** Transmisión, comentarios y reseña, en forma "Nacional" (República Mexicana), hasta las 20:00 horas.
5 **LOS HURACANES.** Aventuras.
9 **AQUI ESTA LA CHILINDRINA.** Comedia.
13 **PARTIDOS POLITICOS.** P. R. I.
22 **LOS INTREPIDOS.** Reportaje. La Influencia de la Luna en el Cuerpo Humano.
9:30 5 **DIVERTIRISAS.** Comedia.
9 **CACHUN, CACHUN, RA, RA.** Comedia.
11 **PELICULA.** Dulce. (Drama).
13 **ALF.** Dibujos animados
22 **EX-CONVENTO DE ACTOPAN.** Reportaje. Patrimonio Restaurado.
10:00 2 **EN DOMINGO, AL DESPERTAR.** Noticias, deportes, variedades, invitados especiales. Guillermo Ortega Ruiz, Angélica Mejía, Mayra Saucedo, Antonio de Valdés, Javier Alarcón, Raúl Orvañanos.
5 **PIRATAS DE LAS AGUAS TENEBROSAS.** Dibujos animados.
9 **FUNCION DE LUCHA LIBRE TRIPLE "A" Y EMPRESA MEXICANA DE LUCHA LIBRE.** Funciones celebradas en distintos escenarios del D.F., e interior de la República, con los encuentros en todas las modalidades del pancracio. Comentarios: Miguel Linares, Alfonso Morales, Raúl Sarmiento, Arturo Rivera, Leobardo Magadán.
13 **EL NIÑO PROBLEMA.** Dibujos animados.
22 **LAS ARTES.** Reportaje. Paisajes del Siglo XIX.
10:30 5 **T-REX.** Aventuras.
13 **CABALLEROS DEL ZODIACO.** Dibujos animados.

Domingo

AGO. 4 MAÑANA/TARDE

22 **VIVIR JUNTOS.** Reportaje. Un Paisaje que se Transforma.
11:00 2 **UN NUEVO DIA.** Con César Costa, Rebeca de Alba e invitados. Edición Especial.
5 **PELICULA.** La Pandilla de Pícaros en Japón. (Acción).
13 **MOTORATONES DE MARTE.** Dibujos animados.
22 **BIOGRAFIAS.** Reportaje. Grace Kelly.
11:30 11 **AVENTURAS EN EL MEDITERRANEO** Aventuras. Las Aguilas del Este. Segunda parte. Joshua y sus sobrinos viajan a Alemania para tratar de salvar a las águilas marinas que están muriendo inexplicablemente.
13 **SAILOR MONN.** Dibujos animados.
22 **DEUTSCHE WELLE.** Reportaje. El Periódico Semanal Die Zeit.
11:50 2 **FUTBOL SOCCER NACIONAL. PARTIDO ESPECIAL.** Desde el estadio Azteca, en Tlalpan, Distrito Federal. "LOS RAYOS" DEL NECAXA Vs. "LOS ASES" DEL FUTBOL NACIONAL. Homenaje a los jugadores destacados durante la Temporada 95-96. Encuentro previo a la Entrega de los Citlallis 1996.
12:00 11 **MOCHILA AL HOMBRO.** Reportajes. Taxco, Guerrero. Una de las ciudades coloniales más típicas y bellas de nuestro México, con sus callejones, tejabanes, e intricados caminos y plazas de un pueblo minero.
TARDE
13 **PELICULA.** Triple función.
22 **CONCIERTO DE MUSICA CLASICA.** Don Quijote.
12:30 11 **ESTA SEMANA EN LA CULTURA.** Reportajes.
1:00 5 **PELICULA.** Locura en la Playa. (Comedia).
9 **LA CRIADA BIEN CRIADA.** Comedia.

¡TELE-GUIAS!

MADURA.- *"No temo a la vejez, pues he sabido evolucionar y asimilar el paso del tiempo. Disfruto cada una de las etapas de mi vida, veo pasar los años como un proceso natural y por eso nunca he tenido conflictos emocionales por la edad".* **CLAUDIA ISLAS.**

Ahora, ¡a analizar!

1. En los Estados Unidos hay varios programas religiosos en la televisión los domingos por la mañana. ¿Cuántos programas religiosos hay en la televisión mexicana según *Tele∗Guía?* ¿Cuáles son?
2. ¿Hay programas para niños los domingos por la mañana? ¿Cuántos puedes nombrar?
3. ¿A qué hora se dan las noticias de la mañana? ¿Cómo se llama el programa noticiero? ¿Cuánto tiempo dura?
4. ¿Hay progamas deportivos? ¿Cuáles son?
5. ¿Por qué ponen Atletismo a las 18:05 horas antes de las competiciones a las 10:00, a las 13:00 y las 12:00 en «Lo mejor del día»?

Al hablar de las noticias del día

cigarrillos	robo	incendio	asesino
Calle 25-6	cliente	tienda	cenar
sospechan	muerto	Calle 6-25	arrestó
dueño	policía	dos mujeres	ambulancia

____

____

Esta mañana el gobernador regresó de su viaje al lago Atitlán, donde la policía informó que más de cien personas perdieron su vida en el vuelo 113 de Aerolíneas Maya.

En el campeonato de fútbol, Chichicastenango jugó contra Antigua y ganó 3 a 0. En béisbol los Gigantes de Quetzaltenango vencieron a los Cardenales de Huehuetenango, 6 a 4. Y aquí en la capital, anoche en fútbol, el equipo Maya Quiché empató al equipo Federal, 2 a 2.

Ahora, ¡a hablar!

A. Las noticias nacionales. Tú eres el (la) locutor(a) de Univisión y estás preparándote para dar las noticias nacionales. ¿Qué vas a decir?

Modelo anoche / policía / capturar / tres ladrones

Anoche la policía capturó a tres ladrones.

1. esta mañana / policía / encontrar / un avión / montañas
2. ayer / policía / arrestar / dos vendedores de cocaína

3. ayer / presidente de Telex / llegar / la capital
4. anoche / hombre / asesinar / cinco personas
5. hoy / presidente / Casa Blanca / hablar / la economía
6. anoche / presidente / recibir / primer ministro del Japón

B. Personas famosas. En las noticias siempre hay información sobre las actividades de personas famosas. Usando tu imaginación, di qué hicieron estas personas ayer.

Modelo Gloria Estefan cantó en México ayer.

				Nueva York
el rey *(king)* de España		salir		Estados Unidos
Fidel Castro		cantar		Inglaterra
el presidente de los EE.UU.	+	viajar	+	España
Rigoberta Menchú		llegar		Europa
el presidente de Guatemala				volver Rusia
¿... ?		¿... ?		¿... ?

C. Los deportes. Ahora imagínate que eres locutor(a) de deportes de una estación de televisión. Prepara un anuncio de los resultados de la semana.

Deporte	**¿Quién?**	**Resultado**
en fútbol	(sus equipos o atletas favoritos)	ganar
en baloncesto		perder
en béisbol		jugar
en ¿... ?		empatar

Y ahora, ¡a conversar!

A. Gente famosa. Escoge una persona famosa y contesta las siguientes preguntas. Luego hazle estas preguntas a tu compañero(a) para saber algo de la persona que él (ella) escogió.

1. ¿Es hombre o mujer?
2. ¿Dónde vive?
3. ¿Cuál es su profesión?
4. ¿Salió en el periódico (revista, televisión) recientemente? ¿Por qué?
5. ¿... ?

B. ¿Y tú? Ahora imagínate que tú eres una persona muy famosa y estás leyendo *Gente,* una revista que informa a sus lectores sobre las actividades de gente famosa. ¿Qué dice de ti y de tus actividades durante el fin de semana pasado?

1. ¿Dónde pasaste el fin de semana? ¿Con quién lo pasaste?
2. ¿Alguien te visitó? ¿te llamó?
3. ¿Visitaste tú a algunas personas? ¿Llamaste a alguien?
4. ¿Saliste el viernes o el sábado por la noche? ¿Con quién? ¿Qué hiciste *(did you do)*?

5. ¿A qué hora regresaste a tu casa el sábado por la noche?
6. Si no saliste el sábado por la noche, ¿qué hiciste?
7. ¿... ?

C. Para los lectores hispanos. Un día por semana, el periódico de tu universidad publica una sección en español con noticias locales, nacionales y mundiales. En grupos de tres o cuatro, preparen esa sección con las noticias de esta semana.

D. Noticias en nuestra clase. La clase de español va a publicar un periódico con noticias importantes de cada alumno de la clase. Para conseguir la información necesaria, primero indica si hiciste algo interesante o si te pasó algo interesante este año en estos lugares. Luego pídeles la misma información a dos compañeros(as) de clase y anótala.

Preguntas	Yo	Amigo(a) 1	Amigo(a) 2
En la universidad			
En casa			
En el trabajo			
En tu vida personal			

¡Luz! ¡Cámara! ¡Acción!

A. Reportaje. Tú y tres compañeros de clase son locutores del noticiero de las seis de la noche. Preparen las noticias del día y preséntenlas a la clase. Uno debe hablar sobre las noticias mundiales, otro sobre las noticias nacionales, otro sobre las noticias locales y otro sobre los deportes.

B. ¿Qué pasó? Anoche en el noticiero de las seis, oíste algo muy interesante en las noticias. Ahora estás contándole a un(a) amigo(a) lo que pasó. Tu amigo(a) quiere saber todos los detalles y te hace muchas preguntas. Dramatiza la conversación con un(a) compañero(a) de clase.

¿Comprendes lo que se dice?

Estrategias para escuchar. *When speaking, especially when providing extensive information as in news reports, the speaker must decide where to stop to take a breath. The words that are said before the speaker pauses to take a breath are called "breath groups." Learning to form logical breath groups is central to speech in all languages. As you hear the following news broadcast about Nobel Peace Prize winner, Rigoberta Menchú, listen to the breath groups the speakers form as they stop sometimes at the end of sentences, other times in the middle of sentences. Do you note any logic to where the speakers stop to take a breath as they report the news?*

Noticiero especial. Escucha este noticiero especial de Radio Capital de Ciudad Guatemala con noticias sobre Rigoberta Menchú, la indígena maya-quiché que, en 1992, fue galardonada con el Premio Nóbel de la Paz. Luego selecciona la frase que mejor completa cada oración.

1. Rodrigo Lagunas y Marta Cajillas son...
   a. hermanos de Rigoberta Menchú.
   b. miembros de un comité de derechos humanos.
   c. locutores de Radio Capital.
2. Según el noticiero, Rigoberta Menchú simboliza...
   a. el sufrimiento de los indígenas guatemaltecos a manos del gobierno.
   b. el Premio Nóbel de la Paz.
   c. el Comité de Justicia Social y Derechos Humanos.
3. El noticiero especial dice que Rigoberta anunció hoy que...
   a. el gobierno guatemalteco respeta los derechos humanos.
   b. el comité de derechos humanos está dando buen resultado.
   c. el comité de derechos humanos no está dando buen resultado.
4. Rigoberta demandó...
   a. la renuncia *(resignation)* del presidente.
   b. ser nombrada miembro del comité del presidente.
   c. la eliminación del comité del presidente.

NOTICIERO CULTURAL

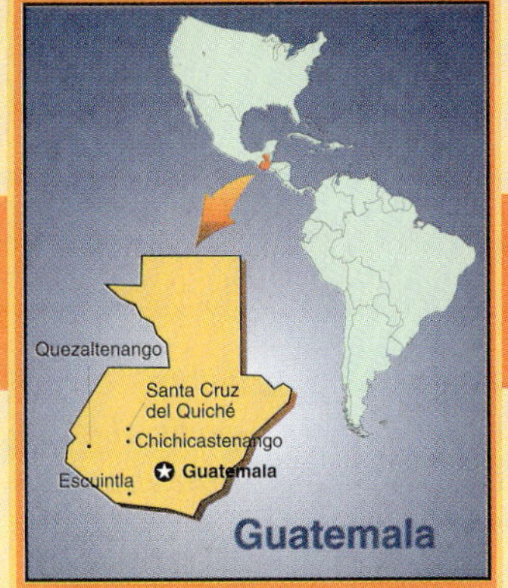

LUGAR... GUATEMALA

Antes de empezar, dime...

1. ¿Adónde en los EE.UU. se puede viajar para conocer el pasado indígena del país? ¿el pasado colonial?
2. ¿Hay una población indígena en los EE.UU. actualmente? ¿Más o menos qué porcentaje es de la población del país?
3. ¿Hay inmigrantes recientes de otros países en tu estado? ¿De qué países?
4. ¿Cómo clasificas la vida de los inmigrantes recientes en tu estado? Explica tu clasificación.

❑ lujosa ❑ muy cómoda ❑ cómoda
❑ difícil ❑ muy difícil ❑ pésima

Indígenas maya-quiché de Guatemala

La cultura maya

Se dice que viajar a Guatemala es «viajar al pasado». En su territorio tuvo esplendor una de las civilizaciones más extraordinarias del continente americano: la cultura maya. Esta cultura estaba dividida en cuatro grandes centros: Tikal en Guatemala, Palenque y Calakmul en México y Copán en el noroeste de Honduras.

Tikal, Guatemala

Actualmente la población indígena representa el 55 por ciento de los habitantes de Guatemala. Muchos de ellos todavía viven en pequeños pueblos donde se dedican a la agricultura o a la artesanía, como hacían sus antepasados *(ancestors)*. Esto, tanto como las impresionantes ruinas precolombinas de la cultura maya, siguen fascinando tanto a los arqueólogos como a los turistas.

Desafortunadamente, al igual que en la mayoría de muchas comunidades indígenas, las condiciones de vida en el campo son muy deficientes, por lo cual muchos de ellos se van a vivir a la ciudad e incluso a otros países, como México y los EE.UU. En esos países los indígenas inmigrantes con frecuencia encuentran una vida aún más difícil debido a que están en culturas extrañas donde a veces ni hablan la lengua ni pueden encontrar trabajo.

Y ahora, dime...

Contesta estas preguntas con un(a) compañero(a) de clase.

1. ¿Por qué se dice que viajar a Guatemala es «viajar al pasado»?
2. Usa estos cuadros para comparar a los mayas en tiempos precolombinos con los mayas actualmente.

LOS MAYAS

Tiempos precolombinos	Actualmente
1.	1.
2.	2.
3.	3.

El español en otras disciplinas: Artesanía

Artesanía. Así como el arte, la artesanía *(handicrafts)* es también una parte importante de las culturas del mundo. ¿Qué sabes tú de la artesanía? ¿Cuál es la diferencia entre el arte y la artesanía? En grupos de dos o tres, preparen una lista de ideas que distinguen lo que es arte de lo que es artesanía. Después, compartan sus ideas con la clase.

Proyecto: Trae a la clase algún objeto favorito de artesanía. Explica su origen, uso, significado, etc. ¡En español, claro!

¡Co-o-o-mpre El Universal!

TAREA Antes de empezar este ***Paso***, estudia **En preparación** 7.2 y haz por escrito los ejercicios de **¡A practicar!** También escucha ***Paso 2 ¿Qué se dice...?*** del Capítulo 7 en el CD del estudiante.

¿Eres buen observador?

Urge "aterrizar" el plan económico: IP; debe cambiar: clero

EL UNIVERSAL

EL GRAN DIARIO DE MEXICO

Incompleta, la reforma electoral: López Obrador

Es todavía la democracia

EL UNIVERSAL

ESTADOS

Inundaciones en dos estados; un muerto

Se desbordan un dique y tres ríos en Juárez y Frontera; decenas de viviendas dañadas

EL UNIVERSAL

INTERNACIONAL

Luchan indígenas de América por sus derechos a la tierra

EL UNIVERSAL

ESPECTACULOS

Más bella que la Sra. Presidenta

Eternamente Collins

EL UNIVERSAL

NUESTRA CIUDAD

Ofrecen 20,000 becas a rechazados

¿Qué necesitaban para entrar?

Desolador, el estado de los

EL UNIVERSAL

NUESTRO MUNDO

Esfera Humana

Enrique Castillo Pesado

LOS PROTAGONISTAS

EL UNIVERSAL

CULTURAL

LA HERENCIA DE LOS POETAS MALDITOS

Subsidio para la

EL UNIVERSAL

DEPORTES

(2)

CAMPEONES

EL UNIVERSAL

AVISO OPORTUNO

(2)

Buscan las rusas pareja en "agencias"

PLANTA INDUSTRIAL

VENTA, RENTA O PERMUTA

AVALUOS

Ahora, ¡a analizar!

1. ¿Cómo se llama este periódico?
2. ¿Cuántas secciones principales tiene? ¿Cuáles son?
3. ¿Cuál es la diferencia entre las noticias de la primera plana, la sección «Internacional» y la sección «Estados»?
4. ¿En qué sección podrías encontrar información sobre películas? ¿noticias de la nación? ¿quién ganó el partido de fútbol anoche? ¿casas en venta? ¿las noticias más importantes del día? ¿la novela más reciente de... ?
5. ¿Te sorprenden las noticias principales en la sección «Internacional»? ¿Por qué?

¿Qué se dice...?

Al leer el periódico del día

Escribe el nombre de cada sección del periódico que los cuatro estudiantes leen: «Espectáculos», «Deportes», «Avisos», «Estados», «Internacional», la primera plana.

Norma tiene mucho interés en quién ganó y quién perdió en el mundo de los deportes. Pero a Meche le interesa más lo que ocurrió recientemente en el mundo, en la nación y en su propia ciudad. Mientras tanto Eduardo prefiere hablar de las películas, obras de teatro y exhibiciones de arte que están presentándose. Él también es muy aficionado a los programas de televisión. En cambio, Jorge no puede pensar en nada más que las buenas gangas de las tiendas. A él le gusta comprar, comprar y comprar.

¿Sabías que... ?

El *Popol Vuh* es el libro más importante de la literatura maya. Es un libro mágico y poético que describe la mitología quiché con respecto a la formación del mundo, los dioses, los héroes y el hombre del pueblo quiché. El nombre «quiché» viene del nombre del lugar donde vivían: el bosque. El sacerdote español fray Francisco Ximénez copió el *Popol Vuh* en el original quiché. Luego, en columnas paralelas, también lo tradujo a una versión en español. El original de fray Francisco se conserva actualmente en la Biblioteca Newberry de Chicago.

Ahora, ¡a hablar!

A. Un siglo interesantísimo. ¿Cuáles fueron algunas de las noticias más interesantes del siglo XX? Identifícalas.

Modelo 1914 / empezar / primera guerra mundial
En mil novecientos catorce empezó la primera guerra mundial.

1. 1918 / terminar / primera guerra mundial
2. 1939 / empezar / segunda guerra mundial
3. 1945 / explotar / primera bomba atómica
4. 1959 / tomar control de Cuba / Fidel Castro
5. 1968 / asesinar (ellos) / Martin Luther King, Jr.
6. 1969 / llegar / Apollo 11 / la luna
7. 1986 / ocurrir / desastre nuclear en Chernobyl
8. 1990 / empezar / reunificación de Alemania
9. 1991 / comenzar / guerra del golfo Pérsico
10. 1992 / empezar / Olimpíadas en Barcelona
11. 1995 / explotar / bomba / Ciudad de Oklahoma
12. este año / ¿... ?

B. ¿Qué pasó en el año 1996? ¿Cuáles fueron las noticias principales de los Estados Unidos en el año 1996?

Modelo enero / terminar / huelga / empleados del gobierno
En enero terminó la huelga de los empleados del gobierno.

1. febrero / cubanos / atacar / dos aviones civiles / EE.UU.
2. abril / la FBI / arrestar / hombre sospechoso de ser / «Unabomber» / Montana
3. abril / accidente de avión / matar / niña piloto / siete años
4. mayo / ocurrir / terrible accidente de avión / Everglades / Florida
5. junio / la FBI / arrestar / miembros del grupo «Freemen» / Montana
6. julio / empezar / Juegos Olímpicos / Atlanta
7. julio / bomba / explotar / durante / Juegos Olímpicos / Atlanta
8. julio / vuelo 800 / TWA / desaparecer / océano Atlántico
9. ¿... ?

C. En 1995. ¿Qué pasó en Latinoamérica en el año 1995? Cambia los tiempos de los verbos del presente al pretérito.

Modelo **diciembre** La presidenta de **Nicaragua,** Violeta Barrios de Chamorro, firma una nueva constitución.
En diciembre, la presidenta de Nicaragua, Violeta Barrios de Chamorro, firmó una nueva constitución.

enero **Chile** y **Bolivia** expresan el deseo de unirse a Mercosur *(Southern Common Market).*

febrero La guerra entre **Perú** y **Ecuador** empieza en la frontera de los dos países.

marzo El gobierno implica al hermano del ex presidente de **México** en el asesinato del secretario general del PRI.

abril En **Guatemala** acusan al gobierno de los Estados Unidos y la CIA de intervención militar en el país desde 1980.

mayo En **Argentina**, el presidente peronista Carlos Saúl Menem, gana las elecciones para la presidencia una vez más.

junio En **Colombia**, la policía arresta a Gilberto Rodríguez Ojuela, el líder del Cartel de Cali.

julio Las fuerzas armadas del gobierno matan a más de 30 personas en el estado de Guerrero, **México**.

agosto En **Colombia**, el ministro de Defensa, Fernando Botero, renuncia a su cargo después de acusaciones de tráfico de drogas.

septiembre **Cuba** reacciona al embargo económico de los Estados Unidos.

octubre Inglaterra y **Argentina** firman un acuerdo sobre los derechos al petróleo en las aguas de las islas Malvinas *(Falkland Islands)*.

noviembre En **Bolivia**, el ex general Mario Vargas Salinas revela el sitio de entierro *(burial site)* de Che Guevara.

D. Este año. ¿Qué pasó este año en el mundo? En grupos de tres o cuatro, recuerden eventos que ocurrieron durante el año.

Y ahora, ¡a conversar!

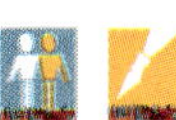

A. De la niñez a la adolescencia. Entrevista a un(a) compañero(a) para saber algo de su niñez y adolescencia. Anota todas sus respuestas.

1. ¿Dónde naciste? ¿En qué año naciste?
2. ¿En qué año empezaste la escuela primaria? ¿Dónde?
3. ¿Dónde viviste los diez primeros años de tu vida?
4. ¿Dónde trabajaste por primera vez?
5. ¿En qué año empezaste a manejar? ¿Cuál fue el primer coche que compraste?
6. ¿En qué año terminaste la escuela secundaria?
7. ¿Cuándo decidiste venir a esta universidad?

B. ¡Ésta es tu vida! Ahora hazle cinco preguntas a tu compañero(a) sobre su vida aquí en la universidad. Anota sus respuestas y con lo que ya tienes del ejercicio anterior, escribe un resumen de la vida de tu compañero(a).

C. Tiempo en cápsula. En grupos de tres o cuatro preparen una descripción breve de los cinco eventos más importantes de los últimos veinte años. Ustedes consideran estos eventos tan importantes que van a poner su lista en una cápsula de tiempo para guardarlos para las futuras generaciones.

D. ¡Noticias fantásticas! Tú y dos amigos(as) trabajan para un periódico que se dedica a reportar noticias fantásticas (tipo *Enquirer*). Preparen los títulos de la primera plana para la próxima edición.

¡Luz! ¡Cámara! ¡Acción!

A. ¿Leíste las noticias de hoy? Tú y dos amigos(as) hablan de las noticias en el periódico de hoy. Cada uno hace un resumen breve de un artículo que leyó y los(las) otros(as) reaccionan. Trabajando en grupos de tres, dramaticen esta situación.

B. ¿Yo, reportero? Tú trabajas para la revista *Hola.* Hoy vas a entrevistar a una persona muy famosa. Quieres saber muchas cosas de su pasado. En parejas dramaticen esta situación.

¿Comprendes lo que se dice?

Estrategias para ver y escuchar. *As you listen to this commercial for Guatemala, pay close attention to how the narrators divide their sentences into logical breath groups.*

¡De Guatemala a guatemejor! Mira este anuncio sobre Guatemala. Luego, con un(a) compañero(a), preparen una lista de razones por qué Guatemala es el lugar ideal para las vacaciones de una familia. Comparen su lista con la de dos otros grupos.

NOTICIERO CULTURAL

GENTE... RIGOBERTA MENCHÚ

Antes de empezar, dime...

Contesta estas preguntas sobre personas marginadas en tu país.

1. ¿Qué grupo o instituciones conoces que ayuden a las personas marginadas?
2. ¿Conoces a personajes históricos marginados que lucharon con éxito por alguna causa? Nómbralos y explica.
3. ¿Conoces a alguna persona de la actualidad que se dedica a ayudar a personas marginadas? Explica.
4. ¿Participas tú en algún tipo de causa o trabajo voluntario? Explica.

Rigoberta Menchú

Rigoberta Menchú

Rigoberta Menchú, indígena maya-quiché, nació el 9 de enero de 1959, en un pueblo llamado Chinel, al norte de Guatemala.

Al igual que todos los campesinos pobres, desde muy niña, empezó a trabajar con sus padres en las cosechas de algodón y café, ganando un bajísimo salario. Más tarde, siguiendo la tradición de muchas mujeres de las zonas rurales, se trasladó a la capital para trabajar en el servicio doméstico.

Pero muy pronto la vida de Rigoberta cambió radicalmente. La muerte violenta de sus padres y un hermano, crímenes atribuidos a las fuerzas del gobierno guatemalteco, la hicieron reaccionar y continuar la tarea social comenzada por su familia. Rigoberta se dedicó entonces a defender a su gente, los indígenas y los de las clases menos favorecidas.

Por esta intensa labor, Rigoberta recibió el Premio Nóbel de la Paz en 1992, premio que le permitió crear una fundación que apoya su causa en Guatemala.

Como toda persona famosa, Rigoberta Menchú no ha escapado a la controversia. Pero sea como sea, su persona sirvió para darle voz a un sector de la población marginada por mucho tiempo.

Y ahora, dime...

Usa un diagrama Venn como éste para hacer un paralelo entre la vida de Rigoberta Menchú y un personaje histórico de los EE.UU., como Martin Luther King, Jr. o César Chávez, que dedicó su vida a la gente marginada.

Rigoberta Menchú	Ambas personas	{Nombre}
1.	1.	1.
2.	2.	2.
3.	3.	3.
4.	4.	4.
5.	5.	5.
. . .	. . .	. . .

Antes de escribir
Estrategias para escribir: Orden cronológico

Generalmente al escribir una autobiografía, el escritor narra su vida en orden cronológico, es decir, eventos de la niñez primero, luego la juventud, luego su vida como adulto. Nota que la breve biografía de Rigoberta Menchú está narrada en orden cronológico. Prepárate ahora para escribir tu autobiografía en orden cronológico.

Ahora, ¡a escribir!

A. En preparación. Decide cuáles fueron los eventos más importantes en tu vida. Escribe un grupo de ideas de todos los eventos que podrías incluir, por ejemplo, datos de nacimiento, dónde vivió tu familia durante los primeros años, escuela primaria, etc. Prepara una lista de todos los eventos principales de tu vida desde tu nacimiento hasta el presente.

B. El primer borrador. Ahora organiza la información en tu lista en orden cronológico y prepara un primer borrador de tu autobiografía. Incluye toda la información de tu lista que consideres relevante.

C. Ahora, a compartir. Comparte tu primer borrador con dos o tres compañeros. Comenta sobre el contenido y el estilo de las composiciones de tus compañeros y escucha los comentarios de ellos sobre tu autobiografía.

D. Ahora, a revisar. Si necesitas hacer cambios basados en los comentarios de tus compañeros, hazlos ahora. Antes de preparar la versión final de tu autobiografía, comparte tu borrador con dos compañeros de clase para que te digan si hay errores de ortografía, gramática o puntuación. Presta atención particular al uso del pretérito.

E. La versión final. Prepara la versión final de tu autobiografía y entrégala. Escribe la versión final a máquina o en la computadora siguiendo el formato recomendado.

F. Ahora, a publicar. En grupos de cinco o seis, junten sus autobiografías en un volumen. Elijan *(Choose)* un título creativo para su volumen, algo como: *Autobiografías de seis estudiantes extraordinarios* o *Cómo llegar a la universidad: seis versiones.*

¿Qué pasó ayer?

TAREA

Antes de empezar este **Paso**, estudia **En preparación** 7.3 y 7.4 y haz por escrito los ejercicios de **¡A practicar!** También escucha **Paso 3 ¿Qué se dice... ?** del Capítulo 7 en el CD del estudiante.

¿Eres buen observador?

Estos son los TV-programas + vistos

Cañaveral de pasiones, *firme en la cúspide...*

Con toda el alma *cerró con buen rating*

***HORARIO MATUTINO** (De 6:00 a 12:00 hrs.)*

Preferencias:	menciones
1.- Al despertar	287
2.- Un nuevo día	256
3.- Cine de la mañana	176
4.- Hola, México	118
5.- Café express	76
Otros con menos de 30 menciones:	35
Total:	**888**

De 1,500 personas encuestadas:
* 612 no ven TV en la mañana
* 888 sí ven TV en la mañana

HOLA, MEXICO

***HORARIO VESPERTINO** (De 13:00 a 19:00 hrs.)*

Preferencias:	menciones
1.- ¡Pácatelas!	310
2.- Canción de amor	235
3.- La sombra del otro	183
4.- La niñera	161
5.- Confidente de secundaria	128
Otros con menos de 30 menciones:	86
Total:	**1,103**

De 1,500 personas encuestadas:
* 397 no ven TV en la tarde
* 1,103 sí ven TV en la tarde

CANCION DE AMOR

Ahora, ¡a analizar!

1. ¿Cuántas personas participaron en esta encuesta? ¿Qué tipo de encuesta es?
2. ¿Cuántas de las personas que participaron tenían opiniones específicas acerca de los programas? ¿Por qué no expresaron opiniones las otras personas?
3. ¿A qué hora del día o de la noche se dan los programas que fueron evaluados? ¿Cuál programa es el más popular? ¿el menos popular?
4. ¿Qué tipo de programa crees que es el más popular? ¿Por qué crees eso? ¿Hay otros programas del mismo tipo entre los diez mencionados? ¿Cuáles? ¿Por qué crees eso?

¿Qué se dice...?

Al hablar de tu telenovela favorita

¿Quién hizo esto: la madre (M), el padre (P), la madre de la telenovela (MT) o el padre de la telenovela (PT)?

_______ 1. Recibió flores.

_______ 2. Descubrió una venta de libros.

_______ 3. Recibió una botella de vino.

_______ 4. Quiere saber qué pasó en *Vidas y sueños* ayer.

MADRE ¡Ay, mira! No lo dejó entrar. Pero, ¿por qué no?

HIJA Luz María descubrió que Roberto no trabajó el sábado por la noche. Ella lo vio en el coche con Lola. Ahora va a explicar por qué salió con Lola.

PADRE Se solicita carpintero a media jornada, hijo. A lo mejor debes solicitar. Siempre dices que necesitas más dinero.

HIJO Papá, ¡ahora no! ¡No ves que miramos la tele!

MADRE ¿Ya terminó? Yo quiero saber qué mentira va a inventar ahora.
HIJO Pero, mamá, no va a decirle una mentira. Dijo que quería decirle la verdad.
MADRE ¡Ay, hijo! ¡Qué inocente estás tú hoy día!
PADRE Aquí dice que se alquila un…
HIJO ¡Ay! ¿Otra vez?
HIJA ¡Ya! ¡Por Dios, papá!

Ahora, ¡a hablar!

A. Robo. En el episodio del programa de televisión *El detective,* el inspector Matamoscas interroga a dos testigos sobre el robo de un banco. ¿Qué dicen los dos testigos?

Modelo **TESTIGO 1** yo / lo / ver / todo
Yo lo vi todo.

1. un coche / parar / enfrente de / banco
2. dos hombres / entrar / banco
3. un hombre / ir / caja
4. el hombre / sacar / pistola
5. el cajero / no decir / nada
6. los hombres / escapar / con / dinero

Modelo **TESTIGO 2** no / ser / así
No, no fue así.

7. tres hombres / salir / coche
8. dos hombres / ir / caja
9. un hombre / decir / algo / cajero
10. el cajero / sacar / todo / dinero / caja
11. los tres hombres / salir / corriendo

B. El sábado. ¿Qué hiciste tú el sábado pasado?

Modelo **En la mañana dormí hasta tarde, hice ejercicio, fui al supermercado, limpié la casa, estudié y…**

1. En la mañana
salir a correr / tomar café / escribir cartas / ir al centro / mandar cartas / limpiar la casa / ver la televisión / descansar / llamar a mis padres
2. En la tarde
ir de compras / caminar a... / hacer la tarea / mirar deportes en la televisión / escuchar la radio / dormir un poco / practicar deportes / ir a la biblioteca / ¿... ?

3. En la noche
ir a una fiesta / salir con amigos / mirar televisión / leer una novela / comer en un restaurante / ir a un concierto / alquilar un video / invitar a unos amigos a casa / ir al cine / ¿... ?

C. Buena impresión. Tú tienes una entrevista para un empleo en una compañía importante. ¿Sabes qué se hace o qué no se hace para dar una buena impresión?

Modelo llevar blue jeans
No se lleva blue jeans.

1. llevar ropa de colores vivos
2. hablar mal de su empleo anterior
3. fumar durante la entrevista
4. mirar a la persona que entrevista
5. hablar claramente
6. decir mentiras
7. llegar a tiempo
8. ¿... ?

D. ¡Necesito dinero urgentemente! ¿Qué puedo hacer? Una solución es vender algunas cosas que no necesito. Prepara unos anuncios de cosas que quieres vender.

Y ahora, ¡a conversar!

A. ¿Quién es? En grupos de tres o cuatro escojan una persona famosa del mundo de la política o del espectáculo. Digan las cosas más importantes que hizo esa persona. El resto de la clase tiene que adivinar quién es. Se permite hacer preguntas para saber más detalles.

Gloria Estefan

Antonio Banderas

Edward James Olmos

Cristina Saralegui

Fidel Castro

Eva Perón

B. ¿Y tú? Ahora tu propia vida va a servir de guión *(screenplay)* para una telenovela. En grupos de tres o cuatro, escriban el guión para un día dramático que tuviste.

C. Necesitamos dinero. Estos individuos necesitan dinero urgentemente. En parejas, ayúdenles a preparar anuncios clasificados para vender algún objeto apropiado. Sean creativos.

Modelo Antonio Banderas

Se vende tambor *(drum)*. **Excelente para música de mambo. Se puede usar como objeto decorativo. $250,00.**

1. Oprah Winfrey
2. Jon Secada
3. Geraldo Rivera
4. Linda Ronstadt
5. ¿... ?

¡Luz! ¡Cámara! ¡Acción!

A. ¡Hace diez años! Tú y un(a) amigo(a) de la escuela secundaria se encuentran después de un largo tiempo. Cuéntense lo que pasó en sus vidas respectivas.

B. Señores y señoras... Ustedes trabajan en el departamento de publicidad para la estación de televisión XELO. En grupos de cuatro o cinco preparen una publicidad para su producto favorito y dramatícenla.

Antes de leer
Estrategias para leer: Adelantarse al tema

A. Adelántate. *Before reading, we frequently try to anticipate* **(adelantar)** *what a reading will be about by focusing on external clues, such as the visual(s) accompanying the reading or the title or subtitles of the reading, or simply by drawing on previous knowledge we may have about the topic of the reading.*

Practica el adelantarte a esta lectura leyendo solamente los títulos, en este caso, las palabras en negrilla *(bold type)* y en imprenta grande. ¿Cuáles de estos temas son muy obvios, cuáles son menos obvios y cuáles probablemente no aparecen en estos anuncios?

1. programadores de computadoras
2. mecánicos
3. ingenieros
4. médicos
5. electricistas
6. guardias de seguridad
7. sirvientas para limpiar la casa
8. secretarias bilingües

B. Prepárate para leer. Adelántate y lee sólo los títulos de los anuncios de la lectura. En una hoja de papel, escribe brevemente dos cosas que crees que cada anuncio va a mencionar. Luego, después de leer los avisos, vuelve a lo que escribiste y confirma tus respuestas.

- Computadoras JCN
- Conserje
- Ingeniero civil
- Ingeniero electrónico

Avisos limitados

JCN *Computadoras JCN*

Para trabajar en su Departamento de seguridad, IBM de Guatemala

Solicita personal calificado que cumpla con los siguientes requisitos:

- Título de técnico superior en seguridad industrial o estudiante universitario, con experiencia previa en el área de seguridad.
- Conocimiento del idioma inglés.

Las personas interesadas deberán dirigirse a la siguiente dirección: Edificio *JCN*, planta baja, Av. Ernesto Blohm

Se solicita

Conserje

(Matrimonio)

Edificio Comercial situado en Lomas Norte, solicita los servicios de un matrimonio para el cuidado, mantenimiento y limpieza del mismo.

Se requiere una pareja joven, dinámica, sin hijos y con buena experiencia en similares trabajos y excelentes referencias por escrito.

Interesados favor de presentarse el lunes 11 de septiembre en el Edf. Centro Lomas, Torre Oeste, Piso 3, Ofic. Núm. 1 y preguntar por la Srta. Agostina.

Importante Empresa del sector de la construcción solicita

Ingeniero Civil

Para incorporarse a una organización dinámica con grandes perspectivas de expansión.

Se ofrece:

- Excelente remuneración
- Beneficios sociales
- Caja de ahorro
- Seguro de vida y hospitalización

Requisitos:

- Experiencia no indispensable
- Disponibilidad de residencia en el interior del país
- Deseos de superación en una compañía corporativa
- Habilidad en el manejo de personal

Favor de enviar curriculum vitae con foto al Apartado Postal Nos. 10 y 203, Cd. Guatemala

Profesores bilingües

(Español/Inglés)

Prestigioso colegio en Col. Lomas está entrevistando a profesores capacitados para el período 1998–99 para trabajar en los niveles de pre-escolar y primaria.

Requisitos indispensables:
•Título docente •Dominio del inglés •Experiencia comprobada •Con preferencia nacionalidad americana, británica o canadiense (no indispensable).

La institución ofrece estabilidad laboral y salario promedio mensual 72.000 Q.

Interesados comunicarse por tele. 256 66 46

Importante Línea Aérea Internacional

Requiere para su Departamento de Reservaciones cinco candidatas(os).

Requisitos:

- Inglés indispensable
- Edad 18 a 25 años
- Bachilleres

Enviar hoja de vida con foto reciente al Anunciador No. 1277, EL TIEMPO.

A ver si comprendiste

Contesta estas preguntas a base de los *Avisos limitados* que leíste.

1. ¿Cuántos puestos requieren experiencia previa? ¿Cuáles son?
2. ¿Cuáles puestos requieren título universitario?

3. ¿Cuántos puestos requieren conocimiento de dos lenguas? ¿Cuáles son?
4. ¿Se puede solicitar por escrito a todos estos puestos? Explica tu respuesta.
5. ¿Cuál de estos puestos te interesa a ti? ¿Por qué?

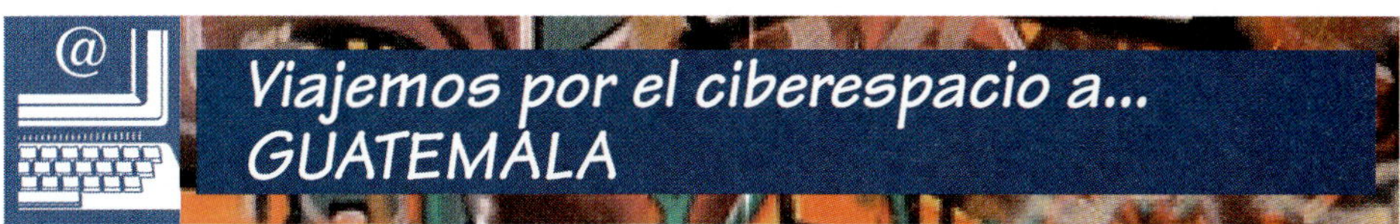

Expand your horizons! *Let's travel through cyberspace to* **Guatemala** where . . .

- through the Internet, you can visit Guatemala's dense jungles, arid deserts, and breathtaking volcanoes, as well as its beautiful beaches on both the Atlantic and Pacific coastlines.
- you can see an abundant variety of plant and animal life, ranging from thousands of species of orchids to the rare national bird, the quetzal.
- in addition to its natural beauty, you can experience the diverse cultures of Guatemala, where the majority of its inhabitants are indigenous, and where over 30 languages and many more regional dialects are spoken.
- you can visit the **Arte Maya Tz'utuhil Museum,** where you can appreciate the work of contemporary self-taught Mayan artists living in towns on Lake Atitlán around San Pedro la Laguna.

If you are a cyberspace browser, join us in **Viajemos por el ciberespacio a... Guatemala,** by trying the following important addresses.

Universidad del Valle de Guatemala
http://www.uvg.edu.gt/

Fundación Rigoberta Menchú Tum
http://ourworld.compuserve.com/homepages/rmtpaz/

Periódicos y revistas
http://www.pronet.net.gt/gweekly/
http://www.prensalibre.com/

Arte Maya:
http://www.artemaya.com/

Because addresses are likely to change without notice, the following key words will guarantee that **Viajemos por el ciberespacio a... Guatemala** will get you to your desired destination:

Palabras clave

Guatemala
Periódicos de Guatemala
Turismo en Guatemala
Arte Maya
Rigoberta Menchú
Radio en vivo Guatemala

http//www.hrwcollege.com

Vocabulario

Asesinatos

arrestar *to arrest*
asesinar *to assassinate*
atacar *to attack*
bomba *bomb*
capturar *to capture*
escapar *to escape*
explotar *to explode*
guerra *war*
huelga *strike*
informar *to inform*
ladrón *thief*
matar *to kill*
pistola *gun*
policía (*f.*) *police force*
policía (*m./f.*) *(male/female) police officer*
robar *to rob; to steal*
robo *robbery*
sospechar *to suspect*

Viajar

aerolínea *airline*
avión (*m.*) *airplane*
viaje (*m.*) *trip*
vuelo *flight*

Deportes

atleta (*m./f.*) *athlete*
baloncesto *basketball*
campeonato *championship*
deporte (*m.*) *sport*
empatar *to tie (in games and elections)*
equipo *team*
ganar *to win*
jugar (ue) *to play*
partido *game*
vencer *to conquer*

Periódicos

aviso *advertisement, classified ad*
espectáculo *movie/theater section of newspaper*
noticias *news*
primera plana *front page*
titular (*m.*) *headline*

Negocios

caja *cash register*
empleo *employment*
entrevista *interview*
experiencia *experience*
negocios *business*
profesión *profession*
puesto *job, position*

Sustantivos

escuela primaria *elementary school*
escuela secundaria *high school*
gobierno *government*
interés (*m.*) *interest*
lago *lake*
llave (*f.*) *key*
mentira *lie*
revista *magazine*
siglo *century*
verdad (*f.*) *truth*
vez (*f.*) *time*
vida *life*

Verbos

celebrar *to celebrate*
comenzar (ie) *to begin*
dejar *to leave behind*
desaparecer *to disappear*
descubrir *to discover*
empezar (ie) *to begin*
entrar *to enter*
fumar *to smoke*
llegar *to arrive*
mandar *to send*
manejar *to drive*
nacer *to be born*
ocurrir *to occur*
ofrecer *to offer*
parar *to stop*
perder (ie) *to lose*
reaccionar *to react*
recibir *to receive*
solicitar *to apply*
terminar *to finish; to end*

Adjetivos

espectacular *spectacular*
fantástico(a) *fantastic*
internacional *international*
local *local*
nacional *national*
propio(a) *own, one's own*
vivo(a) *bright, lively*

Adverbios

anoche *last night*
ayer *yesterday*
durante *during*
esta mañana/tarde/noche *this morning / afternoon / evening*
menos *less*
recientemente *recently*

Otras palabras

¡Escúchame! *Listen to me!*

En preparación 7

7.1 Preterite of Regular Verbs

Providing and requesting information about past events

Spanish has two simple past tenses: the preterite and the imperfect. In this chapter you will study various uses of the preterite. Following are the preterite verb endings for regular verbs.

-AR Verb endings

yo	**-é**	nosotros(as)	**-amos**
tú	**-aste**	vosotros(as)	**-asteis**
Ud.	**-ó**	Uds.	**-aron**
él, ella	**-ó**	ellos, ellas	**-aron**

Encontrar

encontr**é**	encontr**amos**
encontr**aste**	encontr**asteis**
encontr**ó**	encontr**aron**

-ER, -IR Verb endings

yo	**-í**	nosotros(as)	**-imos**
tú	**-iste**	vosotros(as)	**-isteis**
Ud.	**-ió**	Uds.	**-ieron**
él, ella	**-ió**	ellos, ellas	**-ieron**

Vender		**Recibir**	
vend**í**	vend**imos**	recib**í**	recib**imos**
vend**iste**	vend**isteis**	recib**iste**	recib**isteis**
vend**ió**	vend**ieron**	recib**ió**	recib**ieron**

A. The preterite is used to describe an act that has already occurred; it focuses on the beginning, the end, or the completed aspect of an act. The preterite is translated in English as the simple past or as *did* + verb.

Encontré los boletos. { *I found the tickets.* / *I did find the tickets.* }

¿**Vendiste** el coche? { *You sold the car?* / *Did you sell the car?* }

B. Note that the first- and third-person singular endings of regular verbs *always* require a written accent in the preterite.

Regresé a eso de las once. *I returned at about 11:00.*
La policía lo **arrestó** anoche. *The police arrested him last night.*

C. Note also that the first-person plural endings of **-ar** and **-ir** verbs are identical to the present indicative endings. Context determines whether the verb is in the past, the present, or the future.

Mañana **jugamos** en Nueva York; ayer **jugamos** en Miami. *Tomorrow we play in New York; yesterday we played in Miami.*

D. All stem-changing **-ar** and **-er** verbs in the present tense are *regular* in the preterite. Stem-changing **-ir** verbs in the preterite will be discussed in **Capítulo 10.**

Encontraron el avión en las montañas.	*They found the plane in the mountains.*
¿**Entendiste** las noticias?	*Did you understand the news?*
Perdieron el campeonato, ¿verdad?	*They lost the championship, right?*

¡A practicar!

A. Noticias. Paula está leyéndole las noticias a su esposo mientras él prepara el desayuno. ¿Qué le dice ella? Al contestar, completa estas oraciones con el pretérito.

1. La policía ______________ (arrestar) al famoso asesino.
2. El presidente y su esposa ______________ (recibir) al presidente de Guatemala.
3. Unos niños ______________ (encontrar) un millón de dólares.
4. Los Cardenales ______________ (jugar) contra los Gigantes.
5. Una actriz ______________ (vender) sus diamantes.
6. Dos hombres ______________ (asesinar) a un policía.

B. Me interesan los detalles. El marido de Paula está muy interesado en lo que ella dice y pide más información. ¿Qué le pregunta a Paula?

1. ¿Dónde ______________ (encontrar) la policía al asesino?
2. ¿Cuándo ______________ (llegar) los representantes de Guatemala?
3. ¿Dónde ______________ (descubrir) los niños tanto dinero?
4. ¿Quiénes ______________ (ganar), los Cardenales o los Gigantes?
5. ¿Es la misma actriz que ______________ (dejar) a su esposo el mes pasado?
6. ¿Cómo ______________ (matar) ellos al policía?

7.2 Preterite of Verbs with Spelling Changes

Describing in past time

A. To maintain the consonant sound of the infinitive, verbs that end in **-car, -gar,** and **-zar** undergo a spelling change in the preterite. (These rules apply not only to verbs in the preterite but to verbs in any tense whenever the following circumstances occur.)

1. **-car: c** changes to **qu** in front of **e**
   sacar: sa**qué,** sacaste, sacó...
   buscar: bus**qué,** buscaste, buscó...
2. **-zar: z** changes to **c** in front of **e**
   empezar: empe**cé,** empezaste, empezó...
   comenzar: comen**cé,** comenzaste, comenzó...

3. **-gar: g** changes to **gu** in front of **e**
   llegar: lle**gu**é, llegaste, llegó...
   jugar: ju**gu**é, jugaste, jugó...

B. Whenever an unstressed **i** occurs between two vowels, it changes to **y**. Note that these verbs require a written accent in all persons except the third-person plural.

leer		creer		oír	
leí	leímos	creí	creímos	oí	oímos
leíste	leísteis	creíste	creísteis	oíste	oísteis
le**y**ó	le**y**eron	cre**y**ó	cre**y**eron	o**y**ó	o**y**eron
le**y**ó	le**y**eron	cre**y**ó	cre**y**eron	o**y**ó	o**y**eron

¡A practicar!

A. ¡Qué día! Ayer Angélica tuvo (*had*) un día terrible. ¿Qué pasó?

Ayer yo ______________ (empezar) el día con el pie izquierdo *(left foot)*. Cuando ______________ (comenzar) a preparar un café, ______________ (oír) sonar el teléfono. Era mi mamá. Ella ______________ (hablar) más de una hora. Luego ______________ (buscar) las llaves *(keys)* de mi auto pero no las ______________ (encontrar). Las ______________ (buscar) en todas partes pero sin suerte *(luck)*. Finalmente yo ______________ (decidir) tomar el autobús, pero ______________ (llegar) muy tarde a la parada. Yo ______________ (regresar) a casa y no ______________ (salir) el resto del día.

B. Norberto. Por lo general, Norberto lleva una vida muy aburrida. ¿Qué pasó ayer en su vida?

Ayer Norberto ______________ (llegar) tarde a clase. Después de clase ______________ (practicar) fútbol por dos horas. Cuando ______________ (volver) a casa, ______________ (preparar) la cena y ______________ (leer) el periódico. Por la noche no ______________ (empezar) a hacer su tarea hasta que ______________ (llegar) su amigo Ricardo. Norberto y Ricardo ______________ (estudiar) dos o tres horas. De repente *(Suddenly)*, Ricardo ______________ (oír) un ruido *(noise)*. Norberto ______________ (buscar) por todas partes pero no ______________ (encontrar) a nadie. ¡Parece que Ricardo tiene una imaginación muy activa!

7.3 Preterite of *ir, ser, decir,* and *hacer*

Narrating in past time

ir / ser		decir		hacer	
fui	fuimos	dije	dijimos	hice	hicimos
fuiste	fuisteis	dijiste	dijisteis	hiciste	hicisteis
fue	fueron	dijo	dijeron	hizo	hicieron
fue	fueron	dijo	dijeron	hizo	hicieron

A. The preterite forms of **ser** and **ir** are identical. Context will clarify the meaning.

Anoche **fuimos** a ver la película *Lo que el viento se llevó.*	*Last night we went to see the movie* Gone with the Wind.
Vivien Leigh **fue** la actriz principal.	*Vivien Leigh was the leading actress.*
Fuimos solos.	*We went alone.*

B. Note that these irregular verbs do not have written accents in the preterite.

¿Quién **hizo** eso?	*Who did that?*
Te **dije** que yo lo **hice.**	*I told you I did it.*

¡A practicar!

A. En busca de empleo. Completa el párrafo que sigue para saber qué pasó ayer cuando Martín tuvo una entrevista con el supervisor del periódico escolar.

Ayer yo ______________ (ir) a solicitar un trabajo al periódico de la universidad. Todos ______________ (ser) muy amables. El supervisor me ______________ (hacer) escribir una carta en la computadora y luego otras personas me ______________ (hacer) algunas preguntas más técnicas. Finalmente la secretaria me ______________ (decir) que me van a informar del resultado la semana próxima. Espero tener suerte.

B. Cumpleaños. Según Alicia, ¿cómo celebran el cumpleanos de Jaime?

Ayer ______________ (ser) el cumpleaños de Jaime. Jorge, su compañero de cuarto, ______________ (organizar) una fiesta para él. Marta y yo ______________ (ir) a la tienda para comprar champán. Carmen ______________ (hacer) un pastel delicioso. Isabel y Juana ______________ (hacer) unos sándwiches. Todos nosotros ______________ (ir) a la casa de Jorge y esperamos a Jaime. Cuando Jaime ______________ (llegar) todos ______________ (decir): «¡Felicitaciones!» La fiesta ______________ (ser) estupenda. Jaime ______________ (decir): «Es la mejor fiesta de cumpleaños de mi vida».

7.4 The Pronoun *se*: Special Use

Making announcements

In notices such as classified ads, placards, recipes, and signs on windows or walls, the pronoun **se** is employed in Spanish.

Se alquilan bicicletas.	*Bicycles for rent.*
Se necesita secretaria.	*Secretary wanted.*
Se habla inglés aquí.	*English spoken here.*
Se prohíbe estacionar.	*No parking.*

Note that the verb form following **se** is in the third-person singular when followed by a singular noun or infinitive **(secretaria, estacionar)** and in the third-person plural when it is followed by a plural noun **(bicicletas).**

¡A practicar!

A. Anuncios. Imagínate que tú trabajas en el departamento de anuncios clasificados en las oficinas de un periódico de tu ciudad. Prepara algunos anuncios.

Modelo vender / bicicleta nueva
Se vende bicicleta nueva.

1. ofrecer / buen puesto
2. vender / televisor en buen estado
3. buscar / persona competente
4. vender / casa grande
5. necesitar / dos mecánicos
6. desear / camarero competente

B. Ventas. Varios estudiantes están escribiendo anuncios clasificados para poner en el periódico escolar. ¿Qué dicen sus anuncios?

1. vender / libros usados
2. ofrecer / auto en buen estado
3. necesitar / alquilar casa cerca de la universidad
4. comprar / computadoras usadas
5. buscar / persona dinámica para trabajar con niños
6. reparar / bicicletas

CAPÍTULO 8

¡A comer!

Cultural Topics

- **¿Sabías que…?**
  Nombres de comidas en el Cono Sur
  El menú del día
- **Noticiero cultural**
  Lugar: *Chile: Retorno a la democracia*
  Gente: *Salvador Allende*
- **Lectura:** *Crem Helado*

Writing Strategies

- *Descripción de un evento*

Reading Strategies

- *Dar un vistazo*

En preparación

- 8.1 Indirect Object Nouns and Pronouns
- 8.2 The Verb **gustar**
- 8.3 Double Object Pronouns
- 8.4 Review of **ser** and **estar**
- 8.5 The Verb **dar**

In this chapter, you will learn how to …

- request a table at a restaurant.
- order a meal.
- describe your favorite foods.
- get a waiter's attention.

Mercado al aire libre, Santiago de Chile

Familia chilena: ¡A comer!

Restaurante en Santiago de Chile

Lo que ya sabes...

1. ¿Adónde vas para hacer las compras de comestibles (*groceries*)? ¿Vas a veces a los mercados al aire libre? ¿Por qué?
2. ¿Es la familia en la segunda foto como tu familia? ¿Por qué?
3. ¿De qué crees que está hablando esta familia? ¿Conversa mucho tu familia a la hora de comer? ¿De qué?
4. ¿Es el comer una actividad especial para ti o es simplemente algo necesario para alimentar el cuerpo? ¿Prefieres comer solo o en compañía? ¿Por qué?
5. ¿Con qué frecuencia comes en lugares que sirven «comida rápida»? ¿Crees que los lugares que sirven «comida rápida» son muy populares en los países latinos? ¿Por qué?

CHILE

¿Tienen una mesa reservada?

TAREA Antes de empezar este **Paso**, estudia **En preparación** 8.1 y 8.2 y haz por escrito los ejercicios de **¡A practicar!** También escucha **Paso 1 ¿Qué se dice...?** del Capítulo 8 en el CD del estudiante.

¿Eres buen observador?

Ahora, ¡a analizar!

1. ¿Cuáles son las ocho verduras en este jugo? ¿Cuántas puedes nombrar en inglés? ¿Cuáles no puedes nombrar?
2. ¿Cuáles son los ocho premios que se van a dar? ¿Quién o qué ha sido nominado para mejor actuación? ¿para mejor coloración? ¿mejor nutrición?
3. El «**Jugo de 8 Verduras**» tiene un paralelo en Estados Unidos. ¿Cuál es? ¿Lo tomas tú? ¿Te gusta?
4. ¿Por qué crees que dice que es «el auténtico»? ¿Por qué dice que está hecho con amor?
5. ¿Cuál es tu jugo de verdura favorito?

¿Qué se dice...?

Al llegar a un restaurante

¿Para cuántas personas es la reservación? ______________________________

¿A quién esperan? ______________________________

Más o menos, ¿qué hora es? ______________________________

DUEÑO ¿Dónde prefieren sentarse?

LOLA Por favor, una mesa cerca de la ventana.

DUEÑO ¿Les gusta esta mesa?

SRA. RÍOS Si es posible, la mesa del rincón, por favor.

DUEÑO Sí, cómo no. Les puedo preparar la mesa del rincón en seguida. Si son tan amables de esperarme un momento, por favor.

¿Sabías que... ?

Hay mucha variedad en los nombres de las comidas en distintas regiones de las Américas, por ejemplo, entre México y Centroamérica y los países del Cono Sur: Chile, Argentina, Uruguay y Paraguay.

Frutas y verduras	El Cono Sur	México y Centroamérica
avocado	palta	aguacate
beans	porotos	frijoles
string beans	porotos verdes	ejotes
chili pepper	ají	chile
corn	choclo	maíz
peach	melocotón	durazno
peanut	maní	cacahuate
peas	arvejas	chícharos
pineapple	ananá	piña
potato	patata	papa

Ahora, ¡a hablar!

A. ¡Nos gusta comer! A todos nos gusta comer, pero no nos gustan las mismas comidas a todos. Trabajando en parejas, pregúntense si les gustan estas comidas.

Modelo manzana

TÚ **¿Te gustan las manzanas?**
COMPAÑERO(A) **Sí, me gustan muchísimo.**

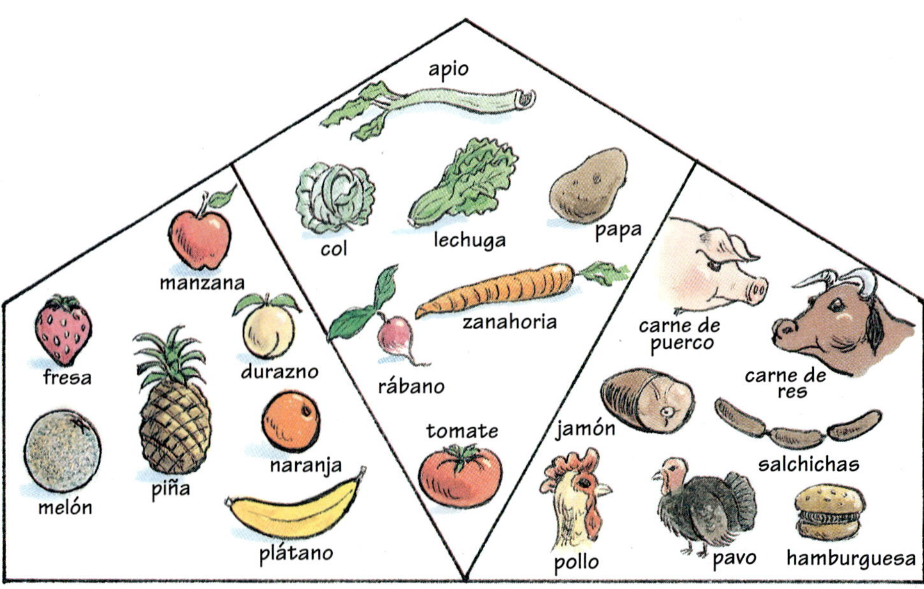

Frutas	Verduras	Carnes
fresa	apio	carne de puerco
manzana	col	carne de res
durazno	lechuga	jamón
melón	papas	salchicha
piña	rábanos	hamburguesa
plátano	tomate	pavo
naranja	zanahorias	pollo

B. Preferencias. No a todos nos gustan las mismas comidas. En grupos de cuatro, decidan a quiénes les gustan o no les gustan estas comidas e informen a la clase de los gustos del grupo.

Modelo **A todos nos gustan los huevos menos a (*nombre*).** o
A nadie *(no one)* le gustan los calamares.

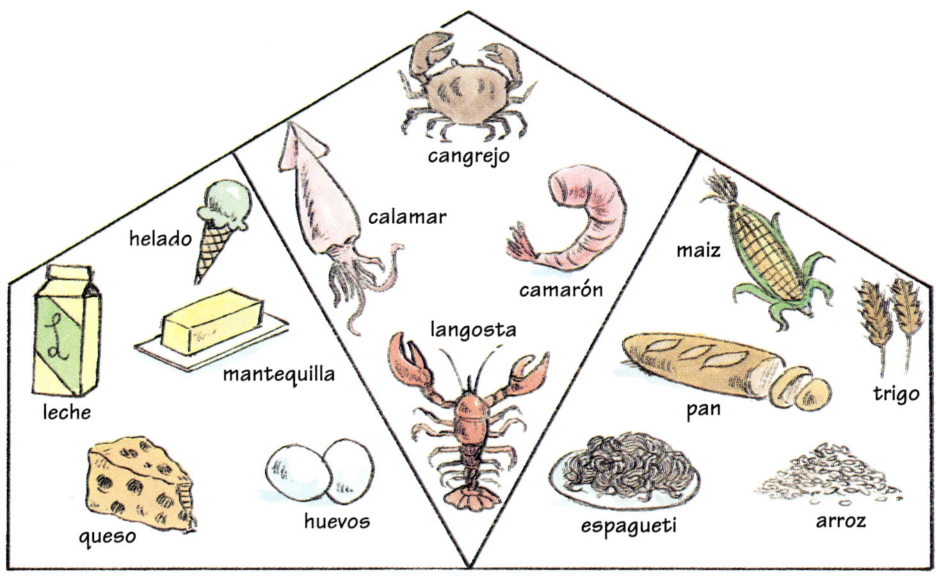

Productos lácteos y otros	Pescados y mariscos	Cereales y pastas
leche	cangrejo	maíz
helado	langosta	pan
mantequilla	camarón	trigo
queso	calamar	espagueti
huevos		arroz

C. Cumpleaños. Invitas a un(a) amigo(a) a tu casa para su cumpleaños. ¿Qué haces para esta persona?

Modelo preparar una fiesta
Le preparo una fiesta.

1. preparar una cena especial
2. hacer un pastel
3. servir la comida
4. decir «Feliz cumpleaños»
5. comprar algo especial
6. dar un abrazo y un beso
7. dar una tarjeta especial
8. servir el pastel

D. Promesas. Carmen y Roberto son novios y piensan casarse pronto. ¿Qué le pregunta Carmen a su futuro esposo? ¿Qué le pregunta él a ella? ¿Qué contesta cada uno?

Modelo preparar el desayuno

CARMEN **¿Vas a prepararme el desayuno todas las mañanas?**
ROBERTO **Sí, te voy a preparar el desayuno.** o
No, no te voy a preparar el desayuno.

Carmen a Roberto

1. traer flores de vez en cuando
2. servir el desayuno en la cama
3. hacer un postre especial los fines de semana
4. ¿... ?

Roberto a Carmen

5. decir siempre palabras de amor
6. hacer pan una vez a la semana
7. preparar comidas especiales
8. ¿... ?

Y ahora, ¡a conversar!

A. ¿Comes bien? Entrevista a un(a) compañero(a) sobre su dieta.

1. ¿Comes carne de res? ¿de puerco? ¿Cuántas veces por semana?
2. ¿Tomas leche? ¿Comes huevos? ¿Cuántas veces por semana?
3. ¿Tomas agua? ¿Cuántos vasos por día?
4. ¿Cuánto pescado comes a la semana? ¿Comes mariscos? ¿Cuánto pan comes generalmente?
5. ¿Cuántas verduras comes a la semana? ¿Tomas desayuno, almuerzo y cena todos los días?
6. En tu opinión, ¿comes bien? ¿mal? ¿Qué necesitas cambiar?

B. ¿Qué recomiendas? ¿Qué comidas les recomiendas a las siguientes personas?

Modelo Elena es vegetariana.
Le recomiendo comer frutas y vegetales.

1. Pablo está muy gordo.
2. Sancho está muy delgado.
3. Enrique tiene diabetes.

4. Victoria tiene el estómago *(stomach)* delicado.
5. Elena es vegetariana.
6. Elías hace mucho ejercicio y quema *(he burns up)* muchas calorías.

C. Hábitos culinarios. ¿Qué conexión hay entre lo que comes y cuándo, dónde y con quién comes? Para saberlo, completa este cuadro con información sobre lo que comiste ayer. Luego, comparen sus formularios en grupos de tres y contesten las preguntas que siguen.

	¿Qué comiste?	¿Dónde comiste?	¿Con quién comiste?	¿De qué hora a qué hora?
desayuno				
bocadillo *(snack)*				
almuerzo				
bocadillo				
cena				
bocadillo				

1. ¿Cuál es la comida más popular para el desayuno? ¿el almuerzo? ¿la cena? ¿los bocadillos *(snacks)*?
2. ¿Dónde y con quién comes con más frecuencia?
3. ¿Cuánto tiempo toman para comer el desayuno? ¿el almuerzo? ¿la cena?
4. ¿Qué hora es la más popular para comer un bocadillo?

¡Luz! ¡Cámara! ¡Acción!

A. Buenas noches, señores. Tú y un(a) amigo(a) llegan a un restaurante. Hay mucha gente pero ustedes tienen una reservación. Explíquenle al (a la) mesero(a) que tienen reservación y díganle dónde prefieren sentarse.

B. Bienvenidos. Tú y un(a) amigo(a) llegan a un restaurante. Tienen una reservación pero llegan media hora tarde y el (la) mesero(a) dice que ya no hay mesas. Dramaticen la situación en grupos de tres.

Estrategias para escuchar. *Linking is the combining of the final sound of one word with the beginning sound of the word that follows. Linking is common to all languages. In English, for example, "What did you eat?" becomes something similar to "Whadjeet?" when final and initial word sounds are linked. In Spanish, linking occurs most frequently under the following conditions.*

1. *Linking always occurs when a word ends with a vowel or consonant sound identical to the vowel or consonant sound that begins the following word.*

   L**a ha**mburgues**a a**yer fue la mejor.

   E**l l**imón y la**s z**anahorias son los ingredientes más importantes de la**s s**opas.

2. *Linking also occurs when a word ends with a vowel sound and the following word begins with a vowel sound.*

   Tengo much**a ha**mbre. ¿A cuánt**o e**st**á e**l bistec grande?

Understanding linking can help you when you are trying to distinguish individual words within a breath group. Now pay particular attention to linking as you listen to Claudio Téllez and Elena Contreras who have just arrived at their favorite restaurant in Santiago.

¿Un aperitivo? Claudio Téllez y Elena Contreras, dos estudiantes de la Universidad de Santiago, están celebrando su primer aniversario de ser novios en Canto del Agua, un nuevo restaurante en Santiago. Escucha su conversación, y luego indica quién hace lo siguiente: el mesero **(M),** Elena **(E)** o Claudio **(C).**

_______ 1. Los lleva a una mesa.

_______ 2. Pregunta si prefieren una mesa cerca de la ventana.

_______ 3. Ofrece un aperitivo.

_______ 4. Pide un vaso de agua.

_______ 5. Pide un vino tinto.

_______ 6. Los deja ver la carta.

_______ 7. Sugiere una ensalada de zanahorias.

_______ 8. Dice que no le gustan las zanahorias.

_______ 9. Recomienda una sopa de mariscos.

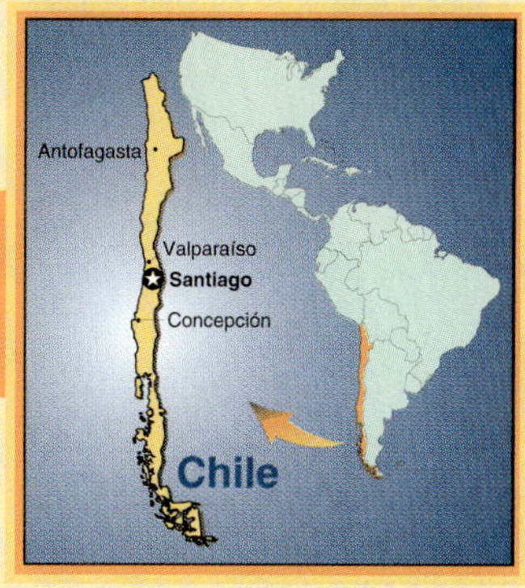

NOTICIERO CULTURAL

LUGAR... CHILE

Antes de empezar, dime...

1. ¿Cuál es el origen del nombre de tu ciudad? ¿de tu estado? ¿de los EE.UU.?
2. ¿Sabes cuántos americanos nativos había en el suroeste de los EE.UU. antes de comenzar los anglosajones a establecer colonias? Compara ese número con el número de americanos nativos que hay en el país ahora.
3. ¿Hay algún período en la historia de los EE.UU. en el que nuestro gobierno no fue democrático? ¿Alguna vez tomaron control del gobierno de los EE.UU. los militares del país?
4. ¿Hay algún producto exclusivo del cual depende la economía de los EE.UU.? ¿Es bueno o no depender de un sólo producto? ¿Por qué?

Patricio Aylwin, presidente de Chile

Chile: Retorno a la democracia

Chile está en el extremo suroeste de Sudamérica. Su nombre viene de la palabra *aymará chilli* que significa «confines de la Tierra», porque este país está prácticamente aislado del resto de Sudamérica por la cordillera de los Andes.

Cuando llegaron los españoles, en el territorio chileno habitaban alrededor de 500.000 indígenas: los *atacameños* y *diaguitas* en la zona norte y los *mapuches* (llamados *araucanos* por los españoles) en la zona sur. Durante el período de los españoles exterminaron a muchos indígenas. Actualmente la población indígena del país es un diez por ciento de la población total.

El Volcán Osorno

Chile se caracteriza en Latinoamérica por tener gobiernos constitucionales democráticos y civiles, excepto dos gobiernos militares. El más reciente ocurrió en 1973, cuando las fuerzas armadas, al mando del General Augusto Pinochet, tomaron el poder. El presidente socialista Salvador Allende murió durante el ataque al palacio presidencial. En 1990, asumió un presidente elegido democráticamente, Patricio Aylwin, después de perder Pinochet un referéndum en 1988.

Hasta la década de los 70 la economía de Chile dependió principalmente de un solo producto de exportación: cobre. Gracias a una exitosa estrategia económica durante la década de los 80, el país pasó a depender de las exportaciones de una variedad de productos agrícolas: frutas, verduras y vino, entre otros. Gracias a las diferencias de estaciones climáticas, el mercado de estos productos chilenos se extiende ahora no sólo a los EE.UU. y Europa sino a otros lugares del mundo.

Y ahora, dime...

Con un(a) compañero(a) de clase haz la siguiente comparación.

	CHILE	EE.UU.
1. Geografía		
2. Población indígena		
3. Sistema de gobierno		
4. Productos de exportación		

El español en otras disciplinas: Alimentación mundial

Frutas y verduras. El éxito *(success)* comercial llegó a Chile en la década de los 80, cuando se empezó a exportar una variedad de frutas y verduras a varios países, en particular a los EE.UU. y Europa. Con temporadas del año opuestas a las de los EE.UU. y Europa, una gran cantidad de las frutas y verduras que los estadounidenses y europeos compran en sus supermercados durante el invierno son importadas de Chile. ¿Qué productos exporta tu estado a otros países? ¿A qué países? Discutan estas preguntas en grupos de tres e informen a la clase de lo que decidieron.

Proyecto: Selecciona un país hispanohablante e investígalo en la enciclopedia para ver qué productos exporta. Prepara un breve informe para la clase sobre lo que encuentres.

¿Qué se les ofrece?

TAREA Antes de empezar este **Paso**, estudia **En preparación** 8.3 y haz por escrito los ejercicios de **¡A practicar!** También escucha el **Paso 2 ¿Qué se dice... ?** del Capítulo 8 en el CD del estudiante.

¿Eres buen observador?

Ahora, ¡a analizar!

1. ¿Para qué compañía es esta propaganda, para «Otra» o para «Casera»?
2. ¿Qué tipos de productos producen «Otra» y «Casera»? ¿Cuáles de esos productos usas tú? ¿Te gustan todos?
3. ¿Cuál es la diferencia entre los productos de «Otra» y los de «Casera»? ¿Es una diferencia importante? ¿Por qué?
4. Explica el título de este anuncio: «La sal está en otras». Explica también la expresión «Salud y conveniencia» en relación a este producto.
5. ¿Cuál usarías tú, «Otra» o «Casera»? ¿Por qué?

LA SAL ESTA EN OTRAS.

Y NO EN CASERA.

Porque Casera envasa una línea de productos sin sal añadida, para aquellos que cuidan de su salud: Salsa de tomate, habichuelas y garbanzos en agua. Todos con la calidad Casera, y sin sal añadida.

SALUD Y CONVENIENCIA CON CASERA SIN SAL.

Al pedir la comida

cóctel de camarones
pescado a la parrilla
bistec a la parrilla
carne asada
pescado frito
langosta
vaso de agua
pollo frito
calamares

CAMARERO ¿Y usted, señorita? A la orden.

LOLA Yo quisiera algo ligero. Tal vez un cóctel de camarones... o, mejor, la ensalada de mariscos.

CAMARERO Y a ustedes, señores, ¿qué les puedo servir?

SR. RÍOS Para mí, el pollo asado, por favor.

PEPE Y yo quisiera probar los camarones al ajillo.

SR. RÍOS Y para beber, una botella de vino blanco para nosotros dos y agua mineral con gas para todos.

CAMARERO A sus órdenes.

SR. RÍOS	(*Al hijo*) ¿Me pasas la sal y la pimienta, por favor? Y, camarero, tráigame un tenedor limpio.
SRA. RÍOS	Y un cuchillo para la mantequilla, por favor. Y una cuchara para el café.
LOLA	¡Ay! Me puede traer una servilleta limpia, por favor.
CAMARERO	¡Cómo no, señorita! Con mucho gusto.

¿Sabías que... ?

Muchos restaurantes europeos y latinoamericanos siempre ofrecen un menú del día. Éste generalmente incluye sopa, ensalada, plato principal, postre y bebida. Esta comida siempre se ofrece a buen precio pero no se permiten sustituciones.

Ahora, ¡a hablar!

A. ¿Qué les puedo servir? Tú y unos amigos están en Coco Loco, un restaurante chileno. Tú pides para todos. ¿Qué dices?

Modelo a mi amiga / pescado frito

A mi amiga Gloria le trae el pescado frito, por favor.

1. a mi padre / camarones
2. a mi madre / bistec
3. al bebé / leche
4. a mí / carne asada
5. a mis hijos / sopa de tomate
6. a todos / agua mineral

B. ¡Por favor! Ahora tú y todos tus amigos ya están comiendo. Pero tú necesitas que tus amigos te pasen varias cosas. ¿Qué les dices?

Modelo una amiga / la sal

Gloria, la sal… ¿me la pasas, por favor?

1. un amigo / el pan
2. una amiga / la cuchara
3. una amiga / la mantequilla
4. un amigo / la servilleta
5. un amigo / el tenedor
6. una amiga / la pimienta

C. Gustos particulares. El padre de Margarita es muy particular y siempre insiste en que le preparen la comida de cierta manera. ¿Cómo se la preparan?

Modelo el pescado / a la parrilla

Siempre se lo preparan a la parrilla.

1. los huevos / revueltos
2. los camarones / al ajillo
3. el bistec / a la parrilla
4. la carne / asada
5. el pollo / frito
6. las papas / asadas

D. ¡Le falta sabor! Trabajando en parejas, pregúntale a tu compañero(a) qué le pone a estas comidas cuando les falta sabor *(they lack flavor)*.

Modelo papas fritas

TÚ **¿Qué les pones a las papas fritas?**
COMPAÑERO(A) **Les pongo sal y salsa de tomate.**

1. huevos	mayonesa o mostaza
2. papas fritas	sal y pimienta
3. hamburguesa	azúcar (*sugar*) o leche
4. té	mantequilla o margarina
5. pescado frito	salsa picante (*hot sauce*)
6. pan francés	limón
	salsa de tomate

Y ahora, ¡a conversar!

A. Entrevista. ¿Cuáles son algunos de los hábitos de comer de tu compañero(a)? Pregúntale a tu compañero(a)...

1. a qué hora desayuna. ¿almuerza? ¿cena?
2. si le gustan los bocadillos. ¿Cuáles?
3. cuándo tiene más hambre.
4. cuándo come más.
5. si come cuando estudia. ¿en el trabajo? ¿viendo televisión?
6. si come platos congelados *(frozen)*. ¿Con qué frecuencia?

B. ¿Tu favorito? Indica tu favorito en cada categoría. Luego en grupos pequeños, prepárense para decirle a la clase si tienen algunos gustos en común.

1. Entremeses:
   a. cóctel de mariscos b. jamón c. queso d. otro: ________
2. Ensalada:
   a. de papas b. verde c. mixta d. otra: ________
3. Sopa de:
   a. pollo b. verduras c. pescado d. otra: ________
4. Plato principal:
   a. bistec b. pollo c. pescado d. otra: ________
5. Bebidas:
   a. café b. vino c. leche d. otra: ________
6. Postre:
   a. helado b. fruta c. pastel d. otro: ________

C. ¡Cuatro estrellas! Clasifica cinco restaurantes de la ciudad de tu universidad usando esta escala de cuatro estrellas. Compara los resultados con el resto de la clase.

Restaurante	Tipo de comida	Especialidad	Calidad	Servicio
	americana			
	mexicana			
	china			
	francesa			
	italiana			

★★★★ Excelente ★★★ Muy bueno ★★ Bueno ★ Aceptable

¡Luz! ¡Cámara! ¡Acción!

A. ¡Mozo! Tú y dos amigos(as) están en su restaurante favorito, estudiando el menú y tratando de decidir qué van a pedir. Dramaticen la situación con un(a) cuarto(a) amigo(a) que hará el papel de camarero(a).

B. ¡A comer! Tú y dos amigos(as) están comiendo en un restaurante pero cada uno necesita que los otros les pasen algunas cosas (la sal, un tenedor, etc.). También tienen que pedirle al (a la) mesero(a) que les traiga varias cosas. Dramaticen la situación.

¿Comprendes lo que se dice?

Estrategias para ver y escuchar. *In the previous* **Paso** *you learned that linking is the combining of the final sound of one word with the beginning sound of the word that follows. As you view this commercial, listen for the linking that takes place in the song. Later you will be asked to identify some of it in writing.*

¡Fundo El Clarín! ¿Te gustan las frutas? ¿Las comes durante todo el año? Al mirar este anuncio, piensa en tus frutas favoritas. Luego, en parejas, contesten las preguntas a continuación.

1. ¿Qué es el Fundo El Clarín?
2. ¿En qué país está el Fundo El Clarín?
3. ¿Por qué dice la fresa que es «deliciosa todo el verano, de diciembre hasta abril»? Explica tu respuesta.
4. A continuación están los primeros versos de la canción que canta la fresa. Indiquen cuáles vocales o consonantes finales se ligan con las vocales o consonantes iniciales.

> Soy la fresa que está más fresca
> que todas las demás,
> deliciosa todo el verano
> de diciembre hasta abril.

NOTICIERO CULTURAL

GENTE...

SALVADOR ALLENDE

Antes de empezar, dime...

Contesta estas preguntas sobre ex presidentes de los EE.UU.

1. Según tu opinión, ¿cuáles son los presidentes más importantes dentro de la historia de los EE.UU.?
2. ¿Qué presidentes de los EE.UU. fueron asesinados en el oficio de presidente?
3. ¿Hay presidentes de los EE.UU. que no pudieron terminar su gobierno debido a otras razones? Explica.

Salvador Allende

Salvador Allende (1908–1973)

Dentro de la historia de Chile, el presidente Salvador Allende forma parte de un capítulo importante.

Nació en Valparaíso y estudió medicina en la Universidad de Chile, donde cultivó sus ideas progresistas que comenzaron ya en la escuela secundaria. Fue uno de los fundadores del Partido Socialista de Chile, en 1933. Participó activamente en la vida política del país, como diputado y más tarde como senador. Después de varios intentos, en 1970 obtuvo la presidencia del país.

Allende quería intentar una transición pacífica al socialismo, incluyendo mejoras sociales para las clases menos favorecidas. Pero la nacionalización de las minas de cobre, el reparto de tierras a familias campesinas y otras medidas causaron el descontento de varios sectores de las clases media y alta del país como también de algunos países del extranjero, inclusive los EE.UU. A esto también contribuyeron el deterioro económico y la hiperinflación.

Allende murió el 11 de septiembre de 1973, durante el bombardeo a la casa de gobierno, La Moneda. Y como otros personajes de la historia, su muerte también es objeto de misterio y polémicas: para algunos fue suicidio, para otros, asesinato.

Por razones de censura política, Allende fue enterrado en una tumba anónima. Sólo en el año 1990, con la vuelta de la democracia, Salvador Allende recibió un homenaje nacional y sus restos fueron enterrados en el Cementerio General, en el panteón de su familia, ante la presencia de cientos de miles de chilenos que ofrecían su último tributo a la memoria de un gran hombre.

Y ahora, dime...

Usa un diagrama Venn como éste para hacer un paralelo entre la vida del presidente Salvador Allende y un presidente de los EE.UU. Tú decide el presidente que quieras comparar.

Salvador Allende	Ambos presidentes	{Nombre}
1.	1.	1.
2.	2.	2.
3.	3.	3.
4.	4.	4.
5.	5.	5.
...	...	...

Antes de escribir
Estrategias para escribir: Descripción de un evento

Orden cronológico. Las descripciones usualmente incluyen muchos detalles y se hacen siguiendo el orden cronológico del evento. Este tipo de descripción es importante particularmente en algunas profesiones como las de policías, abogados y periodistas.

La lista que sigue incluye todos los detalles de un incidente que ocurrió en Coco Loco, un restaurante chileno muy elegante. Ocurrió cuando el reportero de la serie *Los mejores restaurantes de Santiago* fue a cenar allí. El problema es que la lista no está en orden cronológico. Reorganízala, numerando las oraciones de 1 a 11, para que esté en el orden apropiado. Las primeras oraciones ya están indicadas.

______ a. El cocinero llamó al gerente.
______ b. El camarero se sorprendió y llamó al cocinero.
______ c. Mis amigos pidieron una ensalada y pescado frito.
__2__ d. Un camarero nos preguntó si teníamos una mesa reservada.
______ e. Yo pedí una sopa de mariscos.
__3__ f. Le dije que sí, a nombre de Gabriel Ramos.
______ g. Nos llevó a una mesa y nos dio la carta.
______ h. Yo dije:—¡Porque no tengo una cuchara!
______ i. Cuando me sirvieron la sopa, dije: —No la puedo comer.
__1__ j. Mis amigos y yo fuimos al restaurante a comer.
______ k. El gerente dijo:—No está fría, no está salada. ¿Por qué no se la puede comer?

Ahora, ¡a escribir!

A. Ahora, a precisar. El periódico estudiantil de tu universidad va a publicar una serie sobre los mejores restaurantes de la ciudad. Vas a contribuir con una descripción de tu restaurante favorito. Puedes describir algún incidente interesante que te ocurrió allí o tu última visita al restaurante. Empieza por hacer una lista de ideas sobre todo lo que puedes decir de tu restaurante favorito.

B. El primer borrador. Ahora prepara un primer borrador de tu artículo. Incluye la información en la lista de ideas que preparaste en la sección previa.

C. Ahora, a compartir. Comparte tu primer borrador con dos o tres compañeros. Comenta sobre el contenido y el estilo de la descripción de tus compañeros y escucha los comentarios de ellos sobre tu descripción. ¿Comunican bien? ¿Hay bastantes detalles o necesitan más? ¿Es lógica la organización del artículo?

D. El segundo borrador. Haz los cambios necesarios a partir de los comentarios de tus compañeros de clase. Luego prepara un segundo borrador.

E. A compartir, una vez más. Comparte tu segundo borrador con dos o tres compañeros. Esta vez comenta sobre errores de estructura, ortografía o puntuación. Concéntrate específicamente en el uso de complementos directos e indirectos. ¿Los usan cuando deben usarlos? ¿Los ponen frente al verbo o después de y conectados a infinitivos, mandatos o participios presentes? Indica todos los errores de los artículos de tus compañeros y luego decide si necesitas hacer cambios en tu artículo basado en los errores que ellos te indicaron a ti.

F. La versión final. Prepara la versión final de tu artículo y entrégalo. Escribe la versión final a máquina o en la computadora siguiendo el formato recomendado por tu instructor(a).

G. Ahora, a publicar. En grupos de seis, preparen una página titular que diga *Los mejores restaurantes de* (*su ciudad*) y guarden todas las descripciones allí. Decidan entre ustedes cuál de las descripciones va a convencer más al público y léansela a la clase.

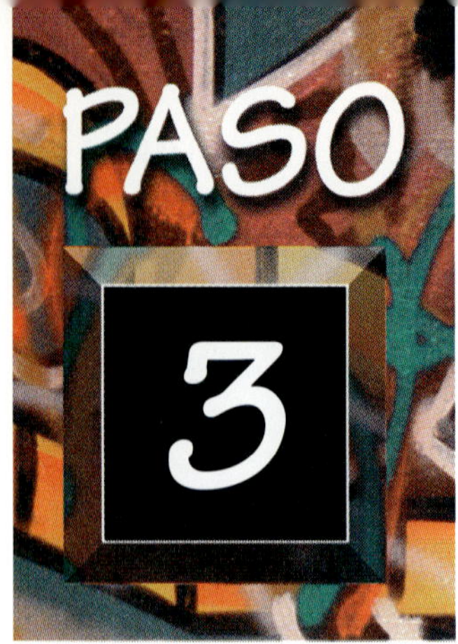

¡Para chuparse los dedos!

TAREA

Antes de empezar este **Paso**, estudia **En preparación** 8.4 y 8.5 y haz por escrito los ejercicios de **¡A practicar!** También escucha el **Paso 3 ¿Qué se dice... ?** del Capítulo 8 en el CD del estudiante.

¿Eres buen observador?

Ahora, ¡a analizar!

1. ¿Cuál es el propósito de este anuncio? ¿el producto principal?
2. ¿Qué vas a aprender a hacer si compras este producto?
3. ¿Dónde se puede comprar este producto?
4. Explica la expresión «Para chuparse los dedos». ¿Cuál es una expresión similar en inglés?
5. Explica la expresión «los manjares más exquisitos».

Al hablar de la comida

¿Quién haría estos comentarios: la madre (M) o la hija (H)?

______ 1. Soy alérgica a los mariscos.

______ 2. El pollo está buenísimo.

______ 3. No puedo comer postres; estoy a dieta.

______ 4. ¡Ay, no! Si tomo café no duermo.

El señor Ríos hace una señal con los dedos y llama al camarero diciendo:—¡Psst, psst! La cuenta, por favor— . Luego le pregunta a su señora:—¿Cuánto le doy de propina?— Ella dice que no necesita darle nada porque la propina va incluida en la cuenta.

Al salir del restaurante los Ríos se encuentran con sus amigos los Ordaz. La señora Ordaz le pregunta a la señora Ríos qué opina de la comida de este restaurante. La señora Ríos dice que la comida es pésima, la ensalada no está fresca y el pollo no tiene sabor. Pero Lola le cuenta a su amiga que las ensaladas son fresquísimas. También le recomienda el pescado, los mariscos y el pollo. —En efecto —dice —hasta los camareros, uno en particular, son exquisitos.

Ahora, ¡a hablar!

A. ¿Y para ti? Para ti, ¿cómo son los siguientes platos?

Modelo el cangrejo

Me gusta mucho. Es sabroso.

Vocabulario útil

pésimo	no muy bueno	bueno	buenísimo
sabroso	delicioso	exquisito	riquísimo

1. la sopa de pollo
2. la carne de puerco
3. el pollo
4. el pescado
5. el café
6. los calamares
7. el arroz
8. el apio

B. ¡Está riquísimo! ¿Qué le dice Lola al camarero cuando él le pregunta cómo está la comida?

Modelo vino / rico

El vino está riquísimo.

1. sopa / rica
2. pescado / sabroso
3. postre / bueno
4. calamares / sabrosos
5. langosta / fresca
6. arroz / bueno

C. ¡Hoy es una excepción! Hoy el señor Ríos está tomando el desayuno en la cafetería del edificio donde trabaja. ¿Qué opina de lo que le sirven?

Modelo el jugo de naranja

Generalmente es pésimo, pero hoy está riquísimo.

1. las frutas
2. el café con leche
3. los huevos revueltos
4. las salchichas
5. el pan
6. el bistec

D. Propinas. ¿Quiénes dan propinas a estas personas: tú, tus padres o todos ustedes?

Modelo el peluquero *(barber)*

Mi padre le da propina al peluquero.

1. taxistas
2. chófer de autobús
3. peluquera (*hairdresser*)
4. dependientes
5. camareros
6. niños que distribuyen el periódico

Y ahora, ¡a conversar!

A. Entrevístense. Entrevista a un(a) compañero(a) y luego que él (ella) te entreviste a ti.

1. ¿Eres alérgico(a) a algún tipo de comida? ¿Cuál?
2. ¿Sabes cocinar? ¿bien? ¿mal?
3. ¿Para quién te gusta cocinar?
4. ¿Qué platos prefieres preparar?
5. ¿Cuál es tu especialidad?
6. ¿Te gusta comer en restaurantes o prefieres comer en tu casa? ¿en la casa de tus padres?
7. ¿Te gusta comer en restaurantes de «comida rápida» (*fast food*)? ¿Por qué?

B. Adivinanzas. ¿Puedes identificar estas bebidas y comidas? Hazlo con dos o tres compañeros. Cuando terminen, díganle a su profesor(a).

1. un líquido caliente que se toma con cuchara
2. un líquido transparente que no tiene sabor
3. un líquido que se toma para no dormir
4. una fruta amarilla, larga, tropical
5. un líquido que los ingleses toman mucho
6. un marisco grande, rojo y bastante caro
7. un plato de lechuga y tomate

C. La Fonda. Tú y tu compañero(a) son dueños del restaurante La Fonda. Su restaurante es muy popular porque ofrece un menú nuevo cada semana. Ahora tienen que preparar el menú para la semana próxima. Incluyan por lo menos tres opciones en cada categoría.

La Fonda

Entremeses

__________ __________

__________ __________

Platos principales

__________ __________

__________ __________

__________ __________

Bebidas

__________ __________

__________ __________

Postres

__________ __________

__________ __________

D. ¿Son generosos? ¿Son generosos tus amigos? Pregúntales a quién le dan estas cosas y bajo qué circunstancias.

Modelo flores

TÚ **¿A quién le das flores y cuándo se las das?**

COMPAÑERO(A) **Se las doy a mi mamá el Día de las Madres.**

1. dinero
2. una sonrisa *(a smile)*
3. propina
4. tu amor
5. consejos
6. tu tiempo
7. cumplidos *(compliments)*
8. ¿... ?

¡Luz! ¡Cámara! ¡Acción!

A. ¡Exquisito(a)! Tú y tu mejor amigo(a) van a un restaurante a cenar. Resulta que su mesero(a) es guapísimo(a). Ustedes empiezan a competir por su atención. ¿Quién gana *(wins)?* Ustedes lo van a decidir en su dramatización.

B. ¡A cenar! Tus padres vienen a visitarte en la universidad, y tú y tu mejor amigo(a) los llevan a cenar a un restaurante elegante. Dramatiza la situación con cuatro compañeros. Decidan quién va a hacer el papel de mamá, papá, hijo(a), mejor amigo(a) y mesero(a). Cada persona debe pedir una comida completa y su camarero(a) debe contestar sus preguntas sobre varias opciones.

Antes de leer
Estrategias para leer: Dar un vistazo

A. Dar un vistazo. *In Chapter 5 you learned to scan by quickly reading a text. It is an especially useful strategy when reading reference texts such as indexes, road maps, dictionaries, classified ads, menus, or any article with long lists because their format allows the reader to concentrate on the information needed and to ignore extraneous material.*

Ahora da un vistazo al menú de Crem Helado en la página 310 y decide si estas declaraciones son ciertas o falsas. Si son falsas, corrígelas.

1. Los huevos con tocineta cuestan $330.
2. El plato más caro del menú es el de langostinos fritos.
3. El plato de pescado más barato del menú es la sopa de pescado.
4. Se puede pedir un sandwich y algo de tomar por menos de $225.
5. No sirven ensaladas en este restaurante.
6. Sirven jugos sólo con helado.
7. La hamburguesa más cara es la «Cow boy».
8. Las gaseosas no cuestan tanto como la leche.
9. La comida más barata del menú cuesta $120.
10. Sólo hay pastelitos de fresa y de limón.

B. Prepárate para leer. Consulta el menú de Crem Helado. Usa los subtítulos y el formato para contestar las preguntas que siguen.

1. A base del arte en el menú, ¿qué tipo de restaurante crees que es Crem Helado? ¿Por qué crees eso?
2. ¿Hay restaurantes en los Estados Unidos con menús similares? ¿Cuáles?
3. ¿Qué crees que es un «cow boy a caballo»? ¿una cerveza o «sifón»? ¿«tinto o aromática»? ¿«milo» caliente o frío? ¿«ponqué»? ¿«salpicón»?

Lectura

Crem Helado

SOPAS:	
Sopa de pescado	480
Crema de champiñones	420
Crema de tomate	370
Consomé de pollo	250
Consomé de pollo con huevo	300
CARNE, POLLO, PESCADO Y OTROS:	
Baby beef	800
Bistec de lomito	800
Steak de jamón	800
Pollo en canasta - 3 piezas	700
Pollo en canasta - especial	800
Róbalo frito	880
Langostinos fritos	1.550
Chuletas de cerdo ahumadas	880
Chili con carne y frijoles	490
EXQUISITAS HAMBURGUESAS DE PURA CARNE:	
Cow boy (Chili con carne)	600
Cow boy a caballo	660
Especial (Tomate-cebolla)	500
Especial a caballo	560
Con queso caliente "Cheeseburger"	430
Sencilla	320
Sencilla a caballo	380
SANDWICHES:	
Steak de lomito	550
De jamón ahumado (Especial)	550
Róbalo frito (Florida)	550
De pollo caliente	600
De pollo frío	500
De jamón	320
De jamón y queso (Combinado)	380
De queso	320
De atún	390
De huevo frito	250
Perro caliente	180
Cochinito silbando	330
Chili dog	330
PLATOS FRIOS:	
Con salchichas	500
Con jamón	520
PORCIONES ADICIONALES Y OTROS:	
2 huevos (A la orden)	120
2 huevos con jamón (A la orden)	330
2 huevos con tocineta (A la orden)	350
Porción de anillos de cebolla	170
Porción de papa a la francesa	170
Porción de papa chips	170
Porción de papa a la americana	180
Tostada, mermelada y mantequilla	130
BEBIDAS:	
Cervezas o Sifón	140
Cervezas lata	190
Gaseosas	40
Tinto o aromática	50
Café con leche	100
Milo caliente o frío	145
Té con limón o leche	100
Leche pasteurizada	100
Malteadas (Varios sabores)	240
POSTRES Y HELADOS:	
Copa de helado (Varios sabores)	190
Sundae con salsas (Varios sabores)	330
Peach melba	400
Banana split	400
Pastelitos (Fresa o Limón)	280
Pastelitos con helado (Fresa o Limón)	350
Ponqué de chocolate	280
Ponqué de chocolate con helado	350
Pie (Manzana o Piña)	280
Pie con helado (Manzana o Piña)	350
Rollo de helado con salsas (Varios sabores)	350
Jugos varios (con o sin leche)	210
Jugos varios con helado	280
Salpicón	280
Salpicón con helado	330

A ver si comprendiste

¡Decide, por favor! La familia Díaz Duque está en Crem Helado un domingo por la tarde. Cada miembro de la familia tiene gustos muy particulares. Decide qué va a pedir cada persona, cuánto les va a costar la comida y cuánta propina deben dejar.

El señor Díaz Duque: Siempre toma unas cervezas con la comida y normalmente tiene buen apetito. Él siempre pide una sopa, un plato de carne y de postre algo dulce con un cafecito.

La señora Díaz Duque: Siempre celebra una comida en un restaurante con algún plato de pescado. Y como siempre está a dieta, no toma nada con la comida.

La hija: Come muchísimo. A ella le encanta la comida gringa. Toma leche en grandes cantidades también. No le gustan los postres.

El hijo menor: Come poco y esto es problemático. Le gustan los perros calientes y a veces el pollo. Lo que sí le gusta mucho es todo lo que lleve fruta y helado.

Expand your horizons! *Let's travel through cyberspace to* ***Chile*** where . . .

- through the Internet, you can visit this prosperous South American country and witness the great economical activity taking place there.
- you can share the emotionally charged feelings Chileans have for their recent bouts with socialism and military dictatorship and the optimism with which they view the future.
- you can chat with Spanish-speaking university students in Santiago and other Chilean cities.
- you can visit Easter Island, one of the most unique places you will ever encounter, where the complete island is an open-air museum, home to a truly fascinating but unfortunately lost culture. There, the friendly Rapanui people and the amazing landscape formed by volcanic craters, lava formations, sandy beaches, brilliant blue water, and mysterious archaeological sites await you.

If you are a cyberspace browser, join us in **Viajemos por el ciberespacio a... Chile** by trying the following important addresses.

Universidad de Chile
http://www.uchile.cl

Universidad de Santiago de Chile
http://www.usach.cl/

Teatro Municipal de Santiago
http://www.municipal.cl/

Fundación Pablo Neruda
http://www.uchile.cl/WWW/NERUDA/Fundacion/fundacion.html

Periódicos:

Diario El Mercurio
http://www.mercurio.cl/

Diario La Época
http://www.reuna.cl/laepoca/

Diario Estrategia
http://www.reuna.cl/estrategia/

Because addresses are likely to change without notice, the following key words will guarantee that **Viajemos por el ciberespacio a... Chile** will get you to your desired destination.

Palabras clave

Chile
Importación-exportación Chile
Pablo Neruda
Salvador Allende
Turismo Chile
Santiago de Chile
Negocios de Chile
Gabriela Mistral
Teatro Municipal de Santiago
Isla de Pascua

http://www.hrwcollege.com

Vocabulario

Verduras

apio *celery*
col *(f.)* *cabbage*
lechuga *lettuce*
papa *potato*
tomate *(m.)* *tomato*
vegetal *(m.)* *vegetable*
verduras *greens, vegetables*
zanahoria *carrot*

Carnes y aves

bistec *steak*
carne *(f.)* *meat*
carne de puerco *pork*
carne de res *beef*
jamón *(m.)* *ham*
pavo *turkey*
pollo *chicken*
salchicha *sausage*

Mariscos y pescados

calamar *(m.)* *squid*
camarón *(m.)* *shrimp*
cangrejo *crab*
langosta *lobster*
marisco *seafood, shellfish*
pescado *fish*

Fruta

durazno *peach*
fresa *strawberry*
fruta *fruit*
manzana *apple*
melón *(m.)* *melon*
naranja *orange*
piña *pineapple*
plátano *banana*

Condimentos

azúcar *(m.)* *sugar*
mantequilla *butter*
mayonesa *mayonnaise*
mostaza *mustard*
pimienta *pepper*
sal *(f.)* *salt*
salsa *sauce*

Otras comidas

arroz *(m.)* *rice*
bocadillo *snack*
ensalada *salad*
entremés *(m.)* *appetizer*
flan *caramel custard*
helado *ice cream*
huevo *egg*
pan *(m.)* *bread*
postre *(m.)* *dessert*
sopa *soup*

Bebidas

jugo *juice*
vino blanco *white wine*
vino tinto *red wine*

En un restaurante

camarero(a) *waiter / waitress*
cuenta *bill*
en seguida *right away*
mesero(a) *waiter / waitress*
propina *tip*
reservación *reservation*

Preparación y condición de comidas

a la parrilla *grilled*
al ajillo *sautéed in garlic*
asado(a) *roasted*
delicioso(a) *delicious*
exquisito(a) *exquisite*
fresco(a) *fresh*
frito(a) *fried*
para chuparse los dedos *finger-licking good*
pésimo(a) *very bad*
revuelto *scrambled*
sabroso(a) *tasty, delicious*

Cubiertos

copa de vino *wineglass*
cuchara *spoon*
cuchillo *knife*
plato *plate, dish*
servilleta *napkin*
tenedor *(m.)* *fork*
vaso *glass*

Comidas principales

almuerzo *lunch*
cena *dinner*
desayuno *breakfast*

Verbos

contar (ue) *to count; to tell*
dar *to give*
desayunar *to eat breakfast*
gustar *to like*
opinar *to express an opinion*
quisiera *would like*
sugerir (ie, i) *to suggest*

En preparación 8

8.1 Indirect Object Nouns and Pronouns

Stating to whom and for whom people do things

A. You learned in **Capítulo 7** that direct objects answer the question *Who?* or *What?* in relation to the verb of the sentence. Indirect objects answer the questions *To whom / what?* or *For whom / what?* in relation to the verb.

Identify the direct and indirect objects in the following sentences. Note that in English the words *to* and *for* are often omitted. Check your answers below.*

1. She doesn't want to tell me the price.
2. No, I will not buy any more bones for your dog!
3. We'll write you a letter.
4. Give us the keys and we'll leave the door open for you.

Now identify the indirect objects in the following Spanish sentences. Check your answers below.†

1. Bueno, ¿van a traernos el menú, o no?
2. Me puedes invitar a tomar un café.
3. ¿Te sirvo algo más?
4. Voy a pedirte un aperitivo, ¿está bien?

B. Study this chart of indirect object pronouns in Spanish.

Indirect Object Pronouns

to me, for me	**me**	**nos**	*to us, for us*
to you, for you (fam.)	**te**	**os**	*to you, for you* (fam.)
to you, for you (formal) *to her, for her* *to him, for him*	**le**	**les**	*to you, for you* (formal) *to them, for them*

In Spanish, both the indirect object pronoun and the indirect object noun may be included in a sentence for *emphasis* or for *clarity* when using **le** or **les.** The preposition **a** always precedes the indirect object noun.

¿**Le** pido más café **al camarero?**	*Shall I ask the waiter for more coffee?*
A ustedes les voy a servir un postre muy especial.	*I'm going to serve you a very special dessert.*

*ANSWERS: **1.** D.O. = price, I.O. = me **2.** D.O. = bones, I.O. = dog **3.** D.O. = letter, I.O. = you **4.** D.O. = keys, door, I.O. = us, you

†ANSWERS: 1. **nos** 2. **Me** 3. **Te** 4. **te**

C. Like direct object pronouns, indirect object pronouns in Spanish are placed in front of conjugated verbs. They may also be attached to the end of infinitives and present participles. Note the placement of the object pronouns in the following sentences and indicate if a change in word order is possible.

Check your answers below.*

1. ¿Qué puedo servirle, señorita?
2. Les recomiendo la sopa de mariscos. ¡Está exquisita!
3. Están preparándonos algo muy especial.
4. ¿Nos puede traer una botella de vino tinto, por favor?

When object pronouns are used with affirmative commands, they also follow and are attached to the verb, which usually requires a written accent to keep the original stress of the verb.

Pregúntele si quiere café o té.	*Ask him / her if he / she wants coffee or tea.*
Dígame si quiere más.	*Tell me if you want more.*

¡A practicar!

A. En un restaurante chileno. La familia Carrillo está en su restaurante preferido. ¿Qué les sirve la camarera?

Modelo a nosotros / nachos
Nos sirve nachos.

1. a mí / camarones al ajillo
2. a mi papá / sopa de mariscos
3. a mis hermanos / pescado frito
4. a todos / té helado
5. a mi mamá / calamares fritos
6. a mis hermanas / ensalada de camarones

B. Regalos para todos. Ramón acaba de regresar de un viaje y trae regalos para todos sus familiares y amigos. ¿Qué les trae?

Modelo a Paloma / un reloj
A Paloma le trae un reloj.

1. a su mamá / una blusa de seda
2. a ti / un diccionario
3. a su papá / dos botellas de vino
4. a ustedes / camisetas
5. a mí / un libro de historia
6. a Pepe y a Paco / unos discos compactos

8.2 The Verb *gustar*

Talking about likes and dislikes

The verb **gustar** means *to be pleasing to* and is the Spanish equivalent of *to like.* The forms of **gustar** are *always preceded* by an indirect object pronoun.

Me gusta la sopa.	*I like soup. (Soup is pleasing to me.)*
No **me gustan** las hamburguesas.	*I don't like hamburgers. (Hamburgers are not pleasing to me.)*

*ANSWERS: 1. **¿Qué le puedo servir...?** 2. **No change.** 3. **Nos están preparando...** 4. **¿Puede traernos...?**

Notice that with the verb **gustar,** what or who is liked will always be the *subject* of the sentence; the person who does the liking will always be the *indirect object* of the sentence.

Identify the subjects and objects in the following examples. Check your answers below.*

1. Nos gusta el pescado.
2. ¿Le gustan los mariscos a usted?
3. Me gustan las ensaladas pero no me gustan con tomate.

If what is liked is an action (**cantar, leer, trabajar,** etc.) or a series of actions, the singular form of **gustar** is generally used.

Me **gusta** viajar.	*I like to travel.*
Nos **gusta** leer y salir a caminar.	*We like to read and to go for a walk.*

¡A practicar!

A. ¡Qué rico! ¿A todos les gusta la comida que les sirve la camarera?

Modelo a nosotros / mariscos
Nos gustan mucho los mariscos. o
No nos gustan.

1. a mí / carne de puerco
2. a nosotros / salchicha
3. a mi mejor amigo(a) / calamares
4. a mis compañeros(as) de cuarto / ensalada de zanahorias
5. a mi mamá / pescado frito
6. a mis hermanos / ensalada

B. Gustos. ¿Conoces los gustos de tus familiares y amigos? ¿Y qué no les gusta?

Modelo abuela: postre sí, verduras no
A mi abuela le gusta el postre. No le gustan las verduras.

1. hermano: jugar al fútbol sí, estudiar no
2. hermana: el verano sí, el invierno no
3. papá: el tomate sí, la lechuga no
4. mamá: las flores sí, el vino no
5. mejor amigo(a): lavar platos sí, cocinar no
6. ¿y a mí?: los postres sí, el pescado no

8.3 Double Object Pronouns

Referring indirectly to people and things

A. When both a direct and an indirect object pronoun are present in a sentence, a specific word order must be maintained. The two pronouns must always be together, with the indirect object pronoun preceding the direct object pronoun.

*ANSWERS: 1. S = **pescado,** I.O. = **nos** 2. S. = **mariscos,** I.O. = **le (a usted)** 3. S. = **ensaladas,** I.O. = **me**

Nothing may separate them. As with single object pronouns, the double object pronouns are placed directly in front of conjugated verbs, or after conjugated verbs and attached to infinitives, present participles, and affirmative commands.

Te lo recomiendo.	*I recommend it to you.*
Ella va a traér**noslo.**	*She is going to bring it to us.*

Remember that the first pronoun in the sentence is not always the subject of the verb. As subject pronouns are often not stated in Spanish, the first pronoun in a sentence may well be the object of the verb.

Translate the following sentences. Check your answers below.*

1. Prefiero la sopa del día, pero me la sirve caliente.
2. Y la cuenta, ¿cuándo nos la van a traer?
3. ¿Es posible? ¿Todavía están preparándotelo?
4. Sírvamelo con el postre, por favor.
5. ¿Puedes pasármelos, por favor?

B. Notice in examples 3, 4, and 5 above, that whenever two object pronouns are attached to a present participle, an affirmative command, or an infinitive, the original stress of the verb form is maintained by a written accent, which is always necessary.

Indicate where written accents need to be placed on the italicized verb forms of the following sentences. Check your answers below.†

1. *Sirvanosla* bien caliente, por favor.
2. ¿Piensas *devolvernoslo* esta tarde?
3. Por favor, *compramelo.*
4. ¿Están *preparandomelo* ahora mismo?

C. In Spanish, whenever two object pronouns beginning with the letter **"l"** occur together in a sentence, the indirect object pronoun **(le, les)** changes to **se.**

	lo		lo
~~le~~	la	~~les~~	la
se	los	**se**	los
	las		las

—El vino «Casillero del diablo» es exquisito.

—~~Les~~ lo recomiendo. → **Se** lo recomiendo.

—¿Vas a comprar dos botellas?

—Sí, voy a regalár~~le~~ las a papá. → Sí, voy a regalár**se**las a papá.

---

*ANSWERS: **1.** I prefer the soup of the day, but serve it to me hot **2.** And the bill, when are they going to bring it to us? **3.** Is it possible? They are still preparing it for you? **4.** Serve it to me with the dessert, please. **5.** Can you pass them to me, please?

---

†ANSWERS: 1. **Sírvanosla** 2. **devolvérnoslo** 3. **cómpramelo** 4. **preparándomelo**

Since **se** may refer to **le** or **les,** it is often necessary to use the preposition **a** plus a noun or prepositional pronoun to clarify its meaning.

Voy a regalár**se**las **a papá.**	*I'm going to give them to Dad.*
Se lo recomiendo **a ustedes.**	*I recommend it to you.*

¡A practicar!

A. Tenemos hambre. Tomás y sus amigos están en un café. ¿Qué les sirve el camarero?

Modelo servir arroz a Mariano
El camarero le sirve arroz a Mariano.
Se lo sirve a Mariano.

1. traer el menú a nosotros
2. traer los entremeses a Mariano y a Juanita
3. traer jamón a mí
4. servir vino blanco a nosotros
5. servir ensalada a Juanita
6. servir sopa de verduras a Mariano y a mí

B. ¡Ay, qué sabroso! La camarera conoce bien los gustos de cada miembro de la familia Gamboa. ¿A quiénes les recomienda estos platos?

Modelo el pescado frito / al señor Gamboa
Se lo recomienda al señor Gamboa.

1. la sopa de tomate / a papá y a mí
2. los calamares / a mi hermana mayor
3. los huevos fritos / a mi hermanito
4. el arroz blanco / a toda la familia
5. el arroz con pollo / a mí
6. el helado / a mi hermana menor

C. ¿Tantos regalos? Paquito, el hermanito de Ramón, quiere saber para quién son todos los regalos. ¿Qué le dice Ramón?

Modelo ¿Para quién son los discos compactos? ¿Para Paloma?
Sí, se los traigo a Paloma.

1. ¿Para quién es la blusa? ¿Para mamá?
2. ¿Para quién son las camisetas? ¿Para mí?
3. ¿Para quién son las dos botellas de vino? ¿Para papá?
4. ¿Para quién es el libro? ¿Para Miguel?
5. ¿Para quiénes son los chocolates? ¿Para nosotros?
6. ¿Para quién son los casetes? ¿Para ti?

8.4 Review of *ser* and *estar*

Describing, identifying, expressing origin, giving location, and indicating change

A. **Ser** is used

- with adjectives to describe physical attributes, personality, and inherent characteristics.
- to identify people or things.
- to express origin and nationality.
- to tell of what material things are made.
- to tell time.
- with impersonal expressions.

B. **Estar** is used

- with adjectives to describe temporal evaluation of states of being, behavior, and conditions.
- to indicate location.
- to form the progressive tense.

¡A practicar!

A. Nuevos amigos. Completa esta carta con la forma correcta de **ser** o **estar** para saber qué le escribe Rebecca a sus padres.

Queridos papás:

¿Cómo ______________ ustedes? Recibí su carta y yo ______________ muy contenta porque vienen a visitarme este domingo. Hace tres semanas que vivo en el nuevo apartamento y mis compañeras ______________ simpatiquísimas. Rosa ______________ alta y morena como yo; siempre nos preguntan si ______________ hermanas. Marina siempre ______________ ocupada porque ______________ una estudiante muy diligente. Toni, el hermano de Marina, y Rosa son novios. Él ______________ muy tímido y cuando nos visita siempre ______________ muy nervioso.

Me despido ahora porque Marina y Rosa me ______________ diciendo: —Rebecca, tú ______________ muy perezosa hoy. ¿Cuándo vas a preparar la comida?

Hasta pronto,
Rebecca

B. ¡En Santiago! Ahora Rebecca está en Chile durante las vacaciones de primavera. Completa su carta a una prima con la forma correcta de **ser** o **estar.**

Querida prima:

¿Cómo ______________ tú? Yo ______________ muy bien y ______________ contentísima aquí en Santiago. La gente aquí ______________ muy simpática.

Todos los chilenos ______________ amistosos y siempre dicen que ______________ impresionados con mi español. Ahora unos amigos y yo ______________ aprendiendo a hablar español muy bien. Todos nosotros ______________ estudiantes en un colegio privado.

¿Conoces a Julio Iglesias? Él ______________ aquí en Santiago ahora. Él ______________ el mejor cantante de España, en la opinión de muchos. No ______________ mi cantante favorito pero me gusta escucharlo.

Bueno, ya ______________ las 10:00 de la noche y yo ______________ muy cansada. Buenas noches y hasta pronto.

Rebecca

8.5 The Verb *dar*

Telling what people give

Dar

to give	
doy	**damos**
das	**dais**
da	**dan**

¡A practicar!

A. La propina. Tú y unos amigos salieron a cenar juntos esta noche. Ahora están decidiendo cuánto deben dejarle de propina al camarero. ¿Cuánto le da cada uno?

Modelo Antonio / $1,25

Antonio le da un dólar y veinticinco centavos.

1. Pablo / $1,00
2. María y Juan / $1,50
3. Yo / $1,50
4. Ana / $1,75
5. Carmen y Pedro / $1,25
6. En total, / ¿... ?

B. ¿Qué se dan? De acuerdo con los gustos de las siguientes personas, ¿qué regalos se dan para la Navidad o para su cumpleaños?

Modelo tú / papá

Yo le doy una pipa a papá. Él me da una camisa.

Vocabulario útil

unas vacaciones	un pastel	un teléfono	una corbata
un televisor	un vestido	unas flores	un suéter
un perro	un perfume	una pipa	una camisa

1. mamá / papá
2. tú / hermano(a)
3. tú y tus hermanos / abuelos
4. tú / mamá
5. tu mejor amigo(a) / tú
6. tú / ¿... ?

CAPÍTULO 9

Un día común y corriente

Cultural Topics

- **¿Sabías que…?**
  Popularity of small, family-owned businesses
- **Noticiero cultural**
  Lugar: *Estados Unidos: Los hispanos… ¿quiénes son?*
  Gente: *Sandra Cisneros, Jon Secada, Rosie Pérez*
- **Lectura:** *Poema: «Una pequeña gran victoria»*

Writing Strategies

- *Organización de una biografía*

Reading Strategies

- *Falta de puntuación en poesía*

En preparación

- 9.1 Weather Expressions
- 9.2 **Mucho** and **poco**
- 9.3 Reflexive Verbs
- 9.4 **Por** and **para:** A Second Look
- 9.5 Affirmative **tú** Commands

In this chapter, you will learn how to …

- *discuss the weather and how it affects you.*
- *describe your daily routine.*
- *ask for and give directions.*
- *describe a typical weekend.*

Calle Misión en San Francisco, California

Knowledge is Power, mural en Chicago del artista puertorriqueño Dzine.

Miami, o sea, la Pequeña Habana en la Florida

Lo que ya sabes...

1. ¿Es la calle Misión de San Francisco una calle típica de los EE.UU.? Explica tu respuesta.
2. En Miami hay un grupo de hispanos muy grande. ¿De dónde es la mayoría? ¿Qué otros grupos de hispanos se encuentran en Miami?
3. ¿Dónde hay una gran concentración de puertorriqueños en los EE.UU. continentales? ¿Por qué crees que seleccionan ir allí?
4. ¿Qué opinas del mural de Dzine *Knowledge is Power*? ¿Qué bandera (*flag*) aparece en el mural?

ESTADOS UNIDOS

Huy, ¡qué frío hace!

TAREA

Antes de empezar este **Paso**, estudia **En preparación** 9.1 y 9.2 y haz por escrito los ejercicios de **¡A practicar!** También escucha **Paso 1 ¿Qué se dice... ?** del Capítulo 9 en el CD del estudiante.

¿Eres buen observador?

Monitor Atmosférico

VERIFICACIÓN VEHICULAR

5 y 6

7 y 8

En esta semana

Nivel máximo diario del ozono.

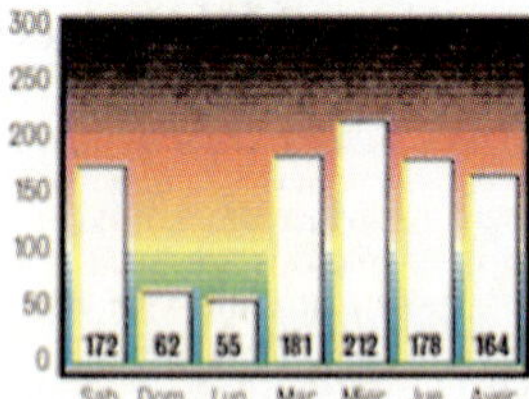

DOBLE NO CIRCULA

Lunes	5 y 6	3 y 4
Martes	7 y 8	1 y 2
Miércoles	3 y 4	9 y 0
Jueves	1 y 2	5 y 6
Viernes	9 y 0	7 y 8

Para los fines de semana se alternarán los autos de una contingencia a otra.

Sábado	Números nones
Domingo	Pares, cero y permisos

A Presión Alta B Presión Baja

Frentes: Tibio Estacionario Frío

Temperaturas: ◂Frío Caliente▸

Golfo de California — Golfo de México — Océano Pacífico

AIR ROUTING INTERNATIONAL CORPORATION

Norteamérica	MAX	MIN
Chicago	28	17
Dallas	38	26
Denver	35	16
Houston	37	26
Las Vegas	41	26
Los Angeles	27	18
Miami	32	26
Montreal	23	14
Nueva York	28	21
Orlando	33	24
San Antonio	38	25
San Diego	23	19
San Francisco	18	13
Toronto	26	14
Tucson	37	25
Vancouver	20	13
Washington D.C.	29	22
Latinoamérica		
Buenos Aires	22	8
Bogotá	19	8
Caracas	31	25
Guatemala	24	16
La Habana	30	23
Lima	18	11
Managua	32	23
Montevideo	21	10
Panamá	33	24
Quito	22	9
Rio de Janeiro	22	14
San José, C.R.	30	21
San Salvador	32	24
Santiago	15	11
Santo Domingo	33	25
Europa		
Amsterdam	23	14
Atenas	37	24
Berlin	26	17
Copenague	24	14
Estocolmo	21	14
Ginebra	29	16
Lisboa	30	17
Londres	23	10
Madrid	36	18
Moscú	24	12
Paris	26	14
Roma	30	21
Asia/Oceanía		
Hong Kong	31	26
Jerusalem	34	19
Sydney	20	12
Tokio	32	26

Ahora, ¡a analizar!

1. ¿Hace frío, calor o buen tiempo en la Cd. de México, de día? ¿de noche?
2. ¿Qué tiempo hace de día y de noche en Acapulco? ¿en Tijuana? ¿Cancún?
3. Hay sol con un poco de nubes en Del Río, Texas. Nombra otras ciudades donde hay sol con un poco de nubes.
4. Llueve en Cd. Juárez. ¿En cuál ciudad de los Estados Unidos llueve? ¿Llueve en la Cd. de México?
5. ¿En cuáles ciudades de Norteamérica hace frío de noche? ¿En cuáles ciudades de Latinoamérica hace frío de día y de noche?
6. ¿En cuál ciudad de Europa hace más calor de día? ¿más frío de noche? ¿En cuáles de Asia / Oceanía?

Al hablar del clima

_______ **1.** Phoenix		**a.**	Está nevando.
_______ **2.** Los Ángeles		**b.**	Hace frío y hay neblina.
_______ **3.** Las montañas		**c.**	Está nublado con llovizna.
_______ **4.** San Francisco		**d.**	Hace calor y está despejado.

En Cuba hoy hay sol pero en el este vemos que hace mucho viento y se acerca una tormenta impresionante. En la Florida ya está lloviendo bien fuerte.

Ahora, ¡a hablar!

A. ¿Qué tiempo hace? ¿Qué tiempo hace generalmente donde vives en los siguientes días de fiesta?

Modelo Navidad *(Christmas)*

En Navidad hace frío.

1. Pascua Florida *(Easter)*
2. Día de Acción de Gracias
3. Navidad
4. Día de San Valentín
5. el 4 de julio
6. Día de las Madres
7. el día de tu cumpleaños

B. Actividades. ¿Qué te gusta hacer bajo las siguientes condiciones?

Modelo está nevando

Cuando está nevando me gusta esquiar.

1. está lloviendo
2. hace mucho calor
3. hay neblina
4. hace viento
5. hace buen tiempo
6. hace mucho frío

C. ¿Cómo se siente? Describe el clima en los siguientes dibujos y explica cómo se sienten las personas en cada dibujo.

Modelo

Hace mucho sol y el señor tiene mucho calor.

1. 

2. 

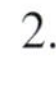

3. 

4. 

5. 

6. 

Y ahora, ¡a conversar!

A. Preferencias. Entrevista a un(a) compañero(a) para saber algo sobre sus preferencias.

1. ¿Qué tiempo prefieres?
2. ¿Cuál es tu estación favorita? ¿Por qué?
3. ¿Cuál es tu mes favorito? ¿Por qué?
4. ¿En qué estación es tu cumpleaños? ¿Qué tiempo hace generalmente en ese día?
5. ¿Cuáles son tus deportes favoritos para cada estación?

B. ¡Abrígate bien! ¿Qué ropa llevarías *(would you wear)* bajo estas condiciones?

Modelo Está nevando.
Llevaría un abrigo, una bufanda, guantes y botas.

Vocabulario útil

1. Está lloviendo.
2. Hace mucho calor y hay sol.
3. Hace calor pero el cielo está nublado y parece que va a llover.
4. Hace mucho viento y la temperatura está a 45 grados Fahrenheit.
5. Es un día estupendo. No hace ni frío ni calor.

C. Pronóstico. Mira el periódico y di cuál es el pronóstico para hoy, para mañana, para el fin de semana.

¡Luz! ¡Cámara! ¡Acción!

El pronóstico del día. Ustedes son locutores del Canal 31. En grupos de tres, prepárense para dar el pronóstico del día. Cada uno debe hacerlo sobre una de estas regiones de los Estados Unidos.

El noreste   La costa del oeste   El suroeste

¿Comprendes lo que se dice?

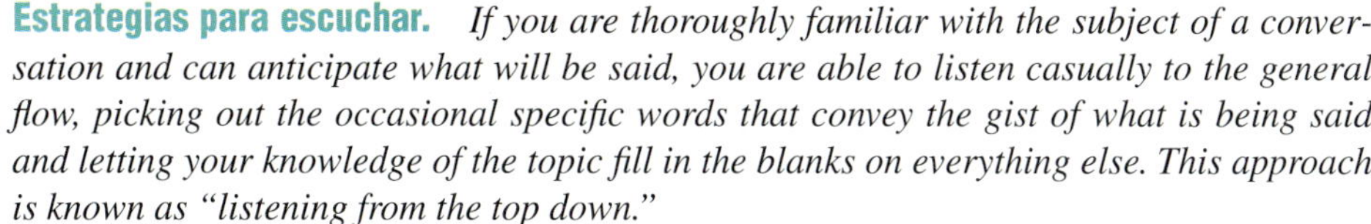

Estrategias para escuchar. *If you are thoroughly familiar with the subject of a conversation and can anticipate what will be said, you are able to listen casually to the general flow, picking out the occasional specific words that convey the gist of what is being said and letting your knowledge of the topic fill in the blanks on everything else. This approach is known as "listening from the top down."*

To familiarize yourself with San Francisco summer weather, read the following paragraph about a typical summer day in San Francisco, then "listen from the top down" to the forecast for July 15.

Si viajas a San Francisco en el verano vas a darte cuenta de que un día típico empieza con neblina, especialmente en los barrios junto a la costa. Más tarde, en la mañana, la neblina se disipa y la temperatura puede ser muy agradable bajo cielos despejados. No obstante, alrededor de las cuatro de la tarde la neblina reaparece, y ya por la noche puede hacer bastante frío y viento. En efecto, puede hacer tanto frío que Mark Twain dijo que nunca había sufrido un invierno tan horrible como el verano en San Francisco.

Pronóstico para San Francisco. Escucha el pronóstico del tiempo en San Francisco para el 15 de julio. Luego con un(a) compañero(a), decidan cómo la información en la columna **B** se combina con la información en la columna **A** según el pronóstico que escucharon.

	A	**B**
_______	1. 25° C	a. máximo del día
_______	2. brisas ligeras	b. termina la neblina
_______	3. 31° C	c. temperatura por la noche
_______	4. neblina	d. vientos fuertes
_______	5. media mañana	e. por la tarde
_______	6. al anochecer	f. en la costa

NOTICIERO CULTURAL

LUGAR... ESTADOS UNIDOS

Antes de empezar, dime...

Contesta estas preguntas para ver cuánto sabes de los hispanos en los EE.UU.

1. ¿De qué países viene la mayoría de los hispanos que hay en los EE.UU.?
2. ¿Qué porcentaje de la población de los EE.UU. representan los hispanos en este país?
3. ¿Qué influencia han tenido los hispanos en la cultura estadounidense? Da ejemplos.

Los hispanos... ¿quiénes son?

Se espera que para el año 2000 el número de hispanos en los EE.UU. llegará a un 20 por ciento. La mayoría de este grupo viene de México (63%), y el resto de Puerto Rico (12%), de Cuba (5%) y de otros países de Centroamérica y de Sudamérica. Vemos la influencia de

October 1996, HISPANIC BUSINESS Magazine

estos grupos en todos los aspectos de la vida en los EE.UU.: la arquitectura, la pintura, la literatura, la música, la cocina, la vestimenta, el cine y mucho más. Los hispanos estadounidenses participan activamente en estos tiempos en el arte, la política y las áreas más importantes del campo nacional. ¿Quién no reconoce los nombres de Henry Cisneros, Secretario de Vivienda y Desarrollo Urbano en el Gabinete del presidente Bill Clinton, o el de Antonia Novello, la Cirujana General de los EE.UU., o el de César Chávez, el gran líder del movimiento obrero?

Por otra parte, el impacto de novelistas como Rudy Anaya, Rolando Hinojosa Smith, Oscar Hijuelos y Sandra Cisneros, de poetas como Alurista, Lorna Dee Cervantes, Jorge Argueta y Francisco Alarcón y de dramaturgos como Luis Valdez y Gregorio Nava, se ha sentido tanto en los EE.UU. como en las Américas y Europa.

La música que han creado los hispanos es incomparable y ha alcanzado enorme popularidad. Todo el mundo conoce la canción *La Bamba* y la música de Gloria Estefan, Jon Secada y Rubén Blades, para nombrar a sólo tres cantantes hispanos. Los actores de origen hispano también están conquistando el público de los Estados Unidos en el cine y en la televisión. Junto a grandes estrellas como César Romero, Anthony Quinn, Rita Moreno, Raúl Julia y Andy García estamos viendo a nuevos actores hispanos como Edward James Olmos, Rosie Pérez, Antonio Banderas, Emilio Estévez, Daphne Zúniga, Cristina Saralegui, Jimmy Smits y muchos más.

Podemos seguir nombrando a hispanos sobresalientes en las artes visuales, la arquitectura, la moda, la cocina, los deportes y otros campos. Sólo en este último sobresalen nombres como Fernando Valenzuela, Nancy López, Chi Chi Rodríguez, José Canseco, Roberto Clemente, los Alomar, Lee Treviño, Tony López, Rudy Galinda, Mary Jo Fernández... La lista de hispanos profesionales en los deportes en este país parece no tener fin.

Los hispanos de los Estados Unidos son un grupo multicolor, cada vez con más confianza en un futuro mejor y en su capacidad de poder unir como en un arco iris *(rainbow)* cultural lo mejor de los Estados Unidos y Latinoamérica.

Y ahora, dime...

Con un(a) compañero(a) de clase haz la siguiente comparación. Indica cuál es la actividad o profesión que tienen estos famosos hispanos estadounidenses.

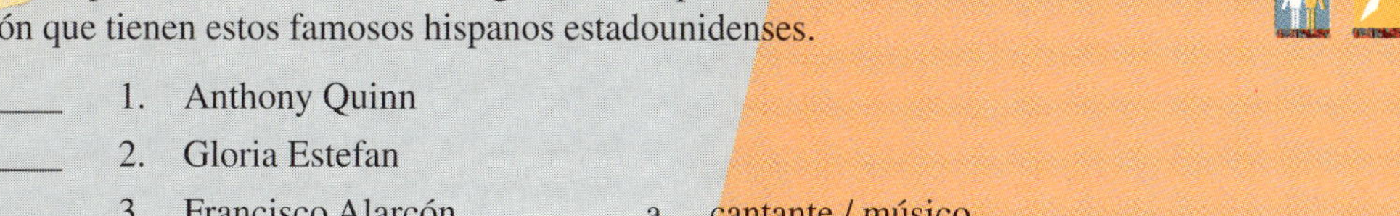

_______ 1.	Anthony Quinn		
_______ 2.	Gloria Estefan		
_______ 3.	Francisco Alarcón	a.	cantante / músico
_______ 4.	Sandra Cisneros	b.	político(a)
_______ 5.	Henry Cisneros	c.	poeta
_______ 6.	Rosie Pérez	d.	actor / actriz de televisión
_______ 7.	Fernando Valenzuela	e.	actor / actriz de cine
_______ 8.	Rolando Hinojosa Smith	f.	novelista
_______ 9.	César Chávez	g.	deportista
_______ 10.	Edward James Olmos		
_______ 11.	Rubén Blades		
_______ 12.	Cristina Saralegui		

El español en otras disciplinas: Meteorología

La temperatura: Así como en distintos países se hablan distintas lenguas, también con frecuencia se usan distintos sistemas para medir la temperatura. En los EE.UU. se usa el sistema Fahrenheit (grados Fahrenheit); en cambio, en los países hispanos se usa el sistema Celsius (grados centígrados). En el pronóstico de San Francisco que escuchaste en **¿Comprendes lo que se dice?,** dijeron que la temperatura máxima y mínima del día eran 31° y 25° C. Con un(a) compañero(a), usando una de estas fórmulas, conviertan esas temperaturas a grados Fahrenheit.

	Grados Fahrenheit	Grados Celsius
Temperatura exacta	(grado C x 1.8) + 32	$\frac{\text{grado F} - 32}{1.8}$
Temperatura aproximada (más fácil de calcular)	(grado C x 2) + 32	$\frac{\text{grado F} - 32}{2}$

Proyecto: Decide a qué país hispano te gustaría ir de vacaciones en el verano y a cuál durante el invierno a esquiar. ¿A qué ciudades irías en esos países? Busca en la enciclopedia la temperatura media en los países y dos de las ciudades que visitarías e informa a la clase de las temperaturas medias en centígrados y en Fahrenheit.

¡El sábado duermo hasta tarde!

TAREA

Antes de empezar este **Paso**, estudia **En preparación** 9.3 y haz por escrito los ejercicios de **¡A practicar!** También escucha **Paso 2 ¿Qué se dice...?** del Capítulo 9 en el CD del estudiante.

¿Eres buen observador?

PHILISHAVE

El rastrillo es cosa del pasado.

Si tú te afeitas con rastrillo... es que todavía no conoces la nueva línea de rasuradoras eléctricas Philishave de Philips; diseñadas para ti que además de ser práctico, quieres la mejor rasurada.
El sistema de 2 y 3 cabezas, rotatorio y de microcorte exclusivo de Philishave, te da una rasurada suave y continua. Con nuevos microsurcos que permiten obtener un afeitado más al ras.
Hay un modelo para cada quien.
Philishave de Philips, para ti que prefieres, la mejor rasurada.

Juntos hacemos tu vida mejor.

PHILIPS

Ahora, ¡a analizar!

1. ¿Qué crees que es un rastrillo? ¿Para qué se usa un rastrillo? ¿Por qué dice este anuncio que es cosa del pasado?
2. ¿Tú usas rastrillo o rasuradora (afeitadora) eléctrica? ¿Por qué?
3. ¿Cuál es la ventaja del sistema rotatorio de Philishave?
4. Explica la expresión «un afeitado más al ras».
5. ¿Hay sólo un modelo de Philishave? ¿Cómo lo sabes? Explica.
6. Explica la frase «Juntos hacemos tu vida mejor».

¿Qué se dice...?

Al describir la rutina diaria

_______ Se afeita.	_______ Se levanta.	_______ Se peina.
_______ Se despierta.	_______ Se ducha.	_______ Oye el despertador.

Generalmente no desayuna porque tiene prisa. Su primera clase es a las siete.

Después de las clases, Mario llega a casa muy cansado. Primero se quita el suéter y los pantalones y luego se pone unos vaqueros. Después de cenar se sienta a ver la tele un rato. Se acuesta a eso de las once y se duerme en seguida.

Ahora, ¡a hablar!

A. Un sábado típico. La rutina de Lupe y Ángel es diferente durante el fin de semana porque no trabajan. ¿Qué hacen los sábados por la mañana, según Ángel?

1. yo / levantarse / 9:00 / mañana
2. también / preparar / desayuno
3. mi esposa / quedarse / cama
4. después / ella / levantarse / y ducharse
5. nosotros / tomar / desayuno / juntos
6. después / nosotros / ir / centro comercial

B. Planes. Ángela tiene planes para este fin de semana. ¿Qué va a hacer?

Modelo levantarse tarde
Ella va a levantarse tarde. o
Ella se va a levantar tarde.

1. despertarse tarde
2. desayunar en la cama
3. bañarse muy tarde
4. no vestirse hasta las doce
5. ir de compras
6. salir con sus amigos
7. divertirse mucho
8. acostarse tarde

C. ¿Mi rutina? Tu compañero(a) quiere saber algo sobre tu rutina diaria. ¿Qué te pregunta y qué le contestas?

Modelo despertarse temprano todos los días

COMPAÑERO(A) **¿Te despiertas temprano todos los días?**
TÚ **Me despierto a las siete todos los días menos los sábados y domingos.**

1. levantarse en seguida
2. ir a clase todos los días
3. hacer la tarea todos los días
4. acostarse temprano
5. divertirse los fines de semana
6. estudiar en la biblioteca

D. Con frecuencia. ¿Con qué frecuencia a la semana haces lo siguiente?

Modelo despertarse temprano
Me despierto temprano cada día.

cada día ● tres veces ● dos veces ● una vez ● nunca

1. ducharse
2. peinarse
3. afeitarse
4. acostarse muy tarde
5. dormirse en la clase
6. sentarse a mirar la televisión
7. levantarse muy temprano

Y ahora, ¡a conversar!

A. ¿Qué haces tú? Hazle preguntas a un(a) compañero(a) de clase para saber cómo pasa el fin de semana.

Pregúntale...

1. a qué hora se acuesta los viernes por la noche. ¿los sábados? ¿los domingos?
2. a qué hora se levanta los domingos por la mañana. ¿Qué hace después de levantarse? ¿de ducharse?
3. si desayuna los sábados y domingos. ¿Qué come? ¿Quién le prepara el desayuno?
4. si generalmente se queda en casa los sábados y domingos o si sale con sus amigos. ¿Qué hace durante el día?
5. qué hace de noche.
6. ¿... ?

B. Consejos. Tú eres muy desorganizado(a) y un poco perezoso(a). Quieres cambiar pero no puedes. Ahora hablas con un(a) consejero(a). Dile tus problemas para que te dé consejos.

Modelo

TÚ **Me levanto muy tarde todos los días.**
CONSEJERO(A) **Debes levantarte más temprano. ¿A qué hora te acuestas?** etc.

C. Un buen fin de semana. Contesta las preguntas en la primera columna de este formulario y luego entrevista a dos compañeros(as) de clase para saber cuáles son sus actividades favoritas. Anota sus respuestas en las columnas apropiadas.

	Yo	Estudiante 1	Estudiante 2
¿Qué haces un sábado normal por la mañana?	1. 2. 3.	1. 2. 3.	1. 2. 3.
¿Qué haces un sábado normal durante el día?	1. 2. 3.	1. 2. 3.	1. 2. 3.
¿Y por la noche?	1. 2. 3.	1. 2. 3.	1. 2. 3.
¿Con quién prefieres estar un sábado por la noche?	1. 2. 3.	1. 2. 3.	1. 2. 3.
¿Cuáles son tus actividades favoritas de un domingo normal?	1. 2. 3.	1. 2. 3.	1. 2. 3.
¿Qué haces durante un fin de semana lluvioso?	1. 2. 3.	1. 2. 3.	1. 2. 3.
(Haz una pregunta original.)			

¡Luz! ¡Cámara! ¡Acción!

A. ¡De vacaciones! Tú estás de vacaciones con dos amigos en la Florida durante las vacaciones de primavera. Hace dos días que están allí y tú decides llamar a tus padres por teléfono. Ellos te hacen muchas preguntas acerca de tu rutina diaria y la de tus amigos. Dramatiza la situación con un(a) compañero(a), quien hará el papel de tu padre o madre.

B. ¡Dificilísimo! Tú estás tratando de convencer a un(a) amigo(a) de que la vida en tu universidad es más difícil que la vida en su universidad. Dramatiza esta situación con un(a) compañero(a). Comparen sus rutinas diarias al hacerlo.

¿Comprendes lo que se dice?

Estrategias para ver y escuchar. *In the previous* **Paso** *you learned that when you are very familiar with the message being communicated, you can anticipate what will be said and therefore understand much more easily. The same is true with what you see and hear on video. Use the knowledge you already have about the evils of cigarette smoking to anticipate what this message about smoking is likely to be. Then listen to the tape and see if you anticipated correctly.*

¿Fumar? Fumar es un placer pero ¿es bueno para la salud? Decide tú mientras ves y escuchas este anuncio irónico. Luego contesta las preguntas que siguen.

1. ¿Quién pagó por este anuncio? ¿Cuál es el mensaje del anuncio?
2. Este anuncio usa la ironía para comunicar un mensaje muy importante. La ironía está entre lo que la mujer dice de fumar en su canción, y cómo el fumar la ha afectado *(has affected her)* en realidad. Con un(a) compañero(a), usen este diagrama para señalar la ironía entre lo que la mujer dice en la canción y la realidad de la situación.

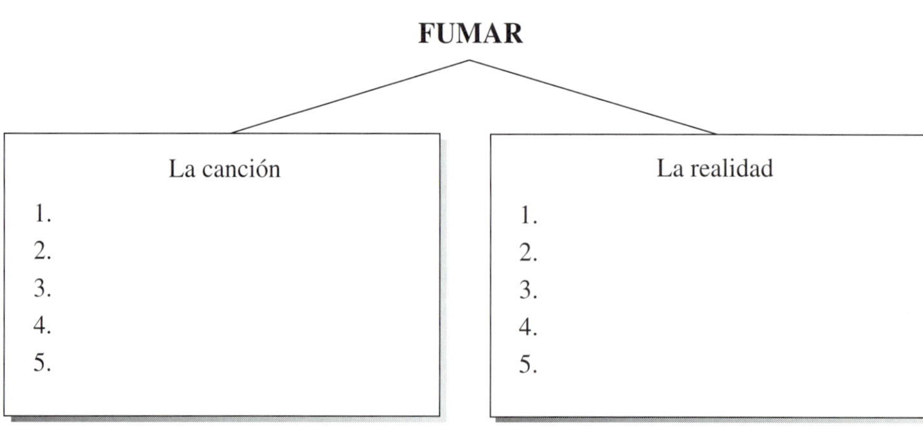

NOTICIERO CULTURAL

GENTE... SANDRA CISNEROS, JON SECADA Y ROSIE PÉREZ

Antes de empezar, dime...

Contesta estas preguntas sobre hispanos famosos de los EE.UU.

1. ¿Has leído *(Have you read)* un libro o cuento de un autor hispano de los EE.UU.? ¿Cuál? ¿Te gustó? ¿Por qué?
2. ¿Tienes algún cantante hispano favorito? ¿Quién es? ¿Cuál es tu disco favorito de este cantante?
3. ¿Quiénes son tus actores hispanos favoritos? ¿En que películas actuaron?

Tres hispanos sobresalientes en los EE.UU.

Sandra Cisneros

Esta poeta y cuentista chicana escribe en inglés pero incorpora mucho español a sus cuentos y poesía. Su libro *The House on Mango Street*, recibió el "American Book Award" en 1985. Como la mayoría de sus cuentos y poesía, este libro está lleno de humor de la realidad de una joven chicana. Ahora, Sandra vive en San Antonio, Texas.

Jon Secada

Este cantante cubanoamericano es bilingüe: graba sus canciones tanto en inglés como en español. Y no importa en qué lengua esté cantando, la venta de sus discos tiende siempre a llegar a más de un millón. Pero Jon Secada no sólo es cantante, sino también compositor y arreglista. Su música se destaca por su sensualidad y pasión.

Rosie Pérez

Esta joven actriz nació en un barrio puertorriqueño en Brooklyn. Es una mujer muy dedicada a su profesión. Sus primeras películas fueron *Do the Right Thing, White Men Can't Jump* y *Fearless.* A pesar de ser de una familia muy grande y de limitados recursos, Rosie Pérez ya ha demostrado que el éxito está al alcance de todos los que actúan con determinación y dedicación.

Y ahora, dime...

Usa un diagrama Venn como éste para comparar a uno de estos hispanos sobresalientes con tu escritor(a), cantante o actor (actriz) favorito(a).

Sandra Cisneros, Jon Secada o Rosie Pérez	Lo que tienen en común	Mi escritor, cantante o actor favorito
1.	1.	1.
2.	2.	2.
3.	3.	3.
4.	4.	4.
5.	5.	5.
. . .	. . .	. . .

¿Te gusta escribir?

Antes de escribir
Estrategias para escribir: Organización de una biografía

A. La biografía. Una biografía es la historia de la vida de una persona. Puede estar organizada en forma cronológica desde el nacimiento hasta los últimos años o puede estar organizada destacando algunas actividades importantes de la vida de la persona que se describe. Es fácil ver la organización de una biografía al ver las preguntas que la biografía contesta. Por ejemplo, la biografía de Sandra Cisneros (en la página 337) contesta las siguientes preguntas.

1. ¿Quién es Sandra Cisneros?
2. ¿Dónde vive?
3. ¿De qué nacionalidad es?
4. ¿Escribe en inglés o en español?
5. ¿Cuál es su obra más conocida?
6. ¿De qué se trata esta obra?

Trabajando con un(a) compañero(a), vuelvan a las breves biografías de Jon Secada y Rosie Pérez y preparen una lista de las preguntas que esas biografías contestan.

B. Preguntas clave. Ahora, con tu compañero(a) preparen una lista de preguntas que debe contestar una persona que esté pensando en escribir una biografía.

Ahora, ¡a escribir!

A. En preparación. Piensa en alguien sobre quien te gustaría escribir la biografía. Puede ser una persona de tu familia, un(a) cantante, escritor(a) o actor (actriz) del que te resulte interesante comunicar su historia a los demás estudiantes. Para empezar, basándote en las preguntas anteriores, escribe una lista de la información que vas a necesitar para escribir una biografía que destaque la cronología y las actividades importantes de la persona.

B. El primer borrador. Ahora usa toda esa información para formar la base de la historia. Tu biografía debe tener un formato similar al orden de las preguntas que hiciste: ***(Nombre)*** **nació el... , en... Vivió sus primeros años en... Estudió en... y en... Hizo sus estudios superiores en... Cuando terminó sus estudios se dedicó a... Después...**

C. Ahora, a compartir. Intercambia tu biografía con dos o tres compañeros. Comenta sobre el contenido y el estilo de las de tus compañeros y escucha los comentarios de ellos sobre tu biografía. Si hay errores de ortografía o de gramática, menciónalos.

D. Ahora, a revisar. Agrega a tu biografía la información que consideres necesaria, basada en los comentarios de tus compañeros. Revisa los errores de gramática, de puntuación y de ortografía.

E. La versión final. Escribe ahora la última versión de tu historia y entrégasela a tu profesor(a).

F. Ahora, a publicar. En grupos de cuatro o cinco lean las biografías que les dará su profesor(a) y decidan cuál es la más interesante. Descríbanla a la clase mencionando las actividades más importantes de la persona que aparece en ella.

¿Y cómo llegó?

TAREA Antes de empezar este **Paso**, estudia **En preparación** 9.4 y 9.5 y haz por escrito los ejercicios de **¡A practicar!** También escucha **Paso 3 ¿Qué se dice... ?** del Capítulo 9 en el CD del estudiante.

¿Eres buen observador?

CENTRO DE LA CIUDAD ● **Lugares de interés**

1. Centro histórico
2. Palacio de los Gobernadores
3. Capitolio
4. La iglesia y la casa más antigua de los EE.UU. continentales
5. La Catedral de San Francisco
6. Zapatería Robles
7. Museo de Bellas Artes
8. Supermercado Garduño
9. Librería El Lector
10. Café Paloma Blanca

Ahora, ¡a analizar!

1. Si en una zapatería se venden zapatos, ¿qué se vende en una frutería? ¿librería? ¿carnicería? ¿papelería? ¿perfumería? ¿tabaquería?
2. Si el Museo de Bellas Artes está a la izquierda del Palacio de los Gobernadores, ¿qué está a la derecha del Palacio de los Gobernadores?
3. ¿Dónde está el Centro Histórico, en frente o detrás del Palacio de los Gobernadores?
4. ¿Dónde está el Supermercado Garduño, en frente o detrás de la Librería El Lector? ¿y el Café Paloma Blanca?
5. ¿Está lejos o cerca del Capitolio, la iglesia más antigua de los EE.UU.? ¿y la casa más antigua? ¿la Catedral de San Francisco?
6. ¿Qué calle va alrededor de toda la ciudad?

¿Sabías que... ?

Por lo general el comercio en los países de habla española es muy especializado; los negocios se dedican a la venta de «un» artículo—de ahí la carnicería, panadería, pastelería, zapatería, mueblería *(furniture store)*, etc. Últimamente se han popularizado los centros comerciales, aunque cada negocio mantiene su independencia. Las tiendas grandes tales como «Sears» o «JC Penney» existen sólo en las grandes ciudades.

¿Qué se dice...?

Si deseas saber cómo llegar a...

1. ¿Adónde va Memo? ______________________
2. ¿Qué autobús debe tomar? ______________________
3. ¿Por dónde pasa el autobús? ______________________

MEMO ¿En qué calle debo bajarme?

PEPE Bájate en la parada que está al lado del Palacio, frente al Museo de Bellas Artes.

MARTA No, no. La parada está detrás del Palacio, en la calle Marcy.

MEMO Y de ahí, ¿para dónde sigo?

PEPE Sigue por la calle Lincoln a la calle San Francisco. Dobla a la izquierda y está a una cuadra y media.

MARTA Sigue derecho por esa calle. Queda en la esquina.

PEPE No. La catedral está a media cuadra. Hay que doblar a la derecha en la calle Catedral.

Ahora, ¡a hablar!

A. ¿Para qué? ¿Para qué van las siguientes personas a esos lugares?

Modelo Marcelo / zapatería

Marcelo va a la zapatería para comprar zapatos.

1. Adela / supermercado
2. Pamela / librería
3. Anselmo / biblioteca
4. Cristina / farmacia
5. Bárbara / panadería
6. Marcelo / papelería
7. Javier / carnicería
8. yo / ¿... ?

B. Transporte. ¿Qué medio de transporte prefieres para llegar a los siguientes lugares?

Modelo al supermercado

Para ir al supermercado prefiero viajar en coche.

Vocabulario útil:

avión	tren	barco	coche
a pie	moto	autobús	bicicleta

1. México
2. la universidad
3. Europa
4. Hawai
5. Canadá
6. la casa de mi mejor amigo(a)
7. visitar a mis padres

C. Opiniones. ¿Qué opinan tú, tu familia y tus amigos de los varios tipos de transporte?

Modelo **Para mí, es importante no manejar cansado.**

	Es importante tener un coche en buenas condiciones.
mis padres	Es peligroso viajar en avión.
yo	Es importante no manejar *(drive)* borracho.
toda mi familia	Es bueno poder manejar a los 16 años.
mis amigos	Es necesario tener límite de velocidad.
mis amigos y yo	Es mejor viajar de noche que de día.
	Es mejor viajar en tren que en coche.
	¿... ?

D. ¿Cómo llego? Ricardo quiere ir a la casa de Patricia pero no sabe dónde vive. ¿Qué le dice Patricia?

Modelo llamarme primero

Llámame primero.

1. venir a las 8:00
2. salir de tu casa a las 7:00
3. tomar el autobús 5
4. bajarte en la parada de la calle Bolívar
5. seguir derecho por esta calle
6. doblar a la izquierda
7. tocar la puerta
8. subir al tercer piso

Y ahora, ¡a conversar!

A. ¿Dónde queda? Imagínate que tu hermano(a) menor acaba de llegar a la universidad. Hoy tú vas a ayudarlo(la) a conocer el lugar. En este momento tú y tu hermano(a) están en tu cuarto. Dile cómo llegar a estos sitios.

Modelo la biblioteca
Para llegar a la biblioteca, sal por esa puerta y dobla a la izquierda. Sigue derecho hasta llegar a un edificio muy alto. Ése es.

1. la biblioteca
2. la piscina
3. el gimnasio
4. la librería
5. el edificio de la administración
6. el laboratorio de idiomas

B. Lugar misterioso. El instructor va a dibujar o va a traer un plano de la comunidad. Luego te va a dar instrucciones para llegar a un lugar misterioso. Sigue sus instrucciones y marca con una X el lugar misterioso.

C. Problemas anónimos. Comparte con la clase un problema que tienes (o uno imaginario). El resto de la clase va a darte consejos para solucionar el problema. Escribe tu problema en una hoja de papel pero no la firmes. Todos los problemas van a ser anónimos.

¡Luz! ¡Cámara! ¡Acción!

A. ¿Podría decirme... ? Tú vas caminando por tu ciudad cuando un(a) estudiante nuevo(a) te pide información sobre cómo llegar a algún lugar. Dramatiza la situación con tu compañero(a).

Estudiante	**Tú**
■ Pregúntale a una persona que camina por la calle si sabe dónde está la estación de policía.	■ Contesta que sí y explícale cómo llegar. Pídele que repita las instrucciones para ver si entendió bien.
■ Repite las instrucciones y dale las gracias. Luego pregúntale cómo se llega a algún otro lugar. Sé cortés.	■ Responde y deséale buena suerte.
■ Despídete.	

B. Ven a casa. Tú y un(a) amigo(a) necesitan estudiar juntos este fin de semana en un proyecto para la clase de biología. Tú invitas a tu amigo(a) a estudiar en tu casa pero él (ella) no sabe dónde vives. Tienes que explicarle cómo llegar a tu casa. Dramatiza la situación con un(a) compañero(a).

Antes de leer
Estrategias para leer: Falta de puntuación en la poesía

A. Falta de puntuación. La poesía tradicional se escribía con letras mayúsculas al empezar una oración y punto final al terminar la oración. Además, también usaba otra puntuación: comas, signos de interrogación o de exclamación, comillas *(quotation marks)*, etc. La poesía moderna con frecuencia no tiene puntuación. Algunos poetas como Francisco X. Alarcón, el poeta chicano que escribió el poema aquí incluido, nunca usa puntuación. Sin embargo, todos sus poemas tienen oraciones completas —sólo falta la puntuación. Si tienes dificultad en leer poesía, a veces sólo con ponerle la puntuación que falta, ayuda mucho a entender lo que dice.

B. Si falta, se la ponemos. En parejas, lean el poema y decidan dónde falta la puntuación. Pongan las letras mayúsculas que faltan, los puntos finales, las comas y las comillas. Si es necesario, escriban el poema de nuevo.

Lectura

El poeta Francisco Xavier Alarcón nació en Wilmington, California, pero se crió tanto en los EE.UU. como en México. Un verdadero bilingüe, se educó en escuelas primarias y secundarias en East Los Ángeles y en Guadalajara, México. Empezó sus estudios universitarios en East Los Ángeles College y terminó su licenciatura en la Universidad Estatal de California en Long Beach. Hizo sus estudios graduados en la Universidad de Stanford. Poeta, crítico y editor chicano, ha publicado nueve colecciones de poemas: *Tattoos* (1985); *Ya vas, Carnal* (1985); *Quake Poems* (1989); *Body in Flames / Cuerpo en llamas* (1990); *Loma Prieta* (1990); *Snake Poems* (1992); *Poemas zurdos* (1992); *No Golden Gate for Us* (1993). Actualmente es catedrático de la Universidad de California en Davis.

Una pequeña gran victoria
por Francisco X. Alarcón

esa noche de verano
mi hermana dijo
    no
ya nunca más
se iba a poner ella
a lavar los trastes° — platos

mi madre sólo
se le quedó viendo
quizás deseando
haberle dicho° — decir
lo mismo
a su propia madre

ella también había odiado° — no le gustaron
sus tareas de "mujer"
de cocinar limpiar siempre estar al tanto° — tener que servir
de sus seis hermanos
y su padre

un pequeño trueno° — sonido fuerte *(thunder)*
sacudió° la cocina — movió
cuando silenciosos
nosotros recorrimos
con los ojos la mesa
de cinco hermanos

el repentino aprieto° — momento incómodo
se deshizo cuando
mi padre se puso
un mandil° y abrió — delantal *(apron)*
la llave del agua
caliente en el fregadero° — lugar para lavar platos

A ver si comprendiste

Contesten estas preguntas en parejas.

1. ¿Dónde estaba el poeta esa «noche de verano»? ¿Quiénes estaban con él? ¿Cuántos eran en total?
2. ¿Quién dijo «no»? ¿A qué y a quiénes dijo «no»? ¿Por qué crees que dijo «no»?
3. ¿Cómo reaccionó la madre? ¿Por qué cree el poeta que su madre reaccionó de esa manera? ¿Estás de acuerdo *(in agreement)* con el poeta? ¿Por qué?
4. Explica por qué el poeta menciona a seis hermanos y luego a cinco hermanos. ¿Es un error?
5. ¿Cómo se solucionó el problema? ¿Quién lavó los platos al final? ¿Qué opinas tú de eso? ¿Podría ocurrir esta situación en tu familia? ¿Por qué?
6. Explica el título del poema.

Viajemos por el ciberespacio a... los EE.UU.

Expand your horizons! *Let's travel through cyberspace to the* ***United States*** *where...*

- in Santa Fe, New Mexico, you can visit the impressive Museum of International Folk Art.

(Ver página siguiente)

- you can visit the **Museo del Barrio** in New York, the only museum in the U.S. entirely devoted to the art and culture of Puerto Rico and Latin America.
- you can access valuable information on Latino holidays being celebrated in the United States.
- through the Internet, you can learn about famous Latinos such as Gloria Estefan, Chita Rivera, and many others.
- you can learn about famous historical Latino figures and Latino leaders today in the United States and elsewhere in the world.
- you can chat with Spanish-speaking people in the United States.

If you are a cyberspace browser, join us in **Viajemos por el ciberespacio a... los EE.UU.** by trying the following important addresses.

La comunidad hispana en EE.UU.
Latino Web
http://www.latinoweb.com/favision/

Hispanos Unidos
http://www.hispunidos.com/

Museo Internacional de Arte Popular, Santa Fe
http://www.state.nm.us/moifa/

Museo del Barrio
http://emall.com/exploreny/ny6.html

Eventos del mundo hispano
http://www.onr.com/sainta/spanish/eventos.html

Agencia de Noticias:
Telemundo
http://telemundo.hispanic.com/

Periódicos:
La opinión (San Antonio, TX)
http://www.laopinion.com/
La oferta review (San Jose, CA)
http://www.laoferta.com/
La prensa (San Diego)
http://www.electriciti.com/theplaza/

Gloria Estefan
http://www.music.sony.com/Music/ArtistInfo/GloriaEstefan.html

Because addresses are likely to change without notice, the following key words will guarantee that **Viajemos por el ciberespacio a... los EE.UU.** will get you to your desired destination.

Palabras clave

Estados Unidos	Cubanoamericanos
Hispanos	Puertorriqueños
Hispanos famosos	Museo del Barrio
Hispanos Unidos	Santa Fe, New Mexico
Latinos	Música Latina
Chicanos	Gloria Estefan

http://www.hrwcollege.com

Clima

centígrados *centigrade*
cielo *sky*
clima ***(m.)*** *climate*
congelado(a) *frozen*
empapado(a) *soaking wet*
estar despejado *to have clear skies*
estar nublado *to be cloudy*
grado *degree*
hacer buen tiempo *to have good weather*
hacer calor *to be hot*
hacer frío *to be cold*
hacer viento *to be windy*
hay sol *it is sunny*
llover (ue) *to rain*
lloviznar *to drizzle, rain lightly*
lluvia *rain*
lluvioso(a) *rainy*
neblina *fog*
nevar (ie) *to snow*
nieve ***(f.)*** *snow*
pronóstico *forecast*
temperatura *temperature*
tiempo *weather*
tormenta *storm*

Ropa

abrigo *coat*
bufanda *scarf*
guantes ***(m. pl.)*** *gloves*
paraguas ***(m. sing. or pl.)*** *umbrella*
traje de baño ***(m.)*** *swimsuit*
vaqueros ***(m. pl.)*** *blue jeans*

Profesiones

actor ***(m.)*** *actor*
actriz ***(f.)*** *actress*
cantante ***(m./f.)*** *singer*
deportista ***(m./f.)*** *athlete*
músico ***(m./f.)*** *musician*
novelista ***(m./f.)*** *novelist*
poeta ***(m./f.)*** *poet*
político ***(m./f.)*** *politician*

Lugares

calle principal ***(f.)*** *main street*
carnicería *butcher shop*
escuela *school*
esquina *corner*
farmacia *pharmacy*
frontera *border*
panadería *bakery*
papelería *stationery store*
pastelería *pastry shop*
zapatería *shoe store*

Transporte

a pie *on foot, walking*
barco *boat*
moto ***(f.)*** *motorcycle*
tren *train*

Puntos cardinales

este *east*
norte *north*
oeste *west*
sur *south*

Rutina diaria

acostarse (ue) *to go to bed*
afeitarse *to shave*
bajarse *to get off; to get down*
bañarse *to bathe*
despertarse (ie) *to wake up*
divertirse (ie) *to have a good time, enjoy oneself*
dormirse (ue) *to fall asleep*
ducharse *to shower, take a shower*
levantarse *to get up*
peinarse *to comb*
quitarse *to take off*
sentarse (ie) *to sit down*
vestirse (i) *to dress, get dressed*

Otros verbos

contestar *to answer*
cortarse *to cut oneself*
doblar *to turn*
preguntar *to ask*
quedarse *to stay; to fit*
repetir (i) *to repeat*
seguir (i) *to continue; to follow*
subir *to go up*
sudar *to perspire, sweat*

Adverbios

al rato *in a short while*
aproximadamente *approximately*
continuamente *continuously*
derecho *straight (ahead)*
en seguida *immediately, at once*
lentamente *slowly*
poco *little*
todo derecho *straight ahead*

Adjetivos

derecho(a) *right*
izquierdo(a) *left*
peligroso(a) *dangerous*
siguiente ***(m./f.)*** *following, next*

Palabras útiles

buena suerte ***(f.)*** *good luck*
despertador ***(m.)*** *alarm clock*
ni… ni *neither . . . nor*
población ***(f.)*** *population*
porcentaje ***(m.)*** *percentage*

En preparación 9

9.1 Weather Expressions

Talking about the weather

A. In Spanish, **hacer, estar,** and the verb form **hay** are commonly used to describe weather conditions.

¿Qué tiempo **hace** hoy?	*What's the weather like today?*
Hace mucho frío.	*It's very cold.*
Sí, pero no **hace** viento.	*Yes, but it's not windy.*
Está lloviendo	*It's raining.*
En el norte **está** nevando.	*In the north it's snowing.*
¿Hay neblina hoy?	*Is there fog today?*
No, pero **hay** mucha contaminación.	*No, but there is a lot of pollution (smog).*

B. The verb **tener** is used to describe how a person feels as a result of the weather conditions.

¿No **tienes** frío?	*Aren't you cold?*
No, en realidad, **tengo** mucho calor.	*No, actually, I'm very hot.*

C. The verb **estar** can also be used to describe a person's condition as a result of the weather.

Estoy congelado.	*I'm frozen.*
Están sudando.	*They are perspiring/sweating.*
Estamos empapados.	*We are soaking wet.*

¡A practicar!

A. ¿Qué tiempo hace? Unos amigos quieren saber qué tiempo hace en diferentes partes de los Estados Unidos. ¿Qué les dices tú?

1. verano en Phoenix, Arizona
2. invierno en Buffalo, Nueva York
3. primavera en Des Moines, Iowa
4. otoño en Boston, Massachusetts
5. todo el año en Chicago, Illinois
6. todo el año en Seattle, Washington

B. Justamente lo opuesto. Y veamos ahora qué tiempo hace en diferentes lugares del mundo, en las siguientes fechas.

1. la Navidad en San Francisco
2. la Navidad en Buenos Aires

3. el 4 de julio en California
4. el 4 de julio en Alaska
5. el Año Nuevo en París
6. el Año Nuevo en Santiago de Chile

9.2 *Mucho* and *poco*

Expressing indefinite quantity

A. **Mucho** and **poco** may describe a noun or a verb. When the former is the case, **mucho** and **poco** act as adjectives and must agree in number and gender with what is being described.

Hay **pocos** carros pero **mucha** contaminación.	*There are few cars but a lot of pollution.*
Hay **mucha** nieve pero hace **poco** frío.	*There is a lot of snow, but it's not very cold.*

B. When **mucho** and **poco** modify a verb, they are adverbs and do not vary in form.

Nieva **mucho** en el invierno.	*It snows a lot in the winter.*
Llueve **poco** aquí en el verano.	*It rains very little here in the summer.*

C. **Muy** is never used to modify **mucho.** Use the word **muchísimo** instead.

Hay **muy poca** nieve pero **muchísima** lluvia.	*There is very little snow but a lot of rain.*

¡A practicar!

A. Así es mi vida. Completa el párrafo con **mucho** o **poco** según tu propio *(your own)* estilo de vida.

Yo tengo ______________ amigas y ______________ amigos y por eso salgo ______________. Este semestre estudio ______________ porque tengo ______________ clases. Trabajo ______________ y gano *(earn)* ______________ dinero. Tengo ______________ tiempo libre. En mi tiempo libre practico ______________ deportes y miro ______________ la televisión. En mi ciudad hay ______________ cosas que hacer.

B. Problemas de un estudiante. ¿Cómo se prepara este estudiante para empezar las clases, después de las vacaciones de verano? Para saberlo, completa el párrafo con **mucho** o **poco.**

El semestre empezó esta semana y yo tuve que comprar ______________ libros. ¡Ay, qué caros son! Por eso, ahora yo tengo muy ______________ dinero. ¡Soy pobre! Además, tengo ______________ clases, pero ______________ energía. Debo organizar mi vida. Necesito trabajar ______________ horas y pasar ______________ tiempo en la biblioteca. Este semestre voy a tener ______________ tarea y ______________ tiempo. ¡Qué horror!

9.3 Reflexive Verbs

Talking about what people do for themselves

Lavarse

to wash			
I wash (myself)	**me** lavo	**nos** lavamos	*we wash (ourselves)*
you wash (yourself) *you wash (yourself)*	**te** lavas **se** lava	**os** laváis **se** lavan	*you wash (yourselves)* *you wash (yourselves)*
he/she/it washes (himself/herself/itself)	**se** lava	**se** lavan	*they wash (themselves)*

A. A verb is called *reflexive* when the subject does the action to or for himself, herself, themselves, etc.; that is, when the subject receives the action of the verb. A reflexive pronoun always accompanies such a verb; it agrees in person and number with the subject of the verb. Reflexive pronouns precede a conjugated verb.

Los niños **se bañan** de noche. — *The children bathe (themselves) at night.*

Yo siempre **me acuesto** a las once. — *I always go to bed at eleven.*

B. Reflexive verbs appear in vocabulary lists with the reflexive pronoun **-se** attached to the infinitive ending. The following is a list of frequently used reflexive verbs. Some of these verbs have been used in previous chapters nonreflexively.

acostarse (ue)	*to go to bed*	levantarse	*to get up; to stand up*
afeitarse	*to shave*	llamarse	*to be named, be called*
bañarse	*to take a bath, bathe*	peinarse	*to comb one's hair*
despertarse (ie)	*to wake up*	ponerse	*to put on* (clothing)
divertirse (ie)	*to have a good time, enjoy oneself*	quitarse	*to take off* (clothing)
dormirse (ue)	*to fall asleep*	sentarse (ie)	*to sit down*
ducharse	*to shower, take a shower*	sentirse (ie)	*to feel*
lavarse	*to wash oneself*	vestirse (i)	*to get dressed*

The reflexive pronoun is necessary only when the subject does something to or for itself.

Mamá **se despierta** primero y luego **despierta** a los niños. — *Mother wakes up first and then wakes up the children.*

Primero **me baño** y luego **baño** a los niños. — *First I bathe, and then I bathe the children.*

C. Reflexive pronouns, like direct and indirect object pronouns, are always placed directly in front of conjugated verbs. They are attached to the end of infinitives, present participles, and affirmative commands. As with object pronouns, a written accent is often necessary to keep the original stress of infinitives, present participles, and affirmative commands when reflexive pronouns are attached.

Siempre **me** afeito antes de ducharme.	*I always shave before taking a shower.*
No vamos a levantar**nos** hasta mediodía.	*We're not going to get up until noon.*
Los jóvenes están divirtiéndo**se** muchísimo.	*The young people are enjoying themselves very much.*
Quíta**te** la ropa y acuésta**te** en seguida.	*Take your clothes off and go to bed right away.*

¡A practicar!

A. Todos los días... ¿Cuál es la rutina en casa de los Chávez según Marta, la hija mayor?

1. Yo ______________ (levantarse) a las 6:30.
2. Yo ______________ (ducharse) rápidamente pero no ______________ (lavarse) el pelo todos los días.
3. Papá ______________ (afeitarse) después de ______________ (ducharse).
4. Mamá ______________ (peinarse) y luego ______________ (peinar) a mi hermanita.
5. Mi hermana y yo ______________ (vestirse) rápidamente.

B. ¡Un pájaro raro! La rutina del profesor Gamboa es muy interesante. Para saber por qué, completa el párrafo con la forma apropiada de los verbos que están entre paréntesis.

Por lo general, el profesor Gamboa ______________ (acostarse) muy temprano, a eso de las 9:30 ó las 10:00 de la noche. ¿Por qué tan temprano? Porque ______________ (levantarse) cuando todo el mundo está durmiendo, a las 4:00 de la mañana. ¿Qué hace a esa hora? Pues, primero ______________ (prepararse) una taza de café. Luego ______________ (sentarse) a trabajar frente a la computadora. No ______________ (bañarse) y no ______________ (afeitarse) hasta las 11:30 porque no tiene que ir a la universidad hasta el mediodía. Ah, ¡y nunca ______________ (peinarse)! Es un pájaro raro *(rare bird)*.

C. ¿Y tú? Responde a las siguientes preguntas sobre tu propia rutina diaria.

1. ¿A qué hora te despiertas diariamente?
2. ¿Prefieres ducharte o bañarte?
3. ¿Cuántas veces a la semana te lavas el pelo?
4. ¿Cuántas veces al día te peinas?
5. ¿A qué hora te levantas los fines de semana?
6. ¿A qué hora te acuestas todos los días?

9.4 *Por* and *para:* A Second Look

Explaining how, when, why, and for whom things are done

In **Capítulo 5** you learned that **por** and **para** have different uses. The following list reviews those uses and introduces several new ones.

Por

- *By, by means of*
  Vinieron **por** avión. — *They came by plane.*
- *Through, along*
  ¿Pasaron **por** aquí? — *Did they pass through here?*
- *Because of*
  Vinieron **por** Gloria Estefan. — *They came because of Gloria Estefan.*
- *During, in*
  Practicaron aquí **por** la mañana y allá **por** la noche. — *They practiced here in the morning and there during the evening.*
- *For: in place of, in exchange for*
  ¿Quién jugó **por** ella? — *Who played for her?*
- *For: for a period of time*
  Jugaron **por** tres horas. — *They played for three hours.*

Para

- *In order to*
  Para ganar, hay que practicar. — *In order to win, it is necessary to practice.*
- *For: compared with, in relation to others*
  Para ser futbolista, no es muy agresivo. — *For a soccer player, he is not very aggressive.*
- *For: intended for, to be given to*
  Compré las entradas **para** tus padres. — *I bought the tickets for your parents.*
- *For: in the direction of, toward*
  De aquí salieron **para** Lima. — *From here they left for Lima.*
- *For: by a specified time*
  Tendremos los resultados **para** mañana. — *We'll have the results by tomorrow.*
- *For: in one's opinion*
  Para nosotros, Maradona es el mejor. — *For us, Maradona is the best.*

¡A practicar!

A. Los planes de Amalia. ¿Qué planes tiene Amalia para el próximo fin de semana? Para saberlo, llena los espacios con **por** o **para.**

1. El sábado voy ______________ la casa de mis padres.
2. ______________ la mañana voy a salir temprano de casa.
3. ¿Por qué? Porque primero debo comprar un regalo ______________ mi madre. Es su cumpleaños.
4. También voy a pasar ______________ la pastelería.
5. Sí, por supuesto, ______________ comprar una rica torta.
6. Pero ¡qué pena! El domingo ______________ la tarde, ya debo regresar a mi casa ______________ prepararme ______________ los exámenes finales.

B. En diciembre, ¡vacaciones! Veamos lo que hace María Teresa en diciembre, completando con **por** o **para.**

Hoy debo estudiar ______________ dos exámenes y el fin de semana voy a escribir mi composición ______________ la clase de filosofía, y después de eso... ¡vacaciones! Salgo ______________ mi casa el lunes ______________ la mañana, y esta vez voy ______________ avión. ¡Sí!, compré el boleto en una oferta. Ahora voy a estar con mi familia ______________ dos semanas completas. ¡Qué suerte!

9.5 Affirmative *tú* Commands

Giving orders and directions

Commands are used to order someone to do or not to do something. **Tú** commands are used with people with whom you are familiar or whom you address as **tú.** There are different forms for affirmative and negative **tú** commands. In this chapter, you will learn only affirmative **tú** commands.

A. In general, the affirmative **tú** command is identical to the third-person singular of the present indicative.

Infinitive	Command
tomar	**Toma** café.
leer	**Lée**lo.
dormirse	**Duérme**te.

Habla con el profesor y **explíca**le tu problema. — *Talk to the professor and explain your problem to him.*

Trae el mapa. — *Bring the map.*

B. There are eight irregular affirmative **tú** command forms. Note that most are derived from irregular first-person singular forms ending with **-go.**

Infinitive	***yo* Present**	***tú* Command**
decir	digo	**di**
poner	pongo	**pon**
salir	salgo	**sal**
tener	tengo	**ten**
venir	vengo	**ven**
hacer	hago	**haz**
ir	voy	**ve**
ser	soy	**sé**

C. Object and reflexive pronouns always follow and are attached to affirmative commands. The placement of pronouns follows this order: reflexive, indirect, direct.

Tráe**melas.**	*Bring them to me.*
Acuésta**te.**	*Go to bed.*
Lléva**selo.**	*Take it to him.*

Notice that whenever pronouns are added to a verb, accents are often necessary in order to maintain the original stress.

¡A practicar!

A. ¡Organízate! El hermano menor de Olga es muy desorganizado. ¿Qué consejos le da Olga a su hermano?

Modelo acostarse / más temprano
Acuéstate más temprano.

1. levantarse / más temprano
2. vestirse / rápidamente
3. poner / la ropa en tu cuarto
4. salir / antes de las 7:30
5. ir / directamente a clase
6. hacer / tu tarea todas la noches

B. ¡Por favor! Tú decides establecer un poco de orden en el uso del baño en tu casa o apartamento. Dile a tu hermano(a) o a tu compañero(a) de cuarto lo que tiene que hacer para evitar que todos quieran usar el cuarto de baño a la vez. Usa mandatos en la segunda persona (**tú**).

1. levantarse temprano
2. ducharse rápidamente
3. vestirse en su cuarto
4. lavarse el pelo por la noche
5. peinarse rápidamente
6. ¿... ?

CAPÍTULO 10

¡Socorro! ¡Llamen a la policía!

Cultural Topics

- **¿Sabías que…?**
  Firefighters in Latin American countries
- **Noticiero cultural**
  Lugar: *Nicaragua: Managua y sus volcanes*
  Gente: *Violeta Chamorro*
- **Lectura:** *Asaltan joyería, mueren 2*

Writing Strategies

- *Conseguir información*

Reading Strategies

- *Anticipar con los titulares*

En preparación

- 10.1 Adverbs Derived from Adjectives
- 10.2 Irregular Verbs in the Preterite
- 10.3 Negative and Indefinite Expressions
- 10.4 Preterite of Stem-changing **-ir** Verbs
- 10.5 **Hacer** and Past Events

In this chapter, you will learn how to …

- ask for help in case of an emergency.
- respond to questions about a crime.
- describe a car accident.
- describe a robbery.

Managua, capital de Nicaragua, situada en una zona de gran actividad sísmica

Después del terremoto de 1972 en Managua, Nicaragua

Marcha del Frente Sandinista de Liberación Nacional (FSLN) en Managua, Nicaragua

Lo que ya sabes...

1. ¿Crees que es peligroso (*dangerous*) construir una ciudad cerca de un volcán? ¿Por qué lo hace la gente?
2. ¿Has sentido (*Have you felt*) un terremoto alguna vez? ¿Cuánto tiempo duró? ¿Cómo debemos protegernos en un terremoto?
3. ¿Por qué hay tantos grupos guerrilleros, como los sandinistas, en unos países latinos? ¿Qué causa que se formen estos grupos? En tu opinión, ¿dan buen o mal resultado estos grupos? ¿Por qué crees eso? Da ejemplos.

NICARAGUA

¡Por favor, vengan pronto!

TAREA Antes de empezar este **Paso**, estudia **En preparación** 10.1 y haz por escrito los ejercicios de **¡A practicar!** También escucha **Paso 1 ¿Qué se dice...?** del Capítulo 10 en el CD del estudiante.

¿Eres buen observador?

Ahora, ¡a analizar!

1. ¿Por qué fue nombrado José Emiliano Avelar «Policía de la semana»? ¿Qué hizo?
2. ¿Es joven o mayor de edad? ¿Cuántos años tiene? ¿Cuánto tiempo ha servido como policía?
3. ¿Qué número de emergencia llamarías en caso de un incendio *(fire)*? ¿en caso de un abuso de drogas? ¿de problemas con un joven delincuente? ¿si necesitaras una ambulancia? ¿en caso de desacuerdos domésticos?
4. ¿Cuáles de estas categorías no reconoces? Pídele ayuda a la clase.

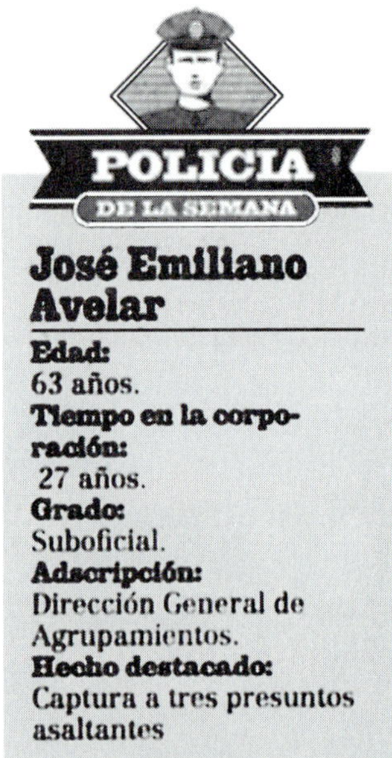
POLICIA
DE LA SEMANA

José Emiliano Avelar

Edad:
63 años.
Tiempo en la corporación:
27 años.
Grado:
Suboficial.
Adscripción:
Dirección General de Agrupamientos.
Hecho destacado:
Captura a tres presuntos asaltantes

TELEFONOS DE EMERGENCIA

5 Adicciones, Grupo Amigos	682 28 18	Cruz Roja	557 57 57
Centro de Integración Juvenil	534 34 34	Centro Antirrábico	549 42 94
Neuróticos Anónimos	539 25 84	Radiopatrullas	06
Bomberos	768 37 00	Robos, asaltos, riñas	08
Locatel	658 11 11	Alcohólicos Anónimos	286 15 93

¿Qué se dice...?

En caso de emergencia

1. Prestar primeros auxilios...
2. Llamar a la policía...
3. Hablar...
4. Actuar...
5. Dar información...
6. Describir... el estado del herido

HEROÍNA ¡Socorro! ¡Auxilio! ¡Incendio! ¡Operadora,... con los bomberos, por favor! Mi casa se está quemando. Hay mucho humo. ¡Llamen inmediatamente a la policía! Es urgente.

OPERADORA Servicio de urgencia. ¿Cuál es su emergencia?

HEROÍNA Necesito una ambulancia urgentemente. ¿Hay un hospital por aquí cerca?

¿Sabías que... ?

La profesión de bombero es de mucha importancia en cualquier ciudad. Los bomberos constantemente corren el riesgo de lastimarse y aún perder la vida. Sin embargo, en algunos países sudamericanos, por ejemplo, esta actividad no es remunerada; es trabajo de voluntarios. El único salario que estos bomberos reciben es la satisfacción de un trabajo bien hecho y también en muchos casos, de salvarle la vida a alguien. En casos de heroísmo, se recompensa a los bomberos con trofeos y condecoraciones.

A propósito...

The ordinal numbers—**primer(o), segundo, tercer(o), cuarto, quinto, sexto, séptimo, octavo, noveno, décimo**—are adjectives and must agree in number and gender with the nouns they modify. When preceding a singular masculine noun, **primero** and **tercero** become **primer** and **tercer.**

Ahora, ¡a hablar!

A. Supervivencia. ¿Sabes algo sobre casos de emergencia? Decide si lo siguiente es verdadero o falso. Si es falso, corrígelo.

1. Una persona que no respira por más de seis minutos puede morirse.
2. Los ataques cardíacos representan la causa principal de la muerte de los adultos mayores de 38 años.
3. Es importante administrar mucha leche a una persona que sufre de envenenamiento *(poisoning).*
4. Si una persona sufre un ataque cardíaco, lo primero que se le debe hacer es la respiración artificial.
5. En caso de dosis excesiva de alguna medicina, debes llamar inmediatamente al servicio de emergencia.
6. Si una persona bebe demasiado alcohol, los efectos no son muy serios.

B. ¿Qué debo hacer? Pregúntale a un(a) amigo(a) lo que debe hacer en estos casos de emergencia.

Modelo Una persona está inconsciente: despertarla / inmediato

TÚ Una persona está inconsciente.

COMPAÑERO(A) **Debes despertarla inmediatamente.**

1. Una persona es víctima de envenenamiento y está inconsciente: llamar al Centro de Control de Venenos / calmado
2. Una persona es víctima de un choque *(shock)* eléctrico: verificar si la víctima respira / normal

3. Una persona sufre de lesiones en la cabeza: observar si hay hemorragia / cuidadoso
4. Una persona sufre de ataque cardíaco: llamar al servicio de emergencia / urgente
5. Una persona se está ahogando *(drowning):* sacarla del agua y empezar a administrar la respiración artificial / rápido

C. ¿Cómo? ¿Cómo haces tú las siguientes cosas?

Modelo estudiar para un examen final (cuidadoso o inteligente)
Estudio cuidadosamente para un examen final.

1. hablar español (rápido o lento)
2. trabajar (duro o tranquilo)
3. ganar dinero (calmado o urgente)
4. manejar (rápido o lento)
5. hacer amigos (fácil o difícil)
6. comunicarse con los padres (frecuente o infrecuente)
7. resolver problemas personales (fácil o difícil)
8. resolver problemas financieros (rápido o lento)

D. Incendio. Di en qué orden y cómo debe hacerse lo siguiente si hay un incendio.

Modelo 1° llamar a los bomberos / inmediato
Primero, se debe llamar a los bomberos inmediatamente.

2° ver si la puerta está caliente / inmediato
3° poner una toalla *(towel)* húmeda debajo de la puerta / rápido
4° caminar por el pasillo / lento
5° buscar la salida más cercana / tranquilo
6° bajar por la escalera / cuidado
7° ayudar a otras personas / cortés

Y ahora, ¡a conversar!

A. Precauciones. Entrevista a tu compañero(a) para saber si ha usado un servicio de emergencia y si está preparado para futuras emergencias.

Pregúntale si…

1. usó alguna vez un servicio de emergencia.
2. te puede explicar cuál fue el caso de emergencia.
3. necesitó esperar mucho.
4. está preparado(a) para ayudar a la víctima de un accidente.
5. está preparado(a) en caso de que ocurra un incendio en su casa o en un edificio.
6. tiene un extintor que funciona.
7. sabe por dónde salir de su casa en caso de incendio.
8. su casa está asegurada.

B. Imprudencias. En el edificio donde vive Carlos ocurrieron seis accidentes el año pasado. Con un(a) compañero(a) explica lo que pasó.

1. la señora Ortiz

2. el señor Jiménez

3. el señor Medina

4. la señorita Valdez

5. Juanito

6. Andrés

C. Accidentes. Dile a un(a) compañero(a) lo que debe hacer en estas situaciones de emergencia.

Modelo chocar en carro con una bicicleta

Si chocas con una bicicleta debes parar el carro inmediatamente y ayudar a la víctima.

1. comer algo contaminado
2. ver a una persona ahogándose
3. caerse de una escalera *(fall from a ladder)*
4. romperse *(break)* una pierna o un brazo
5. recibir un choque (*shock)* eléctrico
6. quemarse

¡Luz! ¡Cámara! ¡Acción!

A. ¡Incendio! Al preparar la comida, tu compañero(a) de cuarto tuvo un accidente y ahora hay un incendio en tu apartamento. Dramatiza la situación con un(a) compañero(a).

B. ¡Auxilio! Tú y un(a) amigo(a) asisten a una clase de primeros auxilios y mañana hay un examen. En preparación para el examen, tu compañero(a) inventa varias situaciones de emergencia para ver si tú sabes qué hacer. Dramatiza la situación con un(a) compañero(a).

¿Comprendes lo que se dice?

Estrategias para escuchar. *In* **Capítulo 9** *you learned that listening is easier when you know something about the subject. However, this is often not the case. When you know nothing about what you are listening to, it is helpful and sometimes necessary to listen for grammatical and linguistic structures that you already know. For example, listening to* verb endings *can tell you not only* who *is carrying out the action, but* when *it is occurring. Listening for* adverbs *derived from adjectives can tell you* how *the action is carried out. This method is known as "listening from the bottom up."*

¿Qué pasó? Escucha este noticiero especial de Radio Managua. Luego con un(a) compañero(a) hagan una lista de por lo menos cuatro cosas que ocurrieron y expliquen con un adverbio o en breves palabras cómo ocurrió cada cosa.

NOTICIERO CULTURAL

Nicaragua
Jinotega
Matagalpa
Corinto
León
Granada
Managua

LUGAR... NICARAGUA

Antes de empezar, dime...

1. Nombra tres bellezas naturales de los EE.UU.
2. ¿Qué tipo de desastres naturales ocurren en los EE.UU.?
3. Haz una lista de los lugares que más sufren desastres naturales en los EE.UU. y al lado de ellos, el tipo de desastre.
4. ¿Por qué sigue viviendo la gente en esos sitios?
5. ¿Cómo reaccionas tú después de estos desastres? Explica.

Managua, Nicaragua

Managua y sus volcanes: Una ciudad que no se deja vencer

Nicaragua es el país más grande de Centroamérica y, con excepción de Belice, el menos poblado. Managua ha sido la capital y el centro comercial de Nicaragua desde el año 1858. Esta ciudad está en la costa sur del lago Managua, uno de los únicos lagos de agua dulce

El centro de Managua despúes del terremoto de 1972

(fresh water) del mundo que tiene tiburones *(sharks)*. Managua presenta al turista los más impresionantes volcanes que pueda ofrecer la madre naturaleza. Pero los mismos volcanes que le dan una inmensa belleza natural, la han destruido completamente varias veces en el pasado.

Managua fue totalmente destruida en marzo del año 1931 por un terremoto. Cinco años más tarde parte de la ciudad desapareció a causa de uno de los incendios más grandes de la historia de Nicaragua. Lentamente se volvió a reconstruir totalmente con las características de una ciudad moderna. En diciembre del año 1972 otro terrible terremoto destruyó el centro de la ciudad, dejando solamente algunos edificios modernos.

Pero esos mismos volcanes que han causado la destrucción de la ciudad en el pasado, le dan una belleza sin igual. Es interesante ver a sólo 16 kilómetros de la ciudad de Managua un cráter de volcán que es uno de los más hermosos lagos donde se puede nadar, pescar, hacer picnic, acampar y dar un paseo en bote. Este lago se llama Laguna de Xiloá.

Parece que Managua vuelve a nacer siempre, de los incendios, terremotos y revoluciones. Por eso, cuando la visitamos, tenemos la sensación de estar ante una ciudad que no se dejará vencer *(conquer)* nunca.

Y ahora, dime...

Con un(a) compañero(a), preparen dos listas: una de razones por qué a mucha gente le gusta vivir en Managua y otra de razones por qué mucha gente rehusa ir a vivir allá.

El español en otras disciplinas: Sismografía

Cultura sísmica. Las experiencias que nos han dejado los sismos (terremotos y temblores) de los EE.UU., México, Colombia, Perú y Chile, entre otros, nos indican que vivimos en un «continente sísmico» y que tenemos que acostumbrarnos a convivir con este tipo de desastres naturales, ya que son fenómenos que van a continuar sucediendo. Por esta razón, es muy importante que «desarrollemos una cultura sísmica» o sea, una cultura que sepa qué hacer antes, durante y después de un terremoto. Con un(a) compañero(a) haz una lista de los «pasos» que ustedes creen que debemos seguir antes, durante y después de este tipo de desastre.

Proyecto: Estudia en la enciclopedia sobre un reciente desastre natural en algún país latino, ya sea un terremoto, una erupción de volcán, un huracán, un tornado, etc., y escribe un breve resumen de cuándo y dónde ocurrió y cómo actuó la gente antes, durante y después del desastre.

¡Yo no tuve la culpa!

TAREA

Antes de empezar este **Paso,** estudia **En preparación** 10.2 y 10.3 y haz por escrito los ejercicios de **¡A practicar!** También escucha **Paso 2 ¿Qué se dice... ?** del Capítulo 10 en el CD del estudiante.

¿Eres buen observador?

Ahora, ¡a analizar!

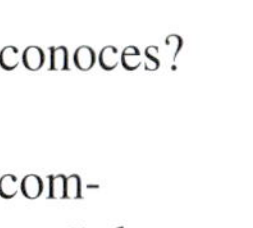

1. ¿Cuáles de estas señales de tráfico reconoces? Explícale el significado de diez a tu compañero(a) y escucha mientras tu compañero(a) te explica otras diez. ¡En español, por supuesto!
2. ¿Qué creen ustedes que significan las siguientes señales: **glorieta, puente angosto, vado, alto, ceda el paso**?

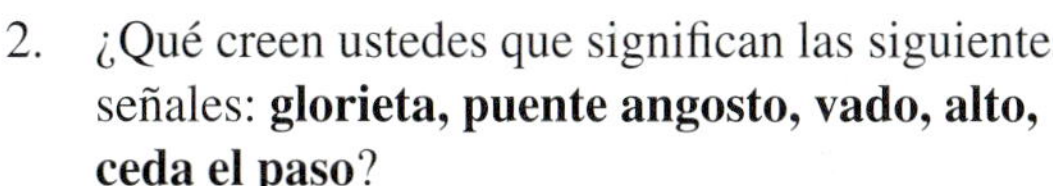

3. Pídele a tu compañero(a) que te explique las que no entiendes. Si no puede, pregúntenle a la clase.

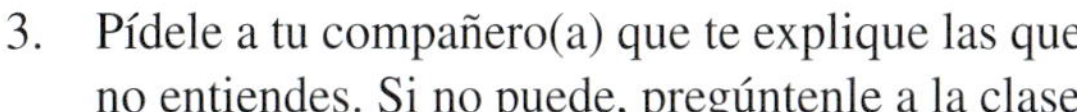

¿Qué se dice...?

Cuando ocurre un accidente automovilístico

_______ 1. Chocó otro coche por detrás.

_______ 2. Trató de frenar.

_______ 3. Le pegó a otro coche por detrás.

_______ 4. Se le reventó una llanta.

_______ 5. Le pegó otro coche.

_______ 6. Lo siente.

SR. BLANCO Mi coche está destrozado.

HEROÍNA ¿Recibieron golpes serios? ¿Hay heridos? *(al Sr. Blanco)* ¿Está usted herido?

SR. BLANCO No lo creo.

HEROÍNA *(al Sr. Rojo)* ¿Cómo se siente usted?

SR. ROJO Pues, no sé. No muy bien.

HEROÍNA ¿Hubo algún testigo?

LOS DOS SRES. No, ninguno.

Ahora, ¡a hablar!

A. ¡Un accidente! Hubo un accidente en la carretera principal de la ciudad. ¿Qué dijeron los chóferes cuando llegó la policía a investigar? Cambia los verbos entre paréntesis al pretérito.

Chófer #1 Yo no tuve la culpa porque…

1. no (poder) ver el otro coche.
2. no (tener) tiempo para frenar.
3. (hacer) todo lo posible por evitar el accidente.

Chófer #2 El otro chófer tuvo la culpa porque…

4. (perder) control del coche.
5. (chocarme) por detrás.
6. (decir) que no me (ver).

B. ¿Qué pasó aquí? Hubo un accidente y tres coches chocaron. ¿Qué dicen los chóferes y los testigos?

Modelo yo / no tener la culpa / él / ser el culpable
Yo no tuve la culpa; él fue el culpable.

Chóferes

1. yo / hacer todo lo posible / pero / no poder frenar
2. ella / parar el coche de repente / y / yo / chocarla
3. yo / perder control del coche / y / pegarle por detrás

Testigos

4. yo / ver el accidente / y / venir a ayudar inmediatamente
5. mi esposa / ayudar a los heridos / mientras yo / llamar a la policía
6. el chófer del coche rojo / tener la culpa / porque / no frenar a tiempo

C. ¿Yo? ¡Nunca! ¿Es tu compañero(a) un(a) conductor(a) modelo? Pregúntale si alguna vez hizo lo siguiente.

nunca — de vez en cuando — a menudo — siempre

Modelo dejar la licencia en casa

COMPAÑERO(A) **¿Dejaste la licencia en casa alguna vez?**
TÚ **Yo nunca dejo la licencia en casa.** o
Yo dejo la licencia en casa de vez en cuando.

1. estar borracho(a) al manejar
2. tener una multa *(ticket)*
3. estacionar en una zona prohibida
4. no decir la verdad a la policía
5. tener un accidente
6. ser testigo de un accidente
7. ¿… ?

D. La última vez. ¿Mantiene tu compañero(a) su coche en buen estado para evitar accidentes? Pregúntale cuándo fue la última vez que hizo lo siguiente.

Modelo limpiar el interior del coche

TÚ **¿Cuándo fue la última vez que limpiaste el interior del coche?**

COMPAÑERO(A) **Lo limpié en octubre.**

1. cambiar el aceite
2. revisar *(check)* el motor
3. echarle agua al radiador
4. inflar las llantas *(tires)*
5. revisar la batería
6. llenar el tanque de gasolina
7. rotar las llantas
8. ¿... ?

Y ahora, ¡a conversar!

A. Mi primer coche. ¿Recuerdas tu primer coche? Entrevista a un(a) compañero(a). Pregúntale sobre su primer coche y háblale del tuyo.

1. ¿En qué año obtuviste tu licencia de manejar? ¿Dónde la obtuviste?
2. ¿Cuál fue tu primer coche? ¿Cuánto costó?
3. ¿En qué año compraste tu primer coche? ¿Quién lo pagó, tú o tus padres?
4. ¿Por cuánto tiempo lo tuviste?
5. ¿Tuviste algún accidente con ese coche? ¿Qué pasó?
6. ¿Qué pasó con ese coche?

B. Mecánicos. ¿Es tu compañero(a) buen(a) mecánico(a)? Léele estas definiciones para ver si, usando el diagrama de un coche en la página A-6, te puede decir el nombre de estas partes del coche. Anótalas y al terminar, verifiquen sus respuestas.

1. Es donde nos sentamos, pero no es una silla.
2. Los coches tienen cuatro. Siempre necesitan aire.
3. Es un espejo *(mirror)* pequeño situado dentro o fuera del coche que se usa para ver si hay otro coche o algún objeto detrás del coche.
4. Sólo se usan de noche para ver mejor.
5. Protege el coche cuando va a chocar contra otro coche.
6. Es esencial para determinar la dirección del movimiento del coche.
7. Protege del viento al chófer y al pasajero. También permite al chófer ver qué hay enfrente del coche.
8. Es una fuente de energía eléctrica.
9. Son esenciales para parar el movimiento del coche.

C. Nueva póliza de seguros. Tú eres agente de seguros *(insurance)*. Tu compañero(a) va a hacer el papel de un(a) cliente que acaba de tener un accidente automovilístico. Para darle una nueva póliza de seguros tienes que conseguir esta información. Entrevístalo(la).

1. edad
2. dirección
3. empleo
4. tipo de coche
5. multas previas: ¿cuántas y por qué?
6. accidentes: ¿cuántos? ¿culpable o no?
7. ¿… ?

¡Luz! ¡Cámara! ¡Acción!

A. ¡Yo no tuve la culpa! Hubo un accidente de dos carros (o dos bicicletas). Los chóferes tienen opiniones muy distintas de cómo ocurrió y quién es el (la) culpable. Un testigo vio todo y puede resolver la discusión. Dramatiza la situación con dos compañeros(as).

B. ¡Idiota! Hubo un accidente entre un coche y una moto. No hubo heridos pero la moto está destrozada. El (La) motociclista está furioso(a). La policía llega y los dos chóferes cuentan su versión de lo que pasó. Dramatiza la situación con dos compañeros(as).

¿Comprendes lo que se dice?

¡Me siento nuevo! Escucha este anuncio que combina elementos de exageración, humor y nacionalismo para vender el producto. Luego da varios ejemplos de cómo se usan estos tres elementos en el anuncio.

NICAR AGUA

Exageración	Humor	Nacionalismo
1.	1.	1.
2.	2.	2.
3.	3.	3.
4.	4.	4.
5.	5.	5.
. . .	. . .	. . .

NOTICIERO CULTURAL

GENTE... VIOLETA CHAMORRO

Antes de empezar, dime...

1. Nombra a tres mujeres famosas en la historia de los EE.UU.
2. Nombra a tres mujeres famosas en la actualidad en los EE.UU.
3. Da ejemplos de mujeres que se destacan en la política de los EE.UU. actualmente.
4. Según tu opinión, ¿están listos los estadounidenses para tener una mujer como presidenta? Justifica tu respuesta.

Violeta Chamorro

Violeta Chamorro

Violeta Barrios de Chamorro, política y empresaria nicaragüense, nació en 1930. Se casó en 1950 con Pedro Joaquín Chamorro, editor del periódico *La Prensa*, quien fue un destacado opositor a la dictadura de la familia Somoza, que estuvo en control desde 1937 hasta 1979. La señora de Chamorro asumió la dirección del periódico después del asesinato de su esposo en 1978. Después de la caída del último Somoza, formó parte de la junta revolucionaria que tomó el poder desde julio de 1979 a abril de 1980. Cuando en 1984 Daniel Ortega, líder del Frente Sandinista de Liberación Nacional (FSLN) fue elegido presidente de Nicaragua, Violeta Chamorro pasó a la oposición y empezó a actuar más activamente en la política de su país.

En 1990 derrotó en elecciones libres a Daniel Ortega, el candidato del movimiento sandinista y se convirtió así en la primera mujer presidenta de esta nación latinoamericana. Su gobierno reestableció relaciones con los EE.UU. y ha logrado también una cierta reconciliación con los frentes opositores. Últimamente, como todo personaje famoso, ha sido objeto de controversias, debido al interés de algunos familiares de participar más directamente también en el gobierno nicaragüense, incluso en el mando del país.

Y ahora dime...

1. Anota lo que sabes de la presidenta Violeta Chamorro.

LA VIDA DE VIOLETA CHAMORRO

Antes de 1978	Después de 1978
1.	1.
2.	2.
3.	3.
4.	4.
5.	5.
. . .	. . .

2. La prensa y la política hicieron un papel muy importante en la vida de Violeta Chamorro. En grupos de tres o cuatro, discutan el papel de la prensa en la política de los EE.UU. ¿Existe una verdadera «libertad de prensa»? ¿Hay necesidad de «censura de prensa»? Informen a la clase de sus conclusiones.

Antes de escribir
Estrategias para escribir: Conseguir información

A. En preparación. Una composición es un trabajo escrito que requiere dos cosas:

1. conseguir información sobre el tema y
2. comunicar esa información por escrito de una manera clara y organizada.

Para conseguir la información necesaria puedes usar varios recursos: entrevistas, libros de referencia como la enciclopedia, revistas, periódicos, etc. Para comunicar la información de una manera clara y organizada debes seguir el proceso de redacción *(writing)* que has usado en estas escrituras desde el principio.

Una buena composición siempre contesta preguntas específicas sobre el tema. En este capítulo has leído dos composiciones en las secciones **Noticiero cultural**, una sobre Managua y sus volcanes y otra sobre Violeta Chamorro. Mira cómo la composición sobre Violeta Chamorro contesta ciertas preguntas específicas.

1. ¿Quién es Violeta Chamorro?
2. ¿Cuándo nació?
3. ¿Qué hizo antes de 1979? ¿después de 1979?
4. ¿Cuándo subió a la presidencia?
5. ¿Qué se logró *(was accomplished)* durante su presidencia?

B. Preguntas clave. Ahora, con un(a) compañero(a) preparen una lista de las preguntas que contesta la composición sobre Managua y sus volcanes.

Ahora, ¡a escribir!

A. La idea principal. Piensa ahora en un tema relacionado con Latinoamérica que te gustaría investigar para escribir una composición. Puede ser sobre un país, una ciudad o región, una persona o un evento histórico. Prepara preguntas apropiadas a tu tema que crees que debes contestar en tu composición. Si necesitas ayuda, mira como guía, las preguntas que preparaste sobre Managua y sus volcanes. Usa varios recursos para encontrar la información necesaria para contestar tus preguntas sobre el tema.

B. El primer borrador. Usa la información que preparaste en **A** para escribir un primer borrador. Pon toda la información relacionada con la misma pregunta en un párrafo.

C. Ahora, a compartir. Comparte tu primer borrador con dos o tres compañeros. Comenta sobre el título, el contenido y el estilo de las composiciones de tus compañeros y escucha los comentarios de ellos sobre tu noticia. Si hay errores de ortografía o de gramática, menciónalos.

D. Ahora, a revisar. Si necesitas hacer unos cambios, a partir de los comentarios de tus compañeros, hazlos ahora.

E. La versión final. Prepara una versión final de tu composición y entrégala.

F. Publicación. En grupos de cuatro o cinco lean las composiciones que les dará su profesor(a) y decidan cuál es la más interesante. Descríbanla a la clase mencionando la información más importante que aparece en ella.

TAREA

Antes de empezar este **Paso**, estudia **En preparación** 10.4 y 10.5, y haz por escrito los ejercicios de **¡A practicar!** También escucha **Paso 3 ¿Qué se dice... ?** del Capítulo 10 en el CD del estudiante.

¿Eres buen observador?

Asalto y captura

Un policía y un civil muertos, dos presuntos asaltantes detenidos y un botín no cuantificado, fue el saldo de una balacera ocurrida en una joyería ubicada en la esquina de Isabel la Católica y 16 de Septiembre, en el Centro Histórico, ayer a las 13:20 horas.

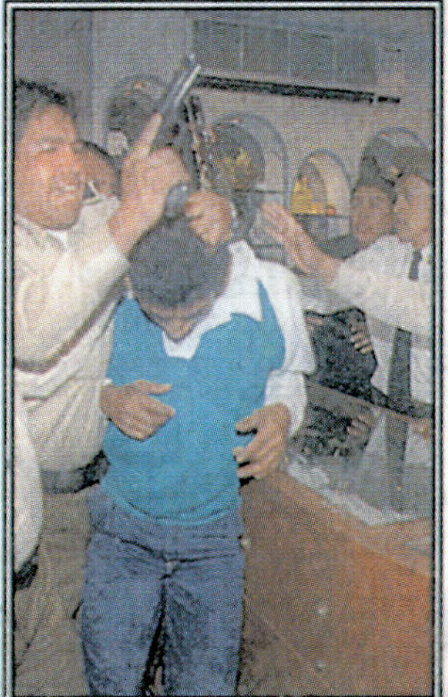

Ahora, ¡a analizar!

1. ¿Dónde ocurrió este asalto? ¿A qué hora? ¿En qué tipo de negocio?
2. ¿Cuántos asaltantes hubo? ¿Fueron todos capturados?
3. ¿Hubo heridos o muertos? ¿Cuántos? ¿Quiénes fueron?
4. ¿Qué es una balacera?
5. ¿Qué es un botín? ¿En qué consiste el botín?

¿Qué se dice...?

Al describir un robo

Hora del robo:	2:00 AM	2:00 PM	4:00 PM
Primero vio al ladrón:	en el banco	en su coche	en la estación
Lo sintió a su lado:	en el banco	en su coche	en la estación

HEROÍNA ¿Puede identificar al ladrón? ¿Cómo es?

VÍCTIMA Es un hombre feo. Es alto con pelo negro y bigotes.

HEROÍNA ¿Qué le robó?

VÍCTIMA Sacó una pistola y me pidió la cartera. Y cuando se la di, se rió de mí. Tuve mucho miedo y no pude hacer nada.

HEROÍNA ¿Por dónde se fue... ?

PROFESORA ¡Margarita! ¡Margarita! ¿Qué te pasa? Presta atención a la clase.

Ahora, ¡a hablar!

A. ¿Qué pasó aquí? Mario fue víctima de un robo. Ahora él le está describiendo a la policía lo que le pasó. ¿Qué dice?

Modelo en el restaurante / yo / despedirme de mis amigos
En el restaurante, yo me despedí de mis amigos.

1. al salir / yo / sentir a una persona detrás de mí
2. esa persona / seguirme al coche
3. yo / pedir ayuda / pero / nadie / oírme
4. el ladrón / pedirme la cartera / y / reírse
5. él / darme un golpe en la cabeza / y / irse
6. alguien / verlo / y / llamar a la policía

B. ¡Mentira! La policía acaba de arrestar al ladrón. Él tiene su propia versión de lo que pasó. ¿Qué dice él? ¿Lo crees?

Modelo yo / ver / hombre borracho salir / restaurante
Yo vi a un hombre borracho salir del restaurante.

1. hombre / caminar / coche / porque / sentirse mal
2. yo / seguirlo / y / ofrecerle / ayuda
3. él / tener miedo / y / empezar a / gritar
4. yo / querer / calmarlo / pero / no / poder
5. yo / no pegarle / hombre
6. hombre / acusarme de / robar / cartera
7. yo / irme / para evitar problemas

C. ¡Solo en Nueva York! El detective Buscapistas trabaja en Nueva York donde siempre pasan cosas extrañas. ¿Qué cosas extrañas pasaron el mes pasado?

Modelo Un ladrón (perseguir) a un policía para devolverle su cartera.
Un ladrón persiguió a un policía para devolverle su cartera.

1. Un gorila (conseguir) una pistola y (asaltar) un banco.
2. Un policía (pedirle) ayuda a un ladrón.
3. Una mujer (asaltar) un banco y (pedir) cinco dólares.
4. Un turista (robarle) la cartera a un ladrón famoso.
5. Un restaurante (servirle) a una familia de extraterrestres.
6. Un borracho (bañarse) en una fuente y luego (vestirse) en público.

D. Hace dos meses que... ¿Cuánto tiempo hace que ocurrieron estos eventos en tu vida?

Modelo oír a alguien gritar «¡Socorro!»
Hace dos meses que oí a alguien gritar «¡Socorro!»

1. ver una película policíaca
2. leer de un incendio
3. ser testigo de un robo
4. ser víctima de un robo o un asalto
5. lastimarte

Y ahora, ¡a conversar!

A. Honesto. Ser completamente honesto no es siempre fácil. Entrevista a un(a) compañero(a) y decide si es completamente honesto(a) o si sólo lo es de vez en cuando.

nunca ——— una vez ——— varias veces

Modelo mentir en una declaración de impuestos *(tax return)*

TÚ **¿Mentiste en alguna declaración de impuestos?**

COMPAÑERO(A) **No. Yo nunca mentí.** o **Sí, mentí una vez.** o **Sí, mentí varias veces.**

1. mentir en una solicitud *(application)* de trabajo
2. pedirle dinero a un(a) amigo(a) y luego no pagarle
3. hacer trampa *(cheat)* en un examen
4. faltar al trabajo
5. inventar pretextos para no salir con una persona
6. inventar rumores sobre una persona
7. hablar mal de un(a) amigo(a)
8. no cumplir con una promesa importante
9. reírse a espaldas de una persona *(behind someone's back)*
10. repetir un secreto importante

B. Extraño. ¿De vez en cuando haces algo totalmente fuera de lo normal? Comparte estos momentos con tus compañeros en grupos de tres o cuatro.

Modelo dormir… horas

Generalmente duermo 8 horas pero un día dormí 15 horas para poder estudiar 24 horas seguidas para un examen de química.

1. no mentir
2. pedir dinero
3. reírse en clase
4. seguir a una persona
5. conseguir un trabajo
6. vestirse de manera extravagante
7. ¿… ?

C. ¡Asalto! Tú y tu compañero(a) son reporteros muy famosos. Esta mañana asaltaron un banco y ustedes dos lo vieron todo. Tomaron algunas fotos que acaban de revelar. Ahora necesitan narrar lo que pasó y describir cada foto.

1.

2.

3. 

4. 

5. 

6. 

7. 

¡Luz! ¡Cámara! ¡Acción!

A. ¡Ladrones! Tú y tu amiga acaban de ser víctimas de un robo. Un grupo de motociclistas le robó la bolsa a tu amiga. Ahora ustedes le están explicando a un policía lo que pasó. Trabajando en grupos de tres, dramaticen esta situación.

B. ¡Socorro! Tú y tu amigo(a) acaban de salir de su discoteca favorita. Son las dos de la mañana. De repente un hombre con una pistola les pide las carteras. ¿Qué hacen? Dramaticen la situación.

Antes de leer
Estrategias para leer: Predecir con titulares

A. Titulares. Siempre que leemos las noticias de un periódico lo primero que leemos son los titulares. La información que nos dan los titulares nos hace decidir si leemos el artículo o buscamos otro de mayor interés para nosotros. Por eso, es esencial seleccionar cuidadosamente cada palabra de los titulares.

1. ¿Qué sabes definitivamente al leer los titulares de este artículo?
2. ¿Cuáles son las tres cosas que crees que se van a mencionar en este artículo?
   a. ______________________________
   b. ______________________________
   c. ______________________________

B. Prepárate para leer. En grupos de tres o cuatro, hagan dos listas: una de los problemas que pueden ocurrir en un asalto y otra de las posibles soluciones. La primera ya está hecha.

Problemas	Soluciones
1. Los ladrones pueden tener como rehénes *(hostage)* a varios clientes de la joyería.	1. La policía puede negociar con los ladrones la libertad de los rehenes.
______________________	______________________
______________________	______________________
______________________	______________________

Lectura

Asaltan joyería; mueren 2

Por Arturo Sánchez

UN POLICÍA Y UN CIVIL MUERTOS, DOS presuntos asaltantes detenidos y un botín no cuantificado, fue el saldo de una balacera ocurrida en una joyería ubicada en la esquina de Isabel la Católica y 16 de Septiembre, en el Centro Histórico, ayer a las 13:20 horas.

Tomando posiciones.

Según versión de testigos, dos hombres y una mujer, quienes aparentaron ser clientes, se introdujeron en la joyería «El Aderezo S. A.», que era custodiada por Antonio Peralta Barrón, placa 9443, elemento de la Policía Bancaria e Industrial.

«Vimos que una mujer salió de la joyería con una bolsa bajo del brazo y que se subía a un taxi, luego oímos dos o tres balazos y nada más. Entonces el policía que estaba afuera corrió para decirnos que llamáramos por teléfono a la joyería, y como no contestaron, avisamos al 08 y a la base Catedral de T 2000», relató la encargada de una tienda contigua.

La balacera duró cerca de 5 minutos.

«Los policías les decían que salieran y que se rindieran porque estaban rodeados, pero uno de ellos quería salir tomando como rehén a la encargada y le apuntaba con una pistola a la cabeza. Entonces cuando un policía rompió un aparador con un pedazo de madera, la señora salió corriendo y se soltó una balacera que duró como 5 minutos», narró un comerciante.

En el interior del edificio fueron detenidos Juan Osorio González, de 33 años de edad; y Arcadio Vázquez, de 30, a quienes les fue decomisada una pistola tipo escuadra calibre 45 milímetros, marca Colt Commander; mientras que una mujer identificada como Karina Neri, presuntamente se dio a la fuga con el producto del robo.

A ver si comprendiste

Un buen artículo informativo sobre un incidente como éste siempre contesta las preguntas más esenciales: ¿quiénes?, ¿qué?, ¿cuándo?, ¿dónde?, ¿cómo?, ¿por qué? y ¿cuánto? ¿Contesta este artículo todas estas preguntas? ¿Cuáles son las respuestas a cada una?

Expand your horizons! *Let's travel through cyberspace to **Nicaragua*** where . . .

- you can visit dozens of volcanoes, many still active, and enjoy their magnificent landscape and beauty.
- you can witness the history of a small country capable of challenging the odds in search of a future that will end the conflict and bring peace and justice.
- you can visit the imposing **Lago Nicaragua.**
- you can read the masterpieces of renowned Nicaraguan poets.
- you can learn about the many earthquakes that continually shake this tiny but vibrant country.

If you are a cyberspace browser, join us in **Viajemos por el ciberespacio a... Nicaragua** by trying the following important addresses:

Universidad Centroamericana
http://165.98.12.3/

Universidad Americana
http://www.uam.rain.ni/

Rubén Darío
http://users.deltanet.com/~drx/ruben.htm
http://sashimi.wwa.com/~roustan/dario.html
http://www.fciencias.unam.mx/~emg/dario.html

Gioconda Belli
http://www.ibw.com.ni/~dlabs/lit/gioconda.html

Periódicos:
El ciberdiario
http://www.ciberdiario.com.ni/ultima.htm
La Prensa
http://www.laprensa.com.ni/

Volcanes: Cerro Negro
http://www.unige.ch:80/cgi-bin/hazards/imagemap/world-map/67,229#Cerro

Lago Nicaragua
http://users.deltanet.com/~drx/nic_lake.htm
http://www.worldheadquarters.com/nicalake.html

Because addresses are likely to change without notice, the following key words will guarantee that **Viajemos por el ciberespacio a... Nicaragua** will get you to your desired destination.

Palabras clave

Nicaragua
Política en Nicaragua
Volcanes de Nicaragua
Comida Nicaragüense
Lago Nicaragua
Daniel Ortega
Violeta Chamorro
Rubén Darío
Gioconda Belli
Cerro Negro

http://www.hrwcollege.com

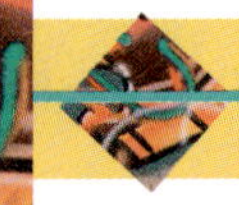

Vocabulario

Emergencias

accidente *(m.)*	*accident*
ataque cardíaco *(m.)*	*heart attack*
caerse	*to fall down*
clínica	*clinic*
emergencia	*emergency*
herido(a)	*wounded, injured*
humo	*smoke*
incendio	*fire*
inconsciente *(m. / f.)*	*unconscious*
morirse (ue, u)	*to die*
muerte *(f.)*	*death*
quemarse	*to burn (up)*
romperse	*to break, shatter*
sufrir	*to suffer*
terremoto	*earthquake*
urgente *(m. / f.)*	*urgent*
víctima *(m. / f.)*	*victim*

Auxilios

ambulancia	*ambulance*
¡Auxilio!	*Help!*
ayuda	*help, assistance*
bombero (a)	*firefighter*
calmarse	*to calm oneself*
hospital *(m.)*	*hospital*
primeros auxilios	*first aid*
proteger	*to protect*
respiración artificial *(f.)*	*artificial respiration*
respirar	*to breathe*
¡Socorro!	*Help!*

Crimen

acusar	*to accuse*
asaltar	*to assault*
culpable *(m. / f.)*	*guilty, culpable*
disparar	*to fire (a gun)*
golpe *(m.)*	*hit, blow*
gritar	*to cry out; to shout*
lastimar	*to injure*
mentir (ie, i)	*to tell a lie*
pegar	*to hit*
perseguir (i, i)	*to follow*
sospechoso(a)	*suspicious*
tener (ie) la culpa	*to be at fault*
testigo	*witness*

Automóvil

asiento	*seat*
automóvil *(m.)*	*automobile*
batería	*battery*
cambiar una llanta	*to change a tire*
carretera	*highway*
carro	*car*
chocar	*to collide*
estacionar	*to park*
frenar	*to apply the brakes (of a car)*
licencia	*license*
llanta	*tire*
mecánico(a)	*mechanic*
motor *(m.)*	*motor*
multa	*fine, ticket, parking ticket*
reventar (ie) una llanta	*to have a blowout*
revisar el motor	*to check the motor*
semáforo	*traffic light*
tanque *(m.)*	*tank*
volante *(m.)*	*steering wheel*

Partes del cuerpo

bigote *(m.)*	*mustache*
brazo	*arm*
cabeza	*head*
espalda	*back*
pierna	*leg*

Verbos

comunicar	*to communicate*
denunciar	*to denounce*
describir	*to describe*
devolver (ue)	*to return (something)*
enchufar	*to plug in*
evitar	*to avoid*
faltar	*to lack; to need; to be missing*
funcionar	*to function, run (a motor)*
identificar	*to identify*
notar	*to notice, take note*
obtener (ie)	*to obtain*
reírse (i, i)	*to laugh*
resolver (ue)	*to resolve*
reventar (ie)	*to burst*
saltar	*to jump*
seguir (i, i) un curso	*to take a class*
sentir (ie, i)	*to feel*
tratar de	*to try, attempt*

Adjetivos

cortés *(m. / f.)*	*courteous*
cuidadoso(a)	*careful*
detallado(a)	*detailed*
duro(a)	*hard, difficult*
honesto(a)	*honest*
lento(a)	*slow*
preciso(a)	*precise*
rápido(a)	*rapid, fast*
seguro(a)	*sure, certain*

Adverbios

con calma	*calmly*
con precisión	*precisely*
cortésmente	*courteously*
de repente	*suddenly*
precisamente	*precisely*
pronto	*quickly, rapidly, fast*
rápidamente	*rapidly, fast*
tranquilamente	*tranquilly, calmly*

Expresiones negativas e indefinidas

alguien	*someone, anyone*
alguna vez	*sometime*
alguno(a)	*some, any*
jamás	*never*
nada	*nothing*
ni… ni	*neither . . . nor*
ninguno(a)	*none, not any*
o… o	*either . . . or*
tampoco	*neither*

Palabras útiles

callejón *(m.)*	*alley*
cartera	*purse, wallet*
estufa	*stove*
operador(a)	*operator*
promesa	*promise*
toalla	*towel*
veneno	*poison*

En preparación 10

10.1 Adverbs Derived from Adjectives

Expressing how an event happened

In **Capítulo 5** you learned that adverbs are words that qualify or modify an adjective, a verb, or another adverb. In this chapter, you will learn how to form adverbs from adjectives.

A. Adverbs are commonly formed from adjectives by adding **-mente** to the feminine singular form of the adjective. This is equivalent to adding **-ly** in English. Written accents on adverbs formed this way are required only if they appear on the adjective form.

tranquilo(a)	**tranquilamente**	*tranquilly, calmly*
lento(a)	**lentamente**	*slowly*
rápido(a)	**rápidamente**	*rapidly, fast*

B. Adjectives that do not have a separate feminine form add **-mente** to the singular form.

total	**totalmente**	*totally*
cortés	**cortésmente**	*courteously*
fuerte	**fuertemente**	*strongly, loudly*

C. When two or more adverbs occur in a series, only the last one takes the **-mente** ending; the others use the feminine (or singular) form of the adjective.

Yo caminaba **cuidadosa y lentamente** cuando lo vi.	*I was walking carefully and slowly when I saw him.*

D. Remember that adverbs are normally placed before adjectives or after the verb they modify.

Lo golpearon **violentamente.**	*They beat him violently.*
El tren es **bastante** rápido.	*The train is quite fast.*

¡A practicar!

A. ¡Es buenísimo! ¿Por qué dicen todos que Ernesto Trujillo es un policía muy bueno? Cambia los adjetivos entre paréntesis por adverbios al contestar.

1. Ernesto trabaja ______________ (serio).
2. Cuando hay una emergencia él llega ______________ (inmediato).
3. Se dedica ______________ (total) a su trabajo.

4. Ernesto siempre sabe ______________ (exacto) qué hacer en una emergencia.
5. Hace ______________ (rápido) todo lo que sus jefes le piden.
6. Siempre habla con el público muy ______________ (cortés).
7. Él siempre piensa ______________ (cuidadoso y lógico) antes de actuar.
8. En una emergencia, Ernesto actúa ______________ (inteligente y eficaz).

B. ¡Qué susto! Completando con el adverbio apropiado, lee lo que dice un periodista al informar de un robo en un restaurante.

La policía llegó ______________ (rápido) y capturó al ladrón ______________ (inmediato). Luego salieron todos del restaurante ______________ (tranquilo), pero al subir al carro policial, el ladrón reaccionó ______________ (violento). El jefe de la policía habló ______________ (cortés) con los periodistas y los clientes del restaurante. Luego agradeció *(expressed appreciation)* ______________ (fuerte) la cooperación de los trabajadores del lugar.

PASO 2

10.2 Irregular Verbs in the Preterite

Describing what already occurred

In **Capítulo 7,** you learned the preterite of **ir, ser, decir,** and **hacer.** The following is a more complete list of irregular verbs in the preterite. Note that all have irregular stems as well as unstressed first- and third-person singular verb endings. Note that with **hacer** the **c** changes to **z (hizo).**

i-stem verbs

hacer:	**hic-**	**-e, -iste, -o, -imos, -isteis, -ieron**
querer:	**quis-**	
venir:	**vin-**	

Venir

vine	vinimos
viniste	vinisteis
vino	vinieron
vino	vinieron

u-stem verbs

andar:	**anduv-**	**-e, -iste, -o, -imos, -isteis, -ieron**
estar:	**estuv-**	
haber:	**hub-**	
poder:	**pud-**	
poner:	**pus-**	
saber:	**sup-**	
tener:	**tuv-**	

Poder

pude	pudimos
pudiste	pudisteis
pudo	pudieron
pudo	pudieron

j-stem verbs

conducir:	**conduj-**	
decir:	**dij-**	
producir:	**produj-**	**-e, -iste, -o, -imos, -isteis, -eron**
traducir:	**traduj-**	
traer:	**traj-**	

Decir

dije	dijimos
dijiste	dijisteis
dijo	dijeron
dijo	dijeron

A. Note that any verb whose stem ends in **j** drops the **i** in the third-person plural ending of the preterite: **dijeron, trajeron,** etc.

B. The preterite of **hay** is **hubo** *(there was, there were).* As in the present indicative, it has only one form for both singular and plural.

Hubo un accidente en la carretera esta mañana.	*There was an accident on the highway this morning.*
¿**Hubo** muchos heridos?	*Were there many injured?*
Afortunadamente no **hubo** heridos.	*Fortunately no one was injured.*

¡A practicar!

A. ¡Hubo un accidente! ¿Cómo ocurrió? Completa estas oraciones con el pretérito de los verbos entre paréntesis.

Elena y Esteban ______________ (estar) en un accidente ayer. Esteban ______________ (perder) el control del coche y no ______________ (poder) parar a tiempo. Ellos ______________ (chocar) con otro coche. La policía ______________ (venir) y ______________ (decir) que el otro chófer no

_______________ (tener) la culpa *(was not at fault)*. Por suerte no _______________ (haber) heridos. Ellos _______________ (tener) que dejar el coche allí y _______________ (andar) a casa.

B. ¡Fue terrible! Ahora Esteban está explicándole a su agente de seguros cómo ocurrió el accidente. Cambia los verbos entre paréntesis al pretérito para saber qué le dice Esteban.

¡ _______________ (Ser) terrible! El chófer delante de mí _______________ (parar) de repente. Yo _______________ (hacer) todo lo posible para evitarlo pero no _______________ (poder) parar a tiempo. _______________ (Yo / perder) totalmente el control del coche. La policía _______________ (decir) que fue mi culpa. Mi señora _______________ (estar) muy nerviosa por varios días después. Ah, _______________ (yo / traer) la descripción del accidente que nos pidió escribir.

10.3 Negative and Indefinite Expressions

Denying information and referring to non-specific people and things

Negative and Indefinite Expressions

nada	*nothing*	algo	*something, anything*
nadie	*no one, nobody*	alguien	*someone, anyone*
ninguno	*none, not any*	alguno	*some, any*
nunca } jamás }	*never*	alguna vez	*sometime, ever*
		siempre	*always*
tampoco	*neither*	también	*also*
ni… ni	*neither . . . nor*	o… o	*either . . . or*

A. **Alguno** and **ninguno** are adjectives and therefore must agree with the words they modify. As with all numbers ending in **uno,** the **-uno** ending becomes **-ún** when it precedes a masculine singular noun: **algún, ningún.**

¿Tiene usted **algunos** amigos bomberos?	*Do you have any friends who are firefighters?*
No, no tengo **ningún** amigo bombero.	*No, I don't have any friends who are firefighters.*
¿Conoce usted a **alguna** persona en esta foto?	*Do you know anyone in this photo?*

B. Unlike English, a double negative construction is quite often used in Spanish. Whenever a negative word follows the verb, another negative word (usually **no)** must precede the verb.

Ni oí **nada, ni** vi a **nadie.**	*I neither heard anything nor did I see anyone.*
No recuerdo **ningún** momento.	*I don't remember (even) one moment.*
Nadie está en la casa.	*No one is in the house.*
No hay **nadie** en la casa.	*There isn't anyone in the house.*

¡A practicar!

A. Primeras informaciones. Para saber cuáles son las primeras preguntas que hacen los bomberos, completa estas preguntas con apropiadas expresiones indefinidas.

1. ¿Hay ______________ en el interior?
2. ¿Está seguro que no haya ______________ persona en el interior?
3. ¿Hay aquí ______________ testigo?
4. Señor, ¿usted vio ______________ sospechoso?
5. ¿Está seguro que no vio a ______________ sospechoso?
6. Señora, ¿está segura que no vio a ______________ ladrón?

B. ¡Contradicciones! El problema con los testigos es que con frecuencia se contradicen *(they contradict each other)*. ¿Cómo contradice Salvador a Lupe? ¿Qué dice?

LUPE Vi a alguien cerca de la casa.
SALVADOR Yo no vi ____
LUPE Noté algo extraño.
SALVADOR ____
LUPE Vi a algunas personas en la calle.
SALVADOR ____
LUPE Yo sé que hay algunos testigos.
SALVADOR ____
LUPE Oí algo extraño a las diez y media.
SALVADOR ____
LUPE Vi a un hombre o a un muchacho entrar en el edificio.
SALVADOR ____

10.4 Preterite of Stem-changing *-ir* verbs

Talking about past events

In the previous chapter, you learned that **-ar** and **-er** stem-changing verbs in the present indicative tense are regular verbs in the preterite. However, all **-ir** verbs whose stem changes in the present indicative also have a stem change in the *third-person* singular and plural forms of the preterite. In these verbs, there is only a one-vowel change: **e → i** or **o → u.** Following are some frequently used stem-changing **-ir** verbs. Note that the present-tense stem change is given first, then the preterite stem change.

Seguir

seguí	seguimos
seguiste	seguisteis
siguió	**siguieron**
siguió	**siguieron**

Dormir

dormí	dormimos
dormiste	dormisteis
durmió	**durmieron**
durmió	**durmieron**

conseguir (i, i)	*to obtain*	preferir (ie, i)	*to prefer*
despedir (i, i)	*to fire, discharge*	reírse* (i, i)	*to laugh*
divertirse (ie, i)	*to have a good time*	repetir (i, i)	*to repeat*
dormir (ue, u)	*to sleep*	seguir (i, i)	*to follow, continue*
mentir (ie, i)	*to lie*	sentir (ie, i)	*to feel, to hear*
morir (ue, u)	*to die*	servir (i, i)	*to serve*
pedir (i, i)	*to ask (for)*	vestirse (i, i)	*to get dressed*
perseguir (i, i)	*to pursue*		

¡A practicar!

A. ¡Con el pie izquierdo! Jaime dice que ayer se levantó con el pie izquierdo. Veamos qué dice él…

Modelo anoche / acostarme / muy tarde
Anoche me acosté muy tarde.

1. no / dormir / muy bien
2. casi / no conseguir / descansar
3. por la mañana / no oír / despertador
4. vestirse / rápidamente
5. preferir / ir / universidad / autobús
6. llegar / tarde a la parada y / perder / el autobús
7. cuando / llegar / finalmente / ver / que era sábado
8. cuando / regresar / casa / compañeros / reírse / de mí

B. ¡Un día fatal! A veces es mejor no levantarse por la mañana. Ayer fue uno de esos días para Francisco. Completa el párrafo con la forma correcta del verbo entre paréntesis para saber por qué.

Anoche Francisco ______________ (dormir) muy mal. Por la mañana ______________ (perder) el autobús para ir al trabajo y no ______________ (conseguir) un taxi hasta las nueve y media. Obviamente, ______________ (llegar) tarde al trabajo. Después de un día dificilísimo, al regresar a casa un ladrón *(thief)* lo ______________ (seguir) y le ______________ (pedir) la cartera. Se la ______________ (llevar) con todo su dinero y documentos de identidad. Francisco casi ______________ (morirse) de miedo.

C. ¡Sí, hay justicia! Ahora la policía está interrogando al ladrón que robó a Francisco. Completa el párrafo con la forma correcta del verbo entre paréntesis para saber qué dice el ladrón.

¡Fue facilísimo! Yo ______________ (repetir) lo que siempre hago cuando veo a una víctima fácil. ______________ (Yo / seguir) al señor por dos cuadras. Como no había *(there was)* nadie en la calle, le ______________ (decir) que tenía una pistola y le ______________ (pedir) la cartera. Cuando él ______________(sentir) mi

*Note that **reír** drops an **e** in the third person singular and plural: **rio, rieron.**

pistola a su lado, casi ______________ (morirse) de miedo. Yo ______________ (reírme) de lo fácil que fue y ______________ (despedirme) cortésmente. Desafortunadamente, ustedes ______________ (seguirme) y aquí estoy.

10.5 *Hacer* and Past Events

Expressing time relationships with *ago*

In **Capítulo 4** you learned to describe an action that began sometime in the past and is still going on with the following formula.

Hace + (time expression) + **que** + (present tense verb)

To describe the time that has lapsed since an event occurred, Spanish uses another formula.

Hace + (time expression) + **que** + (past tense/preterite verb)

Hace dos horas **que comí.**	*I ate two hours ago.*
Hace un mes **que** ellos **llegaron.**	*They arrived a month ago.*

Note that the English equivalent pairs up the past tense and the word *ago*.

¡A practicar!

A. ¡Hace poco! You have been working and studying so much lately that your friends are starting to say that you never do anything else. What do you tell them when they make the following comments?

Modelo ¿Cuándo fue la última vez que fuiste al cine? (dos semanas)
Hace dos semanas que fui al cine.

1. ¿Cuándo fue la última vez que saliste a comer con tus amigos? (dos meses)
2. ¿Cuándo fue la última vez que invitaste a tus amigos a beber una cerveza? (tres semanas)
3. ¿Cuándo fue la última vez que fuiste a cenar con tus amigos? (tres meses)
4. ¿Cuándo fue la última vez que viste la televisión? (una semana)
5. ¿Cuándo fue la última vez que llamaste a tus padres? (un mes)

B. ¿Y cuánto tiempo hace que... ? ¿Cuánto tiempo hace que hiciste lo siguiente?

Modelo llegar a esta ciudad
Hace un año que llegué a esta ciudad.

1. graduarte de la escuela secundaria
2. comenzar a trabajar
3. dejar de vivir con tus padres
4. aprender a conducir
5. empezar a estudiar en esta universidad

CAPÍTULO 11

Y tú, ¿qué hacías?

Cultural Topics

- **¿Sabías que… ?**
  ¿Quiénes asisten a la universidad en los países hispanos?
- ***La dinastía del amor***
  Cross-cultural perceptions regarding teen dating habits and teens having their own apartments
- **Noticiero cultural**
  Lugar: *Costa Rica: Un país que vive la democracia*
  Costumbres: *Los «ticos»*
- **Lectura:** *La leyenda de Iztarú*

Writing Strategies

- *Especificar los hechos*

Reading Strategies

- *Encontrar la idea principal*

En preparación

- 11.1 Imperfect of Regular Verbs
- 11.2 Uses of the Imperfect
- 11.3 Imperfect of **Ser, ir,** and **ver**
- 11.4 Preterite and Imperfect: Completed and Continuous Actions
- 11.5 Preterite and Imperfect: Beginning / End and Habitual / Customary Actions
- 11.6 Present Perfect

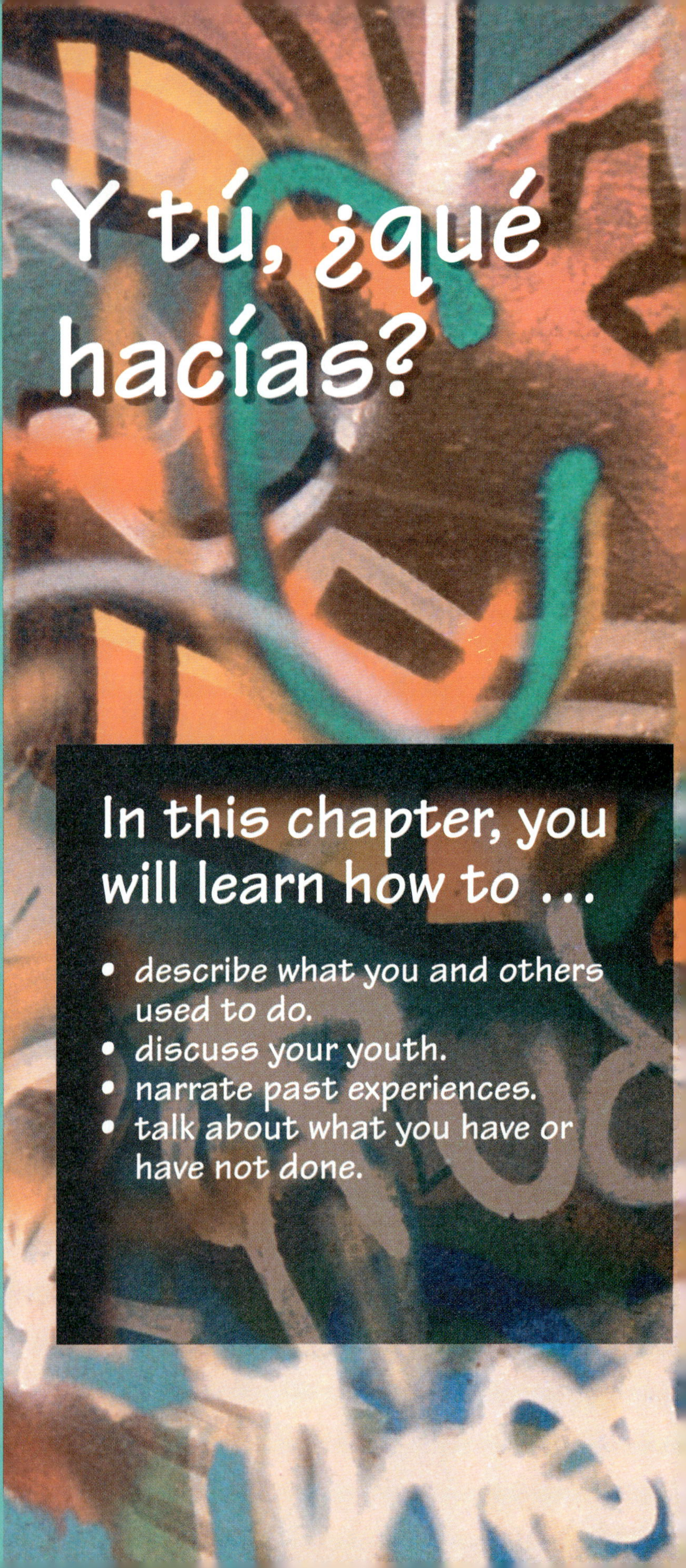

In this chapter, you will learn how to …

- describe what you and others used to do.
- discuss your youth.
- narrate past experiences.
- talk about what you have or have not done.

De niño, yo jugaba al fútbol con mis amigos.

De niña, yo siempre jugaba con mis muñecas.

Nosotros asistíamos a la escuela en Costa Rica.

Lo que ya sabes...

1. ¿Jugabas tú al fútbol cuando eras niño(a)? ¿Jugabas al fútbol en la calle o en otro lugar?
2. Nombra dos o tres juegos que eran muy populares entre los niños cuando tú eras niño(a). ¿Cuáles jugabas tú?
3. Muchos juguetes (*toys*) de niños son universales. ¿Puedes nombrar algunos?
4. ¿Tenías un juguete favorito cuando eras niño(a)? ¿Qué era?
5. ¿Era tu escuela como esta escuela en Costa Rica? Compáralas.

COSTA RICA

Jugaba mucho y estudiaba poco

TAREA

Antes de empezar este **Paso**, estudia **En preparación** 11.1, 11.2 y 11.3 y haz por escrito los ejercicios de **¡A practicar!** También escucha **Paso 1 ¿Qué se dice... ?** del Capítulo 11 en el CD del estudiante.

¿Eres buen observador?

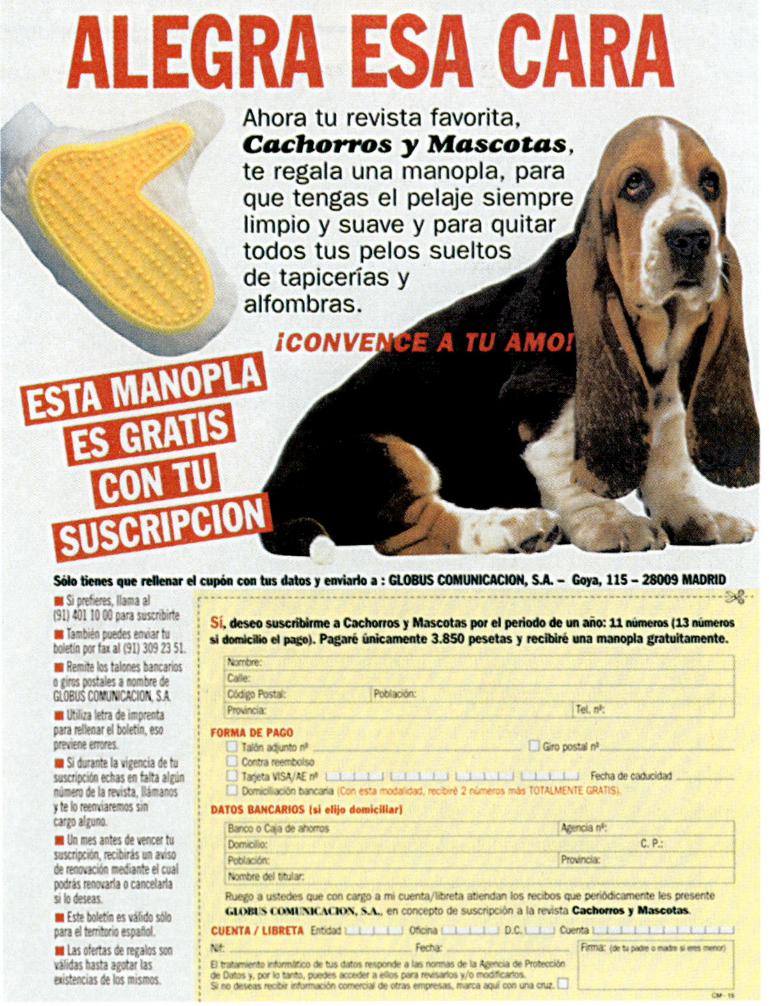

Ahora, ¡a analizar!

1. ¿Para qué es esta propaganda? ¿Para qué producto?
2. ¿Qué vas a recibir gratis si pides este producto?
3. ¿Qué es un cachorro? ¿una mascota?
4. ¿Tienes un cachorro u otra mascota ahora? ¿Dónde está? ¿Tenías un cachorro u otra mascota cuando eras niño(a)? ¿Cómo se llamaba?
5. Explica el título de este anuncio. Explica también la expresión: «¡Convence a tu amo!»

¿Qué se dice...?

Al hablar del pasado

Como buen estudiante yo...

1. ____________________
2. ____________________
3. ____________________

También era popular porque...

4. ____________________
5. ____________________

JORGE Dirigía una banda de música rock y tocaba los tambores y címbalos. También tocaba la trompeta en la orquesta de mi escuela. Mi hermano tocaba el clarinete y el saxofón.

JORGE Casi nunca veía la tele por la noche porque cuando no tenía que practicar al fútbol, iba a trabajar en un supermercado después de las clases.

¿Sabías que... ?

En muchos países hispanos cuesta muy poco o no cuesta nada asistir a una universidad, pero es muy difícil ser aceptado. Hay que aprobar *(pass)* un examen largo y dificilísimo. Cada año hay más postulantes que vacantes y sólo aceptan a los mejores estudiantes. Una vez aceptados, pueden trabajar de ayudantes para ganar experiencia en la carrera elegida.

Ahora, ¡a hablar!

A. ¡Sigue mi ejemplo! El presidente de una compañía de computadoras le está explicando a su hijo cómo llegó a ser presidente. ¿Qué dice que hacía cuando estaba en la escuela secundaria?

Modelo estudiar / cuatro horas / todo / días

Yo estudiaba cuatro horas todos los días.

1. trabajar / tienda / todo / días / después / clases
2. siempre / ayudar / mamá / por / noche
3. no / salir / amigos / fines / semana
4. no / tomar / bebidas / alcohólico
5. leer / mucho / libros
6. jugar / mucho / deportes / y / tocar / banda / mi escuela
7. no / fumar / y / no / usar / drogas

B. Recuerdos. Durante los años de la escuela secundaria generalmente se vive una vida muy activa. ¿Con qué frecuencia hacían tú y tus amigos lo siguiente?

Modelo hablar por teléfono

Nosotros hablábamos por teléfono todos los días.

1. jugar con amigos
2. estudiar juntos
3. ver deportes en la televisión
4. hablar por teléfono
5. salir juntos
6. comer en la cafetería
7. hacer fiestas
8. ¿... ?

C. En la primaria. Cuando estabas en la escuela primaria, tu vida era diferente. Compara tu vida actual con la de tu infancia.

Modelo Ahora trabajo mucho.
Antes no trabajaba nunca.

1. Ahora sufro de estrés.
2. Ahora tengo muchas responsabilidades.
3. Ahora necesito ganar dinero.
4. Ahora duermo *(¿... ?)* horas.
5. Ahora trabajo mucho.
6. Ahora soy muy responsable.
7. Ahora veo poca televisión.
8. Ahora ¿... ?

Y ahora, ¡a conversar!

A. La escuela secundaria. Pregúntale a tu compañero(a)...

1. si estudiaba mucho y tenía mucha tarea en la escuela secundaria.
2. si participaba en muchas actividades. ¿Cuáles?
3. cómo se llamaba su maestro(a) favorito(a) y por qué le gustaba tanto.
4. si le gustaban los deportes y cuáles jugaba.
5. si le gustaba la música y si tocaba algún instrumento.
6. qué hacía después de las clases y si trabajaba.

B. Y tú, ¿qué hacías? La vida constantemente cambia. ¿Qué pasaba en tu vida hace unos tres o cuatro años? Escribe cinco cosas que hacías y compártelas con un(a) compañero(a).

Modelo **En 1996 yo asistía a la escuela secundaria. Vivía en Trenton y trabajaba en un supermercado los fines de semana...**

C. Me recuerda... Para la próxima clase, trae un objeto que te haga recordar tus años de la escuela secundaria. Puede ser un objeto, un animal de peluche *(stuffed animal),* una joya, un artículo de ropa, una foto, un libro, etc.

En grupos de tres o cuatro...

- presenten su objeto.
- descríbanlo en detalle.
- expliquen cuántos años tenían cuando lo obtuvieron.
- expliquen qué importancia tenía para ustedes.

¡Luz! ¡Cámara! ¡Acción!

A. ¿Mis padres? Tú y tu mejor amigo(a) están hablando de cómo eran sus padres cuando eran jóvenes. Dramaticen la situación. Mencionen algunas de las cosas divertidas que hacían.

B. ¡Yo nunca hacía eso! Ahora eres padre o madre y quieres dar un buen ejemplo a tu hijo(a). Le dices lo que hacías cuando asistías a la universidad. Acuérdate que tienes que mostrar un buen ejemplo; exagera lo bueno si es necesario y no hables de lo malo. Dramatiza la situación con un(a) compañero(a) de clase.

¿Comprendes lo que se dice?

La dinastía del amor: Episodio 1

Ahora ustedes van a conocer a la familia Gómez, de Monterrey, México. Todos los martes a las nueve de la noche ellos se sientan *(sit down)* frente al televisor para ver *La dinastía del amor,* una versión en español de la nueva telenovela *(soap opera)* que viene directamente desde los Estados Unidos. La familia incluye al padre, don Sergio Gómez, arquitecto de 48 años; su esposa doña María Luisa de Gómez, profesora de 45 años, y sus dos hijos, Luisita y Juan Pedro. Luisita tiene 16 años y está en su último año de la escuela secundaria. Juan Pedro tiene 20 años y asiste a la Universidad de Arizona en los Estados Unidos.

En el episodio anterior Natalie decide hacer una fiesta en su casa. Este nuevo episodio empieza la noche de la fiesta, a las siete y media. Escúchalo y luego contesta las preguntas a continuación.

A través de dos culturas

Telenovela

1. ¿Dónde se filmó *La dinastía del amor?* ¿Se filmó en español originalmente? Explica.
2. ¿Quiénes llegan a casa de Natalie? ¿A qué hora llegan?
3. ¿Por qué está contenta Natalie?
4. ¿Quién es Eric?
5. ¿Es ésta la primera vez que Sharon y Eric se reúnen *(meet)*?
6. ¿Qué hacen Natalie y Rod?
7. ¿Adónde va Sharon? ¿Quién va con ella?
8. ¿Qué insinúa Kathy al final?

Televidentes

9. ¿Cuál es el nombre, la edad y la profesión de Sergio, María Luisa, Luisita y Juan Pedro?
10. ¿Estás de acuerdo con don Sergio Gómez? ¿Crees que la gente joven cada día está peor? ¿Por qué sí o por qué no?
11. ¿Crees que las ideas de don Sergio y doña María Luisa son anticuadas? Explica.
12. ¿Reaccionan don Sergio y su señora de una manera muy diferente a cómo reaccionarían los padres de una familia estadounidense?
13. ¿Es verdad lo que dice Juan Pedro? ¿Cambian los jóvenes estadounidenses de novio todos los días? ¿y los jóvenes hispanos? Explica.

NOTICIERO CULTURAL

LUGAR... COSTA RICA

Antes de empezar, dime...

1. ¿Qué opinas de la pena de muerte *(death penalty)*? ¿Crees que puede eliminarse en civilizaciones avanzadas o no? ¿Por qué?
2. ¿Hasta qué edad es gratuita *(free)* la educación en los EE.UU.? ¿Crees que debe extenderse esa edad? ¿Por qué?
3. En tu opinión, ¿es posible la democracia sin un ejército para defenderla? ¿Hay países sin ejército donde se practica la democracia? ¿Cuáles?
4. ¿Hay algunas ventajas en no tener ejército? Explica tu respuesta.
5. ¿Qué es el Premio Nóbel de la Paz? ¿Puedes nombrar a alguien que lo recibió recientemente?

Niños costarricenses se preparan para un desfile *(parade)*.

Una democracia sin armas

El sistema de gobierno y la constitución de Costa Rica son algunos aspectos que la hacen muy diferente de otros países hispanos y de los Estados Unidos. En un mundo de violencia, este pequeño país, situado entre Nicaragua y Panamá, da lecciones de democracia a todo el mundo.

Oscar Arias Sánchez

Costa Rica siempre ha sido un país progresista, un líder entre las naciones democráticas. En la constitución de 1949, Costa Rica estableció la educación obligatoria y gratuita *(free)* para todos los costarricenses y creó impuestos *(taxes)* para financiarla. En 1882 eliminó la pena de muerte. Y en 1948 eliminó el ejército. A pesar de la inestabilidad de los países vecinos, Nicaragua y El Salvador, Costa Rica sigue siendo la única democracia sin ejército en Norte y Sudamérica.

El mejor ejemplo del importante papel que tiene la democracia en este pequeño país es que en el año 1987, el presidente de Costa Rica ganó el Premio Nóbel de la Paz. El señor Oscar Arias Sánchez ganó la notable distinción por sus esfuerzos para lograr la paz en Centroamérica. El presidente Arias fue autor del llamado «Plan para la paz en Centroamérica», que fue firmado por cinco repúblicas centroamericanas en 1987, como uno de los mayores intentos para eliminar la violencia y el terrorismo en Centroamérica.

Y ahora, dime...

Usa este diagrama Venn para comparar a Costa Rica y los EE.UU. Indica las diferencias y lo que tienen en común.

Costa Rica

1.
2.
3.
4.
5.
6.
. . .

Costa Rica y Estados Unidos

1.
2.
3.
4.
5.
6.
. . .

Estados Unidos

1.
2.
3.
4.
5.
6.
. . .

El español en otras disciplinas: Música

Música latina. Latino américa se caracteriza por el uso de distintos instrumentos musicales que le dan un «sabor latino» muy especial a su música. Además de los instrumentos de cuerda, percusión y viento, como por ejemplo la guitarra, el tambor o el saxofón, la música latina incorpora una serie de instrumentos muy peculiares como la **marimba,** el **cuatro,** el **guitarrón** y las **maracas**. Más aún, la música andina incluye entre otros el **charango**, las **quenas** y **zampoñas**, las **flautas** y **pitos** y, por supuesto, el «grave» **bombo**. Con un(a) compañero(a), preparen una explicación de dos de estos instrumentos. Si es necesario, consulten un diccionario o una enciclopedia. Presenten sus explicaciones en grupos pequeños.

Proyecto: Trae a la clase algún tipo de música latina y habla de su origen/cultura y de los instrumentos utilizados. Si puedes traer y hablar de un instrumento específico (o una foto de él), ¡aún mejor!

¡No te vi! ¿Dónde estabas?

TAREA Antes de empezar este **Paso**, estudia **En preparación** 11.4 y 11.5 y haz por escrito los ejercicios de **¡A practicar!** También escucha **Paso 2 ¿Qué se dice... ?** del Capítulo 11 en el CD del estudiante.

¿Eres buen observador?

COSTA RICA "A TU MEDIDA"

❖ VOLCANES EN ERUPCION, BOSQUES Y PLAYAS, QUETZALES Y PEREZOSOS, TORTUGAS Y TUCANES, CAIMANES Y GARZAS, ATLANTICO Y PACIFICO, CORCOVADO Y TORTUGUERO...

❖ VIAJES DE NOVIOS, DE AVENTURA, BUCEO, TREKKING, PESCA, OBSERVACION DE AVES... LO QUE TU QUIERAS.

❖ SUITES DE 12.000 PTS. LA NOCHE Y ENCANTADORES HOTELITOS DE 2.500 PTS, EN COCHE CON CONDUCTOR, COCHE DE ALQUILER, TRANSPORTE PUBLICO O COMBINANDO TODAS LAS OPCIONES... Ponemos toda la información a tu alcance para que TU SEAS QUIEN ELIJA ENTRE LAS MULTIPLES OPCIONES QUE OFRECE COSTA RICA.

ESPECIALISTAS EN COSTA RICA

INFORMACION Y RESERVAS:
Pº de la Castellana, 166 - 5º D.
Madrid. Telf.: 350 18 00
Fax: 350 21 51

OCHO
exclusivas suites en las afueras de San José

HOTEL EUROPA CENTRO
En el corazón de San José. Clásico y con un magnífico restaurante

En el Pacífico Central

CARIBBEAN MAGIC
ECO-LODGE
TORTUGUERO

Solicite información detallada, sin compromiso.

Ahora, ¡a analizar!

1. ¿Quién crees que hace esta propaganda? ¿Dónde crees que va a aparecer este anuncio?
2. ¿Cuántos animales puedes ver en Costa Rica según este anuncio? ¿Cuáles son? ¿Sabes qué son todos? Si no, ¿cuáles no identifican?
3. ¿Cuántas actividades distintas puedes hacer en Costa Rica según este anuncio? ¿Cuáles te interesan a ti?
4. ¿Cómo se puede viajar en Costa Rica? ¿Dónde se puede hospedar?
5. Explica el título de este anuncio.

Al hablar de lo que pasó

1. Pensaba ir a su clase, pero...
   a. no se despertó a tiempo.
   b. su carro no funcionó.

2. Mientras se bañaba,...
   a. su mamá preparó el desayuno.
   b. sonó el teléfono.

JORGE La semana pasada no pude comprar el manual de ciencias porque no tenía bastante dinero. ¡Cuesta $75! Llamé a la profesora inmediatamente para quejarme del precio, pero no estaba. Por eso dejé la clase.

JORGE El lunes de la semana pasada me llamó mi amiga Lidia para invitarme a una fiesta el sábado. Pero le dije que no podía aceptar porque ya tenía planes de ir al cine con Abelardo. Eso no era verdad y terminé pasando el sábado solo y aburrido en casa mirando la televisión.

Ahora, ¡a hablar!

A. ¡No dormí toda la noche! Marcos faltó a todas sus clases esta mañana. Para saber por qué, selecciona el verbo correcto en cada oración.

1. Yo (dormí/dormía) cuando un sonido muy fuerte me (despertó/despertaba).
2. El sonido que (oí/oía), (fue/era) la sirena de un coche de policía.
3. Yo (cerré/cerraba) los ojos para dormirme otra vez cuando (sonó/sonaba) el teléfono.
4. Me (levanté/levantaba) para contestar el teléfono pero la llamada no (fue/era) para mí.
5. Como (tuve/tenía) mucho sueño, me (acosté/acostaba) otra vez.
6. Luego el perro de mi vecino (empezó/empezaba) a ladrar *[bark]* y me (desperté/despertaba) otra vez.
7. Cuando (sonó/sonaba) el despertador, yo no lo (oí/oía) porque (dormí/dormía) profundamente.

B. Interrupciones. Ernesto tenía la intención de hacer muchas cosas ayer, pero una serie de interrupciones no le dejaron terminar nada. ¿Qué pasó?

Modelo yo / estudiar: teléfono / sonar
Yo estudiaba cuando el teléfono sonó.

1. escribir / composición: computadora / dejar de funcionar
2. ordenar / cuarto: amigo / llegar
3. leer / libro muy interesante: novia / llamarme
4. manejar / tienda: llanta *(tire)* / pincharse
5. preparar / cena: amigos / invitarme a comer
6. nosotros mirar / televisión: electricidad / cortarse

C. ¡No era perfecto! Jaime era un adolescente bueno y por lo general era responsable, pero, como todos los jóvenes, también hacía algunas cosas malas. ¿Qué hacía generalmente? ¿Qué cosas malas hizo?

Modelo Generalmente (estudiar) mucho antes de un examen pero una vez no (abrir) el libro.
Generalmente estudiaba mucho antes de un examen pero una vez no abrió el libro.

1. Siempre (ser) buen estudiante pero un día (sacar) una F.
2. Siempre (respetar) el límite de velocidad pero un día (manejar) demasiado rápido.
3. Normalmente no (faltar) a clase pero una semana (decidir) no ir a la escuela.
4. Siempre (decir) la verdad pero una vez les (mentir) a sus padres.
5. Nunca (tomar) bebidas alcohólicas pero una noche (emborracharse).
6. Siempre (respetar) a los adultos pero un día (insultar) a su vecino.

D. ¡No fue mi culpa! Juanito es muy mal estudiante. Siempre llega tarde o falta a las clases y siempre tiene un pretexto. ¿Qué le pasó la semana pasada? ¿Qué excusas encontró?

Modelo lunes: llegar tarde / la llanta pincharse

Llegué tarde porque la llanta del coche se pinchó.

1. lunes: llegar tarde / el despertador / no sonar
2. martes: no ir a clase / en la mañana / enfermarme
3. miércoles: faltar a / la clase de matemáticas / perder el libro
4. jueves: no asistir / la primera clase / perder el autobús
5. viernes: no ir a clase / tener emergencia en casa

E. ¿Qué hicieron ayer? Un alumno quiere saber qué hicieron en la clase que se perdió ayer. ¿Qué le dice su amiga?

Para empezar, el profesor ______________ (perder) el autobús y ______________ (llegar) con veinte minutos de retraso. ¡Él ______________ (estar) furioso! Pero él ______________ (enojarse) más cuando ______________ (ver) que cinco estudiantes no ______________ (estar) en la clase. Entonces ______________ (darnos) un examen muy difícil. Por suerte, mientras nosotros ______________ (hacer) el examen, ______________ (sonar) una alarma y todos ______________ (tener) que salir rápidamente. Obviamente, no ______________ (poder) terminar el examen.

Y ahora, ¡a conversar!

A. ¿Mejores excusas? ¿Qué excusas dan ustedes? Trabajando en grupos de tres, preparen una lista de posibles excusas para estas situaciones.

Modelo ¿Por qué no fuiste al laboratorio ayer?

Estaba demasiado cansado. Tuve que preparar un trabajo *(paper)* **para la clase de inglés.**

1. ¿Por qué no hiciste la tarea anoche?
2. ¿Por qué no asististe a clase ayer?
3. ¿Por qué llegaste tan tarde a clase hoy?
4. ¿Por qué no estudiaste para el examen?
5. ¿Por qué faltaste al último examen?

B. ¿Y en tu clase? Trabajando en parejas, pregúntale a tu compañero(a)...

1. cuál fue su primera clase ayer. ¿A qué hora empezó?
2. cómo estaba el (la) profesor(a). ¿Cómo se sentía él (ella)?
3. si estaba preparado(a). ¿Cómo se preparó?
4. si le gustó la clase. ¿Cuál fue el tema de la clase? ¿Lo presentó bien el (la) profesor(a)?
5. si tuvieron un examen. ¿Pasó algo interesante? ¿Qué? Descríbelo.

C. La Cenicienta. Los siguientes dibujos narran parte del famoso cuento de hadas *(fairy tale) La Cenicienta.* Narra el cuento completo con la ayuda de tu compañero(a) que tiene, en la página A-6, los dibujos que faltan.

Vocabulario útil

la madrastra	*stepmother*	la hermanastra	*stepsister*
el príncipe	*prince*	los ratoncitos	*little mice*
la chimenea	*fireplace*	el hada madrina	*fairy godmother*
la calabaza	*pumpkin*	la carroza	*carriage*
la zapatilla	*slipper*	el cristal	*glass, crystal*
la escalera	*stairway*	el paje	*valet*
probar (ue)	*to try on*	de rodillas	*kneeling*

1. Había una vez una muchacha que se llamaba Cenicienta...

3. La Cenicienta no...

5. El hada madrina dijo...

7. Cuando la Cenicienta...

D. Ésta es mi vida. Tu vida va a servir de base para un cuento moderno. Escribe tu versión personal de tu propia vida. Luego compártela con un(a) compañero(a).

Modelo Había una vez un(a) muchacho(a) que se llamaba... Vivía en...

¡Luz! ¡Cámara! ¡Acción!

A. ¡No pude ir! Anoche hubo una fiesta y tú no pudiste ir. Claro, ahora tú quieres saber todos los detalles: ¿quiénes fueron? ¿qué hicieron? ¿si fue una persona muy especial? ¿qué hizo esa persona? ¿con quién bailó?... Dramatiza la conversación con un(a) amigo(a) que te pueda dar toda la información.

B. ¡Pobre mamá (papá)! Ayer fue el cumpleaños de tu mamá (papá) y lo olvidaste completamente. ¡No la (lo) llamaste! ¡No le mandaste ni una tarjeta! Sabes que tu mamá (papá) va a sentirse muy mal. Ahora hablas con ella (él) por teléfono para explicarle por qué no llamaste ayer. Dramatiza la situación con tu compañero(a).

¿Comprendes lo que se dice?

La dinastía del amor: Episodio 2

Son las nueve de la noche del martes y la familia Gómez se prepara para ver otro episodio de la popular telenovela *La dinastía del amor.* En este nuevo episodio Eric, acompañado de Sharon, examina un apartamento que quiere alquilar. Escucha el episodio y luego contesta las preguntas que siguen.

A través de dos culturas

Telenovela

1. ¿Cómo es el apartamento que encuentra Eric?
2. ¿Dónde está el apartamento?
3. ¿Qué dice Sharon sobre el apartamento?
4. ¿Por qué cree Eric que a Natalie le va a gustar el apartamento?
5. ¿Crees que Natalie y Sharon son buenas amigas? ¿Por qué?

Televidentes

6. Don Sergio y doña Luisa insinúan que los jóvenes ahora hacen muchas cosas que no se permitían en sus tiempos. ¿Cuáles son algunas de estas cosas?
7. ¿Trata de la misma manera don Sergio a su hijo y a su hija? ¿Crees que las hijas deben tener los mismos privilegios y responsabilidades que los hijos? Explica. ¿Cuáles son otros problemas que los padres tienen con los hijos?
8. ¿Es común que los estudiantes universitarios vivan en apartamentos en los EE.UU.?
9. ¿Crees que don Sergio y doña Luisa le van a permitir a Luisita vivir en su propio apartamento?
10. ¿Por qué le permite don Sergio a su hijo vivir en un apartamento?

NOTICIERO CULTURAL

COSTUMBRES... COSTA RICA

Antes de empezar, dime...

1. En los EE.UU. como en todos los países la pronunciación varía en diferentes zonas del país. ¿Cuántas de estas zonas o pronunciaciones puedes distinguir tú? ¿Puedes imitar algunas?
2. A veces no sólo la pronunciación varía sino el vocabulario también. En Boston, por ejemplo, hablan de un *"elastic"* mientras que en California dicen *"rubber-band."* ¿Puedes pensar en otras palabras que identifiquen distintas partes de los EE.UU.? Prepara una lista.
3. ¿Cómo son diferentes el inglés de Inglaterra y el de los EE.UU.? Explica y da ejemplos.

Los «ticos»

Dos muchachas conversan en un café de San José. Rosalía es de Costa Rica y Mercedes es de Uruguay.

ROSALÍA Si vamos a ir juntas al cine esta tarde tienes que esperarme un poquitico porque tengo otras cosas que hacer antes de las dos.

MERCEDES Sí, perfecto. No hay problema. ¿Te gustaría pasar a tomar algo antes de la película?

ROSALÍA Sí, buena idea. Conozco un sitio chiquitico cerca de aquí que te va a encantar.

MERCEDES Me encanta como hablas. Suena tan bonito. ¿Es una nueva costumbre de todos los jóvenes usar eso de «tico»?

Pasatiempo favorito

Y ahora, dime...

¿Por qué usa Rosalía tanto el diminutivo **«-tico»**?

1. A los jóvenes de Costa Rica, como a los de todo el mundo, les gusta tener su propia jerga *(slang)* y el diminutivo **«-tico»** es la jerga que está actualmente de moda entre la juventud costarricense.
2. El español de Costa Rica es muy diferente del español de otros países del hemisferio. A veces es difícil comunicarse con los costarricenses.
3. El diminutivo **«-tico»** es parte del dialecto costarricense. No sólo los jóvenes sino también los niños y los adultos usan este diminutivo.

En el Apéndice A, mira el número que corresponde a la respuesta que seleccionaste.

Antes de escribir
Estrategias para escribir: Especificar los hechos

Reportaje. En el capítulo anterior aprendiste que las composiciones siempre contestan ciertas preguntas clave. Lo mismo ocurre con el reportaje periodístico. Para escribir un reportaje periodístico es necesario partir de hechos específicos. Es importante que el reportaje conteste siempre a las preguntas esenciales: **¿qué?, ¿cuándo?, ¿dónde?, ¿cómo?, ¿quiénes?, ¿cuánto tiempo?** y **¿cuáles fueron los resultados?**

Ahora, ¡a escribir!

A. La idea principal. Elige un incidente reciente apropiado para reportar en el periódico de tu universidad. Puede ser un accidente, un partido, una fiesta, un incidente en una clase, en la biblioteca, en la cafetería, en la residencia, etc.

B. Al especificar. Pensando en el incidente que vas a reportar, contesta las siete preguntas de **Reportaje** en la sección anterior. Luego añade otra información pertinente a cada respuesta.

C. El primer borrador. Usa la información que preparaste en **B** para escribir un primer borrador. Pon toda la información relacionada con la misma idea en un párrafo. No te olvides de poner un título que informe sobre lo que va a decir tu artículo.

D. Ahora, a compartir. Comparte tu primer borrador con dos o tres compañeros. Comenta sobre el contenido y el estilo de los reportajes de tus compañeros y escucha los comentarios de ellos sobre tu noticia. Fíjate, en particular, en cada uso del pretérito y del imperfecto. Si hay errores, menciónalos.

E. Ahora, a revisar. Si necesitas hacer cambios, basados en los comentarios de tus compañeros, hazlos ahora.

F. La versión final. Prepara una versión final de tu composición y entrégala.

G. Publicación. Preparen un periódico con todos los artículos de sus compañeros de clase y cuélguenlo *(hang it)* en la pared donde todo el mundo pueda leerlo.

¡No he hecho nada!

TAREA

Antes de empezar este **Paso**, estudia **En preparación** 11.6 y haz por escrito los ejercicios de **¡A practicar!** También escucha **Paso 3 ¿Qué se dice... ?** del Capítulo 11 en el CD del estudiante.

¿Eres buen observador?

Nadie sabe el bien que tiene... hasta que lo ve perdido.

Conserva la naturaleza, hoy. Recibe Ocelotl.

Pronatura te invita a conocer, con la revista Ocelotl, las bellezas naturales de México.
Con sólo N$100.00, además de recibir Ocelotl por un año, apoyarás nuestros proyectos de conservación que van desde las exuberantes selvas tropicales hasta el maravilloso Mar de Cortés.
Porque quieres conservar la naturaleza.
Tu donativo es deducible de impuestos.

Envía este cupón a Pronatura, A.C. Camino al Ajusco Nº 124, 5º Piso.
Fracc. Jardines en la Montaña C.P. 14210 México, D.F.
Tel.: 630 11 33. Fax: 631 57 27.

Nombre ____________________
Teléfono __________ Fax __________
Dirección a donde se enviará la revista ____________________
____
Colonia ____________________
C.P. ______ Ciudad ______ Estado ______
Forma de pago:
Giro postal ☐ Giro bancario ☐ Cheque personal ☐
Tarjeta:
Carnet ☐ Bancomer ☐ Banamex ☐
No. ____________________
Válida hasta ____________________
Firma ____________________
Autorización ____________________

No. de Afiliación Pronatura 4986378
Por este pagaré me obligo incondicionalmente a pagar a la orden del Banco emisor de la tarjeta descrita en este documento, el importe de este título. Este pagaré procede del contrato de apertura de crédito que el Banco emisor y el tarjetahabiente tienen celebrado y representa las disposiciones que del crédito concedido hace el suscriptor.
Tanto la restitución de la suma dispuesta, como los intereses que causara dicha suma, se determinarán y calcularán en la forma, términos y condiciones convenidos en el contrato referido.

Ahora, ¡a analizar!

1. ¿Qué tipo de revista es *Ocelotl*? ¿Dónde se publica?
2. ¿Cuánto cuesta suscribirse a *Ocelotl*? ¿Más o menos cuánto es en dólares?
3. Lo que pagas por una suscripción se usa para varias causas. ¿Cuáles son?
4. ¿Hay organizaciones en los EE.UU. que, como *Ocelotl*, tienen una publicación pero usan el dinero de las suscripciones para proyectos de conservación? Nombra algunas.
5. ¿Estás suscrito a algunas de estas organizaciones? ¿A cuáles?

¿Qué se dice...?

Al hablar de lo que (no) has hecho

1. ______________ ha dejado de llamarlo.
2. ______________ se ha enojado con Jorge.
3. ______________ lo han abandonado.

JORGE Y fíjese, doctor,... le confieso que por primera vez en la vida he recibido una mala nota. Mi profesora de música me ha dado una D y los otros profesores me han amenazado con malas notas también si sigo faltando a mis clases.

JORGE ¡Caramba, doctor! No sé qué me pasa. Siempre he sido un buen estudiante... he estudiado mucho y he trabajado todos los días. He cumplido con mis deberes (*responsibilities*) y he tratado de ser amable con todos. ¿Qué cree usted, doctor? ¿Qué me recomienda?

Ahora, ¡a hablar!

A. Consecuencias. Todos sufrimos las consecuencias de nuestras acciones. ¿Por qué sufren estas personas ahora? ¿Qué han hecho para causar sus problemas?

Modelo Marcos está enfermo porque (comer) demasiado.
Marcos está enfermo porque ha comido demasiado.

1. Marcos está enfermo porque (beber) mucho.
2. Patricio tiene una F en su clase de inglés porque no (escribir) las composiciones.
3. Josefina no tiene electricidad en su casa porque no (pagar) la cuenta.
4. El coche de Andrés no funciona porque él no le (poner) aceite al motor.
5. Los padres de Carolina no le creen porque ella les (decir) muchas mentiras en el pasado.
6. Carlos no entiende la lección porque no (hacer) la tarea.
7. Yo... porque ¿... ?

B. ¡Falta tiempo! Lidia y Jorge se están preparando para los exámenes finales. ¿Qué dicen que les falta hacer?

Modelo leer el último capítulo para la clase de historia
Todavía no hemos leído el último capítulo para la clase de historia.

1. estudiar el vocabulario para la clase de español
2. escribir la última composición para la clase de inglés
3. hacer el proyecto para la clase de química
4. terminar los ejercicios en el manual de laboratorio
5. resolver los últimos problemas de química
6. ver el video para la clase de historia

C. ¿Qué has hecho hoy? Pregúntale a un(a) compañero(a) si ha hecho lo siguiente.

Modelo desayunar

TÚ **¿Has desayunado ya?**
COMPAÑERO(A) **No, todavía no he desayunado.**

1. hacer ejercicio
2. almorzar
3. hacer la cama
4. ponerle gasolina al coche
5. ir a la biblioteca
6. oír las noticias
7. leer el periódico
8. ver esta película

D. ¡Inolvidable! Hay experiencias que dejan una impresión más profunda que otras. ¿Qué has hecho este año que consideras inolvidable?

Modelo leer

He leído *El ingenioso hidalgo, Don Quijote de la Mancha.*

1. leer
2. viajar
3. conocer
4. participar
5. ver
6. ir
7. aprender
8. hacer

Y ahora, ¡a conversar!

A. Y tú, ¿qué has hecho? Trata de recordar todo lo que has hecho esta semana. Prepara una lista y luego léesela a dos compañeros(as). Escriban en la pizarra todo lo que los (las) tres hayan hecho en común.

B. Confesiones. Trabajando en grupos de tres o cuatro mencionen una cosa que cada uno ha hecho que nadie más en el grupo ha hecho y una cosa que han hecho todos en el grupo menos tú.

¡Luz! ¡Cámara! ¡Acción!

A. ¡Eres famoso(a)! Tú has llegado a ser una persona muy famosa. Ahora un(a) reportero(a) te va a entrevistar para saber los secretos de tu éxito. Cuéntale cómo has llegado a ser tan famoso(a). Dramatiza la situación con un(a) compañero(a).

B. ¡Tres medallas! Tú has ganado tres medallas de oro en los Juegos Olímpicos. Un(a) reportero(a) de una revista de deportes te entrevista sobre lo que has hecho para prepararte para esta competición. Dramatiza la situación con un(a) compañero(a).

¿Te gusta leer?

Antes de leer
Estrategias para leer: Encontrar la idea principal

La idea principal. Generalmente, cada párrafo comunica una idea principal. Con frecuencia esa idea se expresa en la primera oración del párrafo y se desarrolla más en detalle en las oraciones que siguen. «**La leyenda de Iztarú**» tiene cuatro párrafos. A continuación, expresamos en pocas palabras la idea principal del primer y del último párrafo. Lee sólo la primera oración del segundo y tercer párrafo y escribe brevemente la idea principal de esos dos párrafos. Luego lee la leyenda completa y verifica si identificaste las ideas principales correctamente.

Párrafo 1: los líderes indígenas del norte y del sur de Costa Rica
Párrafo 2: ______________________________
Párrafo 3: ______________________________
Párrafo 4: los habitantes de Guarco reciben una maldición *(curse)*

Lectura. Esta hermosa leyenda, parte del rico folklore de Costa Rica, trata de explicar un fenómeno natural del país, el volcán Irazú.

El volcán Irazú

La leyenda de Iztarú

Hace muchos años, antes de la llegada de los españoles a Costa Rica...

La parte Norte era gobernada por un cacique llamado Coo, de gran poder y de aplicación a la agricultura. La parte Sur la gobernaba Guarco, cacique déspota invasor.

Guarco y Coo sostenían una lucha por el dominio de todo el territorio (Valle Central del Guarco). La lucha fue grande; poco a poco, Guarco iba derrotando° la resistencia de Coo, hasta que éste murió y dejó en mando° a Aquitaba, un enérgico y fuerte guerrero. Cuando vio que iba a ser derrotado por Guarco, tomó a su hija Iztarú, la llevó al monte más alto de la parte Norte de la región y la sacrificó a los dioses, implorando la ayuda para la guerra.

Estando en una dura batalla con Guarco, Aquitaba imploró la ayuda de «Iztarú» sacrificada; del monte más alto salió fuego, ceniza, piedra° y cayeron sobre los guerreros de Guarco que huyeron.° Del costado° del monte salió un riachuelo° que se convirtió en agua caliente destruyendo los palenques° de Guarco.

Una maldición cundió° y se decía que los habitantes de Guarco trabajarían la tierra, haciendo con ella su propio techo (teja°); el pueblo se llamó luego Tejar de Cartago, la región Norte Cot, y el monte alto volcán Irazú.

defeating
en control
stone
ran away; lado; río pequeño; *defensive fences*
se extendió
tile

A ver si comprendiste

1. Compara a los tres personajes principales.

Coo	Guarco	Aquitaba
1.	1.	1.
2.	2.	2.
3.	3.	3.
4.	4.	4.
5.	5.	5.

2. ¿Quién era Iztarú? ¿En qué se transformó?
3. ¿Qué efecto tuvo esa transformación en los habitantes de Guarco?
4. La leyenda explica la existencia de ciertos lugares en la Costa Rica moderna. ¿Cuáles son esos lugares?

Expand your horizons! *Let's travel through cyberspace to* **Costa Rica** *where you can . . .*

- visit the exceptional National Parks of Costa Rica, indication of the strong national commitment towards the preservation of existing rain forests and natural habitats of a wide variety of plant and animal life.
- stroll through a country that provides shelter for almost 12,000 varieties of plants, 237 species of mammals, 848 types of birds, and 361 different amphibians and reptiles, all native to Costa Rica.
- get to know the "ticos," the people of Costa Rica, and, through the Internet, talk to any number of them.
- learn about the different brands of Costa Rican coffee and how Costa Rican coffee beans are processed to acquire a truly outstanding quality.
- go bird watching as you work your way through hundreds of amazing pictures of birds, from the very tiny to some of the largest, most colorful birds you've ever seen.

If you are a cyberspace browser, join us in **Viajemos por el ciberespacio a... Costa Rica** by trying the following important addresses.

Costa Rica home page
http://www.cr./.

Universidad de Costa Rica
http://www.ucr.ac.cr/

Universidad Latina
http://www.ulatina.ac.cr/

Museo de arte costarricense
http://www.cr./arte/musearte/musearte.htm

Periódicos: La Nación
http://www.nacion.co.cr/

Tico Times
http://infoweb.magi.com/calypso/ttimes.html

Semanario Universidad
http://cariari.ucr.ac.cr/~semana/univ.html

Instituto Nacional de Biodiversidad
http://www.inbio.ac.cr/INBioInfo/Espanol/biodiv.html

Because addresses are likely to change without notice, the following key words will guarantee that **Viajemos por el ciberespacio a... Costa Rica** will get you to your desired destination.

Palabras clave

Museos de Costa Rica
Museo de arte costarricense
Periódico La Nación (San José)
Tico/a (Costarricense)
Avifauna de Costa Rica
Biodiversidad Costa Rica
Organizaciones medioambientalistas
Pájaros de Costa Rica
Parques naturales de Costa Rica

http:///www.hrwcollege.com

Vocabulario

Música

banda	*band*
címbalos	*cymbals*
clarinete *(m.)*	*clarinet*
instrumento	*instrument*
saxofón *(m.)*	*saxophone*
tambor *(m.)*	*drum*
trompeta	*trumpet*

Gobierno

abogado(a)	*lawyer*
ciudadano(a)	*citizen*
democracia	*democracy*
derecho	*law*
ejército	*army*
fuerzas armadas	*armed forces*

Emociones

enojarse	*to get angry*
quejarse	*to complain*
sentirse (ie, i)	*to feel*
soñar (ue)	*to dream*
sufrir de estrés	*to be under stress*

La televisión

episodio	*episode*
filmar	*to film*
telenovela	*T.V. soap opera*

Acciones ofensivas

abandonar	*to abandon*
amenazar	*to threaten*
emborracharse	*to get drunk*
faltar a clase	*to miss class*
insinuar	*to insinuate*
insultar	*to insult*

Adjetivos

anticuado(a)	*very old, antiquated*
último(a)	*latest*

Adverbios

antes	*before*
gratis	*free*
por suerte	*fortunately*
ya	*already*

Verbos

cumplir	*to carry out, realize*
desenchufar	*to unplug (electricity)*
dejar de	*to stop (doing something)*
dirigir	*to direct*
echar de menos	*to miss*
librar	*to free, liberate*
montar	*to get on, ride*
participar	*to participate*
pincharse	*to get a flat tire; to puncture*
sacar buenas notas	*to get good grades*
salir juntos	*to date, go out together*
sonar (ue)	*to ring*

Palabras y expresiones útiles

animal de peluche *(m.)*	*stuffed animal (toy)*
¡caramba!	*good heavens!*
culpa	*fault*
deberes	*responsibilities*
había una vez	*once upon a time*
¡fíjese!	*just imagine!*
gasolinera	*gas or filling station*
joya	*jewel*
Premio Nóbel	*Nobel Prize*
precio	*price*
responsabilidad *(f.)*	*responsibility*

En preparación 11

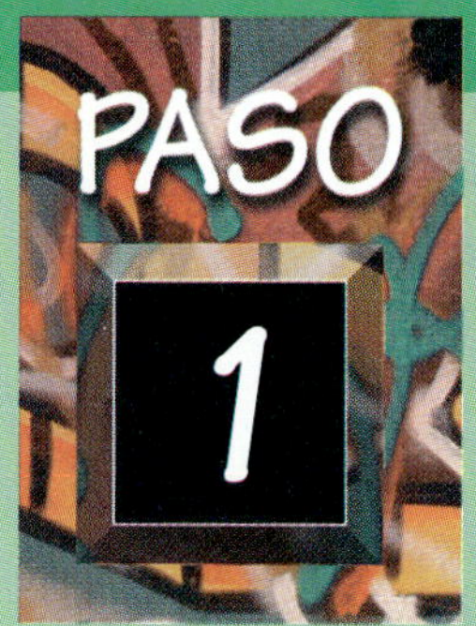

11.1 Imperfect of Regular Verbs

Talking about past events

In **Capítulo 10**, you learned about the preterite. In this chapter, you will learn about another aspect of the past tense: the imperfect. You will also learn how to distinguish between the preterite and imperfect.

-ar Verb endings	Trabajar
-aba	trabajaba
-abas	trabajabas
-aba	trabajaba
-ábamos	trabajábamos
-abais	trabajabais
-aban	trabajaban

-er, -ir Verb endings	Saber	Escribir
-ía	sabía	escribía
-ías	sabías	escribías
-ía	sabía	escribía
-íamos	sabíamos	escribíamos
-íais	sabíais	escribíais
-ían	sabían	escribían

Note that the first- and third-person singular endings are identical. Also *all* the imperfect **-er** and **-ir** endings require a written accent.

A. There are no stem-changing verbs in the imperfect.

B. The imperfect of **hay** is **había** *(there was, there were, there used to be),* from the infinitive **haber.**

C. There are only three irregular verbs in the imperfect: **ser, ir,** and **ver.** They are presented in section 11.3.

11.2 Uses of the Imperfect

Talking about what we used to do

A. The imperfect has several English equivalents.

Trabajaba todos los días. { *I worked every day.* / *I was working every day.* / *I used to work every day.* / *I would work every day.* }

B. Like the preterite, the imperfect is used to talk about an act that has already occurred. However, the imperfect focuses on the continuation of an act or on an act in progress rather than on the completed act. Continuation includes repeated habitual action, background action, actions in progress, and certain physical, mental, or emotional states.

Repeated habitual action

Viajaba mucho en el invierno.	*I would travel a lot in the winter.*
Nunca **dormía** más de ocho horas al día.	*I never slept more than eight hours a day.*

Actions in progress

El bebé **dormía** en el otro cuarto.	*The baby was sleeping in the other room.*
Escuchaba mi disco favorito mientras **limpiaba** la casa.	*I was listening to my favorite record while I cleaned the house.*

Background action

Hacía mucho calor pero todos **estaban** trabajando.	*It was very hot, but everyone was working.*

Physical, mental, or emotional states

En esos días **estábamos** muy enamorados.	*In those days we were very much in love.*
Me **gustaban** mucho las exhibiciones de arte.	*I used to like art exhibits a lot.*

11.3 Imperfect of *ser, ir,* and *ver*

Describing how you used to be, where you used to go, what you used to see

There are three irregular verbs in the imperfect.

Ser		Ir		Ver	
era	éramos	iba	íbamos	veía	veíamos
eras	erais	ibas	ibais	veías	veíais
era	eran	iba	iban	veía	veían
era	eran	iba	iban	veía	veían

¡A practicar!

A. Hace diez años. ¿Quiénes en el pasado hacían lo siguiente: tus padres, tú, tú y tus hermanos, etc.?

1. ______________ vivía con mis padres.
2. ______________ no estudiábamos en la universidad.
3. Algunos de ______________ creíamos en Santa Claus.
4. ______________ me daban dinero.
5. ______________ no conducía un coche.
6. ¿Y ______________? ¿Qué hacías hace diez años?

B. Gente famosa. Las personas famosas no tienen vida privada. Todos sabemos lo que hacen y dicen a cada minuto. ¿Qué hacían estas personas hace unos años?

Modelo 1950 / Ronald Reagan / filmar películas
En 1950 Ronald Reagan filmaba películas.

1. 1960 / Martin Luther King, Jr. / protestar contra / discriminación racial
2. 1965 / los Beatles / cantar por todo el mundo
3. 1969 / Richard Nixon / dirigir el país
4. 1969 / Neil Armstrong / trabajar en la NASA
5. 1989 / alemanes / celebrar / comienzo / Alemania unida
6. 1990 / sudafricano Nelson Mandela / viajar / como hombre libre
7. 1991 / ejército de los Estados Unidos / estar / golfo Pérsico
8. 1996 / Bill Clinton / servir de / Presidente de los EE.UU.

C. ¡Cómo nos cambia la vida! Completa los espacios en blanco para saber cómo era la vida de esta típica estudiante universitaria.

Antes, cuando ______________ (yo / vivir) con mis padres, todo ______________ (ser) más fácil. Primero, ______________ (yo / ser) buena estudiante y nunca ______________ (tener) problemas de dinero. Tampoco ______________ (tener) que trabajar. Bueno, es verdad que ahora nada es fácil, pero también sé que ahora soy una persona muy responsable.

D. ¡Cuántos sacrificios! Marta y Ramiro Roque se conocieron en la universidad. Lee este párrafo que cuenta cómo era la vida estudiantil de ellos. Cambia los verbos al imperfecto.

Nosotros ______________ (ser) estudiantes de medicina y ______________ (trabajar) en un hospital. Marta ______________ (ser) estudiante de ginecología y yo ______________ (estudiar) cirugía. Nosotros ______________ (ir) al hospital dos o tres veces por semana pero no nos ______________ (ver) mucho porque ______________ (trabajar) en diferentes secciones. A pesar de que ______________ (ser) novios, no ______________ (poder) salir mucho juntos porque ______________ (tener) que estudiar día y noche.

11.4 Preterite and Imperfect: Completed and Continuous Actions

Describing completed actions and actions in progress in the past

You have learned that both the preterite and the imperfect are used to talk about the past, but there is a difference in how the two tenses are used. Compare the following.

A. The preterite is used to describe completed past actions.

La conferencia **duró** dos horas. — *The lecture lasted two hours.*
Hablé con mis padres anoche. — *I spoke with my parents last night.*

B. The imperfect is used to focus on continuation or actions in progress and background actions. It is also used to tell time in the past.

Siempre **charlábamos** por horas. — *We always used to chat for hours.*
El teléfono **sonaba** continuamente. — *The phone would ring continuously.*
Eran las seis. — *It was 6:00.*

C. When the preterite and imperfect are used in the same sentence, the imperfect often describes a continuous background action that is interrupted by a completed action expressed in the preterite.

Miraba televisión cuando **llamaste.** — *I was watching television when you called.*
Nos lo **dio** mientras **comíamos.** — *He gave it to us while we were eating.*

D. The imperfect may be used to focus on a future event related to a situation planned in the past.

Debo irme. Tita dijo que la clase **empezaba** a las ocho. — *I must leave. Tita said the class would begin (was going to begin) at 8:00.*

¡A practicar!

A. ¡Qué día! Esta alumna tuvo un día muy malo ayer. Según ella, ¿qué le pasó? Para saberlo, pon los verbos entre paréntesis en el pasado.

Ayer ______________ (ser) un día terrible. Para empezar, yo ______________ (estar) furiosa porque mi novio no me ______________ (llamar) la noche anterior. Luego, cuando yo ______________ (salir) de casa, ______________ (estar) lloviendo a cántaros. ______________ (Buscar) mi paraguas pero no lo ______________ (encontrar). Luego, ______________ (perder) el autobús y ______________ (tener) que esperar el siguiente. Cuando finalmente ______________ (llegar) a clase la secretaria ______________ (anunciar) que la profesora ______________ (estar) enferma. ¡Qué día!

B. ¡No más! Tomás decidió no ir a clase esta mañana. Para saber por qué, pon los verbos en el pasado.

1. ya / ser tarde / cuando / despertarme
2. preparar / desayuno / cuando / teléfono / sonar
3. mientras / bañarse / agua / cortarse
4. cuando / salir / casa / gato / escapar
5. estar manejando / de repente / llanta / pincharse
6. mientras / cambiar / llanta / empezar a / llover
7. finalmente / decidir / regresar / casa

C. ¿De veras? ¿Qué le dice el alumno a su mejor amigo cuando éste quiere saber por qué no fue a clase? Para saberlo, pon todos los verbos en el pasado.

Es verdad. Anoche mi computadora ______________ (dejar) de funcionar. ______________ (Ser) las diez y yo ______________ (estar) preparando la tarea cuando ______________ (sonar) el teléfono. ______________ (Ser) mi madre, y nosotros ______________ (hablar) por una hora, más o menos. Cuando ______________ (regresar) a la computadora, no ______________ (haber) imagen en la pantalla. ______________ (Apretar) varias teclas *(keys)* pero sin ningún resultado. No ______________ (descubrir) hasta esta mañana que mi compañero de cuarto la ______________ (desenchufar).

11.5 Preterite and Imperfect: Beginning/End and Habitual/Customary Actions

Describing the beginning or end of actions and habitual past actions

In the previous section, you learned that the preterite focuses on completed actions and the imperfect focuses on actions in progress.

A. Since the preterite focuses on completed actions, it often emphasizes the beginning or end of an act.

Cuando **vi** a Carlota, **corrí** a saludarla.	*When I saw Carlota, I ran to greet her.*
Salieron corriendo.	*They left running. (They took off running.)*
De repente la computadora no **funcionó.**	*Suddenly the computer did not work. (It just stopped.)*
Me **sentí** muy mal después de la clase de informática.	*I felt very sick after computer science class. (But I got over it.)*

B. The imperfect is used to describe habitual or customary actions or events in progress.

Siempre **daba** la misma excusa.	*I always gave the same excuse.*
Yo nunca **iba** a la biblioteca de noche.	*I never used to go to the library at night.*

¡A practicar!

A. ¡Excusas! Fulano Embustero no trata bien a su novia pero siempre tiene una excusa. ¿Qué le dice a su novia?

1. Esta mañana cuando tú (llamaste / llamabas) yo no (contesté / contestaba) porque (estuve / estaba) en el baño.
2. Yo no te (llamé / llamaba) la semana pasada porque (desconectaron / desconectaban) mi teléfono.
3. La llanta de mi coche (se pinchó / se pinchaba) y por eso (llegué / llegaba) tarde a nuestra cita.
4. Anoche (trabajé / trabajaba) hasta tan tarde que (decidí / decidía) no llamarte para no despertarte.
5. El sábado pasado no (fui / iba) a tu casa porque mi coche no (funcionó / funcionaba).
6. Ayer no te (invité / invitaba) a la fiesta porque tú no (conociste / conocías) a nadie.

B. ¿Qué le voy a decir? Este alumno no fue a su clase de química ayer. ¿Por qué? Para contestar, pon en el pasado los verbos entre paréntesis.

¡Qué horror! No _______________ (acostarme) hasta muy tarde anoche. Esta mañana cuando _______________ (despertarme), ya _______________ (ser) las 9:55. Mi clase de química _______________ (empezar) en cinco minutos. _______________ (Decidir) no ir a clase. Más tarde _______________ (hablar) con un compañero de clase y él _______________ (decirme) que el profesor _______________ (estar) furioso porque yo no _______________ (ir) a clase. Ahora no sé qué le voy a decir al profesor.

C. ¡Aguafiestas! Pon los verbos entre paréntesis en el pasado para saber lo que pasó el sábado pasado en la fiesta de Enrique.

El sábado pasado Enrique ______________ (organizar) una fiesta en su casa. Sus padres no ______________ (estar) y el ______________ (invitar) a muchísima gente. Todos nuestros amigos ______________ (venir) y también ______________ (llegar) gente desconocida. ______________ (Haber) mucha comida y muchas cervezas. Todos ______________ (bailar) y ______________ (cantar) cuando a eso de la una de la mañana unos vecinos ______________ (llamar) a la policía. La policía nos ______________ (obligar) a terminar la fiesta. Enrique no les ______________ (decir) nada a sus padres.

11.6 Present Perfect

Talking about what people have or haven't done

As in English, the present perfect tense in Spanish is a compound past tense. It is formed by combining the present indicative of the auxiliary verb **haber** *(to have)* with the past participle.

Present Indicative

Haber	*to have**
he	hemos
has	habéis
ha	han
ha	han

Present Perfect Tense

Sentir	*to feel*
he sentido	hemos sentido
has sentido	habéis sentido
ha sentido	han sentido
ha sentido	han sentido

A. The past participle of most verbs in English is formed by adding *-ed* to the verb; for example, to travel → *traveled,* to study → *studied,* to open → *opened.* In Spanish, past participles are formed by adding **-ado** to the stem of **-ar** verbs and **-ido** to the stem of **-er** and **-ir** verbs.

Viajar		Querer		Sentir	
viaj**ado**	*traveled*	quer**ido**	*wanted*	sent**ido**	*felt*

The past participle of all **-er** and **-ir** verbs whose stem ends in **-a, -e,** or **-o** requires a written accent: **leído, traído, creído,** etc.

B. As in English, some Spanish verbs have irregular past participles; the following are those most frequently used.

abrir	**abierto**	hacer	**hecho**	resolver	**resuelto**
cubrir	**cubierto**	imprimir	**impreso**	romper	**roto**
decir	**dicho**	morir	**muerto**	ver	**visto**
escribir	**escrito**	poner	**puesto**	volver	**vuelto**

* Do not confuse the auxiliary verb **haber** with the verb **tener,** which is used to express possession and/or obligation.

Note that the past participles of verbs related to those above are also irregular: **descubrir** *(to discover)* → **descubierto, maldecir** *(to curse)* → **maldicho, devolver** *(to return something)* → **devuelto,** etc.

C. In general, the use of the present perfect tense in Spanish parallels its use in English.

No me **he sentido** bien.	*I haven't felt well.*
Han estado muy enfermos.	*They have been very sick.*
Todavía no **se ha levantado.**	*He hasn't gotten up yet.*
No **hemos devuelto** los libros a la biblioteca.	*We haven't returned the books to the library.*

Note that when used in the present perfect, the past participle is invariable; it does not agree in number or in gender with the noun. Reflexive and object pronouns are always placed before the conjugated form of the verb **haber.**

D. With few exceptions, **haber** functions only as an auxiliary verb. The verb **tener** is used to indicate possession or obligation.

No **me he sentido** nada bien.	*I haven't felt well at all.*
Tengo que llamar al médico.	*I have to call the doctor.*

¡A practicar!

A. ¡Qué organizado! Cuando una persona organizada viaja, siempre prepara listas de lo que le queda por hacer. ¿Qué dice esta persona de lo que todavía no ha hecho?

Modelo escribirles a mis tíos en Kansas

Todavía no les he escrito a mis tíos en Kansas.

1. ver el monumento a la entrada del parque
2. ir al parque zoológico
3. sacar fotos de la plaza
4. viajar al sur del país
5. hacer compras en el mercado al aire libre
6. visitar el museo de arte moderno

B. ¡No he hecho nada! Inevitablemente cuando llega el domingo por la tarde, descubrimos que no hemos hecho algunas cosas que pensábamos hacer durante el fin de semana. Pon los verbos en tiempo perfecto para ver unos ejemplos típicos.

1. Miguel no ______________ (ir) de compras.
2. José no ______________ (hacer) la tarea.
3. Yo no les ______________ (escribir) a mis padres.
4. Miguel y José no ______________ (lavar) la ropa.

5. Nosotros no ______________ (poder) limpiar el garaje.
6. Yo no ______________ (abrir) los libros para estudiar.
7. Tú no ______________ (limpiar) tu cuarto.
8. Ustedes no ______________ (llamar) a sus padres.

CAPÍTULO 12

¡Qué vacaciones!

Cultural Topics

- **¿Sabías que… ?**
  Los quechuas
  El cui
- ***La dinastía del amor***
  Cross-cultural perceptions regarding marriage with / without family consent and communication between parents and children.
- **Noticiero cultural**
  Lugar: *Cuzco: El corazón del imperio inca*
  Gente: *Mario Vargas Llosa*
- **Lectura:** *Machu Picchu: La ciudad escondida de los incas*

Writing Strategies

- *Puntos de vista*

Reading Strategies

- *Pistas de contexto*

En preparación

- 12.1 Summary of Preterite and Imperfect
- 12.2 Future Tense of Regular Verbs
- 12.3 Future Tense of Verbs with Irregular Stems
- 12.4 **Tú** Commands: A Second Look

In this chapter, you will learn how to …

- *describe problems you had on a trip.*
- *describe what you did and saw while on vacation.*
- *describe what you will do in the future.*
- *give advice and instructions.*
- *give orders.*

Decoración de oro y turquesa descubierta recientemente en las Tumbas Reales de Sipán

La fortaleza de Sacsahuamán en Cuzco

Terrazas agrícolas en Machu Picchu

Lo que ya sabes...

1. Hay tres figuras en la decoración de oro y turquesa. ¿Qué representan: dioses, reyes o guerreros? ¿Por qué crees eso?
2. ¿Crees que toda la gente de esta civilización vestía de oro, como la figura central de la decoración de oro y turquesa? Explica tu respuesta.
3. ¿Cómo crees que fue construida esta gran fortaleza? ¿Qué crees que usaron para mover y cortar estas gigantescas rocas?
4. Perú es una tierra de muchos terremotos. ¿Cómo crees que han sobrevivido estas impresionantes construcciones por cientos y cientos de años? ¿Tenían los incas mejores arquitectos que los nuestros de hoy en dia?
5. ¿Por qué crees que construyeron estas terrazas agrícolas? ¿Para qué crees que se usaban? ¿Cómo regaban (*irrigate*) las terrazas?

PERÚ

¡Imagínate... nosotros en Lima!

TAREA Antes de empezar este **Paso**, estudia **En preparación** 12.1 y haz por escrito los ejercicios de **¡A practicar!** También escucha **Paso 1 ¿Qué se dice... ?** del Capítulo 12 en el CD del estudiante.

¿Eres buen observador?

Ahora, ¡a analizar!

Un buen arqueólogo tiene que ser un excelente observador porque tiene que interpretar los restos *(remains)* de civilizaciones antiguas. Veamos a qué conclusiones puedes llegar tú sobre la civilización que dejó los restos que aparecen en estas fotografías.

1. ¿Qué talentos tenían las personas que crearon la cerámica con dos picos?
2. ¿Qué crees que son los objetos de oro? ¿Para qué se usaban? ¿Tenían un propósito decorativo o práctico? ¿Qué puedes asumir de una sociedad que producía y usaba este tipo de objetos?
3. ¿Cómo crees que se construyó este lugar? ¿Qué necesitaban saber sus arquitectos? ¿Qué tipo de máquinas y herramientas *(tools)* crees que usaron? ¿Cuántos trabajadores crees que necesitaron?

Machu Picchu

¿Sabías que... ?

Los quechuas eran los indígenas que controlaban la cordillera *(mountain range)* andina desde Ecuador hasta Argentina cuando los españoles llegaron a Perú en 1531. Los quechuas llamaban a su rey o emperador «el Inca». La sociedad quechua o incaica estaba dividida en cuatro clases: los gobernantes, los nobles, la gente común y los esclavos. Esta sociedad mantuvo grandes ejércitos *(armies)* muy organizados, construyó edificios impresionantes y estableció un sistema de carreteras *(highways)* que se extendía de un extremo al otro del imperio incaico. Actualmente, sus descendientes viven en el altiplano de Ecuador, Bolivia y Perú, donde la lengua quechua todavía se habla extensamente.

Al hablar de lo que hiciste u olvidaste hacer

1. ______________________

2. ______________________

3. ______________________

4. ______________________

OLGA Ay, olvidé mis gafas de sol... ¿O las puse en la maleta? No sé. Recuerdo que abrí la maleta, saqué la pasta dental y el cepillo de dientes para lavarme la boca y... ¡Dios mío! Creo que las dejé en el baño.

ENRIQUE ¡Caramba, mujer! ¿En qué pensabas cuando hiciste la maleta?

OLGA La verdad es que estaba muy nerviosa cuando empaqué, Enrique.

Ahora, ¡a hablar!

A. ¡Problemas típicos! Generalmente, cuando viajamos tenemos algunos problemas. Completa las oraciones para saber qué les pasó a Enrique y a Olga durante su viaje a Lima.

Modelo Olga / no dormir bien / porque / la cama / no ser cómoda

Olga no durmió bien porque la cama no era cómoda.

1. el segundo día / Olga / no bañarse / porque / no haber agua caliente
2. Enrique / no afeitarse / porque / la corriente / ser diferente
3. el tercer día / ellos / no cambiar dinero / porque / dejar los pasaportes en el hotel
4. ellos / no poder ir al cine / porque / Enrique / olvidar sus lentes en el hotel
5. ellos / perderse / porque / no tener un mapa de la ciudad
6. ellos / no poder / comprar un mapa / porque / tiendas / estar cerradas

B. ¿Turistas típicos? ¿Son Enrique y Olga turistas típicos? Decide después de completar este párrafo, poniendo los verbos entre paréntesis en el pasado.

Cuando Enrique y Olga Ballesteros ______________ (llegar) al Hotel Colonial en Lima el mes pasado, ______________ (tener) muchos problemas. Primero, Enrique no ______________ (poder) abrir la maleta de Olga porque ______________ (perder) la llave. Cuando Enrique ______________ (tener) que romper la cerradura *(lock),* Olga ______________ (ponerse) furiosa. Luego Olga ______________ (descubrir) que el cepillo de dientes, el champú y un par de zapatos no ______________ (estar) en la maleta. Desafortunadamente, ya ______________ (ser) demasiado tarde para ir de compras. Todas las tiendas ______________ (estar) cerradas. Por eso, Olga ______________ (acostarse) sin lavarse ni los dientes ni el pelo. Al día siguiente ellos ______________ (ir) de compras muy temprano.

C. Mis vacaciones. Y para ti, ¿cómo fueron las últimas vacaciones? ¿Qué pasó? ¿Por qué?

Modelo dormir (bien / mal) porque…

Dormí mal porque la cama era dura.

1. dormir (bien / mal) porque...
2. comer (bien / mal) porque...
3. (no) estar cansado(a) porque...
4. pagar (mucho / poco) porque...
5. visitar (mucho / poco) la ciudad porque...
6. ir (mucho / poco) de excursión porque...

D. ¡Perú mágico! Carla y César pasaron las vacaciones en Perú. ¿Qué hicieron en los diferentes lugares en que estuvieron?

Paracas: Nosotros solamente ______________ (quedarnos) un día. ______________ (Hacer) mucho calor y ______________ (estar) muy húmedo.

Arequipa: ______________ (Pasar) tres semanas allí. Cada mañana ______________ (ir) al mercado para comprar algo. ______________ (Haber) mucha artesanía.

Lago Titicaca: Nosotros ______________ (sacar) muchas fotos mientras el guía nos ______________ (explicar) cómo ______________ (vivir) los quechuas antes de la llegada de los conquistadores.

Cuzco: Yo ______________ (viajar) a Cuzco por tren y ______________ (ver) unas hermosas vistas panorámicas en camino. El segundo día en Cuzco, nosotros ______________ (hacer) una excursión por el valle del río Urubamba.

Machu Picchu: Cuando ______________ (llegar) a Machu Picchu, yo ______________ (saber) que ______________ (estar) en un país mágico.

Y ahora, ¡a conversar!

A. ¿Pingüinos? ¿En Lima? Enrique y Olga tuvieron unas experiencias estupendas durante su viaje a Perú, pero sin duda, la más interesante fue la de Enrique un día que paseaba por la ciudad. Para saber lo que le pasó, estudia estos dibujos mientras que tu compañero(a) estudia los que se encuentran en el Apéndice A. Cuéntale a tu compañero(a) la primera parte del incidente basándote en estos dibujos y él (ella) te va a contar el final basándose en sus dibujos.

1. Un día iba en mi carro por el parque cuando...

2. Paré el carro al lado del pingüino y...

3. Paseábamos en el carro cuando el pingüino dijo que...

4. El policía me preguntó por qué...

B. ¡Qué interesante! Tu compañero(a) hizo un viaje muy interesante recientemente. Pregúntale adónde fue y hazle muchas preguntas acerca de lo que hizo allá.

Modelo ¿A qué hora te acostabas?

C. Viaje a Machu Picchu. Tú y un(a) compañero(a) están viajando por Sudamérica, visitando y explorando diferentes lugares. Ahora están en las famosas cataratas del Iguazú y quieren viajar por Uruguay, Argentina, Chile y Bolivia para llegar al famoso Machu Picchu. Piensan hacer ocho escalas *(stopovers)* en su viaje. ¿Quién va a llegar primero? Para avanzar una escala, tienes que contestar la pregunta de tu compañero(a) correctamente. Tus preguntas están aquí, las de tu compañero(a) están en el Apéndice A.

1. ¿Cuál es la capital de Bolivia?
2. ¿Cuál es la capital de Ecuador?
3. Nombra tres países en la cordillera de los Andes.
4. Nombra dos de los vecinos de Colombia.
5. ¿De qué país era Eva Perón?
6. ¿Quién escribió ***¡Dímelo tú!***? Nombra uno de los autores.
7. ¿Cuántos países de habla española hay en Centroamérica?
8. ¿Cómo se llama la capital de Perú?
9. ¿Cuál es el país de habla española más pequeño de Sudamérica?
10. Nombra dos culturas indígenas de México.
11. ¿En qué país hablan de **chinas** y **guaguas?**
12. Nombra cinco países de Sudamérica y sus capitales.

¡Luz! ¡Cámara! ¡Acción!

A. ¡Ay, qué vacaciones! Tú acabas de regresar de unas vacaciones fantásticas donde tuviste varias experiencias muy interesantes. Ahora le estás contando todos los detalles a tu mejor amigo(a). Tu amigo(a) te hace muchas preguntas también. Dramatiza la situación con un(a) compañero(a) de clase.

B. ¡Puedo explicarlo! Anoche tú no regresaste a casa hasta las cuatro de la mañana. Ahora tus padres están furiosos. Dramatiza esta situación con dos compañeros(as) de clase.

¿Comprendes lo que se dice?

La dinastía del amor: Episodio 3

Esta noche la familia Gómez nuevamente se reúne para ver la telenovela del momento. En este nuevo episodio Sharon va a descubrir un secreto de su hermana mayor. Escucha este episodio y luego contesta las preguntas que siguen.

Vocabulario útil

el sobre	*envelope*
certificado de matrimonio	*marriage certificate*
¡Cállate!	*Be quiet!*

A través de dos culturas

Telenovela

1. ¿Cuál es la relación entre Rod y Betty?
2. ¿Qué le trae Rod a Betty?
3. ¿Qué hay en el sobre?
4. ¿Qué quiere hacer Sharon?
5. ¿Crees que Betty se casó?
6. ¿Qué crees que le pasó a Sharon en la fiesta?

Televidentes

7. ¿Cómo reacciona Luisita Gómez a la situación en la telenovela?
8. ¿Crees que tiene razón Juan Pedro?
9. ¿Qué opinas del comentario de don Sergio?
10. ¿Por qué dice doña Luisa que su hija en particular debe hablar con los padres antes de casarse?
11. ¿Es muy diferente la reacción que tiene don Sergio a la que tendrían tus padres? ¿Existe un gran respeto familiar en los Estados Unidos?
12. ¿Es aceptable en los Estados Unidos que los hijos se casen sin pedirles permiso a los padres?

NOTICIERO CULTURAL

LUGAR... PERÚ

Antes de empezar, dime...

1. ¿Cuál fue el antiguo centro de cultura estadounidense antes de la llegada de los europeos? ¿Existen ruinas de esa época? ¿Dónde? ¿Cómo son? Descríbelas.
2. ¿Cuál es la ciudad más antigua de los EE.UU.? ¿Cuál es el origen y el significado de su nombre?
3. En los Estados Unidos hay muchos rascacielos *(skyscrapers)* impresionantes. ¿Cuánto tiempo crees que van a durar *(last)*? ¿Cuántas personas trabajan para construir uno de esos edificios? ¿Qué maquinaria y herramientas usan?

Vista panorámica de la ciudad de Cuzco

Cuzco: El corazón del imperio inca 

La zona de Cuzco, la capital del imperio de los incas, está situada en las mesetas andinas, al sureste de Lima, en el «corazón» mismo del antiguo imperio. Debido a su rol crucial, esta antigua capital incaica está rodeada de una gran riqueza arqueológica. Cuzco es una palabra quechua que significa ombligo *(navel)* en español y hace referencia a su localidad en el centro del universo. La ciudad fue construida entre 1438 y 1471 durante el apogeo del imperio incaico y se encuentra a una altura de 3.399 m *(11,152 ft.)* sobre el nivel del mar. Su altura hacía de ella una capital difícil de alcanzar y por la misma razón, un lugar muy incómodo para los españoles.

La calle Hatunrumlyoc

La ciudad y sus alrededores contienen innumerables ruinas preincaicas e incaicas que incluyen fortalezas como Sacsahuamán y el Templo del Sol. En la construcción de estas fortalezas se observa un ejemplo incomparable de cantería *(stone cutting):* los bloques de granito están colocados uno sobre el otro sin haber utilizado cemento. Los expertos en el tema han llegado a decir que no existe otro tipo de construcción similar que pueda compararse con ésta en cuanto a su calidad.

En la actualidad los únicos habitantes de estos increíbles testimonios del pasado son las llamas y vicuñas y, claro, los turistas que vienen de todos los rincones del mundo.

Y ahora, dime...

1. Usa este diagrama Venn para comparar a Cuzco con la capital de los EE.UU. o la capital de tu propio estado. Indica las diferencias y lo que tienen en común.

Capital de los EE.UU. o de mi propio estado	Ambas capitales	Cuzco: Capital del imperio incaica
1.	1.	1.
2.	2.	2.
3.	3.	3.
4.	4.	4.
5.	5.	5.
6.	6.	6.
. . .	. . .	. . .

2. ¿Qué quiere decir «Cuzco» en español? Explica su significado.

El español en otras disciplinas: Arqueología

Sitios arqueológicos. Cuando se habla de arqueología inmediatamente pensamos en Egipto, Grecia e Italia, entre otros y, por supuesto, en América. El continente americano es una fuente constante de investigación de norte a sur. Hay lugares que son centros constantes de estudio, como las Tumbas Reales de Sipán, que fueron científicamente excavadas en Perú entre 1987 y 1990. También hay otros que van surgiendo, o descubriéndose casi «por casualidad», como sucedió el 21 de febrero de 1978 en Ciudad de México, con el descubrimiento del Templo Mayor del antiguo Tenochtitlán. Con frecuencia, como fue el caso en Sipán, el descubrimiento de estos sitios arqueológicos implica la destrucción de antiguas tumbas. ¿Qué opinas tú de eso? ¿Crees que los arqueólogos tienen el derecho de entrar en cualquier tumba para sacar sus riquezas? En grupos de tres o cuatro, discutan sus opiniones e informen a la clase sobre sus conclusiones.

Decoración de oro y turquesa encontrada en las Tumbas Reales de Sipán

Proyecto: Investiga en la biblioteca de tu universidad las excavaciones de Sipán en Perú e infórmale lo que encontraste a la clase. Si es posible, trae un libro con fotos de la excavación y del tesoro que se descubrió.

PASO 2 ¿Adónde iremos mañana?

TAREA

Antes de empezar este **Paso**, estudia **En preparación** 12.2 y 12.3 y haz por escrito los ejercicios de **¡A practicar!** También escucha **Paso 2 ¿Qué se dice... ?** del Capítulo 12 en el CD del estudiante.

¿Eres buen observador?

Ahora, ¡a analizar!

1. ¿Dónde comienza el río Amazonas?
2. ¿Se sabe si es el río más largo del mundo? Explica.
3. ¿Qué longitud tiene el río Nilo de Egipto? ¿el río Amazonas?
4. ¿Cuál se sospecha que es la longitud verdadera del río Amazonas? ¿Cómo se piensa comprobarlo?
5. Si las cuentas no fallan, ¿cómo cambiará el *ranking* de los dos ríos?

El Amazonas metro a metro

Se sabe que comienza en la provincia arequipeña de Caylloma, en Perú, y el próximo cinco de julio se certificará si es el río más largo del mundo. Una expedición científica que contará con la participación de varios países pretende establecer su verdadera longitud. En la actualidad está reconocido como el segundo río más largo (6.437 kms), después del Nilo (6.671 kms), pero si no les fallan las cuentas, en breve se demostrará que cuenta con más de 7.000 kms y cambiará el *ranking* de los ríos.

J.M. Miranda

Una expedición científica pretende establecer la verdadera longitud del Amazonas.

¿Qué se dice...?

Al hablar de lo que harás y lo que verás

1. ______________________ Piensa que el hotel es carísimo.
2. ______________________ Pasará todo el día sacando fotos.
3. ______________________ Tendrá que cargar miles de recuerdos.
4. ______________________ Podrá dormir la siesta en el tren.

ENRIQUE Y después de Cuzco, ¿a Lima dijiste? ¿Será caro el hotel donde nos alojaremos? ¿Tendrá agua caliente?

OLGA ¡Por supuesto, Enrique! Lima es la capital y es una ciudad fabulosa.

ENRIQUE ¿Y qué comeremos? Ya no quiero comer más cui. ¡No me importa si es el plato nacional!

OLGA Enrique, en Lima hay montones de restaurantes buenos y baratos donde no tendrás que comer cui. Y si no dejas de quejarte, la próxima vez te dejo en casa.

¿Sabías que... ?

El **cui** o **cuy** (**cuis, cuises** o **cuyes** en el plural) es un conejillo de Indias *(guinea pig)* que se come frito o asado a la parrilla en Perú. Junto con los anticuchos, que se preparan con corazón de res, ají, achiote y vinagre, se consideran como platos indígenas nacionales en Perú. La palabra **cui** viene del quechua, idioma de los incas que siguen hablando muchos indígenas del Perú hoy en día.

Ahora, ¡a hablar!

A. ¡Cuzco! Enrique está muy preocupado y quiere saber todos los detalles de lo que harán en Cuzco. Crea un itinerario para él y su esposa de la información que sigue.

Modelo domingo: empacar las maletas / y / acostarse temprano

El domingo empacarán las maletas y se acostarán temprano.

1. lunes: llegar 17:30 / y / dormir dos o tres horas / porque / ser necesario para evitar el soroche *(altitude sickness)*
2. lunes: por la tarde / ver la piedra de los doce ángulos / salir a comer / y / pasar por el mercado a comprar recuerdos
3. martes: visitar las iglesias coloniales: La Merced, El Triunfo, la Catedral, San Blas, Santo Domingo y La Compañía de Jesús / y / conocer el Palacio de Manco Cápac
4. martes: por la tarde / ir a la casa del inca Garcilaso de la Vega (1539–1615), hijo de un capitán español y de una princesa / y / leer sus memorias
5. miércoles: despertarse a las seis / y / viajar en tren a Lima otra vez

B. ¡Machu Picchu! Ahora Enrique y Olga están conversando sobre sus planes para Machu Picchu. ¿Qué dice Olga que harán ellos?

Modelo miércoles / llegar por la tarde / ir al hotel

El miércoles llegaremos por la tarde e iremos al hotel.

1. quedarse dos días / Hotel del Gobierno
2. caminar por las ruinas / ver cómo los incas construían terrazas para cultivar la tierra
3. subir a Huayna Picchu / observar todas las ruinas desde arriba
4. el guía / explicarnos / historia de Machu Picchu
5. a las 7:00 / comer en el restaurante del hotel / escuchar música andina

C. Mis próximas vacaciones. Entrevista a un(a) compañero(a) de clase para saber cómo y dónde pasará las próximas vacaciones.

1. ¿Adónde irá? ¿Cómo viajará? ¿en avión? ¿en tren? ¿en auto?
2. ¿Viajará solo(a)?
3. ¿Dónde se quedará? ¿Cuánto le costará la vivienda *(housing)*?
4. ¿Cuánto tiempo estará de vacaciones? ¿Se quedará en el mismo lugar o viajará a otros sitios?

5. ¿Dónde comerá? ¿Comerá comida típica?
6. ¿Qué hará durante el día? ¿y de noche?
7. ¿Sacará muchas fotos? ¿Comprará muchos recuerdos?

D. ¡Qué futuro! El futuro está siempre lleno de promesas, de proyectos y de sueños. ¿Cómo ves tu propio futuro? ¿Cuáles son tus proyectos? ¿Será tu vida mejor que ahora? Con un(a) compañero(a), compara tu vida de ahora con la que piensas que podrá ser dentro de diez años.

Modelo trabajo
Ahora trabajo sólo de mesero; dentro de diez años seré director(a) de un banco.

1. trabajo
2. estudios
3. familia
4. esposo(a) e hijos
5. vivienda (casa o apartamento)
6. bienes (coches, casas, propiedad, etc.)

Y ahora, ¡a conversar!

A. Resoluciones. En enero siempre empezamos nuestras resoluciones tradicionales. ¿Cuáles serán tus resoluciones para el año próximo? Discútelas con un(a) compañero(a) y escucha mientras él (ella) te dice las suyas.

B. Bola de cristal. Tú y tus compañeros trabajan para un periódico que se dedica a las noticias extravagantes e increíbles. Ésta es la edición al final del año y, como hacen todos los años, tienen que predecir el futuro más improbable para personas en estos puestos. En grupos de tres escriban sus predicciones. Compártanlas con otro grupo de tres.

1. en el mundo político
2. en el mundo del espectáculo
3. en el mundo del deporte
4. en el mundo del arte

C. ¡El año 2005! El siglo nuevo y un nuevo milenio se están acercando. En grupos de tres o cuatro, digan que creen que estarán haciendo en el año 2010. Decidan quién tendrá el futuro más interesante y cuéntenselo a la clase.

¡Luz! ¡Cámara! ¡Acción!

A. Quiromancia. Tú sabes practicar el arte de la quiromancia *(palm reading)*. Tu compañero(a) quiere saber lo que le espera en el futuro. Lee su futuro y contesta todas las preguntas que él (ella) te haga. (Todas las respuestas están en la palma de la mano, ¡por supuesto!)

B. Compañeros de cuarto. Tú y tu compañero(a) han decidido compartir una casa. Ahora necesitan organizar su vida en común. Entre los dos, planeen lo que cada uno hará para contribuir a la armonía de la casa.

¿Comprendes lo que se dice?

La dinastía del amor: Episodio 4

Esta noche después de la comida, como de costumbre, se reúne la familia Gómez para seguir un nuevo episodio de la telenovela del momento: *La dinastía del amor.* En el último episodio, Sharon, después de encontrar el certificado de matrimonio, acusó a su hermana Betty de haberse casado y dijo que se lo iba a contar a su madre. Betty respondió que también tenía algo que contarle a su madre con respecto a Sharon. Escuchen ahora la continuación y luego contesten las preguntas que siguen.

Vocabulario útil

asustar	*to scare, frighten*	darse cuenta (de)	*to realize*
asustado(a)	*frightened*	ocultar	*to hide*
permiso	*permission*	ponerse al día	*to be up-to-date*

A través de dos culturas

Telenovela

1. ¿Dónde estaba Rod cuando supo que Betty lo buscaba?
2. ¿Por qué cree Betty que Sharon no va a decirle a su mamá lo del certificado de matrimonio?
3. ¿Por qué estaba llorando Betty?
4. ¿Cuál es el secreto de Betty?
5. ¿Por qué no ha hablado la madre de Betty con el padre sobre el secreto de su hija?

Televidentes

6. ¿Estás de acuerdo con el comentario de la señora Luisa? ¿Se casan ahora los jóvenes sin pedirles permiso a los padres?
7. ¿Es verdad lo que dice don Sergio? ¿Consulta la gente joven con sus padres?
8. ¿Por qué no le cuenta Luisita sus problemas a su padre?
9. ¿Por qué se molesta tanto doña Luisa con el comentario de Rod?
10. En tu opinión, ¿cree don Sergio que sus hijos confían en él?
11. ¿Es descortés el comentario de Luisita a su padre?

NOTICIERO CULTURAL

GENTE...

MARIO VARGAS LLOSA

Antes de empezar, dime...

Los buenos escritores. Piensa en los grandes escritores que tú conoces al contestar estas preguntas.

1. En tu opinión, ¿es necesaria una educación universitaria para llegar a ser un gran escritor? Explica tu respuesta.
2. ¿De dónde sacan los grandes escritores sus ideas para contar experiencias tan variadas? ¿Crees que siempre cuentan sus propias experiencias?
3. ¿Tienen que llevar los grandes escritores una vida muy variada? ¿Es necesario que viajen mucho? ¿Es importante que pasen cierto tiempo viviendo en el extranjero? Explica tus respuestas.
4. ¿A qué edad crees que debe empezar a escribir una persona que desea ser un gran escritor? ¿Crees que debe dedicar toda su vida a escribir, y nada más? ¿Por qué?

Mario Vargas Llosa

Mario Vargas Llosa nació en Arequipa, Perú, en el año 1936. Cursó sus primeros estudios en Cochabamba, Bolivia, y los secundarios en Lima y Piura. Se graduó en Letras en la Universidad de San Marcos de Lima y más tarde se doctoró en la Universidad de Madrid. Este famoso escritor peruano ha vivido muchos años en París, Londres y Barcelona.

Empezó a escribir en los años 50, pero no logró su fama hasta 1963 cuando escribió su gran novela *La ciudad y los perros.* Esta novela fue traducida inmediatamente a más de veinte idiomas y recibió el Premio Biblioteca Breve y el Premio de la Crítica (1963). En el año 1966 apareció su segunda gran obra, *La casa verde,* que también obtuvo el Premio de la Crítica (1966) y el Premio Internacional de Literatura Rómulo Gallegos (1967).

Posteriormente ha publicado el cuento *Los cachorros* (1968), y las novelas *Conversación en la Catedral* (1970) y *Pantaleón y las visitadoras* (1973). Vargas Llosa, aparte de ser un escritor que ha alcanzado gran fama internacional, también ha tenido activa participación en la vida política de su país, Perú. Fue candidato a la presidencia en las elecciones de 1990.

Y ahora, dime...

Con un(a) compañero(a) de clase indica los hechos más importantes en la vida de Mario Vargas Llosa, el hombre y el escritor.

MARIO VARGAS LLOSA

El hombre	El escritor
1.	1.
2.	2.
3.	3.
4.	4.
5.	5.
. . .	. . .

¿Te gusta escribir?

Antes de escribir
Estrategias para escribir: Puntos de vista

A. Puntos de vista. Cuando escribimos, es importante pensar cuidadosamente sobre el punto de vista que vamos a tomar. El punto de vista afecta muchísimo el resultado final de lo que escribimos. Por ejemplo, ¿crees que el chófer responsable por el accidente va a describir el accidente de la misma manera que el chófer víctima o algún espectador? ¡Es dudable! Lo más probable es que va a haber tres versiones distintas y las cortes tendrán que decidir el caso.

Ahora vuelve al **Noticiero cultural** del **Paso 1** de este capítulo, *Cuzco: El corazón del imperio inca.* ¿Desde qué punto de vista se escribió esta lectura? ¿Quién es el narrador?

B. Cambiando el punto de vista. Piensa cómo cambiaría esa lectura si el punto de vista fuera distinto. Por ejemplo, indica en una o dos oraciones cómo crees tú que las siguientes personas describirían la conquista de Cuzco. Luego compara tu trabajo con el de dos compañeros de clase.

Un conquistador español	Un inca en Perú ahora	Atahualpa, el último rey de los incas
1. 2. 3. 4. ...	1. 2. 3. 4. ...	1. 2. 3. 4. ...

Ahora, ¡a escribir!

A. Ahora, a planear. Prepara una lista de tres distintas características de Cuzco. Luego descríbelas desde el punto de vista de un conquistador español, de un indígeno inca en Perú ahora o de Atahualpa, el rey inca.

Características	Punto de vista de un conquistador	Punto de vista de un quechua ahora	Punto de vista de Atahualpa
1.	1.	1.	1.
2.	2.	2.	2.
3.	3.	3.	3.

B. El primer borrador. Usa la información que preparaste en la actividad anterior para decidir si vas a escribir sobre Cuzco desde el punto de vista de un conquistador español o de Atahualpa, el último rey de los incas. Escribe el primer borrador de una breve composición titulada «Cuzco: El centro del universo inca». No olvides que todo lo que relates tiene que ser desde el punto de vista de tu personaje.

C. Ahora, a compartir. Comparte tu primer borrador con dos o tres compañeros. Comenta sobre el contenido y el punto de vista de las composiciones de tus compañeros y escucha sus comentarios sobre tu trabajo. ¿Es lógico y consistente el punto de vista?

D. El segundo borrador. Haz los cambios necesarios a partir de los comentarios de tus compañeros de clase. Luego prepara un segundo borrador.

E. A compartir, otra vez. Comparte tu segundo borrador con dos o tres compañeros. Esta vez comenta los errores de estructura, ortografía o puntuación. Fíjate específicamente en el uso del pretérito, del imperfecto y del futuro. Indica todos los errores de tus compañeros y luego decide si necesitas hacer cambios en tu composición teniendo en cuenta los errores que ellos te indiquen a ti.

F. La versión final. Prepara la versión final de tu composición y entrégasela a tu profesor(a). Escribe la versión final a máquina o en la computadora siguiendo el formato recomendado por tu instructor(a).

G. Ahora, a publicar. En grupos de cuatro o cinco, junten sus lecturas en un volumen titulado *Cuzco: Varios puntos de vista.* Su profesor(a) va a guardar sus libros en la sala de clase para que todos puedan leerlos cuando tengan un poco de tiempo libre.

¡No olvides nada!

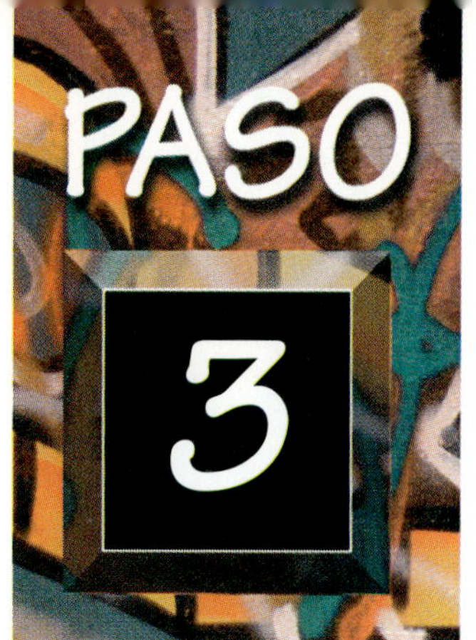

TAREA Antes de empezar este **Paso**, estudia **En preparación** 12.4 y haz por escrito los ejercicios de **¡A practicar!** También escucha **Paso 3 ¿Qué se dice... ?** del Capítulo 12 en el CD del estudiante.

¿Eres buen observador?

SI TE DUELE LA ESPALDA AL VIAJAR...

A veces, cuando viajamos, sufrimos de dolores de espalda. Estos pueden ser causados por estar sentados demasiado tiempo, dormir en camas incómodas o caminar demasiado. Tú sabrás que tienes este problema si de repente sientes un dolor intenso y constante en la parte baja de la espalda. Pero no lo pienses dos veces. Simplemente haz los ejercicios que aquí te sugerimos. El dolor va a desaparecer... Y tú podrás continuar en tu viaje felizmente.

1 Siéntate en una silla dura. Deja caer tu cuerpo lentamente hasta que tu cabeza esté entre tus piernas. Vuelve a tu posición anterior (sentado) y contrae, a la vez, tus músculos abdominales. Relájate y repite el ejercicio.

2 Párate derecho y apoya tus manos en una mesa o silla. Agáchate, doblando las piernas, y levántate nuevamente. Relájate y repite el ejercicio.

¡Advertencia! No hagas demasiados ejercicios, especialmente al principio. Empieza haciendo los ejercicios lenta y cuidadosamente. Si los ejercicios te producen una incomodidad que dure más de 15 ó 20 minutos, detente y no hagas más ejercicios hasta que veas a tu médico.

Ahora, ¡a analizar!

1. ¿Qué puede causar dolores de espalda *(backaches)* cuando viajamos? ¿Crees que los estudiantes también sufren de este problema? ¿Por qué?
2. ¿Cómo sabemos que tenemos dolores de espalda?
3. Dile a un(a) compañero(a) lo que debe hacer si le duele la espalda. Luego que te diga a ti lo que tú puedes hacer. ¡Y háganlo!
4. ¿Qué opinas de estos dos ejercicios? ¿Podrías usarlos?
5. ¿Qué debes hacer si estos ejercicios te causan más dolores de espalda?

¿Qué se dice...?

Al hablar de lo que queda por hacer

1. _______ Escucha.
2. _______ Ve y compra tarjetas postales.
3. _______ Termina el café.
4. _______ No me molestes.
5. _______ Ve tú sola.
6. _______ No gastes mucho dinero.

OLGA ¡Es terrible cómo pasa el tiempo! No he tenido tiempo ni de escribir en mi diario. Pero, por lo menos he hecho mucho ejercicio.

ENRIQUE Eso sí. Hemos caminado millas y millas y millas... y yo siempre cargado con tus maletas.

OLGA Creo que con tanto caminar he perdido peso. ¿Qué te parece, Enrique?

ENRIQUE Estás igual, Olga.

OLGA Bueno, por suerte no me estoy quejando siempre como tú. Oye, no te olvides de comprar algún recuerdo típico.

ENRIQUE No quiero recordar. Además, ¿quién crees que ha pagado todo lo que tú has comprado?

OLGA No seas cruel, Enrique. Eres un viejo gruñón *(grouch)* que se pasa la vida quejándose. Pero, a pesar de todo, te quiero.

Ahora, ¡a hablar!

A. ¡Libre! Ángela va a estudiar en Lima y va a estar sin su familia por primera vez. ¿Qué le recomienda su mamá?

Modelo llamar cada semana
Llama cada semana.

1. salir siempre con otros estudiantes
2. escribir con frecuencia
3. ser muy prudente
4. hacer siempre la tarea
5. quedarse en casa por la noche
6. divertirse

B. ¡No bebas el agua! Su papá también le da consejos. ¿Qué le dice?

Modelo no beber el agua
No bebas el agua.

1. no salir de noche
2. no hablar con extraños *(strangers)*
3. no acostarse tarde
4. no ir a los clubes sola
5. no ser imprudente
6. no llegar tarde a tus clases

C. ¡Vamos al extranjero! Tú vas a hacer tu primer viaje al extranjero. ¿Qué consejos te dan tus padres?

1. no salir solo / noche
2. no beber / agua
3. no comer / vegetales
4. no gastar / dinero en un lugar
5. comprarnos / regalo interesante
6. divertirte

D. El viaje de la vida. ¿Qué le aconsejas a un amigo que quiere triunfar en la vida?

Modelo trabajar
Trabaja mucho. o **No trabajes mucho.**

1. ser responsable
2. casarte
3. salir mucho
4. divertirte
5. tomar drogas
6. ¿... ?

Y ahora, ¡a conversar!

A. ¡Cuídate! Un amigo que viaja contigo en Perú se enferma después de tomar el agua y quiere saber qué debe hacer para mejorarse. Aconséjalo.

Modelo **No comas nada sólido.**

Sugerencias

cerrar las ventanas	no beber más agua	pedir sopa de pollo
beber té caliente	tomar aspirina	no salir del cuarto

B. ¡Lima de noche! Durante tu visita a Lima con tu familia, conoces a un(a) joven de tu edad que ofrece enseñarte Lima de noche. Antes de salir, tus padres te dan varios consejos. ¿Qué te dicen?

C. A tus órdenes. En un viaje a Perú compraste una lámpara muy vieja. Ahora al limpiarla, aparece un genio *(genie)* que dice que está a tus órdenes. Te dice que puede concederte tres deseos. Decide cuáles van a ser tus tres deseos y díselos a la clase.

Modelo **Tráeme mucho dinero, ...**

¡Luz! ¡Cámara! ¡Acción!

A. Turista profesional. Tú acabas de regresar de un viaje al extranjero y ahora todos tus amigos te consideran un turista profesional. Tu mejor amigo(a) piensa visitar el mismo lugar que tú visitaste y te pide consejos. Dramatiza la situación con un(a) compañero(a).

B. El bebé. Tu hermano(a) menor va a empezar su primer año en la universidad el año próximo. ¿Qué consejos le das para que no cometa los mismos errores que tú cometiste? Dramatiza la situación con un(a) compañero(a).

Antes de leer
Estrategias para leer: Pistas de contexto

A. Pistas. En un capítulo previo aprendiste a usar pistas de contexto *(context clues)* cuando no sabes el significado de una palabra. Aprendiste que varias cosas te pueden ayudar a entender una palabra clave desconocida:

- el contenido de la oración
- no preocuparse por saber el significado específico; basta con tener una idea general del significado
- fijarse en la puntuación y la estructura
- identificar las palabras clave y no preocuparse por palabras desconocidas que no son clave

Ahora lee las dos oraciones que siguen.

Una teoría dice que sirvió de refugio a los últimos incas que huían de la dominación española. Sea cual fuere su origen, la ciudad fue construida en las cumbres de la cordillera de los Andes.

1. Identifica las palabras desconocidas en cada oración. ¿Cuántas hay? ¿Cuáles son?
2. ¿Hay algunas palabras clave entre las palabras desconocidas? ¿Cuáles son? ¿Por qué crees que son clave?

B. ¡A descifrar! Con la ayuda de un(a) compañero(a), trata de descifrar las palabras desconocidas de las dos listas. Si tú sabes el significado de las de su lista, no se lo digas. Simplemente ayúdale a adivinar siguiendo uno de los procesos mencionados.

Machu Picchu: La ciudad escondida de los incas

Machu Picchu

No se sabe con certeza cuándo fue construida Machu Picchu. Una teoría dice que la ciudad fue anterior a los incas y desconocida por ellos. Otra dice que fue construida por los incas, pero abandonada antes de la llegada de los españoles. Aún otra teoría dice que sirvió de refugio a los últimos incas que huían de la dominación española. Sea cual fuere su origen, la ciudad fue construida en las cumbres de la cordillera de los Andes a una altura de 1.400 pies sobre el río Urubamba.

No se sabe con seguridad si Machu Picchu fue encontrada por los conquistadores españoles. Si llegaron a conocerla, pronto la olvidaron porque permaneció escondida en las montañas por más de cuatro siglos. En 1911 Hiram Bingham, un profesor de historia de la Universidad de Yale, hizo una expedición al Perú en la que descubrió las ruinas de la ciudad. Desde ese momento aumentó el interés por conocer a fondo los elementos de la cultura incaica.

Algunos investigadores creen que Machu Picchu fue construida como fortaleza para defenderse del ataque enemigo. Otros piensan que fue un santuario de gran importancia mágico-religiosa para los incas. También se cree que fue un centro de trabajadoras femeninas, un convento donde se fabricaba la ropa que vestía el Inca. Lo más probable es que fuera un centro religioso donde se practicaban sacrificios en honor a los dioses.

Machu Picchu es también un laboratorio de la cultura incaica. Allí puede observarse el método que utilizaban para cultivar la tierra por medio de terrazas que permitían la mejor explotación del terreno montañoso. Hay también un sistema de canales para la irrigación agrícola y el consumo humano. Pero lo más impresionante de todo es el empleo de la piedra labrada en la construcción de las casas, templos y otros edificios. El resultado es una arquitectura en armonía con la naturaleza que la rodea. Todo en ella nos hace recordar el esplendor y el rigor de una civilización perdida.

A ver si comprendiste

1. ¿Cuáles son las varias teorías sobre el origen y el propósito de Machu Picchu? ¿Cuál es la más probable, en tu opinión? Explica tu respuesta.
2. ¿Por qué se dice que Machu Picchu es un laboratorio de la cultura incaica? Explica con detalle.
3. ¿Qué es lo más impresionante de Machu Picchu para ti? ¿Por qué?

Viajemos por el ciberespacio a... PERÚ

Expand your horizons! *Let's travel through cyberspace to* ***Peru*** where . . .

- through the Internet, you can visit the land of the astonishing Inca Empire: a land where the shadow of the majestic condor lives on.
- you can peer into the depths of **Cañón de Colca**, the deepest canyon in the world. Find out interesting facts about this impressive work of nature.
- you can visit the beautiful and highest navigable lake in the world: **lago Titicaca.**
- you can take lessons in Quechua, obtain Quechua fonts for your computer to allow you to write Quechua, and browse through lots of software related to this ancient yet living language.
- you can talk to Peruvians living in the United States and have any questions about their country answered directly.

If you are a cyberspace browser, join us in **Viajemos por el ciberespacio a... Perú** by trying the following important addresses.

Universidad Católica del Perú
http://www.pucp.edu.pe/

Universidad de Lima
http://ulima.edu.pe/

Vargas Llosa
http://www.clark.net/pub/jgbustam/famosos/vargasll.html

Machu Picchu
http://ekeko.rcp.net.pe/promperu/TURISMO/machu-picchu.html
http://ekeko.rcp.net.pe/peru/cusco/machupichu.html

Periódicos y revistas:

Ilustración peruana
http://ekeko.rcp.net.pe/CARETAS/

La República
http://ekeko.rcp.net.pe/LaRepublica/

Diario El Comercio
http://ekeko.rcp.net.pe/ELCOMERCIO//

Because addresses are likely to change without notice, the following key words will guarantee that **Viajemos por el ciberespacio a... Perú** will get you to your desired destination.

Palabras clave:

Lago Titicaca
Lima, Perú
Machu Picchu
Cañón de Colca
Peruanos
Quechua
Reserva de Biosfera del Manu
Vargas Llosa

http://www.hrwcollege.com

Viajes

alojarse	*to lodge, to stay overnight*
empacar	*to pack (a suitcase)*
espectáculo	*show, special event*
extranjero	*abroad, a foreign country*
gafas de sol *(f.)*	*sunglasses*
pasaporte *(m.)*	*passport*
regalo	*gift*
ruinas	*ruins*
sello	*stamp (for mail)*
terraza	*terrace*

En el baño

cepillo de dientes *(m.)*	*toothbrush*
champú *(m.)*	*shampoo*
jabón *(m.)*	*soap*
máquina de afeitar *(f.)*	*electric shaver*
pasta dental *(f.)*	*toothpaste*

Verbos

cargar	*to load; to carry*
cometer un error	*to make a mistake*
doler (ue)	*to hurt*
enfermarse	*to get sick*
enviar	*to send*
estar harto(a) de (algo)	*to be fed up with (something)*
estar seguro(a) de (algo)	*to be sure, certain of (something)*
gastar	*to spend*
hacer ejercicio	*to exercise*
hacer la cama	*to make the bed*
hacer la siesta	*to take a nap, rest*
molestar	*to bother*
olvidar	*to forget*
perder (ie) peso	*to lose weight*

Sustantivos

bolso	*purse, pocketbook*
competición *(f.)*	*competition*
corriente *(f.)*	*electrical current*
deseo	*desire, wish*
diario	*diary*
empresa	*company, firm*
esperanza	*hope*
fábrica	*factory*
forma	*form*
lentes de contacto	*contact lens*
memoria	*memory, remembrance*
montón *(m.)*	*a bunch, lots*
origen *(m.)*	*origin*
parrilla	*grill*
uso	*use*
valor *(m.)*	*valor, bravery*
vecino(a)	*neighbor*
vejez *(f.)*	*old age*

Adjetivos

cruel	*cruel*
gruñón (-ona)	*grouchy, grumpy*
igual	*same*
puntual	*punctual*

Adverbios

además	*besides*
todavía	*still*

Palabras útiles

a pesar de todo	*in spite of everything*
ni siquiera	*not even*
No te preocupes.	*Don't worry.*

En preparación 12

12.1 Summary of Preterite and Imperfect

Talking about past events

You have learned that both the preterite and the imperfect are used to talk about an event that took place at some time in the past. The preterite focuses on the beginning or end of the event or on the completed act. The imperfect focuses on the event or action while it was in progress. Visually, this may be illustrated as follows.

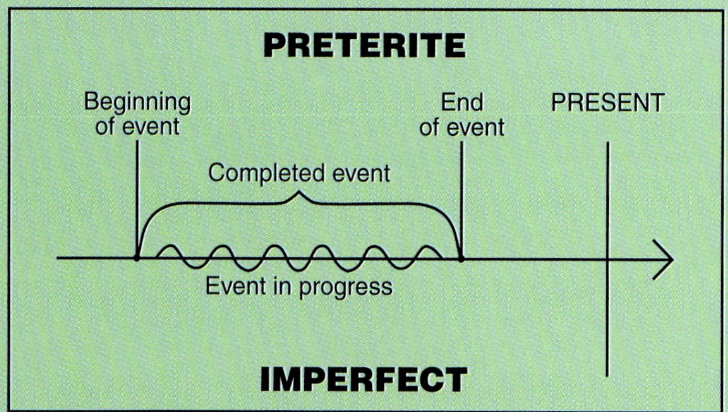

Preterite	**Imperfect**
A. Focus on beginning	Focus on event in progress
En ese momento, **sonó** el teléfono. *At that moment, the phone rang (started to ring).*	**Sonaba** el teléfono. *The phone was ringing. (It wouldn't stop.)*
B. Focus on ending	Habitual or customary acts
Me **quedé** allí una semana. *I stayed there a week. (And then left.)*	Siempre me **quedaba** allí. *I always stayed there. (It was customary.)*
C. Verbs with changed meaning	Certain physical or mental states
Ese día los **conocí.** *I met them that day.*	No me **sentía** bien. *I wasn't feeling well.*

D. Focus on completed act

El presidente afirmó que las clases **empezaron** sin problemas.
The president affirmed that classes started without problems.

Focus on future event within a past context

El presidente confirmó que las clases **empezaban** a fin de mes.
The president confirmed that classes would start at the end of the month.

E. Series of completed acts

Cuando **llegué,** me **tomé** dos aspirinas y me **acosté** en seguida.
When I arrived, I took two aspirin and went to bed right away.

Series of habitual acts

De noche **cenábamos** en un buen restaurante y luego **íbamos** a bailar.
At night we used to dine at a good restaurant and afterwards we'd go dancing.

¡A practicar!

A. ¡Viaje a Perú! El verano pasado Josefina Valle y su esposo viajaron al Perú. ¿Cuál fue su primera impresión? Para saberlo, pon los verbos entre paréntesis en el pasado.

El verano pasado mi esposo y yo ______________ (decidir) hacer un viaje al Perú. ______________ (Ser) la primera vez que yo ______________ (viajar) a Sudamérica. Nosotros ______________ (quedarse) tres semanas. En ese breve tiempo yo ______________ (aprender) mucho. Cada día nosotros ______________ (descubrir) algo nuevo e interesante. Con frecuencia ______________ (ir) a los mercados al aire libre y siempre ______________ (encontrar) algo interesante para comprar y además, los precios ______________ (estar) muy bajos. En Cuzco, nosotros ______________ (visitar) muchos lugares históricos y ______________ (sacar) muchas fotos. Cuando ______________ (tener) que regresar, yo ______________ (estar) un poco triste.

B. De vacaciones en los EE.UU. No a todos les gusta viajar al extranjero durante las vacaciones. Pon los verbos entre paréntesis en el tiempo pasado para saber qué hizo esta familia el verano pasado.

Nosotros ______________ (decidir) viajar al oeste. Papá ______________ (querer) conocer Nuevo México. Lo más interesante del viaje para mí ______________ (ser) Santa Fe, la capital. Es una ciudad interesantísima donde nosotros ______________ (ver) cosas muy interesantes. Por ejemplo, frente al antiguo Palacio del Gobernador ______________ (haber) muchos indios que ______________ (vender) joyas de plata *(silver)* y turquesa. Los precios ______________ (ser) muy buenos y los turistas ______________ (comprar) de todo. De noche, todos ______________ (ir) a cenar a restaurantes que ______________ (servir) comida típica. Una noche mamá ______________ (conseguir) boletos para la Ópera de Santa Fe. ______________ (Ser) muy especial porque ellos ______________ (presentar) la ópera al aire libre. Me gustaría regresar a Santa Fe alguna vez.

12.2 Future Tense of Regular Verbs

Talking about the future

A. In English, the future is usually expressed with the auxiliary verbs *will* or *shall: I will / shall see you later.* The future tense in Spanish is formed by adding the endings **-é, -ás, -á, -emos, -éis,** and **-án** to the infinitive of most **-ar, -er,** and **-ir** verbs.

Estar		**Ser**		**Ir**	
estar**é**	estar**emos**	ser**é**	ser**emos**	ir**é**	ir**emos**
estar**ás**	estar**éis**	ser**ás**	ser**éis**	ir**ás**	ir**éis**
estar**á**	estar**án**	ser**á**	ser**án**	ir**á**	ir**án**

Este verano no **viajaré**. — *This summer I will not travel.*
En el invierno **iremos** a esquiar en Utah. — *In the winter we will go skiing in Utah.*

B. There are other ways to talk about future time in Spanish. Remember that the present indicative and **ir a** + *infinitive* are also used to express future time.

Carlos **llega** mañana a las diez. — *Carlos arrives tomorrow at ten.*
Te **veo** más tarde. — *I'll see you later.*
Vamos a verla esta noche. — *We are going to see her tonight.*
Ella **va a traer**los. — *She is going to bring them.*

¡A practicar!

A. ¡Qué planes tengo! Andrés acaba de graduarse y antes que nada quiere pasar las vacaciones en el Perú. ¿Qué planea hacer?

Modelo yo / pasar / vacaciones / Perú
Yo pasaré las vacaciones en Perú.

1. primero, yo / ir a descansar / playas / Santa María
2. estar / Lima / dos semanas
3. divertirme / todas las noches / discotecas
4. visitar Cuzco / donde poder ver / fortaleza de Sacsahuamán
5. caminar / toda la ciudad / y ver / mucho de la antigua capital
6. regresar / Estados Unidos / agosto

B. ¡Me escaparé! Unos amigos están hablando de lo que harán después de graduarse. Cambia los verbos al futuro para saber lo que dicen.

1. Yo _______________ (ir) a Cuba por tres semanas con mi novia.
2. Alicia y yo _______________ (descansar) y _______________ (tomar) sol en las hermosas playas de La Habana.
3. Gloria y María _______________ (viajar) a Machu Picchu.
4. José _______________ (quedarse) aquí para descansar.
5. Cecilia y Roberto _______________ (volver) a Argentina durante el verano.
6. Fernando dice que _______________ (visitar) a sus parientes en Puerto Rico. _______________ (Estar) allá un mes entero.

12.3 Future Tense of Verbs with Irregular Stems

Talking about the future

The future tense of the following verbs is formed by adding the future tense endings to irregular stems.

decir:	**dir-**	
haber:	**habr-**	
hacer:	**har-**	
poder:	**podr-**	**–é**
poner:	**pondr-**	**–ás**
querer:	**querr-**	**–á**
saber:	**sabr-**	**–emos**
salir:	**saldr-**	**–éis**
tener:	**tendr-**	**–án**
valer:	**valdr-**	
venir:	**vendr-**	

Poder

podré	podremos
podrás	podréis
podrá	podrán

Note that with the exception of **decir** and **hacer,** the irregular stems are derived by eliminating the vowel of the infinitive ending or replacing it with a **d.**

Tendremos que ver al sacerdote.	*We will have to see the priest.*
Los invitados **vendrán** de todas partes.	*The guests will come from all over.*
Tus futuros suegros te **harán** una despedida de soltera.	*Your future in-laws will give you a bridal shower.*

¡A practicar!

A. ¡Hay tanto que hacer! Eva y Adolfo se casarán dentro de un mes. Ahora, Eva está explicándole a su mejor amiga lo que todavía le queda por hacer. ¿Qué dice Eva? Para saberlo, pon los verbos en el futuro.

Yo ______________ (tener) que comprar el vestido muy pronto. Adolfo, yo y nuestros padres ______________ (hacer) la lista de los invitados esta noche. Mamá ______________ (poner) el anuncio de la boda en el periódico. Mis tías ______________ (darme) una despedida de soltera la semana antes de la boda. Adolfo ______________ (poder) hablar con el sacerdote esta semana. Y mis abuelos dicen que ______________ (venir) de Miami.

B. ¡Los días pasan volando! La mejor amiga de Eva tiene algunas ideas de cómo ayudarla. Pon los verbos entre paréntesis en el futuro para saber qué le sugiere.

Yo ______________ (poder) ir contigo a comprar el vestido. Podemos ir mañana por la tarde porque yo ______________ (salir) del trabajo a las dos de la tarde. También nosotras ______________ (tener) tiempo de ir a casa a cenar. Te ______________ (hacer) una cena especial. Probablemente no ______________ (haber) otra oportunidad de estar solas antes de la boda.

12.4 *Tú* Commands: A Second Look

Requesting, advising, and giving orders to people

A. In **Capítulo 9,** you learned that affirmative **tú** commands are identical to the third-person singular of the present indicative.

Llama al médico.	*Call the doctor.*
Bebe muchos líquidos.	*Drink a lot of liquids.*
Pide sopa de pollo.	*Ask for chicken soup.*

You have also learned that there are eight irregular affirmative **tú** commands: **di, pon, sal, ten, ven, haz, ve,** and **sé.**

B. To form a negative **tú** command, drop the final **-o** from the first-person singular of the present indicative and add **-es** to **-ar** verbs and **-as** to **-er** and **-ir** verbs.

Negative *Tú* Commands

tomar:	tomo	No **tomes** cerveza.	*Don't drink beer.*
comer:	como	No **comas** nada.	*Don't eat anything.*
dormir:	duermo	No **duermas** aquí.	*Don't sleep here.*
salir:	salgo	No **salgas** hoy.	*Don't go out today.*

C. Reflexive and object pronouns *must* precede the verb in negative commands and follow and be attached to the verb in affirmative commands. When two pronouns are present in a sentence, the reflexive pronoun always comes first, and the indirect object pronoun always precedes the direct object pronoun.

Acuéstate en seguida y no **te levantes** hasta mañana.	*Go to bed right away and don't get up until tomorrow.*
¡Ah, las pastillas! **Cómpramelas**, por favor.	*Oh, the pills. Buy them for me, please.*

¡A practicar!

A. ¡Sigue mis consejos! Tu compañero(a) de cuarto está enfermo(a). ¿Qué consejos le das?

1. quedarte / en casa
2. no comer / nada
3. tomar / mucho jugo
4. descansar / todo el día
5. no hacer / la tarea / y / no mirar / la televisión
6. acostarte / y / no levantarte
7. dormir / todo el día
8. si suena el teléfono / no contestarlo

B. ¡Estás enfermo(a)! Ahora tu compañero(a) de cuarto está hablando por teléfono con su mamá. ¿Qué le dice ella?

1. no comer / nada
2. no mirar / televisión
3. no leer / mucho
4. no tomar / cerveza
5. no salir / al frío
6. no hacer / ejercicios pesados

C. ¡Instrucciones! Los padres del (de la) enfermo(a) tienen instrucciones muy específicas para ti. ¿Qué te dicen?

Modelo servirle sopa de pollo dos veces al día
Sírvele sopa de pollo dos veces al día. o
Sírvesela dos veces al día.

1. tomarle la temperatura cada cuatro horas
2. no hablarle si se siente cansado(a)

3. darle una aspirina cada seis horas
4. no despertarlo(la) si suena el teléfono
5. prepararle té calientito todo el día
6. servirle un vaso de agua fresca cada media hora

CAPÍTULO 13

Mente sana, cuerpo sano

Cultural Topics

- **¿Sabías que… ?**
  Influencia árabe en la lengua española
- ***La dinastía del amor***
  Cross-cultural perceptions regarding a woman's honor and the issue of adoption vs. abortion.
- **Noticiero cultural**
  Lugar: *Panamá: Puente del Atlántico al Pacífico*
  Gente: *Rubén Blades: Salsero, político y panameño «de corazón»*
- **Lectura:** *El primer escalador con cascada de hielo particular* y *Sumergirse entre barcos naufragados*

Writing Strategies

- *Al persuadir*

Reading Strategies

- *Sumarios*

En preparación

- 13.1 Present Subjunctive: Theory and Forms
- 13.2 Subjunctive with Expressions of Persuasion
- 13.3 **Usted** and **ustedes** Commands
- 13.4 **Ojalá** and Present Subjunctive of Irregular Verbs
- 13.5 Present Subjunctive of Stem-Changing Verbs
- 13.6 Present Subjunctive of Verbs with Spelling Changes

In this chapter, you will learn how to …

- give advice.
- lead a group in aerobic exercise.
- tell someone what to do or not do.
- suggest and make recommendations.

Dos enamorados en la Ciudad de Panamá

Pasatiempo favorito de los panameños: un cafecito o una cerveza, unos cigaros para fumar y buenos amigos...

Club de ejercicios en la capital de Panamá

Lo que ya sabes...

1. ¿Quiénes crees que son las personas en la primera foto: solteros, casados, amantes? ¿Por qué crees eso?

2. ¿Qué importancia tiene el mantenerse en buena forma para ti? ¿Qué haces para estar en buena condición física? ¿Vas a un club de ejercicios?

3. ¿Qué opinas de los pasatiempos de estas personas? ¿Son saludables? ¿Por qué?

4. ¿Por qué crees que tantos jóvenes tienen estos vicios? ¿Es posible dejarlos para siempre? ¿Cómo?

PANAMÁ

¡El exceso es malo para la salud!

TAREA

Antes de empezar este **Paso**, estudia **En preparación** 13.1 y 13.2 y haz por escrito los ejercicios de **¡A practicar!** También escucha **Paso 1 ¿Qué se dice... ?** del Capítulo 13 en el CD del estudiante.

¿Eres buen observador?

Ahora, ¡a analizar!

1. ¿Cuál es el propósito de este anuncio? ¿Por qué dice que tú puedes esperar? ¿Qué debes esperar?
2. ¿Cómo se dice SIDA en inglés?
3. ¿Por qué dice que la abstención o protección son tus mejores armas? ¿Abstención de qué? ¿Protección de qué?
4. ¿Qué es una «Línea de Auxilio»? ¿Siempre son confidenciales? ¿Por qué? ¿Cuál es el número de la línea de auxilio que recomiendan?
5. Explica el lema: «En control de tu cuerpo y tu vida».

¿Qué se dice...?

Al dar consejos

El médico recomienda que Jaime...

1. _______ tome mucha leche.
2. _______ no fume.
3. _______ coma muchas verduras.
4. _______ pierda peso.
5. _______ no beba alcohol.
6. _______ no coma mucha carne.
7. _______ no duerma tanto.
8. _______ camine o corra cada día.
9. _______ beba mucha agua.
10. _______ coma pollo y pescado.

PACO A ver, nada de alcohol, nada de fumar, litros de agua, mucha verdura, correr y caminar. Es una vida ideal... para caballos. ¿Y la medicina para los nervios que tú le pediste?

JAIME No me quiso dar nada.

PACO Pues estos médicos siempre son iguales, Jaime. Siempre recomiendan que la gente haga más ejercicios en el gimnasio y que coman más verduras. Pero en fin no saben nada. ¿Sabes lo que yo opino, amigo?

JAIME No, dime.

PACO Yo sugiero que dejes de ser un teleadicto y que pongas más atención a tus libros en vez de a las telenovelas. De esa forma estarás mejor preparado y no vas a estar tan nervioso en las clases. Eso es lo que tú necesitas. ¿Qué te parece?

Ahora, ¡a hablar!

A. ¡Estoy rendido! Adrián está cansadísimo de tanto estudiar y trabajar. ¿Qué recomiendas para que se relaje? Forma por lo menos ocho recomendaciones originales.

Modelo **Recomiendo que haga un viaje.**

	hacer un viaje
	olvidar el trabajo
aconsejar	descansar todo el domingo
insistir en	tener una fiesta
sugerir	salir más
recomendar	conocer a nuevos amigos
	no preocuparse tanto
	¿... ?

B. El primer semestre. Cuando se empieza la universidad, el primer semestre puede ser una experiencia llena de presiones. ¿Qué consejos tienes para un(a) nuevo(a) estudiante que acaba de entrar en la universidad?

Modelo estudiar cada día un poco

Recomiendo que estudie cada día un poco.

1. no dejar las cosas para después
2. no perder la calma en los exámenes
3. siempre hacer la tarea a tiempo
4. estudiar con otras personas
5. hacer ejercicio con frecuencia
6. no faltar a clase
7. hablar con los consejeros
8. ¿... ?

C. ¡El primer coche! Jaime acaba de recibir su licencia de manejar. Según él, ¿qué consejos recibe de su familia?

Modelo mamá insistir en / nunca / manejar borracho

Mamá insiste en que nunca maneje borracho.

1. padres / recomendar / siempre usar / cinturón de seguridad *(seatbelt)*
2. papá / insistir en / siempre observar los límites de velocidad
3. hermano mayor / recomendar / siempre poner / coche / garaje
4. hermana / insistir en / nunca / beber alcohol
5. papá / recomendar / lavar / coche / con frecuencia
6. padres / insistir en / siempre tener / llanta de auxilio
7. abuela / recomendar / ¿... ?

D. El director. El señor López es el director de una escuela secundaria en una ciudad grande. Él es una persona que siempre tiene que estar en control de todo. ¿Cómo controla a los estudiantes?

Modelo no permitir: los estudiantes llevar ropa controversial
El señor López no permite que los estudiantes lleven ropa controversial.

1. insistir en: los estudiantes no usar drogas
2. no permitir: los estudiantes traer bebidas alcohólicas a la escuela
3. insistir en: los estudiantes no fumar en los baños
4. insistir en: los estudiantes mantener limpia la escuela
5. insistir en: los estudiantes no correr en los pasillos *(halls)*
6. no permitir: los estudiantes comer en los pasillos

Y ahora, ¡a conversar!

A. Doctor Sabelotodo. Tú y tu compañero(a) trabajan para el doctor Sabelotodo, un señor que da consejos en un periódico de su comunidad. ¿Qué consejos puede darles a estas personas? Sugieran varios consejos para cada situación.

Vocabulario útil

aconsejar	preferir	insistir
recomendar	sugerir	permitir

1. Una pareja quiere saber cómo puede tener un matrimonio feliz.
2. Una joven de 18 años necesita conseguir un buen trabajo inmediatamente.
3. Tres compañeros de cuarto quieren saber cómo conseguir buenas notas. ¡Es urgente!
4. Dos amigos quieren vivir juntos; necesitan consejos para poder vivir sin problemas.
5. Un(a) joven acaba de divorciarse. Está muy deprimido(a).

B. ¿Nosotros? ¿consejeros? Todos tenemos problemas: de salud, de dinero, de trabajo o de lo que sea. En grupos de tres, preparen una descripción por escrito de dos o tres problemas típicos de estudiantes universitarios y dénsela a su profesor(a). Él (Ella) va a redistribuir las listas para que cada grupo haga varias recomendaciones para solucionar los problemas de su nueva lista.

C. Sueños. Todos tenemos sueños que queremos realizar algún día. Con un(a) compañero(a) comparte tus sueños. Tu compañero(a) va a darte algunos consejos que te ayuden a lograr *(attain)* lo que quieras.

Modelo

TÚ **Yo quiero vivir en una mansión grande y elegante.**

COMPAÑERO(A) **Sugiero que trabajes mucho y ahorres *(save)* mucho dinero.**

¡Luz! ¡Cámara! ¡Acción!

A. ¿Qué me recomiendas? Es la última semana de exámenes y un(a) amigo(a) que está sufriendo mucho del estrés viene a hablar contigo y con tu compañero(a) de cuarto. ¿Qué consejos le dan ustedes? Dramatiza la situación con dos compañeros(as) de clase.

B. Consejos. Tú y tu compañero(a) de cuarto están hablando con un(a) amigo(a) que tiene problemas serios debido al exceso de alcohol (drogas o cigarrillos). ¿Qué consejos le dan? Dramatiza la situación con dos compañeros(as) de clase.

¿Comprendes lo que se dice?

La dinastía del amor: Episodio 5

Es martes, son las nueve de la noche y una vez más la familia Gómez se reúne para ver la telenovela del momento. En el episodio anterior aprendimos el secreto de Betty, la hermana mayor. En este nuevo episodio vamos a descubrir el secreto de Sharon. Escucha este episodio y luego contesta las preguntas que siguen.

A través de dos culturas

Telenovela

1. ¿Por qué usó Sharon un nombre falso?
2. ¿Tiene Sharon diecinueve años en realidad?
3. ¿Qué teme Sharon que le diga el médico?
4. ¿Qué solución al problema ofrece Eric?

Televidentes

5. ¿Por qué dice Juan Pedro que Eric es tonto?
6. ¿Por qué cree don Sergio que Eric está obligado a casarse con Sharon? ¿Estás de acuerdo con él?
7. ¿Qué solución ofrece Luisita? ¿Estás de acuerdo? ¿Por qué sí o por qué no?
8. ¿A qué soluciones se refiere Juan Pedro?
9. ¿Por qué reacciona don Sergio tan fuertemente?
10. ¿Está Luisita tratando de proteger a su hermano al sugerir otra interpretación?

NOTICIERO CULTURAL

LUGAR... PANAMÁ

Antes de empezar, dime...

1. ¿Cómo puede influir la situación geográfica de un país en su destino o futuro? ¿Puedes dar ejemplos de esto?
2. ¿Qué influencia ha tenido en los EE.UU. el hecho de que México sea el vecino inmediato en la frontera del sur y Canadá en la frontera del norte? ¿Qué influencia ha tenido esta situación geográfica en México y Canadá?
3. ¿Dónde hay fortificaciones antiguas en los EE.UU.? ¿Cuándo fueron construidas? ¿A quiénes protegían estas fortificaciones?

La Ciudad de Panamá

Panamá: Puente del Atlántico al Pacífico

Panamá es un istmo, o sea, tierra angosta que une dos continentes. Es un país pequeño; de este a oeste mide unas 480 millas y de sur a norte varía entre 28 y 120 millas. El futuro de Panamá se determinó en el año 1513 cuando Balboa vio por primera vez el Pacífico. Reconocido muy pronto como el cruce más importante del Atlántico al Pacífico, el destino de este país ha sido determinado en gran parte por su situación geográfica.

La población de Panamá es de aproximadamente 2.655.000 habitantes. Está compuesta por comunidades europeas, indígenas, negras y una minoría de origen asiático. La población de Panamá crece anualmente un 2,2 por ciento.

Su capital, la Ciudad de Panamá, es una impresionante metrópoli de modernos rascacielos *(grandes edificios)* que actualmente tiene una población de 1.200.000. Fundada en 1519, fue de gran importancia para los españoles, siendo el puerto principal de donde salían las expediciones de la Conquista. En el año 1673, esta ciudad tuvo que ser reconstruida después de ser saqueada por el pirata inglés Henry Morgan. Al ser reconstruida, fue fortificada tan efectivamente por los españoles que nunca pudo ser atacada con éxito por el enemigo. Esta fortificación se conserva hasta hoy en la sección de la ciudad llamada «Casco Viejo», uno de los hermosos ejemplos de la arquitectura antigua del mundo hispano.

Y ahora, dime...

Explica con un(a) compañero(a), cómo influyó la situación geográfica de la ciudad de Panamá en su pasado y cómo sigue influyendo en su presente.

INFLUENCIA DE SITUACIÓN GEOGRÁFICA

Pasado	Presente
1.	1.
2.	2.
3.	3.
4.	4.
...	...

El español en otras disciplinas: Ingeniería

Grandes obras de ingeniería. La ingeniería es una parte importantísima de nuestra era. En todos los países del mundo vemos su resultado en los grandes rascacielos, puentes y carreteras, por nombrar algunos. Pero si la ingeniería moderna es impresionante, es aún más impresionante cuando la observamos en antiguas construcciones como las pirámides y templos de México y Guatemala; las hermosas ciudades de los incas, los mayas y los aztecas; los caminos andinos precolombinos, y también los castillos e iglesias medievales españoles. Todas son obras que dan testimonio de la magnífica ingeniería de épocas anteriores.

Y tú, ¿cuánto sabes de proyectos de ingeniería? Con un(a) compañero(a), prepara una lista de los tres proyectos de ingeniería del mundo hispanohablante que ustedes consideran los más importantes. Pueden ser tanto del mundo antiguo como del mundo moderno. Compartan su lista con el resto de la clase para ver cuáles obras se repiten más.

Proyecto: Con un(a) compañero(a), prepara un informe sobre uno de estos proyectos—en español ¡por supuesto! Si es posible, agreguen fotos o dibujos y mencionen el objetivo de la obra, cuánto tiempo llevó construirla, quién la construyó, cuál fue el costo y en qué condiciones está actualmente.

Salten uno, dos, tres...

TAREA Antes de empezar este **Paso**, estudia **En preparación** 13.3 y 13.4 y haz por escrito los ejercicios de **¡A practicar!** También escucha **Paso 2 ¿Qué se dice...?** del Capítulo 13 en el CD del estudiante.

¿Eres buen observador?

Ahora, ¡a analizar!

1. ¿Para qué es esta propaganda? Explica el título de este anuncio. ¿En qué país y ciudad tienes que estar para poder usar este producto?
2. De los servicios que ofrecen, ¿cuántos reconoces? ¿Los has usados alguna vez? ¿Cuáles no reconoces?
3. En el «*Day Spa*» se puede comer tres comidas al día. ¿Cuáles son?
4. Explica lo que son los distintos servicios en el «*Day Spa*».
5. ¿Hay algunos tratamientos que te interesarían a ti? ¿Cuáles?

¿Qué se dice...?

Al hablar de tonificar el cuerpo

Doblen	en un pie.
No respire	vuelta las manos.
Estiren	el ritmo.
Den	por la boca.
Salten	los brazos.
Sigan	las rodillas.

LETICIA ¡Huy! Estoy muerta. Ojalá que sea más fácil mañana.

PACO Estoy molido *(exhausted)*.

JAIME Yo también.

IRENE ¡Ay, qué flojos están todos! Les digo que tienen que sufrir un poco si quieren tonificar el cuerpo. Ojalá pongan más esfuerzo mañana.

TODOS ¡Bu! ¡Vaya! ¡A otro perro con ese hueso! ¡Cállate!

¿Sabías que... ?

La expresión **ojalá** viene de una expresión árabe que invocaba a su dios Alá. La influencia árabe en la lengua y cultura española abunda porque los musulmanes *(Moslems)* controlaron grandes partes de España por casi ochocientos años (711–1492). Siempre cuando dos lenguas conviven por un extenso período de tiempo, la una acaba por influir a la otra y viceversa. Por ejemplo, un gran número de sustantivos que empiezan con **al-** en español vienen directamente del árabe: **alfombra, almohada** *(pillow)*, **algodón** *(cotton)*, **alfalfa, álgebra, almuerzo...** ¿Puedes pensar en palabras en inglés que vienen directamente del español debido a la convivencia de estas dos lenguas en los EE.UU., en particular en el suroeste del país?

Ahora, ¡a hablar!

A. Anatomía. ¿Cuánto saben del cuerpo humano? En grupos de tres, digan para qué sirven las siguientes partes del cuerpo.

Modelo La boca sirve para comer y para hablar.

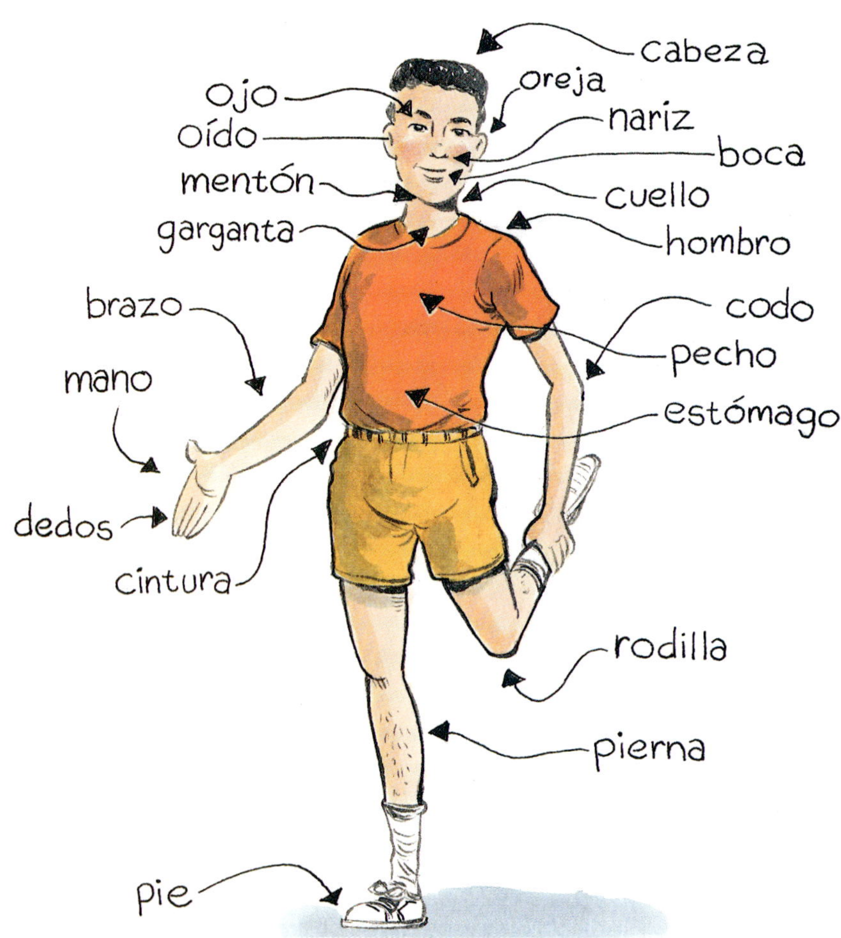

1. las manos
2. la nariz
3. los oídos
4. los dedos
5. los pies
6. los brazos
7. los ojos
8. la boca
9. las piernas
10. ¿... ?

B. ¿Yo, instructor(a) de aeróbicos? Tú eres instructor(a) de ejercicios aeróbicos. ¿Qué les dices a tus alumnos al empezar?

Modelo relajarse / respirar profundamente

Relájense y respiren profundamente.

1. con el ritmo de la música / levantar los brazos / bajarlos
2. estirar los brazos / doblarlos contra el pecho
3. todos juntos / doblar la cintura lentamente a la izquierda / derecha
4. subir la pierna izquierda / bajarla
5. levantar los brazos / dar vuelta las manos
6. subir los hombros / bajarlos

C. ¡Excesos! Los excesos son malos para la salud. ¿Qué le aconsejas a una persona que hace lo siguiente?

Modelo fumar dos paquetes de cigarillos por día

No fume tanto. O simplemente: **No fume.**

1. tomar mucho café
2. gritar *(scream)* mucho
3. correr sin zapatos
4. levantar cosas pesadas
5. leer con poca luz
6. beber mucho vino
7. salir al frío sin abrigo
8. escuchar música fuerte

D. ¡Ya no aguanto! Después de la clase de aeróbicos, Martín está molido. ¿Qué esta pensado?

Modelo espalda: ojalá no ser nada grave

¡Ay la espalda! Ojalá no sea nada grave.

1. cuello: ojalá no tener que ir al médico
2. piernas: ojalá poder caminar al coche
3. cabeza: ojalá / instructora darme una aspirina
4. pies: ojalá no estar hinchados *(swollen)*
5. brazos: ojalá poder abrir la puerta del coche
6. cuerpo: ojalá no tener que ir al hospital

Y ahora, ¡a conversar!

A. «¿Aeroteleadicto?» Hay personas no muy activas que prefieren mirar televisión todo el día en vez de hacer ejercicio. ¿Pueden tú y dos compañeros crear un programa de ejercicio diseñado especialmente para ese tipo de gente? Sean creativos al diseñar ejercicios «aeroteleadictos».

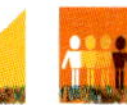

B. Cuerpo ideal. En una hoja de papel escribe el nombre de una persona famosa que, según tú, tiene un cuerpo ideal y está en excelente condición física. Da tu papelito a tu instructor(a) que va a redistribuirlos. Ahora en grupos de tres, lean los nombres de las personas famosas y digan qué consejos pueden darles a personas que deseen tener un cuerpo similar.

Modelo Arnold Schwarzenneger

Para tener un cuerpo como Arnold, levanten pesas cada día, corran una a tres millas cada dos días y...

C. La salud y el ambiente. El ambiente en el que vives y trabajas afecta mucho la salud. Entrevista a un compañero(a) sobre el ambiente en el que vive y trabaja. Usa este cuestionario y anota sus respuestas. Luego aconséjalo(la) acerca de lo que debe hacer o no hacer para mantenerse en forma.

1. ¿Cuáles son los problemas ambientales del lugar donde vives?
   - ❑ pesticidas
   - ❑ asbestos
   - ❑ gases
   - ❑ polen
   - ❑ carcinógenos
   - ❑ humo diesel
2. Lugar de residencia:
   - ❑ campo
   - ❑ suburbio
   - ❑ ciudad
3. Calidad del agua de tu área:
   - ❑ potable
   - ❑ contaminada
   - ❑ muy contaminada
   - ❑ no sabe
4. Nivel de ruido *(noise)*:
   - ❑ muy poco
   - ❑ un poco
   - ❑ mucho
5. Tipo de ruido:
   - ❑ niños
   - ❑ tráfico
   - ❑ trenes
   - ❑ perros
   - ❑ música
   - ❑ aviones
6. ¿Trabajas? Si dices que sí, ¿qué tipo de trabajo haces?
   - ❑ oficina
   - ❑ profesional
   - ❑ manual
   - ❑ intelectual
   - ❑ casa
   - ❑ no trabaja
7. Nivel de crimen:
   - ❑ no existente
   - ❑ muy poco
   - ❑ mucho
8. Lugar de trabajo:
   - ❑ casa
   - ❑ fábrica
   - ❑ oficina
   - ❑ hospital
9. Área donde trabajas:
   - ❑ fumadores
   - ❑ no fumadores
10. Nivel de estrés:
    - ❑ regular
    - ❑ alto
    - ❑ altísimo

¡Luz! ¡Cámara! ¡Acción!

A. ¡Necesito consejos! Tú eres un(a) instructor(a) de ejercicios aeróbicos. Ahora estás dándole consejos a uno(a) de tus estudiantes. Estás diciéndole exactamente cuáles ejercicios debe hacer para tonificar el cuerpo. Trabajando en parejas, dramaticen esta situación. El (La) instructor(a) debe insistir en que el (la) estudiante haga todos los ejercicios para ver si entiende lo que se le dice.

B. ¡Estoy hecho pedazos! Tú y un(a) amigo(a) acaban de terminar su primera clase de ejercicios aeróbicos y los dos están hechos pedazos. Están tan cansados que reconsideran si deben continuar con la clase. Dramatiza la situación con un(a) compañero(a). Hablen de cómo se sienten y de si deben continuar o no.

¿Comprendes lo que se dice?

La dinastía del amor: Episodio 6

Esta noche Luisita salió con unas amigas, pero los otros miembros de la familia se preparan para ver la telenovela del momento, *La dinastía del amor.* En el último episodio dejamos a Sharon y a Eric en la clínica hablando con el doctor Davis. Fueron allí para ver si Sharon estaba embarazada. Escucha ahora y luego contesta las preguntas que siguen.

Vocabulario útil

casado(a)	*married*	en camino	*on the way*
casarse	*to get married*	barbaridad	*nonsense*
criar	*to raise, rear (children)*		

A través de dos culturas

Telenovela

1. ¿Cuál es el problema de Sharon y Eric?
2. ¿Cómo sabe el médico que Sharon y Eric no son esposos?
3. ¿Ofrece Eric una solución al problema?
4. ¿Qué piensa Sharon de esta solución?
5. ¿Qué consejos le da el médico a Sharon?

Televidentes

6. ¿Crees que Juan Pedro tiene razón? ¿Es inocente Eric?
7. ¿Cuál es la única solución, según doña Luisa? ¿Qué opinas de esta solución?
8. ¿Por qué dice don Sergio que la muchacha es tonta? ¿Estás de acuerdo?
9. ¿Cuáles son las soluciones que propone Juan Pedro?
10. ¿Por qué dice la madre que es mejor que Luisita no esté en casa esta noche?
11. En tu opinión, ¿qué haría Juan Pedro si fuera Eric? ¿Se casaría? ¿Favorecería la adopción? ¿el aborto? ¿Viviría con su novia sin casarse?
12. ¿Por qué dice Juan Pedro que Eric es un «don Juan» y que Sharon debe dejarlo?
13. ¿Crees que es posible conseguir un aborto en los países hispanos? ¿Por qué sí o por qué no?

NOTICIERO CULTURAL

GENTE... RUBÉN BLADES

Antes de empezar, dime...

Artistas multitalentuosos. Piensa en los grandes artistas de cine, teatro, arte, música o baile que tú conoces al contestar estas preguntas.

1. ¿Te gustaría seguir la carrera de artista? ¿Por qué? Explica tu respuesta.
2. ¿Por qué será que muchas veces cuando los jóvenes deciden seguir la carrera de artista, ya sea músico, actor o actriz, pintor o bailarín, sus padres se oponen a que sigan esa carrera?
3. ¿Cuántos artistas puedes nombrar que fueron no sólo artistas sino también grandes políticos? ¿Por qué crees que se interesan los artistas en seguir carreras políticas? ¿Hacen buenos políticos los artistas, en tu opinión? Explica tu respuesta.

Rubén Blades: Salsero, político y panameño «de corazón»

Rubén Blades, abogado, músico, actor y político, nació en Panamá en 1948. Sus padres también se dedicaban a la música pero no deseaban ese futuro, a veces difícil, para su hijo. Así lo animaron para que estudiara y terminara su carrera de leyes, cosa que Blades cumplió en la universidad de Harvard en los EE.UU. pero sin dejar de lado su otra pasión, la música. Cuando Blades decidió salir de Panamá e irse a Nueva York en plan de desarrollar esa pasión musical, ya era un «salsero» reconocido en su propio país y ya había completado sus estudios de abogado.

En Nueva York, como les ocurre a tantos que vienen del extranjero a esta gran ciudad, la vida no le fue fácil desde el principio, pero con el tiempo fue haciendo buenos contactos hasta llegar a trabajar «mano a mano» con uno de los grandes: Willie Colón y su orquesta. Fue así, trabajando con Colón, que de veras llegó a ser bien conocido no sólo en los EE.UU. sino en la comunidad hispana del mundo entero.

Entre sus numerosos éxitos, se destaca uno en especial, «Pedro Navaja», apellido que alude al compositor y cantante mismo. Esta canción se encuentra en su LP de salsas *Siembra,* y trata el tema de crítica social, un tema ampliamente conocido en los barrios latinoamericanos y que ha servido de inspiración a otras canciones, películas y obras de teatro.

Esta preocupación por lo social, junto a su formación en derecho, lo llevaron a participar en política dentro de su país en 1993 cuando fue candidato a la presidencia. Aunque no ganó el puesto, el fervor con el cual sigue sus metas nos da una visión del sentido de la vida de este salsero político y panameño «de corazón», como él dice.

Como si su fama de salsero y político no fuera suficiente, Blades también es conocido como excelente actor de cine. Entre sus muchas películas están *Super* con Joe Pesci, *Fatal Beauty* con Whoopi Goldberg, *The Two Jakes* con Jack Nicholson, *Milagro Beanfield War* con Freddie Fender, y la película que lanzó a Rubén en el cine, *Crossover Dreams,* el drama de las experiencias de un salsero neoyorquino.

Y ahora, dime...

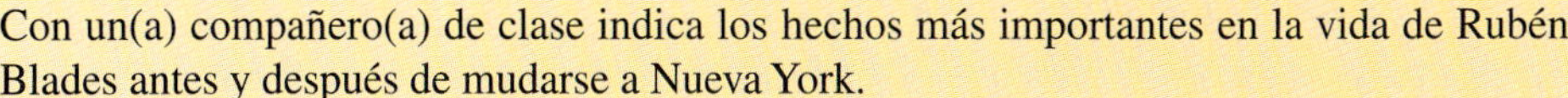

Con un(a) compañero(a) de clase indica los hechos más importantes en la vida de Rubén Blades antes y después de mudarse a Nueva York.

RUBÉN BLADES

Antes de Nueva York	Después de Nueva York
1.	1.
2.	2.
3.	3.
4.	4.
...	...

Antes de escribir
Estrategias para escribir: Al persuadir

A. Persuadir. Muchas veces necesitamos escribir un artículo o un pequeño ensayo para dar información sobre un tema y al mismo tiempo para persuadir a los lectores sobre el aspecto positivo o negativo de nuestras ideas. Al escribir este tipo de ensayo necesitamos presentar ambos argumentos, el positivo y el negativo, y después indicar por qué uno tiene más valor (*validity*) que el otro. Normalmente los temas más controvertidos son los que inspiran este tipo de escritura.

Júntate con dos compañeros y hagan una lista de temas de la actualidad que son interesantes en el momento de escribir este tipo de composición. Algunas sugerencias son: fumar, beber bebidas alcohólicas, eutanasia, etc.

B. Las dos caras de la moneda. Ahora en los mismos grupos, decidan y escriban algunos puntos a favor y en contra sobre dos de los temas en la lista que acaban de hacer.

Ahora, ¡a escribir!

A. En preparación. De los dos temas seleccionados en el ejercicio anterior decide cuál te interesa más —defender o atacar. Basándote en las respuestas dadas a favor o en contra, organiza la explicación de cada punto. Cuando termines tendrás cuatro listas: una que da puntos a favor y una que explica el por qué, y otra que da puntos en contra y una cuarta que también explica el por qué. Por ejemplo:

En favor	¿Por qué?	En contra	¿Por qué?
1. Bueno para la imagen 2. Conformidad 3. ...	1. Es más adulto. Muestra independencia. 2. Todo los amigos fuman. 3. ...	1. Malo para la salud. 2. Ofende a muchas personas. 3. ...	1. Causa cáncer. Puedes morir. 2. No se permite en muchos lugares. Afecta dónde puedes sentarte. 3. ...

B. El primer borrador. Basándote en la lista que tienes del ejercicio anterior decide cuál es tu opinión personal sobre el tema. Ahora organiza la información que tienes en párrafos, enfatizando la parte que tú crees que tiene más valor. Agrega una oración como conclusión al final de la composición para cerrar la escritura y convencer una vez más al lector de tu posición. Puedes usar frases como las siguientes.

- Para terminar yo creo que...
- Antes de terminar quiero repetir que...
- Personalmente no me cabe la menor duda de que...
- Tenemos que tener conciencia sobre...
- Lo más importante es aceptar que...

C. Ahora, a compartir. Intercambia tu composición con dos compañeros para saber su reacción. Cuando leas las de tus compañeros dales sugerencias sobre posibles cambios para mejorar sus puntos de persuasión. Si encuentras errores, menciónalos.

D. Ahora, a revisar. Agrega la información que consideres necesaria para tu composición. No te olvides de revisar los errores que mencionaron tus compañeros(as).

E. La versión final. Ahora que tienes todas las ideas revisadas y las correcciones hechas, saca una copia en limpio y entrégasela a tu profesor(a).

F. Mesa redonda. Sepárense en grupos de cinco o seis estudiantes y lean en voz alta las redacciones. Seleccionen la composición que, en su opinión, mejor logró la meta de persuadir.

El lunes empiezo... ¡Lo juro!

TAREA Antes de empezar este **Paso**, estudia **En preparación** 13.5 y 13.6 y haz por escrito los ejercicios de **¡A practicar!** También escucha **Paso 3 ¿Qué se dice... ?** del Capítulo 13 en el CD del estudiante.

¿Eres buen observador?

Ahora, ¡a analizar!

1. ¿A quiénes se dirige este anuncio? ¿a niños? ¿a jóvenes? ¿a hombres? ¿a mujeres? ¿a todos?
2. ¿Qué es Leche Desnatada Pascual?
3. ¿Quiénes crees que van a tomar esta leche? ¿Por qué crees eso?
4. Explica las expresiones «mantenerte en forma» y «cuidar tu línea».
5. ¿Usarías tú este producto? ¿Por qué?

Al sugerir y recomendar

Paco necesita ______________________________

Jaime quiere ______________________________

Leticia recomienda ______________________________

PACO Dudo que Jaime pueda aguantar (*stand*) un día más sin una hamburguesa o pollo frito, papas fritas...

IRENE ¡Ay! Es imposible que no piense en comer si ustedes no hablan de nada más.

LETICIA Obviamente todos estamos pensando en la misma cosa. Sugiero que olvidemos la dieta y que vayamos a almorzar juntos. Podemos ir al Pollo Tropical.

PACO ¡Ay, vamos! ¡Ya estoy harto de verduras! Me muero por pollo frito, puré de papas con mucha mantequilla, y...

JAIME Y yo pediré un montón de papas fritas. ¡Vámonos!

Ahora, ¡a hablar!

A. Recomendaciones. Selecciona la recomendación más apropiada para cada problema indicado aquí.

Problemas	Recomendaciones
1. estrés	a. El médico sugiere que no coma mucha carne.
2. cáncer	b. El médico recomienda que coma más verduras.
3. alta presión	c. El médico recomienda que tome ocho vasos de agua diarios.
4. ataque al corazón	d. El médico aconseja que trabaje menos.
5. necesitar perder peso	e. El médico aconseja que corra o camine al menos una hora al día.
6. problemas respiratorios	f. El médico insiste en que no fume.
	g. Insiste en que no beba alcohol.

B. ¡Necesitas un cambio! ¿Qué le sugieres a un(a) amigo(a) que está deprimido(a) y que sufre mucho del estrés?

Modelo buscar un trabajo nuevo

Sugiero que busques un trabajo nuevo.

1. no pensar tanto en las responsabilidades
2. pedir unas vacaciones
3. empezar un programa de ejercicio
4. tomar una clase de yoga
5. jugar más
6. salir más el fin de semana
7. dormir lo suficiente

C. ¡Me siento fatal! Con frecuencia, cuando no nos sentimos bien, todo el mundo quiere darnos consejos. ¿Qué consejos te dan estas personas?

Modelo un amigo / recomendar / hacer ejercicios

Un amigo recomienda que haga ejercicios.

1. mis padres / insistir / correr todos los días
2. mi novia(o) / sugerir / ir al médico
3. el médico / preferir / no comer carne
4. mi hermano / recomendar / tomar vitaminas
5. mi madre / insistir / dejar de fumar
6. mi mejor amigo(a) / aconsejar / bajar de peso

D. ¡No puedo hacerlo! No estamos siempre dispuestos a hacer sacrificios, ni siquiera cuando se trata de mejorar nuestra salud. Con un(a) compañero(a), decidan qué les pueden aconsejar a estas personas que dicen que no pueden cambiar.

Modelo «No puedo tomar ocho vasos de agua cada día. ¡No me gusta el agua»!

Sugerimos que pongas un poco de limón al agua.

1. «No me gusta hacer ejercicio. Prefiero ver la televisión».
2. «No puedo comer verduras ¡Las detesto»!
3. «No puedo seguir una dieta rígida. ¡Me encanta comer»!
4. «No puedo correr. Hace demasiado calor en el verano y demasiado frío en el invierno».
5. «No puedo hacer ejercicio regularmente. Estoy muy ocupado. Simplemente no tengo tiempo».
6. «No puedo dormir ocho horas al día. Tengo muchas obligaciones sociales».

Y ahora, ¡a conversar!

A. Buena salud. ¿Están tú y tus amigos en buena salud? Para saberlo, primero completa **Yo** en este cuestionario. Luego entrevista a dos amigos(as) y comparen todos los resultados.

Modelo

TÚ **¿Cuánto mides?**

AMIGO(A) **Mido un metro y ochenta y cinco centímetros.**

Medidas aproximadas: 1 centímetro = 0,4 pulgadas
1 metro = 3,3 pies
1 kilo = 2,2 libras

Yo	Amigo(a) #1	Amigo(a) #2
Altura	**Altura**	**Altura**
_____ metro _____ cm.	_____ metro _____ cm.	_____ metro _____ cm.
Peso _____ kilos	Peso _____ kilos	Peso _____ kilos
Ejercicio	**Ejercicio**	**Ejercicio**
Tipo _____________	Tipo _____________	Tipo _____________
Nivel de dificultad	Nivel de dificultad	Nivel de dificultad
❑ bajo	❑ bajo	❑ bajo
❑ medio	❑ medio	❑ medio
❑ alto	❑ alto	❑ alto
Frecuencia __________	Frecuencia __________	Frecuencia __________
Duración __________	Duración __________	Duración __________
Fumar	**Fumar**	**Fumar**
Frecuencia __________	Frecuencia __________	Frecuencia __________
Cantidad __________	Cantidad __________	Cantidad __________
Alcohol	**Alcohol**	**Alcohol**
Frecuencia __________	Frecuencia __________	Frecuencia __________
Estrés	**Estrés**	**Estrés**
En casa	En casa	En casa
❑ bajo	❑ bajo	❑ bajo
❑ medio	❑ medio	❑ medio
❑ alto	❑ alto	❑ alto
En el trabajo	En el trabajo	En el trabajo
❑ bajo	❑ bajo	❑ bajo
❑ medio	❑ medio	❑ medio
❑ alto	❑ alto	❑ alto
En la universidad	En la universidad	En la universidad
❑ bajo	❑ bajo	❑ bajo
❑ medio	❑ medio	❑ medio
❑ alto	❑ alto	❑ alto
Estado mental	**Estado mental**	**Estado mental**
❑ positivo	❑ positivo	❑ positivo
❑ indiferente	❑ indiferente	❑ indiferente
❑ negativo	❑ negativo	❑ negativo

B. Para mejorar. Ahora, en los mismos grupos de tres, den consejos a cada persona en su grupo según los problemas indicados en la entrevista del ejercicio anterior. Hagan varias recomendaciones sobre lo que pueden hacer para mejorar su condición física.

C. Problemas sociales. Somos animales sociales y como tales a veces tenemos problemas con la gente que nos rodea (*surrounds us*). ¿Qué problemas tienes con las siguientes personas? Comparte tus problemas con dos compañeros(as). Tus compañeros(as) te van a ayudar a resolver los problemas dándote consejos útiles.

1. jefe
2. compañeros de trabajo
3. compañeros de clase
4. padres
5. esposo(a) o novio(a)
6. profesores
7. amigo(a)
8. vecino(a)

¡Luz! ¡Cámara! ¡Acción!

A. ¡Ayúdenme! Tú estás aburrido(a) de todo: tus clases, tus amistades, la vida universitaria... Pídeles consejos a tus amigos. Dramatiza la situación con dos compañeros(as) de clase.

B. Problemas matrimoniales. Dos amigos que sólo llevan tres meses de casados te confiesan que ya están cansados de la rutina del matrimonio. Escucha sus problemas y aconséjalos.

¿Te gusta leer?

Antes de leer
Estrategias para leer: Sumarios

A. Sumarios. Generalmente cuando leemos artículos informativos, tratamos de recordar lo que leímos. Los sumarios nos ayudan a entender y recordar lo que leemos.

La forma más fácil de hacer un sumario de un artículo corto es escribir una oración que lo resuma.

Prepara ahora un sumario de la primera lectura, «El primer escalador con cascada de hielo particular». Empieza por leer el artículo una vez sin parar, para tener una idea general del contenido. Luego léelo detenidamente, haciéndote estas preguntas cada vez:

¿De qué se trata esta lectura?
¿Cómo comienza?
¿Cómo se desarrolla y cómo termina?

Luego haz una cuadrícula como la siguiente, recogiendo la información necesaria al leer la lectura por tercera vez.

Tema	Comienzo	Desarrollo	Conclusiones
Lectura 1	Chris Schmick practica su deporte en una cascada de hielo artificial.	De un largo y estrecho tanque perforado sale el agua en días de mucho frío y se congela.	Chris y sus estudiantes practican escalar el hielo en el tanque.
Sumario de una oración:			

B. Resumen. Usa la información en tu cuadrícula para escribir un sumario, de una oración. Luego compara tu sumario con el de dos o tres compañeros. Revisa tus sumarios si encuentras que no incluiste alguna información importante o si incluiste alguna información insignificante.

Lectura

El primer escalador con cascada de hielo particular

Chris Schmick, dueño de un gimnasio especializado para escaladores en la localidad de Bloomington (Illinois, EE.UU.), cuenta desde hace algún tiempo con una cascada de hielo artificial para practicar su deporte favorito sin desplazarse de su lugar de trabajo. La parte trasera de su gimnasio está formada por un tanque estrecho y alargado de unos 10 metros de alto que recoge agua. Chris ha perforado y tapado estratégicamente el tanque para que en los días de mucho frío pueda salir el agua poco a poco, con el volumen suficientemente para que al día siguiente se haya formado una cascada lo suficientemente resistente para poder ascender. Incluso los días de fuerte lluvia y frío la cascada llega a ser espectacular. Chris, que no es egoísta, comparte su posesión con los alumnos del gimnasio.

Sumergirse entre barcos naufragados

Siempre resulta misterioso y excitante para un submarinista explorar un barco hundido. Historias olvidadas vuelven a renacer entre camarotes, cabinas y viejos salones. En el Caribe, se pueden encontrar cientos de navíos hundidos, entre los que destaca el RMS Rhone. Sumergido frente a las costas de las Islas Vírgenes británicas, está considerado como el barco naufragado más bonito y mejor conservado del Caribe. Hundido por un huracán en 1867, mantiene la mitad de su casco intacto, por lo que se puede bucear en su interior. A lo anterior se une el atractivo de las preciosas capas de coral que lo recubren, así como la gran variedad de peces y flora tropical que en él se encuentran. Además, está considerado como uno de los lugares del mundo más idóneos para inmersiones nocturnas.

A ver si comprendiste

Sigue el mismo proceso que usaste para hacer el sumario de la primera lectura con la segunda, «Sumergirse entre barcos naufragados».

Tema	Comienzo	Desarrollo	Conclusiones
Lectura 2:			
Sumario de una oración:			

Viajemos por el ciberespacio a... PANAMÁ

Expand your horizons! *Let's travel through cyberspace to* **Panamá** where you can. . .

- visit Panama, a country that claims to be, and is, more than a mere Canal.
- travel to the **archipiélago** of the San Blas Islands, the home of the Cuna Indians and **molas**.
- visit the Panama Canal.
- learn about a country that has transformed its economy into a system of world service, as proclaimed in its national motto: *Pro Mundi Beneficio.*
- chat with Panamanians.
- visit **Isla Barro Colorado,** the largest section of the canal, now a biological reserve for scientific research.

If you are a cyberspace browser, join us in **Viajemos por el ciberespacio a... Panamá** by trying the following important addresses.

Universidad Tecnológica de Panamá
http://www.utp.ac.pa/

Universidad de Santa María la Antigua
http://www.usma.ac.pa/

Organización para la organización de la naturaleza ANCON
http://www.ancon.org/

Turismo en Panamá
http://www.pananet.com/turismo/Intro/introi.html

Periódicos:
Diario La Prensa
http://www.gbm.net/prensa/

El siglo
http://www.elsiglo.com/

Servidores de Panamá:
Cybermundo Panamá
http://www.pty.com/

Sinfonet Panamá
http://www.sinfo.net/

Because addresses are likely to change without notice, the following key words will guarantee that **Viajemos por el ciberespacio a... Panamá** will get you to your desired destination.

Palabras clave

Ciudad de Panamá
Universidad de Panamá
Panameños
Canal de Panamá
Archipiélago de San Blas
Molas
Isla Barro Colorado
Parque Nacional Darién
Parque Nacional Portobelo
El Parque Nacional Volcán Barú
Refugio de Vida Silvestre Isla Iguana
Refugio de Vida Silvestre Taboga

http://www.hrwcollege.com

Salud

cáncer *(m.)*	*cancer*
enfermedad *(f.)*	*illness*
estrés *(m.)*	*stress*
fiebre *(f.)*	*fever*
presión *(f.)*	*pressure*
salud *(f.)*	*health*
sangre *(f.)*	*blood*
SIDA *(m.)*	*AIDS*
vitamina	*vitamin*

Ejercicio

adentro	*in, inside*
afuera	*out, outside*
aguantar	*to endure, stand*
bajar	*to go down; to lower*
dar vuelta	*to turn*
doblar	*to bend*
durar	*to last*
estar molido(a)	*to be exhausted*
estar muerto(a)	*to be dead*
estirar	*to stretch*
flojo(a)	*to be lazy*
gimnasia	*gymnastics, calisthenics*
levantar	*to raise, to lift*
pesar	*to weigh*
pesas	*weights*
relajarse	*to relax*
teleadicto(a)	*couch potato*
tonificar	*to tone; to strengthen*

El cuerpo

boca	*mouth*
brazo	*arm*
cabeza	*head*
cintura	*waist*
codo	*elbow*
cuello	*neck*
cuerpo	*body*
dedo	*finger*
diente *(m.)*	*tooth*
espalda	*back*
estómago	*stomach*
hombro	*shoulder*
mano *(f.)*	*hand*
nariz *(f.)*	*nose*
oído	*inner ear*
ojo	*eye*
oreja	*outer ear*
pecho	*chest*
pie *(m.)*	*foot*
piel *(f.)*	*skin*
pierna	*leg*
rodilla	*knee*
tobillo	*ankle*

Consejos

aconsejar	*to advise*
consejo	*advice*
cuidar	*to take care of*
deprimido(a)	*depressed*
deprimirse	*to be depressed*
preocupar	*to worry*

Verbos

dudar	*to doubt*
insistir (en)	*to insist (on)*
medir (i, i)	*to measure*
ojalá	*I hope*
recetar	*to prescribe*

Palabras y expresiones útiles

¡A otro perro con ese hueso!	*Go tell it to the Marines!*
caballo	*horse*
¡Cállate!	*Be quiet!*
de vez en cuando	*once in a while*
embarazada	*pregnant*
profundamente	*profoundly, deeply*
ritmo	*rhythm*

En preparación 13

13.1 Present Subjunctive: Theory and Forms

Giving advice and making recommendations

A. The tenses you have learned up to now—present, present progressive, present perfect, preterite, and imperfect—are all part of the indicative mood. The indicative mood is used in statements or questions that reflect factual knowledge or certainty.

B. A second system of tenses, the subjunctive mood, is used for statements or questions that reflect doubt, desire, emotion, or uncertainty. The subjunctive is so named because it is usually *subjoined* or *subservient* to another dominating idea. Because of its subservient nature, the subjunctive tenses normally occur in a secondary or dependent clause (a group of words with a subject and a verb) of a sentence, and are often introduced by **que**. The verb in the main clause is usually in the indicative.

main clause (indicative) +	**que** +	dependent clause (subjunctive)
Mamá quiere	**que**	ustedes **coman** con nosotros esta noche.

C. To form the present subjunctive, personal endings are added to the stem of the **yo** form of the present indicative. The present subjunctive of **-ar** verbs take endings with **-e,** while **-er** and **-ir** verbs take endings with **-a**.

-ar	Preparar
-e	prepar**e**
-es	prepar**es**
-e	prepar**e**
-emos	prepar**emos**
-éis	prepar**éis**
-en	prepar**en**

-er, -ir	Correr	Asistir
-a	corr**a**	asist**a**
-as	corr**as**	asist**as**
-a	corr**a**	asist**a**
-amos	corr**amos**	asist**amos**
-áis	corr**áis**	asist**áis**
-an	corr**an**	asist**an**

D. Since the personal endings of the present subjunctive are always added to the stem of the **yo** form of the present indicative, verbs that have an irregular stem in the first person (e.g., **conozco, digo, hago, oigo, pongo, salgo, tengo, traigo, vengo, veo**) maintain that irregularity in all forms of the subjunctive.

Tener	Venir	Conocer	Ver
tenga	venga	conozca	vea
tengas	vengas	conozcas	veas
tenga	venga	conozca	vea
tengamos	vengamos	conozcamos	veamos
tengáis	vengáis	conozcáis	veáis
tengan	vengan	conozcan	vean

13.2 Subjunctive with Expressions of Persuasion

Persuading

Whenever the verb in the main clause expresses a request, a suggestion, a command, or a judgment, the verb in the dependent clause is expressed in the subjunctive, provided there is a subject change. This is because the action in the dependent clause is nonfactual and yet to occur.

main clause (indicative) + **que** + dependent clause (subjunctive)

El médico recomienda	que yo **corra** todos los días.
The doctor recommends	*that I run every day.*
También aconseja	que **comamos** menos carne.
He also advises	*that we eat less meat.*
Insiste en	que yo **deje** de fumar.
He insists	*that I stop smoking.*

The following are some frequently used verbs of persuasion.

aconsejar	*to advise*	preferir	*to prefer*
insistir (en)	*to insist*	recomendar	*to recommend*
permitir	*to permit*	sugerir	*to suggest*

¡A practicar!

A. ¡Problemas en el paraíso! Paco y Lupita tienen problemas en su matrimonio. ¿Qué les sugiere el consejero?

Modelo recomendar / cambiar la rutina
Él recomienda que cambien la rutina.

1. sugerir / salir más
2. aconsejar / no quedarse / casa / fines de semana
3. recomendar / tener / más paciencia

4. sugerir / no mirar / tanto / televisión
5. recomendar / hacer / viaje juntos
6. aconsejar / regresar / hablar con él una vez / semana

B. ¡Primer baile! Ángela va a asistir a su primer baile. ¿Qué le dicen sus padres?

1. tu madre y yo insistir / tú regresar / antes de la medianoche
2. yo recomendar / tú no beber / alcohol / fiesta
3. mamá y yo / insistir / ustedes / decir no a las drogas
4. tu madre preferir / tu amigo conducir / el coche al baile
5. yo insistir / tú no fumar
6. nosotros querer / ustedes llamarnos / en caso de emergencia

13.3 *Usted* and *ustedes* Commands

Telling people what to do or not to do

The present subjunctive is used to form both affirmative and negative **usted** and **ustedes** commands.

Respiren profundamente.	*Breathe deeply.*
Eva, no **baje** los brazos.	*Eva, don't lower your arms.*
Levanten las piernas.	*Raise your legs.*
Levántenlas.	*Raise them.*
Eva, no las **doble.**	*Eva, don't bend them.*

Remember that object pronouns always precede negative commands but are attached to the end of affirmative commands.

¡A practicar!

A. ¡Con el médico! El médico de Matilde insiste en que ella coma mejor. ¿Qué le aconseja?

Modelo dejar inmediatamente el café
Deje inmediatamente el café.

1. comer muchas verduras
2. tomar ocho vasos de agua todos los días
3. hacer algún deporte
4. no consumir ni sal ni azúcar
5. no ponerle aceite a las ensaladas
6. no comer nada frito
7. venir a verme en dos semanas

B. ¡Levanten los brazos! Los instructores de ejercicios aeróbicos tienen ciertas rutinas que siempre siguen. Cambia los verbos a mandatos para aprender una de estas rutinas.

Modelo levantar la pierna izquierda
Levanten la pierna izquierda.

1. levantar los brazos
2. respirar profundamente
3. doblar las rodillas
4. estirar las piernas
5. hacerlo otra vez
6. estirar los brazos al frente
7. abrir los brazos
8. escuchar el ritmo
9. correr con el ritmo de la música
10. tomar un descanso

13.4 *Ojalá* and Present Subjunctive of Irregular Verbs

Expressing doubt

A. The following six verbs have irregular subjunctive forms.

Dar	Estar	Haber	Ir	Saber	Ser
dé	esté	haya	vaya	sepa	sea
des	estés	hayas	vayas	sepas	seas
dé	esté	haya	vaya	sepa	sea
demos	estemos	hayamos	vayamos	sepamos	seamos
deis	estéis	hayáis	vayáis	sepáis	seáis
den	estén	hayan	vayan	sepan	sean

The accents on the first- and third-person singular forms of **dar** are necessary in order to distinguish them from the preposition **de.**

B. **Ojalá** *(I hope, God grant)* is *always* followed by the subjunctive. **Tal vez** *(perhaps)* and **quizá(s)** *(maybe)* are followed by the subjunctive when the speaker wishes to express doubt about something.

Quizá **vayamos** al centro mañana. — *Maybe we'll go downtown tomorrow.*
Ojalá (que) me **llame** esta noche. — *I hope he calls me tonight.*

Note that **que** does not usually follow the expressions **tal vez** or **quizá(s)**; however, the use of **ojalá** versus **ojalá que** varies from one region to another and is a matter of personal choice.

¡A practicar!

A. ¡Ejercicios aeróbicos! Hoy Martín asiste a su primera clase de ejercicios aeróbicos. ¿Qué está pensando?

Modelo no ser muy difícil
Ojalá no sea muy difícil.

1. no cansarme mucho
2. saber hacer todos los movimientos
3. haber buena música
4. no estar molido después de la clase
5. la instructora darnos instrucciones claras
6. no tener que correr

B. ¡Ya no aguanto! ¿Qué recomendaciones hace el instructor de ejercicios aeróbicos a sus estudiantes al terminar la clase?

1. recomiendo que ustedes / ir al jacuzzi
2. insisto en que ustedes / estar aquí al empezar la clase
3. sugiero que ustedes / ser más consistentes y / no faltar tanto
4. ojalá ustedes / saber los movimientos / semana próxima
5. sugiero que ustedes / traer agua fresca a la clase
6. insisto en que ustedes / venir a tiempo

13.5 Present Subjunctive of Stem-changing Verbs

Suggesting and requesting

A. Stem-changing **-ar** and **-er** verbs follow the same pattern of stem changes in the present subjunctive as in the present indicative. Therefore, the stems of the **nosotros** and **vosotros** forms do not change.

Contar (ue)

cuente	contemos
cuentes	contéis
cuente	cuenten

Perder (ie)

pierda	perdamos
pierdas	perdáis
pierda	pierdan

B. Stem-changing **-ir** verbs follow the same pattern in the present subjunctive, except for the **nosotros** and **vosotros** forms, which undergo a one-vowel change: **e → i** or **o → u.**

Morir (ue)

m**ue**ra	m**u**ramos
m**ue**ras	m**u**ráis
m**ue**ra	m**ue**ran

Preferir (ie)

pref**ie**ra	pref**i**ramos
pref**ie**ras	pref**i**ráis
pref**ie**ra	pref**ie**ran

Pedir (i)

p**i**da	p**i**damos
p**i**das	p**i**dáis
p**i**da	p**i**dan

¡A practicar!

A. ¡Deprimida! La pobre Anita está atravesando *(going through)* momentos difíciles en su vida. ¿Qué le sugiere su mejor amiga?

Modelo sugerir / nosotras / desayunar juntas
Sugiero que desayunemos juntas.

1. recomendar / tú / contarme tus problemas
2. sugerir / nosotras / salir / este fin de semana
3. aconsejar / tú / ir / consejero
4. recomendar / tú / pedir unas vacaciones
5. recomendar / tú / volar a visitar / padres / Miami
6. insistir en / tú / dormir más

B. ¡Qué viejo me siento! Ricardo se siente mucho más viejo que su edad. Su amigo le da unos consejos para que se sienta mejor. ¿Qué le dice?

1. sugerir / tú / seguir una dieta equilibrada *(balanced)*
2. recomendar / tú / ir de vacaciones
3. sugerir / tú / vestirse más joven
4. insistir en / tú / no fumar tanto
5. aconsejar / tú / hacerte miembro de un club atlético
6. sugerir / tú / no dormir tanto

13.6 Present Subjunctive of Verbs with Spelling Changes

Suggesting and requesting

As in the preterite, verbs that end in **-car, -gar,** and **-zar** undergo a spelling change in the present subjunctive in order to maintain the consonant sound of the infinitive.

-car:	**c** changes to **qu** in front of **e**
buscar:	bus**que**, bus**ques**, bus**que**...
-zar:	**z** changes to **c** in front of **e**
almorzar:	almuer**ce**, almuer**ces**, almuer**ce**...
-gar:	**g** changes to **gu** in front of **e**
jugar:	jue**gue**, jue**gues**, jue**gue**...

¡A practicar!

A. ¡Y en un año más... ! El médico dice que estamos en buena forma, pero siempre nos hace unas recomendaciones. ¿Qué dice?

Modelo sugiero / desayunar / ligeramente
Sugiero que desayunen ligeramente.

1. aconsejo / buscar / un lugar para correr cada día
2. recomiendo / practicar con las pesas

3. prefiero / no almorzar nada pesado
4. permito / jugar fútbol
5. acepto / comenzar la próxima semana
6. pero insisto / seguir mis consejos

B. ¿Qué me recomiendas? Tu compañero(a) de cuarto está muy aburrido(a) con su rutina diaria. ¿Qué le recomiendas?

1. recomendar / tú conocer / nuevo / amigos
2. sugerir / tú buscar / trabajo / inmediato
3. sugerir / tú llegar / clase o al trabajo temprano / de vez en cuando
4. insistir en / tú almorzar conmigo / frecuencia
5. recomendar / tú empezar / clase / baile
6. sugerir / tú sacar / dinero / banco y / hacer un viaje

CAPÍTULO 14

¡Árbitro vendido!

Cultural Topics

- **La dinastía del amor**
  Cross-cultural perceptions regarding divorce and pregnancy before marriage.
- **Noticiero cultural**
  Lugar: *Cuba: Nuestro vecino cercano pero más alejado*
  Gente: *Celia Cruz: «Azúcar» de Cuba*
- **Lectura:** *El Mundial de Fútbol*

Writing Strategies

- *Orden cronológico*

Reading Strategies

- *Pistas de tiempo y cronología*

En preparación

- 14.1 Subjunctive with Expressions of Emotion
- 14.2 Subjunctive with Impersonal Expressions
- 14.3 Subjunctive with Expressions of Doubt, Denial, and Uncertainty
- 14.4 Subjunctive with Expressions of Persuasion, Anticipation, and Reaction
- 14.5 Present Subjunctive in Adjective Clauses

In this chapter, you will learn how to ...

- express fears, hopes, and opinions.
- report what others say.
- describe people.
- refer to unknown entities.

El equipo cubano en la Olimpiada de 1996

El segundo deporte más popular en Cuba

El boxeo sigue siendo muy popular en todo el mundo hispanohablante.

Lo que ya sabes...

1. El béisbol es el deporte más popular en Cuba. ¿Por qué crees que es tan popular?
2. En la Olimpiada de 1996 en Atlanta, Cuba jugó contra los EE.UU. en el campeonato de béisbol. ¿Sabes quién ganó la medalla de oro?
3. El fútbol es el deporte más popular en todo el mundo hispanohablante. ¿Por qué crees que no es tan popular en los EE.UU.? ¿Tiene tu universidad un equipo de fútbol? ¿Con qué frecuencia vas tú a partidos de fútbol?
4. En los países latinos el fútbol tiene fama de provocar violencia entre los espectadores. En tu opinión, ¿qué provoca esta violencia?
5. ¿Qué opinas del boxeo? ¿Debería prohibirse ¿Por qué?

CUBA

¡Por favor, vengan pronto!

TAREA Antes de empezar este **Paso**, estudia **En preparación** 14.1 y 14.2 y haz por escrito los ejercicios de **¡A practicar!** También escucha **Paso 1 ¿Qué se dice... ?** del Capítulo 14 en el CD del estudiante.

¿Eres buen observador?

Ahora, ¡a analizar!

1. ¿Qué es *Escalada*? ¿Una revista de deportes? ¿de montañas? ¿de esquí? ¿de alpinismo? ¿de otra cosa?
2. Todos los deportes mencionados en el anuncio están relacionados con una cosa; ¿con qué están relacionados?
3. Explica lo que es cada deporte mencionado empezando con alpinismo.
4. ¿Qué crees que vas a aprender si lees el artículo principal de este número de *Escalada*: «Los mejores destinos del verano»?

¿Qué se dice...?

Al expresar temores, esperanzas y opiniones

Es necesario...	que no nos derroten.
Espero...	que avancemos al campeonato.
Es una lástima...	que ganemos.
Es necesario...	que no pueda jugar.

SRA. MEDINA Espero que este año ganemos el campeonato.

SR. MEDINA Con este último jonrón, es seguro que ganamos.

HIJO Me sorprende que Ricardo Javier no esté de lanzador en este partido tan importante.

SR. MEDINA Siento mucho que Ricardo Javier no pueda jugar hoy. Se lesionó en el último partido y temo que no pueda jugar por el resto del año.

HIJO ¡Qué lástima! Es mi jugador favorito. Le deseo mucha suerte de todos modos.

JAVIER ¿Es verdad que va a llover?

EDUARDO Lo dudo. Pero es mejor que nos vayamos temprano. Tengo una cita esta noche con Melisa.

¿Sabías que... ?

En Hispanoamérica, el béisbol es un deporte muy popular, en particular en Cuba, México, Venezuela y toda la América Central. En efecto, todos los equipos de las grandes ligas estadounidenses mandan a sus reclutadores a estos países latinos en busca de nuevos jugadores. En Cuba el béisbol es tan popular que, con frecuencia, hasta Fidel Castro deja el puro *(cigar)* al lado para tomar el bate.

Ahora, ¡a hablar!

A. ¡Viva el deporte! Escucha a tu compañero(a) leer los grupos de palabras en la página 503. Identifica la palabra que no pertenece (*belong*) al grupo y el deporte que se asocia con las otras tres.

Modelo

COMPAÑERO(A) pelota, bate, salvavidas, lanzador

TÚ **Salvavidas no pertenece; béisbol es el deporte.**

1. bate, pelota, lanzador, patear
2. nieve, esquí, boxeador, invierno
3. boxeo, cesto, jugador, pelota
4. tenis, bate, red, cancha
5. arquero, cesto, patear, arco
6. piscina, lanzador, zambullirse, salvavidas

B. Temores. José Antonio es reportero de fútbol para la televisión. Ahora está en los vestuarios *(locker room)* de uno de los equipos que van a jugar esta tarde. Es un partido importantísimo y todos están muy nerviosos. ¿Cuáles son sus temores?

Modelo director técnico / tener miedo / mejor jugador / lastimarse

El director técnico tiene miedo de que el mejor jugador se lastime.

1. entrenador / sentir / mejor jugador / estar enfermo
2. entrenador / sorprenderse / equipo contrario / jugar mejor
3. él también / temer / nuestro arquero / cometer / error fatal
4. nosotros / temer / nuestro equipo / perder / partido
5. árbitro / tener miedo / jugadores / no seguir / órdenes
6. jugadores / esperar / árbitro / ser imparcial

C. ¡Me siento muy nervioso! El entrenador de los Pumas está muy nervioso porque esta noche se decide el campeonato de béisbol en su región. En una entrevista esta mañana, expresó sus temores y sus esperanzas. ¿Qué dijo en la entrevista?

Modelo yo temer: los Pumas no jugar bien sin Ricardo Javier

Yo temo que los Pumas no jueguen bien sin Ricardo Javier.

1. nosotros sentir mucho: Ricardo Javier estar enfermo
2. nuestros lanzadores temer: los Tigres derrotarnos
3. yo desear: mis bateadores jugar bien
4. mi equipo esperar: árbitro ser justo
5. nosotros tener miedo: llover esta noche
6. yo esperar: el mejor equipo ganar

D. Es bueno. Marcos es el entrenador de un equipo de baloncesto. En parejas, digan qué piensa Marcos que deben hacer los jugadores antes, durante y después de un partido.

Modelo llevarse bien

Es importante que los jugadores se lleven bien.

Vocabulario útil

es urgente	es importante	es fácil	es difícil
es bueno	es malo	es excelente	es necesario

Antes

1. no tomar bebidas alcohólicas
2. escuchar las instrucciones de otros jugadores
3. descansar bien la noche anterior
4. calmarse

Durante

5. concentrarse en el partido
6. no ser demasiado agresivo
7. jugar bien
8. mantener la calma

Después

9. felicitar al otro equipo
10. saber perder
11. festejar la victoria
12. entrenarse para el próximo partido

Y ahora, ¡a conversar!

A. Adivinanzas. En grupos de dos o tres escojan un deporte y anoten la siguiente información sobre el deporte escogido. Luego den la información al resto de la clase para ver quién puede adivinar el deporte.

1. la estación del año en la cual se practica
2. el lugar donde se practica
3. si es un deporte individual o de equipo
4. el número de jugadores que forman un equipo
5. cómo es el aficionado típico
6. nombres de jugadores(as) importantes

B. Mis deportes favoritos. Entrevista a un(a) compañero(a) sobre sus gustos en deportes y dale la misma información sobre tus gustos. ¿Comparten los mismos gustos?

1. deportes favoritos
2. deporte(s) que practica
3. con qué frecuencia practica su deporte
4. deporte(s) que prefiere ver en el estadio
5. con qué frecuencia va al estadio para ver un partido
6. deporte(s) que mira en la televisión
7. con qué frecuencia mira los deportes en la televisión

C. Expertos. Tú y tus compañeros son expertos en deportes y mucha gente les pide consejos sobre cómo pueden llegar a ser buenos atletas. ¿Qué le dicen ustedes a una persona que quiere practicar los siguientes deportes?

Modelo el fútbol

Es bueno que sepas correr rápidamente. Es necesario que tengas buen sentido de coordinación. Es importante que…

1. el fútbol
2. el fútbol americano
5. el béisbol
6. el voleibol

3. el tenis
4. el boxeo
7. el baloncesto
8. el ciclismo

¡Luz! ¡Cámara! ¡Acción!

A. ¡Campeonato! Tú eres el (la) entrenador(a) de un equipo. (Tú decides de qué deporte.) Mañana tu equipo tiene un partido importante. Ahora un(a) reportero(a) del periódico escolar te va a entrevistar para saber qué temores y esperanzas tienes para el partido de mañana. Dramatiza la situación con un(a) compañero(a) de clase que hará el papel de reportero(a).

B. ¡La última oportunidad! Tú y un(a) amigo(a) van a representar a tu universidad en el campeonato de natación de mañana. Están conversando ahora sobre sus esperanzas y temores con respecto al partido. Dramaticen su conversación.

¿Comprendes lo que se dice?

La dinastía del amor: Episodio 7

Este nuevo episodio tiene lugar en la casa de Betty y Sharon. La madre de las muchachas está hablando con el socio *(business partner)* de su esposo. Con este episodio vemos una tragedia más en la vida de esta familia. Escucha el episodio y luego contesta las preguntas que siguen.

A través de dos culturas

Telenovela

1. ¿Quién es el señor Robertson?
2. ¿Dónde estaba Betty?
3. ¿Por qué volvió tan temprano a casa?
4. ¿Cómo reacciona la señora Kennedy al ver a su hija?
5. ¿Cuál es la relación entre la señora Kennedy y el señor Robertson?
6. ¿Cuándo van a verse nuevamente el señor Robertson y la señora Kennedy? ¿Por qué?

Televidentes

7. ¿Por qué dice Juan Pedro que es probable que el adulterio no dure mucho tiempo?
8. ¿Cuál es la actitud de Luisita ante el matrimonio?
9. ¿Por qué dice la señora Gómez que sus padres se morirían si oyeran a sus nietos *(grandchildren)* hablar así?
10. Comenta las posibles reacciones de la familia Gómez frente a la posibilidad de un divorcio.

NOTICIERO CULTURAL

LUGAR... CUBA

Antes de empezar, dime...

1. En superficie, ¿con qué estado se compara Cuba: con Texas, con Ohio o con Maine?
2. ¿Qué países fueron los participantes principales en la guerra hispanoestadounidense y cuál fue el resultado de esta guerra?
3. ¿Qué tipo de gobierno tiene Cuba ahora: democrático, socialista o comunista? Explica por qué ha seleccionado Cuba esta forma de gobierno.

La Habana, Cuba

Cuba, nuestro vecino cercano más alejado

La República de Cuba tiene una superficie total de 42.804 millas cuadradas y una población de 11.064.000 habitantes. Existe una gran diversidad étnica y cultural entre su gente, mayormente de origen español y africano.

Cuba y Puerto Rico fueron las últimas colonias de España en América. Ambos países fueron cedidos a los EE.UU. como resultado de la guerra de 1898. La primera mitad del siglo XX significó un período de mucha inestabilidad política y social para Cuba. Durante la segunda mitad del siglo XX Cuba llegó a ser conocida como «la madre del extranjero y la madrastra del cubano» debido al favoritismo que el gobierno cubano, bajo el poder del dictador militar Fulgencio Batista, dio a los intereses extranjeros, en particular a los Estados Unidos. Fue en oposición a Batista que se estableció el movimiento guerrillero dirigido por el joven abogado Fidel Castro, quien tomó control del gobierno el 31 de diciembre de 1958. Dos años más tarde, proclamó a Cuba como una república socialista.

Desde entonces, cerca de un diez por ciento de la población ha dejado el país, concentrándose la mayoría en Miami, Florida. Entre los inmigrantes, abandonaron el país una mayoría de profesionales: abogados, médicos, arquitectos, ingenieros, etc. Esto, junto con el embargo impuesto por los EE.UU. y la caída de los gobiernos comunistas de la Unión Soviética, ha dejado el futuro del país muy nebuloso. Últimamente el gobierno de Castro parece contar sólo con el apoyo de los países latinoamericanos y algunos europeos que apoyan la autonomía de los países en cuestiones gubernamentales.

Mientras tanto, es irónico que La Habana, la ciudad capital latinoamericana más cercana geográficamente de los EE.UU., es la que al mismo tiempo se encuentra más alejada políticamente.

Y ahora, dime...

Contesten estas preguntas en parejas.

1. ¿Por qué crees que hay tanta gente de origen africano en Cuba?
2. ¿Ha sido Cuba siempre un estado socialista? Explica tu respuesta.
3. ¿Por qué es significativo que casi un diez por ciento de la población salió de Cuba?
4. ¿Por qué es irónico que Cuba y los EE.UU. estén tan alejados políticamente?

El español en otras disciplinas: Deportes

El béisbol. El béisbol es considerado por muchos el deporte nacional de los EE.UU., pero a la vez, debemos notar también que es el deporte favorito de muchas naciones. En el mundo hispanohablante, por ejemplo, es el deporte favorito de tres naciones caribeñas: Cuba, Puerto Rico y la República Dominicana. También despierta pasiones entre los aficionados de México, Venezuela, Colombia y los países centroamericanos. Pero no sólo es popular en nuestro continente, sino que también hay gran interés en este deporte en Japón, Taiwán y Corea del Sur, entre otros países. En grupos de tres o cuatro, hagan una lista de todos los jugadores de béisbol de origen hispano en las ligas norteamericanas. ¿Cuántos pueden nombrar? ¿Pueden indicar la nacionalidad de cada uno?

Proyecto: Escribe un pequeño informe sobre uno de los jugadores de béisbol que identificaste en la actividad anterior, por supuesto ¡en español! Si es posible, incluye fotos del individuo.

¡Es increíble que te guste!

TAREA Antes de empezar este **Paso**, estudia **En preparación** 14.3 y 14.4 y haz por escrito los ejercicios de **¡A practicar!** También escucha **Paso 2 ¿Qué se dice... ?** del Capítulo 14 en el CD del estudiante.

¿Eres buen observador?

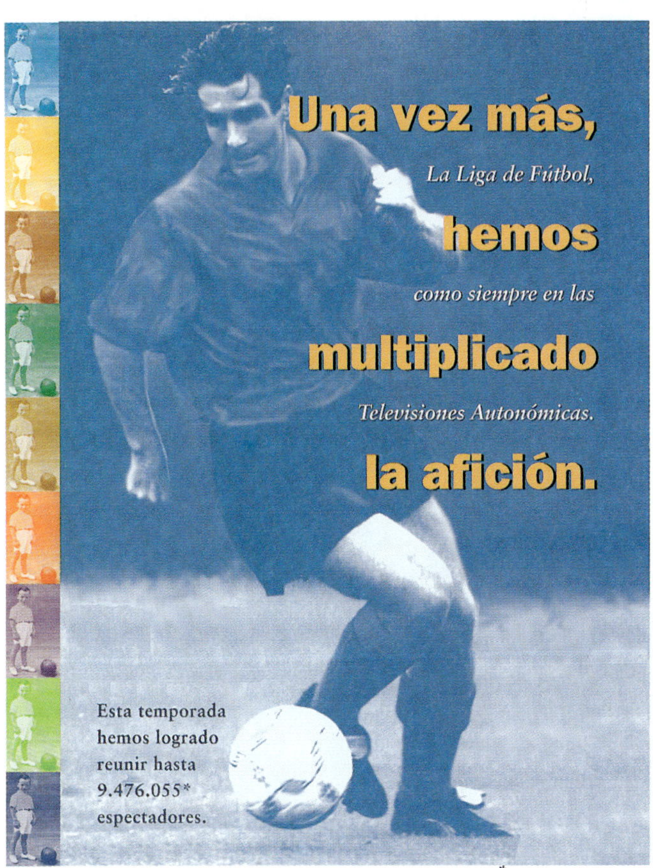

Ahora, ¡a analizar!

1. ¿Para qué es esta propaganda?
2. ¿Qué afición han multiplicado?
3. ¿Qué son las Televisiones Autonómicas? ¿Qué programas pueden verse en las Televisiones Autonómicas?
4. ¿Cuántos espectadores han logrado reunir? ¿Cuánto tiempo fue necesario para reunirlos? ¿Qué han visto estos espectadores? ¿Dónde lo han visto?
5. ¿Qué deportes miras tú en la televisión? ¿Con qué frecuencia?

¿Qué se dice...?

Al expresar opiniones e informar sobre lo que otros dicen

1. _______ Es increíble que te guste el boxeo.
2. _______ Es cierto que el boxeo es un poco violento.
3. _______ Yo creo que es un deporte como cualquier otro.
4. _______ Ese peinado es violento.

EDUARDO Hola, Melisa. Hola, Dino. ¡Pero qué hermosa estás, mi amor!

MELISA ¿Te gusta mi peinado?

EDUARDO Sí, es... interesante. Oye, Dino. ¿Quién va ganando la pelea?

DINO Bueno, en este momento Ruiz está golpeando bien fuerte a Martí. Pero dudo que gane.

EDUARDO Yo tampoco creo que pueda ganar. Martí es el mejor boxeador.

DINO ¿Y quién ganó el partido de béisbol?

EDUARDO Pues, tuve que salir antes de terminar el partido para estar a tiempo con Melisa. Pero es probable que ganemos.

MELISA Vámonos Eduardo, ya es tarde.

EDUARDO Hasta pronto, Dino.

DINO Buenas. Diviértanse.

Ahora, ¡a hablar!

A. Boxeo. Un matrimonio está viendo una pelea de boxeo en la televisión. A él no le gusta mucho el boxeo. ¿Qué le dice a su esposa?

Modelo ser verdad / no gustarme / mucho / boxeo

Es verdad que no me gusta mucho el boxeo.

1. yo / creer / boxeo / ser inhumano
2. ser obvio / los golpes / dañar / la cabeza
3. yo / no pensar / ser / un deporte justo
4. ser cierto / las peleas / estar / arregladas *(fixed)*
5. ser imposible / un boxeador / no terminar / medio loco
6. ser verdad / los organizadores / ganar / todo el dinero
7. yo / no dudar / los boxeadores / sufrir / dolores de cabeza

B. ¿Y tú? ¿Qué opinas del boxeo? Expresa tu opinión sobre lo siguiente.

Modelo Las peleas están arregladas.

Yo pienso que las peleas están arregladas. o
Dudo que las peleas estén arregladas.

Vocabulario útil

(no) creer	ser obvio	ser posible	ser verdad
(no) pensar	ser cierto	ser imposible	(no) dudar

1. El boxeo es malo para la salud.
2. Los golpes dañan el cerebro *(brain)*.
3. Las peleas de boxeo siempre están arregladas.
4. Todos los deportistas son materialistas.
5. El boxeo es el deporte más cruel de todos.
6. El boxeo es más cruel que la corrida *(bullfighting)*.
7. ¿... ?

C. Los Juegos Olímpicos. Pregúntale a tu compañero(a) de clase qué piensa de los Juegos Olímpicos.

Modelo Son demasiado políticos.

TÚ **¿Crees que los Juegos Olímpicos sean demasiado políticos?**

COMPAÑERO(A) **Es posible que sean un poco políticos pero no creo que sean demasiado políticos.**

1. ¿... ? Unen más a las naciones del mundo.
2. ¿... ? Provocan incidentes políticos violentos.
3. ¿... ? Provocan sentimientos patrióticos positivos.
4. ¿... ? Se toman demasiado en serio.
5. ¿... ? Son un paso positivo hacia la paz mundial.
6. ¿... ? Son simplemente un medio más de publicidad para algunos productos multinacionales.

D. Las Olimpiadas. Tú y un(a) compañero(a) de clase son entrenadores(as) del equipo olímpico de béisbol. Es necesario que sus atletas mantengan cierta disciplina para poder estar en óptimas condiciones. ¿Qué exigen de sus atletas? Decídelo con un(a) compañero(a).

Modelo **Exigimos que se acuesten temprano y que duerman ocho horas cada noche.**

1. Exigimos que...
2. Insistimos en que...
3. Les decimos que...
4. No les permitimos que...
5. Les aconsejamos que...
6. No dejamos que...
7. Preferimos que no...

Y ahora, ¡a conversar!

A. ¡Debate! ¿Es la competencia buena o mala para los niños? En grupos de tres preparen una lista de argumentos o a favor o en contra. Luego, en grupos de seis, lleven a cabo su debate. Informen a la clase quién ganó y cuáles fueron los argumentos más válidos.

B. ¡Más debate! Trabajen en grupos de cuatro. Dos de cada grupo deben defender las opiniones que aparecen a continuación y los otros dos deben oponerse. Al terminar, cada grupo debe decidir quién ganó el debate o si empataron.

1. El béisbol es aburridísimo.
2. La corrida de toros combina el atletismo y el arte.
3. El fútbol americano es muy violento.
4. El tenis es un deporte sólo para los ricos.
5. El golf es aburrido y absurdo.

C. Excursión invernal. Ustedes y sus compañeros(as) trabajan para una asociación voluntaria que se ocupa de los adolescentes. Este año deciden llevar a los chicos a las montañas por una semana. Ahora ustedes necesitan establecer algunas reglas para que no resulte una excursión infernal. En grupos de tres o cuatro decidan lo que van a permitir y lo que van a prohibir.

Permitimos que... **Se prohibe que...**

D. ¿Qué me recomiendas? Trabajando en grupos de tres o cuatro, supongan que van a tener cuatro días de vacaciones juntos. Cada uno debe sugerir varias actividades posibles y luego decidir qué sugerencias van a aceptar.

Modelo Sugiero que vayamos a esquiar a las montañas.
Yo prefiero que nos quedemos a descansar aquí.

¡Luz! ¡Cámara! ¡Acción!

A. Entrenador(a). Tú eres el (la) entrenador(a) de un equipo de (tú decides qué deporte). En una semana tu equipo va a participar en el campeonato estatal. Ahora estás dándoles instrucciones a los (las) dos mejores jugadores(as) de tu equipo. Ellos(as), claro, tienen varias preguntas para ti. Dramatiza la situación con dos compañeros(as) de clase.

B. Decisiones, decisiones. Eres un jugador de béisbol en Cuba y acabas de ser invitado a jugar con una liga de los EE.UU. Hoy un(a) reportero(a) cubano te entrevista para saber si te vas a ir a los EE.UU. o no. Dramatiza la situación con un(a) compañero(a).

¿Comprendes lo que se dice?

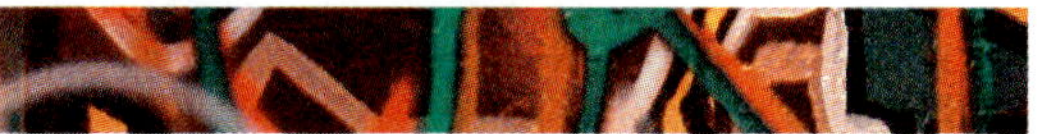

La dinastía del amor: Episodio 8

Nos encontramos una vez más en la sala de la familia Gómez frente al televisor. En este nuevo episodio se revela el secreto de Sharon y Eric. Escucha el episodio y contesta las preguntas que siguen.

A través de dos culturas

Telenovela

1. ¿Qué noticia le da Sharon a su madre?
2. ¿Cómo reacciona la madre?
3. ¿Cuál es la solución que ofrece Sharon?
4. ¿Qué preocupa a la madre?
5. ¿Quién interrumpe la conversación?

Televidentes

6. ¿Está de acuerdo don Sergio Gómez con la solución de Sharon y Eric? ¿Por qué?
7. ¿Qué es más importante para Juan Pedro?
8. ¿Qué opina Luisita?
9. ¿Por qué piensa doña Luisa que sus hijos han cambiado? ¿Tiene razón ella?
10. ¿Quién es más razonable frente a este problema? Explica.
11. ¿Sería diferente la reacción de tus padres a la de don Sergio y doña Luisa? Explica.

NOTICIERO CULTURAL

GENTE... CELIA CRUZ

Antes de empezar, dime...

1. ¿Qué influencia han tenido los afroamericanos en la música de los EE.UU.? ¿Tienes algún músico afroamericano favorito? ¿Por qué te gusta?
2. ¿Qué influencia han tenido los afroamericanos en los ritmos bailables de los EE.UU.? ¿Cuáles son algunos bailes que tú consideras exclusivamente afroamericanos?
3. Prepárate para explicarle a la clase cómo bailar uno de los bailes que consideras típicamente afroamericano.

Celia Cruz: «Azúcar» de Cuba

Los ritmos tropicales y los bailes de origen afrocubano: la *rumba*, el *mambo*, el *chachachá*, han tenido un gran impacto en el gusto musical de generaciones tanto en Latinoamérica como en los EE.UU.

Celia Cruz es la cantante cubana que ha sido reconocida por todos como la reina de la rumba, la contagiosa música que en su última reencarnación es llamada *salsa* y vibra de costa a costa tanto en los EE.UU. como en Latinoamérica, y actualmente hasta en los países más lejanos como Suiza, Suecia y Japón. La biografía de Celia Cruz es muy sencilla: de su humilde niñez un día se despertó estrella. Aunque ya había establecido su carrera en Cuba, como tantos otros de su patria emigró a los EE.UU., donde su gracia y habilidad como cantante la han llevado al éxito y la fama.

Sin duda, Celia está entre los artistas hispanos más reconocidos y con frecuencia aparece con ellos. En uno de sus últimos discos, *Azúcar Negra,* canta duos con Gloria Estefan y Jon Secada. Éste, como lo han sido todos sus discos, ya ha alcanzado un éxito fenomenal. Como se dijo de la reina de la salsa en la sección de Gente en la revista *Más:* «Ayer grande, hoy gigante y mañana, si Dios y los santos quieren, ¡colosal!»

Instrucciones para bailar. Sigue la clave del ritmo agitando las caderas *(hips)* y los brazos, al mismo tiempo que mueves los pies con agilidad y elegancia. Echa por la ventana las inhibiciones. Siéntete el rey o reina del salón de baile. No les pongas mucha atención a las miradas de los presentes, sin duda que se están muriendo de envidia *(envy).* Diles en voz alta, como dice Celia Cruz al terminar una canción: **¡azúcar!**

Y ahora, dime...

Contesten estas preguntas en parejas.

1. Nombra algunos ritmos afrocubanos. Nombra también algunos ritmos afroamericanos.
2. Explica la cita de la revista *Más* que se menciona en esta lectura.
3. ¿Cuáles son los tres adjetivos que usarías para describir la salsa?
4. ¿Qué necesitas no tener para bailar bien la salsa?
5. Explica el título de esta lectura.

¿Te gusta escribir?

Antes de escribir
Estrategias para escribir: Orden cronológico

A. La cronología. Cuando escribimos ensayos históricos, como la breve historia de Cuba en el **Noticiero cultural** del **Paso 1,** usualmente seguimos un orden cronológico. Es decir, empezamos con el primer incidente que ocurrió, luego mencionamos el segundo, el tercero, etc., hasta el final. Después del final expresamos alguna opinión personal y global sobre el tema.

¿Es éste el proceso que usó el autor del **Noticiero cultural** del **Paso 1?** Para decidir si lo es, contesten las preguntas que siguen en grupos de tres o cuatro.

1. ¿Empieza la lectura con el primer incidente que ocurrió? Si es así, ¿cuál es?
2. ¿Continúa con el segundo, el tercero, el cuarto, etc.? Prepara una lista de todos los incidentes que se mencionan en el mismo orden. ¿Es un orden cronológico?
3. ¿Incluye todos los incidentes importantes en la historia de Cuba? Si no, ¿cómo lo sabes?
4. ¿Qué criterio crees que usó el autor para decidir qué partes de la cronología iba a incluir y qué partes tendría que excluir?

B. Lista de ideas. Ahora en los mismos grupos, preparen una lista de temas apropiados para ensayos históricos. Mencionen por lo menos diez temas. Luego cada persona debe seleccionar uno de los temas para desarrollar en las siguientes secciones.

Ahora, ¡a escribir!

A. En preparación. Decide cuál de los temas vas a desarrollar y prepara una lista de todos los incidentes importantes relacionados con tu tema. Pon la lista en orden cronológico.

B. El primer borrador. Basándote en la lista que tienes del ejercicio anterior decide cuál es la información más importante y desarróllala en varios párrafos, dando detalles donde te parezca apropiado. Agrega algunas oraciones expresando tus opiniones como conclusión para cerrar la escritura.

C. Ahora, a compartir. Intercambia tu ensayo con otros dos compañeros para saber su reacción. Cuando leas los de tus compañeros dales sugerencias sobre posibles cambios para mejorar su desarrollo cronológico. Si encuentras errores, menciónalos.

D. Ahora, a revisar. Agrega la información que consideres necesaria para tu ensayo. No te olvides de revisar los errores que mencionaron tus compañeros.

E. La versión final. Ahora que tienes todas las ideas revisadas y las correcciones hechas, saca una copia en limpio y entrégale la composición a tu profesor(a).

F. Mesa redonda. Sepárense en grupos de cinco o seis estudiantes y lean en voz alta las redacciones. Decidan cuál ensayo histórico les pareció más interesante y explíquenle a la clase por qué lo seleccionaron.

¡Qué golazo!

TAREA

Antes de empezar este *Paso*, estudia **En preparación** 14.5 y haz por escrito los ejercicios de **¡A practicar!** También escucha **Paso 3 ¿Qué se dice... ?** del Capítulo 14 en el CD del estudiante.

¿Eres buen observador?

Los Juegos Olímpicos, hoy

ATLETISMO

Hombres Maratón, 7:00

BASQUETBOL

Mujeres:
Partido por la medalla de bronce 9:30.
Partido por la medalla de oro.

BOXEO

Mosca, Pluma, Welter Ligero, Mediano Ligero, Semipesado, Super Pesado, finales 13:30.

CANOTAJE

Hombres Kayak doble 500 final, 9:00.
Hombres canoa single 500 final.
Mujeres kayak single 500 final.
Hombres kayak single 500 final.
Hombres canoa doble 500 final.
Mujeres kayak doble 500 final.

ECUESTRES

Salto individual, semifinal 10:00.
Salto individual, final.

GIMNASIA RITMICA

Individual finai, 13:00.

HANDBOL

Hombres partido por la medalla de bronce, 15:30.
Hombres partido por la medalla de oro.

VOLEIBOL

Hombres partido por la medalla de bronce 12:00.
Hombres partido por la medalla de oro 14:30.

CLAUSURA

Clausura de los Juegos Olímpicos de Atlanta 1996 a las 18:00 horas.

Ahora, ¡a analizar!

1. ¿Para qué es este horario? ¿Dónde tuvieron lugar estas competencias?
2. ¿Para qué día de las competencias es el horario? ¿para el primero? ¿para el segundo? ¿para el... ? ¿para el último? ¿Cómo lo sabes?
3. ¿Cuántas competencias para mujeres hay por la mañana? ¿por la tarde? ¿Cuáles son?
4. ¿A qué hora es la primera competencia? ¿la última?
5. Explica lo que es canotaje, ecuestres y gimnasia rítmica.
6. ¿Cuántas categorías de boxeo más bajas en peso que el Welter hay? ¿Cuáles son? ¿Cuántas más altas en peso que el Welter hay? ¿Cuáles son?

¿Qué se dice...?

Al referirse a alguien o algo desconocido

¿Quién puede patear la pelota como Ramón Ángel? ______________________

¿A qué le tiene miedo Ramón Ángel? ______________________

LOURDES Lo que necesitamos es un árbitro que sea imparcial.

MELISA ¡Claro! ¡Que sea imparcial y que sepa algo de fútbol!

EDUARDO Dino, ¿crees que el año que viene encontrarán a un entrenador que tenga tanta experiencia como Germán?

DINO La experiencia no es la única cosa necesaria. Buscan a alguien que sepa ser buen líder también.

EDUARDO Yo no creo que tengan dificultad en encontrar a alguien. El puesto está muy bien pagado.

Ahora, ¡a hablar!

A. ¡Qué desastre! Hoy tu equipo está jugando muy mal y está perdiendo. ¿Qué dice el público?

Modelo no hay nadie / estar en forma
No hay nadie que esté en forma hoy.

1. no hay nadie / jugar bien
2. necesitamos un delantero / saber correr
3. no hay ningún defensor / ser capaz de / parar / pelota
4. el equipo necesita un arquero / defender mejor el arco
5. no hay nadie / manejar / bien / pelota
6. necesitan buscar un entrenador / tener / más experiencia

B. ¡Victoria! Los fanáticos del equipo vencedor *(winning team)* están muy orgullosos de la actuación de sus jugadores. ¿Cuáles son sus comentarios?

Modelo tenemos un equipo / ser verdaderamente superior
Tenemos un equipo que es verdaderamente superior.

1. tenemos un arquero / no dejar pasar la pelota
2. hay muchos jugadores / saber patear bien
3. tenemos un capitán / dirigir muy bien
4. el equipo tiene un entrenador / preparar bien a los jugadores
5. tenemos muchos defensores / jugar a nivel profesional
6. tenemos un equipo / poder ganar el campeonato

C. Se solicita... Eres director(a) del departamento de educación física en tu universidad. Necesitan nuevos empleados para el nuevo curso escolar. ¿Qué tipo de experiencia requieres tú para cada puesto?

Modelo profesor(a) de golf: tener 10 años de experiencia
Buscamos un(a) profesor(a) de golf que tenga diez años de experiencia.

Vocabulario útil
se solicita necesitamos buscamos

1. entrenador(a) para el equipo de fútbol: haber jugado en ligas profesionales
2. profesor(a) de tenis: tener experiencia en otras universidades
3. profesor(a) de educación física: interesarse en entrenar a los incapacitados *(handicapped)*
4. entrenador(a) para el equipo de béisbol: estar dispuesto(a) a viajar mucho
5. médico(a): tener 5 o más años de experiencia con atletas
6. dos secretarios(as): poder trabajar noches, sábados y domingos

D. Atletas. Tú quieres saber si tu compañero(a) conoce personalmente a atletas de talento. Hazle las siguientes preguntas.

Modelo ser campeón mundial de tenis

TÚ **¿Conoces a alguien que sea campeón mundial de tenis?**
COMPAÑERO(A) **Sí, conozco a alguien que es campeón mundial de tenis.** o **No, no conozco a nadie que sea campeón mundial de tenis.**

1. practicar alpinismo
2. participar en maratones
3. ser entrenador(a) profesional
4. jugar al fútbol profesionalmente
5. haber ganado una medalla olímpica
6. ser boxeador profesional
7. practicar el judo
8. ¿... ?

Y ahora, ¡a conversar!

A. Gimnasio. Tú y unos(as) amigos(as) deciden abrir un nuevo gimnasio y necesitan emplear a mucha gente. En grupos de tres o cuatro, decidan qué tipo de empleados necesitan y qué experiencia debe tener cada uno.

Modelo **Necesitamos algunos instructores de ejercicios aeróbicos que sepan animar a la gente.**

B. ¡Revolución! Imagínate que tú y tus compañeros(as) tienen el poder de cambiar todo lo que no les gusta de su universidad. En grupos de tres o cuatro decidan qué tipo de personas van a formar parte de su nueva universidad.

1. Queremos un presidente que...
2. Buscamos profesores que...
3. Ofrecemos becas *(scholarships)* a estudiantes que...
4. Necesitamos atletas que...
5. No queremos a nadie que...

C. En el futuro. Piensa en quién serás en unos quince años: ¿Dónde trabajarás? ¿Con quién vivirás? ¿Qué harás?... Luego hazle preguntas a tu compañero(a) para ver qué tipo de persona será y contesta las preguntas que él (ella) te haga a ti.

Modelo

TÚ **¿Serás una persona que trabaje día y noche?**
COMPAÑERO(A) **Es probable que trabaje día y noche.**

¡Luz! ¡Cámara! ¡Acción!

A. Necesito más ayuda. El (La) director(a) de una escuela secundaria se reúne con los jefes de los departamentos de música, historia, matemáticas y lenguas extranjeras. Cada jefe explicará sus necesidades para el próximo año y el (la) director(a) decidirá cuántos nuevos puestos habrá. Dramaticen esta situación en grupos de cinco.

B. Hospital. Tú eres el (la) administrador(a) de un hospital. Te reúnes con las personas encargadas de la cafetería, de la lavandería, de los conserjes y de la farmacia. Cada persona va a explicar sus necesidades de personal para el próximo año. Tú tendrás que decidir qué se puede hacer y qué no se puede hacer.

Antes de leer
Estrategias para leer: Pistas de tiempo y cronología

A. Pistas de tiempo. El reconocer las pistas de tiempo, por ejemplo **tercera, el 9 de agosto, luego, ayer...,** al leer es muy importante. Las pistas de tiempo ayudan al lector a establecer la cronología de los acontecimientos de la lectura. Como tal ofrecen cierto sentido de unidad y coherencia a la lectura. Lee el párrafo a continuación e identifica todas las pistas de tiempo.

> La primera Copa Mundial de Fútbol se jugó en Montevideo, Uruguay, en julio de 1930. Allí los grandes rivales fueron los argentinos contra los uruguayos, venciendo y ganando la copa el equipo uruguayo. En 1934, se jugó en Italia y ganó el equipo local. Italia triunfó cuatro años más tarde en Francia. Luego el campeonato se suspendió, debido al comienzo de la segunda guerra mundial. Se reinició en 1950 en Brasil.

B. Cronología. En parejas, preparen una lista del orden cronológico de todos los eventos que se mencionan en la lectura que sigue. Los primeros eventos ya están indicados.

Eventos

1. F.I.F.A. creada por Jules Rimet
2. 1930 primera Copa Mundial
3. 1934 Italia gana

El Mundial de Fútbol

Mucho se ha dicho de y escrito sobre de todo lo relacionado con al campeonato mundial de fútbol. El campeonato es dirigido por la Federación Internacional del Fútbol Asociado (F.I.F.A.). La federación fue creada por el señor Jules Rimet, quien dio su nombre a la copa.

La primera Copa Mundial de Fútbol se jugó en Montevideo, Uruguay, en julio de 1930. Allí los grandes rivales fueron los argentinos contra los uruguayos, venciendo y ganando la copa el equipo uruguayo. En 1934, se jugó en Italia y ganó el equipo local. Italia volvió a triunfar cuatro años más tarde en Francia. Luego el campeonato se suspendió, debido al comienzo de la segunda guerra mundial. Se reinició en 1950 en Brasil.

En 1958, la Copa se jugó en Suecia, donde por primera vez triunfó el equipo brasileño. Fue en esa ocasión en la que apareció la máxima figura del fútbol de todos los tiempos: el famoso Pelé. Edson Arantes do Nacimiento tenía sólo 17 años. Pelé era un joven delgado y sonriente que entró al juego cuando, en un partido en que su equipo se enfrentaba a la entonces Unión Soviética, otro jugador del equipo brasileño se lastimó.

Cuatro años más tarde, en Santiago de Chile, Brasil obtuvo su segunda victoria. En México, en 1970, Brasil logró, con la ayuda de Pelé, quedarse definitivamente con la deseada copa «Jules Rimet» al ganar por tercera vez. Al vencer, Brasil frustró las ambiciones de Italia, que tuvo que esperar hasta 1982 para ganar su tercer campeonato.

Ganadores de la Copa "Jules Rimet"

Partido en la Copa Mundial de Fútbol

El campeonato mundial de fútbol continúa congregando, al igual que los Juegos Olímpicos, a la comunidad internacional. Es una manifestación de confraternidad internacional por medio de un deporte excepcional.

A ver si comprendiste

1. El Mundial empezó en 1930 y se juega cada cuatro años. Pero hubo una temporada en que no se jugó. ¿Cuál fue? ¿Por qué se suspendió? ¿Por cuánto tiempo se suspendió?
2. ¿Quién es Jules Rimet? Explica su importancia.
3. ¿Quién es Pelé? Explica su importancia.
4. ¿Hay alguien en la clase que haya visto el Mundial en persona alguna vez? ¿en la televisión?
5. ¿Por qué crees que el fútbol no es tan popular en los EE.UU. como en el resto del mundo?

Viajemos por el ciberespacio a... CUBA

Expand your horizons! *Let's travel through cyberspace to **Cuba*** where you can . . .

- visit this small island otherwise off limits to U.S. citizens.
- view the streets of Havana, the exuberant capital of Cuba.
- stroll through many wonderfully preserved colonial cities.
- enjoy hundreds of miles of unspoiled beaches.
- listen to great music.
- appreciate Cuba's rich literary tradition.
- penetrate the mysteries of the mystic **santería** religion.

If you are a cyberspace browser, join us in **Viajemos por el ciberespacio a... Cuba,** by trying the following important addresses.

Universidad de La Habana
http://www.web.net/cuba_university

Cuba en la Internet:
Cubaweb
http://www.cubaweb.cu/

Habaguanet ciboney
http://members.icanect.net/~ciboney//

Sobre cuestiones cubanas:
Center for International Policy
http://www.us.net/cip/cuba.htm

La Fundación Nacional Cubano Americana
http://www.canfnet.org/

Periódicos y revistas:

Periódico Granma
http://www.cubaweb.cu/granma/index.html

Prensa Latina: Agencia de Noticias de Cuba
http://www.prensa-latina.org/

Discursos de Fidel Castro
gopher://lanic.utexas.edu:70/11/la/Cuba/Castro

Because addresses are likely to change without notice, the following key words will guarantee that **Viajemos por el ciberespacio a... Cuba** will get you to your desired destination.

Palabras clave

Universidad de La Habana
República de Cuba
La Habana
Medicina en Cuba
Música cubana
Celia Cruz
Escritores cubanos
Silvio Rodríguez
Playa del Varadero
Malecón
Fidel Castro

http://www.hrwcollege.com

Vocabulario

Deportes

alpinismo	*mountain climbing*
boxeo	*boxing*
ciclismo	*cycling*
esquí (*m.*)	*skiing*
fútbol	*soccer*
fútbol americano (*m.*)	*football*
natación (*f.*)	*swimming*

Jugadores y oficiales

árbitro	*umpire, referee*
arquero	*goalie, goalkeeper*
bateador(a)	*batter (baseball)*
capitán (capitana)	*captain*
defensor(a)	*guard*
delantero(a)	*forward*
entrenador(a)	*coach*
lanzador(a)	*pitcher*

Fútbol

arco	*goal*
estadio	*stadium*
gol (*m.*)	*goal*
golpe de cabeza (*m.*)	*hitting (the ball) with one's head*
patear	*to kick*
pelota	*ball*

Béisbol

bate (*m.*)	*bat*
jonrón (*m.*)	*homerun*
liga	*league*

Baloncesto

cancha	*court*
cesto	*basket*
red (*f.*)	*net*

Misceláneo de deportes

campeón (campeona)	*champion*
competencia	*competition*
derrotar	*to defeat, beat*
estar en forma	*to be in shape*
juego	*game*
lastimarse	*to hurt oneself*
lesionarse	*to get hurt, get injured*
maratón (*m.*)	*marathon*
pelea	*fight*
pista	*lane; (ski) trail*
salvavidas (*m. / f.*)	*lifeguard, lifesaver*
tener cuidado	*to be careful*

Verbos

apoyar	*to aid, support*
concentrarse	*to concentrate*
dañar	*to damage, hurt*
dejar	*to allow, permit*
enumerar	*to enumerate*
exigir	*to demand*
felicitar	*to congratulate*
manejar	*to manage; to control*
prohibir	*to prohibit, forbid*
provocar	*to provoke*
sorprender	*to surprise*
temer	*to fear*
unir	*to unite*
zambullirse	*to dive, jump in (the water)*

Adjetivos

absurdo(a)	*absurd*
agresivo(a)	*aggressive*
contrario(a)	*opposite, opposing*
imparcial	*impartial*
justo(a)	*just, fair*
obvio(a)	*obvious*
político(a)	*political*

Palabras y expresiones útiles

calma	*calm*
de todos modos	*anyway*
estar dispuesto(a) a	*to be inclined to*
lástima	*pity, shame*
líder (*m. / f.*)	*leader*
mantener la calma	*to stay calm*
nivel (*m.*)	*level*
paz (*f.*)	*peace*
público	*public*
ser capaz de	*to be capable of*
tomar el pelo	*to pull one's leg, tease*

En preparación 14

14.1 Subjunctive with Expressions of Emotion

Expressing emotion

Whenever an emotion such as fear, joy, sadness, pity, or surprise is expressed in the main clause of a sentence, the subordinate clause will be expressed in the subjunctive mood.

Main Clause	Subjunctive Clause
Tememos	que Ricardo Javier no **pueda** jugar hoy.
Me alegro (de)	que **estemos** aquí.
Siento mucho	que nuestro mejor jugador **esté** enfermo.
Les **sorprende**	que el árbitro **sea** tan joven.

A. If the subject of both clauses is the same, an infinitive is used instead of a subjunctive clause.

¿Te sorprende **ganar** el premio del mejor jugador?	*Are you surprised to win the best player award?*
Me alegro de **poder** estar aquí.	*I am glad to be able to be here.*

B. The following are some frequently used expressions of emotion.

alegrarse (de)	*to be glad*
esperar	*to hope*
estar contento(a) (de)	*to be happy*
estar furioso(a)	*to be furious*
sentir (ie, i)	*to regret, feel sorry*
sorprenderse (de)	*to be surprised*
temer	*to fear*
tener miedo (de)	*to be afraid*

¡A practicar!

A. ¡Uno más! Si gana el partido de esta noche, su equipo va a ir al campeonato. ¿Qué dicen ustedes?

1. Espero que el equipo ______________ (ganar).
2. Elodia teme que ellos ______________ (tener) el mejor equipo.
3. Nos sorprende que su mejor jugador ______________ (ser) Andrés Salazar.
4. Estoy contenta de que todos nuestros jugadores ______________ (estar) aquí.
5. Me alegro de que su mejor jugador no ______________ (poder) jugar hoy.
6. Temo que ustedes ______________ (beber) demasiado en el partido.

B. ¡Televidentes! Eduardo y Dino se preparan para ver el partido de fútbol en la televisión. ¿Qué piensan?

1. Eduardo alegrarse de / dar el partido en la tele
2. Dino sentir / su jugador favorito / no poder jugar hoy
3. ellos temer / no haber bastante cerveza
4. Eduardo tener miedo de / el árbitro / no ser imparcial
5. Dino esperar / el partido / ser limpio
6. Eduardo sorprenderse / haber cambiado de capitán

14.2 Subjunctive with Impersonal Expressions

Expressing opinions

Most impersonal expressions are formed with the third-person singular of the verb **ser** followed by an adjective; for example, **es importante, era triste,** and **fue bueno.** Note that in impersonal expressions, the subject *it* is understood.

A. If an impersonal expression in the main clause expresses a certainty, such as **es cierto, es seguro, es verdad, es obvio,** then the indicative is used in the following clause.

Es obvio que nuestro equipo **va** a ganar.	*It's obvious that our team is going to win.*
Es verdad que el entrenador **está** enfermo.	*It's true that the coach is sick.*

The following are some frequently used impersonal expressions of certainty.

Es obvio	Es indudable	Es cierto
Es verdad	Es seguro	Es evidente

B. All other impersonal expressions are followed by the subjunctive when there is a change of subject in the subordinate clause. If no change of subject occurs, then the infinitive is used.

Es increíble que **tengan** jugadores tan altos.	*It's incredible that they have such tall players.*
Es mejor que yo no **vaya** al partido.	*It's better that I not go to the game.*
Es imposible ganar ahora.	*It's impossible to win now.*

Note that in the first two examples, the focus of the dependent clause is on different subjects; in the third example the focus is on an event or a statement.

Some frequently used impersonal expressions often followed by the subjunctive include the following.

Es necesario	Es mejor	Es natural
Es lógico	Es probable	Es posible
Es imposible	Es importante	Es una pena
Es increíble		

¡A practicar!

A. ¡Campeonato de béisbol! ¿Qué opinan los cubanos de sus jugadores y de los del equipo contrario?

1. Es imposible que ellos _______________ (ganar) con ese entrenador.
2. Es obvio que nosotros _______________ (ir) a ganar.
3. Es mejor que nuestro equipo _______________ (ser) más agresivo.
4. Es evidente que nosotros _______________ (tener) excelentes oportunidades de ganar la copa.
5. Es indudable que nuestro capitán _______________ (ser) el mejor.
6. Es evidente que nuestro equipo _______________ (ser) excelente.

B. ¡Soy fanático! ¿Qué les dice un cubano fanático del béisbol a sus amigos antes del partido?

Modelo ser importante / nosotros ganar
Es importante que nosotros ganemos.

1. no ser bueno / nosotros tener un entrenador nuevo
2. ser increíble / el otro equipo ser tan bueno
3. no ser bueno / hacer tanto calor hoy
4. ser ridículo / las entradas ser tan caras
5. ser obvio / el estadio no ir a llenarse *(to fill up)* hoy
6. ser cierto / nuestro equipo tener excelentes jugadores

14.3 Subjunctive with Expressions of Doubt, Denial, and Uncertainty

Expressing doubt, denial, and uncertainty

A. When the main clause of a sentence expresses doubt, denial, or uncertainty, the subjunctive must be used in the subordinate clause whenever there is a change of subject.

Main Clause	Subjunctive Clause
Dudo	que **podamos** ir con ustedes.
No creo	que ellos **tengan** las entradas.
Es probable	que yo no **vaya.**

In spoken Spanish it is becoming acceptable to use the subjunctive even when there is no change of subject.

Dudo que **(yo) pueda** hacerlo esta tarde.

B. Remember that expressions of certainty, including those denying doubt, are followed by the indicative mood or an infinitive.

Estoy seguro de que **llegan** hoy.	*I'm sure they arrive today.*
No dudamos que **tienes** el dinero.	*We don't doubt that you have the money.*

C. The verbs **creer** and **pensar** are usually followed by the subjunctive when they are negative or in a question. They are followed by the indicative when used in the affirmative.

No creo que **estén** bien entrenados.	*I don't believe they are well trained. (They don't appear to be and probably aren't.)*
¿Crees que lo **acepten** los aficionados?	*Do you believe that the fans will accept him? (They may not.)*
Pienso que **están** en el partido.	*I think (believe) they are at the game.*

¡A practicar!

A. Domingo deportivo. Melisa está mirando su programa favorito, *Domingo deportivo,* en la tele. Ella es muy aficionada a los deportes. ¿Qué dice cuando mira los diferentes eventos?

Modelo no creer / su entrenador / ser tan bueno como el nuestro
No creo que su entrenador sea tan bueno como el nuestro.

Fútbol
1. yo dudar / nuestro equipo / estar en forma para este partido
2. ser increíble / árbitros / ser tan injustos

Fútbol americano
3. yo no creer / ese equipo / ganar hoy
4. ser increíble / ellos / jugar tan mal

Boxeo
5. ser cierto / Cuba / tener excelentes boxeadores
6. yo no dudar / esta pelea / terminar en un empate *(tie)*

Béisbol
7. ser lógico / el equipo cubano / tener tanto éxito
8. ser probable / nuestro equipo / ganarle a los EE.UU. en la Olimpiada.

B. ¡Cálmate! Tú estás muy nervioso(a) por el partido esta noche. ¿Qué estás diciendo?

1. ser obvio / el número ocho no saber nada
2. ser probable / el árbitro recibir dinero del otro equipo

3. ser posible / nuestro equipo ya estar cansado
4. yo dudar / su entrenador ser bueno
5. ¿creer tú / ellos tener mejores jugadores?
6. nosotros no dudar / ese jugador ser excelente

14.4 Subjunctive with Expressions of Persuasion, Anticipation, and Reaction

Persuading, anticipating, and reacting

Whenever the main clause in a sentence expresses desire, command, request, suggestion, permission, or prohibition, the verb in the subordinate clause is expressed in the subjunctive provided there is a subject change.

Main Clause	Subjunctive Clause
No **quiere**	que **esquiemos** solos.
Recomiendan	que **subamos** en las sillas dobles.
Aconsejan	que **nos pongamos** las gafas.
Insiste en	que **practiquemos** juntos.

A. The following frequently used expressions denote persuasion, anticipation, and reaction.

aconsejar	*to advise*	permitir	*to permit*
decir (i)	*to tell (command)*	preferir (ie, i)	*to prefer*
desear	*to desire*	prohibir	*to prohibit, forbid*
insistir (en)	*to insist*	querer (ie)	*to want*
mandar	*to order (command)*	recomendar (ie)	*to recommend*
pedir (i, i)	*to ask*	sugerir (ie, i)	*to suggest*

B. Certain expressions may either express a command or convey information. The subjunctive is used *only* when a command is being expressed.

Dice que **bajemos** despacio.	*He tells us to come down slowly.*
Dice que **bajamos** despacio.	*He says we came down slowly.*
Insiste en que no **doblemos** las rodillas.	*He insists that we not bend our knees.*
Insiste en que no **doblamos** las rodillas.	*He insists (on the fact) that we are not bending our knees.*

C. As with expressions of emotion, the subjunctive is used after expressions of persuasion, anticipation, and reaction only when there is a subject change. If there is no change of subject, an infinitive is used.

Quiero **aprender** a esquiar bien.	*I want to learn to ski well.*
Quiero que todos **aprendan** a esquiar bien.	*I want everyone to learn to ski well.*

Es importante **saber** frenar.	*It's important to know how to brake (stop).*
Es importante que **sepan** frenar.	*It's important that you know how to brake.*

¡A practicar!

A. Vacaciones de invierno. Unos amigos quieren hacer algo diferente durante estas vacaciones de invierno. ¿Qué sugiere cada persona que hagamos todos nosotros?

Modelo Ramón / sugerir / hacer un viaje largo en tren
Ramón sugiere que hagamos un viaje largo en tren.

1. yo / recomendar / ir a esquiar
2. Tina / sugerir / aprender a patinar *(skate)*
3. Tomás / querer / quedarnos en casa
4. Enrique / preferir / hacer un viaje por la costa
5. Ramona / aconsejar / pasar un fin de semana en Colorado
6. Olga / insistir / alquilar una cabaña en las montañas
7. Tomás / insistir / no gastar demasiado dinero
8. él / decir / ser mejor ahorrar nuestro dinero

B. ¡Y más consejos! ¿Qué dice David de los consejos que él recibe de sus profesores, amigos y familiares?

1. Mi consejero ______________ (decirme) que sólo ______________ (yo / tomar) ocho unidades el próximo año.
2. Él ______________ (decir) que yo siempre ______________ (tomar) muchas unidades.
3. Mis padres ______________ (preferir) que yo no ______________ (trabajar) el próximo año.
4. Ellos ______________ (creer) que yo ______________ (trabajar) demasiado.
5. Mis amigos ______________ (sugerirme) que ______________ (yo / salir) con ellos.
6. Ellos ______________ (pensar) que yo no ______________ (salir) nunca de casa.

C. Los planes de David. ¿Y cuáles son los deseos de David?

1. David querer: ser ingeniero
2. él querer: sus padres no trabajar más
3. él desear: terminar pronto sus estudios universitarios

4. él desear: sus hermanos estudiar en la universidad también
5. también él insistir en: practicar deportes con frecuencia
6. él insistir en: su novia practicar algún deporte también

14.5 Present Subjunctive in Adjective Clauses

Referring to unfamiliar persons, places, and things

Sometimes a clause is used as an adjective to describe a person, place, or thing. For example, in the following sentence the adjective clause describes **mujer.**

	Adjective Clause
Conozco a una mujer	que ganó cinco medallas de oro.

The verb of the adjective clause may be in the subjunctive or in the indicative.

A. If the antecedent—the person, place, or thing being described—is indefinite (either nonexistent or not definitely known to exist), the verb in the adjective clause must be in the subjunctive.

Busco un entrenador que **hable** ruso.	*I am looking for a coach who speaks Russian. (I'm not sure the person exists.)*
Necesitamos una secretaria que **sepa** taquigrafía.	*We need a secretary who knows shorthand.*

B. If, on the other hand, the antecedent is known to exist, then the verb in the adjective clause must be in the indicative.

Busco al entrenador que **habla** ruso.	*I am looking for the coach who speaks Russian. (I know the person.)*
Contratamos a un secretario que **sabe** taquigrafía y contabilidad.	*We hired a secretary who knows shorthand and bookkeeping.*
Voy a solicitar el puesto que **ofrece** el mejor salario.	*I'm going to apply for the job that offers the highest salary.*

Note that the mood used in adjective clauses indicates whether the speaker is talking about a fact or something hypothetical or abstract.

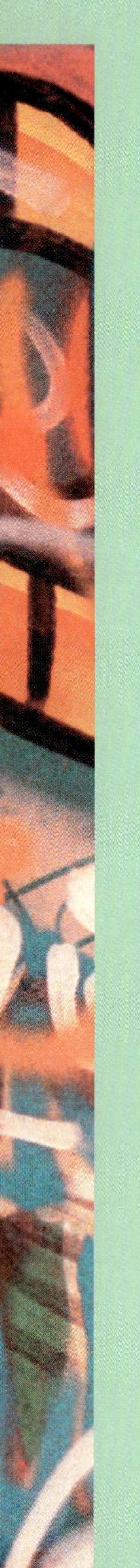

C. Negative antecedents always refer to the nonexistent. Therefore, the verb in an adjective clause modifying a negative antecedent must be in the subjunctive.

No hay nadie que **esté** dispuesto a trabajar los fines de semana.	*There isn't anyone who is willing to work on weekends.*
No encuentro a ningún solicitante que **sepa** hablar japonés.	*I can't find any applicant who knows how to speak Japanese.*

The personal **a** is not usually used before an indefinite direct object. **Nadie** and **alguien,** however, always take the personal **a** when used as direct objects.

¡A practicar!

A. Nuevo personal. Los socios de un club deportivo están discutiendo los contratos de nuevo personal. ¿Qué dicen ellos?

1. necesitamos / entrenador / ser muy enérgico
2. necesitamos / entrenador / dirigir a los Atléticos
3. buscamos / lanzador / tener experiencia
4. buscamos / lanzador / jugar ahora por los Gigantes
5. contratamos / bateadores / venir de los juveniles
6. contratamos / bateadores / ya tener fama

B. Club deportivo. Un amigo está hablando con su consejero sobre la necesidad de fundar un club deportivo para estudiantes graduados. Según él, ¿qué tipo de personas necesitan para administrar el club?

1. necesitamos un presidente que / poder trabajar bien con el profesorado y los estudiantes
2. tenemos que encontrar un vicepresidente que / ser responsable y / trabajar bien con el presidente
3. para tesorero *(treasurer)*, necesitamos a alguien que / saber contabilidad *(bookkeeping)* y que / ser honesto
4. y para secretario necesitamos una persona que / escribir a máquina y / saber usar la computadora
5. también queremos nombrar a alguien que / representarnos en las reuniones del departamento

C. La universidad nos apoya. Ahora su amigo está contándoles a sus compañeros lo que dijo el consejero. ¿Qué les dice?

Dice que la universidad estará a favor de que ______________ (nosotros / organizar) un club que ______________ (preocuparse) de los intereses deportivos de los estudiantes graduados. Cree que debemos nombrar una persona que ______________ (hablar) con la administración en seguida. Dice que hay una persona en la administración que ______________ (tener) experiencia en esos asuntos *(matters)*. Y como yo soy una persona que ______________ (conocer) el sistema político de la universidad, yo puedo ser el representante por el momento. Él cree que debemos elegir un representante que ______________ (ser) muy activo y que no ______________ (tener) miedo de defender los intereses del grupo.

CAPÍTULO 15

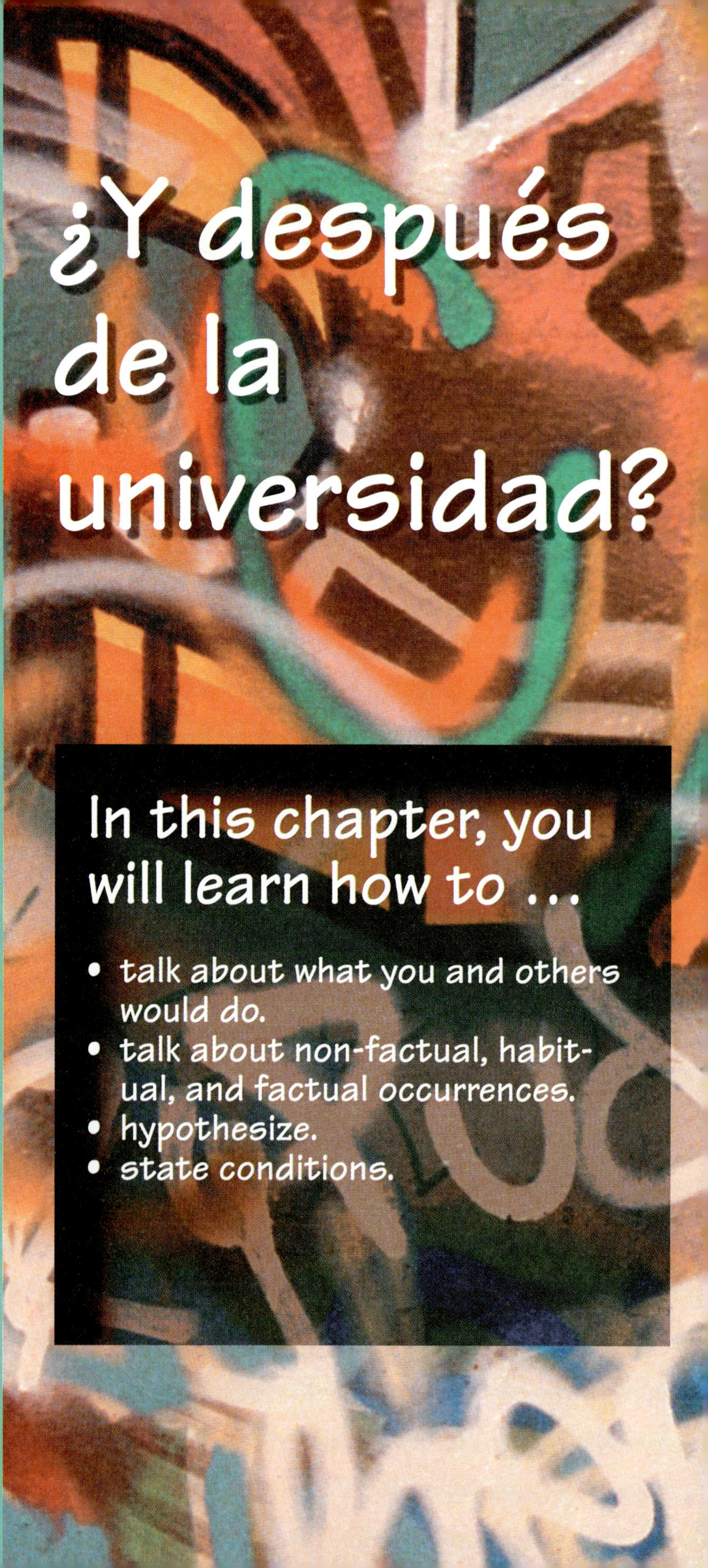

¿Y después de la universidad?

Cultural Topics

- **¿Sabías que…?**
  Seguro de trabajo y la mujer profesional latinoamericana
- **La dinastía del amor**
  Cross-cultural perceptions regarding maintaining a mistress and the issue of machismo.
- **Noticiero cultural**
  Lugar: *Ecuador: Las islas Galápagos*
  Gente: *La mujer en Ecuador*
- **Lectura:** *Mitos y realidades*

Writing Strategies

- *Hacer un análisis*

Reading Strategies

- *Inferencia*

En preparación

- 15.1 Conditional of Regular and Irregular Verbs
- 15.2 Subjunctive in Adverb Clauses
- 15.3 Past Subjunctive: Conditional Sentences with **si** Clauses

In this chapter, you will learn how to …

- talk about what you and others would do.
- talk about non-factual, habitual, and factual occurrences.
- hypothesize.
- state conditions.

¿El padre hispano del siglo XXI?

Joven ecuatoriana en busca de empleo

Boda en una iglesia en Quito, Ecuador.

Lo que ya sabes...

1. En tu opinión, ¿existen quehaceres domésticos (*household chores*) que solamente la mujer debe hacer? ¿Cuáles? ¿Existen quehaceres domésticos que solamente el hombre debe hacer? ¿Cuáles?
2. ¿Crees que las mujeres deben quedarse en casa si tienen hijos preescolares? ¿Por qué? ¿Qué opinas de los hombres que se quedan en casa mientras sus esposas trabajan?
3. ¿Es fácil encontrar trabajo donde tú vives? ¿Cuáles son las fuentes principales de trabajo en tu estado?
4. ¿Aceptarías mudarte a otra ciudad o a otro estado para conseguir trabajo? Si no, ¿por qué no?
5. ¿Crees que es importante casarse en una iglesia? ¿Por qué?
6. ¿Qué opinas de las parejas que viven juntas sin casarse?

ECUADOR

¿Harías algo por mí?

TAREA Antes de empezar este **Paso**, estudia **En preparación** 15.1 y haz por escrito los ejercicios de **¡A practicar!** También escucha **Paso 1 ¿Qué se dice...?** del Capítulo 15 en el CD del estudiante.

¿Eres buen observador?

Ahora, ¡a analizar!

1. ¿Por qué es diferente el detergente «Micolor»?
2. ¿Para qué ropa debe usarse? ¿En qué se especializa?
3. ¿Comprarías tú un detergente que no lava más blanco? ¿Por qué?
4. Explica el lema: «Al blanco lo que es del blanco y al color, Micolor».

EL ÚNICO DETERGENTE QUE NO LAVA MÁS BLANCO.

¿Para qué quieres blancura en tu ropa de color?. Los detergentes que "lavan más blanco" son demasiado agresivos con los colores. Utiliza Micolor, el auténtico especialista del color. Gracias a su fórmula con protectores, Micolor elimina la suciedad más rebelde y conserva los colores siempre como nuevos, lavado tras lavado. Prueba Micolor y notarás la diferencia.

Al blanco lo que es del blanco y al color, Micolor.

¿Qué se dice...?

Al hablar de lo que tú y otras personas harían

1. ¿Qué tipo de ayuda quiere Alicia? _______________
2. ¿Qué sugieres tú que haga Raúl?

- ❑ sacar la basura
- ❑ preparar la comida
- ❑ lavar el carro
- ❑ limpiar la casa
- ❑ lavar los platos
- ❑ cambiar los pañales del bebé
- ❑ cortar el césped
- ❑ mantener el carro

RAÚL Sí, cómo no, vida mía, ¿qué sugieres que yo haga?

ALICIA Bueno, me parece que podrías cambiar los pañales del bebé de vez en cuando y si lavaras los platos todas las noches y plancharas la ropa una vez a la...

RAÚL Espera, espera, mi amor. Si yo acepto hacer todo eso, ¿sacarías tú la basura cada dos días? ¿Y cortarías el césped los fines de semana? ¿Lavarías el carro todos los domingos y lo mantendrías lleno de gasolina?

ALICIA ¡Ay, Raúl! ¿Por qué te pones tan machista cada vez que hablamos de quehaceres domésticos?

Ahora, ¡a hablar!

A. Te ayudaría en todo. Javier quiere convencer a Josefina que se case con él. ¿Qué promesas le hace? ¿Qué dice que haría por ella?

Modelo ayudarte en todo

Te ayudaría en todo.

1. lavar la ropa
2. limpiar el baño
3. sacar la basura
4. ir de compras
5. estar siempre contigo
6. ser siempre muy romántico
7. traerte flores a menudo

B. La pareja ideal. En tu opinión, ¿haría el esposo ideal lo siguiente o no? ¿y la esposa ideal?

Modelo salir siempre con los amigos (las amigas)

Él nunca saldría con los amigos. o
Ella siempre saldría con las amigas.

1. ir solo(a) de vacaciones
2. decir mentiras al (a la) cónyuge *(spouse)*
3. tener su cuenta privada en el banco
4. tomar decisiones sin consultar al (a la) cónyuge
5. hacer muchos viajes solo(a)
6. vivir en otra ciudad por razones de trabajo
7. poner siempre la música que le gusta a la otra persona
8. sacrificarse totalmente por la otra persona

C. Amistad. La amistad es tan sagrada *(sacred)* como el matrimonio y los amigos ideales no son fáciles de encontrar. Pregúntale a tu compañero(a) si cree que los amigos verdaderos harían lo siguiente.

Modelo llamarse con frecuencia

TÚ **¿Crees que los amigos verdaderos se llamarían con frecuencia?**

COMPAÑERO(A) **Sí, creo que se llamarían con frecuencia.** o
No, no creo que se llamarían con frecuencia.

1. escucharse siempre con paciencia
2. visitarse en el hospital
3. pedirse siempre dinero
4. escribirse a menudo
5. decirse mentiras
6. ayudarse ante las dificultades

D. Y mucho más. Dile a un(a) compañero(a) lo que harías por un amigo verdadero y pregúntale qué haría él (ella).

Modelo hacer…

Yo haría cosas especiales para un amigo. Y tú, ¿qué harías?

1. decir...
2. tener...
3. hacer...
4. estar...
5. dar...
6. ir...
7. salir...
8. ¿...?

Y ahora, ¡a conversar!

A. Debate. Los Estados Unidos no ha tenido nunca a una mujer como presidenta. ¿Debería una mujer llegar a ser presidenta? Trabajando en grupos de cuatro, cada pareja debe tomar una posición opuesta y defenderla.

B. Todo sería diferente. ¿Cómo sería el mundo si tú y tus compañeros(as) fueran presidentes de unas grandes superpotencias? ¿Qué harían para mejorar el mundo? Trabajando en grupos de tres o cuatro, decidan lo que harían y cómo sería su mundo. Presenten a la clase un resumen de sus conclusiones.

C. ¿Qué harías si...? Con frecuencia nos vemos en situaciones difíciles debido a tener que vivir dentro de un presupuesto fijo *(fixed budget)*. Trabajando en grupos de tres o cuatro, decidan qué harían ustedes si se vieran en las siguientes situaciones. Comparen sus respuestas con las de los otros grupos.

1. Mañana es el cumpleaños de un amigo y como estamos a fines de mes, no tienes dinero para comprarle un regalo.
2. Hay que pagar el alquiler, pero tú y tus compañeros(as) de cuarto no tienen el dinero para pagarlo.
3. Tú y tu novio(a) están en un restaurante muy elegante celebrando su cumpleaños. Pensabas que tenías bastante dinero pero él (ella) decidió pedir el plato más caro y no te va a alcanzar el dinero.
4. Acabas de comprar un carro nuevo y después de sólo dos meses de tenerlo, te despiden del trabajo. Si te atrasaras *(fail to make)* un pago más, perderías el carro.

¡Luz! ¡Cámara! ¡Acción!

A. ¡La pobreza! Aunque los Estados Unidos es un país de mucha riqueza, todavía existe también mucha pobreza. Tú y tu compañero(a) creen que es necesario que desaparezca la pobreza en este país. Dramaticen una conversación discutiendo posibles soluciones al problema.

B. ¡Emergencia! En grupos de tres o cuatro, dramaticen lo que harían en caso de una emergencia (ustedes decidan qué tipo de emergencia) para asegurarse del bienestar de su familia, de sus vecinos y de su comunidad. ¿Cuáles serían sus prioridades?

¿Comprendes lo que se dice?

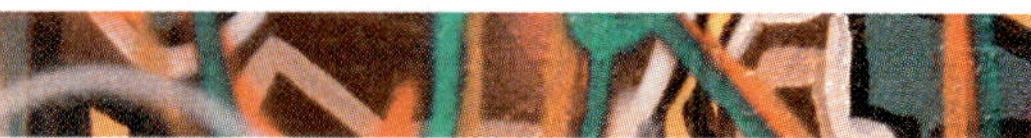

La dinastía del amor: Episodio 9

La familia Gómez, como de costumbre, espera el comienzo de la telenovela del momento. La semana pasada los televidentes quedaron pendientes de varios asuntos: ¿Cómo dirá Betty a su familia que se casó? ¿Se casará Sharon con Eric? Escucha este episodio y luego contesta las preguntas que siguen.

Vocabulario útil

aguantar	*to bear, tolerate*	hacer daño	*to harm, to damage*
casamiento	*marriage*	un mal rato	*a bad time*

A través de dos culturas

Telenovela

1. ¿Dónde estaba la señora Kennedy?
2. ¿Qué problemas tienen Sharon y Betty?
3. ¿Qué dice Betty de los problemas de la familia?
4. ¿Quién es el culpable, según el señor Kennedy? ¿Por qué lo cree?
5. ¿Por qué vino Eric a casa de los Kennedy?
6. ¿Por qué le pide Betty a Eric que se calle?
7. ¿Qué hace Betty al final del episodio?
8. ¿Qué le pasa al padre?

Televidentes

9. ¿Es sincero don Sergio Gómez cuando dice que él se moriría si sus hijos actuaran como los Kennedy?
10. ¿Crees que Luisita tiene razón? ¿Es un crimen casarse sin avisar a nadie?

NOTICIERO CULTURAL

LUGAR... ECUADOR

Antes de empezar, dime...

1. Nombra algunas de las bellezas naturales de los EE.UU.
2. Nombra lugares de los EE.UU. en los que se preservan especies en peligro de extinción. Nombra también esas especies.
3. Nombra algunos parques nacionales de tu país.

Ecuador: Las islas Galápagos

Las islas Galápagos, llamadas oficialmente el archipiélago de Colón, se extienden al norte y al sur de la línea ecuatorial, a 600 millas de la República del Ecuador. Fueron descubiertas en 1535 por un obispo español, Tomás de Berlanga, siendo redescubiertas años más tarde por piratas y bucaneros ingleses, quienes las usaron de refugio y base para sus ataques. Ya, en los siglos XVIII y XIX fueron punto de interés de balleneros y otros navegantes, los que llegaban atraídos por la carne y el aceite de las enormes tortugas terrestres llamadas galápagos.

Estas islas son mundialmente reconocidas como un verdadero laboratorio viviente, destacándose por su exótica belleza y por la riqueza de su fauna y flora. Aunque los primeros visitantes introdujeron especies domésticas, los verdaderos «señores» son las especies más raras, como las manadas de leones marinos, los álbatros dómines, cierto tipo de pingüinos llegados de la Antártica, las iguanas y otras especies que al migrar se han ido adaptando al hábitat de las islas.

Leones marinos

Albatros dómines

Pingüinos

Iguanas

Y fue de su corta visita (36 días) a estas islas que Charles Darwin, que viajó como naturalista del buque de investigación *HMS Beagle,* publicó en 1859, después de veinte años de reflexión, *El origen de las especies.* Esta obra revolucionó al mundo, cambiando el concepto que la humanidad tenía de sí misma. Darwin basó su teoría de la evolución de las especies, en los cambios experimentados por animales y plantas al adaptarse al ambiente en el cual se desarrollarían más tarde.

Al conmemorarse el centenario de la publicación de *El origen de las especies,* el gobierno de Ecuador, conjuntamente con un consorcio multinacional de organizaciones científicas y de conservación, establecieron el Parque Nacional de las Islas Galápagos, santuario mundial.

Y ahora, dime...

El viaje de Darwin a las islas Galápagos tuvo un impacto muy grande. Usa este diagrama araña con un(a) compañero(a) para indicar qué descubrió Darwin en las islas y el impacto que esos descubrimientos tuvieron en el mundo.

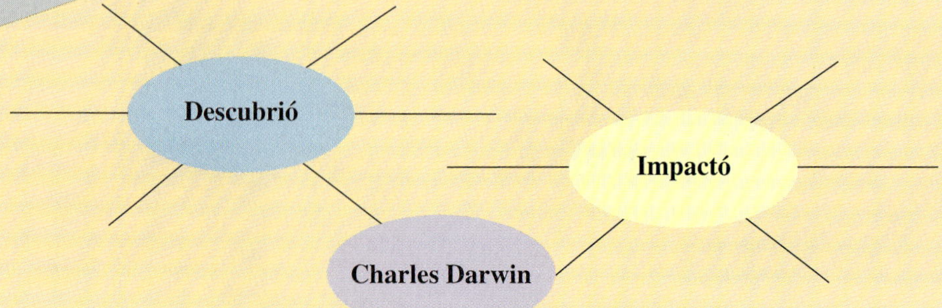

El español en otras disciplinas: Ecología

La selva tropical. Uno de los mayores problemas que afecta al medio ambiente actualmente, además de la contaminación, es el problema de la deforestación y el peligro constante en que se debaten las reservas biológicas y las riquezas naturales del planeta. Con un(a) compañero(a) hablen entre sí y decidan cómo asignarle un número a cada uno de los problemas o peligros de la siguiente lista, otorgándole el número 1 al problema que les parece más serio, el 2 al siguiente más serio y así hasta el 8 al menos serio. Luego en grupos de cuatro, hagan una tabla de estadística con los resultados.

_____ Deforestación
_____ Pesticidas y fumigantes
_____ Intereses del petróleo
_____ Contaminación
_____ Especies en peligro de extinción
_____ Búhos en los bosques
_____ Ganado en los bosques
_____ Desechos radioactivos

Proyecto. Haz un breve informe sobre algún problema ecológico en un país hispano. Tendrás que buscar información en los periódicos o revistas sobre la ecología. Describe el problema e indica lo que el país está haciendo para solucionarlo.

Aceptaré la oferta con tal que...

TAREA

Antes de empezar este **Paso**, estudia **En preparación** 15.2 y haz por escrito los ejercicios de **¡A practicar!** También escucha **Paso 2 ¿Qué se dice...?** del Capítulo 15 en el CD del estudiante.

¿Eres buen observador?

Ahora, ¡a analizar!

1. ¿Son todos estos puestos para personas con título universitario? ¿Cuáles requieren otros requisitos?
2. ¿Solicitarías tú algunos de estos puestos? Explica.
3. ¿Cuál de estos puestos tiene más requisitos? ¿Cuál tiene menos?
4. ¿Cuál crees que pagará más? ¿Por qué crees eso?
5. Explica lo que quiere decir «Se garantiza confidencialidad» en el tercer anuncio.

EL DIARIO
SOLICITA
INSPECTOR DE SEGURIDAD

Requisitos:
- Bachiller
- Conocimientos en Seguridad Industrial y Protección contra Incendios
- Dispuesto a trabajar en turno rotativo
- Nacionalidad norteamericana
- Edad entre 24 y 35 años (no limitativo)
- Residencia en el área metropolitana

Interesados: Favor dirigirse con currículum vitae y foto reciente, a la siguiente dirección: Mesa St. Edificio Diario de El Paso. Horario: 8:30 am a 11:00 am y 1:30 pm a 4:30 pm.

Empresa Internacional
SOLICITA
CONDUCTORES

Requisitos:
- Licencia de conducir
- Carta de referencias de trabajos anteriores (2)
- Una foto de frente tipo carnet reciente
- Certificado médico
- 6º grado de instrucción primaria aprobado

Interesados dirigirse a: Calle Industrial, Edificio Importados Latinoamérica. Solicitar al Sr. Ricardo San Martín en horas de oficina.

EMPRESA DISTRIBUIDORA DE PRODUCTOS DE CONSUMO MASIVO
SOLICITA
JEFE(A) ADMINISTRATIVO(A)

- Graduado universitario
- Experiencia en el área Administrativa, Personal, Crédito y Cobranzas
- Edad entre 25 y 35 años
- Capacidad de Planificación, Organización con dinamismo e iniciativa propia
- Conocimientos generales en manejo de microprocesadores

SE GARANTIZA CONFIDENCIALIDAD

Enviar currículum vitae a la Caja Postal 7077, indicando aspiraciones de sueldo y foto reciente

Seguros *LA SEGURIDAD*
SOLICITA
ANALISTAS DE PERSONAL

Orientamos nuestra búsqueda hacia un joven dinámico, egresado de una Universidad o Instituto Universitario como Técnico Superior, Licenciado en Relaciones Industriales o carrera afín, con experiencia. Es esencial tener habilidad para establecer buenas relaciones interpersonales y facilidad para expresarse oralmente.

Interesados favor dirigirse a nuestra oficina en la Av. Universidad esq. con El Paseo, con currículum vitae y dos fotografías recientes tamaño carnet.

¿Qué se dice...?

Al hablar de hechos ciertos e inciertos

1. No sabe si quiere empleo en ______________________
2. No dejará su puesto actual hasta que ______________________
3. El ambiente es muy agradable aunque ______________________
4. La experiencia de la entrevista ayudará aunque ______________________

RAÚL Cuando acepten mis condiciones, firmaré el contrato, y no antes.

ALICIA Tan pronto como te ofrezcan el puesto, nos mudaremos.

RAÚL Es cierto que después de que me den un trabajo tendremos que tomar muchas decisiones. Pero, ¡no te adelantes! El problema es que todavía no me han ofrecido nada.

ALICIA No hay problema, Raúl. Tengo mucha confianza en ti. Espera hasta que recibas dos ofertas, entonces sí que tendremos un problema.

¿Sabías que... ?

En muchos países hispanos, la mujer cuenta con importante y excelente protección por su condición de madre de familia. Por ejemplo, a la mujer embarazada le permiten un reposo de casi un mes y medio antes —y de casi tres meses después— del nacimiento de su bebé. Además, el seguro de trabajo de la mujer le garantiza el cuidado gratuito o casi gratuito (de acuerdo a su salario) de los hijos en edad preescolar (de tres meses a cuatro años). En Chile, por ejemplo, una empresa o institución con un número superior a veinticinco empleadas tiene que crear, por decreto de ley, una guardería (*day-care center*).

Ahora, ¡a hablar!

A. Decisiones. Juan Carlos se va a graduar este verano y quiere viajar durante unos seis meses antes de empezar su vida profesional. Ahora está pensando en las ventajas y desventajas de viajar por un período tan largo. ¿Qué piensa?

Modelo viajar a menos que: ofrecerme un buen puesto
Viajaré a menos que me ofrezcan un buen puesto.

1. salir antes de que: mi novia y yo decidir casarnos
2. poder ir con tal de que: mi padre prestarme dinero
3. no ir solo a menos de que: mi amigo Jorge no poder viajar
4. visitar a mis parientes para que: mis padres estar contentos conmigo
5. no hacer planes antes de que: todos mis papeles estar en orden
6. no confirmar mis reservaciones sin que: mi amigo y yo estar seguros de ir

B. ¿Me aceptarán? Óscar mandó una solicitud de trabajo hace una semana, pero todavía no ha recibido ninguna respuesta. A pesar de todo, como es tan optimista, ya está haciendo planes. ¿En qué está pensando?

Modelo aceptaré en cuanto / recibir la oferta
Aceptaré en cuanto reciba la oferta.

1. me mudaré tan pronto como / firmar el contrato
2. compraré un auto nuevo después de que / recibir el primer sueldo
3. haré un viaje a Europa cuando / tener mis primeras vacaciones
4. aceptaré aunque el trabajo / estar lejos
5. tendré que comprar muebles tan pronto como / mudarme
6. pero seguiré con mi vida diaria hasta que ellos / contestar mi carta

C. ¡Felicitaciones! Óscar, por fin, recibe las noticias. Le han hecho una excelente oferta, pero en otra ciudad. Ahora está hablando por teléfono con un amigo que trabaja allá. ¿Qué le dice el amigo?

Modelo aunque el lugar / estar lejos / ser un buen puesto
Aunque el lugar está lejos, es un buen puesto.

1. tan pronto como tú / llegar / tener que llamarme
2. cuando una persona nueva / llegar / siempre / nosotros hacer una recepción
3. en cuanto tú / pasar unos días aquí / todo ser fácil
4. aunque la empresa / ser grande / todo el mundo / conocerse
5. aunque tú siempre / estar ocupado / el ambiente / ser agradable
6. cuando tú / tener problemas / alguien ayudarte

D. ¿Para qué? Los seres humanos tenemos la capacidad de complicarnos la vida por diferentes razones. Dile a tu compañero(a) para qué haces lo siguiente y escucha mientras te dice para qué lo hace él (ella).

Modelo trabajar

Yo trabajo para que mis hijos coman bien. o
Yo trabajo para comprarme un coche nuevo.

1. hacer ejercicio
2. trabajar
3. estudiar
4. comprar una casa
5. (no) estar a dieta
6. tener tarjetas de crédito
7. pagar impuestos
8. ¿... ?

Y ahora, ¡a conversar!

A. Problemas con el presupuesto. Tu universidad tiene problemas serios con el presupuesto y está considerando aumentar el precio de la matrícula de los estudiantes. Tú y dos compañeros(as) de clase están en un comité estudiantil que va a hacer recomendaciones a la administración indicando bajo qué condiciones es aceptable aumentar la matrícula. ¿Qué recomendaciones hacen ustedes?

B. ¡Por fin! Tú y tus amigos van a graduarse en menos de un mes. En grupos de tres o cuatro discutan todo lo que piensan hacer.

Modelo **Tan pronto como me gradúe, viajaré a Sudamérica.**
Viajaré por tres meses a menos que...

C. Pasos importantes. El matrimonio no es el único paso importante en la vida. Hay otras decisiones que nos esperan a lo largo de la vida. ¿Qué harán tú y tu compañero(a) en las siguientes situaciones?

Modelo Cuando consigamos trabajo...

Cuando consigamos trabajo podremos comprarnos carros nuevos.

1. Tan pronto como nos graduemos...
2. Cuando tengamos bastante dinero...
3. En cuanto consigamos un buen puesto de trabajo...
4. Hasta que tengamos bastante dinero...
5. En cuanto terminemos los estudios de posgrado
6. Después de que nos jubilemos *(retire)*...

¡Luz! ¡Cámara! ¡Acción!

A. Necesito un aumento de sueldo. Tú estás hablando con tu supervisor(a) en el trabajo. Acaba de decirte que te van a dar un aumento de sueldo *(raise)* pero vas a tener que trabajar de noche, de las once de la noche hasta las siete de la mañana. Tú necesitas el aumento pero el horario no te conviene. Ofreces otras alternativas. Dramatiza la situación con un(a) compañero(a).

B. ¡Ay, los padres! Tus padres quieren que tú consigas un trabajo después de graduarte, pero quieres continuar con los estudios de posgrado. Ellos tienen sus razones y tú tienes las tuyas. Dramatiza esta situación con dos compañeros de clase.

¿Comprendes lo que se dice?

La dinastía del amor: Episodio 10

Estamos en el mes de abril y esta noche la familia Gómez verá el último episodio de la temporada. El señor Kennedy ha muerto. Sharon y Eric están casados y la señora Kennedy se prepara para casarse con el señor Robertson, el socio de su finado *(late)* esposo. Escucha ahora el último episodio y luego contesta las preguntas que siguen.

Vocabulario útil

malagradecido	*ungrateful*	vergüenza	*shame*
mentira	*lie*	engañar	*to deceive*
SIDA *(m.)*	*AIDS*	merecer	*to deserve*

A través de dos culturas

Telenovela

1. ¿Qué noticias acaba de dar Betty a su madre?
2. ¿Por qué se comporta de manera tan insolente Betty con su madre?
3. ¿Cómo reacciona la señora Kennedy?
4. Según Betty, ¿por qué se casó? ¿Cómo reacciona la madre?
5. ¿Con quién acaba de hablar Sharon? ¿Qué le dijo?
6. ¿Cuál fue la causa de la muerte de su marido, según la señora Kennedy?
7. ¿Por qué le dice Betty a su madre que «todo se paga en este mundo»?
8. ¿Cómo reacciona Sharon?

Televidentes

9. ¿Por qué cree Luisita Gómez que el señor Kennedy merecía ser engañado por su esposa?
10. ¿Qué opina Juan Pedro de una mujer que engaña a su marido? ¿y de un hombre que engaña a su esposa?
11. ¿Y qué opina don Sergio? ¿y doña Luisa?
12. ¿Tiene razón doña Luisa al decir que don Sergio y Juan Pedro son machistas? Explica.

NOTICIERO CULTURAL

GENTE... LA MUJER EN ECUADOR

Antes de empezar, dime...

1. ¿Cuándo logró el voto la mujer en los EE.UU.?
2. ¿En qué década tuvo su apogeo el Movimiento de Liberación Femenina en los EE.UU.?
3. ¿Están protegidos bajo la ley la mayor parte de derechos femeninos o todavía está la mujer estadounidense luchando por esos derechos? Explica tu respuesta.

Quito, Ecuador.

La mujer en Ecuador

Muy poco sabemos de la mujer ecuatoriana, y lo que sabemos siempre está rodeado del estereotipo de la mujer indígena, pasiva, trabajadora, obediente y experta en la artesanía manual. Aunque Ecuador no figura en muchas estadísticas mundiales, los cambios que se han producido en el país relacionados a la mujer son muchos. En primer lugar, Ecuador fue el primer país de Sudamérica en permitir el divorcio y el primero en darle el derecho del voto a las mujeres en el año 1929.

Más recientemente en los años 70, se empezó a organizar el movimiento feminista con grupos de mujeres que pertenecían a la clase trabajadora. El propósito principal fue lograr más alimentos, mejores condiciones de salud y cuidado infantil, especialmente en las zonas rurales. En el año 1975 el grupo de mujeres que organizó el Comité de Solidaridad para los conflictos laborales, publicó la revista *La Pachacama* que sirvió de voz en muchos cambios sociales de miles de personas de todo el país.

En 1976 se organizó la Brigada de Mujeres Universitarias que logró cambios en los sectores de la construcción, el comercio, los servicios y la industria textil. Después de formarse el Grupo Autónomo de Mujeres, la Unión de Mujeres Trabajadoras y la Unión Nacional de Mujeres Ecuatorianas, la Oficina Nacional de la Mujer junto a la Asociación Jurídica Femenina de Guayaquil, propusieron nuevas leyes al gobierno que lograron uno de los más importantes cambios en las leyes que protegen los derechos de la mujer de Ecuador. Estas leyes, que no permiten nuevas discriminaciones en contra del sexo femenino en el país, han sido propuestas por las Naciones Unidas como ejemplo para muchos otros países del mundo.

Y ahora, dime...

Contesten estas preguntas en parejas.

1. ¿Cuál es el estereotipo que rodea a la mujer ecuatoriana? Nombra dos o tres datos que contradigan este estereotipo.
2. ¿Quién dio primero el derecho del voto a la mujer, Argentina o Ecuador? ¿EE.UU. o Ecuador?
3. ¿En qué año se empezó a formar el movimiento femenino en Ecuador? ¿Con qué propósito?
4. ¿Qué es *La Pachacama*?
5. ¿Cuáles son algunas organizaciones femeninas en los EE.UU.?
6. ¿Cómo puede ayudar a las mujeres de los EE.UU. el modelo de leyes propuesto por las Naciones Unidas?

Antes de escribir
Estrategias para escribir: Hacer un análisis

A. Generalizaciones equivocadas. En la escritura, como en el habla, hay una tendencia a generalizar y, con frecuencia, estas generalizaciones no son válidas. Por eso, siempre es bueno analizar cualquier generalización. Cuando analizamos por escrito, es importante presentar todos los hechos que apoyen o que contradigan la generalización.

Mira la generalización que se hizo de la mujer ecuatoriana a principios del **Noticiero cultural** sobre «La mujer en Ecuador».

1. ¿Qué datos contradicen este estereotipo?
2. ¿Qué publicación contradice esta generalización?
3. ¿Qué agrupaciones contradicen esta generalización?
4. ¿Qué puedes deducir, entonces, después de leer este texto de la mujer ecuatoriana?

B. ¡No es verdad! Tanto como la prensa en los EE.UU. tiende a generalizar equivocadamente a Hispanoamérica, la prensa hispanoamericana también tiende a hacer lo mismo con los EE.UU. Con dos compañeros(as) de clase, preparen una lista de generalizaciones equivocadas que ustedes saben o creen que los latinoamericanos tienen de los ciudadanos de los EE.UU. Un ejemplo es: *Todos los americanos son ricos.*

Ahora, ¡a escribir!

A. En preparación. En los mismos grupos que prepararon la lista de generalizaciones en el ejercicio anterior, seleccionen cuatro o cinco de sus generalizaciones y, para cada una, preparen una lista de hechos que contradigan la generalización.

B. El primer borrador. Basándose en las listas que acaban de preparar, desarrollen un análisis de un párrafo para cada generalización. Cada análisis debe incluir varios hechos específicos y una o dos oraciones para llamar atención a lo incorrecto de la generalización.

C. Ahora, a compartir. Intercambien su análisis con otro grupo para saber su reacción. Lean el análisis de sus compañeros y denles sugerencias sobre posibles cambios para mejorar su análisis. Si encuentran errores, menciónenlos.

D. Ahora, a revisar. Ahora agreguen la información que consideren necesaria para su análisis. No olviden revisar los errores que mencionaron sus compañeros.

E. La versión final. Saquen una copia en limpio y entréguensela a su profesor(a).

F. Publicación. En grupos de nueve, comparen sus análisis, en particular cuando escribieron sobre las mismas generalizaciones. Informen a la clase sobre las generalizaciones que los tres grupos tuvieron en común.

Si me dieran $600,00 mensuales...

TAREA Antes de empezar este **Paso**, estudia **En preparación** 15.3 y haz por escrito los ejercicios de **¡A practicar!** También escucha **Paso 3 ¿Qué se dice...?** del Capítulo 15 en el CD del estudiante.

¿Eres buen observador?

Ahora, ¡a analizar!

1. ¿Para qué es esta propaganda?
2. ¿Cuántas categorías distintas de seguros ofrece esta compañía? ¿Cuáles son?
3. ¿Cuáles de estos seguros son apropiados para niños? ¿adultos? ¿familias? ¿compañías o empresas?
4. ¿Qué tipos de seguros tienes tú? ¿Cuáles de estas categorías de seguros te gustaría conseguir?

INSTINTO DE PROTECCION

Sede Social: Plaza de España, 15 - Tel. 541 93 87 - 28008 Madrid

SEGUROS:

ACCIDENTES:
- INDIVIDUALES
- FAMILIAR
- GRUPO

AGRARIOS COMBINADOS
SANTA LUCIA ASISTENCIA
COMBINADO DE:
- COMERCIOS Y OFICINAS
- DECESOS Y ACCIDENTES
- EDIFICIOS Y COMUNIDADES DE VIVIENDAS
- HOGAR
- INCENDIO - ROBO
- TALLERES E INDUSTRIAS
- ROBO Y EXPOLIACION

CRISTALES
INCENDIOS:
- RIESGOS SENCILLOS
- RIESGOS INDUSTRIALES

RESPONSABILIDAD CIVIL:
- GENERAL
- OBLIGATORIO CAZADOR
- VOLUNTARIO CAZADOR

VIDA:
- PLAN DE AHORRO JUVENIL
- PLAN DE JUBILACION 6000 MIXTOS, VIDA ENTERA, TEMPORALES Y
- ANUALIDADES CAPITAL DIFERIDO CON REEMBOLSO DE PRIMAS
- RENTA VITALICIA
  - DIFERIDA
  - INMEDIATA

VIDA DE GRUPO:
- PARA CASOS DE MUERTE PARA CASOS DE VIDA

CAPITAL, RESERVAS Y PROVISIONES TECNICAS: 74.371.277.281 Ptas.

¿Qué se dice...?

Al formar hipótesis y declarar condiciones

- ❑ Podrían comprar un carro nuevo.
- ❑ Tendrían que mudarse.
- ❑ Podrían pagar todas las deudas.
- ❑ No podrían invertir en la bolsa *(stock market)*.
- ❑ Alicia tendría que buscar empleo de tiempo completo.
- ❑ Alicia podría ir a la escuela tiempo completo.

RAÚL Amor mío, no has entendido. Me ofrecen $1.625.000 sucres mensuales. Y con eso pienso pagar nuestras deudas, comprar un coche nuevo e invertir en la bolsa a la vez. Ahora te vuelvo a preguntar, si te diera a ti $325.000 al mes, ¿cómo vivirías?

ALICIA En ese caso, viviría un poco mejor. Podría pagar algunas cuentas y compraría los libros para mis clases. Pero si la cantidad que me piensas dar fuera un poquito más grande, también ahorraría para esas vacaciones en Europa que siempre me estás prometiendo.

Ahora, ¡a hablar!

A. Si tuviera un buen puesto. María Antonia no gana mucho en su trabajo actual. Por eso acaba de solicitar empleo en otras compañías más importantes. ¿Qué dice María Antonia sobre la posibilidad de conseguir uno de estos puestos?

Modelo (estar) muy contenta si me ofrecieran un mejor puesto
Yo estaría muy contenta si me ofrecieran un mejor puesto.

1. (mudarme) si fuera necesario
2. (poder) comprarme un auto nuevo si me pagaran bien
3. (ser) difícil decidir si recibiera dos ofertas buenas
4. (tener) que adaptarme a otro ambiente si otra compañía me ofreciera un puesto
5. (adquirir) buena experiencia si cambiara de trabajo
6. mis padres (estar) orgullosos si una compañía importante me ofreciera un puesto

B. ¡Todo es posible! ¿Qué harías tú si te vieras en estas situaciones?

Modelo Si ganaras un millón de dólares en la lotería...
Lo invertiría, la mitad en la bolsa y la otra mitad en bienes raíces *(real estate).*

1. Si tuvieras que reducir tu presupuesto en un cincuenta por ciento...
2. Si el alquiler de tu apartamento aumentara en un cincuenta por ciento...
3. Si ganaras un millón de dólares en la lotería...
4. Si un pariente rico te ofreciera un viaje gratuito alrededor del mundo empezando la semana que viene...
5. Si tu novio(a) te abandonara por una persona rica...

C. ¡Decisiones! Al recibir una oferta de trabajo, con frecuencia nos vemos obligados a tomar decisiones. Dile a un(a) compañero(a) lo que dirías si te vieras en estas circunstancias y escucha lo que él (ella) diría.

Modelo Si me ofrecieran un trabajo en el extranjero, yo...
Si me ofrecieran un trabajo en el extranjero, yo lo aceptaría.

1. Si el salario fuera bueno pero la empresa pequeña, yo...
2. Si me dieran buenas posibilidades de ascenso pero un horario difícil, yo...
3. Si el puesto requiriera viajar mucho, yo...
4. Si el puesto estuviera en una ciudad muy grande, yo...
5. Si el puesto se encontrara en un pueblo pequeño, yo...
6. Si el ambiente en el trabajo no fuera ideal, yo...

D. Condiciones. ¿Bajo qué condiciones harías lo siguiente?

1. Dejaría mi puesto actual si...
2. Compraría un coche nuevo si...
3. Trabajaría menos si...
4. Viviría en otro país si...
5. Me mudaría a otra ciudad si...
6. Cambiaría mi estilo de vida si...
7. Sería más feliz si...
8. ¿...?

Y ahora, ¡a conversar!

A. ¡Ay! ¡La conciencia no me lo permite! Trabajando en grupos de tres o cuatro, decidan qué harían ustedes en estas situaciones. Comparen sus respuestas con las de los otros grupos.

1. ¿Qué harían tú y dos amigos si al dar a la cajera del supermercado un billete de $20,00 ella se equivocara y les diera cambio de $50,00?
2. ¿Qué harían ustedes si, caminando por la calle, vieran a un hombre grande y fuerte asaltar a una mujer?
3. ¿Qué harían si al recibir su estado de cuentas del banco vieran un error de $137,00 a su favor?
4. ¿Qué harían si hoy tuvieran que pagar el alquiler y tú y tus compañeros(as) de apartamento no tuvieran el dinero?
5. ¿Qué harías si sólo dos meses después de comprar un carro nuevo te despidieran del trabajo?

B. Si fuera así... ¿Qué pasaría si tú y tus compañeros(as) tuvieran que adaptarse a algunas situaciones totalmente diferentes? ¿Qué harían ustedes en estas tres situaciones?

1. si tuvieran que vivir un año en la selva
2. si fueran los únicos habitantes de una isla
3. si encontraran un tesoro

C. Sería diferente. Ahora inventen tres situaciones en las que se necesitaría hacer cambios radicales y pregunten a otros grupos lo que harían.

¡Luz! ¡Cámara! ¡Acción!

A. Organización de las Naciones Unidas. Trabajando en grupos de cuatro o cinco, imagínense que ustedes son miembros de un comité de profesionales de la Organización de las Naciones Unidas. La misión del comité es decidir qué harían si pudieran efectuar cualquier cambio para mejorar el mundo. Dramaticen la primera reunión de su comité.

B. Gobierno estudiantil. Trabajando en grupos de tres o cuatro, imagínense que ustedes son miembros del gobierno estudiantil de su universidad. El (La) presidente(a) de su universidad les ha pedido que le digan qué harían ustedes si la universidad tuviera que reducir su presupuesto en un quince por ciento. Dramaticen su primera reunión.

¿Te gusta leer?

Antes de leer
Estrategias para leer: Inferencia

A. Inferir. Inferir es sacar una consecuencia o una conclusión de una cosa o, dicho de otra manera, «leer entre líneas». Un buen lector hace inferencias constantemente al leer. Por ejemplo:

> *¿Ha visto usted alguna vez las imágenes de Hispanoamérica que proyecta la televisión estadounidense o las fotos de los países hispanos en los periódicos y revistas de este país?*

Al leer estas líneas, el lector podría inferir o llegar a la conclusión de que el autor va a hablar de imágenes o negativas o positivas de Hispanoamérica. En este punto, cualquiera inferencia sería posible. Continuemos.

> *Parece que las noticias siempre son malas y que el mundo sólo se interesa en los países hispanos cuando ocurre un desastre natural o político.*

Nuestra primera inferencia ya se aclara y nos lleva a concluir que el autor va a hablar de imágenes negativas.

Ahora, escribe una inferencia válida para cada comentario a continuación. Luego, en grupos de cuatro, comparen sus inferencias.

1. En los anuncios de las agencias de viaje sólo vemos playas tropicales pobladas de hermosos hoteles de lujo, donde la gente de dinero es atendida por gente de piel morena y sonrisas blancas.

   Inferencia: ____

   ____

2. ¡Mire usted a su alrededor! En los EE.UU. vive una población hispana mayor que la de Venezuela. La ciudad de Nueva York tiene más habitantes hispanohablantes que La Habana, Cuba.

   Inferencia: ____

   ____

3. En Perú, de cada tres habitantes, uno habla quechua o aymará. En Paraguay, casi el noventa por ciento de la población habla guaraní en combinación con el español.

   Inferencia: ____

   ____

B. Entre líneas. Decide si las inferencias que acabas de hacer son correctas o no. Después de leer «Mitos y realidades», vuelve a tus inferencias y cámbialas si es necesario.

Mitos y realidades

¿Ha visto usted alguna vez las imágenes de Hispanoamérica que proyecta la televisión estadounidense o las fotos de los países hispanos en los periódicos y revistas de este país? Parece que las noticias siempre son malas y que el mundo sólo se interesa en los países hispanos cuando ocurre un desastre natural o político. Por el contrario, en los anuncios de las agencias de viaje sólo vemos playas tropicales pobladas de hermosos hoteles de lujo, donde la gente de dinero (casi siempre anglos) es atendida por gente morena.

¿Sabe usted cuál es la verdadera Hispanoamérica? Para ver qué sabe de sus vecinos al sur, analicemos cinco percepciones del mundo hispano. Primero califique estas percepciones como verdaderas o falsas, y luego lea el análisis de cada una para ver cuánto sabe usted de sus vecinos.

V F 1. Los hispanos viven en España y al sur de la frontera con los Estados Unidos.

V F 2. El español es la lengua común de los países hispanos.

V F 3. Los hispanos son gente baja, de piel morena y pelo negro.

V F 4. En los países hispanos predomina lo antiguo y lo tradicional.

V F 5. Los países hispanos son pobres y subdesarrollados.

Percepción 1 *Los hispanos viven en España y al sur de la frontera con los Estados Unidos.*
Análisis 1 ¡Mire usted a su alrededor! En los EE.UU. vive una población hispana mayor que la de Venezuela. La ciudad de Nueva York tiene más habitantes hispanohablantes que La Habana, Cuba. ¡Los EE.UU. es el quinto país que tiene más hispanohablantes del mundo! Sus vecinos hispanos no están muy lejos. ¡Están al otro lado de la calle!

Percepción 2 *El español es la lengua común de los países hispanos.*
Análisis 2 No cabe duda que el español es la lengua de los países hispanos. Sin embargo, el número de personas que hablan un idioma indígena alcanza a los veinte millones o más, ¡y va creciendo! En México, por ejemplo, más de cinco millones de personas hablan una lengua indígena. En Perú, de cada tres habitantes, uno habla

quechua o aymará. En Paraguay, casi el noventa por ciento de la población habla guaraní en combinación con el español. En Bolivia y Guatemala, más de la mitad de la población habla lenguas indígenas como el aymará y el quiché.

Percepción 3 *Los hispanos son gente baja, de piel morena y pelo negro.*
Análisis 3 No todos los hispanos son morenos. En tres países —Argentina, Uruguay y Costa Rica— la población es casi exclusivamente blanca, en su mayoría de ascendencia europea. En algunos países, como Guatemala, Bolivia o Ecuador, predomina la población indígena, aunque sería difícil clasificarla como raza pura. En otros países, en particular en Cuba, Puerto Rico, la República Dominicana y por toda la costa del Caribe también hay mucha gente de descendencia africana y personas de sangre mixta llamados mulatos, una combinación de sangre negra y sangre europea. Pero en la mayor parte de Latinoamérica, como es el caso en México y Paraguay, la mayoría de la gente se podría clasificar como una mezcla de indio y europeo que dio como resultado el mestizaje. Los mestizos son los que dan la imagen popular a Hispanoamérica, pero en las grandes ciudades se distinguen también los descendientes de diversos grupos de inmigrantes, incluyendo a chinos, judíos, italianos, árabes, alemanes, ingleses, japoneses... en fin, gente de todo el mundo.

Percepción 4 *En los países hispanos predomina lo antiguo y lo tradicional.*
Análisis 4 Los hispanos representan una cultura de tradiciones muy antiguas, pero en la actualidad la población hispana es extraordinariamente joven. En casi todos los países hispanos, más de la mitad de los habitantes son menores de 25 años. En Honduras, Bolivia y Paraguay, por ejemplo, sólo un habitante de cada tres es mayor de 25 años. ¡En México, esto llega a tal extremo que un habitante de cada cuatro tiene menos de 10 años! Sin duda, ¡la juventud de Hispanoamérica es su futuro!

Percepción 5 *Los países hispanos son pobres y subdesarrollados.*
Análisis 5 Esta cuestión tiene muchas interpretaciones. Los problemas de Hispanoamérica son indiscutiblemente grandes, pero también es necesario señalar el tremendo potencial de esta cultura y lo que ya ha hecho. México es uno de los líderes del mundo en la extracción de la energía termal y tiene expertos internacionales en el cultivo de xerófilos *(drought-tolerant plants)*. Cuba posee una de las industrias ganaderas más avanzadas del mundo y Colombia sobresale en el desarrollo de las técnicas de cirugía óptica. España en la actualidad disfruta de sus propias marcas nacionales de computadoras y automóviles. En el mundo hispano sobran los recursos naturales y humanos, pero el tiempo y el dinero son escasos. Si los hispanos llegaran a responder a las crisis con lo mejor de su cultura, podrían enseñarnos soluciones a los problemas más grandes de nuestro mundo.

A ver si comprendiste

Con un(a) compañero(a), indica las inferencias que se pueden hacer de cada una de estas cinco percepciones, y luego anoten los hechos que contradicen esas inferencias.

Percepción	Inferencia	La verdad
1. Los hispanos viven en España y al sur de la frontera con los Estados Unidos.		
2. El español es la lengua común de los países hispanos.		
3. Los hispanos son gente baja, de piel morena y pelo negro.		
4. En los países hispanos predomina lo antiguo y lo tradicional.		
5. Los países hispanos son pobres y subdesarrollados.		

Viajemos por el ciberespacio a... ECUADOR

Expand your horizons! *Let's travel through cyberspace to* ***Ecuador*** where . . .

- you can visit one of the most interesting ecotravel Internet sites in the world.
- through the Internet, you can visit three scenically and culturally diverse regions of Ecuador: the coast, the Andes, and the Amazon basin.
- through the Internet, you can actually visit the many varied Galapagos Islands.
- you can also learn about the ongoing struggle of the indigenous people of Ecuador and its Afro-Ecuadorian population.

If you are a cyberspace browser, join us in **Viajemos por el ciberespacio a... Ecuador** by trying the following important addresses.

Universidades:
Escuela Politécnica Nacional
gopher://sis.poli.edu.ec/

Universidad Católica de Santiago de Guayaquil
http://mia.lac.net/ucsg/

Ministerio de Turismo de Ecuador
http://mia.lac.net/mintur/

Periódicos:
Diario Hoy
http://www.ecnet.ec/hoy/hoy.htm

El Comercio
http://www.elcomercio.com

El Universo
http://www.eluniverso.com/

Revista Vistazo
http://www.vistazo.com.ec

Because addresses are likely to change without notice, the following key words will guarantee that **Viajemos por el ciberespacio a... Ecuador** will get you to your desired destination.

Palabras clave

Ecuador	Indígenas Ecuador
Quito	Mujeres Ecuador
Fiestas de Quito	Otavalo
Galápagos	Puerto Lago
Guayaquil	Cabañas Cotococha

http://www.hrwcollege.com

Quehaceres domésticos

cambiar los pañales *change diapers*
cortar el césped *to cut the grass*
planchar *to iron*
sacar la basura *to take out the trash*

Economía

bolsa *stock market*
contrato *contract*
crédito *credit*
cuenta *account*
deuda *debt*
desempleo *unemployment*
ganar *to earn*
impuestos *taxes*
prestar *to lend*
presupuesto *budget*
salario *salary*
seguro *insurance*
sueldo *salary, pay*
tiempo completo *full time*

Conjunciones

a menos que *unless*
antes (de) que *before*
aunque *although*
con tal (de) que *provided (that)*
en caso (de) que *in case*
en cuanto *as soon as*
para que *so that*
sin que *unless, without*
tan pronto como *as soon as*

Verbos

adelantarse *to get ahead; to go forward*
adquirir (ie) *to acquire*
ahorrar *to save*
atender (ie) *to take care of, pay attention to*
aumentar *to augment, increase*
despedir (i, i) *to dismiss; to fire (from a job)*
engañar *to deceive, trick*
graduarse *to graduate*
hacer daño *to hurt, damage*
invertir (ie, i) *to invest*
jubilarse *to retire*
mantener (ie) *to maintain*
merecer *to deserve, be worthy of*
portarse bien *to behave*
sacrificarse *to sacrifice oneself*
tener confianza *to trust*
tomar decisiones *to make decisions*

Palabras útiles

ambiente *(m.)* *surroundings, ambience*
casamiento *marriage*
cónyuge *(m. / f.)* *spouse*
isla *island*
lotería *lottery*
malagradecido(a) *ungrateful, unappreciative*
nota *grade*
oferta *offer*
selva *jungle*
tesoro *treasure*
un mal rato *a bad time*

En preparación 15

15.1 Conditional of Regular and Irregular Verbs

Stating what you would do

A. The conditional is used to state conditions under which an action may be completed. In English, the conditional is expressed with *would: I would go if . . .* In Spanish, the conditional is formed by adding the endings **-ía, -ías, -ía, -íamos, -íais,** and **-ían** to the infinitive of most **-ar, -er,** and **-ir** verbs.

Estar		Ser		Ir	
estar**ía**	estar**íamos**	ser**ía**	ser**íamos**	ir**ía**	ir**íamos**
estar**ías**	estar**íais**	ser**ías**	ser**íais**	ir**ías**	ir**íais**
estar**ía**	estar**ían**	ser**ía**	ser**ían**	ir**ía**	ir**ían**
estar**ía**	estar**ían**	ser**ía**	ser**ían**	ir**ía**	ir**ían**

Yo **llevaría** a los heridos al hospital.	*I would take the injured to the hospital.*
Allí **recibirían** la atención médica necesaria.	*There they would receive the necessary medical attention.*

B. The conditional of the following verbs is formed by adding the conditional endings to irregular stems. Note that the irregular stems of these verbs are identical to those of the irregular future tense verbs.

decir: **dir-**
haber: **habr-**
hacer: **har-**
poder: **podr-**
poner: **pondr-**
querer: **querr-**
saber: **sabr-**
salir: **saldr-**
tener: **tendr-**
valer: **valdr-**
venir: **vendr-**

–ía
–ías
–ía
–íamos
–íais
–ían

Hacer

haría	haríamos
harías	haríais
haría	harían
haría	harían

Haría todo lo posible para conseguir el puesto. — *I would do everything possible to get the job.*

Mamá **podría** vivir conmigo. — *Mother could live with me.*

¡A practicar!

A. ¡Yo lo haría así! Tu mejor amiga piensa mudarse a un nuevo apartamento. ¿Qué le dices que harías tú si estuvieras en su lugar?

Modelo lavar las ventanas
Antes de mudarme, lavaría las ventanas.

1. comprar camas nuevas
2. cambiar las cortinas del comedor
3. pedir una nueva cocina
4. pintarlo de nuevo
5. no firmar un contrato anual
6. solicitar el cambio de teléfono de inmediato
7. pagar sólo un mes de garantía
8. ¿... ?

B. ¡Me encanta! Al esposo de tu amiga le gustó el apartamento. ¿Qué dicen que harían él y su esposa si decidieran mudarse allí?

Modelo tener que comprar un sofá nuevo
Tendríamos que comprar un sofá nuevo.

1. poner plantas por todos lados
2. tener más espacio para nuestros libros
3. poder tener una gatita aquí
4. salir a correr por el parque que está cerca
5. no querer mudarnos a otra ciudad
6. haber más tranquilidad para estudiar

C. ¡Nunca! Los padres de tu profesor ya son mayores de edad y ahora él está considerando si los llevaría a un hogar de ancianos (*nursing home*). ¿Qué dice él?

Yo jamás ______________ (llevar) a mis padres a un hogar de ancianos. Ellos ______________ (venir) a vivir con nosotros. Mi esposa dice que así, nuestros hijos ______________ (tener) la oportunidad de conocer bien a sus abuelos. Yo los ______________ (cuidar) como ellos me cuidaron a mí. Siempre ______________ (querer) estar con ellos y ______________ (hacer) todo lo posible para darles lo mejor. Ellos ______________ (poder) ayudarnos con los niños. También, con sus muchos años de experiencia, ellos ______________ (saber) aconsejarnos cuando lo necesitáramos.

PASO 2

15.2 Subjunctive in Adverb Clauses

Stating conditions

A. In Spanish, certain conjunctions are *always* followed by the subjunctive. Note that they are used to relate events that may or may not happen. Thus, a doubt is implied, requiring the subjunctive.

a menos que	*unless*	en caso (de) que	*in case*
antes (de) que	*before*	para que	*so that*
con tal (de) que	*provided (that)*	sin que	*without, unless*

Yo sacaré la basura **antes de que regrese** el jefe. — *I'll take out the trash before the boss returns.*

Yo limpiaré el baño **con tal que** tú **cambies** los pañales del bebé. — *I'll clean the bathroom provided you change the baby's diapers.*

B. Certain adverbial conjunctions may be followed by either the subjunctive or the indicative. The subjunctive follows these expressions when describing a future or hypothetical action or something that has not yet occurred. The indicative is used to describe habitual or known facts.

aunque	*although*	en cuanto	*as soon as*
cuando	*when*	hasta que	*until*
después (de) que	*after*	tan pronto como	*as soon as*

Habitual	**Future action**
Siempre lo hace cuando **llega.**	Lo hará cuando **llegue.**
Factual	**Hypothetical**
Lo aceptaré aunque **tendré** que trabajar en otro estado.	Lo aceptaré aunque **tenga** que trabajar en otro estado.

C. When the focus is on an event rather than on a participant, a preposition and an infinitive are used rather than a conjunction and the subjunctive.

Llámame **antes de venir.**	*Call me before coming.*
Lo haré **sin decirle.**	*I'll do it without telling him.*

¡A practicar!

A. Rutina semanal. Antonio y Raúl son compañeros de apartamento. Ellos distribuyen las tareas al principio de cada semana para mantenerlo limpio. ¿Cómo lo hacen esta semana?

1. Yo sacaré la basura (con tal que/sin que) tú laves los platos.
2. Tendremos que limpiar todo el apartamento (con tal que/en caso de que) vengan tus padres.
3. Podemos salir a comer esta noche (a menos que/para que) no tengamos que lavar platos.
4. Prepara el café (antes de que/con tal que) me duerma.
5. No podré lavar las ventanas (para que/sin que) tú me ayudes.
6. Yo puedo preparar la cena esta noche (a menos que/antes de que) tú quieras hacerlo.

B. Vacaciones. Ahora Antonio y Raúl están planeando salir de vacaciones. Antonio, como siempre, es muy organizado y desea dejar todo en orden. ¿Qué le dice a Raúl?

ANTONIO Yo me bañaré antes de que tú ______________ (limpiar) el baño.

RAÚL Bien. Luego yo limpiaré el baño, con tal que tú ______________ (sacar) la basura.

ANTONIO Yo puedo lavar las ventanas a menos que tú ______________ (querer) hacerlo.

RAÚL No. Yo haré el café para que tú ______________ (no dormirte).

ANTONIO Sí, y luego tomaremos un descanso para que nosotros ______________ (poder) cenar.

C. ¡Mi primera oferta! Una estudiante de ingeniería está esperando su primera oferta de trabajo. ¿En qué está pensando?

1. Llamaré a mis padres tan pronto como / recibir una oferta
2. Siempre llamo a mis padres cuando / recibir buenas noticias
3. Aceptaré aunque / tener que mudarme a otro estado
4. Mamá va a ponerse triste en cuanto / saber que voy a mudarme
5. Pero ella siempre se alegra cuando / saber que estoy contenta
6. No me mudaré hasta que / encontrar un buen apartamento allá
7. Me sentiré mejor tan pronto como / encontrar uno
8. Siempre me pongo nerviosa cuando / empezar un trabajo nuevo
9. Cuando ya / estar bien instalada, voy a hacer una fiesta muy grande

15.3 Past Subjunctive: Conditional Sentences with *si* Clauses

Hypothesizing

The past subjunctive of *all* verbs is formed by removing the **-ron** ending from the **ustedes** form of the preterite and adding the past subjunctive verb endings: **-ra, -ras, -ra, -ramos, -rais, -ran.*** Thus, any irregularities in the **ustedes** form of the preterite will be reflected in all forms of the past subjunctive. Note that the **nosotros** form requires a written accent.

Comprar		Tener		Ser	
compra~~ron~~		tuvie~~ron~~		fue~~ron~~	
compra**ra**	comprá**ramos**	tuvie**ra**	tuvié**ramos**	fue**ra**	fué**ramos**
compra**ras**	compra**rais**	tuvie**ras**	tuvie**rais**	fue**ras**	fue**rais**
compra**ra**	compra**ran**	tuvie**ra**	tuvie**ran**	fue**ra**	fue**ran**
compra**ra**	compra**ran**	tuvie**ra**	tuvie**ran**	fue**ra**	fue**ran**

A. The past subjunctive has the same uses as the present subjunctive, except that it generally applies to past events or actions.

Insistieron en que **fuéramos.**	*They insisted that we go.*
Era imposible que lo **terminaran** a tiempo.	*It was impossible for them to finish it on time.*

B. In Spanish, as in English, conditional sentences express hypothetical conditions usually with an *if*-clause: *I would go if I had the money.* Since the actions are hypothetical and one does not know if they will actually occur, the past subjunctive is used in the *if*-clause.

Iría a Perú si **tuviera** el dinero.	*I would go to Peru if I had the money.*
Si **fuera** necesario, pediría un préstamo.	*If it were necessary, I would ask for a loan.*

C. Sentences with *if*-clauses in the present use either the present indicative or the future tense in the main clause and the present indicative in the *if*-clause. The present subjunctive is *never* used in *if*-clauses.

Si me **invitas,** voy contigo.	*If you invite me, I'll go with you.*
Pero no iré si **llueve.**	*But I won't go if it rains.*

*An alternate form of the past subjunctive uses the verb endings -se, -ses, -se, -semos, -seis, -sen. This form is used primarily in Spain and in literary writing, and is not practiced in this text.

¡A practicar!

A. ¡Ay, si tuviera más dinero...! Como bien se sabe, los estudiantes con frecuencia tienen problemas económicos y siempre sueñan con tener más dinero. ¿Qué harían estos estudiantes si tuvieran más dinero?

Modelo Marta / regresar / México
Si tuviera más dinero, Marta regresaría a México.

1. Sonia / ir / Europa / estudiar
2. Mario y Estela / mudarse / apartamento / más grande
3. Emilio / comprar / nuevo / auto
4. Anita y yo / hacer / viaje / Sudamérica
5. María y Alejandro / poder / pagar / todo / deudas
6. Salvador / poner / dinero / banco

B. La realidad es que... Como no todos somos ricos, con frecuencia hay que encontrar otras soluciones a los problemas. ¿Qué soluciones consideran estas personas?

Modelo Marta podría regresar a México si... (padres prestarle el dinero)
Marta podría regresar a México si sus padres le prestaran el dinero.

1. Sonia podría ir a Europa a estudiar si... (la universidad hacerle un préstamo)
2. Mario y Estela podrían mudarse a otro apartamento si… (los dos conseguir trabajo de noche)
3. Emilio podría comprar un nuevo auto si... (darle un aumento en el trabajo)
4. Anita y yo podríamos hacer un viaje a Sudamérica si… (encontrar una excursión más barata)
5. María y Alejandro podrían pagar todas sus deudas si... (sacar el dinero de su cuenta de ahorros)
6. Salvador podría poner más dinero en el banco si... (mudarse a un apartamento más barato)

Y AHORA, ¡A CONVERSAR! Noticiero cultural

Para empezar
Noticiero cultural

Lee el número que corresponde a la respuesta que seleccionaste.

1. Rick greeted the president of the university using the **tú** form, which was totally inappropriate. The **usted** form should always be used with persons with titles such as president, professor, doctor, reverend, etc. This is the correct answer.
2. Most certainly, the president of the university is a very important person and probably does not have time to stop and talk to Rick and Julio. However, the president would not be discourteous. He would always have time to respond **«Muy bien, gracias.»** This is not the correct answer. Read the dialogue once more.
3. It is true that Rick is a first-year student and does not speak Spanish fluently. But the president of the university is a teacher himself and probably has a lot of patience with first-year students. Try another response.

Capítulo 1, Paso 1
Y ahora, ¡a conversar!

C. ¿Son los mismos? Alicia, Carmen, José y Daniel son estudiantes de la clase de español de tu compañero de cuarto. Tú tienes unos amigos que se llaman Alicia, Carmen, José y Daniel. La descripción de tus amigos aparece *(appears)* aquí. La descripción de los amigos de tu compañero aparece en la página 32. ¿Son los mismos? *To decide if they are the same, ask your partner questions. Do not look at each other's descriptions until you have finished this activity.*

Modelo **¿Es Alicia de Venezuela?**

JOSÉ Es de Ecuador. No es muy serio. Es chistoso y muy simpático. Es muy activo y sociable.

DANIEL Es de Quito. Es serio y estudioso. Es muy activo y atlético. También es algo tímido.

ALICIA Es una amiga venezolana. Es de Caracas. Es inteligente, cómica y muy popular. También es muy atlética.

CARMEN Es muy seria. Es inteligente, tímida y muy estudiosa. Es de Venezuela, de la capital. Es sociable pero algo conservadora.

Capítulo 1, Paso 2

Noticiero cultural

Lee el número que corresponde a la respuesta que seleccionaste.

1. Although English is widely spoken in the Spanish-speaking world, the majority of the people still do not speak English. It is not possible to spend the summer in three Spanish-speaking countries and speak only English. Try another response.
2. It is true that Castilian is the Spanish spoken in Castille, a region of Spain. However, Castilian is more like the Spanish spoken in Latin America than British English is like American English. A Spaniard would not have any difficulty understanding the Spanish spoken in Latin America and vice versa. Look for another response.
3. Some people believe that the Spanish spoken in Spain is very different from the Spanish spoken in the Americas. The truth of the matter is that all Spanish-speaking countries, including Spain, speak the same Spanish. True, as you travel from country to country, or even from region to region within a country, there are variations in vocabulary, intonation, and even pronunciation; however, none of these variations keep persons from different countries from understanding each other. Spanish speakers from all over the Spanish-speaking world have less difficulty understanding each other than English speakers from the U.S. have understanding British English.

Capítulo 1, Paso 3

Y ahora, ¡a conversar!

D. ¿Son diferentes? Estos dibujos y los dibujos de la página 47 son muy similares pero hay cinco diferencias. Descríbele este dibujo a tu compañero(a) y él (ella) va a describirte el otro dibujo hasta encontrar las diferencias. No se permite ver el dibujo de tu compañero(a) hasta terminar esta actividad.

Capítulo 2, Paso 2
Noticiero cultural

Lee el número que corresponde a la respuesta que seleccionaste.

1. Teresa is from Spain; she speaks and understands Spanish perfectly. Look for another possibility.
2. This is not so. Spaniards understand Puerto Ricans perfectly. Try another response.
3. There are some vocabulary differences in certain regions of the Spanish-speaking world, which is the case here. This is the correct response. Can you guess the meaning of the words Teresa didn't understand?

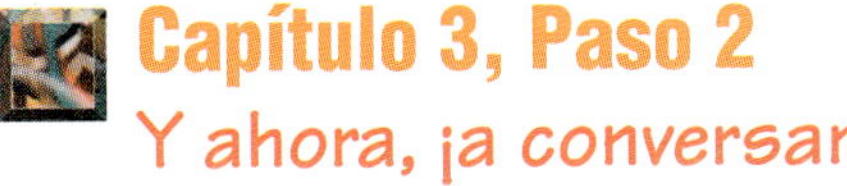

Capítulo 3, Paso 2
Y ahora, ¡a conversar!

C. ¿Qué están haciendo? ¿Cuántas diferencias hay entre este dibujo y el de tu compañero(a), en la página 115? Recuerda que no se permite mirar el dibujo de tu compañero(a) hasta terminar esta actividad.

Modelo **¿Cuántas personas están bailando?**

Capítulo 3, Paso 3
Y ahora, ¡a conversar!

B. ¡Qué cambiados están! Éstos son Daniel y Gloria después de estudiar un año en la Universidad de Salamanca. Tu compañero(a) tiene un dibujo, en la página 124, de Daniel y Gloria antes de ir a estudiar en España. Describan a las personas en sus dibujos para saber cómo han cambiado. No se permite mirar el dibujo de tu compañero(a) hasta terminar esta actividad.

Capítulo 4, Paso 1
Y ahora, ¡a conversar!

C. ¡Robo! *(There was a theft in the* Palacio de Bellas Artes *in Mexico City and you were the only witness.)* Usa este dibujo *(drawing)* para describir a los ladrones *(thieves)*. Tu compañero(a), un(a) artista que trabaja para la policía, va a dibujar a las personas que tú describas.

Capítulo 4, Paso 2
Y ahora, ¡a conversar!

C. En el escaparate. Tú estás de compras en la ciudad de México y quieres comprar todas las prendas de esta lista. Desafortunadamente, muchas prendas no tienen etiqueta *(price tag)*. Pídele a tu compañero(a) los precios que quieres saber y dale los precios que él (ella) necesita. El escaparate *(store window)* de tu compañero(a) está en la página 156. No se permite mirar el escaparate del compañero(a) hasta terminar esta actividad.

Tú quieres comprar:

1. pijamas para tu hermana
2. un traje para ti
3. botas para tu papá
4. pantalones para tu hermano
5. un vestido para tu mamá

Capítulo 6, Paso 1
Y ahora, ¡a conversar!

D. ¿Cuáles son las diferencias? Tu debes usar este dibujo y tu compañero(a) el dibujo en la página 220. Ambos son similares, pero no son idénticos. Describan sus dibujos para descubrir las diferencias. No mires el dibujo de tu compañero(a) hasta descubrir todas las diferencias.

Capítulo 10, Paso 2

Y ahora, ¡a conversar!

B. Mecánicos. ¿Es tu compañero(a) buen(a) mecánico(a)? Escucha las definiciones que tu compañero(a) te va a leer e identifica cada parte que define. Dale el nombre de la parte para que la escriba al lado de la definición. No se permite leer las definiciones, sólo escucharlas.

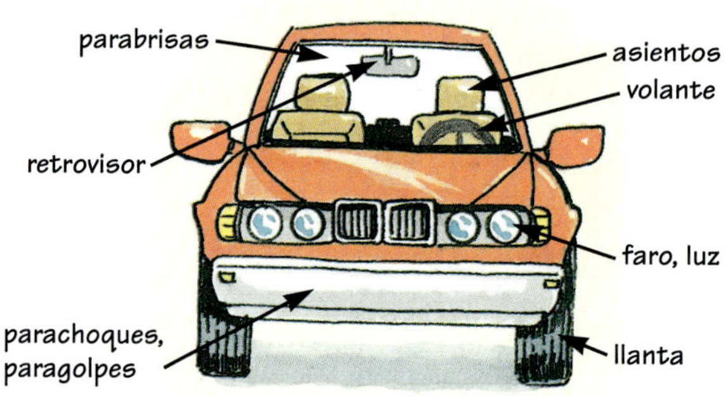

Capítulo 11, Paso 2

Y ahora, ¡a conversar!

C. La Cenicienta. Los siguientes dibujos narran parte del famoso cuento de hadas *(fairytale) La Cenicienta.* Narra el cuento completo con la ayuda de tu compañero(a) que tiene, en la página 405, los dibujos que faltan.

Vocabulario útil

la madrastra	*stepmother*	la hermanastra	*stepsister*
el príncipe	*prince*	los ratoncitos	*little mice*
la chimenea	*fireplace*	el hada madrina	*fairy godmother*
la calabaza	*pumpkin*	la carroza	*carriage*
la zapatilla	*slipper*	el cristal	*crystal*
la escalera	*stairway*	el paje	*valet*
probar (ue)	*to try on*	de rodillas	*kneeling*

2. Un día su madrasta...

4. La pobre muchacha...

6. La Cenicienta...

8. El Príncipe...

Capítulo 11, Paso 2
Costumbres

Lee la respuesta con el mismo número que la que tú seleccionaste.

1. Aunque en todos los países hispanos, al igual que en el resto del mundo, la gente joven usa palabras «nuevas» o «diferentes» en su vocabulario diario normal, en Costa Rica tanto los jóvenes como los adultos y los niños usan el «-tico». Esta respuesta no es la mejor.
2. Es español de Costa Rica es muy similar al español del resto del mundo hispanohablante. Hay variantes, pero nunca son tan drásticas como para impedir la comunicación. Busca otra respuesta.
3. El dialecto costarricense cambia la terminación de los diminutivos por «-tico» en vez de «-ito». Por eso Rosalía en vez de decir *poquito* dice *poquitico* y *chiquitico* en vez de *chiquito*. Esta es la respuesta correcta.

Capítulo 12, Paso 1
Y ahora, ¡a conversar!

A. ¿Pingüinos? ¿En Lima? Enrique y Olga tuvieron estupendas experiencias en su viaje a Perú, pero sin duda, la más interesante fue la de Enrique un día que paseaba por la ciudad. Para saber lo que le pasó, estudia estos dibujos mientras que tu compañero(a) estudia los que se encuentran en la página 432. Escucha a tu compañero(a) mientras él (ella) relata la primera parte del incidente. Luego cuéntale el final.

5. De repente vimos al mismo policía que...

6. El policía me preguntó ¿por qué...?

7. Llevé al pingüino zoológico como ud. sugirió y...

8. Ahora llevo al pingüino a casa porque...

Capítulo 12, Paso 1
Y ahora, ¡a conversar!

C. Viaje a Machu Picchu. Tú y un(a) compañero(a) están viajando por Sudamérica, visitando y explorando diferentes lugares. Ahora están en las famosas cataratas del Iguazú y quieren viajar por Uruguay, Argentina, Chile y Bolivia para llegar al famoso Machu Picchu. Piensan hacer ocho escalas *(stopovers)* en su viaje. ¿Quién va a llegar primero? Para avanzar una escala, tienes que contestar la pregunta de tu compañero(a) correctamente. Tus preguntas están aquí; las de tu compañero(a) están en la página 433.

1. ¿Cuál es la capital de Paraguay?
2. ¿Cuál es la capital de Perú?
3. Nombra el país que es un estado libre asociado.
4. Nombra dos de los vecinos de Perú.
5. ¿De qué país es Diego Rivera?
6. ¿Quién escribió *Cien años de soledad*?
7. ¿Cuántos países de habla española hay en Sudamérica?
8. ¿Cómo se llama la moneda de Paraguay?
9. ¿Cuál es el país más grande de Sudamérica?
10. ¿Cuáles son las dos capitales de Bolivia?
11. ¿En qué país comen *porotos* y *ají*?
12. Nombra cinco países de la América Central y sus capitales.

Appendix B

Accentuation

In Spanish as in English, all words of two or more syllables have one syllable that is stressed more forcibly than the others. The following rules govern where a word is stressed and when words require written accents.

A. Words that end in a vowel (**a, e, i, o, u**) or the consonants **n** or **s** are stressed on the next-to-the-last syllable.

tardes capi**ta**les **gran**de es**tu**dia **no**ches **co**men

B. Words that end in a consonant other than **n** or **s** are stressed on the last syllable.

bus**car** ac**triz** espa**ñol** liber**tad** ani**mal** come**dor**

C. Words that do not follow the two preceding rules require a written accent to indicate where the stress is placed.

ca**fé** sim**pá**tico fran**cés** na**ción** Jo**sé** **Pé**rez

D. Diphthongs, the combination of a weak vowel (**i, u**) and a strong vowel (**e, o, a**) or two weak vowels next to each other, form a single syllable. A written accent is required to separate diphthongs into two syllables. Note that the written accent is placed on the stressed syllable.

seis	**cuo**ta	inte**rior**	**ai**re	**au**to
re**ír**	conti**nú**o	**rí**o	ma**íz**	ba**úl**

Regular Verbs

Infinitive	hablar *to speak*	aprender *to learn*	vivir *to live*
Present Participle	hablando *speaking*	aprendiendo *learning*	viviendo *living*
Past Participle	hablado *spoken*	aprendido *learned*	vivido *lived*

Simple Tenses

Present Indicative *I speak, am speaking, do speak*	hablo hablas habla	aprendo aprendes aprende	vivo vives vive
	hablamos habláis hablan	aprendemos aprendéis aprenden	vivimos vivís viven
Imperfect Indicative *I was speaking, used to speak, spoke*	hablaba hablabas hablaba	aprendía aprendías aprendía	vivía vivías vivía
	hablábamos hablabais hablaban	aprendíamos aprendíais aprendían	vivíamos vivíais vivían
Preterite *I spoke, did speak*	hablé hablaste habló	aprendí aprendiste aprendió	viví viviste vivió
	hablamos hablasteis hablaron	aprendimos aprendisteis aprendieron	vivimos vivisteis vivieron
Future *I will speak, shall speak*	hablaré hablarás hablará	aprenderé aprenderás aprenderá	viviré vivirás vivirá
	hablaremos hablaréis hablarán	aprenderemos aprenderéis aprenderán	viviremos viviréis vivirán
Conditional *I would speak*	hablaría hablarías hablaría	aprendería aprenderías aprendería	viviría vivirías viviría
	hablaríamos hablaríais hablarían	aprenderíamos aprenderíais aprenderían	viviríamos viviríais vivirían

Present Subjunctive *(that) I speak*	hable hables hable	aprenda aprendas aprenda	viva vivas viva
	hablemos habléis hablen	aprendamos aprendáis aprendan	vivamos viváis vivan
Past Subjunctive *(that) I speak,* *might speak*	hablara hablaras hablara	aprendiera aprendieras aprendiera	viviera vivieras viviera
	habláramos hablarais hablaran	aprendiéramos aprendierais aprendieran	viviéramos vivierais vivieran
Commands *informal* *Speak* *formal*	habla (no hables)	aprende (no aprendas)	vive (no vivas)
	hable hablen	aprenda aprendan	viva vivan

Compound Tenses

Present Perfect Indicative *I have spoken*	he has ha	hemos habéis han	hablado	aprendido	vivido
Past Perfect Indicative *I had spoken*	había habías había	habíamos habíais habían	hablado	aprendido	vivido
Present Progressive *I am speaking*	estoy estás está	estamos estáis están	hablando	aprendiendo	viviendo
Past Progressive *I was speaking*	estaba estabas estaba	estábamos estabais estaban	hablando	aprendiendo	viviendo

Stem-changing Verbs

-ar, -er Verbs	1. e → ie		2. o → ue*	
	pensar	perder	contar	volver
Present Indicative	pienso	pierdo	cuento	vuelvo
	piensas	pierdes	cuentas	vuelves
	piensa	pierde	cuenta	vuelve
	pensamos	perdemos	contamos	volvemos
	pensáis	perdéis	contáis	volvéis
	piensan	pierden	cuentan	vuelven
Present Subjunctive	piense	pierda	cuente	vuelva
	pienses	pierdas	cuentes	vuelvas
	piense	pierda	cuente	vuelva
	pensemos	perdamos	contemos	volvamos
	penséis	perdáis	contéis	volváis
	piensen	pierdan	cuenten	vuelvan

-ir Verbs	3. e → ie, i	4. e → i, i	5. o → ue, u
	sentir	pedir	dormir
Present Indicative	siento	pido	duermo
	sientes	pides	duermes
	siente	pide	duerme
	sentimos	pedimos	dormimos
	sentís	pedís	dormís
	sienten	piden	duermen
Present Subjunctive	sienta	pida	duerma
	sientas	pidas	duermas
	sienta	pida	duerma
	sintamos	pidamos	durmamos
	sintáis	pidáis	durmáis
	sientan	pidan	duerman
Preterite	sentí	pedí	dormí
	sentiste	pediste	dormiste
	sintió	pidió	durmió
	sentimos	pedimos	dormimos
	sentisteis	pedisteis	dormisteis
	sintieron	pidieron	durmieron

*Note: The verb **jugar** changes **u → ue.**

Past Subjunctive	sintiera sintieras sintiera	pidiera pidieras pidiera	durmiera durmieras durmiera
	sintiéramos sintierais sintieran	pidiéramos pidierais pidieran	durmiéramos durmierais durmieran
Present Participle	sintiendo	pidiendo	durmiendo

Irregular Verbs

Infinitive	Participles	Present Indicative	Imperfect	Preterite
1. andar *to walk*	andando andado	ando andas anda	andaba andabas andaba	anduve anduviste anduvo
		andamos andáis andan	andábamos andabais andaban	anduvimos anduvisteis anduvieron
2. buscar *to look for*	buscando buscado	busco buscas busca	buscaba buscabas buscaba	busqué buscaste buscó
c → qu before **e**		buscamos buscáis buscan	buscábamos buscabais buscaban	buscamos buscasteis buscaron
3. caer *to fall*	cayendo caído	caigo caes cae	caía caías caía	caí caíste cayó
		caemos caéis caen	caíamos caíais caían	caímos caísteis cayeron
4. conducir *to drive*	conduciendo conducido	conduzco conduces conduce	conducía conducías conducía	conduje condujiste condujo
c → zc before **a, o**		conducimos conducís conducen	conducíamos conducíais conducían	condujimos condujisteis condujeron
5. conocer *to know*	conociendo conocido	conozco conoces conoce	conocía conocías conocía	conocí conociste conoció
c → zc before **a, o**		conocemos conocéis conocen	conocíamos conocíais conocían	conocimos conocisteis conocieron

Future	Conditional	Present Subjunctive	Past Subjunctive	Informal/Formal Commands
andaré	andaría	ande	anduviera	—
andarás	andarías	andes	anduvieras	anda (no andes)
andará	andaría	ande	anduviera	ande
andaremos	andaríamos	andemos	anduviéramos	—
andaréis	andaríais	andéis	anduvierais	—
andarán	andarían	anden	anduvieran	anden
buscaré	buscaría	busque	buscara	—
buscarás	buscarías	busques	buscaras	busca (no busques)
buscará	buscaría	busque	buscara	busque
buscaremos	buscaríamos	busquemos	buscáramos	—
buscaréis	buscaríais	busquéis	buscarais	—
buscarán	buscarían	busquen	buscaran	busquen
caeré	caería	caiga	cayera	—
caerás	caerías	caigas	cayeras	cae (no caigas)
caerá	caería	caiga	cayera	caiga
caeremos	caeríamos	caigamos	cayéramos	—
caeréis	caeríais	caigáis	cayerais	—
caerán	caerían	caigan	cayeran	caigan
conduciré	conduciría	conduzca	condujera	—
conducirás	conducirías	conduzcas	condujeras	conduce (no conduzcas)
conducirá	conduciría	conduzca	condujera	conduzca
conduciremos	conduciríamos	conduzcamos	condujéramos	—
conduciréis	conduciríais	conduzcáis	condujerais	—
conducirán	conducirían	conduzcan	condujeran	conduzcan
conoceré	conocería	conozca	conociera	—
conocerás	conocerías	conozcas	conocieras	conoce (no conozcas)
conocerá	conocería	conozca	conociera	conozca
conoceremos	conoceríamos	conozcamos	conociéramos	—
conoceréis	conoceríais	conozcáis	conocierais	—
conocerán	conocerían	conozcan	conocieran	conozcan

Infinitive	Participles	Present Indicative	Imperfect	Preterite
6. construir *to build* **i → y,** **y** inserted before **a, e, o**	construyendo construido	construyo construyes construye construimos construís construyen	construía construías construía construíamos construíais construían	construí construiste construyó construimos construisteis construyeron
7. continuar *to continue*	continuando continuado	continúo continúas continúa continuamos continuáis continúan	continuaba continuabas continuaba continuábamos continuabais continuaban	continué continuaste continuó continuamos continuasteis continuaron
8. creer *to believe*	creyendo creído	creo crees cree creemos creéis creen	creía creías creía creíamos creíais creían	creí creíste creyó creímos creísteis creyeron
9. dar *to give*	dando dado	doy das da damos dais dan	daba dabas daba dábamos dabais daban	di diste dio dimos disteis dieron
10. decir *to say, tell*	diciendo dicho	digo dices dice decimos decís dicen	decía decías decía decíamos decíais decían	dije dijiste dijo dijimos dijisteis dijeron
11. empezar *to begin* **z → c** before **e**	empezando empezado	empiezo empiezas empieza empezamos empezáis empiezan	empezaba empezabas empezaba empezábamos empezabais empezaban	empecé empezaste empezó empezamos empezasteis empezaron

Future	Present Conditional	Past Subjunctive	Informal/Formal Subjunctive	Commands
construiré	construiría	construya	construyera	—
construirás	construirías	construyas	construyeras	construye (no construyas)
construirá	construiría	construya	construyera	construya
construiremos	construiríamos	construyamos	construyéramos,	—
construiréis	construiríais	construyáis	construyerais	—
construirán	construirían	construyan	construyeran	construyan
continuaré	continuaría	continúe	continuara	—
continuarás	continuarías	continúes	continuaras	continúa (no continúes)
continuará	continuaría	continúe	continuara	continúe
continuaremos	continuaríamos	continuemos	continuáramos	—
continuaréis	continuarías	continuéis	continuarais	—
continuarán	continuarían	continúen	continuaran	continúen
creeré	creería	crea	creyera	—
creerás	creerías	creas	creyeras	cree (no creas)
creerá	creería	crea	creyera	crea
creeremos	creeríamos	creamos	creyéramos	—
creeréis	creeríais	creáis	creyerais	—
creerán	creerían	crean	creyeran	crean
daré	daría	dé	diera	—
darás	darías	des	dieras	da (no des)
dará	daría	dé	diera	dé
daremos	daríamos	demos	diéramos	—
daréis	daríais	deis	dierais	—
darán	darían	den	dieran	den
diré	diría	diga	dijera	—
dirás	dirías	digas	dijeras	di (no digas)
dirá	diría	diga	dijera	diga
diremos	diríamos	digamos	dijéramos	—
diréis	diríais	digáis	dijerais	—
dirán	dirían	digan	dijeran	digan
empezaré	empezaría	empiece	empezara	—
empezarás	empezarías	empieces	empezaras	empieza (no empieces)
empezará	empezaría	empiece	empezara	empiece
empezaremos	empezaríamos	empecemos	empezáramos	—
empezaréis	empezaríais	empecéis	empezarais	—
empezarán	empezarían	empiecen	empezaran	empiecen

Infinitive		Present Participles	Indicative	Imperfect	Preterite
12.	esquiar	esquiando	esquío	esquiaba	esquié
	to ski	esquiado	esquías	esquiabas	esquiaste
			esquía	esquiaba	esquió
			esquiamos	esquiábamos	esquiamos
			esquiáis	esquiabais	esquiasteis
			esquían	esquiaban	esquiaron
13.	estar	estando	estoy	estaba	estuve
	to be	estado	estás	estabas	estuviste
			está	estaba	estuvo
			estamos	estábamos	estuvimos
			estáis	estabais	estuvisteis
			están	estaban	estuvieron
14.	haber	habiendo	he	había	hube
	to have	habido	has	habías	hubiste
			ha (hay)	había	hubo
			hemos	habíamos	hubimos
			habéis	habíais	hubisteis
			han	habían	hubieron
15.	hacer	haciendo	hago	hacía	hice
	to make, do	hecho	haces	hacías	hiciste
			hace	hacía	hizo
			hacemos	hacíamos	hicimos
			hacéis	hacíais	hicisteis
			hacen	hacían	hicieron
16.	ir	yendo	voy	iba	fui
	to go	ido	vas	ibas	fuiste
			va	iba	fue
			vamos	íbamos	fuimos
			vais	ibais	fuisteis
			van	iban	fueron
17.	leer	leyendo	leo	leía	leí
	to read	leído	lees	leías	leíste
			lee	leía	leyó
	i → y;		leemos	leíamos	leímos
	stressed **i → í**		leéis	leíais	leísteis
			leen	leían	leyeron

Future	Conditional	Present Subjunctive	Past Subjunctive	Informal/Formal Commands
esquiaré	esquiaría	esquíe	esquiara	—
esquiarás	esquiarías	esquíes	esquiaras	esquía (no esquíes)
esquiará	esquiaría	esquíe	esquiara	esquíe
esquiaremos	esquiaríamos	esquiemos	esquiáramos	—
esquiaréis	esquiaríais	esquiéis	esquiarais	—
esquiarán	esquiarían	esquíen	esquiaran	esquíen
estaré	estaría	esté	estuviera	—
estarás	estarías	estés	estuvieras	está (no estés)
estará	estaría	esté	estuviera	esté
estaremos	estaríamos	estemos	estuviéramos	—
estaréis	estaríais	estéis	estuvierais	—
estarán	estarían	estén	estuvieran	estén
habré	habría	haya	hubiera	—
habrás	habrías	hayas	hubieras	—
habrá	habría	haya	hubiera	—
habremos	habríamos	hayamos	hubiéramos	—
habréis	habríais	hayáis	hubierais	—
habrán	habrían	hayan	hubieran	—
haré	haría	haga	hiciera	—
harás	harías	hagas	hicieras	haz (no hagas)
hará	haría	haga	hiciera	haga
haremos	haríamos	hagamos	hiciéramos	—
haréis	haríais	hagáis	hicierais	—
harán	harían	hagan	hicieran	hagan
iré	iría	vaya	fuera	—
irás	irías	vayas	fueras	ve (no vayas)
irá	iría	vaya	fuera	vaya
iremos	iríamos	vayamos	fuéramos	—
iréis	iríais	vayáis	fuerais	—
irán	irían	vayan	fueran	vayan
leeré	leería	lea	leyera	—
leerás	leerías	leas	leyeras	lee (no leas)
leerá	leería	lea	leyera	lea
leeremos	leeríamos	leamos	leyéramos	—
leeréis	leeríais	leáis	leyerais	—
leerán	leerían	lean	leyeran	lean

Infinitive		Participles	Present Indicative	Imperfect	Preterite
18.	oír	oyendo	oigo	oía	oí
	to hear	oído	oyes	oías	oíste
			oye	oía	oyó
	i → y		oímos	oíamos	oímos
			oís	oíais	oísteis
			oyen	oían	oyeron
19.	pagar	pagando	pago	pagaba	pagué
	to pay	pagado	pagas	pagabas	pagaste
			paga	pagaba	pagó
	g → gu		pagamos	pagábamos	pagamos
	before **e**		pagáis	pagabais	pagasteis
			pagan	pagaban	pagaron
20.	poder	pudiendo	puedo	podía	pude
	can, to	podido	puedes	podías	pudiste
	be able		puede	podía	pudo
			podemos	podíamos	pudimos
			podéis	podíais	pudisteis
			pueden	podían	pudieron
21.	poner	poniendo	pongo	ponía	puse
	to place,	puesto	pones	ponías	pusiste
	put		pone	ponía	puso
			ponemos	poníamos	pusimos
			ponéis	poníais	pusisteis
			ponen	ponían	pusieron
22.	querer	queriendo	quiero	quería	quise
	to like	querido	quieres	querías	quisiste
			quiere	quería	quiso
			queremos	queríamos	quisimos
			queréis	queríais	quisisteis
			quieren	querían	quisieron
23.	reír	riendo	río	reía	reí
	to laugh	reído	ríes	reías	reíste
			ríe	reía	rió
			reímos	reíamos	reímos
			reís	reíais	reísteis
			ríen	reían	rieron

Future	Conditional	Present Subjunctive	Past Subjunctive	Informal/Formal Commands
oiré	oiría	oiga	oyera	—
oirás	oirías	oigas	oyeras	oye (no oigas)
oirá	oiría	oiga	oyera	oiga
oiremos	oiríamos	oigamos	oyéramos	—
oiréis	oiríais	oigáis	oyerais	—
oirán	oirían	oigan	oyeran	oigan
pagaré	pagaría	pague	pagara	—
pagarás	pagarías	pagues	pagaras	paga (no pagues)
pagará	pagaría	pague	pagara	pague
pagaremos	pagaríamos	paguemos	pagáramos	—
pagaréis	pagaríais	paguéis	pagarais	—
pagarán	pagarían	paguen	pagaran	paguen
podré	podría	pueda	pudiera	—
podrás	podrías	puedas	pudieras	—
podrá	podría	pueda	pudiera	—
podremos	podríamos	podamos	pudiéramos	—
podréis	podríais	podáis	pudierais	—
podrán	podrían	puedan	pudieran	—
pondré	pondría	ponga	pusiera	—
pondrás	pondrías	pongas	pusieras	pon (no pongas)
pondrá	pondría	ponga	pusiera	ponga
pondremos	pondríamos	pongamos	pusiéramos	—
pondréis	pondríais	pongáis	pusierais	—
pondrán	pondrían	pongan	pusieran	pongan
querré	querría	quiera	quisiera	—
querrás	querrías	quieras	quisieras	quiere (no quieras)
querrá	querría	quiera	quisiera	quiera
querremos	querríamos	queramos	quisiéramos	—
querréis	querríais	queráis	quisierais	—
querrán	querrían	quieran	quisieran	quieran
reiré	reiría	ría	riera	—
reirás	reirías	rías	rieras	ríe (no rías)
reirá	reiría	ría	riera	ría
reiremos	reiríamos	riamos	riéramos	—
reiréis	reiríais	riáis	rierais	—
reirán	reirían	rían	rieran	rían

Infinitive		Participles	Present Indicative	Imperfect	Preterite
24.	saber *to know*	sabiendo sabido	sé sabes sabe	sabía sabías sabía	supe supiste supo
			sabemos sabéis saben	sabíamos sabíais sabían	supimos supisteis supieron
25.	salir *to leave*	saliendo salido	salgo sales sale	salía salías salía	salí saliste salió
			salimos salís salen	salíamos salíais salían	salimos salisteis salieron
26.	seguir *to follow*	siguiendo seguido	sigo sigues sigue	seguía seguías seguía	seguí seguiste siguió
	gu → **g** before **a, o**		seguimos seguís siguen	seguíamos seguíais seguían	seguimos seguisteis siguieron
27.	ser *to be*	siendo sido	soy eres es	era eras era	fui fuiste fue
			somos sois son	éramos erais eran	fuimos fuisteis fueron
28.	tener *to have*	teniendo tenido	tengo tienes tiene	tenía tenías tenía	tuve tuviste tuvo
			tenemos tenéis tienen	teníamos teníais tenían	tuvimos tuvisteis tuvieron
29.	traer *to bring*	trayendo traído	traigo traes trae	traía traías traía	traje trajiste trajo
			traemos traéis traen	traíamos traíais traían	trajimos trajisteis trajeron

Future	Conditional	Present Subjunctive	Past Subjunctive	Informal/Formal Commands
sabré	sabría	sepa	supiera	—
sabrás	sabrías	sepas	supieras	sabe (no sepas)
sabrá	sabría	sepa	supiera	sepa
sabremos	sabríamos	sepamos	supiéramos	—
sabréis	sabríais	sepáis	supierais	—
sabrán	sabrían	sepan	supieran	sepan
saldré	saldría	salga	saliera	—
saldrás	saldrías	salgas	salieras	sal (no salgas)
saldrá	saldría	salga	saliera	salga
saldremos	saldríamos	salgamos	saliéramos	—
saldréis	saldríais	salgáis	salierais	—
saldrán	saldrían	salgan	salieran	salgan
seguiré	seguiría	siga	siguiera	—
seguirás	seguirías	sigas	siguieras	sigue (no sigas)
seguirá	seguiría	siga	siguiera	siga
seguiremos	seguiríamos	sigamos	siguiéramos	—
seguiréis	seguiríais	sigáis	siguierais	—
seguirán	seguirían	sigan	siguieran	sigan
seré	sería	sea	fuera	—
serás	serías	seas	fueras	sé (no seas)
será	sería	sea	fuera	sea
seremos	seríamos	seamos	fuéramos	—
seréis	seríais	seáis	fuerais	—
serán	serían	sean	fueran	sean
tendré	tendría	tenga	tuviera	—
tendrás	tendrías	tengas	tuvieras	ten (no tengas)
tendrá	tendría	tenga	tuviera	tenga
tendremos	tendríamos	tengamos	tuviéramos	—
tendréis	tendríais	tengáis	tuvierais	—
tendrán	tendrían	tengan	tuvieran	tengan
traeré	traería	traiga	trajera	—
traerás	traerías	traigas	trajeras	trae (no traigas)
traerá	traería	traiga	trajera	traiga
traeremos	traeríamos	traigamos	trajéramos	—
traeréis	traeríais	traigáis	trajerais	—
traerán	traerían	traigan	trajeran	traigan

Infinitive	Participles	Present Indicative	Imperfect	Preterite
30. valer	valiendo	valgo	valía	valí
to be worth	valido	vales	valías	valiste
		vale	valía	valió
		valemos	valíamos	valimos
		valéis	valíais	valisteis
		valen	valían	valieron
31. venir	viniendo	vengo	venía	vine
to come	venido	vienes	venías	viniste
		viene	venía	vino
		venimos	veníamos	vinimos
		venís	veníais	vinisteis
		vienen	venían	vinieron
32. ver	viendo	veo	veía	vi
to see	visto	ves	veías	viste
		ve	veía	vio
		vemos	veíamos	vimos
		veis	veíais	visteis
		ven	veían	vieron
33. volver	volviendo	vuelvo	volvía	volví
to return	vuelto	vuelves	volvías	volviste
		vuelve	volvía	volvió
		volvemos	volvíamos	volvimos
		volvéis	volvíais	volvisteis
		vuelven	volvían	volvieron

Future	Conditional	Present Subjunctive	Past Subjunctive	Informal/Formal Commands
valdré	valdría	valga	valiera	—
valdrás	valdrías	valgas	valieras	val (no valgas)
valdrá	valdría	valga	valiera	valga
valdremos	valdríamos	valgamos	valiéramos	—
valdréis	valdríais	valgáis	valierais	—
valdrán	valdrían	valgan	valieran	valgan
vendré	vendría	venga	viniera	—
vendrás	vendrías	vengas	vinieras	ven (no vengas)
vendrá	vendría	venga	viniera	venga
vendremos	vendríamos	vengamos	viniéramos	—
vendréis	vendríais	vengáis	vinierais	—
vendrán	vendrían	vengan	vinieran	vengan
veré	vería	vea	viera	—
verás	verías	veas	vieras	ve (no veas)
verá	vería	vea	viera	vea
veremos	veríamos	veamos	viéramos	—
veréis	veríais	veáis	vierais	—
verán	verían	vean	vieran	vean
volveré	volvería	vuelva	volviera	—
volverás	volverías	vuelvas	volvieras	vuelve (no vuelvas)
volverá	volvería	vuelva	volviera	vuelva
volveremos	volveríamos	volvamos	volviéramos	—
volveréis	volveríais	volváis	volvierais	—
volverán	volverían	vuelvan	volvieran	vuelvan

Supplemental Structures

The following structures are not actively taught in ***¡Dímelo tú!,*** but are presented here for reference.

Perfect Tenses

In **Capítulo 11** you learned that the present perfect tense is formed by combining the present indicative of the verb **haber** with the past participle. Similarly, the past perfect, future perfect, and conditional perfect tenses are formed by combining the imperfect, future, and conditional, respectively, of **haber** with the past participle.

Past perfect	Future perfect	Conditional perfect
había **habías** **había** **habíamos** **habíais** **habían** } + past participle	**habré** **habrás** **habrá** **habremos** **habréis** **habrán** } + past participle	**habría** **habrías** **habría** **habríamos** **habríais** **habrían** } + past participle

In general, the use of these perfect tenses parallels their use in English.

Dijo que **había vivido** allí seis años.	*He said he had lived there six years.*
Para el año 1998, **habremos terminado** nuestro estudios aquí.	*By the year 1998, we will have finished our studies here.*
Yo lo **habría hecho** por ti.	*I would have done it for you.*

The present perfect subjunctive and past perfect subjunctive are likewise formed by combining the present subjunctive and past subjunctive of **haber** with the past participle.

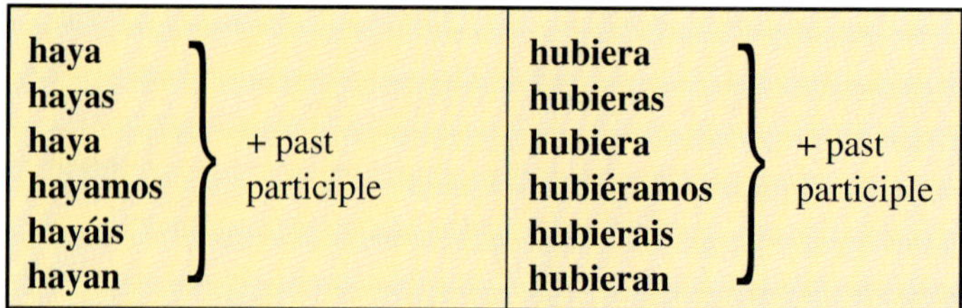

Present perfect subjunctive	Past perfect subjunctive
haya **hayas** **haya** **hayamos** **hayáis** **hayan** } + past participle	**hubiera** **hubieras** **hubiera** **hubiéramos** **hubierais** **hubieran** } + past participle

These tenses are used whenever the independent clause in a sentence requires the subjunctive and the verb in the dependent clause represents an action completed prior to the time indicated by the independent clause verb. If the tense of the verb in the independent clause is present or future, the present perfect subjunctive is used; if the tense is past or conditional, the past perfect subjunctive is used.

Dudo que lo **hayan leído.** — *I doubt that they have read it.*
Si **hubieras llamado,** no tendríamos este problema ahora. — *If you had called, we would not have this problem now.*

Past Progressive Tense

In **Capítulo 3** you learned that the present progressive tense is formed with the present indicative of **estar** and a present participle. The past progressive tense is formed with the imperfect of **estar** and a present participle.

Past progressive tense

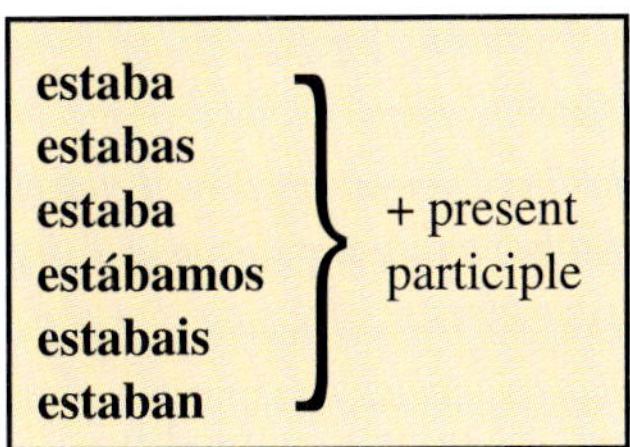

estaba
estabas
estaba
estábamos
estabais
estaban
} + present participle

The past progressive tense is used to express or describe an action that was in progress at a particular moment in the past.

Estábamos comiendo cuando llamaste. — *We were eating when you called.*
¿Quién **estaba hablando** por teléfono? — *Who was talking on the phone?*

Another past progressive tense can also be formed with the preterite of **estar** and the present participle. However, its use is of much lower frequency in Spanish.

Probability in the Past and in the Future

Spanish uses both the future and conditional tenses to express probability or conjecture about present or past events or states of being.

¿Qué hora es? — *What time is it?*
No sé; **serán** las 8:00. — *I don't know; it's probably 8:00.*
¿Qué **estarían** haciendo? — *I wonder what they were doing?*
Estarían divirtiéndose. — *They were probably having a good time.*

Note that the words *probably* and *I wonder* are not expressed in Spanish, as the verb tenses convey this idea.

Stressed Possessive Adjectives and Pronouns

In **Capítulo 2** you learned to express possession using **de** or the possessive adjectives **[mi(s), tu(s), su(s), nuestro(a, os, as), vuestro(a, os, as)].** Possession may also be expressed using the stressed possessive adjectives equivalent to the English *of mine, of yours, of ours, of theirs.*

Stressed possessive adjectives and pronouns

mío	**mía**	*my, (of) mine*	**nuestro**	**nuestra**	*our, (of) ours*
míos	**mías**		**nuestros**	**nuestras**	
tuyo	**tuya**	*your, (of) yours*	**vuestro**	**vuestra**	*your, (of) yours*
tuyos	**tuyas**		**vuestros**	**vuestras**	
suyo	**suya**	*its, his, (of) his,*	**suyo**	**suya**	*their, (of) theirs*
suyos	**suyas**	*hers, (of) hers, your, (of) yours*	**suyos**	**suyas**	*your, (of) yours*

A. As adjectives, the stressed possessives must agree in number and gender with the thing possessed.

Una amiga **mía** viene a visitar hoy.	*A friend of mine is coming to visit today.*
¿Qué hay en las maletas **suyas**, señor?	*What do you have in your suitcases, sir?*
El coche **nuestro** nunca funciona.	*Our car never works.*

Note that stressed possessive adjectives *always* follow the noun they modify. Also note that the noun must be preceded by an article.

B. Stressed possessive adjectives can be used as possessive pronouns by eliminating the noun.

¿Dónde está **la suya**, señor?	*Where is yours, sir?*
El nuestro nunca funciona.	*Ours never works.*

Note that both the article and possessive adjective must agree in number and gender with the noun that has been eliminated.

C. A stressed possessive pronoun may be used without the article after the verb **ser**.

Esta maleta no **es mía**, señor.	*This suitcase is not mine, sir.*
¿Es suya, señora?	*Is it yours, ma'am?*

Prepositional Pronouns

Pronouns used as objects of a preposition are identical to the subject pronouns with the exception of **mí** and **ti**.

Prepositional pronouns

mí	*me*	**nosotros(as)**	*us*
ti	*you* (fam.)	**vosotros(as)**	*you* (fam.)
usted	*you*	**ustedes**	*you*
él	*him*	**ellos**	*them*
ella	*her*	**ellas**	*them*

Esta carta no es **para ella**, es **para ti.**	*This letter is not for her, it's for you.*
Habló **después de mí.**	*She spoke after me.*
¿Es posible que terminen **antes de nosotros**?	*Is it possible they will finish before us?*

Note that **mí** has a written accent to distinguish it from the possessive adjective **mi.**

A. The prepositional pronouns **mí** and **ti** combine with the preposition **con** to form **conmigo** (*with me*) and **contigo** (*with you*).

Si tú estudias **conmigo** esta noche, yo iré **contigo** al médico.	*If you study with me tonight, I'll go with you to the doctor.*

B. The subject pronouns **yo** and **tú** follow the prepositions **entre, excepto,** and **según** instead of **mí** and **ti.**

Según tú, yo no sé nada.	*According to you, I don't know anything.*
Entre tú y yo, tienes razón.	*Between you and me, you are right.*

Demonstrative Pronouns

Demonstrative adjectives may be used as pronouns. In written Spanish, an accent mark always distinguishes a demonstrative pronoun from its demonstrative adjective counterpart.

Esta novela es excelente; **ésa** es aburridísima.	*This novel is excellent; that one is extremely boring.*
Ese señor es el jefe, y **aquéllos** son sus empleados.	*That gentleman is the boss, and those are his employees.*

The neuter demonstratives **esto, eso**, and **aquello** are used to refer to a concept, an idea, a situation, a statement, or an unknown object. The neuters do not require written accents.

¡**Esto** es imposible!	*This is impossible!*
¿Qué es **eso**?	*What is that?*

Past Participles Used as Adjectives

The past participle may be used as an adjective, and like all adjectives in Spanish, it must agree in number and gender with the noun it modifies.

Los coches **hechos** en Hungría y en Corea son más baratos.	*Cars made in Hungary and Korea are cheaper.*
Sí, pero yo prefiero uno **hecho** y **comprado** en los EE.UU.	*Yes, but I prefer one made and bought in the U.S.*

Frequently the past participle is used as an adjective with the verb **estar.**

Mira, tus lentes **están rotos.**	*Look, your glasses are broken.*
El despertador **estaba puesto.**	*The alarm was turned on.*

Spanish-English Vocabulary

This vocabulary includes all the words and expressions listed as active vocabulary in ***¡Dímelo tú!***. The number following the English meaning refers to the chapter and **paso** in which the word or phrase was first used actively. (The first number is the chapter; the number after the decimal is the **paso.**)

All words are alphabetized according to the 1994 changes made by the **Real Academia: ch** and **ll** are no longer considered separate letters of the alphabet. Stem-changing verbs appear with the change in parentheses after the infinitive: **(ie), (ue), (i), (ie, i), (ue, u),** or **(i, i)**.

Most cognates, conjugated verb forms, and proper nouns used as passive vocabulary in the text are not included in this glossary.

The following abbreviations are used.

adj.	adjective	*n.*	noun
adv.	adverb	*pl.*	plural
art.	article	*pp.*	past participle
conj.	conjunction	*poss.*	possessive
dir. obj.	direct object	*prep.*	preposition
f.	feminine	*pron.*	pronoun
fam.	familiar	*refl.*	reflexive
form.	formal	*rel.*	relative
indir. obj.	indirect object	*s.*	singular
interj.	interjection	*subj.*	subject
m.	masculine		

A

a to **5.1**; **a la(s)** + *time* at (time) o'clock **2.3**; **a la derecha** to the right **5.1**; **a la izquierda** to the left **5.1**; **a la parrilla** grilled **8.2**; **a menos que** unless **15.1**; **a otro perro con ese hueso** go tell it to the Marines **9.3**; **a partir de** starting in; **a pesar de** in spite of **12.3**; **a pie** on foot, walking **9.3**; **a veces** sometimes, at times **1.3**
abandonar to abandon **11.3**
abarcar to embrace, cover, include
aborto *(m.)* abortion
abogado(a) lawyer **11.3**
abrigo *(m.)* coat **13.2**
abril April **2.3**
abrir to open **2.1**
absurdo(a) absurd **14.2**
abuelo(a) grandfather / grandmother **5.1**
abuelos grandparents **5.1**
aburrido(a) boring **1.2**
acá here, over here
académico(a) academic
acampar to camp, go camping
accidente *(m.)* accident **10.1**
acción *(f.)* action
aceite *(m.)* oil
aceptar to accept **6.1**
acera *(f.)* sidewalk
acerca de about, concerning
acompañar to accompany **6.1**
aconsejar to advise **13.1**
acordarse (ue) to remember, recall
acordonar to cordon off
acostarse (ue) to go to bed **9.2**
actitud *(f.)* attitude
actividad *(f.)* activity
activo(a) active **1.1**
actor *(m.)* actor **9.3**
actriz *(f.)* actress **9.3**
actuación *(f.)* behavior, performance
actualmente currently
actuar to act; to behave
acudir to go to the aid of
acusar to accuse **10.3**
adelantarse to get ahead, go forward **15.2**
además besides **12.3**
adentro in, inside **13.2**
adiós good-bye **PE**
adivinanza *(f.)* riddle
adivinar to guess
administrador(a) administrator **2.1**
admirar to admire **6.3**
adolescencia *(f.)* adolescence
¿adónde? (to) where? **3.1**
adorar to adore **6.3**
adquirir (ie) to acquire **15.3**
aerolínea *(f.)* airline **7.2**
aeropuerto *(m.)* airport
afeitarse to shave **9.2**
afición *(f.)* liking, fondness
aficionado(a) fan *(of sporting events)* **6.1**
afuera out, outside **13.2**; abroad
agosto August **2.3**

agresivo(a) aggressive **14.1**
agua *(f.)* water **4.3**
aguantar to endure, stand **13.3**
ahogarse to drown
ahora now **5.1**
ahorrar to save **15.3**
aire *(m.)* air
aislado(a) isolated
al (a + el) to the + *(m. noun)* **1.3**; **al ajillo** sauteed in garlic **8.2**; **al alcance** within reach; **al fondo** in the back **8.1**; **al lado** beside **5.1**; **al rato** in a short while **9.2**
alargado(a) elongated
alcalde *(m.)*, **alcaldesa** *(f.)* mayor
alcanzar to reach; to attain
alcoba *(f.)* bedroom **3.1**
alcohólico(a) alcoholic
alejado(a) distant, remote
alemán, alemana German **4.1**
alérgico(a) allergic
alfombra *(f.)* carpet **5.2**
algo something **6.1**
algodón *(m.)* cotton **4.2**
alguien someone, anyone **10.2**
alguna vez sometime **10.2**
algúno, alguna some, any **10.2**
almohadilla *(f.)* mouse pad **2.1**
almorzar (ue) to have lunch **4.1**
almuerzo *(m.)* lunch **8.1**
alojarse to lodge, room; to stay overnight **12.2**
alpinismo *(m.)* mountain climbing **14.3**
alquiler *(m.)* to rent **2.2**
alrededor around
alternativa *(f.)* alternative
altiplano *(m.)* highlands
alto(a) tall **3.2**
allí there
amable nice, amiable
amar to love **6.3**
amarillo(a) yellow **4.1**
ambicioso(a) ambitious
ambiente *(m.)* surroundings, ambience **15.2**
ambos both
ambulancia *(f.)* ambulance **10.1**
amenaza *(f.)* threat
amigo(a) friend **PE**
amistad *(f.)* friendship
amo(a) owner, proprietor
amoroso(a) loving, affectionate
ampliamente widely
amueblado(a) furnished **5.1**
añadir to add; to increase
análisis *(m.)* analysis
anaranjado(a) orange **4.1**
anatomía *(f.)* anatomy
andino(a) Andean
angosto(a) narrow
animal de peluche *(m.)* stuffed animal (toy) **11.1**
animar to encourage
año *(m.)* year **4.1**
anoche last night **7.1**
anotar to jot down
anterior previous
antes de *(prep.)* before **11.1**; **antes (de) que** *(conj.)* before **15.1**
anticipar to anticipate
anticuado(a) very old, antiquated
antiguo(a) antiquated, old-fashioned
antipático(a) disagreeable **3.3**
antropólogo(a) anthropologist
anuncio *(m.)* announcement
apagar to turn off
aparecer to appear
aparentar (ie) to pretend, feign
apartamento *(m.)* apartment **2.1**
aparte apart
apellido *(m.)* last name **5.1**
apetito *(m.)* appetite
apio *(m.)* celery **8.1**
apoyar to aid; to support **14.1**
apreciar to appreciate
aprender to learn **2.2**
apretar (ie) to tighten; to squeeze
aprobar (ue) to pass *(a class)*
apropiado(a) appropriate
aproximadamente approximately **9.1**
¡apúrese! hurry up! **4.3**
aquí here **3.2**
árbitro *(m.)* umpire, referee **14.1**
árbol *(m.)* tree
arco *(m.)* goal **14.1**
arco iris *(m.)* rainbow
arena *(f.)* sand
arqueólogo(a) archaeologist
arquero *(m.)* goalie, goalkeeper **14.1**
arquitecto(a) architect
arquitectura *(f.)* architecture
arrasar to level, smooth
arreglar to fix **11.2**
arrestar to arrest **7.1**
arrogante arrogant
arroz *(m.)* rice **8.3**
arte *(m.)* art **1.2**
artesanía *(f.)* handicrafts, crafts
artista *(m. / f.)* artist **3.1**
asado(a) roasted **8.2**
asaltar to assault **10.3**
asegurado(a) insured
asegurar to insure; to assure
asesinar to assassinate **7.1**
asiento *(m.)* seat **10.2**
asistir to attend **4.3**
asociación *(f.)* association
asociar to associate
aspiradora *(f.)* vacuum cleaner
aspirina *(f.)* aspirin **4.3**
atacar to attack **7.2**
ataque cardíaco *(m.)* heart attack **10.1**
atender (ie) to take care of; to pay attention to **15.2**
atleta *(m. / f.)* athlete **7.1**
atlético(a) athletic **1.1**
atraer attract
audífono *(m.)* headphones **4.1**
aumentar to augment, increase **15.3**
aún even, even though
aunque although **15.1**
autobús *(m.)* bus **2.1**
automóvil *(m.)* automobile **10.2**
autor(a) author
auxilio *(m.)* assistance, aid; **¡auxilio!** help! **10.1**
avanzar to advance
ave *(f.)* bird
avenida *(f.)* avenue **5.3**
avión *(m.)* airplane **7.1**
aviso *(m.)* advertisement, classified ad **7.2**
¡ay! oh! **5.2**
ayer yesterday **7.1**
ayuda *(f.)* help, assistance **10.1**
ayudar to help **2.2**

azúcar *(m.)* sugar **8.2**
azul blue **4.1**

B

bailar to dance **1.2**
baile *(m.)* dance **6.1**
bajar to go down, lower **13.2**; **bajar de peso** to lose weight
bajarse to get off, get down **9.3**
bajo(a) short **3.3**
ballenero *(m.)* whaler
baloncesto *(m.)* basketball **7.1**
banco *(m.)* bank, bench
banda *(f.)* band
bañarse to bathe **9.2**
baño *(m.)* bathroom **2.2**
barato(a) inexpensive **2.2**
barco *(m.)* boat **9.3**
barranca *(f.)* ravine, gorge
barrio *(m.)* neighborhood
bastante enough **5.3**; **bastante bien** well enough **PE**
bate *(m.)* bat **14.1**
bateador(a) batter *(baseball)* **14.1**
batear to bat
batería *(f.)* battery **10.2**
baúl *(m.)* trunk, chest
bautizo *(m.)* baptism
beber to drink **4.3**
bebida *(f.)* drink **6.2**
beisbolista *(m./f.)* baseball player
belleza *(f.)* beauty
bendición *(f.)* blessing
beso *(m.)* kiss
betabel *(m.)* beet
biblioteca *(f.)* library **1.3**
bicicleta *(f.)* bicycle
bien fine, well; **bien parecido(a)** good-looking; **Bien, gracias** Fine, thank you. **PE**
bienvenido(a) welcome
bigote *(m.)* mustache **10.3**
billete *(m.)* ticket, bill
biología *(f.)* biology
bistec *(m.)* steak **8.1**
blanco(a) white **4.1**
blusa *(f.)* blouse **4.1**
boca *(f.)* mouth **13.2**
bocadillo *(m.)* snack **8.1**
boleto *(m.)* ticket **6.1**
bolígrafo *(m.)* ballpoint pen **1.1**
bolsa *(f.)* stock market **15.3**
bolsillo *(m.)* pocket
bolso *(m.)* purse, pocketbook **12.1**
bomba *(f.)* bomb **7.1**
bombero(a) firefighter **10.3**
borracho(a) drunk **3.1**
borrador *(m.)* eraser
bosque *(m.)* forest
botas *(f.)* boots **4.2**
bote *(m.)* boat
botella *(f.)* bottle **4.3**
botín *(m.)* booty, spoils
botón *(m.)* button
boxeo *(m.)* boxing **14.1**
brazo *(m.)* arm **10.1**
buceo *(m.)* underwater swimming
bueno(a) good **1.2**; **buena suerte** *(f.)* good luck **9.3**; **Buenas noches** Good evening **PE**; **Buenas tardes** Good afternoon **PE**; **Buenos días** Good morning **PE**
bufanda *(f.)* scarf **9.1**
bus *(m.)* bus
buscar to look for **1.3**
butaca *(f.)* armchair, easy chair
buque *(m.)* boat

C

caballo *(m.)* horse **13.1**
cabeza *(f.)* head **10.3**
cabezal *(m.)* pillow, headrest
cacique *(m.)* Indian chief
cada *(adj. m.* or *f.)* every, each **2.3**
caerse to fall down **10.1**
café *(m.)* coffee **1.3**; café **2.1**
cafetería *(f.)* cafeteria
caído *(pp.)* fallen
caja *(f.)* cashier's office **7.3**
cajero(a) cashier **2.1**
calamares *(m.)* squid **8.1**
calculadora *(f.)* calculator **1.1**
calendario *(m.)* calendar
calidad *(f.)* quality
cálido(a) warm, hot
caliente hot
calificado(a) qualified
¡cállate! be quiet! **13.2**
calle *(f.)* street **5.1**; **calle principal** *(f.)* main street **9.3**
callejón *(m.)* alley **10.1**
calma *(f.)* calm
calmarse to calm (oneself) down
caloría *(f.)* calorie
cama *(f.)* bed **5.1**
cámara *(f.)* camera **4.1**; **cámara de diputados** House of Parliament
camarero(a) waiter / waitress **8.3**
camarón *(m.)* shrimp **8.2**
cambiar to change, alter; **cambiar los pañales** to change diapers **15.1**; **cambiar una llanta** to change a tire **10.2**
cambio *(m.)* change
caminar to walk **2.3**
camión *(m.)* bus
camisa *(f.)* shirt **4.1**
camiseta *(f.)* tee shirt **4.1**
campeón *(m.)*, **campeona** *(f.)* champion **14.3**
campeonato *(m.)* championship **7.1**; **campeonato mundial** *(m.)* world championship **7.1**
campesino(a) peasant, farmer
campo *(m.)* camp; campus; country
canal *(m.)* canal; channel
cancelar to cancel
cáncer *(m.)* cancer **13.1**
cancha *(f.)* court (for sports) **14.1**
canción *(f.)* song **3.1**
cangrejo *(m.)* crab **8.3**
cantante *(m./f.)* singer **9.3**
cantar to sing **3.1**
cantidad *(f.)* quantity
capacidad *(f.)* capacity
capitán *(m.)*, **capitana** *(f.)* captain **14.3**
caprichoso(a) capricious, whimsical
capturar to capture **7.1**
cara *(f.)* face
característica *(f.)* characteristic
¡caramba! goodness! good heavens! **11.3**
cargar to load; to carry **12.2**
Caribe *(m.)* Caribbean

carne *(f.)* meat **8.1**; **carne de puerco** *(f.)* pork **8.1**; **carne de res** *(f.)* beef **8.1**
carnicería *(f.)* butcher shop **9.3**
caro(a) expensive **2.2**
carpeta *(f.)* folder
carrera *(f.)* race
carretera *(f.)* highway **10.1**
carro *(m.)* car **5.2**
carta *(f.)* letter **2.2**; menu
cartera *(f.)* purse, wallet **10.1**
casa *(f.)* house **2.2**
casamiento *(m.)* marriage **15.1**
casarse to marry, get married
cascada *(f.)* cascade, waterfall
casco *(m.)* helmet
casete *(m.)* cassette **3.1**
casi almost **4.2**
castellano *(m.)* Castilian, Spanish language
catarata *(f.)* waterfall
categoría *(f.)* category
cedido(a) ceded, handed over
celebración *(f.)* celebration
celebrar to celebrate **7.3**
cementerio *(m.)* cemetery
cena *(f.)* dinner **1.3**
cenar to eat dinner **6.1**
centígrados *(m.)* centigrade **9.1**
centro *(m.)* center, downtown **5.1**; **centro comercial** *(m.)* shopping center, mall **5.3**
cepillo de dientes *(m.)* toothbrush **12.1**
cerca de near **5.1**
cercano(a) near, close
cero zero
cerrar (ie) to close **4.1**
cerveza *(f.)* beer **3.1**
cesto *(m.)* basket **14.1**
chaleco *(m.)* vest
champiñón *(m.)* mushroom
champú *(m.)* shampoo **12.1**
chaqueta *(f.)* jacket **4.1**
cheque *(m.)* check
chico(a) boy / girl **2.3**
chimenea *(f.)* chimney **5.1**
chistoso(a) witty, funny
chocar to collide **10.1**
chocolate *(m.)* chocolate
chófer *(m. / f.)* chauffeur, driver **2.1**
choque eléctrico *(m.)* electric shock
chuletas *(f.)* chops
chupar to suck *(a lemon, candy)*
ciclismo *(m.)* cycling **14.1**
cielo *(m.)* sky **9.1**
ciencias políticas *(f.)* political science **1.2**
cierto(a) true, certain
címbalo *(m.)* cymbal **11.1**
cinco five
cine *(m.)* movie theater **3.2**
círculo *(m.)* circle
cita *(f.)* date **6.1**
ciudad *(f.)* city
ciudadano(a) citizen **11.1**
civilización *(f.)* civilization
clarinete *(m.)* clarinet **11.1**
¡claro que sí! of course! **6.1**
clase *(f.)* class **PE**
clásico(a) classical **6.1**
clausurar to close, bring to a close
clave *(f.)* code, key
cliente *(m. / f.)* client
clima *(m.)* climate **9.1**
clínica *(f.)* clinic **10.1**
cobre *(m.)* copper
coche *(m.)* car **3.2**
cocina *(f.)* kitchen **3.1**
cocinar to cook
cocinero(a) cook **2.1**
coctel *(m.)* cocktail
codo *(m.)* elbow **13.2**
col *(f.)* cabbage **8.1**
colección *(f.)* collection
colgar (ue) to hang, hang up
colocar to place
columna *(f.)* column
collar *(m.)* necklace
comedor *(m.)* dining room **5.1**
comentario *(m.)* commentary
comenzar (ie) to begin **7.2**
comer to eat **1.2**
cometer un error to commit an error **21.3**
cómico(a) comical, funny **1.2**
comida *(f.)* food **2.1**
comité *(m.)* committee
¿cómo? how?, what? **3.1**; **¿cómo estás?** how are you? **PE**; **¡cómo no!** why not! **6.1**; **¿cómo se llama usted? / ¿cómo te llamas?** what's your name? **PE**
cómodo(a) comfortable **5.2**
compañero(a) partner; **compañero(a) de cuarto** roommate **PE**
comparar to compare
compartir to share **2.2**
competencia *(f.)* competition **14.2**
competición *(f.)* competition **12.3**
competir (i, i) to compete
completar to complete
comportarse to behave
comprar to buy **1.3**
computadora *(f.)* computer **2.1**
común common
comunidad *(f.)* community
con with **1.3**; **con calma** calmly; **con frecuencia** frequently **5.1**; **con precisión** precisely **10.1**; **¡con razón!** no wonder! **4.2**; **con relación a** in relation to; **con tal (de) que** provided (that) **15.1**
concentrarse to concentrate **14.1**
conciencia *(f.)* conscience
concierto *(m.)* concert **6.2**
conclusión *(f.)* conclusion
concurso *(m.)* contest
condición *(f.)* condition **5.2**
conducir to drive **6.1**
conexión *(f.)* connection
confesar (ie) to confess
confianza *(f.)* confidence
conflicto *(m.)* conflict
confundir to confuse
congelado(a) frozen **9.1**
conjunto *(m.)* ensemble
conmigo with me
conocer to know **3.3**
conquista *(f.)* conquest
conquistar to conquer
consecuencia *(f.)* consequence
conseguir (i, i) to get, obtain **6.2**
consejero(a) advisor
consejo *(m.)* advice **13.1**
conserje *(m.)* janitor
conservador(a) conservative **1.1**
conservar to conserve

considerar to consider
constitución *(f.)* constitution
contagioso(a) contagious
contaminación *(f.)* contamination, pollution
contaminado(a) contaminated
contar (ue) to count; to tell **8.3**
contenido *(m.)* content
contento(a) happy **3.1**
contestar to answer **9.3**
contigo with you
contiguo(a) adjacent
continente *(m.)* continent
continuamente continuously **9.1**
contrario(a) opposite, adverse **14.1**
contraste *(m.)* contrast
contratar to contract
contrato *(m.)* contract **15.2**
controlar to control **2.2**
controvertido(a) controversial
convencer to convince
convencido(a) convinced
convento *(m.)* convent
conversación *(f.)* conversation **PE**
conversar to converse
cónyuge *(m. / f.)* spouse **15.1**
coordinador(a) coordinator
copa *(f.)* goblet; **copa de vino** glass of wine **8.2**
copia *(f.)* copy
corazón *(m.)* heart **6.3**
corbata *(f.)* necktie **4.2**
cordillera *(f.)* mountain range
correcto(a) correct, proper
corregir (i, i) to correct
correr to run **2.1**
corrida *(f.)* bullfight
corriente *(f.)* electrical current **12.1**; *(adj.)* common, current, up-to-date
cortar to cut; **cortar el césped** to mow the lawn **15.1**
cortarse to cut oneself **9.2**
corte *(f.)* court
corto(a) short *(in length)* **4.1**
cortés courteous, polite **10.1**
cortésmente courteously, politely **10.1**
cosa *(f.)* thing **5.1**
cosecha *(f.)* harvest
costa *(f.)* coast
costar (ue) to cost **4.2**
costo *(m.)* cost
costumbre *(f.)* custom
crear to create
creativo(a) creative
crédito *(m.)* credit **15.2**
crítica *(f.)* criticism
crítico(a) critical
cronología *(f.)* chronology
cruce *(m.)* crossing
crudo(a) raw
cruel cruel **13.3**
cruz *(f.)* cross
cruzar to cross
cuaderno *(m.)* notebook **1.1**
cuadra *(f.)* city block **5.1**
cuadrado *(m.)* square
cuadro *(m.)* painting **4.3**
¿cuál(es)? which one(s)? what?
cualidad *(f.)* quality, characteristic
¿cuándo? when? **3.1**
¿cuánto(a)? how much? **3.1**
¿cuántos(as)? how many? **2.2**
cuarto *(m.)* room; **cuarto de baño** *(m.)* bathroom
cuarto(a) fourth
cubierta *(f.)* cover
cubrir to cover
cuchara *(f.)* spoon **8.2**
cuchillo *(m.)* knife **8.2**
cuello *(m.)* collar
cuenta *(f.)* bill; account
cuentista *(m. / f.)* short-story writer
cuento de hadas *(m.)* fairytale
cuerpo *(m.)* body **13.2**
cuestión *(f.)* question, issue
cuestionario *(m.)* questionnaire
cuidadoso(a) careful **10.2**
cuidar to take care of; **cuidar a los niños** to babysit, care for the children **15.1**
¡cuídate! take care!
culpa *(f.)* fault **11.2**
culpable guilty, culpable **10.3**
cumpleaños *(m. s.* and *pl.)* birthday **3.2**
cumplir to carry out, realize **11.3**
cuñado(a) brother-in-law / sister-in-law
curioso(a) curious

D

dama *(f.)* lady **4.2**
dañar to damage, hurt **14.2**
dar to give **8.3**; **dar vuelta** to turn **13.2**
dato *(m.)* fact
de from, about; **de repente** suddenly **10.2**; **de todos modos** anyway **14.1**; **de veras** really; **de vez en cuando** once in a while **13.3**
debajo de under **5.1**
debate *(m.)* debate
deberes *(m. pl.)* responsibilities **11.3**
decano(a) dean
decidir to decide **2.1**
decir (i) to say **6.2**
decisión *(f.)* decision
decorar to decorate **3.2**
dedicación *(f.)* dedication
dedicar to dedicate
dedo *(m.)* finger **13.2**
defender to defend
defensor(a) guard *(soccer)* **14.3**
dejar to leave behind **7.1**; to allow, permit **14.2**; **dejar de** to stop *(doing something)* **11.3**
delante de in front of **5.1**
delantero(a) forward *(soccer)* **14.3**
delgado(a) thin **3.3**
delicioso(a) delicious **8.3**
demasiado(a) too much **6.1**
democracia *(f.)* democracy **11.1**
dentista *(m. / f.)* dentist
denunciar to denounce **10.1**
dependiente *(m. / f.)* store clerk, salesperson **2.1**
deporte *(m.)* sport **7.2**
deportista *(m. / f.)* sportsman, sportswoman **9.3**
deprimido(a) depressed **13.1**
deprimirse to be depressed
derecho *(adv.)* straight (ahead); *(m.)* law
derecho(a) right **9.3**
derrotar to defeat, beat **14.1**
desaparecer to disappear **7.2**
desarrollar to develop
desarrollo *(m.)* development

desastre *(m.)* disaster
desayunar to eat breakfast **8.1**
desayuno *(m.)* breakfast **8.1**
descansar to rest **3.2**
descendiente *(m. / f.)* descendant
descortés discourteous
describir to describe **10.1**
descripción *(f.)* description
descubrimiento *(m.)* discovery
descubrir to discover **7.3**
deseado(a) desired
desear to desire **4.3**
desempleo *(m.)* unemployment **15.1**
desenchufar to unplug *(electricity)* **11.1**
deseo *(m.)* desire, wish **12.1**
desesperado(a) desperate
desierto *(m.)* desert
desocupado(a) unoccupied **5.1**
desorganizado(a) disorganized **1.3**
despedida good-bye, farewell
despedir (i, i) to dismiss, fire *(from a job)* **15.3**
despedirse (i, i) to take leave, say good-bye
despertador *(m.)* alarm clock **9.2**
despertarse (ie) to wake up **9.2**
después de after **5.1**
destino *(m.)* destiny, fate
destruir to destroy
desventaja *(f.)* disadvantage
detallado(a) detailed **10.2**
detalle *(m.)* detail
determinar to determine
destacarse to stand out
detestar to detest **6.3**
detrás de behind **5.1**
deuda *(f.)* debt **15.3**
devolver (ue) to return (something) **10.3**
día *(m.)* day **2.3**; **de día** during the day **2.3**; **Día de Acción de Gracias** *(m.)* Thanksgiving Day; **día de la semana** *(m.)* weekday **2.3**; **Día de las Madres** *(m.)* Mother's Day; **Día de San Valentín** *(m.)* Valentine's Day; **Día del Padre** *(m.)* Father's Day **9.1**
diálogo *(m.)* dialogue
diario(a) daily **12.3**
dibujo *(m.)* drawing
diccionario *(m.)* dictionary **1.2**
diciembre December **2.3**
dictadura *(f.)* dictatorship
diente *(m.)* tooth **13.2**
dieta *(f.)* diet
diez ten
diferencia *(f.)* difference
difícil difficult **1.2**
dinámico(a) dynamic
dinastía *(f.)* dynasty
dinero *(m.)* money
dios *(m.)* god
dirección *(f.)* address **5.1**
directamente directly
dirigir to direct **11.1**
disciplina *(f.)* discipline
disco record **3.1**; **disco compacto** *(m.)* compact disc **3.1**
discoteca *(f.)* discotheque
discriminación discrimination
diseñar to design
diseño *(m.)* design
disfrutar to enjoy
disparar to fire *(a gun)* **10.1**
disponible available **5.1**
distinto(a) different
diversidad *(f.)* diversity
diverso(a) diverse
divertido(a) amusing, funny **1.2**
divertir (ie, i) to entertain, show a good time
divertirse (ie, i) to have a good time, enjoy oneself **9.2**
dividir to divide **2.1**
doblar to turn **9.3**; to bend **13.2**
doble double **14.3**
docena *(f.)* dozen
dólar *(m.)* dollar **5.1**
doler (ue) to hurt **12.2**
dolor *(m.)* pain, ache; **dolor de cabeza** *(m.)* headache
dominación *(f.)* domination
domingo Sunday **2.3**
donar to donate
¿dónde? where? **3.1**
dormir (ue, u) to sleep **1.2**
dormirse (ue, u) to fall asleep **9.2**
dormitorio *(m.)* bedroom **5.1**
dos two
dramatizar to role-play
dramaturgo(a) playwright
ducharse to shower, take a shower **9.2**
duda *(f.)* doubt
dudar to doubt **13.3**
dueño(a) owner **5.1**
dulce *(m.)* candy, sweet
durante during **7.1**
durar to last **13.1**
durazno *(m.)* peach **8.1**
duro(a) hard, difficult **10.2**

E

echar de menos to miss *(someone)* **11.1**
ecológico(a) ecological
economía *(f.)* economics **1.2**
edad *(f.)* age **5.3**
edificio *(m.)* building **2.2**
educación física *(f.)* physical education **1.2**
educado(a) educated; raised
efecto *(m.)* effect
eficaz efficient
ejemplo *(m.)* example
ejército *(m.)* army **11.1**
elección *(f.)* election
elegante elegant **1.1**
elegir (i, i) to choose, select; to elect
eliminar to eliminate
embarazada pregnant **13.1**
embarazo *(m.)* pregnancy **13.1**
emborracharse to get drunk **11.2**
emergencia *(f.)* emergency **10.1**
emigrar emigrate
emocionante touching, moving
empacar to pack *(a suitcase)* **12.1**
empapado(a) soaking wet **9.1**
empatar to tie *(in games and elections)* **7.1**
empezar (ie) to begin **7.2**
empleado(a) employee **2.1**
empleo *(m.)* employment, work, job **7.3**
empresa *(f.)* company **12.2**
en on **5.1**; **en caso (de) que** in case **15.1**; **en cuanto** as soon as **15.1**; **en efecto** in

fact **11.2**; **en oferta** on special **4.2**; **en rebaja** reduced **4.2**; **en seguida** immediately, at once **8.2**
enamorado(a) in love **3.3**
enamorarse to fall in love
encantado(a) delighted **PE**
encargado(a) in charge
enchufar to plug in **10.1**
encima de on top of **5.1**
encontrar (ue) to find **4.1**
encuesta *(f.)* survey
energía *(f.)* energy
enero January **2.3**
enfermarse to get sick **12.3**
enfermedad *(f.)* illness **13.3**
enfermo(a) sick **3.1**
enfrente de in front of **5.1**
engañar to deceive; to trick **15.2**
enojarse to get angry **11.2**
enorme enormous
ensalada *(f.)* salad **8.2**
enseñar to teach
entender (ie) to understand **4.1**
entonces then **5.1**
entrada *(f.)* entrance **5.1**
entrar to enter **7.3**
entre between **5.1**
entregar to deliver, hand over
entremés *(m.)* appetizer **8.3**
entrenador(a) coach **14.3**
entrevista *(f.)* interview **7.3**
entrevistar to interview **2.1**
enumerar to enumerate **14.2**
enviar to send **12.3**
envidioso(a) envious, jealous
episodio *(m.)* episode **11.1**
equipaje *(m.)* luggage, baggage
equipo *(m.)* team **7.1**
escala *(f.)* stopover
escapar to escape **7.3**
escaparate *(m.)* store window, display window
escaso(a) scarce
escena *(f.)* scene
escoger to choose, select
escribir to write **1.2**; **escribir cartas** to write letters **1.2**
escritor(a) writer **7.2**
escritorio *(m.)* *(teacher's)* desk **1.2**
¡escúchame! listen to me! **7.3**
escuchar música to listen to music **1.2**
escuela *(f.)* school **9.3**; **escuela primaria** *(f.)* elementary school **7.2**; **escuela secundaria** *(f.)* high school **7.2**
escultura *(f.)* sculpture
ese(a) *(pron. s.)* that **4.1**
esencial essential
esfuerzo *(m.)* effort
esmeralda *(f.)* emerald
eso *(neuter pron.)* that **4.1**
esos(as) those **4.1**
espalda *(f.)* back **10.3**
especial special **1.3**
especialización *(f.)* specialization, major **3.3**
especializarse to specialize, major
específico(a) specific
espectacular spectacular **7.3**
espectáculo *(m.)* movie / theater section *(of a newspaper)* **7.2**; show, special event **12.2**
espejo *(m.)* mirror
esperanza *(f.)* hope **12.2**
esperar to wait for; to expect **3.2**
esposo(a) husband / wife **4.1**
esquema *(f.)* outline
esquí *(m.)* skiing **14.1**
esquiar to ski
esquina *(f.)* corner **9.3**
esta mañana / tarde / noche this morning / afternoon / evening **7.1**
establecer to establish
estación *(f.)* season **2.3**
estacionar to park **10.2**
estadio *(m.)* stadium **14.1**
estado *(m.)* state **3.3**
estar to be **3.1**; **estar despejado** to have clear skies **9.1**; **estar dispuesto(a)** to be inclined to **14.3**; **estar en forma** to be in shape **14.3**; **estar enamorado(a) de** to be in love with **6.3**; **estar harto(a) de** to be fed up with **12.2**; **estar loco(a) por** to be crazy about **6.3**; **estar molido(a)** to be exhausted **13.2**; **estar muerto(a)** to be dead **13.2**; **estar nublado** to be cloudy **9.1**; **estar seguro(a) de** to be sure, certain of **12.2**
estatura *(f.)* height **5.3**
este *(m.) (pron. s.)* east **9.1**
este(a) this **4.1**
estilo *(m.)* style
estirar to stretch **13.2**
esto *(neuter pron.)* this **4.1**
estómago *(m.)* stomach **13.2**
estos(as) *(pron. pl.)* these **4.1**
estratégico(a) strategic
estrecho(a) narrow
estrella *(f.)* star
estrés *(m.)* stress **13.1**
estudiante *(m. / f.)* student **PE**
estudiar to study **1.3**
estudio *(m.)* studio
estudioso(a) studious **1.1**
estufa *(f.)* stove **10.1**
estupendo(a) stupendous **1.2**
eterno(a) eternal
étnico(a) ethnic
evento *(m.)* event **6.1**
evitar to avoid **10.3**
evolución *(f.)* evolution
exacto(a) exact
exagerar to exaggerate
examen *(m.)* exam **2.1**
excelente excellent **PE**
excepción *(f.)* exception
excepcional exceptional
exceso *(m.)* excess
excursión *(f.)* tour **4.1**
excusa *(f.)* excuse
exhibición *(f.)* exhibition **6.1**
exigente demanding
exigir to demand **14.2**
existir to exist
éxito *(m.)* success
experiencia *(f.)* experience **7.3**
explicar to explain **6.1**
explotar to explode **7.2**
expresar to express **6.3**
expresión *(f.)* expression
exquisito(a) exquisite **8.3**
extranjero(a) foreign, alien; **al extranjero** abroad, in a foreign country
extrañar to miss
extraño(a) strange
extremo(a) extreme

F

fábrica *(f.)* factory **12.1**
fabricar to produce
fabuloso(a) fabulous
fácil easy **1.2**
falda *(f.)* skirt **4.1**
falso(a) false
faltar to lack, need, be missing **10.3**; **faltar a clase** to miss class **11.2**
fama *(f.)* fame
familia *(f.)* family **2.2**
familiares *(m. pl.)* extended family members **2.3**
famoso(a) famous **1.1**
fanático(a) fanatic **2.3**
fantástico(a) fantastic **7.2**
farmacia *(f.)* pharmacy **9.3**
fascinante fascinating
fascinar to fascinate **6.3**
favorito(a) favorite **1.2**
febrero February **2.3**
fecha *(f.)* date **5.3**
felicidad *(f.)* happiness
felicitar to congratulate **14.1**
feliz happy **2.3**; **¡Feliz cumpleaños!** Happy birthday! **3.2**
fenomenal phenomenal **3.3**
feo(a) ugly **2.3**
ferrocarril *(m.)* railroad
fiebre *(f.)* fever **13.2**
fiel faithful
fiesta *(f.)* party **3.2**
fijarse to notice; to pay attention
filmar to film **11.1**
filtro *(m.)* filter
fin *(m.)* end; **fin de semana** *(m.)* weekend **2.1**
financiar to finance
firma *(f.)* firm; signature
firmar to sign **6.1**
física *(f.)* physics **1.2**
flan *(m.)* caramel custard **8.2**
flojo(a) lazy **13.2**
flor *(f.)* flower **6.1**
forma *(f.)* form **12.3**
formal formal
fortuna *(f.)* fortune
foto *(f.)* photo **3.3**
fotografía *(f.)* photograph **4.1**
fracasar to fail
francés, francesa French **4.1**
frase *(f.)* phrase
frenar to apply the brakes *(of a car)* **10.2**
fresa *(f.)* strawberry **8.1**
fresco(a) fresh **8.3**
frito(a) fried **8.2**
frontera *(f.)* border **9.1**
frustrado(a) frustrated **3.3**
fruta *(f.)* fruit **8.1**
fuente *(f.)* fountain, source
fuerte strong, loud **5.1**
fuerza *(f.)* strength, force; **fuerzas armadas** *(f. pl.)* armed forces **11.1**
fumador(a) smoker **10.2**
fumar to smoke **7.3**
funcionar to function, run *(a motor)*
fundado(a) founded
furioso(a) furious **3.1**
fútbol *(m.)* soccer **14.1**; **fútbol americano** *(m.)* football
futbolista *(m. / f.)* soccer player **11.2**
futuro *(m.)* future

G

gafas de sol *(f. pl.)* sunglasses **12.1**
ganar to win **7.1**; to earn **15.3**
ganga *(f.)* bargain **4.2**
garaje *(m.)* garage **5.1**
garantizar to guarantee
gaseosa *(f.)* carbonated drink **4.3**
gasolina *(f.)* gasoline
gasolinera *(f.)* gas; filling station **11.1**
gastar to spend **12.3**
gasto *(m.)* expense **6.1**
gatito(a) small cat **5.1**
gato(a) cat **5.1**
genealógico(a) genealogical
generación *(f.)* generation
género *(m.)* gender
generoso(a) generous
genio(a) genius
gente *(f.)* people **3.2**
gerente *(m. / f.)* manager **2.1**
gigantesco(a) gigantic
gimnasia *(f.)* gymnastics, calisthenics **13.1**
gira *(f.)* day trip, tour
gobernar (ie) to govern
gobierno *(m.)* government **7.1**
gol *(m.)* goal **14.3**
golpe *(m.)* hit, blow **14.1**; **golpe de cabeza** *(m.)* hitting the ball with one's head **2.1**; **golpe militar** *(m.)* military coup, *coup d'état*
golpear to hit, beat up **7.2**
goma *(f.)* pencil eraser **1.1**
gordo(a) fat **3.3**
grabar to record
grado *(m.)* degree **9.1**
graduarse to graduate **15.1**
grande big, large **1.2**
gratis *(adv.)* free **11.1**
gris gray **4.1**
gritar to cry out, shout **10.3**
grito *(m.)* shout, scream
gruñón, gruñona grouchy, grumpy **12.3**
grupo *(m.)* group
guante *(m.)* glove **9.1**
guapo(a) good-looking **3.2**
guardar to keep
guardia *(m. / f.)* guard
guerra *(f.)* war
guía *(m. / f.)* guide **4.1**; **guía telefónica** *(f.)* telephone book
guitarra *(f.)* guitar **3.2**
guitarrista *(m. / f.)* guitar player **3.2**
gustar to like **8.1**

H

habitación *(f.)* dwelling, room **2.2**
habitante *(m. / f.)* inhabitant
hábito *(m.)* habit
hablar por teléfono to speak on the phone **1.3**
hacer to make; to do **2.3**; **hacer buen tiempo** to have good weather **9.1**; **hacer calor** to be hot **9.1**; **hacer la cama** to make the bed **12.3**; **hacer daño** to hurt, damage **15.1**; **hacer ejercicio** to exercise **12.3**; **hacer frío** to be cold **9.1**; **hacer el papel** to play the

role; **hacer la siesta** to take a nap, rest **12.2**; **hacer trampas** to cheat **10.3**; **hacer viento** to be windy **9.1**
hacia toward
hamburguesa *(f.)* hamburger **1.3**
hasta until **14.1**; **hasta la vista** good-bye, see you. **PE**; **hasta luego** see you later **PE**; **hasta mañana** see you to-morrow **PE**; **hasta pronto** see you soon **PE**
hay there is, there are
hay sol it is sunny **9.1**
hecho(a) *(adj.)* done; *(n. m.)* fact
helado *(m.)* ice cream
herido(a) wounded, injured **10.1**
hermanastro(a) stepbrother / stepsister **5.1**
hermano(a) brother / sister **5.1**
hermanos *(m. pl.)* siblings **5.1**
hermoso(a) beautiful **3.2**
hielo *(m.)* ice
hijo(a) son / daughter **5.1**
hijos *(m. pl.)* children **5.1**
hispano(a) Hispanic
historia *(f.)* history
hogar *(m.)* home
hoja de papel *(f.)* sheet of paper
¡hola! hello! **PE**
hombre *(m.)* man **3.3**
hombro *(m.)* shoulder **13.2**
honesto(a) honest **10.3**
hora *(f.)* hour, time **2.3**
horno *(m.)* oven
hospital *(m.)* hospital **10.1**
hotel *(m.)* hotel **2.1**
hoy today **5.2**
huelga *(f.)* strike **7.2**
huevo *(m.)* egg **8.1**
huir to run away, escape
humano(a) human
húmedo(a) humid
humo *(m.)* smoke **10.1**
hundido(a) sunken
¡huy! *(interj.)* oh!, ouch!

I

ideal ideal
idéntico(a) identical
identificar to identify **10.3**
idioma *(m.)* language **3.3**
iglesia *(f.)* church **5.1**
ignorar to ignore
igual alike, same **12.3**
igualmente likewise **PE**
ilustrar to illustrate
imagen *(f.)* image
imaginación *(f.)* imagination
imaginar, imaginarse to imagine **6.3**
impaciente impatient **1.1**
imparcial impartial **14.3**
impedir (i, i) to prevent, obstruct
imperio *(m.)* empire
impermeable *(m.)* raincoat **4.2**
importante important **3.2**
imposible impossible
impresión *(f.)* impression
impresionante impressive
impresionar to impress **6.1**
impresora *(f.)* printer **2.1**
improbable improbable
impuestos *(m. pl.)* taxes **15.2**
incaico(a) Inca, Incan
incendio *(m.)* fire **10.1**
incidente *(m.)* incident
incierto(a) uncertain, doubtful
incluir to include
inconsciente unconscious **10.1**
inconveniente inconvenient
increíble incredible, unbelievable
indicar to indicate
índice *(m.)* index
indígena indigenous, native
indio(a) Indian
indiscutible indisputable, unquestionable
indispensable indispensable
individuo *(m.)* individual
industria *(f.)* industry
inestabilidad *(f.)* instability
infancia *(f.)* infancy
influencia *(f.)* influence
información *(f.)* information
informal informal
informar to inform **7.1**
informativo(a) informative
informe *(m.)* report
ingeniería *(f.)* engineering **1.2**
inglés *(m.)* English *(language)* **1.2**
ingresos *(m. pl.)* income, revenue
inhumano(a) inhumane
iniciar to initiate; to begin
inmediatamente immediately **2.3**
inmenso(a) immense
innovador(a) innovative
inocente innocent
inolvidable unforgettable
insinuar to insinuate **11.1**
insistir (en) to insist *(on, upon)*
inspirar to inspire
instrumento *(m.)* instrument
integrar to integrate
inteligente intelligent
intercambio *(m.)* exchange
interés *(m.)* interest **7.2**
interesante interesting **1.1**
internacional international **7.2**
interpretar to interpret
interrumpir to interrupt
íntimo(a) intimate, private
inútil useless
inventar to invent
invertir (ie, i) to invest **15.3**
investigador(a) investigator, researcher
invierno *(m.)* winter **2.3**
invitación *(f.)* invitation
invitado(a) guest **3.1**
invitar to invite **2.3**
invocar to invoke
inyección *(f.)* injection, shot **13.3**
ir de compras to go shopping **4.2**
ironía *(f.)* irony
irónico(a) ironic
irrigación *(f.)* irrigation
irse to go away, leave
isla *(f.)* island **15.3**
itinerario *(m.)* itinerary
izquierdo(a) left **9.3**

J

jabón *(m.)* soap **12.1**
jamás never **10.2**
jamón *(m.)* ham **8.2**
japonés, japonesa Japanese **4.1**
jardín *(m.)* garden
jefe *(m. / f.)* boss, chief

jonrón *(m.)* home run **14.1**
joven *(m. / f.)* young man / woman *(adj.)* young **4.1**
joya *(f.)* jewel **11.1**
jubilarse to retire **15.2**
juego *(m.)* game **14.2**
jueves Thursday **2.3**
jugador(a) player
jugar (ue) to play **7.2**
jugo *(m.)* juice **8.3**; **jugo de naranja** *(m.)* orange juice **8.3**
jugoso(a) juicy
julio July **2.3**
junio June **2.3**
juntarse to get together
junto next to, by **5.3**
justo(a) just, fair **14.1**
juventud *(f.)* youth

L

labor *(f.)* work
laboratorio *(m.)* laboratory **1.3**
ladrón, ladrona thief **7.1**
lago *(m.)* lake **7.1**
lámpara *(f.)* lamp **5.1**
lana *(f.)* wool **4.2**
langosta *(f.)* lobster **8.3**
lanzador(a) pitcher **14.1**
lápiz *(m.)* pencil **1.1**
largo(a) long **4.1**
lástima *(f.)* pity, shame **14.1**
lastimar to injure **10.3**
lastimarse to hurt oneself **14.1**
lavandería *(f.)* laundry
lavaplatos *(m. / f., s. and pl.)* dishwasher **2.1**
lavar to wash **2.2**
le *(indir. obj. pron., s.)* (to, for) him, her, you **8.1**; **le presento a…** I'd like you to meet. . . **PE**
lector *(m.)* reader
lectura *(f.)* reading
leche *(f.)* milk **4.3**
lechuga *(f.)* lettuce **8.1**
leer to read **1.2**
legalmente legally
lejos de far from **5.1**
lengua *(f.)* tongue
lentamente slowly **9.2**
lente *(m)* contact lens **12.1**
lento(a) slow **10.2**
les *(indir. obj. pron., pl.)* (to, for) them, you **8.1**
lesionarse to get hurt, injured **14.1**
lesión *(f.)* lesion, injury
levantar to raise; to lift **13.2**
levantarse to get up **9.2**
ley *(f.)* law
leyenda *(f.)* legend
liberal liberal **1.1**
librar to free, liberate **11.1**
libre free **6.1**
librería *(f.)* bookstore **1.3**
libro *(m.)* book **1.2**
licencia *(f.)* license **10.2**
licenciatura *(f.)* degree *(school)*
líder *(m. / f.)* leader **14.3**
liga *(f.)* league **14.3**
límite *(m.)* limit; **límite de velocidad** *(m.)* speed limit
limón *(m.)* lemon
limonada *(f.)* lemonade **4.3**
limpiar to clean **2.3**
limpio(a) clean
lindo(a) pretty **4.2**
liquidación *(f.)* sale **4.2**
lista *(f.)* list
literatura *(f.)* literature **1.2**
llamada *(f.)* phone call **3.2**
llamar to call **1.3**; **llamar la atención** to call attention to **9.3**
llanta *(f.)* tire **10.2**; **llanta desinflada** *(f.)* flat tire
llave *(f.)* key **12.1**
llegar to arrive **7.1**; to wear **4.3**
lleno(a) de full of
llevar to take **6.1**; **llevar a cabo** to carry out
llevarse bien to get along well **13.3**
llorar to cry **11.2**
llover (ue) to rain **9.1**; **llover a cántaros** to rain cats and dogs **9.1**
lloviznar to drizzle, rain lightly **9.1**
lluvia *(f.)* rain **9.1**
lluvioso(a) rainy **9.2**
¡lo juro! I swear
lo siento I'm sorry **3.2**
local local **7.2**
loco(a) crazy **3.3**
locutor, locutora radio announcer
lograr to get; to achieve
lotería *(f.)* lottery **15.3**
lucha *(f.)* struggle, conflict
luna *(f.)* moon
luego then
lugar *(m.)* place
lujoso(a) luxurious
lunes Monday **2.3**
luz *(f.)* light

M

machista macho, male chauvinist
madera *(f.)* lumber; **de madera** wooden
madrastra *(f.)* stepmother **5.1**
madre *(f.)* mother **5.1**; **madre naturaleza** *(f.)* Mother Nature
malagradecido(a) ungrateful, unappreciative **15.2**
maleta *(f.)* suitcase **1.3**
malo(a) bad **5.2**
mamá *(f.)* mother
manada *(f.)* heard, flock
mandar to send **7.3**
mandato *(m.)* command
manejar to drive **7.3**; to manage, control **14.3**
manera *(f.)* manner
manga *(f.)* sleeve
manifestación *(f.)* demonstration
mano *(f.)* hand **13.2**
mantener (ie) to maintain **15.1**; **mantener la calma (ie)** to keep calm, stay calm **14.1**
mantequilla *(f.)* butter **8.2**
manzana *(f.)* apple **8.1**
mañana *(adv.)* tomorrow; *(n., f.)* morning
máquina *(f.)* machine; **máquina de afeitar** *(f.)* electric shaver **12.1**; **máquina de escribir** *(f.)* typewriter
mar *(m.)* sea
maratón *(m.)* marathon **14.3**
maravilla *(f.)* wonder, marvel
marcar to mark
marcha *(f.)* march

marchar to march
marisco *(m.)* seafood, shellfish
martes Tuesday **2.3**
marzo March **2.3**
más more
máscara *(f.)* mask
matar to kill **7.3**
matemáticas *(f. pl.)* mathematics **1.2**
materiales *(m. pl.)* supplies
matrícula *(f.)* registration
matrimonio *(m.)* married couple
máximo(a) maximum, greatest
mayo May **2.3**
mayonesa *(f.)* mayonnaise **8.2**
mayor older, oldest **5.3**
mayoría *(f.)* majority
me *(dir. obj. pron.)* me **6.1**; *(indir. obj. pron.)* (to, for) me **8.1**; *(refl. pron.)* myself **9.2**; **me encantaría** I would love to **6.1**; **me llamo...** my name is . . . **PE**
mecánico(a) mechanic **10.2**
medalla *(f.)* medal
medias *(f. pl.)* stockings **4.2**
médico(a) doctor
medio ambiente *(m.)* environment
medir (i, i) to measure **13.1**
mejor better **5.2**
mejorarse to get better, improve
melón *(m.)* melon **8.1**
memoria *(f.)* memory, remembrance **12.2**
mencionar to mention
menor younger, youngest **5.3**
menos less
mensaje *(m.)* message
mensual monthly **5.1**
mente *(f.)* mind
mentir (ie, i) to tell a lie **10.3**
mentira *(f.)* lie **7.3**
menú *(m.)* menu
merecer to deserve, be worthy of **15.2**
mermelada *(f.)* marmalade
mes *(m.)* month
mesa *(f.)* table **6.1**
mesero(a) waiter / waitress **2.1**
mi *(poss. adj.)* my **PE**; **mi nombre es...** my name is . . . **PE**
miembro *(m. / f.)* member
mientras while
miércoles Wednesday **2.3**
militar military
mirar to look at, watch **1.3**
misa *(f.)* mass *(religious)*
miserable miserable
miseria *(f.)* misery
mismo(a) same
misterioso(a) mysterious
mitad *(f.)* half
mito *(m.)* myth
mochila *(f.)* backpack **1.1**
moda *(f.)* fashion
modelo *(m. / f.)* model
modesto(a) modest **3.3**
modo *(m.)* manner, way
molestar to bother **12.3**
momento *(m.)* moment **6.1**
moneda *(f.)* coin
mono(a) monkey **5.3**
monólogo *(m.)* monologue
montaña *(f.)* mountain **2.3**
montar to get on, ride **11.3**
monte *(m.)* mountain
montón *(m.)* a bunch, lots **12.2**
moreno(a) dark *(referring to complexion and hair)* **3.3**
morir, morirse (ue, u) to die **10.1**
mostaza *(f.)* mustard **8.2**
mostrador *(m.)* counter
mostrar to show; to demonstrate
motivo *(m.)* motive
moto *(f.)* motorcycle **9.3**
motor *(m.)* motor **10.2**
mucho(a) much, a lot **1.3**; **mucho gusto** pleased to meet you **PE**
mudarse to move
mueble *(m.)* furniture **5.1**
muerte *(f.)* death **10.1**
mujer *(f.)* woman **3.3**
multa *(f.)* fine, ticket, parking ticket **10.2**
mundo *(m.)* world
muralla *(f.)* wall
museo *(m.)* museum
música *(f.)* music **3.1**
músico *(m. f.)* musician **9.3**
muy very **1.2**; **muy bien, gracias** fine, thank you **PE**

N

nacer to be born **7.2**
nacional national **7.2**
nada nothing **10.2**
nadar to swim **1.2**
nadie no one, nobody **3.3**
naranja *(f.)* orange **8.3**
nariz *(f.)* nose **13.2**
narrar to narrate
natación *(f.)* swimming **14.1**
naturaleza *(f.)* nature
naturalmente naturally **3.2**
Navidad *(f.)* Christmas
navío *(m.)* ship, vessel
neblina *(f.)* fog **9.1**
necesitar to need **1.3**
negación *(f.)* negation
negativo(a) negative
negocios *(m. pl.)* business **7.2**
negro(a) black **4.1**
nervioso(a) nervous **3.1**
nevar (ie) to snow **9.1**
nevera *(f.)* refrigerator **5.1**
ni... ni neither . . . nor **10.2**
ni siquiera not even **12.3**
nieve *(f.)* snow **9.1**
ningún (ninguno, ninguna) none, not any **10.2**
niñez *(f.)* childhood
niño(a) child **4.1**
nivel *(m.)* level **14.3**
no no **PE**; **no muy bien** not very well **1.3**; **no te preocupes** don't worry **PE**
nocturno(a) nightly, nocturnal
noche *(f.)* night
nombrar to name
nombre *(m.)* name
norma *(f.)* norm
norte *(m.)* north **9.1**
nota *(f.)* grade, note **15.2**
notar to notice, take note **10.1**
noticias *(f. pl.)* news **7.2**
noticiero *(m.)* news, newscast
novedades *(f. pl.)* latest fashions
novela *(f.)* novel **3.2**
novelista *(m. / f.)* novelist **9.3**
noveno(a) ninth
noviembre November **2.3**
novio(a) boyfriend / girlfriend **1.2**

nueve nine
nuevo(a) new **2.1**
número *(m.)* number
nunca never **1.3**
nutritivo(a) nutritious, nutritive

O

o... o either . . . or **10.2**
obediente obedient
objetivo(a) objective
objeto *(m.)* object, thing
obligación *(f.)* obligation
obligado(a) obligated
obligar to oblige
obligatorio(a) obligatory, compulsory
obra *(f.)* work; **obra de teatro** *(f.)* play *(theater)* **6.1**
obrero(a) laborer, worker
observar to observe
obstáculo *(m.)* obstacle
obtener (ie) to obtain **10.2**
obviamente obviously
obvio(a) obvious **14.1**
ocasión *(f.)* occasion **6.1**
ocho eight
octavo(a) eighth
octubre October **2.3**
ocupado(a) occupied
ocupar to occupy
ocurrir to occur **7.2**
odiar to hate **6.3**
oeste *(m.)* west **9.1**
oferta *(f.)* offer **15.2**
oficina *(f.)* office **2.1**
ofrecer to offer **7.3**
oído *(m.)* inner ear **13.2**
oír to hear **6.1**
ojalá I hope **13.2**
ojo *(m.)* eye **5.3**; **¡ojo!** pay attention!
olvidar to forget **12.1**
opción *(f.)* option
operador(a) operator **10.1**
opinar to express an opinion **8.3**
oponerse to oppose, object to
oportunidad *(f.)* opportunity
oposición *(f.)* opposition
optimista *(m./f.)* optimist
opuesto(a) opposite
orden *(m.)* order
ordenar to organize, put in order; **ordenar el cuarto** to put one's room in order **1.3**
oreja *(f.)* outer ear **13.2**
organización *(f.)* organization
organizar to organize **2.2**
orgullo *(m.)* pride
origen *(m.)* origin **12.3**
orilla *(f.)* border, edge
oro *(m.)* gold
ortografía *(f.)* spelling
os *(dir. obj. pron., fam. pl.)* you **6.1**; *(indir. obj. pron., fam. pl.)* (to, for) you **8.1**; *(refl. pron., fam. pl.)* yourselves
oscuro(a) dark **5.2**
otoño *(m.)* autumn **2.3**
otro(a) other, another **2.1**
¡oye! listen! **6.1**

P

paciencia *(f.)* patience **5.3**
paciente *(m./f.)* patient **1.1**
padecer to suffer; to endure
padrastro *(m.)* stepfather **5.1**
padre *(m.)* father **5.1**
padres *(m. pl.)* parents **5.1**
pagar to pay **2.2**; **pagar la matrícula** to pay registration fees
pagaría I would pay **4.2**
página *(f.)* page
país *(m.)* country
paisaje *(m.)* landscape, countryside
palabra *(f.)* word; **palabras afines** *(f. pl.)* cognates
pan *(m.)* bread **8.1**
panadería *(f.)* bakery **9.3**
pantalones *(m. pl.)* pants, trousers **4.1**; **pantalones cortos** *(m. pl.)* shorts, short pants **4.1**
pañal *(m.)* diaper
pañuelo *(m.)* handkerchief
papa *(f.)* potato **8.1**
papá *(m.)* papa, daddy
papel *(m.)* paper **1.1**; role
papelería *(f.)* stationery store **9.3**
par *(m.)* pair **4.2**
para for, in comparison with, in relation to, in order to **5.3**; intended for, to be given to, toward, by a specified time, in one's opinion **9.3**; **para chuparse los dedos** finger-licking good **8.3**; **para que** so that **15.1**; **para servirle** at your service
parada de autobús *(f.)* bus stop **5.1**
paraguas *(m.s.* and *pl.)* umbrella **9.1**
parar to stop **7.3**
parcialmente partially
parecer to seem, appear like **6.1**
parecido(a) similar, alike
pared *(f.)* wall
pareja *(f.)* pair, couple **3.3**
pariente *(m.)* relative **5.1**
parlantes *(m. pl.)* speakers **2.1**
parque *(m.)* park **5.3**
parrilla *(f.)* grill **12.2**
participar to participate **11.1**
particular private
partido *(m.)* game *(competitive)*; political party
pasado(a) past
pasaporte *(m.)* passport **12.1**
pasar to pass; to spend time **2.3**; to hand over; **pasar el trapo** to dust; **pasar la aspiradora** to vacuum
pasatiempo *(m.)* pastime
Pascua Florida *(f.)* Easter
pasear to walk; to go for a ride
pasillo *(m.)* corridor, passage
pasión *(f.)* passion
paso *(m.)* step, pace
pasta dental *(f.)* toothpaste **12.1**
pastel *(m.)* cake **3.2**
pastilla *(f.)* pill **4.3**
pastoril pastoral
patear to kick **14.1**
patio *(m.)* patio **3.1**
pavo *(m.)* turkey **8.1**
paz *(f.)* peace **14.2**
pecho *(m.)* chest **13.2**
pedir (i, i) to ask for **6.2**
pegar to hit **10.2**
peinarse to comb **9.3**
pelea *(f.)* fight **14.2**

película *(f.)* film **4.1**; **película policíaca** *(f.)* detective movie
peligroso(a) dangerous **9.3**
pelo *(m.)* hair **5.3**
pelota *(f.)* ball **14.1**
peluquero(a) barber, hairdresser
pensamiento *(m.)* thought
pensar (ie) to plan; to think **4.1**
pequeño(a) small, little **3.3**
perder (ie) to lose **7.1**; **perder peso** to lose weight **12.3**
perdido(a) lost
perezoso(a) lazy **1.2**
perfecto(a) perfect
periódico *(m.)* newspaper **2.1**
periodista *(m. / f.)* newspaper reporter **2.1**
permanecer to stay, remain
permitir to permit **5.1**
pero but **6.1**
perro(a) dog **5.1**
perseguir (i, i) to follow **10.3**
persona *(f.)* person
personalidad *(f.)* personality
persuadir to persuade
pertenecer to belong
pesar to weigh **13.1**
pesas *(f. pl.)* weights **13.2**
pescado *(m.)* fish **8.2**
pésimo(a) very bad **8.3**
peso *(m.)* weight **5.3**
petróleo *(m.)* petroleum, oil
piano *(m.)* piano **3.2**
pico *(m.)* beak, sharp point
pie *(m.)* foot **13.2**
piedra *(f.)* rock
piel *(f.)* skin **13.3**; hide
pierna *(f.)* leg **10.1**
pieza *(f.)* piece
pijamas *(m. pl.)* pajamas **4.2**
pimienta *(f.)* pepper **8.2**
piña *(f.)* pineapple **8.1**
pincharse to get a flat tire; to puncture
pingüino *(m.)* penguin
pintor(a) painter
pirata *(m.)* pirate
piscina *(f.)* swimming pool **5.3**
piso *(m.)* floor
pista *(f.)* lane, (ski) run **14.1**; clue
pistola *(f.)* gun **7.3**
pizarra *(f.)* chalkboard **1.2**
planchar to iron **15.1**
planear to plan
planes *(m. pl.)* plans **6.1**
plástico *(m.)* plastic **5.2**
plátano *(m.)* banana **8.1**
plato *(m.)* plate, dish **6.1**
playa *(f.)* beach **2.3**
población *(f.)* population **9.3**
poblado(a) populated
pobreza *(f.)* poverty
poco little **9.1**
poder (ue) to be able, can **4.1**
poderoso(a) powerful
policía *(f.)* police force; *(m.)* police officer *(male)* **7.1**
política *(f.)* politics
político *(m. / f.)* politician **9.3**
político(a) political **14.2**
pollo *(m.)* chicken **8.1**
polución *(f.)* pollution
polvo *(m.)* dust
poner to put **5.1**; **poner la mesa** to set the table **6.1**
ponerse to become **6.3**; to put on *(clothing)*
popular popular **1.1**
popularidad *(f.)* popularity
por by, by means of, through, along, on **5.3**; because of, during, in for, for a period of time, in, in exchange for, in place of **9.3**; **por ciento** percent; **por escrito** in writing, written; **¡por fin!** at last!; **por medio de** by means of; **¿por qué?** why? **3.1**; **por suerte** fortunately, luckily **11.2**; **por supuesto** of course **5.1**
porcentaje *(m.)* percentage **9.3**
porque because
portada *(f.)* facade, front
portarse bien to behave **15.2**
poseer to possess
posibilidad *(f.)* possibility
positivamente positively
positivo(a) positive
posteriormente subsequently, later
postre *(m.)* dessert **8.1**
practicar to practice **3.2**; **practicar un deporte** to play a sport
precaución *(f.)* precaution
precio *(m.)* price **11.2**
precioso(a) precious
preciso(a) precise **10.2**
precolombino(a) pre-Columbian
predecir (i) to predict
preferencia *(f.)* preference
preferir (ie, i) to prefer **4.1**
pregunta *(f.)* question **3.1**
preguntar to ask **9.3**
premio *(m.)* prize; **Premio Nóbel** *(m.)* Nobel Prize **11.1**
prenda *(f.)* garment, article of clothing
prensa *(f.)* press
preocupado(a) preoccupied, worried **3.1**
preocupar to worry **13.1**
preparación *(f.)* preparation
preparar to prepare; **preparar la cena** to prepare dinner **1.3**
presentación *(f.)* introduction, presentation
presión *(f.)* pressure **13.1**
prestar to lend **15.2**; **prestar auxilio** to give assistance, aid **10.1**
presupuesto *(m.)* budget **15.3**
primavera *(f.)* spring **2.3**
primer(o, a) first **6.1**; **primeros auxilios** *(m. pl.)* first aid **10.1**
primo(a) cousin **5.1**
prisionero(a) prisoner
privado(a) private
privilegio *(m.)* privilege
probar (ue) to try; to taste
problemático(a) problematic
proceso *(m.)* process
proclamar to proclaim
producto *(m.)* product
pródigo(a) prodigal, wasteful
profesión *(f.)* profession **7.1**
profesional professional **PE**
profesor(a) professor, teacher **PE**
profundamente profoundly **13.2**
profundo(a) profound

programa *(m.)* program **6.1**
programador(a) programmer
progresista *(adj. m.* or *f.)* progressive
prohibir to prohibit, forbid **14.2**
promesa *(f.)* promise **10.3**
prometer to promise **5.1**
pronóstico *(m.)* *(weather)* forecast **9.1**
pronto quick, rapid, fast **10.1**
propina *(f.)* tip **8.3**
propio(a) own, one's own **7.2**
proponer to propose
proteger to protect **10.3**
protestar to protest
proveer to provide, furnish
provocar to provoke **14.2**
próximo(a) next **2.3**
proyectar to project
proyecto *(m.)* project
psiquiatra *(m. / f.)* psychiatrist
publicación *(f.)* publication
publicar to publish
público *(m.)* public **14.1**; audience
puerta *(f.)* door **2.1**
puesto *(m.)* job, position **7.3**
punto *(m.)* point
puntuación *(f.)* punctuation
puntual punctual **12.1**
pupitre *(m.)* desk *(pupil's)*
puro(a) pure

Q

¿qué? what?, which?. . . **3.1** **¡qué desastre!** what a mess! **5.2**; **¿qué tal?** how are you?. . . **PE** **¿qué te parece…?** what do you think of . . . ?
quedarse to remain, stay; to fit *(clothing)* **9.3**
quejarse to complain **11.2**
quemarse to burn (up) **10.1**
querer (ie) to want **4.1**; to love **6.3**
¿quién(es)? who? **3.1**
química *(f.)* chemistry **1.2**
quinto(a) fifth
quisiera I (he, she) would like **8.2**
quitar to take away
quitarse to take off **9.2**

R

rábano *(m.)* radish
racista *(m. / f.)* racist
radiador *(m.)* radiator
radio *(f.)* radio **1.3**
ramo de flores *(m.)* bouquet
rapero(a) rapper
rápidamente rapidly, fast **10.1**
rápido(a) rapid, fast **10.2**
raro(a) rare, uncommon
rascacielos *(m. s.* and *pl.)* skyscraper
ratón *(m.)* mouse **2.1**
raza *(f.)* race
reaccionar to react **7.2**
realidad *(f.)* reality
realizar to carry out, accomplish
rebaja *(f.)* reduction
recámara bedroom **5.1**
recepcionista *(m. / f.)* receptionist
recetar to prescribe **13.2**
rechazar to turn down, reject **6.1**
rechazo *(m.)* rejection
recibir to receive **7.1**
reciente recent
recientemente recently **7.1**
reclamado(a) reclaimed
recoger to gather, pick up
recomendación *(f.)* recommendation
recomendar (ie) to recommend **4.3**
reconocer to recognize
reconstruir to reconstruct
recordar (ue) to remember **5.3**
rector(a) president *(of a university)* **PE**
recuerdo *(m.)* souvenir **4.1**
recurso *(m.)* resource
red *(f.)* net **14.1**
redondo(a) round
reemplazar to replace
reflejar to reflect
refresco *(m.)* soft drink **1.3**
refugio *(m.)* refuge
regalar to give a gift
regalo *(m.)* gift **12.3**
región *(f.)* region
regla *(f.)* rule
regresar to return **2.3**
reina *(f.)* queen
reírse (i, i) to laugh **10.3**
relación *(f.)* relation
relacionar to relate
relajarse to relax **13.2**
religioso(a) religious
renacer to be reborn
repetir (i, i) to repeat **9.3**
reportar to report
representante *(m. / f.)* representative
representar to represent
reservación *(f.)* reservation **8.1**
reservado(a) reserved
resfriado *(m.)* cold *(illness)*
residencia *(f.)* residence, dorm **2.2**
resolución *(f.)* resolution
resolver (ue) to resolve **10.1**
respetar to respect **6.3**
respeto *(m.)* respect
respiración artificial *(f.)* artificial respiration **10.1**
respirar to breath **10.1**
responder to respond, answer
responsabilidad *(f.)* responsibility **11.1**
respuesta *(f.)* response **PE**
restaurante *(m.)* restaurant **2.1**
restaurar to restore
resto *(m.)* rest
resumen *(m.)* summary
retorno *(m.)* return
reunido(a) reunited, gathered
reunirse to reunite, get together
reunión *(f.)* meeting, gathering
revelar to reveal; to develop *(film)*
reventar (ie) to burst **10.2**; **reventar una llanta** to have a blowout **10.2**
revisar to revise; to review; **revisar el motor** to check the motor **10.2**
revista *(f.)* magazine **7.1**
revolución *(f.)* revolution
revuelto(a) scrambled *(egg)* **8.2**
rey *(m.)* king
rico(a) rich; delicious **3.2**
riguroso(a) rigorous
rincón *(m.)* corner
rin-rin ring-ring *(phone)*

ritmo *(m.)* rhythm **13.2**
robar to rob, steal **7.1**
robo *(m.)* robbery, theft **7.1**
robusto(a) robust
rodear to surround
rodilla *(f.)* knee **13.2**
romántico(a) romantic **1.1**
rojo(a) red **4.1**
romperse to break, shatter **10.1**
ropa *(f.)* clothes
rosa *(f.)* rose
rubio(a) blond
ruinas *(f. pl.)* ruins
ruta *(f.)* route
rutina *(f.)* routine, habit

S

sábado Saturday **2.3**
saber to know *(facts or information)* **3.3**
sabor *(m.)* flavor, taste
sabroso(a) tasty, delicious **8.3**
sacar to take out; **sacar buenas notas** to get good grades **11.3**; **sacar fotografías** to take pictures **4.1**; **sacar la basura** to take out the trash **15.1**
sacrificarse to sacrifice oneself **15.1**
sacudida eléctrica *(f.)* electric shock
sagrado(a) sacred, holy
sal *(f.)* salt **8.2**
sala *(f.)* living room **3.1**; **sala de urgencia** *(f.)* emergency room
salado(a) salty
salario *(m.)* salary **15.3**
salchicha *(f.)* sausage **8.1**
salir to leave, go out; **salir juntos** to date, go out together **11.1**
salsa *(f.)* sauce **8.2**; type of Puerto Rican dance and music **3.3**; **salsa de tomate** *(f.)* ketchup; **salsa picante** *(f.)* hot sauce
saltar to jump **10.1**
salud *(f.)* health **13.1**
saludo *(m.)* greeting
salvavidas *(m. / f., s.* and *pl.)* lifeguard, lifesaver **14.1**
sangre *(f.)* blood **13.2**
sandwich *(m.)* sandwich **4.3**
sano(a) healthy, fit
satisfecho(a) satisfied, full
saxofón *(m.)* saxophone **11.1**
se *(indir. obj. pron.)* to it, to him, to her, to you, to them **8.2**; *(refl. pron.)* himself, herself, itself, themselves **9.2**
secador *(m.)* hair dryer
secretario(a) secretary **2.1**
secreto *(m.)* secret
seda *(f.)* silk **4.2**
seguidor *(m. / f.)* follower
seguir (i, i) to continue; to follow **9.3**; **seguir un curso** to take a class **10.1**
segundo(a) second
seguridad *(f.)* security, safety
seguro *(m.)* insurance **15.3**
seis six
seleccionar to select
sello *(m.)* stamp *(postage)* **12.3**
selva *(f.)* forest, jungle **15.3**
semáforo *(m.)* traffic light **10.2**
semana *(f.)* week **1.3**
semestre *(m.)* semester
sensato(a) sensible, prudent
sensible sentimental, sensitive
sentarse (ie) to sit down **9.2**
sentido *(m.)* sense; **sentido común** *(m.)* common sense; **sentido contrario** opposite direction
sentimientos *(m. pl.)* feelings, sentiments **6.3**
sentirse (ie, i) bien to feel fine **11.2**
señalar to signal, indicate
señor man; Mr.
señora lady; Mrs. **4.1**
señorita young lady, Miss
separar to separate
septiembre September **2.3**
séptimo(a) seventh
ser capaz de to be capable of **14.3**
serie *(f.)* series
serio(a) serious **1.1**
servicios *(m. pl.)* bathroom **4.1**
servilleta *(f.)* napkin **8.2**
servir (i, i) to serve **6.2**
sexto(a) sixth
SIDA *(m.)* AIDS **13.1**
siempre always **1.3**
siete seven
siglo *(m.)* century **7.1**
significado *(m.)* meaning
siguiente following, next **9.3**
sílaba *(f.)* syllable
silla *(f.)* chair **1.2**
simpático(a) pleasant, likeable **1.1**
sin *(prep.)* without **5.1**; **sin embargo** nevertheless; **sin igual** without equal; **sin que** *(conj.)* unless **15.1**
sincero(a) sincere
sirviente *(m. / f.)* servant
sistema *(m.)* system
sitio *(m.)* site
situación *(f.)* situation
situado(a) situated
sobre over, on top of **5.1**; *(n. m.)* envelope
sobrepasar to exceed, surpass
sobresaliente outstanding
sobresalir to excel, be outstanding
sobretodo *(m.)* overcoat
sobrevivir to survive
sociable sociable
sociedad *(f.)* society
¡socorro! help! **10.1**
sofá *(m.)* sofa **5.1**
sol *(m.)* sun
solicitar to apply for; to ask for **7.3**
solicitud *(f.)* application form **7.3**
sólo *(adv.)* only **5.1**
someterse to yield, surrender
sonar (ue) to ring **11.1**
sonreír (i, i) to smile
soñar (ue) to dream **11.3**
sopa *(f.)* soup **8.2**
soportar to support
sorprendente surprising
sorprender to surprise **14.1**
sospechar to suspect **7.1**
sospechoso(a) suspicious **10.3**
soy (*from* **ser**) I am **PE**
subdesarrollado(a) underdeveloped
subir to go up; to get on **9.3**; **subir de peso** to gain weight
subterráneo(a) subterranean
suciedad *(f.)* dirt, filth
sucio(a) dirty **5.2**

sudar to perspire, sweat **9.1**
sudoeste *(m.)* southwest
sudor *(m.)* sweat, perspiration
sueldo *(m.)* salary, pay **15.2**
suelto(a) loose
sueño *(m.)* dream
suéter *(m.)* sweater **4.2**
sufrir to suffer **5.1**; **sufrir estrés** to be under stress **sufrir lesiones** to be injured, wounded
sugerir (ie, i) to suggest **8.2**
sumario *(m.)* summary
superficie *(f.)* surface
supermercado *(m.)* supermarket **5.1**
superpotencia *(f.)* superpower
suponer to suppose, assume
suposición *(f.)* supposition, assumption
sur *(m.)* south **9.1**
suspender to suspend
sustancia *(f.)* substance
sustantivo *(m.)* noun

T

talento *(m.)* talent
taller *(m.)* workshop
tamaño *(m.)* size
también also **1.1**
tambor *(m.)* drum **11.1**
tampoco neither **10.2**
tan so **5.3**; **tan… como** as . . . as **4.2**; **tan pronto como** as soon as **15.1**
tanque *(m.)* tank **10.2**
tanto(a) so much, *(pl.)* so many **2.3**; **tanto(a) como** as much as **4.2**; **tantos(as) como** as many as **4.2**
tapar to cover
tarde late **5.1**; *(n., f.)* afternoon
tarea *(f.)* homework **4.3**
tarjeta *(f.)* card **8.1**
te *(dir. obj. pron.)* you **6.1**; *(indir. obj. pron.)* (to, for) you **8.1**; *(refl. pron.)* yourself *(fam., s.)*; **te presento a…** I'd like you to meet . . . **PE**
té *(m.)* tea **4.3**
teatro *(m.)* theater **1.3**
techo *(m.)* roof
teclado *(m.)* keyboard **2.1**
tele *(f.)* T.V.
teleadicto(a) couch potato **13.2**
teléfono *(m.)* phone **1.3**
telenovela *(f.)* T.V. soap opera **11.1**
televisor *(m.)* T.V. set **5.1**
temer to fear **14.1**
temperatura *(f.)* temperature **9.1**
temporada *(f.)* season
temprano early **5.1**
tendría (*from* **tener**) I would have **4.2**
tenedor *(m.)* fork **8.2**
tener (ie) to have **2.2**; **tener… años** to be . . . years old **4.3**; **tener calor** to be hot **4.3**; **tener confianza** to trust **15.2**; **tener la culpa** to be at fault **10.2**; **tener éxito** to succeed **4.3**; **tener frío** to be cold **4.3**; **tener ganas de** to feel like **4.3**; **tener hambre** to be hungry **4.3**; **tener miedo de** to be afraid of **4.3**; **tener prisa** to be in a hurry **4.3**; **tener que** to have to **4.3**; **tener razón** to be right **4.3**; **tener sed** to be thirsty **4.3**; **tener sueño** to be sleepy **4.3**; **tener suerte** to be lucky **4.3**
teniente *(m. / f.)* lieutenant
teoría *(f.)* theory
tercer(o, a) third
terminar to finish, end **7.1**
terraza *(f.)* terrace **12.2**
terremoto *(m.)* earthquake **10.1**
terreno *(m.)* terrain, ground, land
terrestre terrestrial, earthy
¡terrible! terrible! **PE**
territorio *(m.)* territory
terrorista *(m. / f.)* terrorist
tesoro *(m.)* treasure **15.3**
testamento *(m.)* testament
testigo *(m.)* witness **10.1**
testimonio *(m.)* testimony
tiempo *(m.)* weather **9.1**; time; **tiempo completo** full-time **15.3**
tienda *(f.)* store **2.1**
tímido(a) timid **1.1**
tío(a) uncle / aunt **5.1**
tipo *(m.)* type
titular *(m.)* headline, heading
título *(m.)* title, caption, heading
tiza *(f.)* chalk **1.2**
toalla *(f.)* towel **10.1**
tobillo *(m.)* ankle **13.3**
tocar to play *(an instrument)* **3.2**; **tocar el timbre** to ring the doorbell
todavía still **12.3**
todo(a) all **6.3**; **todo derecho** straight ahead; **todo el día** all day **2.1**; **todo el mundo** everyone, everybody **3.2**; **todos los días** every day **1.3**
tomar to drink; to take; **tomar decisiones** to make decisions **15.1**; **tomar el pelo** to pull one's leg **14.1**
tomate *(m.)* tomato **8.1**
tonelada *(f.)* ton
tonificar to tone, strengthen **13.2**
tono *(m.)* tone
tonto(a) foolish, dumb **1.1**
toque *(m.)* touch
torero(a) bullfighter
tormenta *(f.)* storm **9.1**
tortuga *(f.)* turtle
tostado(a) toasted
trabajador(a) *(adj.)* hard-working **1.2**
trabajar to work **2.1**
trabajo *(m.)* work **2.1**
tradición *(f.)* tradition
traer to bring **6.1**
tráfico *(m.)* traffic **5.3**
traje *(m.)* suit **4.1**; **traje de baño** *(m.)* swimsuit **9.1**
tranquilizante *(m.)* tranquilizer **10.1**
tranquilo(a) tranquil, peaceful **3.3**
transformar to transform
transporte *(m.)* transport, transportation

tras after, behind
trasladarse to move, change residence
trastes *(m. pl.)* dishes
tratado *(m.)* treaty
tratamiento *(m.)* treatment
tratar to treat; to handle; **tratar de** to try, attempt **10.3**; to deal with, be about
tremendo(a) tremendous
tren *(m.)* train **9.3**
tres three
triste sad **3.1**
triunfar to triumph
triunfo *(m.)* triumph, victory
trompeta *(f.)* trumpet **11.1**
tropas *(f. pl.)* troops
tu *(fam. poss. adj.)* your **2.2**
tú *(fam. subj. pron.)* you **PE**
tumba *(f.)* tomb
turista *(m./f.)* tourist
tuyo(a) *(fam. poss. adj.)* your

U

ubicación *(f.)* position, location
úlcera *(f.)* ulcer
último(a) last, ultimate **2.3**; latest **11.3**
un(a) a, an **1.1**; **un mal rato** a bad time **15.1**; **un poco** a little **1.3**
único(a) only, sole, unique, extraordinary
unidad *(f.)* unit, unity
unir to unite **14.2**
universidad *(f.)* university **PE**
universitario(a) pertaining to the university **1.1**
urgente urgent **10.1**
usar to use **4.1**
uso *(m.)* use **12.3**
útil useful
utilizar to utilize, use

V

vacaciones *(f. pl.)* vacation **2.3**
vacío(a) empty
válido(a) valid
valle *(m.)* valley
valor *(m.)* valor, bravery **12.3**; value
vaqueros *(m. pl.)* blue jeans **9.2**
variedad *(f.)* variety
varón *(m.)* male, man **4.2**
vaso *(m.)* glass **8.1**
vecino(a) neighbor **12.1**
vegetal *(m.)* vegetable **8.1**
vegetariano(a) vegetarian
vejez *(f.)* old age **12.2**
vencedor *(m./f.)* conqueror, victor
vencer to conquer **7.1**
vendedor(a) seller, salesclerk **2.1**
vender to sell **2.1**
veneno *(m.)* poison **10.1**
venir (ie, i) to come **2.2**
ventaja *(f.)* advantage
ventana *(f.)* window **5.1**
ver to see **4.1**
verano *(m.)* summer **2.3**
verdad *(f.)* truth **7.3**
verdadero(a) true
verde green **4.1**
verduras *(f. pl.)* greens, vegetables **8.1**
verificar to verify
versión *(f.)* version
vestido *(m.)* dress **4.1**
vestimenta *(f.)* dress
vestirse (i, i) to dress (oneself), get dressed **9.2**
vez *(f.)* time **7.2**
viaje *(m.)* trip **7.1**
vibrar to vibrate
víctima *(f.)* victim **10.1**
victoria *(f.)* victory
vida *(f.)* life **7.1**
viejo(a) old **5.1**
viento *(m.)* wind
viernes Friday **2.3**
vigilar to watch over, guard
vino *(m.)* wine **4.3**; **vino blanco** *(m.)* white wine **8.2**; **vino tinto** *(m.)* red wine **8.2**
violencia *(f.)* violence
violento(a) violent
visitante *(m./f.)* visitor
visitar to visit **2.3**
visita *(f.)* tour **4.1**
vistazo *(m.)* glance
vitamina *(f.)* vitamin **13.3**
vivienda *(f.)* dwelling, housing
vivir to live **2.2**
vivo(a) bright *(colors)*, lively **7.3**
vocabulario *(m.)* vocabulary
volante *(m.)* steering wheel **10.2**
volar (ue) to fly **4.3**
volcán *(m.)* volcano
voluntario(a) volunteer **11.2**
volver (ue) to return **4.1**
voto *(m.)* vote
voz *(f.)* voice; **en voz alta** aloud; **en voz baja** quietly
vuelo *(m.)* flight **7.1**

Y

¿y tú? and you? **PE**
ya already **11.3**
yarda *(f.)* yard
¿yo? me? **PE**

Z

zanahoria *(f.)* carrot **8.1**
zapatería *(f.)* shoestore **9.3**
zapato *(m.)* shoe **4.2**
zoología *(f.)* zoology
zoológico: parque zoológico *(m.)* zoo

English-Spanish Vocabulary

This vocabulary includes all the words listed as active vocabulary in *¡Dímelo tú!* Stem-changing verbs appear with the change in parentheses after the infinitive: **(ie), (ue), (i), (ie, i), (ue, u),** or **(i, i)**.

Most cognates, conjugated verb forms, and proper nouns used as passive vocabulary in the text are not included in this glossary.

The following abbreviations are used.

adj.	adjective	*n.*	noun
adv.	adverb	*pl.*	plural
conj.	conjunction	*pp.*	past participle
dem.	demonstrative	*poss.*	possessive
dir. obj.	direct object	*prep.*	preposition
f.	feminine	*pron.*	pronoun
fam.	familiar	*refl.*	reflexive
form.	formal	*rel.*	relative
indir. obj.	indirect object	*s.*	singular
m.	masculine	*subj.*	subject

A

a un(a); **a bad time** un mal rato; **a little** un poco; **a lot** mucho(a)
abandon abandonar
able capaz; **to be able** poder **(ue)**
abortion aborto *(m.)*
about de, acerca de; **to be about** tratar de
abroad extranjero *(m.)*
absurd absurdo(a)
academic académico(a)
accept aceptar
accident accidente *(m.)*
accompany acompañar
accomplish realizar
account cuenta *(f.)*
accuse acusar
ache dolor *(m.)*
acquire adquirir **(ie)**
act actuar
action acción *(f.)*
active activo(a)
activity actividad *(f.)*
actor actor *(m.)*
actress actriz *(f.)*
add añadir
address dirección *(f.)*
administrator administrador(a)
admire admirar
adolescence adolescencia *(f.)*
adore adorar
advance adelantar, avanzar
advantage ventaja *(f.)*
adverse contrario(a)
advertisement aviso *(m.)*; **classified ad** aviso *(m.)*
advice consejo *(m.)*
advise aconsejar
advisor consejero(a)
affectionate amoroso(a)
afraid of (to be) tener miedo de
after después de
afternoon tarde *(f.)*
age edad *(f.)*
aggressive agresivo(a)
aid auxilio *(m.)*; *(v.)* apoyar; prestar auxilio
AIDS SIDA *(m.)*
air aire *(m.)*
airline aerolínea *(f.)*
airplane avión *(m.)*
airport aeropuerto *(m.)*
alarm clock despertador *(m.)*
alcoholic alcohólico(a)
alike igual *(adj., m.* or *f.)*; parecido(a)
all todo(a); **all day** todo el día
allergic alérgico(a)
alley callejón *(m.)*
allow dejar
almost casi
along por
aloud en voz alta
already ya
also también
alternative alternativa *(f.)*
although aunque
always siempre
ambience ambiente *(m.)*
ambitious ambicioso(a)
ambulance ambulancia *(f.)*
amiable amable *(adj., m.* or *f.)*
amusing divertido(a)
an un(a)

analysis análisis *(m.)*
anatomy anatomía *(f.)*
and y; **and you?** ¿y tú?
Andean andino(a)
angry (to get) enojarse
animal animal *(m.)*; **stuffed animal** *(toy)* animal de peluche *(m.)*
ankle tobillo *(m.)*
announcement anuncio *(m.)*
another otro(a)
answer responder, contestar
anthropologist antropólogo(a)
anticipate anticipar, anticipado
antiquated antiguo(a), anticuado(a)
any algún (alguno, alguna)
anyone alguien
anyway de todos modos
apart aparte
apartment apartamento *(m.)*
appear aparecer; **appear like** parecer
appetite apetito
appetizer entremés *(m.)*
apple manzana *(f.)*
application form solicitud *(f.)*
apply for solicitar
appreciate apreciar
appropriate apropiado(a)
approximately aproximadamente
April abril
archaeologist arqueólogo(a)
architect arquitecto(a)
architecture arquitectura *(f.)*
arm brazo *(m.)*
armed forces fuerzas armadas *(f. pl.)*
army ejército *(m.)*
around alrededor
arrest arrestar
arrive llegar
arrogant arrogante *(adj., m.* or *f.)*
art arte *(m.)*
article of clothing prenda *(f.)*
artificial respiration respiración artificial *(f.)*
artist artista *(m. / f.)*
as . . . as tan… como; **as many as** tantos como; **as much as** tanto como; **as soon as** en cuanto, tan pronto como
ask preguntar; **ask for** pedir **(i, i)** solicitar
aspirin aspirina *(f.)*
assassinate asesinar
assault asaltar
assistance ayuda *(f.)*
associate asociar
association asociación *(f.)*
assume suponer
assumption suposición *(f.)*
assure asegurar
at en; **at last!** ¡por fin!; **at (time) o'clock** a la(s) + *time;* **at night** de noche; **at once** en seguida; **at times** a veces; **at your service** para servirle
athlete atleta *(m. / f.)*
athletic atlético(a)
attack atacar
attain alcanzar
attempt tratar de
attend asistir
attitude actitud *(f.)*
attract atraer
audience público *(m.)*
augment aumentar
August agosto
aunt tía *(f.)*
author autor(a)
automobile automóvil *(m.)*
autumn otoño *(m.)*
available disponible *(adj., m.* or *f.)*
avenue avenida *(f.)*
avoid evitar

B

baby-sit cuidar a los niños
back espalda *(f.)*
backpack mochila *(f.)*
bad malo(a)
bakery panadería *(f.)*
ball pelota *(f.)*
banana plátano *(m.)*
band banda *(f.)*
bank banco *(m.)*
baptism bautizo *(m.)*
barber peluquero(a)
bargain ganga *(f.)*
baseball player beisbolista *(m. / f.)*
basket cesto *(m.)*
basketball baloncesto *(m.)*
bat bate *(m.)* *(v.)* batear
bathe (oneself) bañarse
bathroom baño *(m.)*, cuarto de baño *(m.)*, servicios *(m.)*
batter *(baseball)* bateador(a)
battery batería *(f.)*
be estar; **Be quiet!**; ¡Cállate!
beach playa *(f.)*
beak pico *(m.)*
beat derrotar
beat up golpear
beautiful hermoso(a)
beauty belleza *(f.)*
because porque; **because of** por
become ponerse
bed *(f.)* cama
bedroom alcoba *(f.)*, dormitorio *(f.)*, recámara *(f.)*
beef carne de res *(f.)*
beer cerveza *(f.)*
beet remolacha *(f.)*; betabel *(m.)*
before *(prep.)* antes de; *(conj.)* antes (de) que
begin comenzar **(ie),** empezar **(ie)**
behave actuar; portarse bien
behavior actuación *(f.)*, conducta *(f.)*
behind detrás de
belong pertenecer
bench banco *(m.)*
bend doblar
beside al lado
besides además
better mejor
between entre
bicycle bicicleta *(f.)*
big grande *(adj. m.* or *f.)*
bill cuenta *(f.)*
biology biología *(f.)*
bird ave *(f.)*
birthday cumpleaños *(m.s.* and *pl.)*
black negro(a)
blessing bendición *(f.)*

block cuadro *(m.)*, cubo *(m.)*; **city block** cuadra *(f.)*
blond rubio(a)
blood sangre *(f.)*
blouse blusa *(f.)*
blow golpe *(m.)*
blue azul
boat bote *(m.)*, buque *(m.)*, barco *(m.)*
body cuerpo *(m.)*
bomb bomba *(f.)*
book libro *(m.)*
bookstore librería *(f.)*
boot bota *(f.)*
border frontera *(f.)*
boring aburrido(a)
born (to be) nacer
boss jefe *(m. / f.)*
both ambos
bother molestar
bottle botella *(f.)*
bouquet ramo de flores *(m.)*
boxing boxeo *(m.)*
boy chico
boyfriend novio
brake *(apply the brakes of a car)* frenar
bravery valor *(m.)*
bread pan *(m.)*
break romper
breakfast desayuno *(m.)*
breathe respirar
bright vivo(a)
bring traer
brother hermano
brother-in-law cuñado
budget presupuesto *(m.)*
building edificio *(m.)*
bullfight corrida de toros *(f.)*
bullfighter torero(a)
bunch *(a lot)* montón *(m.)*
burn (up) quemarse
burst reventar **(ie)**
bus autobús *(m.)*, bus *(m.)*; **bus stop** parada de autobús *(f.)*
business negocios *(m. pl.)*
but pero
butcher shop carnicería *(f.)*
butter mantequilla *(f.)*
button botón *(m.)*
buy comprar
by junto, por; **by a specified time** para; **by means of** por medio de

C

cabbage col *(f.)*
café café *(m.)*
cafeteria cafetería *(f.)*
cake pastel *(m.)*
calculate calcular
calendar calendario *(m.)*
calisthenics gimnasia *(f.)*
call llamar; **call attention to** llamar la atención
calm calma *(f.)*; **calm (oneself)** calmarse
calmly con calma
calories calorías *(f. pl.)*
camera cámara *(f.)*
camp acampar
campus campo *(m.)*
can poder (ue)
cancel cancelar
cancer cáncer *(m.)*
candy dulce *(m.)*
capable of (to be) ser capaz de
capacity capacidad *(f.)*
captain capitán *(m.)*, capitana *(f.)*
caption título *(m.)*
capture capturar
car coche *(m.)*, carro *(m.)*, automóvil *(m.)*
caramel caramelo *(m.)*; **caramel custard** flan *(m.)*
carbonated drink gaseosa *(f.)*
card tarjeta *(f.)*
careful cuidadoso(a)
Caribbean Caribe *(m.)*
carpet alfombra *(f.)*
carrot zanahoria *(f.)*
carry cargar
carry out realizar
cashier cajero(a)
cassette casete *(m.)*
cat gato(a); **small cat** gatito(a)
category categoría *(f.)*
celebrate celebrar
celery apio *(m.)*
cemetery cementerio *(m.)*
center centro *(m.)*
centigrade centígrado *(m.)*
century siglo *(m.)*
certain cierto(a); **certain of (to be)** estar seguro(a) de
chair silla *(f.)*
chalk tiza *(f.)*
chalkboard pizarra *(f.)*
champion campeón *(m.)*, campeona *(f.)*
championship campeonato *(m.)*
change cambio *(m.)*; *(v.)* cambiar; **change a tire** cambiar una llanta; **change diapers** cambiar los pañales
channel canal *(m.)*
characteristic característica *(f.)*, cualidad *(f.)*
cheat hacer trampas
check cheque *(m.)*; **check the motor** revisar el motor
chemistry química *(f.)*
chest *(for storage)* baúl *(m.)*; *(body part)* pecho *(m.)*
chicken pollo(a)
child niño(a)
childhood niñez *(f.)*
children hijos *(m.)*, niños *(m.)*
chimney chimenea *(f.)*
chocolate chocolate *(m.)*
choose elegir **(i, i)**, escoger
chops chuletas *(f.)*
Christmas Navidad *(f.)*
church iglesia *(f.)*
circle círculo *(m.)*
citizen ciudadano(a)
city ciudad *(f.)*
civilization civilización *(f.)*
clarinet clarinete *(m.)*
class clase *(f.)*
classical clásico(a)
clean *(adj.)* limpio(a), *(v.)* limpiar
client cliente *(m. / f.)*
climate clima *(m.)*
clinic clínica *(f.)*
close cerrar (ie)
clothes ropa *(f.)*
cloudy (to be) estar nublado
clue pista *(f.)*
coach entrenador(a)

coast costa *(f.)*
coat abrigo *(m.)*
cocktail coctel *(m.)*
coffee café *(m.)*
coin moneda *(f.)*
cold frío *(m.)*; resfriado *(illness) (m.)*; **cold (to be)** hacer frío *(weather)*, tener frío *(person)*
collar cuello *(m.)*
collection colección *(f.)*
collide chocar
column columna *(f.)*
comb peinarse
come venir (ie, i)
comfortable cómodo(a)
comical cómico(a)
committee comité *(m.)*
common común *(m.)*; **common sense** sentido común *(adj., m.* or *f.)*
community comunidad *(f.)*
compact disc disco compacto, CD *(m.)*
company empresa *(f.)*
compare comparar
compete competir **(i, i)**
competition competición *(f.)*, competencia *(f.)*
complain quejarse
complete completar
computer computadora *(f.)*
concentrate concentrarse
concerning acerca de
concert concierto *(m.)*
condition condición *(f.)*
confess confesar **(ie)**
confidence confianza *(f.)*
conflict conflicto *(m.)*
confuse confundir
congratulate felicitar
connection conexión (f.)
conquer conquistar, vencer
conqueror vencedor *(m. / f.)*
conquest conquista *(f.)*
conscience conciencia *(f.)*
consequence consecuencia *(f.)*
conservative conservador(a)
conserve conservar
consider considerar
constitution constitución *(f.)*
contact lens lentes de contacto *(m.)*
contagious contagioso(a)
contamination contaminación *(f.)*
content contenido *(m.)*
contest concurso *(m.)*
continue seguir **(i, i)**
continuously continuamente
contract contrato *(m.)*; *(v.)* contratar
contrast contraste *(m.)*
control controlar; manejar
controversial controvertido(a)
conversation conversación *(f.)*
converse conversar
convince convencer
convinced convencido(a)
cook *(v.)* cocinar; *(n.)* cocinero(a)
copy copia *(f.)*
cordon off acordonar
corner esquina *(f.)*; rincón *(m.)*
correct *(adj.)* correcto(a); *(v.)* corregir (i, i)
corridor pasillo *(m.)*
cost costar **(ue)**
cotton algodón *(m.)*
couch potato teleadicto(a)
count contar **(ue)**
country campo *(m.) (countryside)*; país *(m.) (nation)*
couple pareja *(f.)*
court corte *(f.) (legal)*; cancha *(f.) (sports)*
courteous cortés
courteously cortésmente
cousin primo(a)
cover cubierta *(f.)*, *(v.)* abarcar, cubrir, tapar
crab cangrejo *(m.)*
crafts artesanía *(f.)*
crazy loco(a); **crazy about (to be)** estar loco(a) por
create crear
creative creativo(a)
credit crédito *(m.)*
criticism crítica *(f.)*
cruel cruel *(adj., m.* or *f.)*
cry llorar; **cry out** gritar
curious curioso(a)
currently actualmente
custom costumbre *(f.)*
cut cortar; **cut oneself** cortarse
cycling ciclismo *(m.)*
cymbal címbalo *(m.)*

D

daddy papá *(m.)*
daily diario(a)
damage dañar; hacer daño
dance baile *(m.)*; *(v.)* bailar
dangerous peligroso(a)
dark moreno(a) *(referring to complexion and hair)*; oscuro(a)
date cita *(f.)*; fecha *(f.)*; *(v.)* salir juntos
daughter hija
day día *(m.)*
dead (to be) estar muerto(a)
deal with tratar de
dean decano(a)
death muerte *(f.)*
debate debate *(m.)*
debt deuda *(f.)*
deceive engañar
December diciembre
decide decidir
decision decisión *(f.)*
decorate decorar
dedicate dedicar
defeat derrotar
defend defender
degree grado *(m.) (temperature)*; licenciatura *(f.) (educational)*
delicious delicioso(a), rico(a), sabroso(a)
delighted encantado(a)
deliver entregar
demand exigir
demanding exigente
democracy democracia *(f.)*
demonstration manifestación *(f.)*
denounce denunciar
dentist dentista *(m. / f.)*
depressed deprimido(a); **to be depressed** deprimirse
descendent descendiente *(m. / f.)*
describe describir
description descripción *(f.)*
desert desierto *(m.)*
deserve merecer
design diseñar

desire deseo *(m.)*, *(v.)* desear
desired deseado(a)
desk pupitre *(m.) (pupil's)*, escritorio *(m.) (teacher's)*
dessert postre *(m.)*
destroy destruir
detail detalle *(m.)*
detailed detallado(a)
determine determinar
detest detestar
develop desarrollar; revelar *(film)*
dialogue diálogo *(m.)*
diaper pañal *(m.)*
dictatorship dictadura *(f.)*
dictionary diccionario *(m.)*
die morir **(ue, u)**, morirse **(ue, u)**
diet dieta *(f.)*
difference diferencia *(f.)*
different distinto(a)
difficult difícil *(adj., m.* or *f.)*, duro(a)
dining room comedor *(m.)*
dinner cena *(f.)*; **eat dinner** cenar
direct dirigir
directly directamente
dirt suciedad *(f.)*
dirty sucio(a)
disadvantage desventaja *(f.)*
disagreeable antipático(a)
disappear desaparecer
disaster desastre *(m.)*
discipline disciplina *(f.)*
discotheque discoteca *(f.)*
discourteous descortés *(adj., m.* or *f.)*
discover descubrir
discovery descubrimiento *(m.)*
discrimination discriminación *(f.)*
dish plato *(m.)*; **dishes** trastes *(m. pl)*
dishwasher lavaplatos *(m.s.* or *pl.)*
dismiss despedir **(i, i)**
disorganized desorganizado(a)
distant alejado(a)
diversity diversidad *(f.)*
divide dividir
do hacer
doctor médico(a)
dog perro(a)
dollar dólar *(m.)*
domination dominación *(f.)*
donate donar
don't worry no te preocupes *(fam.)*
door puerta *(f.)*
dorm residencia *(f.)*
double doble *(adj., m.* or *f.)*
doubt duda *(f.)*; *(v.)* dudar
doubtful incierto(a)
downtown centro *(m.)*
dozen docena *(f.)*
drawing dibujo *(m.)*
dream sueño *(m.)*, *(v.)* soñar (ue)
dress vestido *(m.)*, *(v.)* vestirse **(i, i)**
drink bebida *(f.)*; *(v.)* beber, tomar
drive conducir, manejar
driver chófer *(m. / f.)*
drizzle lloviznar
drown ahogarse
drum tambor *(m.)*
drunk borracho(a); **to get drunk** emborracharse
dumb tonto(a)
during durante; por; **during the day** de día
dust polvo *(m.)*, *(v.)* pasar el trapo
dwelling vivienda *(f.)*

E

each cada *(adj., m.* or *f.)*
early temprano *(adv.)*
earn ganar
earthquake terremoto *(m.)*
earthy terrestre *(adj., m.* or *f.)*
east este *(m.)*
Easter Pascua Florida *(f.)*
easy fácil *(adj., m.* or *f.)*
eat comer; **eat breakfast** desayunar
economics economía *(f.)*
educated educado(a)
effect efecto *(m.)*
efficient eficaz *(adj., m.* or *f.)*
effort esfuerzo *(m.)*
egg huevo *(m.)*
eight ocho
eighth octavo(a)
either . . . or o… o
elbow codo *(m.)*
elect elegir **(i, i)**
election elección *(f.)*
electric shaver máquina de afeitar *(f.)*
electric shock choque eléctrico *(m.)*, sacudida eléctrica *(f.)*
electrical current corriente *(f.)*
elegant elegante *(adj., m.* or *f.)*
eliminate eliminar
elongated alargado(a)
embrace abarcar
emerald esmeralda *(f.)*
emergency emergencia *(f.)*
emergency room sala de urgencia *(f.)*
emigrate emigrar
empire imperio *(m.)*
employee empleado(a)
employment empleo *(m.)*
empty vacío(a)
encourage animar
end fin *(m.)*; *(v.)* terminar
endure aguantar
energy energía *(f.)*
engineering ingeniería *(f.)*
English inglés *(m.)*
enjoy disfrutar; **enjoy oneself** divertirse **(ie, i)**
enormous enorme *(adj., m.* or *f.)*
enough bastante *(adj., m.* or *f.)*
enter entrar
entertain divertir **(ie, i)**
entrance entrada *(f.)*
enumerate enumerar
envelope sobre *(m.)*
environment medio ambiente *(m.)*
episode episodio *(m.)*
eraser borrador *(m.)*; goma *(f.)*
escape escapar
essential esencial *(adj., m.* or *f.)*
establish establecer
ethnic étnico(a)
even aún; **even though** aún
event evento *(m.)*
every cada; **every day** todos los días
everybody todo el mundo
everyone todo el mundo
evolution evolución *(f.)*
exact exacto(a)
exaggerate exagerar

exam examen *(m.)*
example ejemplo *(m.)*
exceed sobrepasar
excel sobresalir
excellent excelente *(adj., m.* or *f.)*
exception excepción *(f.)*
exceptional excepcional *(adj., m.* or *f.)*
exchange intercambio *(m.)*
excuse excusa *(f.)*
exercise ejercicio
exhausted (to be) estar molido(a)
exhibition exhibición *(f.)*
expect esperar
expense gasto *(m.)*
expensive caro(a)
experience experiencia *(f.)*
explain explicar
explode explotar
express expresar; **express an opinion** opinar
expression expresión *(f.)*
exquisite exquisito(a)
extended family members familiares *(m. pl.)*
extraordinary único(a)
extreme extremo(a)
eye ojo *(m.)*

F

fabulous fabuloso(a)
facade portada *(f.)*
face cara *(f.)*
fact dato *(m.)*, hecho *(m.)*
factory fábrica *(f.)*
fail fracasar
fair justo(a)
fairytale cuento de hadas *(m.)*
fall caer; **fall asleep** dormirse **(ue, u)**; **fall down** caerse; **fall in love** enamorarse
fallen caído(a)
false falso(a)
family familia *(f.)*
famous famoso(a)
fan *(of sporting events)* aficionado(a)
fanatic fanático(a)
fantastic fantástico(a)
far from lejos de
farmer campesino(a)
fascinate fascinar
fascinating fascinante
fast pronto, rápidamente, rápido(a)
fat gordo(a)
father padre *(m.)*
Father's Day Día del Padre *(m.)*
fault culpa *(f.)*; **to be at fault** tener la culpa
favorite favorito(a)
fear temer
February febrero
fed up (to be) estar harto(a) de
feel sentir **(ie, i)**, sentirse **(ie, i)**; **feel fine** sentirse bien **(ie, i)**; **feel like** tener ganas de
feelings sentimientos *(m. pl.)*
fever fiebre *(f.)*
fifth quinto(a)
fight pelea *(f.)*
filling station gasolinera *(f.)*
film película *(f.)*; *(v.)* filmar
filth suciedad *(f.)*
finance financiar
find encontrar **(ue)**
fine multa *(f.)*; *(adv.)* bien; **fine, thank you** bien, gracias, muy bien, gracias
finger dedo *(m.)*; **finger-licking good** para chuparse los dedos
finish terminar
fire incendio *(m.)*; *(v.)* disparar *(a gun)*; despedir **(i, i)** *(from a job)*
firefighter bombero(a)
firm firma *(f.)*
first primer, primero(a)
first aid primeros auxilios *(m. pl.)*
fish pescado *(m.)*
fit sano(a)
five cinco
fix arreglar
flat tire llanta desinflada *(f.)*
flavor sabor *(m.)*
flight vuelo *(m.)*
floor piso *(m.)*
flower flor *(f.)*
fly volar **(ue)**
fog neblina *(f.)*
folder carpeta *(f.)*
follow perseguir **(i, i)**; seguir **(i, i)**
follower seguidor *(m. / f.)*
following siguiente *(adj., m.* or *f.)*
fondness afición *(f.)*
food comida *(f.)*
foolish tonto(a)
foot pie *(m.)*
football fútbol americano *(m.)*
for para, por
forbid prohibir
force fuerza *(f.)*
forecast pronóstico *(m.) (weather)*
foreign extranjero(a)
forest bosque *(m.)*, selva *(f.)*
forget olvidar
fork tenedor *(m.)*
form forma *(f.)*
formal formal *(adj., m.* and *f.)*
fortunately por suerte
fortune fortuna *(f.)*
forward delantero(a) *(soccer position)*
founded fundado(a)
fountain fuente *(f.)*
free *(adv.)* gratis; libre *(adj., m.* or *f.)*; *(v.)* librar
French francés, francesa
frequently con frecuencia
fresh fresco(a)
Friday viernes
fried frito(a)
friend amigo(a)
friendship amistad *(f.)*
from de
front portada *(f.)*
frozen congelado(a)
fruit fruta *(f.)*
frustrated frustrado(a)
fryer pollo(a)
full satisfecho(a); **full of** lleno(a) de
full-time tiempo completo
function funcionar
funny chistoso(a); cómico(a) divertido(a)
furious furioso(a)
furnish proveer
furnished amueblado(a)
furniture muebles *(m. pl.)*
future futuro *(m.)*

G

gain weight subir de peso
game *(competitive)* partido *(m.);* juego *(m.)*
garage garaje *(m.)*
garden jardín *(m.)*
garment prenda *(f.)*
gas station gasolinera *(f.)*
gasoline gasolina *(f.)*
gather recoger
gathered reunido(a)
gathering reunión *(f.)*
gender género *(m.)*
generation generación *(f.)*
generous generoso(a)
genius genio(a)
German alemán, alemana
get conseguir **(i, i); get ahead** adelantarse; **get along well** llevarse bien; **get down** bajarse; **get hurt** lesionarse; **get off** bajarse; **get on** subir, montar; **get together** juntarse, reunirse; **get up** levantarse
gift regalo *(m.)*
gigantic gigantesco(a)
girl chica
girlfriend novia
give dar; **give a gift** regalar; **give assistance** prestar auxilio
glance vistazo *(m.)*
glass vaso *(m.);* **glass of wine** copa de vino *(f.)*
glove guante *(m.)*
go ir; **go camping** acampar; **go down** bajar; **go for a ride** pasear; **go forward** adelantarse; **go out** salir; **go shopping** ir de compras; **go tell it to the Marines** a otro perro con ese hueso; **go to bed** acostarse **(ue); go up** subir
goal arco *(m.);* gol *(m.)*
goalie arquero *(m.)*
goalkeeper arquero *(m.)*
goblet copa *(f.)*
god dios
goddess diosa
gold oro *(m.)*
good bueno(a); **good afternoon** buenas tardes; **good evening** buenas noches; **good heavens!** ¡caramba! **good luck** buena suerte *(f.);* **good morning** buenos días
good-bye adiós, hasta la vista
good-looking bien parecido(a), guapo(a)
goodness! ¡caramba!
gorge barranca *(f.)*
govern gobernar **(ie)**
government gobierno *(m.)*
grade nota *(f.);* **get good grades** sacar buenas notas
graduate graduarse
grandfather abuelo
grandmother abuela
grandparents abuelos *(m. pl.)*
green verde
greens verduras *(f. pl)*
greeting saludo *(m.)*
gray gris
grill parrilla *(f.)*
grilled a la parrilla
grouchy gruñón, gruñona
ground terreno *(m.)*
group grupo *(m.)*
guarantee garantizar
guard guardia *(m. / f.);* defensor(a); *(v.)* vigilar
guess adivinar
guest invitado(a)
guide guía *(m. / f.)*
guilty culpable *(adj., m.* and *f.)*
guitar guitarra *(f.);* **guitar player** guitarrista *(m. / f.)*
gun pistola *(f.)*
gymnastics gimnasia *(f.)*

H

habit hábito *(m.);* rutina *(f.)*
hair pelo *(m.);* **hair dryer** secador *(m.)*
hairdresser peluquero(a)
half mitad *(f.)*
ham jamón *(m.)*
hamburger hamburguesa *(f.)*
hand mano *(f.);* **hand over** entregar
handicrafts artesanía *(f.)*
handkerchief pañuelo *(m.)*
handle tratar
hang colgar **(ue); hang up** colgar **(ue)**
happiness felicidad *(f.)*
happy feliz; contento(a); **Happy birthday!** ¡feliz cumpleaños!
hard duro(a); **hard-working** trabajador(a)
hate odiar
have tener; **have to** tener que; **have a blowout** reventar (ie) una llanta; **have a good time** divertirse **(ie, i); have clear skies** estar despejado; **have good weather** hacer buen tiempo; **I would have** tendría
head cabeza *(f.)*
headache dolor de cabeza *(m.)*
heading titular *(m.),* título *(m.)*
headline titular *(m.)*
headphones audífono *(m.)*
health salud *(f.)*
healthy sano(a)
hear oír
heart corazón *(m.);* **heart attack** ataque cardíaco *(m.)*
height estatura *(f.)*
hello! ¡hola!
helmet casco *(m.)*
help ayuda *(f.);* **help!** ¡auxilio!, ¡socorro!; *(v.)* ayudar
her *(dir. obj. pron. s.)* ella; *(indir. obj. pron. s.)* le
here acá, aquí
highlands altiplano *(m.)*
highway carretera *(f.)*
him *(dir. obj. pron. s.)* él; *(indir. obj. pron. s.)* le
Hispanic hispano(a)
history historia *(f.)*
hit golpe *(m.);* *(v.)* golpear, pegar
holy sagrado(a)
home hogar *(m.);* **home run** jonrón *(m.)*

homework tarea *(f.)*
honest honesto(a)
hope esperanza *(f.)*
horse caballo *(m.)*
hospital hospital *(m.)*
hot caliente *(adj., m.* or *f.); **hot (to be)** hacer calor *(weather);* tener calor *(person);* **hot sauce** salsa picante
hotel hotel *(m.)*
hour hora *(f.)*
house casa *(f.)*
housing vivienda *(f.)*
how? ¿cómo?; **how are you?** ¿cómo estás? *(fam.)*, ¿qué tal?; **how many?** ¿cuántos(as)?; **how much?** ¿cuánto(a)?
human humano(a)
humid húmedo(a)
hungry (to be) tener hambre
hurry up apúrese; **in a hurry (to be)** tener prisa
hurt dañar; doler **(ue)** hacer daño; **hurt oneself** lastimarse
husband esposo

I

I yo; **I am** soy; **I hope** ojalá; **I'd like you to meet . . .** te presento a...
ice hielo *(m.)*
ice cream helado *(m.)*
ideal ideal *(adj., m.* or *f.)*
identical idéntico(a)
identify identificar
ignore ignorar
illness enfermedad *(f.)*
illustrate ilustrar
image imagen *(f.)*
imagination imaginación *(f.)*
imagine imaginar, imaginarse
immediately en seguida; inmediatamente
immense inmenso(a)
impartial imparcial *(adj., m.,* or *f.)*
impatient impaciente *(adj., m.* or *f.)*
important importante *(adj., m.* or *f.)*
impossible imposible *(adj., m.* or *f.)*
impress impresionar
impression impresión *(f.)*
impressive impresionante *(adj., m.* or *f.)*
improbable improbable *(adj., m.* or *f.)*
in *(prep.)* por, *(adv.)* adentro; **in a short while** al rato; **in case** en caso (de) que; **in charge** encargado(a); **in exchange for** por; **in fact** en efecto; **in front of** delante de, enfrente de; **in love** enamorado(a); **in order to** para; **in place of** por; **in relation to** para; **in spite of** a pesar de; **in the back** al fondo
Incan incaico(a)
incident incidente *(m.)*
inclined to estar dispuesto a...
include incluir
income ingresos *(m.)*
inconvenient inconveniente *(adj., m.* or *f.)*
increase añadir, aumentar
incredible increíble *(adj., m.* or *f.)*
index índice *(m.)*
Indian indio(a)
indicate indicar, señalar
individual individuo *(m.)*
industry industria *(f.)*
inexpensive barato(a)
infancy infancia *(f.)*
influence influencia *(f.)*
inform informar
information información *(f.)*
inhabitant habitante *(m. / f.)*
inhumane inhumano(a)
initiate iniciar
injection inyección *(f.)*
injure lastimar; lesionarse
injured herido(a)
inner ear oído *(m.)*
innocent inocente *(adj., m.* or *f.)*
innovator innovador(a)
inside adentro
insinuate insinuar
insist (on) insistir (en)
inspire inspirar
instability inestabilidad *(f.)*
instrument instrumento *(m.)*
insurance seguro *(m.)*
insure asegurar
insured asegurado(a)
integrate integrar
intelligent inteligente *(adj., m.* or *f.)*
intended for para
interest interés *(m.)*
interesting interesante *(adj., m.* or *f.)*
international internacional *(adj., m.* or *f.)*
interpret interpretar
interview entrevista *(f.); (v.)* entrevistar
intimate íntimo(a)
introduction presentación *(f.)*
invent inventar
invest invertir **(ie, i)**
invitation invitación *(f.)*
invite invitar
iron planchar
ironic irónico(a)
irony ironía *(f.)*
irrigation irrigación *(f.)*
island isla *(f.)*
isolated aislado(a)
it *(dir. obj. pron.)* lo, la; *(indir. obj. pron.)* le; *(subj. pron.)* él, ella; **it is sunny** hay sol
itinerary itinerario *(m.)*

J

jacket chaqueta *(f.)*
janitor conserje *(m.)*
January enero
Japanese japonés, japonesa
jealous envidioso(a)
jeans: blue jeans vaqueros *(m. pl.)*
jewel joya *(f.)*
job puesto *(m.)*
jot down anotar
juice jugo *(m.)*
juicy jugoso(a)
July julio

jump saltar
June junio
just justo(a)

K

keep guardar; **keep calm** mantener **(ie)** la calma
ketchup salsa de tomate *(f.)*
key llave *(f.)*
keyboard teclado *(m.)*
kick patear
kill matar
king rey *(m.)*
kiss beso *(m.)*
kitchen cocina *(f.)*
knee rodilla *(f.)*
knife cuchillo *(m.)*
know conocer; **know facts** saber

L

laboratory laboratorio *(m.)*
laborer obrero(a)
lack faltar
lady dama *(f.)*; señora *(f.)*
lake lago *(m.)*
lamp lámpara *(f.)*
land terreno *(m.)*
lane pista *(f.)*
language lenguaje *(m.)*, idioma *(m.)*
large grande *(adj., m.* or *f.)*
last último(a), *(v.)* durar **last name** apellido *(m.)*; **last night** anoche
late tarde
later posteriormente; más tarde
latest último(a)
laugh reírse **(i, i)**
laundry lavandería *(f.)*
law derecho *(m.)*; ley *(f.)*
lawyer *(m.)* abogado
lazy flojo(a); perezoso(a)
leader líder *(m. / f.)*
league liga *(f.)*
learn aprender
leave salir; **leave behind** dejar
left izquierdo(a)
leg pierna *(f.)*
legally legalmente
lemon limón *(m.)*
lemonade limonada *(f.)*
lend prestar
less menos
letter carta *(f.)*
lettuce lechuga *(f.)*
level nivel *(m.)*
liberal liberal *(adj., m.* or *f.)*
liberate librar
library biblioteca *(f.)*
license licencia *(f.)*
lie mentira *(f.)*
lieutenant teniente *(m. / f.)*
life vida *(f.)*
lifeguard salvavidas *(m. / f.)*
lifesaver salvavidas *(m.)*
lift levantar
light luz *(f.)*
like gustar; **I (he, she, it) would like** quisiera
likeable simpático(a)
likewise igualmente
liking afición *(f.)*
limit límite *(m.)*
list lista *(f.)*
listen! ¡oye!; **listen to me!** ¡escúchame! *(fam.)*
literature literatura *(f.)*
little pequeño(a); poco
live vivir
living room sala *(f.)*
load cargar
lobster langosta *(f.)*
local local *(adj., m.* or *f.)*
location ubicación *(f.)*
long largo(a)
look at mirar; **look for** buscar
loose suelto *(m.)*
lose perder **(ie)**; **lose weight** perder **(ie)** peso
lost perdido(a)
lots montón *(m.)*
lottery lotería *(f.)*
loud fuerte *(adj., m.* or *f.)*
love amar, querer (ie); **in love with (to be)** estar enamorado(a) de; **I would love to** me encantaría
loving amoroso(a)
lower bajar
lucky (to be) tener suerte
luckily por suerte
luggage equipaje *(m.)*
lumber madera *(f.)*
lunch almuerzo *(m.)*; **to have lunch** almorzar **(ue)**

M

machine máquina *(f.)*
macho machista *(m.)*
magazine revista *(f.)*
maintain mantener (ie)
major especialización *(f.)*; *(v.)* especializarse
majority mayoría *(f.)*
make hacer; **make the bed** hacer la cama; **make decisions** tomar decisiones
male varón *(m.)*
mall centro comercial *(m.)*
man hombre *(m.)*; varón *(m.)*
young man joven *(m.)*
manage manejar
manager gerente *(m. / f.)*
manner manera *(f.)*, modo *(m.)*
marathon maratón *(m.)*
March marzo
march marchar
mark marcar
marmalade mermelada *(f.)*
marriage casamiento *(m.)*
marry casarse; **get married** casarse
mathematics matemáticas *(f. pl.)*
May mayo
mayonnaise mayonesa *(f.)*
mayor alcalde *(m.)*, alcaldesa *(f.)*
me *(dir. obj. pron.)* me; *(indir. obj. pron.)* me; *(refl. pron.)* me; **me?** ¿yo?
meaning significado *(m.)*
measure medir **(i, i)**
meat carne *(f.)*
mechanic mecánico(a)
medal medalla *(f.)*
meeting reunión *(f.)*

melon melón *(m.)*
member miembro *(m. / f.)*
memory memoria *(f.)*
mention mencionar
menu menú *(m.)*
message mensaje *(m.)*
military militar *(adj., m.* or *f.)*
milk leche *(f.)*
mirror espejo *(m.)*
miss extrañar, echar de menos; **miss class** faltar a clase
missing (to be) faltar
modest modesto(a)
moment momento *(m.)*
Monday lunes
money dinero *(m.)*
monkey mono(a)
monologue monólogo *(m.)*
month mes *(m.)*
monthly mensual *(adj., m.* or *f.)*
moon luna *(f.)*
more más
morning mañana *(f.)*
mother mamá *(f.),* madre *(f.);* **Mother Nature** madre naturaleza *(f.);* **Mother's Day** Día de las Madres *(m.)*
motor motor *(m.)*
motorcycle moto *(f.)*
mountain climbing alpinismo *(m.)*
mountain montaña *(f.),* monte *(m.)*
mouse ratón *(m.);* **mouse pad** almohadilla *(f.)*
mouth boca *(f.)*
move mudarse
movie theater cine *(m.);* **movie / theater section** *(of newspaper)* espectáculo *(m.)*
mow the lawn cortar el césped
Mrs. señora *(f.)*
much mucho(a)
museum museo *(m.)*
mushroom champiñón *(m.)*
music música *(f.)*
musician músico *(m. / f.)*
mustache bigote *(m.)*
mustard mostaza *(f.)*
my *(poss. adj.)* mi; **my name is . . .** me llamo... , mi nombre es...
mysterious misterioso(a)

N

name nombre *(m.); (v.)* nombrar
napkin servilleta *(f.)*
narrate narrar
narrow angosto(a), estrecho(a)
national nacional *(adj., m.* or *f.)*
native indígena *(adj., m.* or *f.)*
naturally naturalmente
nature naturaleza *(f.)*
near cerca de
necklace collar *(m.)*
necktie corbata *(f.)*
need necesitar
negation negación *(f.)*
negative negativo(a)
neighbor vecino(a)
neighborhood barrio *(m.)*
neither tampoco; **neither . . . nor** ni... ni
nervous nervioso(a)
net red *(f.)*
never jamás, nunca
nevertheless sin embargo
new nuevo(a)
news noticias *(f.)*
newscaster noticiero *(m.)*
newspaper periódico *(m.);* **newspaper reporter** periodista *(m. / f.)*
next próximo(a), siguiente *(adj., m.* or *f.);* **next to** junto a
nice amable *(adj., m.* or *f.)*
night noche *(f.)*
nightly nocturno(a)
nine nueve
ninth noveno(a)
no no; **no one** nadie; **no wonder!** ¡con razón!
Nobel Prize Premio Nóbel *(m.)*
nobody nadie
nocturnal nocturno(a)
none ninguno(a)
north norte *(m.)*
nose nariz *(f.)*
not any ninguno(a); **not even** ni siquiera; **not very well** no muy bien
note nota *(f.)*
notebook cuaderno *(m.)*
nothing nada
notice fijarse, notar
noun sustantivo *(m.)*
novel novela *(f.)*
novelist novelista *(m. / f.)*
November noviembre
now ahora
number número *(m.)*

O

object oponerse
obligated obligado(a)
obligation obligación *(f.)*
oblige obligar
observe observar
obstruct impedir **(i, i)**
obtain conseguir **(i, i);** obtener **(ie)**
obvious obvio(a)
obviously obviamente
occasion ocasión *(f.)*
occupied ocupado(a)
occupy ocupar
occur ocurrir
October octubre
of de; **of course** por supuesto, ¡claro que sí!
offer oferta *(f.); (v.)* **offer** ofrecer
office oficina *(f.);* **cashier's office** caja *(f.)*
oh! *(interj.)* ¡ay!, ¡huy!
oil aceite *(m.),* petróleo *(m.)*
old viejo(a); **to be . . . years old** tener... años; **old age** vejez *(f.);* **old-fashioned** antiguo(a); **very old** anticuado(a)
older mayor
on en, por; **on foot** a pie; **on special** en oferta; **on top of** encima de, sobre
once in awhile de vez en cuando
only *(adv.)* sólo; *(adj.)* único(a)
open abrir
operator operador(a)
opportunity oportunidad *(f.)*
oppose oponerse
opposite opuesto(a), contrario(a); **opposite direction** sentido contrario *(m.)*
opposition oposición *(f.)*

optimist optimista *(m. / f.)*
orange anaranjado(a) *(color);* naranja *(f.) (fruit);* **orange juice** jugo de naranja *(m.)*
order orden *(f.)*
organization organización *(f.)*
organize ordenar, organizar
origin origen *(m.)*
other otro(a)
out afuera
outer ear oreja *(f.)*
outside afuera
outstanding sobresaliente *(adj., m.* or *f.)*; **to be outstanding** sobresalir
oven horno *(m.)*
over sobre; **over here** acá
overcoat sobretodo *(m.)*
own propio(a)
owner amo *(m.)*, dueño(a)

P

pace paso *(m.)*
pack (a suitcase) empacar
page página *(f.)*
pain dolor *(m.)*
painting cuadro *(m.)*
pair par *(m.) (things);* pareja *(f.) (people)*
pajamas pijamas *(m. pl.)*
pants pantalones *(m. pl.)*
papa papá *(m.)*
paper papel *(m.)*
parents padres *(m. pl.)*
park parque *(m.)*; *(v.)* estacionar
parking ticket multa *(f.)*
participate participar
partner compañero(a)
party fiesta *(f.)*
pass pasar; **pass a class** aprobar **(ue)**
passage pasillo *(m.)*
passport pasaporte *(m.)*
past pasado(a)
pastime pasatiempo *(m.)*
pastoral pastoril *(adj., m.* or *f.)*
patience paciencia *(f.)*
patient paciente *(adj., m.* or *f.)*
patio patio *(m.)*
pay attention to atender **(ie)**
pay sueldo *(m.)* *(v.)* pagar; **I would pay** pagaría
peace paz *(f.)*
peaceful tranquilo(a)
peach durazno *(m.)*
pen (ballpoint) bolígrafo *(m.)*
pencil lápiz *(m.)*
people gente *(f.)*
pepper pimienta *(f.)*
percent por ciento
percentage porcentaje *(m.)*
perfect perfecto(a)
performance actuación *(f.)*
permit dejar; permitir
person persona *(f.)*
personality personalidad *(f.)*
perspiration sudor *(m.)*
perspire sudar
persuade persuadir
petroleum petróleo *(m.)*
pharmacy farmacia *(f.)*
phenomenal fenomenal *(adj., m.,* or *f.)*
phone teléfono *(m.);* **phone call** llamada *(f.)*
photo foto *(f.)*
photograph fotografía *(f.)*
physical education educación física *(f.)*
physics física *(f.)*
piano piano *(m.)*
pick up recoger
piece pieza *(f.)*
pill pastilla *(f.)*
pineapple piña *(f.)*
pirate pirata *(m. / f.)*
pitcher lanzador(a) *(baseball)*
pity lástima *(f.)*
place lugar *(m.)*
plan *(v.)* pensar **(ie),** planear
plans planes *(m. pl.)*
plastic plástico *(m.)*
plate plato *(m.)*
play obra de teatro *(f.) (in theater); (v.)* jugar **(ue); play a sport** practicar un deporte; **play an instrument** tocar; **play the role** hacer el papel
player jugador(a)
pleasant simpático(a)
pleased to meet you mucho gusto
plug in enchufar
pocket bolsillo *(m.)*
point punto *(m.)*
poison veneno *(m.)*
police force policía *(f.)*
police officer policía *(m.)*
polite cortés *(adj., m. and f.)*
politely cortésmente
political party partido *(m.)*
political político(a)
political science ciencias políticas *(f. pl.)*
politician político *(m. / f.)*
politics política *(f.)*
pollution contaminación *(f.),* polución *(f.)*
popular popular *(adj., m.* or *f.)*
popularity popularidad *(f.)*
populated poblado(a)
population población *(f.)*
pork carne de puerco *(f.)*
position puesto *(m.)*
positive positivo(a)
positively positivamente
possess poseer
possibility posibilidad *(f.)*
potato papa *(f.)*
poverty pobreza *(f.)*
powerful poderoso(a)
practice practicar
precaution precaución *(f.)*
precious precioso(a)
precise preciso(a)
precisely con precisión
predict predecir **(i)**
prefer preferir **(ie, i)**
preference preferencia *(f.)*
pregnancy embarazo *(m.)*
pregnant embarazada
preoccupied preocupado(a)
preparation preparación *(f.)*
prepare preparar; **prepare dinner** preparar la cena
prescribe recetar
presentation presentación *(f.)*
president *(of a university)* rector(a)
press prensa *(f.)*
pressure presión *(f.)*
pretend aparentar **(ie)**
pretty lindo(a)

previous anterior *(adj., m.* or *f.)*
pre-Colombian precolombino(a)
price precio *(m.)*
pride orgullo *(m.)*
printer impresora *(f.)*
prisoner prisionero(a)
private privado(a)
privilege privilegio *(m.)*
prize premio *(m.)*
problematic problemático(a)
process proceso *(m.)*
proclaim proclamar
prodigal pródigo(a)
product producto *(m.)*
profession profesión *(f.)*
professional profesional *(adj., m.* or *f.)*
professor profesor(a)
profound profundo(a)
profoundly profundamente
program programa *(m.)*
programmer programador(a)
progressive progresista *(m. / f.)*
prohibit prohibir
project proyecto *(m.); (v.)* proyectar
promise promesa *(f.); (v.)* prometer
propose proponer
proprietor amo *(m.)*
protect proteger
protest protestar
provide proveer
provided (that) con tal (de) que
provoke provocar
prudent sensato(a)
psychiatrist psiquiatra *(m. / f.)*
public público *(m.)*
publication publicación *(f.)*
publish publicar
pull one's leg tomar el pelo
punctual puntual *(adj., m.* or *f.)*
punctuation puntuación *(f.)*
pure puro(a)
purse bolso *(m.);* cartera *(f.)*
put poner; **put in order** ordenar; **put one's room in order** ordenar el cuarto

Q

quality calidad *(f.);* cualidad *(characteristic) (f.)*
quantity cantidad *(f.)*
queen reina *(f.)*
question pregunta *(f.)*
quick pronto
quietly en voz baja

R

race carrera *(f.) (car);* raza *(f.) (ethnic)*
racist racista *(m. / f.)*
radiator radiador *(m.)*
radio announcer locutor *(m. / f.)*
radio radio *(f.)*
radish rábano *(m.)*
railroad ferrocarril *(m.)*
rain lluvia *(f.), (v.)* llover **(ue); rain cats and dogs** llover **(ue)** a cántaros; **rain lightly** lloviznar
rainbow arco iris *(m.)*
raincoat impermeable *(m.)*
rainy lluvioso(a)
raise levantar
rapid pronto; rápido(a)
rapidly rápidamente
rapper rapero(a)
rare raro(a)
ravine barranca *(f.)*
raw crudo(a)
reach alcanzar
react reaccionar
read leer
reality realidad *(f.)*
realize cumplir
really de veras
reborn (to be) renacer
recall acordarse **(ue)**
receive recibir
recent reciente *(adj., m.* or *f.)*
recently recientemente
receptionist recepcionista *(m. / f.)*
reclaimed reclamado(a)
recognize reconocer
recommend recomendar **(ie)**
recommendation recomendación *(f.)*
reconstruct reconstruir
record disco *(m.); (v.)* grabar
red rojo(a); **red wine** vino tinto *(m.)*
reduced en rebaja
reduction rebaja *(f.)*
referee árbitro *(m.)*
reflect reflejar
refrigerator nevera *(f.)*
refuge refugio *(m.)*
region región *(f.)*
registration matrícula *(f.)*
reject rechazar
rejection rechazo *(m.)*
relate relacionar
relation relación *(f.)*
relative pariente *(m.)*
relax relajarse
religious religioso(a)
remain permanecer, quedarse
remember acordarse **(ue),** recordar **(ue)**
remembrance memoria *(f.)*
remote alejado(a)
rent alquiler *(m.), (v.)* alquilar
repeat repetir **(i, i)**
replace reemplazar
report informe *(m.); (v.)* reportar
represent representar
representative representante *(m. / f.)*
researcher investigador(a)
reservation reservación *(f.)*
reserved reservado(a)
residence residencia *(f.)*
resolution resolución *(f.)*
resolve resolver **(ue)**
resource recurso *(m.)*
respect respeto *(m.); (v.)* respetar
respond responder
response respuesta *(f.)*
responsibilities deberes *(m. pl.);* responsabilidades *(f. pl.)*
responsibility responsabilidad *(f.)*
rest resto *(m.); (v.)* descansar, hacer la siesta
restaurant restaurante *(m.)*
restore restaurar
retire jubilarse
return retorno *(m.); (v.)* regresar; volver **(ue);** devolver **(ue)** *(something)*
reunite reunirse
reunited reunido(a)

reveal revelar
revenue ingresos *(m. pl.)*
review revisar
revise revisar
revolution revolución *(f.)*
rhythm ritmo *(m.)*
rice arroz *(m.)*
rich rico(a)
riddle adivinanza *(f.)*
ride montar
right derecho(a); **to be right** tener razón
rigorous riguroso(a)
ring sonar **(ue); ring the doorbell** tocar el timbre; **ring-ring** (phone) rin-rin
roasted asado(a)
rob robar
robbery robo *(m.)*
robust robusto(a)
rock piedra *(f.)*
role papel *(m.)*
role-play dramatizar
romantic romántico(a)
roof techo *(m.)*
room cuarto *(m.)*, habitación *(f.)*
roommate compañero(a) de cuarto
rose rosa *(f.)*
round redondo(a)
route ruta *(f.)*
routine rutina *(f.)*
ruins ruinas *(f. pl)*
rule regla *(f.)*
run *(v.)* correr, funcionar (a motor); **run away** huir

S

sacred sagrado(a)
sacrifice oneself sacrificarse
sad triste *(adj., m.* or *f.)*
safety seguridad *(f.)*
salad ensalada *(f.)*
salary salario *(m.)*, sueldo *(m.)*
sale liquidación *(f.)*
salesclerk vendedor(a)
salesperson dependiente *(m. / f.)*
salt sal *(f.)*
salty salado(a)
same igual *(adj., m.* or *f.)*, mismo(a)
sand arena *(f.)*
sandwich sandwich *(m.)*
satisfied satisfecho(a)
Saturday sábado
sauce salsa *(f.)*
sausage salchicha *(f.)*
sautéed in garlic al ajillo
save ahorrar
saxophone saxofón *(m.)*
say decir (i)
scarce escaso(a)
scarf bufanda *(f.)*
scene escena *(f.)*
school escuela *(f.)*; **elementary school** escuela primaria *(f.)*; **high school** escuela secundaria *(f.)*
scrambled *(egg)* revuelto
scream grito *(m.)*
sculpture escultura *(f.)*
sea mar *(m. / f.)*
seafood marisco *(m.)*
season estación *(f.)*; temporada *(f.)*
seat asiento *(m.)*
second segundo(a)
secret secreto *(m.)*
secretary secretario(a)
security seguridad *(f.)*
see ver; **see you later** hasta luego; **see you soon** hasta pronto; **see you tomorrow** hasta mañana
seem parecer
select elegir **(i, i),** escoger; seleccionar
sell vender
seller vendedor(a)
semester semestre *(m.)*
send enviar; mandar
sense sentido *(m.)*
sensible sensato(a)
sensitive sensible *(adj., m. or f.)*
sentimental sensible *(adj., m. or f.)*, sentimental *(adj., m. or f.)*, romántico(a)
sentiments sentimientos *(m. pl.)*
separate separar
September septiembre
series serie *(f.)*
serious serio(a)
servant sirviente *(m. / f.)*
serve servir **(i, i)**
set the table poner la mesa
seven siete
seventh séptimo(a)
shame lástima *(f.)*
shampoo champú *(m.)*
share compartir
sharp point pico *(m.)*
shatter romperse
shave afeitarse
sheet of paper hoja de papel *(f.)*
shellfish marisco *(m.)*
ship navío *(m.)*
shirt camisa *(f.)*; **tee shirt** camiseta *(f.)*
shoe zapato *(m.)*; **shoestore** zapatería *(f.)*
shopping center centro comercial *(m.)*
short bajo(a) *(in height)*; corto(a) *(in length)*; **short pants** pantalones cortos *(m. pl.)*
shorts shorts *(m. pl.)*, pantalones cortos *(m. pl.)*
shoulder hombro *(m.)*
shout grito *(m.)*; *(v.)* gritar
show espectáculo *(m.)*; **show a good time** divertir **(ie, i)**
shower **(take a shower)** ducharse
shrimp camarón *(m.)*
siblings hermanos *(m. pl.)*
sick enfermo(a); **get sick** enfermarse
sidewalk acera *(f.)*
sign firmar
signal señalar
silk seda *(f.)*
similar parecido(a)
sincere sincero(a)
sing cantar
singer cantante *(m. / f.)*
sister hermana
sister-in-law cuñada
sit down sentarse **(ie)**
site sitio *(m.)*
situated situado(a)
situation situación *(f.)*
six seis

sixth sexto(a)
size tamaño *(m.)*
ski esquiar
skiing esquí *(m.)*
skin piel *(f.)*
skirt falda *(f.)*
sky cielo *(m.)*
skyscraper rascacielos *(m. s.* or *pl.)*
sleep dormir **(ue, u)**
sleepy (to be) tener sueño
sleeve manga *(f.)*
slow lento(a)
slowly lentamente
small pequeño(a)
smile sonreír **(i, i)**
smoke humo *(m.); (v.)* fumar
snack bocadillo *(m.)*
snow nieve *(f.), (v.)* nevar **(ie)**
so tan; **so many** tantos(as); **so much** tanto(a); **so that** para que
soap jabón *(m.)*
soccer fútbol *(m.);* **soccer player** futbolista *(m. / f.)*
sociable sociable *(adj., m. or f.)*
society sociedad *(f.)*
sofa sofá *(m.)*
soft drink refresco *(m.)*
sole único(a)
some algún (alguno, alguna)
someone alguien
something algo
sometime alguna vez
sometimes a veces
son hijo
song canción *(f.)*
sorry triste *(adj., m. or f.)*; **I'm sorry** Lo siento.
soup sopa *(f.)*
source fuente *(f.)*
south sur *(m.)*
southwest sudoeste *(m.)*
souvenir recuerdo *(m.)*
speak hablar; **speak on the phone** hablar por teléfono
speakers parlantes *(m.)*
special especial *(adj., m. or f.);* **special event** espectáculo *(m.)*
specific específico(a)
spectacular espectacular *(adj., m. or f.)*
speed limit límite de velocidad *(m.)*
spend gastar *(money);* pasar *(time)*
spoon cuchara *(f.)*
sport deporte *(m.)*
sportsman deportista *(m.)*
sportswoman deportista *(f.)*
spouse cónyuge *(m. / f.)*
spring primavera *(f.)*
square cuadrado *(m.)*
squeeze apretar **(ie)**
squid calamar *(m.)*
stadium estadio *(m.)*
stamp *(for mail)* sello *(m.)*
stand *(put up with)* aguantar
star estrella *(f.)*
state estado *(m.)*
stationery store papelería *(f.)*
stay permanecer, quedarse; **stay calm** mantener **(ie)** la calma; **stay overnight** pasar la noche
steak bistec *(m.)*
steal robar
steering wheel volante *(m.)*
step paso *(m.)*
stepdaughter hijastra
stepfather padrastro *(m.)*
stepmother madrastra *(f.)*
stepson hijastro
still todavía
stock market bolsa *(f.)*
stockings medias *(f.)*
stomach estómago
stone piedra *(f.)*
stop parar; **stop doing something** dejar de
store tienda *(f.);* **store clerk** dependiente; **store window** escaparate *(m.)*
storm tormenta *(f.)*
stove estufa *(f.)*
straight (ahead) derecho
strange extraño(a)
strawberry fresa *(f.)*
street calle *(f.);* **main street** calle principal *(f.)*
strength fuerza *(f.)*
strengthen tonificar
stress estrés *(m.);* **be under stress** sufrir estrés
stretch estirar
strike huelga *(f.)*
strong fuerte *(adj., m. or f.)*
student estudiante *(m. / f.)*
studio estudio *(m.)*
studious estudioso(a)
study estudiar
stupendous estupendo(a)
style estilo *(m.)*
subsequently posteriormente
substance sustancia *(f.)*
subterranean subterráneo(a)
succeed tener éxito
success éxito *(m.)*
suddenly de repente
suffer sufrir
sugar azúcar
suggest sugerir **(ie, i)**
suit traje *(m.)*
suitcase maleta *(f.)*
summary resumen *(m.);* sumario *(m.)*
summer verano *(m.)*
sun sol *(m.)*
Sunday domingo
sunglasses gafas de sol *(f. pl.)*
sunken hundido(a)
supermarket supermercado *(m.)*
superpower superpotencia *(f.)*
supplies materiales *(m. pl.)*
support apoyar, soportar
suppose suponer
supposition suposición *(f.)*
sure (to be) estar seguro(a) de
surface superficie *(f.)*
surpass sobrepasar
surprise sorprender
surprising sorprendente
surrender someterse
surround rodear
surroundings ambiente *(m.)*
survey encuesta *(f.)*
survive sobrevivir
suspect sospechar
suspend suspender
suspicious sospechoso(a)
sweat sudor *(m.); (v.)* sudar
sweater suéter *(m.)*
sweet dulce *(m.)*
swim nadar; **swimsuit** traje de baño *(m.)*

swimming natación *(f.)*; **swimming pool** piscina *(f.)*
syllable sílaba *(f.)*
system sistema *(m.)*

T

table mesa *(f.)*
take tomar, llevar; **take care!** ¡cuídate! **take a class** seguir **(i, i)** un curso; **take a nap** hacer la siesta; **take away** quitar; **take care of** atender **(ie),** cuidar; **take leave** despedirse **(i, i);** **take note** anotar; **take off** quitarse; **take out the trash** sacar la basura; **take pictures** sacar fotografías
talent talento *(m.)*
tall alto(a)
tank tanque *(m.)*
taste sabor *(m.)*; *(v.)* probar **(ue)**
tasty sabroso(a)
tax impuesto *(m.)*
tea té *(m.)*
teach enseñar
team equipo *(m.)*
telephone book guía telefónica *(f.)*
tell contar **(ue);** **tell a lie** mentir **(ie, i)**
temperature temperatura *(f.)*
terrace terraza *(f.)*
terrain terreno *(m.)*
terrestrial terrestre
terrible terrible
territory territorio *(m.)*
terrorist terrorista *(m. / f.)*
testament testamento *(m.)*
testimony testimonio *(m.)*
Thanksgiving Day Día de Acción de Gracias *(m.)*
that *(dem. pron.)* ése(a); *(neuter pron.)* eso
theater teatro *(m.)*
theft robo *(m.)*
them *(dir. obj. pron., pl.)* los *(m.)*, las *(f.)*; *(indir. obj. pron., pl.)* les
then entonces, luego
theory teoría *(f.)*
there allí
these *(dem. adj.)* estos(as)
thief ladrón, ladrona
thin delgado(a)
thing cosa *(f.)*
think pensar **(ie)**
third tercero(a)
thirsty (to be) tener sed
this *(dem. pron.)* este(a), *(neuter pron.)* ésto; **this morning / afternoon / evening** esta mañana / tarde / noche
those *(dem. pron.)* ésos(as), aquéllos(as)
thought pensamiento *(m.)*
threat amenaza
three tres
through por
Thursday jueves
ticket billete *(m.)*, boleto *(m.)*; multa *(traffic)*
tie empatar *(in games and elections)*
tighten apretar (ie)
time hora *(f.)*, tiempo *(m.)*, vez *(f.)*
timid tímido(a)
tip propina *(f.)*
tire llanta *(f.)*
title título *(m.)*
to a; **to the +** *(m. s. noun)* al; **to the left** a la izquierda; **to the right** a la derecha
toasted tostado(a)
today hoy
tomato tomate *(m.)*
tomb tumba *(f.)*
tomorrow mañana *(f.)*
ton tonelada *(m.)*
tone tono *(m.)*, *(v.)* tonificar
tongue lengua *(f.)*
too much demasiado(a)
tooth diente *(m.)*; **toothbrush** cepillo de dientes *(m.)*; **toothpaste** pasta dental *(f.)*
touch toque *(m.)*
tour excursión *(f.)*, gira *(f.)*
tourist turista *(m. / f.)*
tours visitas *(f. pl)*
toward hacia, para
towel toalla *(f.)*
tradition tradición *(f.)*
traffic tráfico *(m.)*; **traffic light** semáforo *(m.)*
trail *(ski)* pista *(f.)*
train tren *(m.)*
tranquil tranquilo(a)
tranquilizer tranquilizante *(m.)*
transform transformar
transport transporte *(m.)*
transportation transporte *(m.)*
treasure tesoro *(m.)*
treat tratar
treatment tratamiento *(m.)*
treaty *(m.)* tratado
tree árbol *(m.)*
tremendous tremendo(a)
trick engañar
trip viaje *(m.)*
triumph triunfo *(m.)*, *(v.)* triunfar
troops tropas *(f.)*
trousers pantalones *(m. pl.)*
true cierto(a), verdadero(a)
trumpet trompeta *(f.)*
trunk baúl *(m.)*
trust tener confianza
truth verdad *(f.)*
try probar (ue), tratar de
Tuesday martes
turkey pavo *(m.)*
turn dar vuelta, doblar; **turn down** rechazar; **turn off** apagar
turtle tortuga *(f.)*
TV televisión *(f.)*; **TV set** televisor *(m.)*; **TV soap opera** telenovela *(f.)*
type tipo *(m.)*
typewriter máquina de escribir *(f.)*

U

ugly feo(a)
ulcer úlcera *(f.)*
ultimate último(a)
umbrella paraguas *(m.s.)*
umpire árbitro *(m.)*
unappreciative malagradecido(a)

unbelievable increíble *(adj., m. or f.)*
uncertain incierto(a)
uncle tío *(m.)*
uncommon raro(a)
unconscious inconsciente *(adj., m. or f.)*
under debajo de
underdeveloped subdesarrollado(a)
understand entender **(ie)**
unemployment desempleo *(m.)*
unforgettable inolvidable *(adj., m. or f.)*
ungrateful malagradecido(a)
unique único(a)
unit unidad *(f.)*
unite unir
unity unidad *(f.)*
university universidad *(f.)*
unless a menos que, sin que
unoccupied desocupado(a)
unplug desenchufar
unquestionable indiscutible *(adj., m. or f.)*
until hasta
urgent urgente *(adj., m. or f.)*
us *(dir. and indir. obj. pron.)* nos; *(prep. pron.)* nosotros(as)
use uso *(m.)*; *(v.)* usar, utilizar
useful útil *(adj., m. or f.)*
useless inútil *(adj., m. or f.)*
utilize utilizar

V

vacation vacaciones *(f. pl.)*
vacuum pasar la aspiradora; **vacuum cleaner** aspiradora *(f.)*
Valentine's Day Día de San Valentín *(m.)*
valid válido(a)
valley valle *(m.)*
valor valor *(m.)*
value valor *(m.)*
variety variedad *(f.)*
vegetable vegetal *(m.)*; **vegetables** verduras *(f. pl.)*
vegetarian vegetariano(a)
verify verificar
version versión *(f.)*
very muy; **very bad** pésimo(a)
vest chaleco *(m.)*
vibrate vibrar
victim víctima *(f.)*
victor vencedor(a)
victory triunfo *(m.)*, victoria *(f.)*
violence violencia *(f.)*
violent violento(a)
visit visitar
visitor visitante *(m. / f.)*
vitamin vitamina *(f.)*
vocabulary vocabulario *(m.)*
voice voz *(f.)*
volcano volcán *(m.)*
volunteer voluntario(a)
vote voto *(m.)*

W

wait esperar
waiter camarero *(m.)*; mesero *(m.)*
waitress camarera *(f.)*; mesera *(f.)*
wake up despertarse **(ie)**
walk caminar, pasear
walking a pie
wall pared *(f.)*, muralla *(f.)*
wallet cartera *(f.)*
want querer **(ie)**
war guerra *(f.)*
warm cálido(a)
wash lavar
watch mirar; **watch over** vigilar
water agua *(f.)*
waterfall cascada *(f.)*, catarata *(f.)*
way modo *(m.)*
wear llevar
weather tiempo *(m.)*
Wednesday miércoles
week semana *(f.)*; **weekday** día de la semana *(m.)*; **weekend** fin de semana *(m.)*
weigh pesar
weight peso *(m.)*
weights pesas *(f. pl.)*
welcome bienvenido(a)
well bien; **well enough** bastante bien
west oeste *(m.)*
wet empapado(a)
whaler ballenero *(m.)*
what? ¿qué?, ¿cómo?, ¿cuál(es)?; **what do you think of . . . ?** ¿qué te parece... ? **what's your name?** ¿cómo se llama usted? / ¿cómo te llamas?
what a mess! ¡qué desastre!
when? ¿cuándo?
where? ¿dónde? **(to) where?** ¿adónde?
which? ¿qué?; **which one(s)?** ¿cuál(es)?
while mientras
white blanco(a)
who? ¿quién(es)?
why? ¿por qué?; **why not!** ¡cómo no!
widely ampliamente
wife esposa
win ganar
wind viento *(m.)*
windy (to be) hacer viento
window ventana *(f.)*
wine vino *(m.)*
winter invierno *(m.)*
wish deseo *(m.)*
with con; **with me** conmigo; **with you** *(fam.)* contigo
without sin; **without equal** sin igual
witness testigo(a)
woman mujer *(f.)*; **young woman** joven *(f.)*
wooden de madera
woods selva *(f.)*
wool lana *(f.)*
word palabra *(f.)*
work trabajo *(m.)*, empleo *(m.)*; obra *(f.) (of art)*; *(v.)* trabajar
worker obrero(a)
workshop taller *(m.)*
world mundo *(m.)*
worried preocupado(a)
worry preocupar
worthy of (to be) merecer

wounded *(adj.)* herido(a); *(v.)* sufrir lesiones
write escribir; **write letters** escribir cartas; **in writing** por escrito
writer escritor(a)
written por escrito

Y

yard patio *(m.)*
year año *(m.)*
yellow amarillo(a)
yesterday ayer
yield someterse
you *(dir. obj. pron.)* te, os, lo, la, los, las; *(indir. obj. pron.)* te, os, le, les, se; *(prep. pron.)* ti, usted, ustedes, vosotros(a); *(subj. pron.);* tú, usted, ustedes, vosotros(as)
younger menor
your *(fam. poss. adj.)* tu; *(poss. adj.)* tuyo(a)
youth juventud *(f.)*

Z

zero cero
zoo zoológico *(m.)*
zoology zoología *(f.)*

Index of Grammar

E

F

G

H

I

L

M

N

O

P

U

V

W

Index of Culture and Functions

D

E

F

G

T

U

V

W

Credits and Acknowledgments

 Literary/Realia Credits

The authors wish to thank publishers and organizations for the use of their material.

Más, Magazine, Univisión Publications
Clara, Publicaciones Sayrols, S.A. de C. V., Mexico, D. F.
Fonogramas & Video, 20th Century Fox
Vuelo, Secretaría de Turismo, México
El Mueble, RBA Revistas Príncipe, Barcelona, Spain
United Airlines Corporation
Sojourn International Magazine, Manzi Editores, Buenos Aires, Argentina
La nación, Buenos Aires, Argentina
Reforma, Asalto y Captura por Arturo Sanchez, 3 de agosto, México, D. F.
Departamento de Agricultura, San Juan, Puerto Rico
Pronatura, Instituto Nacional de Antropología, México, D. F.
Dónde Ir, Editorial Ciudad de México, México, D. F.
Super Pop, Barcelona, Spain
Cachoros y Mascotas, Madrid, Spain
Eres, Centro Cultural Universitario, México, D. F.
Eres, Universidad Anahuac, México, D. F.
Eres, Universidad Tecnológica de México, México, D. F.
Ecología, Amazona Metro a Metro, Madrid, Spain
TV Nota, México, D. F.
Casera, S. A., México, D. F.
*Tele*Guía,* México, D. F.
Micolor S. A., Madrid, Spain
Frugosa, S. A. de C.V., Jumex, México, D. F.
Heredez, S. A. de C.V., México, D. F.
Philips Mexicana, S. A. de C. V.
Oxígeno Urban Spa, Buenos Aires, Argentina
El Universal, México, D. F.
Oficina Central para Asuntos del Sida
TV Nota, Revista #56, México, D. F.
Liga de Fútbol, Juegos Olímpicos
El Universal, México, D. F.
Fútbol Profesional, Madrid, Spain
Leche Desnatada Pascua
Bravo, Madrid, Spain
Hispanic Business magazine
Una Pequena Gran Victoria from Body in Flames by Francisco Alarcon © 1990, published by Chronicle Books.
Crem Helado
Leyendas Costarricenses publicada por la Editorial de la Universidad Nacional
Globus Comunicación © 1997
Hispanic Business Magazine
Manzi Publicidad, S. A., Buenos Aires, Argentina
OKY Agencia de Viajes Dos Mil, S.L, Costa Rica

 Photo Credits

Mark Antman/The Image Works, 3
John Warden/Tony Stone Images, 3
Odyssey/Frerck/Chicago, 3
Francois Gohier/Photo Researchers Inc., 3
Odyssey/Frerck/Chicago, 3
Odyssey/Frerck/Chicago, 3
Odyssey/Frerck/Chicago, 5
Peter Menzel, 13
Chip & Rosa Maria de la Cueva Peterson, 13
Odyssey/Frerck/Chicago, 13
Odyssey/Frerck/Chicago, 14
Peter Menzel/Stock, Boston, 14
John Cancalosi/Stock, Boston, 27
Odyssey/Frerck/Chicago, 27

Beryl Goldberg, 27
Renate Hiller/Monkemeyer Press Photo, 28
Odyssey/Frerck/Chicago, 28
Odyssey/Frerck/Chicago, 28
Odyssey/Frerck/Chicago, 33
Tom McHugh/Photo Researchers Inc, 33
Jackie Foryst/Bruce Coleman Inc., 33
Chris Cheadle/Tony Stone Images, 34
Robert Fried/DDB Stock Photo, 34
Odyssey/Frerck/Chicago, 34
Odyssey/Frerck/Chicago, 34
Chip & Rosa Maria de la Cueva Peterson, 34
Beryl Goldberg, 41
Suzanne Murphy-Larronde, 65
Michael Newman/Photo Edit, 65
Chip & Rosa Maria de la Cueva Peterson, 65
Joan Iaconetti/Bruce Coleman Inc., 72
Odyssey/Frerck/Chicago, 73
Stacy Pick/Stock, Boston, 81
Odyssey/Frerck/Chicago, 82
Beryl Goldberg, 103
Mark Antman/The Image Works, 103
Odyssey/Frerck/Chicago, 103
Odyssey/Frerck/Chicago, 109
Peter Menzel/Stock, Boston, 110
Art Resource, 111
ARS, NY/Art Resource, 111
Art Resource, 117
Ulrike Welsch, 141
Peter Menzel/Stock, Boston, 141
Odyssey/Frerck/Chicago, 141
Doug Bryant/DDB Stock Photo, 142
Albert M. Bender Collection/San Francisco Museum of Modern, 144
The Fine Arts Museums of San Francisco, Gift of Albert M. Bender, 144
Odyssey/Frerck/Chicago, 148
Odyssey/Frerck/Chicago, 149
Art Resource, 150
Odyssey/Frerck/Chicago, 157
Odyssey/Frerck/Chicago, 179
Odyssey/Frerck/Chicago, 179
Beryl Goldberg, 179
Peter Menzel/Stock, Boston, 187
Michael Dwyer/Stock, Boston, 188
Raphael Wollman/Gamma-Liaison, 195
Mark J. Terrill AP/Wide World Photos, 196
Beryl Goldberg, 215
Bob Daemmrich/The Image Works, 215
Odyssey/Frerck/Chicago, 215
Harold & Erica Van Pelt, 222
Odyssey/Frerck/Chicago, 223
Susan Meiselas/MAGNUM Photos, 231
Courtesy of Univision, 251
Gottlieb/Monkmeyer Press Photo, 251
Odyssey/Frerck/Chicago, 258
Odyssey/Frerck/Chicago, 259
Paul S. Howell/Gamma-Liaison, 266
Roger Sandler/Gamma-Liaison, 272
Steve Azzara/Gamma-Liaison, 272
Lee/Archive Photos, 272
Courtesy of Cristina Saralegui, 272
Rob Crandall/Stock, Boston, 272
Raphael Wollman/Gamma-Liaison, 272
Ulrike Welsch, 283
Ulrike Welsch, 283
Chip & Rosa Maria de la Cueva Peterson, 283
Alexis Duclos/Gamma-Liaison, 291
Rob Crandall/Stock, Boston, 292
Corbis/Bettmann, 300
James Prigoff, 321
Odyssey/Frerck/Chicago, 321
James Prigoff, 321
M. Toussaint/Gamma-Liaison, 337
Archive Photos, 337
Westenberger/Gamma-Liaison, 338
Tony Alfaro/DDB Stock Photo, 357
Dr. A.C. Twomey/Photo Researchers Inc., 357
Paolo Bosio/Gamma-Liaison, 357
Larry Luxner/DDB Stock Photo, 364
Dr. A.C. Twomey/Photo Researchers Inc., 365
Brad Markel/Gamma-Liaison, 372
Chip & Rosa Maria de la Cueva Peterson, 391
Ulrike Welsch, 391
Ulrike Welsch, 391
Milton C. Toby/DDB Stock Photo, 397
Milton C. Toby/DDB Stock Photo, 398
Odyssey/Frerck/Chicago, 407
Doug Bryant/DDB Stock Photo, 413
Susan Einstein, 427, 437
Odyssey/Frerck/Chicago, 427
Francis E. Caldwell/DDB Stock Photo, 427
Loren McIntyre/Woodfin Camp & Assoc., 428
Loren McIntyre/Woodfin Camp & Assoc., 428
Odyssey/Frerck/Chicago, 428
Roberto Bunge/DDB Stock Photo, 435
Odyssey/Frerck/Chicago, 436
Reuters/Anibal/Solimano/Archive Photos, 443
Odyssey/Frerck/Chicago, 451
Sonda Dawes/The Image Works, 463
P. Gontier/The Image Works, 463
Chip & Rosa Maria de la Cueva Peterson, 463

Will & Deni McIntyre/Photo Researchers Inc., 469
L. Dematteis/The Image Works, 478
Lloyd Young, The Pantagraph/AP/Wide World Photos, 487
Ralph Oberlander/Stock, Boston, 487
Al Behrman/AP/Wide World Photos, 499
Alan Cave/DDB Stock Photos, 499
AFP/Corbis-Bettmann, 499
Ulrike Welsch, 506
Jack Vartoogian, 514
Gilles Mingasson/Gamma-Liaison, 521
Reuters/Wilson Melo/Archive Photos, 522
Bob Daemmrich/The Image Works, 535
Bob Daemmrich/Stock, Boston, 535
Ulrike Welsch, 535
Andrew J. Martinez/Photo Researchers Inc., 541
Inga Spence/DDB Stock Photos, 541
Rob Crandall/The Image Works, 542
Wolfgang Kaehler, 542
Chip & Rosa Maria de la Cueva Peterson, 549
Chip & Rosa Maria de la Cueva Peterson, 556
Beryl Goldberg, 556
Ulrike Welsch, 557
Chip & Rosa Maria de la Cueva Peterson, 557